Sidney D'Mello   Arthur Graess
Björn Schuller   Jean-Claude M:

Affective Computing and Intelligent Interaction

4th International Conference, ACII 2011
Memphis, TN, USA, October 9-12, 2011
Proceedings, Part II

Springer

Volume Editors

Sidney D'Mello
University of Memphis
202 Psychology Building
Memphis, TN 38152, USA
E-mail: sdmello@memphis.edu

Arthur Graesser
University of Memphis
202 Psychology Building
Memphis, TN 38152, USA
E-mail: a-graesser@memphis.edu

Björn Schuller
Technische Universität München
Arcisstraße 21, 80333, München, Germany
E-mail: schuller@tum.de

Jean-Claude Martin
LIMSI-CNRS
Bâtiment 508, 91403 Orsay Cedex, France
E-mail: martin@limsi.fr

ISSN 0302-9743   e-ISSN 1611-3349
ISBN 978-3-642-24570-1   e-ISBN 978-3-642-24571-8
DOI 10.1007/978-3-642-24571-8
Springer Heidelberg Dordrecht London New York

Library of Congress Control Number: 2011937625

CR Subject Classification (1998): I.4, I.5, I.3, H.5.1-3, I.2.10, J.4, K.3

LNCS Sublibrary: SL 6 – Image Processing, Computer Vision, Pattern Recognition, and Graphics

Typesetting: Camera-ready by author, data conversion by Scientific Publishing Services, Chennai, India

Printed on acid-free paper

Springer is part of Springer Science+Business Media (www.springer.com)

Lecture Notes in Computer Science 6975

Commenced Publication in 1973
Founding and Former Series Editors:
Gerhard Goos, Juris Hartmanis, and Jan van Leeuwen

Editorial Board

Preface

Welcome to the proceedings of the fourth bi-annual International Conference of the Humaine Association on Affective Computing and Intelligent Interaction (ACII 2011), which was held in Memphis, Tennessee from October 9th to 12th, 2011. Since its inception in 2005, the ACII conference series has featured some of the most innovative and fascinating basic and applied research in the burgeoning research area centered on emotions, affective computing, user modeling, and intelligent systems. This tradition of exemplary interdisciplinary research has been kept alive in 2011 as evident through the imaginative, exciting, and diverse set of papers spanning the fields of computer science, engineering, psychology, education, neuroscience, and linguistics.

The ACII 2011 conference program featured a rich tapestry of original research embodied through oral presentations, posters, invited talks, workshops, interactive demos, and a doctoral consortium. In all, we received 196 submissions (124 regular papers and 72 papers for workshops, Doctoral Consortium, and demos). Each paper was reviewed by at least two expert reviewers (most papers received three reviews) and vetted by members of the Senior Program Committee and organizers of various events. Forty-four out of the 124 regular papers were accepted as oral presentations (36 percent), and an additional 35 papers were accepted for poster presentations (an overall acceptance rate of 64 percent).

The conference also featured invited talks by three outstanding researchers: Rosalind Picard (MIT), Arvid Kappas (Jacobs University Bremen), and James Lester (North Carolina State University). The conference was kick-started by a full day of workshops on cutting-edge topics including affective brain-computer interfaces, machine learning for affective computing, emotions in games, as well as the first International Audio/Visual Emotion Challenge and Workshop. The conference also included an interactive events session where a number of researchers traveled the globe to demonstrate their affective interfaces and technologies. In keeping with ACIIs tradition of encouraging and scaffolding the next generation of researchers, the conference featured a Doctoral Consortium where 15 students presented their dissertation research. In all, the proceedings featured 138 papers, 79 regular papers (oral presentations and posters), and 59 additional papers for the workshops, Doctoral Consortium, demos, and invited speaker abstracts.

The ACII 2011 conference would not have been possible without the vision and dedicated effort of a number of people. We are indebted to the Program Committee and the Senior Program Committee for their exceptional work in reviewing the submissions and helping us select the best papers for the conference. We would like to acknowledge Kostas Karpouzis and Roddy Cowie, who along with Jean-Claude Martin, organized the Doctoral Consortium. Thanks to

Ginevra Castellano, who joined Björn Schuller to organize the workshops, and to Rafael Calvo and Tanner Jackson who joined Sidney D'Mello to organize the interactive events. We are grateful to Brendan Allison, Stephen Dunne, Dirk Heylen, and Anton Nijholt for organizing the Affective Brain-Computer Interfaces workshop; Georgios Yannakakis, Ana Paiva, Kostas Karpouzis, and Eva Hudlicka for organizing the Emotion in Games workshop; M. Ehsan Hoque, Dan McDuff, Louis Philippe, and Rosalind Picard for organizing the Machine Learning for Affective Computing workshop; and to Michel Valstar, Roddy Cowie, and Maja Pantic who, along with Björn Schuller, organized the First International Audio/Visual Emotion Challenge and Workshop. We would like to thank members of the Humaine Associations Executive Committee for their advice and support. Finally, thanks to the authors for sending us their best work and to all the attendees who bring ACII to life.

Sidney D'Mello and Art Graesser would also like to thank Cristina Conati for encouraging the Memphis team to host the 2011 conference and Jonathan Gratch for his invaluable support and assistance throughout the year leading up to the conference. We are indebted to the student volunteers from the Institute of Intelligent Systems, particularly Blair Lehman, Caitlin Mills, and Amber Strain, who were invaluable in numerous respects. Thanks to the staff of Conference Planning and Operations at the University of Memphis (with a special acknowledgement to Lauren Coggins) for all the local arrangements. Finally, we would like to thank our sponsors, the Institute for Intelligent Systems, the University of Memphis (Office of the Provost), the FedEx Institute of Technology, and Aldebran Robotics, who generously provided funds to help offset the registration costs for students.

In summary, 2011 appears to be an excellent year for Affective Computing and Intelligent Interaction. The keynotes, oral and poster presentations, live demos, Doctoral Consortium, opening workshops, attendees from all over the world, and the fall weather in Memphis (the Home of the Blues and the birth place of Rock and Roll) undoubtedly made the first ACII conference to be held in North America an intellectually stimulating, enjoyable, and memorable event.

October 2011

Sidney D'Mello
Art Graesser
Björn Schuller
Jean-Claude Martin

Organization

General Conference Chairs

Sidney D'Mello   University of Memphis, USA
Art Graesser   University of Memphis, USA

Program Chairs

Sidney D'Mello   University of Memphis, USA
Art Graesser   University of Memphis, USA
Björn Schuller   Technical University of Munich, Germany
Jean-Claude Martin   LIMSI-CNRS, France

Doctoral Consortium Chairs

Jean-Claude Martin   LIMSI-CNRS, France
Kostas Karpouzis   National Technical University of Athens, Greece
Roddy Cowie   Queen's University, Belfast, UK

Interactive Events (Demos) Chairs

Sidney D'Mello   University of Memphis, USA
Rafael Calvo   University of Sydney, Australia
Tanner Jackson   University of Memphis, USA

Workshop Chairs

Björn Schuller   Technical University of Munich, Germany
Ginevra Castellano   Queen Mary University of London, UK

Organizers of Affective Brain-Computer Interfaces (aBCI 2011) Workshop

Brendan Allison   TU Graz, Austria
Stephen Dunne   Starlab Barcelona, Spain
Dirk Heylen   University of Twente, The Netherlands
Anton Nijholt   University of Twente, The Netherlands

Organizers of Emotion in Games Workshop

Georgios Yannakakis	IT University, Denmark
Ana Paiva	Instituto Superior Técnico/INESC-ID, Portugal
Kostas Karpouzis	National Technical University of Athens, Greece
Eva Hudlicka	Psychometrix Associates, Inc., USA

Organizers of Machine Learning for Affective Computing (MLAC) Workshop

M. Ehsan Hoque	MIT, USA
Dan McDuff	MIT, USA
Louis Philippe	USC, USA
Rosalind Picard	MIT, USA

Organizers of the First International Audio/Visual Emotion Challenge and Workshop (AVEC)

Björn Schuller	Technical University of Munich, Germany
Michel Valstar	Imperial College London, UK
Roddy Cowie	Queen's University Belfast, UK
Maja Pantic	Imperial College London, UK

Senior Program Committee (Oral Presentations and Posters)

Anton Batliner	University of Erlangen-Nuremberg, Germany
Rafael Calvo	University of Sydney, Australia
Jean-Claude Martin	LIMSI-CNRS, France
Ben Du Boulay	University of Sussex, UK
Dirk Heylen	University of Twente, The Netherlands
Eva Hudlicka	Psychometrix Associates, USA
Qiang Ji	Rensselaer Polytechnic Institute, USA
Diane Litman	University of Pittsburgh, USA
Anton Nijholt	University of Twente, The Netherlands
Peter Robinson	University of Cambridge, UK
Nilanjan Sarkar	Vanderbilt University, USA
Björn Schuller	Technical University of Munich, Germany
Georgios Yannakakis	IT University of Copenhagen, Denmark

Program Committee (Oral Presentations and Posters)

Omar Alzoubi	University of Sydney, Australia
Elisabeth André	Augsburg University, Germany
Ivon Arroyo	University of Massachusetts Amherst, USA
Ruth Aylett	Heriot Watt University, UK
Gerard Bailly	CNRS, France
Ryan Baker	Worcester Polytechnic Institute, USA
Anton Batliner	University of Erlangen-Nuremberg, Germany
Christian Becker-Asano	University of Freiburg, Germany
Nadia Bianchi-Berthouze	University College London, UK
Luis Botelho	Superior Institute of Labour and Enterprise Sciences, Portugal
Ioan Buciu	University of Oradea, Romania
Win Burleson	Arizona State University, USA
Roberto Bresin	KTH, Sweden
Antonio Camurri	University of Genoa, Italy
Ginevra Castellano	Queen Mary University of London, UK
Jeffery Cohn	University of Pittsburgh, USA
Darren Cosker	University of Bath, UK
Ellen Cowie	Queen's University Belfast, UK
Kerstin Dautenhahn	University of Hertfordshire, UK
Eugénio De Oliveira	University of Porto, Portugal
Laurence Devillers	LIMS-CNRS, France
Anna Esposito	Second University of Naples, Italy
Kate Forbes-Riley	University of Pittsburgh, USA
Jonathan Gratch	University of Southern California, USA
Hatice Gunes	Imperial College London, UK
Jennifer Healey	Intel, USA
Emile Hendriks	Delft University of Technology, The Netherlands
Keikichi Hirose	University of Tokyo, Japan
Julia Hirschberg	Columbia University, USA
Ian Horswill	Northwestern University, USA
David House	Royal Institute of Technology, Sweden
Kostas Karpouzis	ICCS, Greece
Jarmo Laaksolahti	SICS, Sweden
Brent Lance	University of Southern California, USA
John Lee	The University of Edinburgh, UK
James Lester	North Carolina State University, USA
Henry Lieberman	MIT, USA
Christine Lisetti	Florida International University, USA
Patricia Maillard	Universidade do Vale do Rio dos Sinos, Brazil
Carlos Martinho	Instituto Superior Técnico, Portugal
Cindy Mason	Stanford University, USA
Matteo Matteuci	Politecnico di Milano, Italy

Peter Mcowan	Queen Mary University of London, UK
Scott Mcquiggan	SAS Institute, USA
Rada Mihalcea	University of North Texas, USA
Luís Morgado	ISEL, Portugal
Helen Pain	University of Edinburgh, UK
Ana Paiva	INESC-ID and Instituto Superior Técnico, Lisbon
Ioannis Patras	Queen Mary University of London, UK
Christian Peter	Fraunhofer Institute for Computer Graphics, Germany
Paolo Petta	Austrian Research Institute for Artificial Intelligence, Austria
Mannes Poel	University of Twente, The Netherlands
Frank Pollick	University of Glasgow, UK
Alexandros Potamianos	Technical University of Crete, Greece
Thierry Pun	University of Geneva, Switzerland
Ma. Mercedes T. Rodrigo	Ateneo de Manila University, The Philppines
Matthias Scheutz	Tufts University, USA
Magy Seif El-Nasr	Simon Fraser University, Canada
Hiroshi Shimodaira	University of Edinburgh, UK
Mark Shröder	DFKI, Germany
Stefan Steidl	University of Erlangen-Nuremberg, Germany
Jianhua Tao	Institute of Automation of the Chinese Academy of Sciences, China
Daniel Thalmann	Nanyang Technological University, Singapore
Barry-John Theobald	University of East Anglia, UK
Isabel Trancoso	Instituto Superior Técnico / INESC-ID, Portugal
Jan Treur	Vrije Universiteit Amsterdam, The Netherlands
Matthew Turk	University of California, Santa Barbara, USA
Egon L. Van Den Broek	University of Twente, The Netherlands
Juan Velasquez	MIT, USA
Ning Wang	Arizona State University, USA
Joyce Westerink	Philips Research, The Netherlands
Beverly Woolf	University of Massachusetts Amherst, USA
Chung-Hsien Wu	National Cheng Kung University, Taiwan
Lijun Yin	Binghamton University, USA

Additional Reviewers (Oral Presentations and Posters)

Fiemke Both	Maria-Elena Chavez-Echeagaray
Hana Boukricha	Jeffrey Girard
Guillaume Chanel	Javier Gonzalez-Sanchez
Amber Strain	Hatice Gunes

Kaoning Hu
Md. Sazzad Hussain
Blair Lehman
Chee Wee Leong
Peng Liu
Nataliya Mogles
David Pereira
Hector Perez Martinez
Stefan Rank

Matthew Rosato
Maria Ofelia Clarissa San Pedro
Stefan Scherer
C. Natalie Van Der Wal
Rianne Van Lambalgen
Arlette Van Wissen
Rainer Wasinger
Joyce Westerink

Program Committee (Workshops, Doctoral Consortium, Demos)

Aggelos Pikrakis	University of Piraeus, Greece
Albert Rilliard	LIMSI-CNRS, France
Alessandro Vinciarelli	University of Glasgow, UK
Anton Batliner	University of Erlangen-Nuremberg, Germany
Anton Nijholt	University of Twente, The Netherlands
Ashish Kapoor	Microsoft Research, USA
Athanassios Katsamanis	University of Southern California, USA
Audrey Girouard	Carleton University, Canada
Brent Lance	US Army Research Laboratory - Translational Neuroscience Branch, USA
Carlos Busso	The University of Texas at Dallas, USA
Catherine Pelachaud	CNRS Telecom ParisTech, France
Céline Clavel	LIMSI-CNRS, France
Christian Muhl	University of Twente, The Netherlands
Dan Bohus	Microsoft Research, USA
Egon L. Van Den Broek	University of Twente, The Netherlands
Elisabeth André	Augsburg University, Germany
Felix Burkhardt	Deutsche Telekom, Germany
Femke Nijboer	University of Twente, The Netherlands
Fernando De La Torre	Carnegie Mellon University, USA
Gary Garcia Molina	Philips Research Europe, The Netherlands
George Caridakis	ICCS-NTUA, Greece
Ginevra Castellano	Queen Mary University of London, UK
Gualtiero Volpe	InfoMus Lab - DIST - University of Genoa, Italy
Hatice Gunes	Imperial College London, UK
Hector P. Martinez	IT University of Copenhagen, Denmark
Iain Matthews	Disney Research Pittsburgh, USA
Ioannis Patras	Queen Mary University of London, UK
Jan B.F. Van Erp	TNO Human Factors - Perceptual and Cognitive Systems, The Netherlands

Jianhua Tao	Chinese Academy of Sciences, China
Jonathan Gratch	University of Southern California, USA
Jonghwa Kim	University of Augsburg, Germany
Joris Janssen	Philips, The Netherlands
Julia Hirschberg	Columbia University, USA
Julian Togelius	IT University of Copenhagen, Denmark
Julien Epps	The University of New South Wales, Australia
Kai Kuikkaniemi	HIIT, Finland
Laurence Devillers	LIMSI-CNRS, France
Magalie Ochs	NII, Japan
Magy Seif El-Nasr	Simon Fraser University, Canada
Marc Cavazza	University of Teesside, UK
Marc Schröder	DFKI GmbH, Language Technology Lab, Germany
Marcello Mortillaro	Swiss Center for Affective Sciences, Switzerland
Marian Bartlett	University of California, San Diego, USA
Mashfiqui Rabbi	Bangladesh University of Engineering and Technology, Bangladesh
Matthew Turk	University of California, USA
Matti Pietikainen	University of Ouly, Finland
Mohamed Chetouani	University Pierre and Marie Curie, France
Nadia Berthouze	University College London, UK
Nicolas Sabouret	LIP6, France
Nicu Sebe	University of Trento, Italy
Olga Sourina	Nanyang Technological University, Singapore
Ouriel Grynszpan	CNRS, France
Patricia Jaques	UNISINOS, Brazil
Peter Desain	Radboud University Nijmegen, The Netherlands
Peter Robinson	University of Cambridge, UK
Rafael Bidarra	Delft University of Technology, The Netherlands
Raul Fernandez	IBM Research, USA
Robert Leeb	Ecole Polytechnique Federale de Lausanne (EPFL), Switzerland
Ruth Aylett	Heriot-Watt University, UK
Shri Narayanan	University of Southern California, USA
Simon Lucey	CSRIO-ICT, Australia
Sophie Rosset	LIMSI-CNRS, France
Stefan Kopp	University of Bielefeld, Germany
Stefan Steidl	University of Erlangen-Nuremberg, Germany
Stephen Fairclough	Liverpool John Moores University, UK
Tanja Schultz	Universität Karlsruhe, Germany
Tetsunori Kobayashi	Waseda University, Japan

Thierry Pun	University of Geneva, Switzerland
Thomas J. Sullivan	NeuroSky, USA
Thorsten Zander	TU Berlin, Germany
Touradj Ebrahimi	Ecole Polytechnique Federale de Lausanne (EPFL), Switzerland
Victoria Eyharabide	UNICEN University, Argentina
Winslow Burleson	Arizona State University, USA
Yannick Mathieu	CNRS - Université Paris 7, France

Additional Reviewers (Workshops, Doctoral Consortium, Demos)

Ruth Aylett	Ana Paiva
Florian Eyben	Fabien Ringeval
Gangadhar Garipelli	Marieke Thurlings
Theodoros Giannakopoulos	Felix Weninger
Brais Martinez	Martin Woellmer
Angeliki Metallinou	Ramin Yaghoubzadeh
Antonios Oikonomopoulos	

Steering Committee

Nick Campbell	Trinity College, Ireland
Ginevra Castellano	Queen Mary University of London, UK
Jeffery Cohn	University of Pittsburgh, USA
Cristina Conati	University of British Columbia, Canada
Roddy Cowie	Queen's University Belfast, UK
Jonathan Gratch	University of Southern California, USA
Dirk Heylen	University of Twente, The Netherlands
Arvid Kappas	Jacobs University Bramen, Germany
Kostas Karpouzis	National Technical University of Athens, Greece
Jean-Claude Martin	LIMSI-CNRS, France
Maja Pantic	Imperial College, UK
Catherine Pelachaud	CNRS, TELECOM ParisTech, France
Paolo Petta	Austrian Research Institute for Artificial Intelligence, Austria
Helmut Prendinger	National Institute of Informatics, Japan
Marc Schröder	German Research Center for Artificial Intelligence, Germany
Björn Schuller	Munich University of Technology, Germany
Jianhua Tao	Chinese Academy of Sciences, China

Local Assistance

Lauren Coggins
Blair Lehman
Caitlin Mills
Amber Strain
Staff and Students of the Institute for Intelligent Systems

Sponsors

University of Memphis
HUMAINE Association
FedEx Institute of Technology
Institute for Intelligent Systems
Aldebaran Robotics

Table of Contents – Part II

Poster Papers

Doctoral Consortium

Interactive Event (Demo Papers)

The First Audio/Visual Emotion Challenge and Workshop

Affective Brain-Computer Interfaces Workshop (aBCI 2011)

Emotion in Games Workshop

Machine Learning for Affective Computing Workshop

Table of Contents – Part I

Poster Papers

Emotion Twenty Questions:
Toward a Crowd-Sourced Theory of Emotions

Abe Kazemzadeh, Sungbok Lee, Panayiotis G. Georgiou,
and Shrikanth S. Narayanan*

University of Southern California

Abstract. This paper introduces a method for developing a socially-constructed theory of emotions that aims to reflect the aggregated judgments of ordinary people about emotion terms. *Emotion Twenty Questions* (EMO20Q) is a dialog-based game that is similar to the familiar Twenty Questions game except that the object of guessing is the name for an emotion, rather than an arbitrary object. The game is implemented as a dyadic computer chat application using the Extensible Messaging and Presence Protocol (XMPP). We describe the idea of a theory that is socially-constructed by design, or *crowd-sourced*, as opposed to the *de facto* social construction of theories by the scientific community. This paper argues that such a subtle change in paradigm is useful when studying natural usage of emotion words, which can mean different things to different people but still contain a shared, socially-defined meaning that can be arrived at through conversational dialogs. The game of EMO20Q provides a framework for demonstrating this shared meaning and, moreover, provides a standardized way for collecting the judgments of ordinary people. The paper offers preliminary results of EMO20Q pilot experiments, showing that such a game is feasible and that it generates a range of questions that can be used to describe emotions.

1 Introduction

There are some enterprises in which a careful disorderliness is the true method.
–H. Melville, *Moby Dick*

Science often begins with a good question. One may wonder whether the question a scientist asks is fundamentally different than the question of a non-scientist, or whether they are fundamentally the same. It is usual, in the field of affective computing, for scientists to treat people as experimental subjects when studying

* As we consider the players of *Emotion Twenty Questions* to be contributors to this theory, we would like to acknowledge the players for their contribution: Stephen Bodnar, Theodora Chaspari, Jimmy Gibson, Jangwon Kim, Michelle Koehn, Angeliki Metalinou, Emily Mower, Elly Setiadi, Kurt Weible, and Mary Weible. We also acknowledge the use of Ejabberd and iJab open source software. This work was supported by NSF and DARPA.

S. D′Mello et al. (Eds.): ACII 2011, Part II, LNCS 6975, pp. 1–10, 2011.

emotions. This paper takes a contrary view, where people who would formerly be considered as experimental subjects now function more like theory-generating scientists and the scientists play more of an editorial role. This change of roles is not as substantial as it sounds, but mainly serves to give a new perspective to the study of emotions. This view, we argue, is useful for studying the non-scientific meaning of emotion words as they are used in social contexts. We do not argue against having a controlled, scientific vocabulary for studying emotions, but rather that the study of natural emotions warrants closer attention to how everyday people understand and describe emotions with natural language. This type of study falls under the umbrella terms of *commonsense knowledge* or *folk ontology* [1,2].

One function of natural language is to reference objects, whether real or virtual, using patterns of sound or writing. This system of reference provided by natural language is mainly *socially-constructed* (as opposed to innate), in that the names of things are established by the conventions of shared tradition and consensus of a community of speakers, e.g., speakers of a given language or workers in a specific profession. In some such communities, such as a scientific field, the process of socially constructing a terminology is deliberate, systematic, and precise; in other communities it is not. For example, the world-wide community of English speakers has no editorial board or royal academy to arbitrate the correct usage of words. Though it may seem serendipitous that such a loosely regulated system can function as well as it does, it is in fact due to this loose organization that natural language achieves it's flexibility and scalability. On the other hand, general natural language lacks the precision and conciseness that is necessary for specific purposes, such as scientific discussion.

The linguistic division of labor between everyday language and technical jargon is all very fine and well when the technical terminology is disjoint from common language, but it can become problematic when there is considerable overlap. The field of affective computing is one such example: the scientific terms for emotions overlap with common linguistic usage. Since one of the aims of affective computing is to process natural language, it is necessary to be mindful of the difference between the scientific and common definition of emotional terms. Much of the previous work in affective computing has focused on the scientific definition of emotional terms. Needless to say, these scientific definitions must have a high degree of similarity with the common definitions for them to be meaningful, but the scientific definitions are necessarily limited and may not correspond to everyday usage. This distinction can be seen as a prescriptive versus descriptive focus. However, currently there is a movement towards studying more naturalistic and non-prototypical emotion expression [3,4], which may benefit from a corresponding movement towards using the more natural, socially-defined terminological basis that we aim to discover in the research described by this paper.

To move from the scientific theory of emotions to a theory that explicitly accounts for subjectivity and social construction, we made use of *crowd-sourcing* [5] and *games with a purpose* [6]. Crowd-sourcing aims to gather the collective knowledge of a group and is closely tied to the emergent properties of online social communities and web intelligence [7]. Games with a purpose are a particular way of crowd-sourcing. In our case, we devised a game that we call *Emotion Twenty Questions* (EMO20Q). This game is similar to the ordinary Twenty Questions game except that it is limited to guessing about emotion words. Furthermore, it is implemented as an online chat application using the Extensible Messaging and Presence Protocol (XMPP) so that the games can be recorded and studied. As the introductory quote alludes, we carefully allow open-ended user response within the limited context of the EMO20Q game and the text chat modality.

2   EMO20Q

2.1   Rules

In the game of Emotion Twenty Questions (EMO20Q) there are two players who interact using natural language. In this paper, we consider the case when both players are humans. A game consists of a series of *matches*; in each match one of the players assumes the role of *answerer* and the other, the role of *questioner*. At the beginning of the match, the answerer picks an emotion word, unbeknownst to the questioner, which we call the *emotion in question*. The emotion in question need not be the emotion of answerer's current state and, importantly, the answerer is not forced to choose from a prescribed list of emotions. Once the answerer has picked an emotion, the questioner has twenty *turns* to guess the emotion in question, where a turn is a question posed by the questioner in natural language followed by an answer by the answerer. If the identity of the emotion in question is guessed in twenty or fewer turns, the questioner wins. On the other hand, if the emotion is still unknown to the questioner after twenty turns, then the answerer wins.

Although questioning and answering are the two basic plays of EMO20Q, there are other types of game actions that would best described as dialog acts. For example, a player may ask about rules, give directions, give hints, make clarifications, give-up/resign, or engage in small-talk. Also, as in other games, one player may cheer or jeer the other player to express sportsmanship or competitiveness. At the end of a match there is usually a recapitulation of especially salient turns and at that time the questioner may debate the answers given or whether the emotion in question is actually an emotion. This end-game behavior can be useful for determining fringe cases of words that may or may not be actual emotions and can identify erroneous answers.

There were some rules that were proposed in hindsight after our first pilot tournament. One particular rule is that synonyms should be counted as a correct, game-ending guess if the answerer cannot come up with a distinguishing characteristic (e.g., "brave" and "courageous", and "awe" and "amazement"). As these additional rules may improve the gameplay, the EMO20Q rules committee is considering them for future seasons.

2.2   Motivation

The game of EMO20Q serves to address several issues that arise when considering theories of emotion. First, this theory seeks to understand emotional behavior from the level of the individual player/subject. In Sect. 3 we formulate a general theory of emotions as an aggregation of the personal theories of each player. The questioner in EMO20Q can be seen as testing a hypothesis given his or her personal theory, and the person-independent theory can be seen as the union of the theories of the individual person-specific theories, with contradictions thrown out.

Another motivation of the EMO20Q game is that it allows for spontaneous natural language behavior while constraining the language to the targeted domain we wish to study. Much past work [8,9,10,11,12,13] has focused on eliciting responses from subjects who are presented with words as stimuli. However, the stimuli are predetermined and the responses are constrained, often as a Likert scale or prescribed set of emotion categories. In EMO20Q, potentially any word can be picked as an emotion word and any question can be asked of it; it is only limited by the game's rules and the subjects' good-faith judgment. Thus, in contrast with purely elicited experiments, EMO20Q can be presumed to have higher experimental validity and less experimental bias. The player/subjects of EMO20Q are less constrained by the elicitation methodology and we can assume that their honesty and cooperation is comparable to elicitation experiments, or improved due to the supervision of the other player and their shared communicative goals. There is the possibility of experimental effects due to interactions between players. Thus we can assume to have less experimental effects than in experiments with guided/elicited responses due to the bias from using a fixed set of stimuli and responses.

One drawback of this approach is that it will hard to quantify reliability in the unconstrained interactions of EMO20Q. Reliability can be measured in the amount of agreement between subjects, but this can be difficult because we do not force subjects to pick any particular words, so the words that are in common between users are determined by chance and hence sparse. Because of this, an alternative way to measure reliability could be done in offline question-answering of specific question-emotion pairs, which could be repeated across subjects.

The experimental methodology of EMO20Q has other advantages. Receiving stimulus and giving response using the same modality, natural language, has the potential to be more sensitive than Likert scales or restricting user input to fixed choices. This is because we can assume that natural language has the capabilities of expressing most, if not all, of the *communicable* distinctions between emotions. Even in cases where one is literally "at a loss for words", there are descriptions, like the quoted phrase, that people use to approximate such an emotion. One exception where the natural language modality could be less sensitive is in the case of less fluent subject/players, such as children and non-native speakers. In this case, we can imagine subjects who have conceptual distinctions in their theories of emotions that they are not able to verbally express without the aid of elicitation. The utility of the natural language modality can be seen in the productive, social aspects, and ubiquity of language, as well as the relation to engineering solutions, such as natural language processing.

3   Constructing a Theory from EMO20Q

How does one analyze data from EMO20Q? We use the data collected from the game to construct a theory. Our method uses a stripped-down definition of the term *theory* from mathematical logic which states that a theory Γ is simply a set of sentences in some language $\mathcal{L}$ that is true of a model M [14]. In the case of EMO20Q, Γ is the set of questions that were answered with "yes" and negations of the questions that were answered with "no" for a given emotion, $\mathcal{L}$ is the language of propositional logic, and M is a mental model of emotions, which we assume is only accessible through observation of communicative behavior. In this view, each question in EMO20Q can be represented as a proposition $p \in P$ that can be judged true or false of a given emotion $\varepsilon \in E$ by player $i \in I$ according to that player's mental model, $M_{\varepsilon,i}$. Assuming now that player i is the answerer who has just been asked question p, we can say that $\models_{M_{\varepsilon,i}} p$ if the player answers "yes" or $\models_{M_{\varepsilon,i}} \neg p$ if the player answers "no". The previous notation is read "$p/\neg p$ is satisfied by $M_{\varepsilon,i}$", or equivalently "$M_{\varepsilon,i}$ is a model of $p/\neg p$".

A theory for a specific emotion ε and a specific player i, denoted $\Gamma_{\varepsilon,i}$, is constructed as a Boolean vector of length $|P|$, where $|P|$ is the total number of questions. For every question p_n asked of player i, the n-th position of the vector $\Gamma_{\varepsilon,i}$ will be *true* or 1 if the player has answered yes to p_n when the emotion in question was ε. In this case we can say that p_n is a *theorem* of $\Gamma_{\varepsilon,i}$. Similarly, *false* or 0 is assigned to element n of $\Gamma_{\varepsilon,i}$ if p_n received no as an answer while being questioned while ε was the emotion in question. In this case, $\neg p_n$ is a theorem of Γ. If a contradiction is reached, i.e., if both p_n and $\neg p_n$ are members of the set $\Gamma_{\varepsilon,i}$, then both are removed. In practice, this has not happened and we assume that it will not because a player is consistent with him or herself in normal situations, so such a contradiction would be a warning flag that a player may not be playing consistently.

One can proceed in a similar manner for a person-independent theory Γ_{ε} of a particular emotion ε. In this case, the proposition p_n associated with a particular question is added to Γ_{ε} if any player has answered yes to p_n when questioned about emotion ε, and conversely for $\neg p_n$ when any player has answered no. In the case of a person-independent theory, in general one can expect some contradictions and these would signify when there is disagreement about whether such a proposition is true or false of that particular emotion. In this case, as before for the person-specific case, both propositions should be removed from the theory to prevent contradictions.

If a theory for a specific emotion can be seen as a long list of propositions that are true of it, the theory of a set of emotions can be seen as an matrix Γ indexed by the emotions in one dimension and the questions in the other dimension. If the theory Γ contains emotions ε_m for $1 \leq m \leq |E|$ and propositions p_n for $1 \leq n \leq |P|$, then Γ will be an $|E| \times |P|$ matrix. Ordinarily, Boolean algebra would dictate that this matrix would consist of ones and zeros. Such a representation has been explored under the aegis of *formal concept analysis* [15]. However, we need the matrix to be sparse to represent the fact that not all of the combinations of questions and emotions have been encountered and that there may be some contradiction among subjects. To this end, we propose that the matrix be a $(1, 0, -1)$-matrix, or a *signed matrix/graph* [16], where 1 indicates that the proposition of column-m is true for the emotion of row-n, -1 indicates that it is false, and 0 indicates that it has not been seen or that a contradiction has been encountered.

4   Results

In preliminary experiments, we collected a total of 26 matches from 12 players. Since each match has two players, this averaged about 4 matches per player. The number of matches played by a player ranged from 2 to 12. The mean and median number of questions was 12.04 and 15.5, respectively, when failures to correctly guess the emotion were averaged in as 20 questions.

In the data, a total of 23 unique emotions were chosen, i.e., only three emotions were observed more than once, and these involved related word forms (e.g., "confused" and "confusion"; "frustrated" and "frustration"). The emotions that were played are: *admire, adore$^+$, anger, awe$^+$, boredom, bravery*, calm, confidence*, confusion$^+$, contempt, disgust, enthusiasm$^+$, frustration, gratefulness, jealousy, love, proud, relief, serenity, shame, silly, surprised,* and *thankful.* The starred emotion words were disputed by players after the games and those marked by a plus were emotions that were not successfully guessed. In addition, there were 66 additional emotion words that were referred to in questions that attempt to identify the emotion in question.

There was a total of 313 questions-asking events that received unambiguous yes/no answers. After normalizing the questions for punctuation and case, there was a total of 297 unique questions types with 13 questions types (29 tokens) seen more than once and no questions were seen more than 3 times. Since the surface forms of the questions vary widely and because at the current stage we have not developed natural language processing techniques to extract the underlying semantics of the questions, we used manual preprocessing to standardize the questions to a logical form that is invariant to wording. This logical form converted the surface forms to a pseudo-code language with a controlled vocabulary by converting the emotion names to nouns if possible, standardizing attributes of emotions and the relations of emotions to situations and events. Examples of the standardized questions are shown in Tab. 1. After the standardization, there were a total of 222 question types. We also manually mapped the surface form of the answers to yes/no/other answers. In the future, we will explore how to automate these steps and represent fuzziness in the answers that are not clearly "yes" or "no".

After the manual normalization we found that there were 37 questions types that had been asked at least twice, eight questions types that were asked three

Table 1. Examples of question standardization

Standardized Question	Examples
cause(emptySet,e)	*can you feel the emotion without any external events that cause it?*
	is it an emotion that just pops up spontaneously (vs being triggered by something)?
cause(otherPerson,e)	*is it caused by the person that it's directed at?*
	Do you need someone to pull this emotion out of you or evoke it? if so, who is it?
e.valence==negative	*is it considered a negative thing to feel?*
	2) so is it a negative emotion?
situation(e,birthday)	*would you feel this if it was your birthday?*
	is it a socially acceptable emotion, say, at a birthday party?
e==frustration	*oh, is it frustrated?*
	frustration?

times, four that were asked at least four times (a total of 90 question tokens were repeated at least twice). Examining the normalized questions revealed interesting patterns of question reuse through the social interactions of the players, though more longitudinal data will be needed to rigorously characterize these interactions. Approximately half of the questions were emotion identity questions.

To get a better idea of the relative frequencies of general types of questions, we devised a way of classifying the questions using the following categories: *identity questions* (guessing an emotion), *attribute questions* (asking about dimensional attribute like valence or activation), *similarity/subsethood questions* (asking if the emotion in question is similar to or a type of another emotion), *situational questions* (questions that ask about specific situations associated with the emotion in question), *behavior questions* (questions that are asked about the behavior associated with the emotion in question), *causal questions* (questions about the cause, effect, or dependency of the emotion in question), *social questions* (questions asking about other parties involved in the emotion–this overlaps somewhat with causal questions and situational questions), *miscellaneous questions* (questions that defied classification or had categories with too few examples). Some examples of these categories are given in Tab. 2.

Table 2. Examples of question categories

Question Categories	Examples
identity (42%)	*is it angry?*
	guilt?
attribute (13%)	*is it something one feels for long periods of time?*
	is it a strong emotion?
similarity/ subsethood (10%)	*is the emotion a type of or related to content or zen contentment (is that a word?_)*
	so it's similar to excited?
situational (14%)	*is the emotion more likely to occur when you are tired?*
	would i feel this if my dog died?
behavior (3%)	*you can express it in an obvious way by sighing?*
	do adults usually try to discourage children from feeling this?
causal (7%)	*yes. mynext question is can it harm anyone besides the feeler?*
	I think I know, but I'll ask one more question...does it ever cause children to wake up and cry?
social (8%)	*are you less likely to experience the emotion when around good firiends?*
	13)would you feel that towards someone who is superior to you?
miscelaneous (3%)	*i dont' know if this is a valid question, but does it start with the letter D?*
	or an aspirational emotion?
	does the word function or can be conjugated as anything eles? i.e. can it be a verb too?

5   Discussion

One of the claims we made in Sect. 2.2 was that the methodology of EMO20Q allowed for less experimental effects than other types of elicitation. Another benefit is that one class of experimental effect is easily measurable: influence of one subject's guessing strategies on another subject can be quantified in terms of question reuse. In fact, examining the question reuse revealed interesting patterns that in a different context could be studied in its own right as a social phenomenon over time, as opposed to being considered an extraneous effect, though more longitudinal data will be needed to rigorously characterize these interactions.

There were some experimental effects with hinting behavior. In after-action reviews with the players, there was anecdotal evidence of retribution type experimental effects, where one player who gives only yes/no answers without any hints will be given less hints when it is their turn to be questioner. Furthermore, there is also mercy type experimental effects, whereby more hints are given by the answerer as the questioner approaches the 20 question limit. Since our main focus was the yes/no questions we did not attempt to quantify the hinting behavior as this did not effect the collection of yes/no question/answers for emotion words.

By analyzing the distribution of question types, we can begin to see some general trends in how people describe emotions. The categories we used are a descriptive way of generalizing the data, not precise classes. Certain questions could have been classified into into multiple categories. In particular, the social, behavioral, causal, and situational questions all referred to various types of real-world knowledge and so these categories tended to run together. For example "are you more likely to experience the emotion when around good friends?" was labeled social, whereas "Would you feel this emotion at a birthday party?" was labeled situational, even though these two examples are very closely related. Therefore, these categories should be interpreted in a general, descriptive sense apart from the theory we aim to crowd-source.

The EMO20Q game requires that an emotionally intelligent agent can understand emotions without observing them, thanks to natural language and empathy. Empathy, which we consider to be the ability to understand emotions that are not one's own emotions, is an important aspect of this game. This game explores a computational type of empathy and that can be thought of as empathy removed of its humane connotations. Just as intelligence tests often seek to isolate verbal intelligence from mathematical or creative intelligence, emotional intelligence may have also a verbal aspect and EMO20Q could provide a way to test for such a component of emotional intelligence.

There were a few behaviors and game states that we did not anticipate when formulating the rules, and these will be incorporated in future data collections. One issue was that of synonyms. Several times, a questioner would get a very close word and oscillate between related synonyms, for example "mad" and "angry". In the future, we will deal with this by changing the stopping criteria from guessing the exact word to guessing a synonym that cannot be distinguished by any type of explanation. However, even though it may seem that two words are closely related, there may still be some differences. For example, one player was unsure about whether "proud" and "pride" would be considered equal (native speakers of English generally feel that "pride" has a negative connotation, whereas "proud" has a positive connotation).

6 Conclusion

In this paper, we proposed the EMO20Q game as an experimental methodology to collect *natural language descriptions of emotions*. These descriptions, extracted from the questions asked in the game, were used to construct player-specific theories of emotions. Although we made the distinction of scientific-versus-natural-language descriptions of emotions, we feel that our approach can in fact be used to scientifically study the social behavior of communicative agents, humans or computers, who may have different knowledge, memory, and experience that they draw upon when conveying emotional information to each other.

Automating a computer agent that plays EMO20Q poses many interesting challenges and opportunities. The ultimate test of whether the theories collected with our methodology are valid is if they can enable an automated agent to simulate a human player, as in a Turing test. The main challenge to automating a player of EMO20Q is robust natural language understanding. The questioner agent needs to select questions and process yes/no type answers, but the answerer agent would need to understand an open set of questions that can be asked of any emotion, so we consider the questioner role to be easier to automate than the answerer role. Our initial work on designing a questioner agent is described in [17,18] and [18] includes an interactive demo. For automating the answerer role, the computer would need a way to understand a wide variety of questions. We have undertaken previous research on how to answer questions about dimensional representations for emotions and similarity and subsethood judgments [12,13,19], which, according to our pilot data, make up nearly 25% of the total questions. Moreover, questions about the unknown emotion's identity accounted for a significant portion (42%) of the questions we observed. These emotion identity questions could be understood by template matching questions in the form of "is it X?" or simply "X?". However, the remaining question types in Tab. 2 will be relatively more difficult because they require real world knowledge.

In conclusion, this paper examined how one can experimentally derive a theory of emotions from relatively unconstrained natural language interaction that is focused to the domain of emotions using the EMO20Q game. Our pilot data led to descriptive results that can inform practitioners of affective computing about how people understand emotions and communicate about them with natural language. Our future work will aim to collect more data to expand coverage of emotions, broaden the population of players, and to continue development of automated agents that play EMO20Q. We also endeavor to make our data and methodologies accessible to the community. These can be found at http://code.google.com/p/emotion-twenty-questions/.

References

1. Gordon, A., Kazemzadeh, A., Nair, A., Petrova, M.: Recognizing expressions of commonsense psychology in english text. In: Proceedings of the 41st Annual Meeting on Association for Computational Linguistics, ACL 2003 (2003)
2. Singh, P., Lin, T., Mueller, E.T., Lim, G., Perkins, T., Zhu, W.L.: Open mind common sense: Knowledge acquisition from the general public. In: Chung, S., et al. (eds.) CoopIS 2002, DOA 2002, and ODBASE 2002. LNCS, vol. 2519, pp. 1223–1237. Springer, Heidelberg (2002)
3. Devillers, L., Abrilian, S., Martin, J.-C.: Representing real-life emotions in audio-visual data with non basic emotional patterns and context features. In: Tao, J., Tan, T., Picard, R.W. (eds.) ACII 2005. LNCS, vol. 3784, pp. 519–526. Springer, Heidelberg (2005)
4. Mower, E., Metallinou, A., Lee, C.-C., Kazemzadeh, A., Busso, C., Lee, S., Narayanan, S.: Interpreting ambiguous emotional expressions. In: ACII Special Session: Recognition of Non-Prototypical Emotion from Speech-The Final Frontier?, Amsterdam, Netherlands (2009)
5. Howe, J.: The rise of crowdsourcing. Wired Magazine 14.06 (June 2006)
6. von Ahn, L., Dabbish, L.: Labeling images with a computer game. In: Proceedings of the SIGCHI Conference on Human Factors in Computing Systems (2004)
7. Zhong, N., Liu, J., Yao, Y., Ohsuga, S.: Web intelligence. In: Computer Software and Applications Conference (2000)
8. Whissell, C.M.: The Dictionary of Affect in Language, pp. 113–131. Academic Press, London (1989)
9. Osgood, C.E., Suci, G.J., Tannenbaum, P.H.: The Measurement of Meaning. University of Illinois Press, US (1957)
10. Oudeyer, P.: The production and recognition of emotions in speech: features and algorithms. J. Hum. Comput. Stud. 59, 157–183 (2003)
11. Russell, J.A., Mehrabian, A.: Evidence for a three-factor theory of emotions. Journal of Research in Personality 11, 273–294 (1977)
12. Kazemzadeh, A., Lee, S., Narayanan, S.: An interval type-2 fuzzy logic system to translate between emotion-related vocabularies. In: Proceedings of Interspeech, Brisbane, Australia (September 2008)
13. Kazemzadeh, A.: Using interval type-2 fuzzy logic to translate emotion words from spanish to english. In: IEEE World Conference on Computational Intelligence (WCCI) FUZZ-IEEE Workshop (2010)
14. Enderton, H.B.: A Mathematical Introduction to Logic, 2nd edn. Academic Press, London (2001)
15. Ganter, B., Wille, G.S.R. (eds.): Formal Concept Analysis: foundation and applications. Springer, Berlin (2005)
16. Kunegis, J., Lommatzsch, A., Bauckhage, C.: The slashdot zoo: Mining a social network with negative costs. In: World Wide Web Conference (WWW 2009), Madrid, pp. 741–750 (April 2009)
17. Kazemzadeh, A., Lee, S., Georgiou, P.G., Narayanan, S.: Determining what questions to ask, with the help of spectral graph theory. In: Proceedings of Interspeech (2011)
18. Kazemzadeh, A., Gibson, J., Georgiou, P., Lee, S., Narayanan, S.: Emo20q questioner agent. In: D´Mello, S., et al. (eds.) Proceedings of ACII (Interactive Event), vol. 6975, pp. 313–314. Springer, Heidelberg (2011), The interactive demo http://sail.usc.edu/emo20q/questioner/questioner.cgi
19. Kazemzadeh, A., Lee, S., Narayanan, S.: An interval type-2 fuzzy logic model for the meaning of words in an emotional vocabulary (2011) (under review)

A Pattern-Based Model for Generating Text to Express Emotion

Fazel Keshtkar and Diana Inkpen

School of Electrical Engineering and Computer Science, University of Ottawa,
Ottawa, Canada
{akeshtka,diana}@site.uOttawa.ca

Abstract. In this paper we introduce a novel pattern-based model for generating emotion sentences. Our model starts with initial patterns, then constructs extended patterns. From the extended patterns, we chose good patterns that are suitable for generating emotion sentences. We also introduce a sentence planning module, which provides rules and constraints for our model. We present some examples and results for our model. We show that the model can generate various types of emotion sentences, either from semantic representation of input, or by choosing the pattern and the desired emotion class.

Keywords: Emotion Expression, Pattern-based, Natural Language Generation, Sentiment Analysis, Surface Realization.

1 Introduction

Emotions and feelings connect us with our lives, and affect how we build and maintain the basis for interactions with people in society. These types of phenomena also take place in the virtual communities. Through the virtual environment and social networks, people can stay in touch with their relatives and friends. They exchange experiences, share opinions and feelings, and fulfill their social need for interpersonal communication, using the online world of computer-mediated communications and similar environments. Affect is an important element in social interaction. Over the past decade, issues of recognition, interpretation and representation of affect and emotion have been extensively investigated by researchers in the field of affective computing and emotion analysis. A wide range of modalities have been considered, including affect in speech, facial display, posture and physiological activity. Recently, textual information has increased, and researchers are now interested in studying different kinds of affective phenomena, including sentiment analysis, subjectivity and emotions in text.

Natural Language Generation (NLG) systems produce text or speech from a given nonlinguistic input following, an interpretation, document planning, sentence planning and surface realization tasks [10]. In this work, we focus on surface realization, the task of producing surface word strings from a nonlinguistic input specification. We introduce a pattern-based model; the user can choose a pattern, then based on the pattern variable fields, the tool will generate emotion sentences.

S. D'Mello et al. (Eds.): ACII 2011, Part II, LNCS 6975, pp. 11–21, 2011.

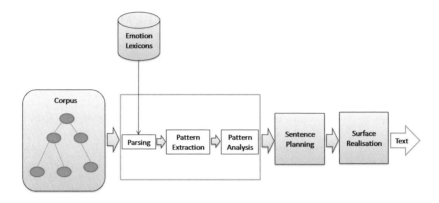

Fig. 1. Our Pattern-based Architecture for Sentence Generation

2   Our Model to Generate Emotion Sentences

The vast amount of text that is becoming available online offers new possibilities for achieving corpus-based approaches to NLG systems. We have developed a 'pattern-based model', a system that generates extraction patterns using untagged text. Our model requires only a pre-classified corpus of relevant and irrelevant texts; nothing inside the texts needs to be tagged in any way. Our goal with this model is to extract emotion patterns from the corpus, then find the best patterns to describe good semantic representations for each emotion category. For input, our model uses a semantic representation of the meaning of the input sentence to be conveyed in a different realization sentence.

During our research, for the paraphrase extraction [5], we recorded the parts-of-speech (PoS) tags, and the words surrounding the emotion seeds. We extracted pronouns and the open-class lexical terms (nouns, verbs, adjectives and adverbs) before and after each seed, for each class of emotion. They have advantages in our model: first, to find paraphrases and context similarity for paraphrase extraction; and second, to find the behavior and the formation of POS and words that surround each emotion word, which is our goal in this paper. This also helps determine the construction of emotion sentences. Figure 1 illustrates the interaction between input semantic values and sentences taken from a corpus, the pattern extraction and analysis, planning the sentence by using a finite state model, and the output text produced by the surface realization engine. Although based on a small set of examples, the combination of sentence, noun, verb, adjective and adverb patterns with the ability to change individual values, could allow the application to generate a range of sentences, broader than the target corpus.

2.1   Data Set

The starting point of our work was to provide a corpus of emotion sentences for the six emotion categories we used in our research (i.e., joy, anger, sadness, fear,

Table 1. The features that we used to extract patterns

Features	Description
F1	Sequence of PoS and Tokens of the Sentence
F2	First Verb before the Seed
F3	First Noun before the Seed
F4	Pronoun before the Seed
F5	Seed
F6	Pronoun after the Seed
F7	First Noun after the Seed
F8	First Verb after the Seed
F9	First Adjective after the Seed
F10	First Adverb after the Seed

surprise and disgust). We used the same data set that we collected for paraphrase extraction (explained in [5]). Each sentence in the target corpus might contain an emotion word, which can be used to produce a pattern of the original sentence.

2.2 Parsing and Tokenization

In our approach, rich feature representations are used to distinguish between emotions expressed toward different targets. In order to generate these representations, we did parts-of-speech tagging using the POS tagger developed by [6]. First we reviewed Table 1, and from the features in this table we used pronoun, noun, verb, adverb and adjective before and after emotion seeds, along with their tokens, for each emotion category. This step produced a syntactic analysis for each sentence. For each POS we introduced some heuristic rules to extract original patterns.

2.3 Pattern Extraction

We extracted the features shown in Table 1, to determine their frequency in the corpus. We transferred the tokenized sentences into the vector space of features. Table 2 displays statistics for four lexical classes of POS. It shows that pronouns, nouns, verbs, adverbs and adjectives are rich representation features in our data set. It also shows that, on average, 65% (out of 100% before seeds) of these features appear before emotion seeds, and 54% (out of 100% after seeds) of the time they appear after emotion seeds. In the table, L (Left) and R (Right) are parts-of-speech or tokens before emotion seeds, and parts-of-speech or tokens after emotion seeds, respectively. Previous research on word sense disambiguation in contextual analysis has identified several features that are good indicators of word properties. These include surrounding words and their POS tags, collocation and keywords in contexts [7].

Table 3 shows the percentages of these features for each emotion category, before and after emotion seeds in our data set. We examined the formation and construction of pronouns, nouns, verbs, adjectives and adverbs for each of the

Table 2. The Frequency of POS for each emotion

Emotion	Total	Pronoun	Verb	Noun	Adjective	Adverb	Total
anger(L)	7727	2061	1178	561	279	1250	5329(69%)
anger(R)	7618	1607	486	1757	190	256	2689(35%)
joy(L)	13340	2544	2275	1080	672	2487	9058(68%)
joy(R)	13542	2415	716	2961	368	877	7337(54%)
fear(L)	11988	2334	2062	952	613	2293	5961(50%)
fear(R)	12229	2177	648	2575	350	832	6582(54%)
disgust(L)	13796	2581	2444	1118	699	2570	9412(68%)
disgust(L)	14005	2441	734	3036	378	921	7510(54%)
sad(L)	16939	2858	3244	1353	905	3204	11564(68%)
sad(R)	17128	2889	881	3642	479	843	8734(51%)
surprise(L)	8406	2111	1316	602	312	1384	5725(51%)
surprise(R)	8314	1688	508	1911	222	290	4619(56%
Total(L)	72196	14489	12519	5666	3480	13188	47049(65%)
Total(R)	72836	13217	3973	15882	1987	4019	39078(54%)

emotion categories. Based on this, we extracted the initial patterns for each emotion category.

2.4   Pattern Analysis

In this section, we analyze the patterns and explain how we can construct "good" patterns from extended patterns by extending the initial patterns. We define the notions of initial patterns, extended patterns, and good patterns.

- **Initial Patterns**
  Based on the statistics shown in the previous sections, we were able to determine *initial pattern* for our system. We considered POS before and after emotion seeds, and we included the emotion seeds in an initial pattern. For example; 'N ES V' (N: Noun, ES: Emotion Seed, V: Verb) is an *initial pattern*. We extracted all initial patterns surrounding the emotion seeds.
- **Extended Patterns**
  Since we intended to generate emotion sentences, and any sentence must have three main components (i.e., subject, verb, and object), it is difficult to construct emotion sentences from the initial patterns. Therefore, we extended them to create larger patterns that were suitable candidates for sentence generation. For example, from the initial pattern |V ES N|, we can construct *extended* patterns such as "N V ES N", "PR V ES N", "N V ES JJ", and many others. However, it became clear that the *extended* patterns may not be suitable candidates for sentence generation, and so we selected *good* patterns from the extended patterns.
- **Good Patterns**
  We call p a good pattern if it can generate a grammatically-correct sentence. For clarification, we explain our method with an example. Let the initial pattern p be "V ES N". We take p and match it to the candidate sentence to

Table 3. The Percentage of POS for each Emotion

Emotion	Pronoun	Verb	Noun	Adjective	Adverb
anger(L)	27%	15%	7%	4%	16%
anger(R)	37%	11%	41%	4%	6%
joy(L)	28%	25%	12%	7%	27%
joy(R)	33%	10%	40%	5%	12%
fear(L)	39%	35%	16%	10%	38%
fear(R)	33%	10%	39%	5%	13%
disgust(L)	27%	26%	12%	7%	27%
disgust(R)	33%	10%	40%	5%	12%
sadness(L)	25%	28%	12%	8%	28%
sadness(R)	33%	10%	42%	5%	10%
surprise(L)	37%	23%	11%	5%	24%
surprise(R)	37%	11%	41%	5%	6%
Total(L)	31%	27%	12%	7%	28%
Total(R)	34%	10%	41%	5%	10%

Table 4. Some initial patterns

Initial Patterns
Noun Emotion-Seed Verb
Verb Emotion-Seed Noun
Pronoun Emotion-Seed Verb
Verb Emotion-Seed Pronoun
Adjective Emotion-Seed Verb
Adverb Emotion-Seed Verb
Verb Emotion-Seed Adjective
Verb Emotion-Seed Adverb

find the extended pattern. From the pattern p we can construct the pattern P_1 "N V ES N". An example of a correct sentence from pattern P_1 is, "Stuff looks like heaven". From p we can also construct pattern P_2 "PR V ES N", and an example of this pattern is, "It was great idea". Finally, in this example, from the initial pattern p we can construct the extended patterns P_1 and P_2, which are *good* patterns. As shown by the examples, the *good* patterns can generate different types of emotion sentences. Figure 2 illustrates the transformation of the construction of some *initial* patterns into *extended* patterns, with examples. We followed the above method and retrieved many *good* patterns from the *extended* patterns.

2.5 Sentence Planner

Sentence planning is one the main tasks of any NLG system. It determines how the information is divided among individual sentences, and which cohesion parts (e.g., pronouns, discourse markers, verbs, etc.) should be added to

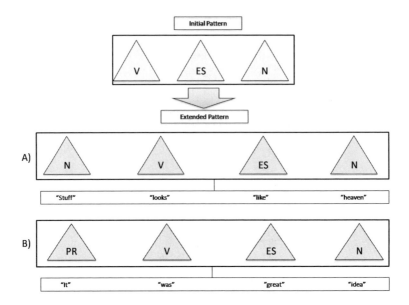

Fig. 2. Constructing Extended Pattern with Examples (ES: Emotion Seed)

Table 5. Some good patterns

Good Patterns	
N V ES N	Amy is happy girl
PR V ES N	She is nice person
PR V ES RB	they lived happily together
PR V RB ES	I am quite upset
PR V ES JJ	I am feeling smart
PR V RB ES	I am pretty good

make the text coherent and smooth [10]. In sentence planning, we define some rules for constructing patterns from the previous section to generate emotion sentences. For example, the pattern "PR V great NN" could generate the sentence "He was great idea", which is not a correct sentence. So, our rules add restrictions in order to choose a correct pronoun for subject of the sentence. We also try for agreement between the pronouns and verbs, and the coherency of the sentence. Sentence planning is a distinct phase of the generation process. It requires computing various aspects, including sentence delimitation, sentence internal organization and references.

Pattern Selection Task

– **Transforming a pattern to a sentence format.** This will manage the chosen pattern to determine the correct format for the sentence structure, in terms of subject, verb and object formation. The user can select a subject and a verb, and the rest will be considered as object by the system. Another option is for the system to identify the subject, verb and object based on a selected pattern, and the user identify the variable parts in the system. For example, in the pattern "Pronoun Verb Emotion-Seed Noun", the Pronoun will be considered as the Subject, the Verb will be the verb and the Emotion-Seed and Noun will be considered as the Object. This will help the sentence realization module to generate an output sentence.

- **Determining correct emotion words.** This task involves selecting different syntactic alternatives for the elements of emotion seeds in the pattern, from a set of semantic representations and equivalent input texts or chosen emotion.
- **Sentence content delimitation.** If the user wants to generate more than one sentence, the sentence planner can allocate the information so that it is distributed into distinct sentences.
- **Internal sentence organization.** Within the sentence, the sentence planner must allocate the subject, specify the adjuncts, determine the order of preposition phrases, determine the subordination of relative clauses, etc.
- **Lexical choice:** This task involves selecting from a set of semantically equivalent but syntactically different alternatives.

Aggregation Task

- **Conjunction and other aggregation.** i.e., transforming (1) to (2):
  1) Amy is happy. Amy is nice.
  2) Amy is happy and nice.
- **Pronominalization and other reference.** i.e., transforming (3) to (4):
  3) Amy is worried. Amy has an exam.
  4) Amy is worried. She has an exam.
- **Introducing discourse markers.** i.e., transforming (5) to (6):
  5) I just saw Amy, she was sick.
  6) I just saw Amy, she was also sick.

The common theme behind these operations is that they do not change the information content of the text; instead they make it more fluent and easier to read. Sentence planning is important if the text needs to read fluently and, in particular, if it should appear to have been written by a human. Otherwise, there is no need to emphasize sentence planning, and the system can perform minimal aggregation.

2.6 Surface Realization

The realizer (the final NLG module) generates actual text based on decisions made by the document planner and the sentence planner (microplanner). A realizer generates individual sentences, typically from a 'deep syntactic' structure [9]. The realizer needs to ensure that the rules of English are followed:

- Punctuation rules: For example, the sentence: "Amy looks great, nice, and beautiful" must end with "." not ","
- Morphology: the plural of *box* is *boxes*, not *boxs*.
- Agreement: For example: "I am happy" instead of "I are happy".
- Reflexive: For example: "Amy made herself happy" instead of "Amy made Amy happy".

There are too many linguistic formalisms and rules which can be incorporated into an NLG Realizer to explain here. Some are general purpose engines such as FUF [3] and Penman [8], which can be programmed with various linguistic rules. We used SimpleNLG [4] and our Authoring Tool NLG System [1] for sentence realization, and to generate sentence. Using the pattern definitions from the previous sections, we designed a simple surface realization component for our model.

We designed a simple surface realization component for our model, using the pattern definitions from the previous section. Our surface realization module can currently accept a template as input (to be taken as a sample structure with inherited default values for the output sentence) and, optionally, parameters representing the alternative semantics of its subject, verb and object constituents. Alternatively, it is possible to specify a sentence from scratch without using an existing template as a basis [2], in a standard pattern format such as "Noun Verb Emotion-Seed Noun" or other pattern formats. We believe the latter option in the system helps to specify simpler sentence structures more conveniently, instead of having to look up an example, or find templates in the corpus. In both the template-based and pattern-based approaches the system selects a target template/pattern, then provides a set of values to fill in the template/pattern variable fields. These input values overwrite the default values provided by the template; that is, those values that were inherited from the corpus data or other lexical sources. If necessary, they are adjusted by basic agreement rules to reestablish grammaticality.

2.7   Examples and Results

Providing Variables for Fields. Depending on the type of template or pattern, our system can support five types of variables: pronouns, nouns, verbs, adjectives and adverbs. The variables for the pronoun fields can be any type of pronouns, based on the pattern or template requirement. The supported variable fields for nouns and noun phrases are: determiner type, gender, number, person, pre and post-modifiers, the noun-phrase head, proposition, or relative clause. Nouns can be chosen by the user, or from the nouns provided in Section 2.3.

For verbs or verb phrases, the variable fields are verb or verb phrase type, and can be finite, infinite, mode, verb tense or adverbial modifiers. The gender and number for verbs are not specified directly, but they can be inherited from the subject by the sentence realizer to avoid a conflicting input specification.

For adverb variable fields, our system can accept different types of adverbs, such as adverbs of manner (e.g., carefully), adverbs of time (e.g., today, next

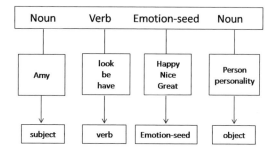

Fig. 3. An example for to generate sentence with pattern for emotion happiness

Table 6. An example of surface realization with the pattern: "Noun Verb Emotion-Seed Noun" for the emotion happiness

Amy looks happy person.
Amy is nice person.
Amy has nice personality.
Stuff looks like heaven.
It was great idea.
They had good time.

week), adverbs of frequency (e.g., usually, occasionally), adverbs of degree (e.g., a lot, so much), and adverbs of comment (e.g., fortunately).

In terms of adjective variable fields, our system can accept different types of adjectives, such as: personal titles (e.g., Mr., Ms, Dr., etc.), possessive adjectives (e.g., my, your, his, our, their, its), demonstrative adjectives (e.g., this, that, these, those), indefinite adjectives (e.g., no, any, many, few, several), and numbers.

To generate sentences with our patterns, the user can 1) choose any pattern, 2) identify the desired emotion category (happiness, anger, fear, sadness, surprise or disgust) and 3) select the variables for pattern fields (in this case, the system can choose automatically as well). The system then 4) transform the semantic representation that is determined by the user to guide sentence formation, and generate different types of emotion sentences.

We describe how a pattern-based example works in our system below (Figure 3). The user selects a favorite pattern; here the selected pattern is "Noun Verb Emotion-Seed Noun", and the desired emotion is "happiness". Then the user can select "Amy" for the first Noun in the pattern, and one of the verbs "look", "be" or "have" as the verb for the variable field Verb in the pattern. As an Emotion-Seed, suppose the user selects "happy", "nice" and "great". For the last field of the pattern, we consider "person" and "personality". To generate the final output, the system will transform the combination of patterns to a sentence format which is `"Subject+Verb+Emotion-Seed+Object"`.

Some fields in the pattern need to be in agreement. For example, agreement between $<Subject, Verb>$ and sometimes $<Subject, Object>$. Also, it needs to select proper emotion seeds to be suitable for the sentence structure, and for fluency in the final output sentence. These constrains are again performed by the sentence planner, agreement rules and the surface realization module.

With this pattern, the system can generate different types of emotion sentences. For example, we can use our Authoring Tool NLG system to generate different types of sentences with various subjects (singular, plural), verbs (with different tenses: present, past, future) and objects. By changing the emotion expression to a different emotion category (e.g., *anger*), the system is able to generate various types of emotion sentences for the *anger* emotion with the same pattern. The final surface realization for this pattern is presented in Table 6. We note here, with one pattern, the system can generate various emotion sentences for different emotion classes, but the type of emotion sentence to be generated is the user's choice.

As any research, our work has some limitations, as well. For example, for the results in Table 6, some sentences might not be perfect English sentences. For example, "Amy looks happy girl" must be "Amy looks a happy girl", or, for the sentence "She is nice person", is better to have "She is a nice person". As we can see, these sentence will be more fluent, if the determiner "a" is added. Our solutions to this are: 1) we can use a language model which can fix this deficiency, 2) we can add an extra module in our system so that the user is able to add the determiner in the generated sentence.

3   Conclusion and Future Work

This paper presented a model for sentence generation to express emotions. Our model started with initial patterns, then constructed extended patterns. From the extended patterns, we chose good patterns suitable for generating emotion sentences. We also introduced a Sentence Planning module, which provides rules and constraints for our model. Sentence Planning will also need a module that ensures that a sentence is coherent, grammatically correct and fluent.

Finally, we presented some examples and results for our model. We showed that the model can generate various types of emotion sentences, either from semantic representation of input, or by choosing the pattern and the desired emotion class. The results indicate that our system generates fluent English emotion sentences, and some that require minor modifications, though they are still usable. For future work, we plan to extend our model to cover more patterns for English sentences, and to include more emotion categories.

References

1. Caropreso, M.F., Inkpen, D., Khan, S., Keshtkar, F.: Automatic generation of narrative content for digital games. In: IEEE NLP-KE 2009, Dalian, China (2009)
2. Caropreso, M.F., Inkpen, D., Khan, S., Keshtkar, F.: Visual development process for automatic generation of digital games narrative content. In: 47th ACL-IJCNLP Workshop, WS4, Singapore, August 2-7 (2009)

3. Elhadad, M.: Using Argumentation to Control Lexicon Choice. Ph.D. thesis, Columbia University, New York, USA (1994)
4. Gatt, A., Reiter, E.: Simplenlg: A realisation engine for practical applications. In: ENLG (2009)
5. Keshtkar, F., Inkpen, D.: A corpus-based method for extracting paraphrases of emotion terms. In: 11th NAACL-HLT 2010 Association for Computational Linguistics-Human Language Technologies, WS2: Computational Approaches to Analysis and Generation of Emotion in Text, Los Angeles, CA (June 2010)
6. Klein, D., Manning, C.D.: Fast exact inference with a factored model for natural language parsing. In: Advances in Neural Information Processing Systems, vol. 15, pp. 3–10. MIT Press, Cambridge (2003)
7. Mihalcea, R.: Co-training and self-training for word sense disambiguation. In: Natural Language Learning (CoNLL 2004), Boston (May 2004)
8. Penman: The penman user guide. Tech. rep., Technical Report, Information Science Institute, Marina Del ray, CA 90292 (1989)
9. Reiter, E.: An architecture for data-to-text systems. In: Proceedings of ENLG 2007, pp. 97–104 (2007)
10. Reiter, E., Dale, R.: Building Natural Language Generation Systems. Studies in Natural Language Processing. Cambridge University, Cambridge (2000)

Interpretations of Artificial Subtle Expressions (ASEs) in Terms of Different Types of Artifact: A Comparison of an on-screen Artifact with A Robot

Takanori Komatsu[1], Seiji Yamada[2], Kazuki Kobayashi[3],
Kotaro Funakoshi[4], and Mikio Nakano[4]

[1] Shinshu University, International Young Researcher Empowerment Center,
3-15-1 Tokida, Ueda 3868567, Japan
tkomat@shinshu-u.ac.jp
[2] National Institute of Informatics/ SOKENDAI/ Tokyo Intitute of Technology,
2-1-2 Hitotsubashi, Tokyo 1018430, Japan
seiji@nii.ac.jp
[3] Shinshu University, Graduate School of Engineering,
4-17 Wakasato, Nagano 3808553, Japan
kby@shinshu-u.ac.jp
[4] HONDA Research Institute Japan,
8-1 Honcho, Wako 3510188, Japan
{funakoshi,nakano}@jp.honda-ri.com

Abstract. We have already confirmed that the artificial subtle expressions (ASEs) from a robot can accurately and intuitively convey its internal states to participants [10]. In this paper, we then experimentally investigated whether the ASEs from an on-screen artifact could also convey the artifact's internal states to participants in order to confirm whether the ASEs can be consistently interpreted regardless of the types of artifacts. The results clearly showed that the ASEs expressed from an on-screen artifact succeeded in accurately and intuitively conveying the artifact's internal states to the participants. Therefore, we confirmed that the ASEs' interpretations were consistent regardless of the types of artifacts.

Keywords: Artificial subtle expressions (ASEs), interpretation, robot, on-screen artifact.

1 Introduction

Many studies concerning human communications have reported that small changes in the expressions of paralinguistic information (e.g., pitch and power of utterances) and nonverbal information (e.g., facial expressions, gaze directions, and gestures) can aid in facilitating smooth human communications especially in conveyance of one's internal states to others [1,2], and such simple information is called subtle expressions [3]. For example, Ward [4] reported that the subtle flections of the pitch information

S. D´Mello et al. (Eds.): ACII 2011, Part II, LNCS 6975, pp. 22–30, 2011.

in speech sounds reflect one's emotional states even when contradicted by the literal meanings of the speech sounds, and Cowell and Ayesh [5] offered a similar argument in terms of facial expressions. Some researchers then tried to implement such humans' subtle expressions in artifacts. For example, Kipp and Gebhard [6] developed a dexterous avatar agent that can slightly change its facial expression according to the user's gaze direction, and Sugiyama et al. [7] created a humanoid robot that can slightly change its behaviors based on its situational recognition. However, it can be easily imagined that these implementations costs were considerably expensive.

On the other hand, we have already found that the simple expressions from artifacts like beeping sounds or blinking LED's play similar roles to such human's subtle expressions [8,9]. Based on the results of these studies, we proposed "Artificial Subtle Expressions (ASEs)" as an intuitive notification methodology used to describe the internal states of artifacts for users [10]. In particular, we stipulated that ASEs are simple and low-cost expressions for artifacts that enable humans to accurately and intuitively estimate the internal states of artifacts, and then we were able to experimentally recognize that such ASEs had succeeded in accurately and intuitively conveying the internal states of a robot (i.e., confidence level of the suggestions) to the participants [10, 11]. We are now planning to implement these ASEs in various types of artifacts requiring communication with users; not only for robots but also for artifacts appearing on the display.

However, various studies have reported that different types of artifacts (e.g., robots vs. on-screen agents) evoke different attitudes or different impressions from users toward these artifacts. For example, Wainer et al. [12] reported that a robot was seen as most helpful, watchful, and enjoyable compared to an on-screen agent, while Shinozawa et al. [13] stated that the appropriate types of artifacts depended on their interactive situations. Thus, the issue of whether the ASEs can be utilized regardless of the types of artifacts still need to be investigated because we only confirmed that the ASEs expressed from a robot (MindStorms robot, LEGO Corporation) were effective in our former study [10].

The purpose of this study is then to investigate whether the ASEs expressed from an artifact appearing on a display (we call this artifact "on-screen artifact") could accurately and intuitively convey its internal states to participants, and to compare the results of this experiment with the ones of our former study. If we could find that the ASEs expressed from an on-screen artifact also succeeded in accurately and intuitively conveying its internal states to the participants like in our former study, we could conclude that the ASEs' interpretation is consistent regardless of the types of artifacts and that the ASEs can be utilized in various types of artifacts.

2   Experiment

2.1   Setting

We used a "driving treasure hunting" video game as an experimental environment to observe the participants' behavior (Figure 1). In this game, the game image scrolls forward on a straight road, which imitates the participant driving a car using a car navigation system (the left bottom of Figure 1), with small hills appearing along the way. A coin is inside one of the three hills, while the other two hills have nothing. The game ends after the participant encounters 20 sets of hills, and the approximate duration of this video game is about three minutes. The purpose is to get as many coins as possible. In this experiment, the participant was awarded 1 point for each coin that they found. The participants in this experiment were informed that 1 point was equivalent to 50 Japanese yen (about 50 US cents) and that after the experiment, they could use their points to purchase some stationery supplies (e.g., a ballpoint pen or mechanical pencil) of equivalent value.

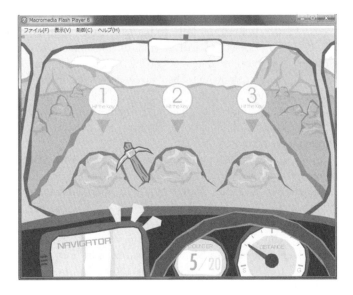

Fig. 1. Screenshot of driving treasure hunting video game

The position of the coin in the three hills was randomly assigned. In each trial, a car navigation system next to the driver's seat on the screen told them in which position it expected the coin to be placed. The navigation informed them of the expected position of the coin using speech sounds. The participants could freely accept or reject the navigation' suggestions. In each trial, even though the participants selected one hill among the three, they did not know whether the selected hill had the coin or not (actually, the selected hill just showed a question mark and a closed treasure box, as depicted in the center of Figure 2). The participants were informed of their total game points only after the experiment.

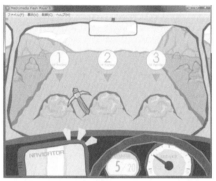

1. Encountering three hills

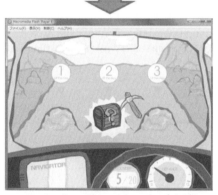

2. Selecting the 2nd hill (but not knowing whether this Selection was right or not)

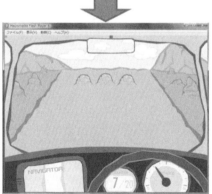

3. Walking to the next three hills

Fig. 2. Procedure of driving treasure hunting video game

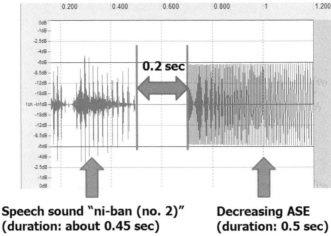

Fig. 3. Speech sound "ni-ban (no.2)" and ASE

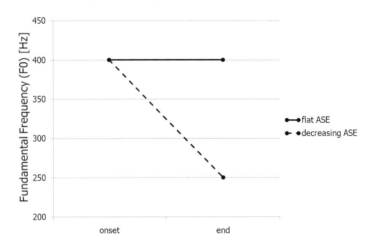

Fig. 4. Flat and decreasing ASEs (duration: 0.5 second)

2.2   Utilized ASE

We utilized the audio ASEs from the navigation system's speech sounds. In this experiment, the navigation system expressed artificial Japanese speech sounds to express the expected position of the coin; that is, "ichi-ban (no. 1)," "ni-ban (no. 2)," and "san-ban (no. 3)." These artificial speech sounds were created by the text-to-speech (TTS) function of the "Document Talker (Create System Development Company)." Just 0.2 seconds after these speech sounds, one of the two simple artificial sounds was played as the ASE (Figure 3). These two ASEs were triangular wave sounds 0.5 seconds in duration, but their pitch contours were different (Figure 4); that is, one was a flat sound (onset F0: 400 Hz and end F0: 400 Hz, called "flat

ASE"), and the other was a decreasing one (onset F0: 400 Hz and end F0: 250 Hz, called "decreasing ASE"). These ASE sounds were created by using "Cool Edit 2000 (Adobe Corporation)."

Actually, these speech sounds and the ASEs were the same as the ones that were used in our former study [10]. In that study, we already confirmed that the speech sounds with decreasing ASEs informed users of the robot's lower confidence in the suggestions given as the robot's internal states.

2.3 Procedure

Twenty Japanese university students (14 men and 6 women; 21 – 24 years old) participated. The driving treasure hunting video game was projected on a 46-inch LCD in front of the participants at a distance between them of approximately 100 cm (Figure 5). The navigation's speech sounds were played on the speaker equipped with this LCD, and the sound pressure of these speech sounds placed at the participants' head level was set to about 50 dB (FAST, A).

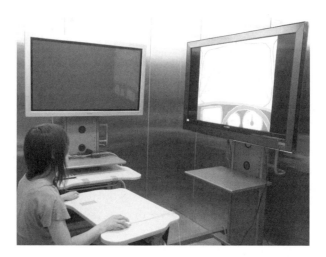

Fig. 5. Experimental Scene

Before the experiment started, the experimenter told the participants the settings and purpose of the game. However, the experimenter never mentioned or explained the ASEs. Therefore, the participants had no opportunity to acquire prior knowledge about the ASEs. Among the 20 trials, the navigation system used the flat ASE 10 times and the decreasing ASE 10 times. The order of expression for these two types of ASEs was counterbalanced among the participants.

For this experiment, the experimental stimuli and its procedure were completely the same as that in our former study [10], while the type of artifact for expressing the speech sounds with the ASEs was the only thing that was different. The purpose of this experiment was to observe the participants' behavior whether they accepted or rejected the navigation's suggestions in terms of the types of ASEs used; because, we already confirmed that the speech sounds with decreasing ASEs informed users of the robot's lower confidence in the suggestions given as the robot's internal states in our former study. Therefore, if we could observe the phenomenon where the participants would accept the navigation's suggestion when the flat ASE was added to the speech sounds while they would reject the suggestion when the decreasing ASE was used, we would be able to recognize that the utilized ASEs had succeeded in accurately and intuitively conveying the navigation's internal states to the participants.

3   Results

3.1   ASEs From an on-screen Artifact

To investigate the effect of the ASEs from the navigation as on-screen artifact on the participants' behavior, we calculated the rejection rate, indicating how many of the navigation's suggestions the participants rejected for the 10 flat ASEs and the 10 decreasing ASEs. For all 20 participants, the average rejection rate of the 10 flat ASEs was 1.75 (SD=1.61), while the rejection rate of the 10 decreasing ASEs was 4.35 (SD=2.76, Figure 6). These rejection rates for the 10 flat ASEs and 10 decreasing ASEs were then analyzed using a one-way analysis of variance (ANOVA) (within-subjects design; independent variable: type of ASE, flat or decreasing, dependent variable: rejection rate). The result of the ANOVA showed a significant difference between the two stimuli ($F(1,19)=8.16$, $p<.05$, (*)); that is, the on-screen artifact's suggestions when utilizing the decreasing ASE showed a significantly higher rejection rate compared to the ones with the flat ASE. Therefore, we could confirm that the ASEs expressed from an on-screen artifact also succeeded in accurately and intuitively conveying the artifact's internal states to the participants.

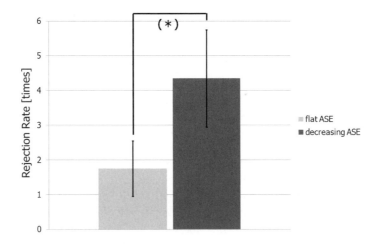

Fig. 6. Rejection rate for ASEs from on-screen artifact for all 20 participants

3.2   Comparison of an on-screen Artifact with a Robot

To investigate how the interpretations of the ASEs from an on-screen artifact were different with the ones from a robot, we compared the results from this experiment with the ones acquired in our former study [10]. In the former study, the average rejection rate of the 10 flat ASEs from the robot was 1.73 (SD=1.51), while the rejection rate of the 10 decreasing ASEs was 4.58 (SD=2.43). Since the participants in this paper did not participate in the former study and the utilized speech sounds and the ASEs were the completely same with ones utilized in the former study, these rejection rates acquired in this experiment and those in the former one were then analyzed using a 2 (independent variable in between-subjects factor: types of artifacts, on-screen artifact or robot) x 2 (independent variable in within-subjects factor: type of ASEs, flat or decreasing) mixed ANOVA (dependent variable: rejection rate). The results showed that there were no significant differences in the interaction effects (F(1,37)=0.04, n.s.) and in the main effect of "types of artifacts" (F(1,37)=0.08, n.s.), while there was a significant difference in the main effect of "types of ASEs" (F(1,37)=20.48, p<.01 (**)) (Figure 7). Thus, we could confirm that the ways of interpretation of the ASEs from the on-screen artifact were the same as the ones from a robot. In other words, the ASEs' interpretation was consistent regardless of the types of artifact.

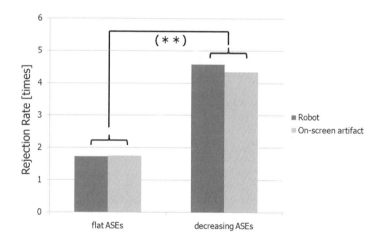

Fig. 7. Rejection rate for ASEs from an on-screen artifact and a robot

4   Discussion and Conclusions

We experimentally investigated whether the ASEs from the on-screen artifacts could convey the artifact's internal states to participants in order to confirm whether the ASEs can be interpreted consistently regardless of the types of artifacts. The results of the experiment clearly showed that the ASEs from an on-screen artifact succeeded in accurately and intuitively conveying its internal states to the participants. In addition, a comparison of the results from this experiment with ones in a former study showed that the ways of interpretations of the ASEs from an on-screen artifact were the same as the ones from a robot. In other words, the ASEs' interpretation was consistent regardless of the types of artifact. These results succeeded in strongly appealing the robustness and consistency of ASEs. Therefore, the experimental investigations in this paper strongly support this practical application of ASEs.

Now we are planning to implement the ASEs in various types of realistic applications requiring communication with their users; e.g., spoken dialogue systems such as ATMs or automatic reservation systems. In particular, we are now focusing on a car navigation system for the target application of ASEs, because current car navigation systems still sometimes present poor driving routes to their users. However, if this navigation system's confidence level regarding the route instruction is not very high, the speech instructions with the ASEs could implicitly convey a lower confidence level. If the ASEs are still effective in such situations, they could be utilized in realistic situations in which the artifacts have to convey their internal states to users.

References

1. Kendon, A.: Do gestures communicate? A Review. Research in Language and Social Interaction 27(3), 175–200 (1994)
2. Cohen, P.R., Morgen, J., Pollack, M.E.: Intentions in Communication. The MIT Press, MA (1990)
3. Liu, K., Picard, W.R.: Subtle expressivity in a robotic computer. In: Proc. CHI 2003 Workshop on Subtle Expressivity for Characters and Robots, pp. 1–5 (2003)
4. Ward, N.: On the Expressive Competencies Needed for Responsive Systems. In: Proc. CHI 2003 Workshop on Subtle Expressivity for Characters and Robots, pp. 33–34 (2003)
5. Cowell, J., Ayesh, A.: Extracting subtle expressions for emotional analysis. In: Proc. 2004 IEEE SMC, vol. (1), pp. 677–681 (2004)
6. Kipp, M., Gebhard, P.: IGaze: Studying reactive gaze behavior in semi-immersive human-avatar interactions. In: Prendinger, H., Lester, J.C., Ishizuka, M. (eds.) IVA 2008. LNCS (LNAI), vol. 5208, pp. 191–199. Springer, Heidelberg (2008)
7. Sugiyama, O., Kanda, T., Imai, M., Ishiguro, H., Hagita, N., Anzai, Y.: Humanlike conversation with gestures and verbal cues based on a three-layer attention-drawing model. Connection Science 18(4), 379–402 (2006)
8. Komatsu, T., Yamada, S.: How do robotic agents' appearances affect people's interpretation of the agents' attitudes? In: Ext. Abstracts CHI 2007, pp. 2519–2524. ACM Press, New York (2007)
9. Funakoshi, K., Kobayashi, K., Nakano, M., Yamada, S., Kitamura, Y., Tsujino, H.: Smoothing human-robot speech interactions by using blinking-light as subtle expression. In: Proc. ICMI 2008, pp. 293–296. ACM Press, New York (2008)
10. Komatsu, T., Yamada, S., Kobayashi, T., Funakoshi, K., Nakano, M.: Artificial Subtle Expressions: Intuitive Notification Methodology of Artifacts. In: Proc. CHI 2010, pp. 1941–1944. ACM Press, New York (2010)
11. Funakoshi, K., Kobayashi, K., Nakano, M., Komatsu, T., Yamada, S.: Non- humanlike Spoken Dialogue: a Design Perspective. In: Proc. SIGDIAL 2010 (2010) (to appear)
12. Wainer, J., Feil-Seifer, D.J., Shell, D.A., Mataric, M.J.: Embodiment and Human-Robot Interaction: A Task-Based Perspective. In: Proc. IEEE ROMAN 2007, pp. 872–877 (2007)
13. Shinozawa, K., Naya, F., Yamato, J., Kogure, K.: Differences in effects of robot and screen agent recommendations on human decision-making. International Journal of Human-Computer Studies 62, 267–279 (2004)

Affective State Recognition in Married Couples' Interactions Using PCA-Based Vocal Entrainment Measures with Multiple Instance Learning

Chi-Chun Lee[1], Athanasios Katsamanis[1], Matthew P. Black[1],
Brian R. Baucom[2], Panayiotis G. Georgiou[1], and Shrikanth S. Narayanan[1,2]

[1]Signal Analysis and Interpretation Laboratory (SAIL), Los Angeles, CA, USA
[2]Department of Psychology, University of Southern California, Los Angeles, CA, USA
http://sail.usc.edu

Abstract. Recently there has been an increase in efforts in Behavioral Signal Processing (BSP), that aims to bring quantitative analysis using signal processing techniques in the domain of observational coding. Currently observational coding in fields such as psychology is based on subjective expert coding of abstract human interaction dynamics. In this work, we use a Multiple Instance Learning (MIL) framework, a saliency-based prediction model, with a signal-driven vocal entrainment measure as the feature to predict the affective state of a spouse in problem solving interactions. We generate 18 MIL classifiers to capture the variable-length *saliency* of vocal entrainment, and a cross-validation scheme with maximum accuracy and mutual information as the metric to select the *best* performing classifier for each testing couple. This method obtains a recognition accuracy of 53.93%, a 2.14% (4.13% relative) improvement over baseline model using Support Vector Machine. Furthermore, this MIL-based framework has potential for identifying meaningful regions of interest for further detailed analysis of married couples interactions.

Keywords: multiple instance learning, vocal entrainment, couple's therapy, behavioral signal processing (BSP), affective recognition.

1   Introduction

There has been an increasing effort in bridging the manual observation coding of human behaviors done in various mental health applications [10], such as couple therapy and autism spectrum disorder diagnosis, with the automatic annotation of abstract human behaviors/states using signal processing techniques, such as emotion recognition, using low level behavioral cues [8,5,13]. Manual observation coding done by the domain experts provides a subjective and detailed analysis of human-human behaviors/interactions in terms of various annotated attributes of interest, while automatic annotation using cues derived directly from observed signals provides a objective and quantitative analysis. Previous works [1,7,12]

S. D'Mello et al. (Eds.): ACII 2011, Part II, LNCS 6975, pp. 31–41, 2011.

have shown the effectiveness of applying machine learning techniques in predicting various behavioral ratings in married couples engaging in problem-solving interactions, e.g., blame, negativity, positivity, approach, avoidance, etc, using different variants of directly observed low level behavioral descriptors. There are two main goals in this present work. The first goal is to apply a suitable machine learning technique using signal-derived measures of vocal entrainment calculated at the speaking turn-level to predict the overall session-level codes of negativity/positivity of a spouse; result of this investigation could provide evidence of engineering utility of such a signal-derived entrainment measure. Second, since entrainment has been shown [3] to play a crucial role in analyzing marital communications, multiple instance learning (MIL) presents itself as an appealing framework because of its ability to identify *saliency* as it performs predictions. This potential advantage when combined with features that carry meaningful insights into the study of marital communication, can offer an opportunity to perform detailed analysis on these salient regions generated through MIL.

Multiple instance learning (MIL) is a widely used machine learning technique that has shown its effectiveness in pattern recognition applications such as drug activity estimation and image retrieval [11,15]. MIL is different from the traditional supervised learning technique, where an instance is associated with a label. In MIL, the label is associated with a bag that consists of multiple instances, and there is no explicit label given to each instance as training. This framework is appealing in working with session-level behavioral code prediction while the individual speaking turn annotation is unavailable. Furthermore, MIL can often be solved in a general way by using Diverse Density introduced in Maron and Lozano-Perez's [11] work. This involves in finding a concept point in the feature space that is close to at least one instance from every positive bag and far away from instances in negative bags. This concept point can be viewed as the *salient* points for a given bag label, and is used to identify the *salient* instances of a bag. This formulation of MIL along with the usage of vocal entrainment features can help identify the meaningful *salient* vocal entrainment measures to offer interpretable insights into regions of interest of couples' interactions while performing prediction on spouse's affective state.

In this work, we focus our recognition task using a vocal entrainment measure on sessions in which the spouse was rated with *high positive* or *high negative* affect. We utilize signal-derived vocal entrainment measures [9] as the only describing feature per instance in a MIL framework. Furthermore, our formulation allows a salient *instance* span not only a single speaking turn but multiple turns. We have applied a leave-one-couple out cross validation within training along with maximum accuracy and mutual information criteria to select the best performing classifier out of multiple MIL-based classifiers trained with different features lengths of *instances* for each training fold. The proposed method obtains a 53.93% accuracy, which is 3.93% (7.86% relative) over chance and 2.14% (4.13% relative) over a baseline Support Vector Machine (SVM) based classifier. This MIL-based classification scheme provides a method for performing classification through identification of a *best* MIL classifier, each classifier is learned with variable-length salient instances of vocal entrainment. The method is able to obtain a fair recognition accuracy with vocal entrainment as the *only* features, and the classification result identifies interpretable saliency.

The paper is organized as follows: section 2 describes the database and research methodology. Experiment setup and results are discussed in section 3, and conclusions are in section 4.

2 Research Methodology

2.1 Database

The data that we are using was collected as part of the largest longitudinal, randomized control trial of psychotherapy for severely and stably distressed couples [2]. A total of 569 sessions consisting of 117 unique real married couples engaging in ten-minute problem solving interactions, in which they discussed a problem in their marriage. The corpus consists of manual word transcriptions, split-screen videos, and a single channel far-field audio of varying quality across sessions. Furthermore, both spouses were evaluated with 33 session-level codes using two standard manual codings, the Social Support Interaction Rating System (SSIRS) and the Couples Interaction Rating System (CIRS), with multiple trained evaluators. Details of this database are described in the previous work [1]. The audio data is automatically aligned with the word-level transcripts using the system *SailAlign* developed at SAIL [6]. *SailAlign* takes in the manual word transcriptions and automatically performs iterative word alignment to the whole session of audio data, and as a result, pseudo-turns are generated with speaker identifications (3 categories: husband, wife, unknown). These automatically aligned pseudo-turns are used as *speaking turns* in our research work. After this automatic process, 372 sessions out of 569 sessions are considered as *good* sessions to be used to conduct research because they meet the criteria of 5 dB signal-to-noise ratio (SNR) and at least 55% of the words within each session are successfully aligned.

The focus of this work is to utilize a quantification measure of vocal entrainment to predict extreme affective state (positive & negative), based on "Global Positive" and "Global Negative" code from SSIRS, of each spouse in married couples' interactions. Instead of working with the original 9-point scale rating, we transform it into a binary classification problem in which we take top 20% of positive and negative rated wife and husband. This results in a total of 140 (70 ratings on husband, 70 ratings on wife) sessions of *high positive* and 140 (70 ratings on husband, 70 ratings on wife) sessions of *high negative*. This accounts for a total of 280 interaction sessions with 81 unique couples, and it is the classification dataset of interest for this paper.

2.2 Multiple Instance Learning

In this section, we describe a brief summary of the multiple instance learning (MIL) in the context of predicting spouses' session-level affective states. MIL is a learning algorithm to handle a classification situation where a label is associated with a bag consisting of multiple unlabeled instances rather than the more common scenario of associating a label with every training instance. The traditional formulation of MIL in a binary classification task (positive (1) vs. negative (0)) is that, a bag is labeled as positive if at least one instance in that bag is positive, and the bag is negative if only all instances are labeled as negative. A general way to solve the MIL problem is with the use of maximization of *Diverse Density* (DD) function [11] with respect to a concept point t – a point in the feature space that is close to at least one instance from every positive bag and far away from instances in negative bags. The maximization of the diverse density function $(DD(t))$ is defined as follows, where B_i^+, B_i^- denote the positive, negative bag, B_{ij}^+, B_{ij}^- denote the jth instance in bag i, and assuming the bag label are indexed as logical 0 and 1.

$$\operatorname*{argmax}_{t} DD(t) = \operatorname*{argmax}_{t} \prod_{i} P(t|B_i^+) \prod_{i} P(t|B_i^-)$$

$$P(t|B_i^+) = 1 - \prod_{j}(1 - P(B_{ij}^+))$$

$$P(t|B_i^-) = \prod_{j}(1 - P(B_{ij}^-))$$

$$P(t|B_{ij}^+) = \exp(-||B_{ij}^+ - t||^2)$$

Since there is no closed-form solution for this optimization, a gradient ascent method is often used to find the local maximum of DD function with respect to this concept point, t. In this work, we utilize a method called Expectation-Maximization Diverse Density (EM-DD) [15], in which the knowledge of which instance determines the label of the bag is modeled using a set of hidden variables that are estimated using the Expectation-Maximization framework.

The crucial assumptions of this MIL framework is that the single *most positive* instance in a bag determines whether a bag is positive, meaning if at least one of the instances in the bag has the probability of being positive > 0.5, the bag is labeled as positive. While there are variants in MIL that relax this assumption, this standard formulation is intuitively appealing. This approach, allows us to perform session-level affective code prediction without explicit labels at individual speaking-turns and also identify the most *salient* instance of vocal entrainment that determines the session-level affective code.

2.3   PCA-Based Signal-Derived Vocal Entrainment Measures

In this work, we used a feature that is based on the quantification of vocal entrainment for each spouse at the turn level using Principal Component Analysis (PCA) on vocal features. We have shown that this signal derived feature is indeed a viable quantification method of the often qualitatively-described vocal entrainment phenomenon [9] during interpersonal interactions. In order to compute the

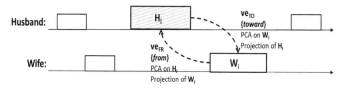

Fig. 1. Example of Computing Two Directions of Vocal Entrainment for Turns H_i

PCA-based vocal entrainment features, there are two major steps: first is to construct the speaking characteristics space, and second is to project the other speaker's vocal features on this constructed vocal characteristic space. There can be two directions (*toward, from*) of vocal entrainment in a dyadic interaction; for example, at a husband's turn seen in Figure 1, H_i, he can be entraining toward wife's speech, denoted as *toward*, and wife's speech can also becoming entraining toward this husband's speech segment, denoted as*from*. Figure 1 shows an example of computing the two directions of vocal entrainment, ve_{TO}, ve_{FR}, for husband's speech at turn H_i in an interaction session. The following is the list of steps in computing the husband's ve_{TO} at turn H_i:

1. Extract appropriate vocal features, X_1, to represent the husband's speaking characteristics at turn H_i.
2. Perform PCA on z-normalized X_1, such that $Y_1^T = D_1 X_1^T$.
3. Predefine a variance level ($v_1 = 0.95$) to select L-subset of basis vectors, D_{1L}.
4. Project the z-normalized vocal features, X_2 extracted from wife's speech at turn W_i, using D_{1L}.
5. Compute the vocal entrainment measure as the ratio of represented variance of X_2, in W_{1L} basis, and the predefined variance level in step 3.

In order to compute the husband's ve_{FR} at turn H_i, we just need to swap X_1 with X_2 of the above steps. The vocal features representing speaking characteristics include polynomial stylization of pitch contour and statistical functionals computed for energy and MFCC per word. Detailed of this data-driven PCA-based vocal entrainment measure can be found another of our paper on analyzing vocal entrainment in marital communication [9].

2.4   MIL Classifiers Setup and Selection

As discussed in Section 2.2, if we treat a *high positive* emotion label as the *positive bag* in the standard MIL framework, a salient vocal entrainment will predict positive emotion, and lack of such salient vocal entrainment will predict negative emotions. It is desirable to retain this framework of understanding saliency especially because the features themselves carry meaningful insights into the analysis of couples' interactions. However, we have made two modifications in an effort to relax the assumption of the standard MIL framework.

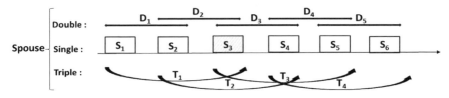

Fig. 2. A Diagram of MIL Classifier Setup

- While a salient instance can be the deciding factor of predicting *high positive* emotion, at the same time, conversely, a salient instance of *high negative* emotion may be the most informative predictor of *high negative* emotion. Hence, for a given fixed set of features, we train two MIL classifiers with bag labels reversed (0 becomes 1, and 1 becomes 0).
- While a *single* turn window of vocal entrainment features can be used to predict the affective state, multiple-length windows of vocal entrainment can be more informative predictors. Hence, we train three MIL classifiers, *single, double, triple* using entrainment features with an instance span of up to three turns.

Figure 2 shows a schematic diagram of the classifiers set up described above: for predicting a spouse's affective rating (a bag), three different turn lengths (defining an instance) of features will be used (shown as *single, double triple*), and within each instance three different types of vocal entrainment features will be used ({*toward*}, {*from*}, {*toward & from*}). For each of this MIL classifier, we swap the bag labels as described above. This in total generate ($3 \times 3 \times 2 = 18$) 18 classifiers. We select the one best performing MIL classifier based on maximum accuracy and mutual information through cross validation within training. As an example of how this framework can be used to locate saliency is referred in Figure 2. Assuming for a testing couple, through this MIL classifier setup and selection, the best performing classifier is based on *single* vocal entrainment features. The selected classifier predicts the spouse as having *high positive* emotion code because S_3 is a salience instance determining the overall bag label of *positive emotion* of the spouse. This saliency, S_3, turn in the session can then be treated as a region of interest for further analyzing for entrainment occurrence.

3   Experiment Setups and Results

Two different experiments were set up to evaluate the effectiveness of the MIL classification framework described in Section 2 in recognizing each spouse's affective state (*high positive* vs. *high negative*). In all of the experiments, the evaluation scheme was based on leave-one-couple-out cross validation (81 folds). The selection of the *best* classifier to be used in performing recognition for each testing fold was based on the leave-one-couple-out cross validation (80 folds) within training. The evaluation metric is the percentage (%) of accurately recognized spouse' affective ratings. EM-DD was trained using the MILL [14] software.

- **Experiment I :** Evaluate the performance of the proposed MIL classification scheme compared to different methods of selecting the *best* classifiers out of the 18 MIL classifiers.
- **Experiment II:** Evaluate the performance of the proposed MIL classification scheme compared to using different lengths of turns as features for each instance.

3.1   Experiment I Setup

The main assumption underlying Experiment I is that since there can be a large variability between each couple as they interact in their own norm, a different classifier is required to perform the recognition of the affective state of each spouse. As described in Section 2.3, 18 different classifiers were trained, and the proposed method of classifier selection was based on maximum accuracy with mutual information as tie breaker. In this experiment, we compared the proposed method with the following classifier selection technique:

- *Baseline*: SVM-based classifier using nine statistical functionals (mean, variance, range, maximum, minimum, 25% quantile, 75% quantile, interquartile range, median) computed per session of one specific type of entrainment measures (*toward*).
- *Voting*: Majority voting on 18 classifiers' results to assign the session label.
- *Same* MIL classifier for entire training folds: pick the classifier that occurs the most (out of 81 folds), in which it obtains the maximum accuracy in each fold. (Denoted in Table 1 by ONE_{maxA}).
- *Different* MIL classifiers for each training fold: pick the classifier according to our selection criterion (Denoted in Table 1 by Proposed).

3.2   Experiment I Result

A summary of the result of Experiment I is in Table 1. Several observations can be made with the results from Experiment I. First is that the absolute recognition rate is not very high, which may have been due to the fact that there is essentially only one type of feature used in this work. It is promising to see that our proposed method based on MIL framework achieves a 3.93% absolute (7.86% relative) improvement over chance and a 2.14% (4.13% relative) improvement over the

Table 1. Summary of Experiment I Result

Classifier	Accuracy (%)
Chance	50.00%
Baseline SVM	51.79%
Majority Voting	44.64%
ONE_{maxA}	50.71%
Proposed	**53.93%**

baseline model although significance testing using difference of proportion does not show the result significantly higher than the baseline at the $\alpha = 0.05$ level.

The results indicate that these signal-derived vocal entrainment measures possess some discriminative power in recognizing the spouse's affective state. Second, the baseline model used nine commonly-used statistical functionals computed at the session level with a SVM (radial basis function kernel), which serves as baseline of *not* using salient instances for prediction. While the comparison is not perfectly fair without optimizing SVM parameters, it is still encouraging that we obtain a better recognition accuracy through this saliency-based classification scheme. Furthermore, the majority voting over 18 classifiers obtains a performance less than chance indicates that a single optimized classifier per interacting couple is essential in achieving better accuracy.

3.3   Experiment II Setup

In this experiment, we examined the idea that a *salient* instance can occur at longer intervals, here measured in number of consecutive turns. The maximum number of turns considered for training of the MIL classifier was three, determined empirically. We compare the the three sets of classifiers (*Single, Double, Triple* as shown in Figure 2 described in Section 2.4 with the proposed combined set of classifiers.

- *Single*: Includes classifiers trained on vocal entrainment features only for one turn for a given rated spouse.
- *Double*: Includes classifiers trained on vocal entrainment features only for two turns for a given rated spouse.
- *Triple*: Includes classifiers trained on vocal entrainment features only for three turns for a given rated spouse.
- *Proposed*: Includes all 18 classifiers

3.4   Experiment II Result

Table 2 shows the accuracies of different sets of classifiers.

There are a few points to be noted by observing Table 2. When we considered the *Single, Double, Triple*-only classifier set, none of the classifier sets by itself is

Table 2. *Summary of Experiment II Results.*

Classifier	Accuracy (%)
Chance	50.00%
Baseline SVM	51.79%
Single	47.50%
Double	45.36%
Triple	47.86%
Proposed	**53.93%**

able to obtain a recognition rate better than chance. However, by considering all three sets of classifiers to perform classifier selection, we achieve the best performance. This bears implication that *salient* instances do span multiple turns, and that they differ from couple to couple. In fact, out of 81 folds cross-validation, 38 folds (46.91%) used *Single* classifier set, 31 folds (38.27%) used *Double* classifier set, and 12 folds (14.81%) used *Triple* classifier set. Experiment II shows that it is beneficial to consider multiple turns of vocal entrainment in this MIL framework to perform the binary classification on affective states of the spouses when working with disjoints set of couples in training and testing.

From Table 1 and Table 2, it is understood that the PCA-based vocal entrainment feature of itself may not be optimal to provide the discriminant power in recognizing affective state. In fact, the study [4] shows that higher-level of entrainment may not actually always correspond to the positive outcome of couples interaction, and it indeed is a complex relationship between entrainment and emotions. It is, however, still encouraging to observe that through the use of vocal entrainment measures with this proposed MIL framework, we are able to retain the original concept of identifying saliency within an interaction and also, through a couple of intuitive modifications, obtain an improved recognition accuracy over the baseline model. Further analysis on what specific roles or any temporal characteristic of these identified *salient* vocal entrainment episodes play in terms of affective states of the married couples will be very important.

4 Conclusion and Future Work

Experts in psychology often derive a set of subjective attributes to annotate specific behavior patterns to understand human interaction dynamics; this process of behavioral coding is an important human analytical instrument. Machine pattern recognition in behavioral signal processing aims to learn from a set of objective signals/cues in order to predict abstract human mental states. In this work, we focus on a specific method in bridging between these two aspects – human and machine analysis of behavior patterns– using a signal-derived vocal entrainment measure to represent an attribute of interest. We apply a multiple instance learning method to learn the salient portion of this attribute in predicting the session-level affective rating of each spouse in a dataset of married couple interactions. A classification scheme based on MIL is used in this paper to utilize salient instances of vocal entrainment measures of variable turn lengths to obtain the best performing classification accuracy. As described in Section 3, through the usage of this MIL framework, we achieve an overall 53.93% recognition rate.

This work has many possible future directions. The first is to gain further improvements through inclusion of other interpretable and meaningful attributes with signal-derived approximations, such as arousal level, expected interacting behaviors and possible deviation from the normal behaviors. This combined with the proposed MIL framework will be essential to provide the region of interest in an interaction and highlight the various attributes that experts in psychology can concentrate to perform their analysis. Furthermore, this MIL framework selects *one* best classifier for each testing couple from the assumption that salient instances happen at variable turn lengths. This can be further relaxed to devise a technique to incorporate such notion in the MIL framework itself instead of performing classifier selection. Pin-pointing *salient* instances, especially in the framework of predicting using meaningful attributes describing an interaction, is essential in the detailed study of deeper understanding of various observation-driven codes that describe human interaction dynamics.

Acknowledgments. This research was supported in part by funds from the National Science Foundation, the Viterbi Research Innovation Fund, and the U.S Army.

References

1. Black, M.P., Katsamanis, A., Lee, C.C., Lammert, A.C., Baucom, B.R., Christensen, A., Georgiou, P.G., Narayanan, S.S.: Automatic classification of married couples' behavior using audio features. In: Proceedings of Interspeech (2010)
2. Christensen, A., Atkins, D., Berns, S., Wheeler, J., Baucom, D.H., Simpson, L.: Traditional versus integrative behavioral couple therapy for significantly and chronically distressed married couples. J. of Consulting and Clinical Psychology 72, 176–191 (2004)
3. Eldridge, K., Baucom, B.: Couples and consequences of the demand-withdraw interaction pattern. In: Positive Pathways for Couples and Families: Meeting the Challenges of Relationships. Wiley-Blackwell (in press)
4. Gottman, J.M.: The roles of conflict engagement, escalation, and avoidance in marital interaction: A longitudinal view of five types of couples. Journal of Consulting and Clinical Psychology 61(1), 6–15 (1993)
5. Grimm, M., Kroschel, K., Mower, E., Narayanan, S.: Primitives-based evaluation and estimation of emotions in speech. Speech Communication 49(10-11), 787–800 (2007)
6. Katsamanis, A., Black, M.P., Georgiou, P.G., Goldstein, L., Narayanan, S.S.: SailAlign: Robust long speech-text alignment. In: Very-Large-Scale Phonetics Workshop (January 2011)
7. Lee, C.C., Black, M.P., Katsamanis, A., Lammert, A.C., Baucom, B.R., Christensen, A., Georgiou, P.G., Narayanan, S.S.: Quantification of prosodic entrainment in affective spontaneous spoken interactions of married couples. In: Proceedings of Interspeech (2010)
8. Lee, C.M., Narayanan, S.S.: Toward detecting emotions in spoken dialogs. IEEE Transactions on Speech and Audio Processing 13(2), 293–303 (2005)
9. Lee, C.C., Katsamanis, A., Black, M.P., Baucom, B.R., Georgiou, P.G., Narayanan, S.S.: An analysis of PCA-based vocal entrainment measures in married couples' affective spoken interactions. In: Proceedings of Interspeech (2011)
10. Margolin, G., Oliver, P., Gordis, E., O'Hearn, H., Medina, A., Ghosh, C., Morland, L.: The nuts and bolts of behavioral observation of marital and family interaction. Clinical Child and Family Psychology Review 1(4), 195–213 (1998)
11. Maron, O., Lozano-Pérez, T.: A framework for multiple-instance learning. In: Advances in Neural Information Processing Systems, pp. 570–576 (1998)

12. Rozgić, V., Xiao, B., Katsamanis, A., Baucom, B., Georgiou, P.G., Narayanan, S.S.: Estimation of ordinal approach-avoidance labels in dyadic interactions: Ordinal logistic regression approach. In: ICASSP (2011)
13. Schuller, B., Batliner, A., Seppi, D., Steidl, S., Vogt, T., Wagner, J., Devillers, L., Vidrascu, L., Amir, N., Kessous, L.: The relevance of feature type for automatic classification of emotional user states: Low level descriptors and functionals. In: Proceedings of Interspeech (2007)
14. Yang, J.: MILL: A multiple instance learning library, http://www.cs.cmu.edu/~juny/MILL/index.html
15. Zhang, Q., Goldman, S.: EM-DD: An improved multiple-instance learning technique. In: Advances in Neural Information Processing Systems, vol. 2, pp. 1073–1080 (2002)

A Comparison of Unsupervised Methods to Associate Colors with Words

Gözde Özbal[1], Carlo Strapparava[1], Rada Mihalcea[2], and Daniele Pighin[3]

[1] FBK, Trento, Italy
[2] UNT, Denton TX, USA
[3] UPC, Barcelona, Spain

Abstract. Colors have a very important role on our perception of the world. We often associate colors with various concepts at different levels of consciousnes and these associations can be relevant to many fields such as education and advertisement. However, to the best of our knowledge, there are no systematic approaches to aid the automatic development of resources encoding this kind of knowledge. In this paper, we propose three computational methods based on image analysis, language models, and latent semantic analysis to automatically associate colors to words. We compare these methods against a gold standard obtained via crowd-sourcing. The results show that each method is effective in capturing different aspects of word-color associations.

1 Introduction

Colors have a significant effect in our daily lives and the way we perceive the world is strongly connected to their presence. Several psycholinguistic studies [9,1,7,15] have demonstrated a deep connection between colors and emotions. This connection is generally not straightforward, in the sense that it is not easy to directly map colors to emotions. On the other hand, we typically build associations between colors and words and, in turn, between words and emotions. As an example, by establishing a connection between *black* and *darkness* or *death*, and by observing that these two words are often associated with *fear*, we could automatically link the color *black* to *fear*. In this respect, the investigation of the relation between words and colors is a very important step towards the automatic connotation of the emotional content of a word.

However, to our knowledge, there is no resource that contains information about the association of words and colors. Such a resource could be important for many applications. For instance, it could be useful for several educational purposes such as attracting attention, facilitating the memorization process by triggering the visual memory in addition to the verbal memory [14]. This resource could also be used for advertising by automatically coloring advertisement texts based on the appropriate colors, according to the common sense knowledge or the emotion that we wish to convey. Word-color associations could also be used as features in algorithms for automatic image tagging [10].

In this paper, we propose three methods to automatically associate colors and words in English, and compare their performances. Each of these three methods

S. D'Mello et al. (Eds.): ACII 2011, Part II, LNCS 6975, pp. 42–51, 2011.

has the potential to emphasize different aspects of the chromatic connotation of words. The first is based on the distribution of colors in images retrieved from the web, and we expect it to effectively capture the visual features that are characteristic of a concept. The second method exploits the point-wise mutual information of words and colors observed in bi-grams extracted from the web. It is able to model the usage of color-words (e.g. "green" or "blue") as attributive modifiers for the words. The last method relies on the calculation of the semantic similarity between words and colors and it can describe more abstract properties of conceptual associations between them. We compare these three methods against a gold standard that we obtain using the crowdsourcing service provided by the Amazon Mechanical Turk.[1]

The rest of the paper is structured as follows. In Section 2, we review previous work relevant to this task. In section 4, we describe the three methods we propose. In section 3, we detail the annotation process and the evaluation framework. In section 5, we discuss the results of the evaluation. Finally, in Section 6, we draw conclusions and outline ideas for possible future work.

2 Related Work

There has been a considerable interest in psycholinguistics addressing the impact of colors on emotions. Among the most notable studies, Kaya [9] tried to investigate the association between colors and emotions by carrying out experiments where college students were asked to indicate their emotional responses to principal, intermediate and achromatic colors, and the reasons for their choices. Alt [1] focused on the topic "emotional responses to colors used in advertisement." The results showed that the color of the advertisement affected the emotional responses of the consumers of a product. It was also observed that ethnicity and culture affected the color preferences of consumers. Following the same direction, Gao et al. [7] analyzed and compared the *color emotions* (the relationships between colors and emotions) of people from seven regions in a psychophysical experiment, with an attempt to clarify the influences of culture and color perception attributes on color emotions. Soriano and Valenzuela [15] investigated why there is often a relationship between color and emotion words in different languages, while Xin et al. [17] compared the color emotional responses which were obtained by conducting visual experiments in different regions based on a set of color samples. Madden et al. [11] focused on the possible power of colors for creating and sustaining brand and corporate images in international marketing. This study explored the favorite colors of consumers from different countries, the meanings they associated with colors, and their color preferences for a logo.

In addition to all these studies focusing on the association of colors and emotions, to the best of our knowledge there is only one [8] focusing on the automatic acquisition of colors associated with words. It attempts to find the typical colors of objects by exploiting co-occurrence data on the web. More specifically, it proposes to concatenate nouns with a set of color words used in image processing.

---

[1] https://www.mturk.com/mturk/welcome

Table 1. Percentage of words in each majority class

majority class	1	2	3	4	5	6	7	8	9	10
% of words	0	0.5	2	10.5	16.5	13	22	15	16.5	4

Thereby, it aims to explore the mapping between the ordinary text and visible color spectrum. The results show that common-sense colors of objects are often reflected by the textual data on the web.

Regarding the automatic association of colors and emotions, Strapparava and Özbal [16] conducted an empirical study to check the similarity of colors and emotions. Their main goal was to explore whether state-of-the-art corpus analysis techniques could give support to psycholinguistic experiments. Thus, they investigated the correlation of their results with the outcomes of a psycholinguistic experiment [1]. Considering that these experiments are very costly since a lot of resources are required for setup and evaluation, employing a corpus-based approach for affective sensing could be much more efficient for any future analyses. To achieve this, they compared the similarities between the representations of colors and emotions in the latent similarity space (see Section 4.3) and obtained a quite high correlation with the psycholinguistic experiment reported in [1].

3 Evaluation Framework

The assignment of color properties to words is an unexplored task, and hence there is no standard evaluation framework that we can use to test our methods. We thus create our own dataset, and also propose a set of evaluation metrics that are appropriate for the task.

3.1 Data

We selected a subset of the words used in the experiments described in [8], which consist of 200 words covering different linguistic aspects (frequent/rare words, different parts-of-speech, concrete/abstract words, etc.)

For the annotation, we used the Amazon Mechanical Turk service, and created a task including all 200 words. Inspired by the work of [13], for each word we asked two questions: a first question meant to verify the quality of the annotation (and thus avoid random spam annotations), and also pinpoint the intended meaning of the word, followed by a second question where the color annotations were requested. The colors used for the second question belonged to the list of 11 basic colors defined by [2], namely white, black, red, green, yellow, blue, brown, pink, purple, orange and grey. For instance, assuming the word *plant* with the meaning of *living organism*, the following questions would be asked:

1. Select the most appropriate word to fill in the blank:
   plant is a: (a) *set*, (b) *living organism*, (c) *message*

2. Select at least one or at most three colors that best represent *plant* among: *white, black, red, green, yellow, blue, brown, pink, purple, orange, gray*

The annotators were instructed to choose all the colors (up to three) that could be associated with a word. If more than three colors were possible, they were asked to choose the three most related ones. If a word has an abstract meaning and does not have a specific color, the annotators were asked to choose the color they think of when they visualize the word in their mind. Finally, for words with more than one meaning, they had to consider the meaning indicated by the correct answer in the first question. The dataset was annotated by ten different annotators. We only considered the annotations for the items where the first question was answered correctly.

To have a concrete idea about the agreement between annotators, we calculated the majority class of each term in our data set. The resulting statistics are shown in Table 1. A word belongs to majority class k if the most frequent annotation for that word was selected by k annotators. For example, the most frequent color assigned to the word *grass* is *green*. Since 9 annotators have selected this color, the word *green* belongs to majority class 9. A large percentage of words belonging to high majority classes is symptomatic of good inter-annotator agreement. Considering that 10 annotators were involved, we can consider as very reliable all the annotations having majority class greater than 5. In fact, in these cases the absolute majority of annotators has selected the same color. By looking at Table 1 we can observe that 70.5% of the annotations fall in this category. This high agreement among annotators suggests that the annotation task was well designed and that the resulting dataset is reliable.

3.2 Evaluation Measures

We define the evaluation framework based on the intuition that a word can be associated with one or more colors. Ideally, there is a single color that "best" defines the word, but there can be also multiple colors that describe features of the target word.

Our evaluation framework is inspired by the lexical substitution task [12], where a system attempts to generate a word (or a set of words) to replace a target word, such that the meaning of the sentence is preserved. Given this analogy, the evaluation metrics used for lexical substitution can be adapted to the evaluation of image tagging. Specifically, we adopt the *best* and out-of-ten (reformulated as out-of-three, *oot*) precision and recall scores from [12]. For a given method, we allow as many colors as the algorithm feels fit for the target word, and the credit is given depending on the number of annotators who picked that color as well as the number of annotator responses for the item, and the number of answers provided by the system.

The *best* scorer gives credit to only one best answer. If the system provides several answers, the credit is divided among them. The *oot* scorer allows up to three system responses and does not divide the credit for an answer by the number of system responses.

Formally, if i is an item in the set of instances I, and T_i is the multiset of gold standard synonym expansions from the human annotators for i, and a system provides a set of answers S_i for i, then the BEST score for item i is:

$$best(i) = \frac{\sum_{s \in S_i} freq(s \in T_i)}{|S_i| \cdot |T_i|} \quad ; \quad oot(i) = \frac{\sum_{s \in S_i} freq(s \in T_i)}{|T_i|} \qquad (1)$$

Precision is calculated by summing the scores for each item and dividing by the number of items that the system attempted whereas recall divides the sum of scores for each item by $|I|$. Thus:

$$precision = \frac{\sum_i score(i)}{|i \in I : defined(S_i)|} \quad ; \quad recall = \frac{\sum_i score(i)}{|I|} \qquad (2)$$

where $score(i)$ can be either $best(i)$ or $oot(i)$.

For both *best* and *oot*, the evaluator provides two operation modes: a *normal* mode and a *strict* mode, in which only test examples for which there is a most frequent annotation are accounted for. In our evaluation, we will assume that the lack of a most frequent annotation is a marker for words with no chromatic characterization. Therefore, we decided not to consider these examples and to report accuracy measured in *strict* mode.

4   Automatic Methods for Associating Colors with Words

In this section we describe in more detail the three methods that we are comparing. Each method is employed to map the same set of words to the set of eleven basic colors as explained in Section 3.1.

4.1   Image Analysis

With this technique, we try to combine the power of text-based image retrieval with very simple image analysis techniques. Thanks to modern search engines, we can easily access a large selection of images conveniently indexed by one or more keywords. The main idea behind this approach is that, statistically, colors that are inherent to a concept will tend to prevail in images indexed with respect to the words describing it.

In the preparation phase of this technique, we queried Google image search engine [2] for each word in our data set by using Google Search API [3] and restricting the results to be in *full color*. Accordingly, we collected the 64 highest ranked results. Then, we analyzed all the images to determine the dominant colors. We first mapped all the colors in each image onto the set of basic colors. Then, we measured the amount of each color present in the images as the number of pixels of that color divided by the total number of pixels. Finally, we conducted a statistical analysis of all the images retrieved for the same word and observed which color was dominant, i.e. the most frequent color on average.

---

[2] http://images.google.com/
[3] http://code.google.com/apis/imagesearch/

As the color space of the most common image formats for the web consists of 2^{24} different values (i.e. 256 values for each primary color), we first needed to find a way of establishing a correspondence between values in this space and our basic color set. To simplify the problem, we decided to adopt a two-step strategy: first, we defined a reduced palette of colors for which a mapping onto the basic color set was known; then, we approximated all the colors in the images to the closest value in the palette, based on the color distance in the RGB space.

We design a palette based on a geometric partition of the RGB color space. The range of each component of the RGB space [0-255] is divided into four equal intervals by defining 5 cut-points at the values 0, 64, 128, 191 and 255. Then, we generate all the colors corresponding to the combinations of these five values for each component, resulting in a set of 125 colors which constitute our palette. Finally, we map each of them onto one of the eleven colors, leaving the initial mapping to two annotators and asking a third annotator to resolve the (very few) ties. For all our image processing needs, we used the `convert` command line utility bundled with the ImageMagick[4] library.

4.2   Language Models on Web Data

The Google Web 1T corpus is a collection of English N-grams, ranging from one to five N-grams, and their respective frequency counts observed on the Web [4]. The corpus was generated from approximately 1 trillion tokens from the Web, predominantly English.

We used a bigram model to measure the likelihood of each color to modify a given target word. We determine the co-occurrence likelihood by using the mutual information between the color and the word.[5] Given a color C and a word W, we calculate the mutual information as:

$$MI(C, W) = \frac{frequency(C, W)}{frequency(C) * frequency(W)} \tag{3}$$

By calculating the mutual information between each of the eleven colors and a given target word, we determine a ranking over the colors.

4.3   Similarity between Colors and Words

There is a relatively large number of word-to-word similarity measures proposed in the literature, ranging from distance-oriented measures computed on lexical repositories (e.g., WordNet) [5], to metrics based on models of distributional similarity learned from large text collections. We chose to exploit a corpus-based measure of word semantic similarity in particular Latent Semantic Analysis (LSA) [6]. Some of our requirements were the capability of comparing similarity among words from different part-of-speeches (e.g., between an adjective

---

[4] http://www.imagemagick.org/
[5] To query Google N-grams, we use a B-tree search implementation, kindly made available by Hakan Ceylan from University of North Texas.

Table 2. Evaluation results

(a) Methods comparison.

Model	Accuracy best	oot
Baseline	13.02	30.18
LSA	16.57	31.95
N-Gram	21.89	53.25
Image	36.69	56.80
N-Gram + Image	37.87	57.25

(b) Aggregated image method results.

Models	best avg	dev	oot avg	dev
50 % cropping	27.22	0.00	55.82	0.68
60 % cropping	28.40	0.59	53.65	0.35
no cropping	33.53	2.80	54.63	2.08
10 images	28.80	2.24	54.83	1.23
20 imgages	29.39	2.79	54.04	1.90
64 images	30.97	5.03	55.23	1.48

and a verb), and the possibility in the future to easily test similarity acquired from specialized or domain-oriented corpora.

For our experiments, LSA was used to acquire, in an unsupervised setting, a vector space from the British National Corpus.[6] In LSA, term co-occurrences in a corpus are captured by means of a dimensionality reduction operated by a singular value decomposition on the term-by-document matrix representing the corpus. LSA can be viewed as a way to overcome some of the drawbacks of the standard vector space model (sparseness and high dimensionality). In fact, the LSA similarity is computed in a lower dimensional space, in which second-order relations among terms and texts are exploited. The similarity in the resulting vector space is then measured with the standard cosine similarity. LSA has the advantage of allowing homogeneous representation and comparison of words, word sets, or text fragments. For representing word sets and texts by means of a LSA vector, it is possible to use a variation of the *pseudo-document* methodology described in [3]. In practice, each document can be represented in the LSA space by summing up the normalized LSA vectors of all the terms contained in it.

For our purposes, we simply compare the similarities among the representations of the basic colors and the words in our dataset. Differently from the syntagmatic association derived from exploiting N-grams, this measure could provide a more "domain-oriented" association among colors and words.

5   Evaluation and Results

We create a baseline assigning random colors to each word in our data set. For the *oot scoring* the number of random colors was set to 3, and for the *best scoring* the first color among the 3 in *oot* was selected.

A comparison among the three methods, sorted by accuracy, is shown in Table 2(a). The second and third column of the table show the accuracy of the models according to *best* and *oot* scores. Since we enforce our methods to always provide

---

[6] BNC is a very large (over 100 million words) corpus of modern English , both spoken and written (see http://www.hcu.ox.ac.uk/bnc/). Other more specific corpora could also be considered to obtain a more domain oriented similarity.

Table 3. Sample output comparison of the three methods against the results published in [8] (*TCoT*). The table shows the best three colors according to each method. Color names have been shortened to the first three letters.

	TCoT	Img	N-grams	LSA	Oracle
dog	red,bla,yel	gre,gra,bro	bro,red,yel	red,pin,pur	bla(9),bro(8),whi(7)
asparagus	whi,gre,pur	gre,gra,whi	gre,whi,pur	ora,gre,pur	gre(9),whi(1),bro(1)
lime	sil,gre,blu	gre,whi,gra	yel,pin,gre	gre,ora,yel	gre(6),whi(3),gra(2)
bread	whi,bro,bla	bro,gre,whi	bro,whi,ora	bro,ora,gre	bro(9),whi(7),ora(2)

at least one answer, the denominator in the precision formula in (2) is always equal to $|I|$, and the precision and recall are always the same.

It can be observed that the best results are achieved by using the image method, while LSA is only slightly better than the baseline. On the *oot* evaluation, the N-Gram model is almost as accurate as the image method. On the *best* evaluation, the image method clearly outperforms all the others, with differences of more than 15 accuracy points. The last line of the table shows the results obtained by combining the image method with the N-Gram model.[7] This combination improves slightly over the results obtained by the individual approaches, but the improvement is only marginal with respect to the performance of images alone. Although the accuracy is not very high, we should consider the very low baseline of the task (i.e. 13.02% and 30.18% for *best* and *oot*, respectively), with respect to which our best models improve considerably. In particular, the results of the image method are very interesting given the difficulty of the task.

After observing that in many images the color of the background was predominant with respect to the subject, we also tried cropping the images at different sizes (no cropping, 50% and 60% cropping). We also investigated the effect of the number of images (64, 20 or 10) used to obtain the statistics. The results of this experiment are shown in Table 2(b), where we report the average (*avg*) and standard deviation (*dev*) of the accuracy for the two measures observed by fixing one of the parameters while variating the other. As an example, the row labeled *50% cropping* shows the average and standard deviation of the accuracy measured by repeating an experiment with the crop factor set to 50% when using 10, 20 and 64 images. By increasing the crop factor, we achieve more stable models (i.e. lower deviation), at the cost of accuracy. This finding may be related to the fact that cropping images makes it easier to focus on the right color when there is a dominant one, while it reduces our ability to handle more difficult subjects. Concerning the number of images, it seems to have a similar effect on the final accuracy.

Table 3 compares a sample of the output of the three methods against the results obtained on the same words with the method described in [8] (column *TCoT*). According to the annotation (column *Oracle*), the most frequent color assigned to *dog* is black (with 9 votes), followed by brown (8) and white (7). All

---

[7] We also considered the combination of all three methods, but the accuracy was lower than the image method in isolation.

the methods provide at least one of these colors among the first three results, with the exception of LSA which suggests red, pink and purple, three colors which have never been selected by any annotator. As for the word *asparagus*, all the methods can associate it with the best color (green, with 9 annotations) within the first three guesses. In the case of *lime*, the best choices according to the annotations are green, white and gray. The image method is the only one which captures all of them, while all the other methods introduce noise. For the last example, *bread*, the annotators selected the colors brown (with 9 preferences), white (with 7) and orange (with 2). In this case, the N-gram method manages to capture all three colors, *Img* and *TCoT* 2 and *LSA* only one.

These observations confirm the empirical evaluation and suggest that the image-based and the N-gram methods are the most effective. On the contrary, LSA performance is generally poor. A possible explanation is that the vector space model, which is very appropriate for modeling position-independent similarity as observed in broad contexts, fails in modeling the relation between a noun and its attributes. As expected, this kind of relation, which is very highly dependent on the vicinity and relative position of the words, is modeled quite accurately by just considering bi-gram statistics.

6   Conclusions and Future Work

In this paper we proposed three computational methods to automatically associate words and colors. We have also described the procedure we followed to create a gold standard via crowdsourcing service provided by Mechanical Turk.

Our results show that the method using image features gives the best results, and the one using a language model on web data performs quite well, while the results obtained by the LSA method calculating the similarity between colors and words are only slightly better than the baseline.

The results are promising even though not conclusive, as the methods that we proposed can be improved in many ways. The image method has a major limitation in the fact that we are not trying to disambiguate word sense during image retrieval, causing a lot of noise (e.g., when retrieving images for *apple* most of the results are related to the popular computer brand rather than the fruit). Concerning the N-Gram method, we could try to exploit more structured information (e.g. dependency structures) to capture relations not limited to co-occurrence in a bi-gram. In the case of LSA, we need to device more tailored representations in order to fully exploit the potential of the vector space. Moreover, we will define confidence intervals for each of the different methods, so as to be able to combine them more robustly. In addition, we will conduct analysis at the word sense level to understand whether different senses of words can be associated to different colors. Finally, we will carry out further experiments to explore the performance of the methods for different languages.

Acknowledgements. Gözde Özbal and Carlo Strapparava were partially funded by a Google research award.

References

1. Alt, M.: Emotional responses to color associated with an advertisement. Master's thesis, Graduate College of Bowling Green State University, Ohio (2008)
2. Berlin, B., Kay, P.: Basic Color Terms Their Universality and Evolution. University of California, Berkeley (1969)
3. Berry, M.: Large-scale sparse singular value computations. International Journal of Supercomputer Applications 6(1), 13–49 (1992)
4. Brants, T., Franz, A.: Web 1T 5-gram version 1. LDC (2006)
5. Budanitsky, A., Hirst, G.: Evaluating WordNet-based measures of lexical semantic relatedness. Computational Linguistics 32(1), 13–47 (2006)
6. Deerwester, S., Dumais, S.T., Furnas, G.W., Landauer, T., Harshman, R.: Indexing by latent semantic analysis. Journal of the American Society for Information Science 41(6), 391–407 (1990)
7. Gao, X., Xin, J., Sato, T., Hansuebsai, A., Scalzo, M., Kajiwara, K., Guan, S., Valldeperas, J., Jose, M.L., Billger, M.: Analysis of cross-cultural color emotion. Color Research and Application 32, 223–229 (2007)
8. Grefenstette, G.: The Color of Things: Towards the Automatic Acquisition of Information for a Descriptive Dictionary. Revue Française de Linguistique Appliquée X, 83–94 (2005)
9. Kaya, N.: Relationship between color and emotion: a study of college students. College Student Journal, 396–405 (2004)
10. Leong, C., Mihalcea, R., Hassan, S.: Text mining for automatic image tagging. In: International Conference on Computational Linguistics, Beijing, China, pp. 647–655 (August 2010)
11. Madden, T.J., Hewett, K., Martin, S.R.: Managing images in different cultures: A cross-national study of color meanings and preferences. Journal of International Marketing 8(4), 90–107 (2000)
12. McCarthy, D., Navigli, R.: The semeval English lexical substitution task. In: Proceedings of the ACL Semeval Workshop (2007)
13. Mohammad, S., Turney, P.: Emotions evoked by common words and phrases: Using mechanical turk to create an emotion lexicon. In: Proceedings of the NAACL HLT 2010 Workshop on Computational Approaches to Analysis and Generation of Emotion in Text, Los Angeles, CA, pp. 26–34 (2010)
14. Özbal, G., Strapparava, C.: MEANS: Moving Affective Assonances for Novice Students. In: Proceedings of the 16th International Conference on Intelligent User Interfaces, IUI 2011, pp. 449–450. ACM, New York (2011)
15. Soriano, C., Valenzuela, J.: Emotion and colour across languages: implicit associations in spanish colour terms. Social Science Information 48, 421–445 (2009)
16. Strapparava, C., Özbal, G.: The color of emotions in texts. In: Proceedings of the 2nd Workshop on Cognitive Aspects of the Lexicon, Coling 2010, Beijing, China, pp. 28–32 (2010)
17. Xin, J., Cheng, K., Taylor, G., Sato, T., Hansuebsai, A.: A cross-regional comparison of colour emotions. part I. quantitative analysis. Color Research and Application 29, 451–457 (2004)

Computer Based Video and Virtual Environments in the Study of the Role of Emotions in Moral Behavior

Xueni Pan[1], Domna Banakou[2], and Mel Slater[1,2]

[1] Department of Computer Science, University College London
Gower Street, London, UK
[2] Event Lab, ICREA-University of Barcelona
Barcelona, Spain
{s.pan,m.slater}@cs.ucl.ac.uk, dbanakou@ub.edu,

Abstract. The role of emotions in moral issues is an important topic in philosophy and psychology. Recently, some psychologists have approached this issue by conducting online questionnaire-based studies. In this paper, we discuss the utility and plausibility of using computer based video and virtual environments to assist the study of moral judgments and behavior. In particular, we describe two studies: the first one demonstrates the use of computer generated visual effects. This was for the design and implementation of an experimental study aiming at observing participants' moral judgment towards an actor's confession of a behavior with doubtful morality, during which the actor either blushed or not. In the second study, we examine people's responses when confronted with a moral dilemma in a Virtual Environment.

Keywords: Moral Psychology, Virtual Reality, Emotions, Blushing, Moral Dilemmas.

1 Introduction

For many years, emotions have been viewed as irrelevant or even an antagonistic factor when making moral judgments [1]: for example, members of jury are commonly reminded that they should not allow emotions to interfere in their judgment [2]. However, recently many moral psychologists and neuroscientists have viewed the role of emotion differently: they view the "quick, automatic affective reactions" that we have towards moral issues as part of our instinct, and that are shaped by natural selection [3, 4]. This theory proposed an obvious challenge to the traditional understanding behind moral psychology, and thereby led to a series of studies in which participants were invited to give their responses to moral dilemmas [3, 5]. The typical protocol of such studies includes a paper-based or internet-based questionnaire that consists of several moral dilemmas presented to participants for their judgment. The results of those studies have contributed to revealing the significant role emotion plays in moral judgment [3, 5]. In this paper we propose the exploitation of computer based videos and Virtual Environments (VEs) as an alternative approach to the study of moral issues, and present results from our studies to support this. The idea of using computer generated graphics in psychological studies is not new, as it could "afford less of a

S. D´Mello et al. (Eds.): ACII 2011, Part II, LNCS 6975, pp. 52–61, 2011.

tradeoff" between ecological validity and experimental control [6]. In this study, we further extend this type of research to situations associated with moral issues. In the following, we first review existing studies on the role of emotions in moral issues. Then we focus on one emotional expression: social blushing and its relation to moral emotions, where we demonstrate the use of computer based special effects in this area of research. In particular, we measure participants' moral judgment towards a video clip of someone making a confession of his actions when confronted with a moral dilemma, while giving the confession he was either blushing or not. Finally, we extended our studies to a VE in which we studied participants' reaction towards a moral dilemma *in vivo*.

2 Emotions and Rationality in Moral Judgments

There are two competing theories on the process of moral judgments: a traditional theory which holds that our moral behaviors are driven by conscious and rational reasoning [7], and a more recent theory that stresses the impact of human intuitions and emotions on our behavior [4]. Under the traditional theory (rational theory), morally matured individuals are capable of justifying their moral conduct with explicit principles. Following this theory, a trained philosophy student stands a better chance of providing more rigorous and precise moral reasoning than a randomly chosen member of the public. In such a process, emotion is something undesirable and thus should be avoided.

Possible reasons as to why emotions should be avoided while making moral judgments are summarized as follows [8]: emotions are partial (one would give more consideration to those they care more for, i.e., judging a harmful act as less serious if carried out by their sibling), arbitrary (favoring a stranger more than others because he wears the same shirt as someone you love), and passive (emotion is involuntary, therefore one cannot be held responsible for his emotional reaction. For instance, nobody would blame someone who just lost a close friend and therefore could not attend an important meeting). However, despite recognizing the irrational aspect of emotions, Pizarro argued that emotions could nevertheless aid reasoning as they "reflect our pre-existing concerns" [8].

Several experimental studies have provided evidence supporting the idea that emotion affects our judgment in decision-making, very often at an subconscious level: Bailenson et al. found that a voter is more likely to vote for candidates with their face manipulated to look similar to the voter's [9]; in a Dictator Game, participants who were informed of the family name of their counterparts gave a larger offer of money, as compared to those who had less information of their counterparts [10]. However, in that same study, the disclosure of family names had no significant effect in the Ultimatum Game. The authors proposed that in the Ultimatum Game, strategic considerations crowded out the empathy triggered by the family name. In this case, the rational side of brain processing outweighed the emotion reaction.

In the context of judgment with a higher moral weight, particularly in moral dilemmas that involve killing or saving people's lives, a similar pattern has been observed. Greene et al. [11] suggested that, depending on its content, different moral dilemmas trigger different levels of emotional engagement. According to this theory, the result of moral judgments is a mixture of rational reasoning and emotional reactions, the proportion of the two varies systematically and could be related to how "personal" the moral dilemma is. Hauser et al. [5] proposed that the "moral attribution" of the action itself influences our moral judgments: even if pushing a switch and pushing a man down the bridge have the same consequences, the majority would find the former morally permissible but not the latter.

Questionnaire studies on moral dilemmas have provided insight on the role of emotions in moral judgment. In this type of study, moral dilemma scenarios are commonly presented as written descriptions. This method is certainly valid if moral judgment operates at a purely rational level. However, if moral judgment is a product from both rational reasoning and emotional intuition, there is a potential flaw: using purely written language, the emotional responses triggered by motor sensors are absent, causing the reader to compensate for this lack of information with their own personal experiences. As a consequence of this, the results from those studies reflect only what people imagine they would feel and do rather than how they would be feeling and what they would do *in vivo*. Moreover, using written scripts restricts the ability to convey certain sensory information that operates at a subconscious level. For instance, in the aforementioned experimental study by Bailenson et al. [9], if the scenario were to be presented with written language, it is unlikely anybody would choose to favor a candidate who is described to have higher similarity in their appearance to the voter. Visual stimuli therefore should be tested visually to reveal their power which happens only at a subconscious level.

However, scenarios involving moral dilemmas were to be presented in physical reality, irresolvable ethical problems would arise since most moral dilemmas involve saving or sacrificing people's lives. Here we propose an alternative approach: using virtual environments (VE) to create those moral dilemma scenarios, and generating visual stimulus that would otherwise be difficult to create in real life (e.g., blushing, which is involuntary). In the following sections we discuss two types of study: one uses computer special effect software to test the relationship between people's moral judgment and blushing; and a series of studies carried out in VE to test people's reaction towards a moral dilemma *in vivo*.

3   Moral Judgment and Blushing: A Pilot Study

3.1   Social Blushing and Morality

During an interpersonal communication, the most observed area of the human body is the face [12], which produces over twenty thousand facial expressions [13], and has been considered to be the channel to express emotions [14]. Among all facial features, blushing has been one of the most studied due to its mysterious nature: it is often considered to be undesirable, and psychologists have debated its function.

Due to its location and color, blushing is a directly observable signal indicating shame or embarrassment, and therefore might appease the observer [15, 16]. Leary and Meadows suggested that "blushing serves to placate others and restore normal relations after a transgression for which the person might otherwise be rejected" [17]. This is consistent with Semin and Manstead's finding that after performing a social transgression, people who displayed embarrassment received more positive evaluation than those who did not [18]. De Jong et al.'s work [19, 20] suggested that blushing serves a remedial function, such as attenuating the negative impression and therefore makes the observer judge the blusher's reason for blushing as less serious. His experimental studies have indicated that people who blushed after violating a social rule received less negative evaluation compared to those who did not blush. However, in this experiment only paper-based scripts were used where an embarrassing situation and the person's reaction to it were *described*. As a visual cue, blushing is very difficult to test under controlled experimental conditions because of its involuntary nature.

In this study we aim to investigate how blushing influenced people's moral judgment. Previously, we tested participants' reaction towards a blushing avatar that blushes after making a small mistake [21]. In this study, we tested their reaction towards something more serious than a small mistake – a moral behavior which could be interpreted as either permissible or not permissible.

During the interview in that previous experiment, many participants mentioned that the lack of facial expressions on the face of the avatar was disturbing, which impacted the effectiveness of blushing. In this new study we took a different approach: in order to achieve highly realistic facial expressions, we used direct recording of a professional actor's performance. Blushing was then added as a special effect. Here we present our experimental design, implementation, and finally discuss our results.

3.2 Experimental Design

Participants were invited to watch a video clip in which an actor told a story of a life-threatening situation that he survived a few years ago. Finally, he made a confession of an action that could be judged as not morally permissible. During the confession, the actor was either blushing or not, depending on the condition. After the presentation, participants were asked to complete a questionnaire regarding whether they found the actor's conduct morality permissible, as well as their judgment of the actor's personality.

The confession made by the actor was a fictitious story based on morality studies [22, 23], where the stories were presented on paper. Our aim was to choose a real "moral dilemma": something that on the average about half of the population would find morally permissible. The chosen script is as follows, a situation that amongst 38 participants, 58% found to be morally permissible in [23]:

"Last summer I was on a cruise when a fire started. We were forced to abandon the ship and use the lifeboats. However, the lifeboats were not designed to carry that many people. The lifeboat I was in was sitting dangerously low in the water-a few inches lower and it would sink. The sea started to get rough, and the boat began to fill with water. If nothing was done, we would all sink before the rescue boats arrived and everyone on board would die. However, on our boat there was an injured person who would certainly die no matter what happened. I knew that if I pushed this person overboard we would stay afloat and the remaining passengers would be saved. To save myself and everyone else, I pushed this person out of the boat."

There were two conditions in the experiment, in condition one (blushing condition) the actor was manipulated to display blushing on his face during his confession. In the condition two (non-blushing condition), the actor narrated his confession with a neutral facial color that remained unchanged throughout the whole video. Apart from the change of the facial color, the two video clips in both conditions are identical to each other. This was implemented by post-editing the facial color of the actor in the video clips. In the next Section, we present the implementation.

Our research questions were: (1) According to psychological studies, blushing serves as a remedial function. However, would the expression of blushing influence the participants' moral judgment towards the blusher? (2) Would blushing influence the participants' judgment of the blusher personality? (3) Would blushing trigger certain emotional response in its observer?

3.3   Implementation

We recorded the short movie with a professional actor, who studied the story in advance and narrated it in front of the camera while displaying a serious and sad expression on his face. Blushing is the reddening of the face, emphasizing the change of tone rather than the just the color of the face. Therefore we post-processed the original video clip with Adobe After Effect to prepare the two video clips used in the experiment. We first prepared the "non-blushing" video clip by adjusting the RGB value of the color on his face to a non blushing level and made it consistent for the whole video clip. Then we added color information abstracted from our "blushing reference" onto this "non-blushing" video to create our "blushing" video (Fig. 1).

(a)

(b)

Fig. 1. (a) Non-blushing Video (b) Blushing Video

Our blushing reference was obtained by recording a short video clip of a person who was known to blush easily. She was informed about our research and agreed to participate. Blushing was induced by confronting her with the camera which was in itself sufficient to trigger embarrassment. In order to abstract color information, we analyzed the video frame by frame. As we were interested in finding how the recorded blusher's facial color changed, we selected a specific area of interest on her cheek and abstracted the color information of this area for each frame. We then applied the change of color from this reference video to the target video using Adobe After Effects frame by frame to create the effect of blushing. As mentioned above, we also produced a video that has a constant color value throughout the whole time, which was used in the non-blushing condition.

3.4 Results

We carried out a study with 24 participants, 12 in each condition (both 6 females and 6 males). The average age was 25 (±3.6 S.D.) years. The experiment was approved by the UCL Ethic Committee. Participants attended the experiment at pre-arranged times. Upon arriving, each participant was given an information sheet to read, and after they agreed to continue they were given a consent form to sign. They were then seated half a meter away from the display of a desktop machine running Windows XP. The experimenter then explained to them that their task was to watch a video clip, and then complete a questionnaire. They were also given a pair of headphones to listen to the video and a mouse to interact with the user-interface. The experimenter then left the participant alone in the room to watch the video. They then played the video clip, answered the questionnaire, and watched a final video clip in which the actor explained that the story was entirely fictional. Finally they went through a debriefing session and were paid 5 pounds for their time.

The post-questionnaire given to the participants consisted of questions regarding participants' judgments about the moral action (pushing a sick person off the boat to save other people) and their feelings towards the actor, and emotions they felt.

Our first concern was whether the display of blushing changed participants' moral judgments. The result showed that 67% of the participants found the action morally permissible, with 58% from the blushing condition and 75% from the non-blushing condition. The difference between the two proportions is not significant ($p = .68$, test of proportions), nor when compared with previous studies presented on paper (58%, 38 participants [23], $p = .48$). When considering the two genders separately, 67% females found it permissible (the same in both conditions), and 50% males found it permissible with the blushing actor, 87% with the non-blushing avatar.

Moreover, we were interested in how the blushing would influence participants' judgments towards the personality of the actor, including: *reliability*, *honesty*, *sympathetic*, and *likability*. We found no difference between two conditions when considering both genders together. However, when looking at two genders separately, we found that the blushing actor received higher rating scores on all four personality measures than the non-blushing one amongst female participants, whilst for male participants it was the opposite: the non-blushing avatar received higher scores on all four measurements. In particular, the blushing actor were judged as more reliable compared to the non-blushing actor ($p=0.04$, One-Way ANOVA) by female participants, and male participants found the non-blushing one more likable compared to the blushing actor ($p = 0.00$). The similar pattern of female participants gave more positive comments on the blushing avatar whilst male participants preferred the non-blushing avatar also applied on other questions: female participants thought the blushing actor's action as more appropriate, more obliged, less shameful, whereas for male participants, the above applied with the non-blushing actor. Our sample size is too small for meaningful statistical tests in comparison of gender by condition, but the results pointed to hypotheses for future research.

Finally, we also asked participants to choose from one of the six basic emotions (happy, sad, angry, surprise, disgust, fear) or nothing to describe their feelings. For male participants, it was almost the same in both conditions that half of them chose "nothing" and the other half chose "sad", apart from one participant who chose "surprise" (blushing condition). For female participants, it was clear that blushing had an impact on their emotions: in the blushing condition, 2 chose "nothing", 2 "sad", and 2 "Angry". In the non-blushing condition, 2 chose "nothing", 2 chose "disgust", 1 "fear", and 1 "sad".

4   From Moral Judgment to Moral Actions

4.1   Moral Actions in VE

It has been frequently demonstrated that VE triggers people's realistic responses. In particular, in an immersive VE, people tend to respond to situations and events as if they were real, despite the fact that they are consciously aware of the situation's artificiality [24-26]. This attribution has made VE an ideal media for the studies of moral dilemmas, since we can recreate scenarios virtually and observe participants' feeling and behaviors *in vivo*. The moral dilemmas scenarios, as mentioned in Section 2, would be difficult to create in real life and certainly would generate great ethical concerns. In our lab we have conducted a series of studies using VE to create social encounters where participants were confronted with difficult choices in their actions. The power of VE has been demonstrated in triggering participants' realistic subjective, behavioral, and physiological responses [24, 25]. For instance, in Slater et al.'s Virtual Obedience experiment, participants were requested by an authority figure to inflict electric shocks on a virtual woman. Despite the fact that they knew the scenario was not real, 6 out of 23 participants (26%) withdrew early from the experiment and participants exhibited signs of stress albeit at a lower intensity than in the original studies by Stanley Milgram [27]. In another experiment, Rovira et al. explored participants' response to a violent event in VR [24]. In this experiment, Participants in a VE witnessed a perpetrator bullying a victim, leading eventually to violence. The results showed that participants became involved in the scenario and many intervened to try to stop the violence or said they wanted to intervene.

4.2   Would You Push the Switch to Save Five in VE?

More recently we conducted an experimental study examining social encounters directly related to moral dilemmas that involve sacrificing or saving people's lives [28], a scenario with a structure similar to that of the classic trolley dilemma used in moral studies. Here in order to achieve clarity (the consequences of participants' action has to be unmistakably understood) and originality (the scenario has to be new to all participants to achieve an unbiased effect), we designed a Virtual Art Gallery scenario in which a gunman started shooting while on a lift which was controlled by the participant. The situation was arranged such that participants were confronted with a moral dilemma: when the gunman started shooting they could either leave the lift where it was or send it down to the floor below. If they did nothing, 5 people would die; if they pushed the switch to bring the lift down, 5 people would be saved but one other person would instead be put in danger (the Action condition, Fig.2. (b)). There was another condition such that when the shooting occurred, if participants did nothing 1 would die but 5 would be saved (the Omission Condition). We have tested the scenario in an Immersive VE (CAVE-like system) and a non-immersive desktop VE. Results from this first pilot showed that participants in the CAVE were more likely to give a utilitarian answer (saving the greatest number of lives) in the post experimental questionnaire. The result also indicated that, in both CAVE and desktop VE, participants' were shocked by the incident and many reported that they panicked and were under pressure in deciding what to do (this is more so for those who experienced the CAVE condition).

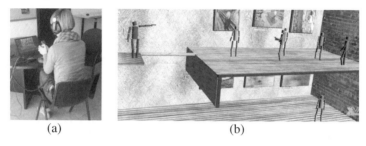

(a)   (b)

Fig. 2. Moral Dilemma in Virtual Environment (a) Participants interact with the scenario through a Joystick (b) Gunman starts shooting at visitors in an art gallery (Action Condition)

In order to gain a better understanding of participants' panic reaction, we conducted a second pilot study that included the Autonomic Perception Questionnaire (APQ) [29] with the scenarios presented on a desktop machine. Here 10 participants attended our study (Fig.2 (a), 5 in the Action Condition, 5 Omission Condition). The APQ questionnaire was given to participants both before and after their experiment in order to observe their physiological changes caused by the scenario. The result suggested that in the Action Condition, the mean post-APQ score was higher than pre-APQ ($p<0.05$). In the Omission Condition, the post-APQ score was also higher than pre-APQ, but not significant ($p = 0.41$). Although the sample size was small, the result indicated that participants perceived increased physiological stress level, especially for those in the Action Condition, as shown in Fig. 3.

Fig. 3. APQ Score from the Action and Omission Conditions

5 Discussion

In the first study presented in this paper, we assessed people's moral judgments towards an actor making a confession about his behavior when confronted with a moral dilemma. We also included an emotional reaction closely related to morality as an extra variable – social blushing. Our results suggested a very interesting pattern: female participants gave more positive judgments towards the blushing actor while male participants were more predisposed to positively evaluate the non-blushing actor. Although there was no evidence that blushing triggered a difference in participants' moral judgment directly, it was clear that blushing had an impact on participants' judgment on the actor's personality, and that blushing triggered different emotions in female participants. In our previous study, the result suggested that the blushing female avatar received more positive evaluations from male participants [21]; a more recent study which included female participants further supported our findings [30]. In our current work, when confronted with a dilemma with heavy moral weight, we have demonstrated that blushing on male triggered different reaction in different genders. However, it is yet to be explored whether such differences were caused by the gender of the blusher or the moral weight associated with the dilemma.

Secondly, we have reviewed a series of experiments conducted in our lab using VE related to moral issues, and described an on-going study investigating participants' reactions towards a moral dilemma *in vivo*. We presented results obtained from our second pilot study. The results suggested that participants had a significant increased level of perceived physiological stress in the Action Condition, which is more of a moral dilemma for the participants, as there was the urge for them to push the switch that would result in the likely shooting of one person who would otherwise be safe. However, the cause and effect is still not clear: is it because the situation makes them more stressed, and therefore they conducted the action (sacrifice 1 to save 5), or is it because they conducted the action, and therefore became more stressed? In future, more studies using VE will be conducted to further investigate this issue.

Both studies have further demonstrated the use of computer based video and Virtual Reality in triggering participants' realistic reaction at a subjective, physiological, and behavior level. Especially in the second study, although our VE set up only presented abstract human figures, participants had a strong reaction towards the moral dilemma as indicated by post experimental discussions with the participants. These two studies, together with previous research as reviewed in this paper, suggest that VEs can play an important part in investigating the role of emotions in moral judgment and behavior.

Acknowledgment. This research is funded by the Leverhulme Trust project "The exploitation of immersive virtual reality for the study of moral judgments". Special thanks to Prof. Marc Hauser for contributing to the experimental design.

References

1. Kant, I.: Groundwork of the Metaphysics of Morals (1785). Practical Philosophy. 49–108 (1996)
2. Feigenson, N.R.: Sympathy and Legal Judgment: A Psychological Anaylsis. Tenn. L. Rev. 65, 1 (1997)
3. Greene, J., Haidt, J.: How (and where) does moral judgment work? Trends in Cognitive Sciences 6, 517–523 (2002)
4. Hauser, M.D.: Moral minds: How nature designed our universal sense of right and wrong. Ecco Pr. (2006)
5. Hauser, M., Cushman, F., Young, L., Kang Xing, J.: A dissociation between moral judgments and justifications. Mind & Language 22, 1–21 (2007)

6. Loomis, J.M., Blascovich, J.J., Beall, A.C.: Immersive virtual environment technology as a basic research tool in psychology. Behavior Research Methods 31, 557–564 (1999)
7. Kohlberg, L.: Stage and sequence: The cognitive-developmental approach to socialization. Rand McNally (1969)
8. Pizarro, D.: Nothing more than feelings? The role of emotions in moral judgment. Journal for the Theory of Social Behaviour 30, 355–375 (2000)
9. Bailenson, J.N., Iyengar, S., Yee, N., Collins, N.A.: Facial similarity between voters and candidates causes influence. Public Opinion Quarterly 72, 935 (2008)
10. Charness, G., Gneezy, U.: What's in a name? Anonymity and social distance in dictator and ultimatum games. Journal of Economic Behavior & Organization 68, 29–35 (2008)
11. Greene, J.D., Sommerville, R.B., Nystrom, L.E., Darley, J.M., Cohen, J.D.: An fMRI investigation of emotional engagement in moral judgment. Science 293, 2105 (2001)
12. Argyle, M.: Bodily communication. Taylor & Francis, Abington (1988)
13. Birdwhistell, R.L.: Kinesics and context: Essays on body motion communication (1970)
14. Ekman, P., Sorenson, E.R., Friesen, W.V.: Pan-cultural elements in facial displays of emotion. Science 164, 86 (1969)
15. Castelfranchi, C., Poggi, I.: Blushing as a discourse: Was Darwin wrong? (1990)
16. Keltner, D.: Signs of appeasement: Evidence for the distinct displays of embarrassment, amusement, and shame. Journal of Personality and Social Psychology 68, 441–441 (1995)
17. Leary, M.R., Meadows, S.: Predictors, elicitors, and concomitants of social blushing. Journal of Personality and Social Psychology 60, 254–262 (1991)
18. Semin, G.R., Manstead, A.: The social implications of embarrassment displays and restitution behaviour. European Journal of Social Psychology 12, 367–377 (1982)
19. De Jong, P.J.: Communicative and remedial effects of social blushing. Journal of Nonverbal Behavior 23, 197–217 (1999)
20. De Jong, P.J., Peters, M.L., De Cremer, D.: Blushing signify guilt: Revealing effects of blushing in ambiguous social situations. Motivation and Emotion 27, 225–249 (2003)
21. Pan, X., Gillies, M., Slater, M.: The Impact of Avatar Blushing on the Duration of Interaction between a Real and Virtual Person. Presence (2008)
22. Greene, J.D., Nystrom, L.E., Engell, A.D., Darley, J.M., Cohen, J.D.: The neural bases of cognitive conflict and control in moral judgment. Neuron 44, 389–400 (2004)
23. Huebner, B., Hauser, M.D., Pettit, P.: How the Source, Inevitability and Means of Bringing About Harm Interact in Folk Moral Judgments. Mind & Language 26, 210–233 (2011)
24. Rovira, A., Swapp, D., Spanlang, B., Slater, M.: The Use of Virtual Reality in the Study of People's Responses to Violent Incidents. Frontiers in Behavioral Neuroscience 3 (2009)
25. Slater, M., Antley, A., Davison, A., Swapp, D., Guger, C., Barker, C., Pistrang, N., Sanchez-Vives, M.V.: A virtual reprise of the Stanley Milgram obedience experiments. PLoS One 1, 39 (2006)
26. Pertaub, D.P., Slater, M., Barker, C.: An experiment on public speaking anxiety in response to three different types of virtual audience. Presence: Teleoperators & Virtual Environments 11, 68–78 (2002)
27. Milgram, S.: Behavioral study of obedience./. abnorm. soc. Psycho. J. 67, 371–378 (1963)
28. Pan, X., Slater, M.: Confronting a Moral Dilemma in Virtual Reality: A Pilot Study. In: BSC Human-Computer Interaction, HCI (2011)
29. Mandler, G., Mandler, J.M., Uviller, E.T.: Autonomic feedback: The perception of autonomic activity. The Journal of Abnormal and Social Psychology 56, 367 (1958)
30. Dijk, C., Koenig, B., Ketelaar, T., de Jong, P.J.: Saved by the blush: Being trusted despite defecting. Emotion 11, 313 (2011)

EmoWisconsin: An Emotional Children Speech Database in Mexican Spanish

Humberto Pérez-Espinosa, Carlos Aleberto Reyes-García,
and Luis Villaseñor-Pineda

Instituto Nacional de Astrofísica Óptica y Electrónica,
Luis E. Erro 1. Tonantzintla, Puebla, 72840, México
humbertop@inaoep.mx, kargaxxi@inaoep.mx, villasen@inaoep.mx

Abstract. The acquisition of naturalistic speech data and the richness of its annotation are very important to face the challenges of automatic emotion recognition from speech. This paper describes the creation of a database of emotional speech in the Spanish spoken in Mexico. It was recorded from children between 7 and 13 years old while playing a sorting card game with an adult examiner. The game is based on a neuropsychological test, modified to encourage dialogue and induce emotions in the player. The audio was segmented at speaker turn level and annotated with six emotional categories and three continuous emotion primitives by 11 human evaluators. Inter-evaluator agreement is presented for categorical and continuous annotation. Initial classification and regression experiments were performed using a set of 6,552 acoustic features.

Index Terms: emotional speech corpus, continuous emotion model.

1 Introduction

Within the affective computing area, the adequate generation of resources is a key factor for the subsequent research and development of new emotion models usable in realistic applications. Several important points must be considered for the creation of emotional speech databases. First, the nature and origin of the captured speech. There are different types of data sources. Traditionally, the most widely used source of emotional data is the acting of emotions. IEMO-CAP [3], Emo-DB [2] and SSE [14] contain acted emotional speech. Another way of acquiring data is through emotions induction. Induction can be done by presenting stimuli, such as images, videos or audio in order to generate an emotional reaction. Induction can also be done by an interaction, where experimenters attempt to generate some emotional reaction by performing an activity. For example, by conducting a Wizard of Oz experiment in which subjects interact with a computer system that they believe to be autonomous, but actually is controlled by a human. EmoTaboo [7], SAL 1 [8], FAU Aibo [23] are some examples of induced emotions databases. Also, there are spontaneous data acquired in real interaction environments, such as television shows or telephone systems for customer service. The databases VAM [11], and EMOTV1 [1] were recorded

S. D'Mello et al. (Eds.): ACII 2011, Part II, LNCS 6975, pp. 62–71, 2011.
© Springer-Verlag Berlin Heidelberg 2011

from TV shows. The databases Genova Airport Lost Luggage Database [20] and CEMO [24] were recorded from telephonic services. Using acted emotional speech oversimplifies the automatic emotion recognition. It is difficult to use recognizers trained with acted data in real world applications, given that, within people's interaction emotions are not expressed as intense and prototypical as an actor usually interprets them[23]. On the other hand, acquiring data in real environments is problematic. It is difficult to obtain the rights to make the data publicly available, the position of microphones and cameras is not ideal, there is noise like acoustic and visual background, there is no control on the emotional content [3]. The current trend is to record spontaneous, naturalistic and realistic speech in an environment with restricted conditions, such as an interview [12].

Another important point to be considered is the annotation scheme. It should be easily understood by the human evaluators in order to reach a high inter-evaluator agreement. The two most used annotation schemes are the categorical, where emotional categories are assigned to the speech samples, and the continuous, where each speech sample is rated with numerical values corresponding to levels of emotion primitives. Continuous annotation can be made statically, for example, using The Self Assessment Mannequin (SAM) [13]. In this way, whole segments are evaluated with the same value. Emotion primitive annotation can also be done time continuously, i.e. tracking a perceived emotional state continuously over time as allowed by the Feeltrace [4] labeling tool. It is also valuable to annotate other information such as linguistic information, events, history, context and other types of emotional and linguistic descriptors. High diversity of age, gender, language, socio-cultural context and, of course, emotional diversity is desirable. For emotion primitives, the ideal is to have enough samples distributed throughout the three-dimensional space. Table 1 shows some of the existing databases annotated with emotion primitives and their most important properties. It is needed to generate more databases in different languages, covering a wider range of emotional phenomena; taking into account relevant points, like spontaneity, rich annotation to enable further study and comparison of results among different acoustic features and classifiers [22].

Table 1. Speech databases annotated with emotion primitives. V = Valencia, A = Activation, D = Dominance, E = Anticipation / Expectation, I = Emotion Intensity

Database	EmoWisconsin (our work)	IEMOCAP	VAM	SAL 1	SEMAINE
Recorded Hours	11:38	12:00	12:00	4:11	6:30
Speakers	28	10	20	4	20
Segmentation	Turns	Turns	Turns	Session	Session
Instances	2,040	10,039	947	4	25
Data Type	Induced	Acted	Spontaneous	Induced	Induced
Language	Spanish	English	German	English	English
Primitives	V,A,D	V,A,D	V,A,D	V,A	V,A,D,E,I
Evaluators	11	3	17	4	4

2   Database Design

The experiment we proposed to build our database was to modify the Wisconsin Card Sorting Test (WCST) [10] to induce emotions in children. The database was designed according to the following considerations: a) Language is Mexican Spanish given our interest in the particularities of our native language and because it will expand the multilingual analysis of emotion primitives. b) Speech is spontaneous, induced and natural. It is spontaneous in order to study phenomena that only occur spontaneously, as mixture and intensity of emotions. It is induced in order to have a controlled environment and to produce our own data which give us the rights to make it available to the scientific community. It is natural because children do not disguise their emotions [23]. c) Annotation of the emotional content was done with emotion primitives and emotion categories in order to compare both approaches and enable comparison with other works. d) We worked with a relatively high number of participants to enable the creation of speaker independent models. e) We worked with a relatively high number of evaluators to cope with the high subjectivity in the annotation of emotions. f) We recorded good quality audio, but it is not noise free, in order to emulate the real applications audio capturing difficulties. g) Emotional diversity. Getting emotional states in the low and high regions of each emotion primitive axes.

2.1   Wisconsin Card Sorting Test

The original WCST was designed to assess the abstract cognitive function of the individual. It consists of four key cards and 128 response cards with geometric figures that vary according to three perceptual dimensions: color, form and number. See Fig. 1 left side. The task requires subjects to find the correct classification principle by trial and error and examiner feedback. The participant is not told how to match the cards; however, he or she is told whether a particular match is right or wrong. The classification principle is a combination of the perceptual dimensions. Once the subject chooses the correct rule they must maintain this sorting principle (or set) across changing stimulus conditions while ignoring the other   now irrelevant   stimulus dimensions. After ten consecutive correct matches, the classification principle changes without warning, demanding a flexible shift in set. The WCST is not timed and sorting continues until all cards are sorted or a maximum of six correct sorting criteria have been reached [15]. The test is carried out with the person administering the test, i.e. the examiner, on one side of the desk facing the participant on the other. The test takes approximately 12 to 20 minutes to carry out and generates a number of psychometric scores, including numbers, percentages, and percentiles of: categories achieved, trials, errors, and perseverative errors. With these results indexes are calculated to diagnose the individual.

2.2   Emotional Wisconsin Card Sorting Test

The idea of this modification to the original WCST is to address it as a game, in which children are deeply involved in its realization. The children's performance and interaction with the examiner trigger reactions that affect their emotional state, which in turn is reflected in their voices. Each child participated in two sessions referred as positive and negative.

Positive Session: A friendly examiner inspires confidence to the child before and during this session. Examiner encourages the child to orally express all their impressions of the game. The game's instructions are clearly explained. The examiner designs classification principles that the child can solve causing satisfaction. At this stage of the test, it is expected that the child begins in a neutral emotional state and is directed toward a high valence, activation, and dominance (see section 5, for the explanation of these terms). We expected emotional states associated with serenity, security, motivation, joy.

Negative Session: When the positive session ends, the examiner tells the children they will participate in the second part of the game. At the beginning of the negative session a grumpy examiner introduces himself to the child. During the game the examiner seems to be annoyed and impatient. At this stage of the test, it is expected that the child starts from a neutral emotional state and change to low valence and low dominance state. Activation may vary from low to high. Initially, emotions similar to nervousness, insecurity, stress and frustration were expected in this session.

As in the original test, the participant is given a stack of cards. The examiner decides on the run, the difficulty of the classification principle according to the child's age, performance in the test and either if it is the positive or negative session. During both sessions conversation with the child is incited. After the recording sessions end, an identification form is filled up with age, sex, duration of each session and completed sequences. Two elements are used for emotion induction: First, the position or personality that the examiner shows by gesticulation, gestures, tone of voice, words of encouragement and pressure. Second child's performance in the game. It is expected that events / factors like the following trigger emotions in children: A very difficult classification principle may cause stress or anxiety. Finding the classification principle could lead to satisfaction, confident. Misunderstandings with the examiner would cause insecurity, uncertainty. Too easy classification principle eventually lead to boredom, tedium. Deception, frustration would be present when failing to find the classification principle. Excitement and enthusiasm would activate when participants realize that he/she has developed a skill for the game. When the examiner applies pressure to solve the game quickly, stress and nervousness would be induced.

Before the final database recording, a pilot test was done with nine children. During this test, we realized that it was important to know the emotional state of children prior to the recording sessions. If they were under painful or stressful personal situation, the negative session challenge became too overwhelming for them. Such children were found too stressed at the end of the sessions. The personality and personal experience of each child plays an important role since some children are more habituated to manage pressure situations and dealing with intimidating adults. For acquiring these important details about children, we briefly interviewed each child before recording sessions. In this interview we delved into their personality and current emotional stability to prevent emotional damage. We always applied first positive session and then negative session in order to gain the trust of the child. Another point observed in the pilot test is that the role the examiners play, friendly or grumpy, is reinforced by his voice and appearance, to achieve the desired effect on the child.

3   Recording

The tests were applied by a group of five recently graduated psychologists who also helped to design the final form of the examination. These examiners were exchanging their roles. We worked with a group of 28 children with the widest range of ages that the test accepts. Eleven girls and seventeen boys ranging between seven and thirteen years old. The recording was made in an environment with little noise, but not completely isolated. It was recorded in a small room using two computers, a desktop microphone and a Sigmatel STAC 9200 sound card. Recordings were mono channel, with 16 bits sample size, 44,100 kHz sample rate and stored in WAV Windows PCM format. We recorded 11:39 hours in 56 sessions, two sessions per child in seven days at the National Institute of Astrophysics Optics and Electronics in Puebla, Mexico.

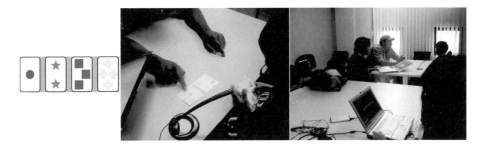

Fig. 1. During the sessions the examiner sits on one side of the desk facing the participant on the other. Two more adults are in the room monitoring the recording.

4   Segmentation

Best segment size is an open problem. Different alternatives as words, speaker turns, sentences, etc. have been tested. It is generally accepted that a speaker turn level segmentation is a good option [23,3]. Segmentation was done manually. After segmentation we obtained a total of 3,098 segments. 1,424 acquired in positive sessions and 1,674 acquired in negative sessions. The criteria instructed for segmentation are as follow: 1) Avoid those segments with more than one voice at the same time that is, examiner's voice overlaps child's voice. 2) Split the turn when it contains long pauses. 3) Include non-linguistic expressions mixed with words. 4) Do not include isolated non-linguistic expressions.

Table 2. Number of segments per emotion category. DNM = Did not match any of the six emotions we were looking for, UD = Undetermined, DF = Doubtful, AY = Annoyed, MT = Motivated, NV = Nervous, NT = Neutral, CF = Confident.

	Segments	DNM	UD	DF	AY	MT	NV	NT	CF
Positive	1,424	525	119	205	5	41	105	11	413
Negative	1,674	533	118	310	12	31	162	10	498
Total	3,098	1,058	237	515	17	72	267	21	911

5   Annotation

We used two annotation schemes to describe the emotional content in our data: categorical and continuous approaches. The categorical approach is based on the concept of basic emotions such as anger, joy, sadness, etc., that are the most intense form of emotions from which all other emotions are generated by variations or combinations of them [6], assuming the existence of universal emotions. On the other hand, the continuous approach represents emotional states using a continuous multidimensional space. Emotions are represented by regions in a n-dimensional space where each dimension represents an emotion primitive. Emotion primitives are subjective properties shown by all emotions. The primitives we used are Valence, Activation and Dominance [21]. Valence describes how negative or positive is a specific emotion. Activation, describes the internal excitement of an individual and ranges from being very calm to be very active. Dominance describes the degree of control that the individual intends to take on the situation, or in other words, how strong or weak the individual seems to be. For continuous annotation we used SAMs and Feeltrace labeling tools. We annotated our data with six emotional categories and transcribed the sessions. To choose the emotional categories, pilot tests were analyzed. It was determined that the six emotional states chosen (Doubtful, Annoyed, Motivated, Nervous, Neutral, Confident) were the most recurrent in children's speech. Annotators were trained, explaining to them the emotional state that each label represented and the meaning of each emotion primitive. For categorical annotation, besides the emotional labels, annotators used a label for segments that did not match any labels and segments they consider as wrongly segmented. Table 2. shows the number of segments per category. Eleven annotators participated in this process. We used the evaluation platform TRUE [19] to annotate our data (Fig. 2).

6   Inter-evaluator Agreement

To estimate the inter-evaluator agreement in the categorical annotation we used *Free-marginal multirater Kappa* [25]. To measure the agreement in the continuous emotion primitives annotation we use the *Cronbach alpha index* [5]. Results are shown in Table 3. As we can see, agreement is low. Mainly for the categorical annotation. However, having many annotators enable the possibility of increasing agreement by eliminating the evaluators with less agreement obtaining a

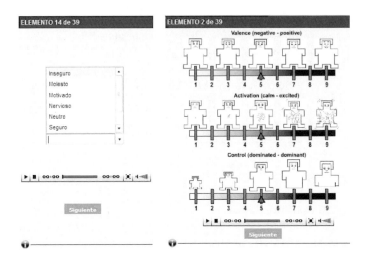

Fig. 2. TRUE online testing platform. Left: Categorical. Right: Continuous evaluation

more reliable final annotation. We calculated final labels from the annotations of all the evaluators using the following criteria. For categorical annotation we counted how many times the sample is annotated with each emotion category. The final label is the emotion that appeared the most. When there is not an unique maximum the sample is labeled as undetermined. Table 2 shows the number of samples annotated per category. For continuous annotation, the final label is the mean of all the annotations.

Table 3. Inter-evaluator agreement. Free-marginal Kappa and Percent of overall agreement were calculated for categorical annotation. Cronbach alpha coefficients were computed for continuous annotation, Valence, Activation, Dominance.

	Categorical Kappa	Categorical Overall	V	A	D
Positive Session	0.2265	0.3443	0.6671	0.7045	0.6480
Negative Session	0.2496	0.3493	0.5765	0.6667	0.6029
Mean	0.2380	0.3468	0.6218	0.6856	0.6254

7   Classification and Regression Experiments

We extracted 6,552 acoustic features per instance using openEAR [9], see Table 4. For emotion primitives we performed a feature selection process based on a wrapper algorithm that evaluates features subsets using Regression Support Vector Machines and a Linear Forward Selection searching method. We ran this algorithm in a Fixed Width modality [26]. For emotion categories we

Table 4. Acoustic Features used for classification and regression tasks

Feature Type	# of Features	Feature Type	# of Features
LOG Energy	117	Zero Crossing Rate	117
Probability of Voicing	117	F0 Contour	234
MFCC	1,521	MEL Spectrum	3,042
Spectral Energy in Bands	469	Spectral Roll Off Point	468
Spectral Flux	117	Spectral Centroid	117
Spectral Max and Min	233	**Total**	**6,552**

Table 5. Classification and regression results. F-measure was calculated for categorical classification and Pearson's correlation coefficient was calculated for emotion primitives estimation. The Sel. Feat. column shows the selected features for 4 classes/7 classes/Valence/Activation/Dominance

Instances	Sel. Feat.	Classes	Categorical	V	A	D
1,764	2,465/17/24/16	4	0.508	0.6152	0.7246	0.6676
2,040	2,622/13/39/29	7	0.407	0.6146	0.7349	0.6744

performed a feature selection process based on Cfs Subset Evaluation using a genetic searching method [26]. In Table 5 we can see the number of selected features. We made experiments with seven (Undetermined, Doubtful, Annoyed, Motivated, Nervous, Neutral, Confident) and four (Doubtful, Motivated, Nervous, Confident) classes. For categorical classification we used a Support Vector Machine algorithm and evaluated with 10-fold cross validation. As expected, results were slightly better using four classes. For continuous estimation, Valence, Activation and Dominance, we used Support Vector Machine for Regression. As in previous experiments we have performed with other databases [16,18,17], it was more difficult to estimate Valence, and easier to estimate Activation.

8   Conclusions

The creation of this database, gives us the possibility of further research on speech automatic emotion recognition and other studies related to the analysis of emotional speech. Given that it is annotated with emotion categories and emotion primitives, it offers to the research community in this field, the possibility of more complete studies in continuous space, field that is growing in importance lately [12], and enable comparison with categorical classification. By means of the experiment we mounted to acquire emotional speech we got valuable emotional data and learned about how to interact with children in this type of experimental setting. We think that its application was successful in general. However, the inter-evaluator agreement was lower than expected. On the other hand, it is good to have a high number of human evaluators; this opens the possibility of selecting the best evaluators and improve the agreement. These difficulties are examples of the high subjectivity of the task. The emotional content was not as diverse as we expected. This corpus is strongly unbalanced, with few samples of some classes. Classification and regression showed similar degree of difficulty than in other continuous annotated databases as VAM and IEMOCAP.

Acknowledgements. The authors wish to express their gratitude for the support given to carry out this research to Conacyt through the postgraduate scholarship 49296 and the project 106013. We also wish to thank to the psychologists, of the psychology faculty of the Autonomous University of Puebla, Indira Sánchez, Liliana I. Meléndez, Nancy C. Hidalgo, Rafael García and Reyna González for their advice and support in the design of the test and the realization of the sessions. We also thank to the programmers Cristina Avelar and Rodolfo Maldonado for their support.

References

1. Abrilian, S., Devillers, L., Buisine, S., Martin, J.C.: Emotv1: Annotation of real-life emotions for the specification of multimodal affective interfaces. In: 11th International Conference Human-Computer Interaction (2005)
2. Burkhardt, F., Paeschke, A., Rolfes, M., Sendlmeier, W., Weiss, B.: A database of german emotional speech. In: Interspeech 2005, Lissabon, pp. 1517–1520. International Speech Communication Association (2005)
3. Busso, C., Bulut, M., Lee, C.-C., Kazemzadeh, A., Mower, E., Kim, S., Chang, J., Lee, S., Narayanan, S.S.: Iemocap: Interactive emotional dyadic motion capture database. Language Resources and Evaluation 42(4), 335–359 (2008)
4. Cowie, R., Douglas-Cowie, E., Savvidou, S., McMahon, E., Sawey, M.: Feeltrace: An instrument for recording perceived emotion in real time. In: ISCA Workshop on Speech and Emotion, pp. 19–24 (2000)
5. Cronbach, L.: Coefficient alpha and the internal structure of tests. Psychometrika 16(3), 297–334 (1951)
6. Dalgleish, T., Power, M.: Handbook of cognition and emotion (March 1999)
7. Devillers, L., Martin, J.-C.: Coding emotional events in audiovisual corpora. In: LREC 2008, pp. 1259–1265 (2008)
8. Douglas-Cowie, E., Cowie, R., Sneddon, Cox, C., Lowry, M., Martin, J.C., Devillers, L., Batliner, A.: The humaine database: addressing the needs of the affective computing community. In: Paiva, A., Prada, R., Picard, R. (eds.) 2nd International Conference on Affective Computing and Intelligent Interaction (ACII'2007), Lisbon, Portugal 12-14 September. pp. 488–500. Springer, LNCS (2007)
9. Eyben, F., Wollmer, M., Schuller, B.: openear - introducing the munich open-source emotion and affect recognition toolkit. In: Proc. 4th International HUMAINE Association Conference on Affective Computing and Intelligent Interaction 2009, pp. 1–6 (2009)
10. Grant, D.A., Berg, E.A.: A behavioral analysis of degree of reinforcement and ease of shifting to new responses in a weigl-type card-sorting problem 38, 404–411 (1948)
11. Grimm, M., Kroschel, K., Narayanan, S.: The vera am mittag german audio-visual emotional speech database. In: Proceedings of the IEEE International Conference on Multimedia and Expo (ICME 2008), pp. 865–868 (2008)

12. Gunes, H., Schuller, B., Pantic, M., Cowie, R.: Emotion representation, analysis and synthesis in continuous space: A survey. In: Proceedings of IEEE International Conference on Automatic Face and Gesture Recognition (FG 2011), EmoSPACE 2011 - 1st International Workshop on Emotion Synthesis, rePresentation, and Analysis in Continuous spacE, Santa Barbara, CA, USA (March 2011)
13. Lang, P.J.: Behavioral treatment and bio-behavioral assessment: Computer applications. In: Sidowski, J.B., Johnson, J.H., Williams, T.A. (eds.) Technology in Mental Health Care Delivery Systems, pp. 119–137. Ablex Pub. Corp., Norwood (1980)
14. Montero, J.: Estrategias para la mejora de la naturalidad y la incorporación de variedad emocional a la conversión texto a voz en castellano. Ph.D. thesis, Universidad Politécnica de Madrid (2003)
15. Nyhus, E., Barcelo, F.: The wisconsin card sorting test and the cognitive assessment of prefrontal executive functions: a critical update. Brain Cogn. 71(3), 437–451 (2009)
16. Pérez-Espinosa, H., Reyes-García, C.A., VillaseñorPineda, L.: Features selection for primitives estimation on emotional speech. In: International Conference on Acoustics, Speech, and Signal Processing (ICASSP 2010), pp. 5138–5141. Institute of Electrical and Electronics Engineers, Dallas (2010)
17. Pérez-Espinosa, H., Reyes-García, C.A., VillaseñorPineda, L.: Acoustic feature selection and classification of emotions in speech using a 3d continuous emotion model. Biomedical Signal Processing and Control (in Press, 2011)
18. Pérez-Espinosa, H., Reyes-García, C.A., VillaseñorPineda, L.: Bilingual acoustic feature selection for emotion estimation using a 3d continuous model. In: Proceedings of IEEE International Conference on Automatic Face and Gesture Recognition (FG 2011), EmoSPACE 2011 - 1st International Workshop on Emotion Synthesis, Representation, and Analysis in Continuous Space, Santa Barbara, CA, USA (March 2011)
19. Planet, S., Iriondo, I., Martínez, E., Montero, J.A.: True: an online testing platform for multimedia evaluation. In: Proceedings of the Second International Workshop on EMOTION: Corpora for Research on Emotion and Affect at the 6th Conference on Language Resources & Evaluation (LREC 2008), Marrakech, Morocco (2008)
20. Scherer, K.R., Ceschi, G.: Lost luggage: A field study of emotion-antecedent appraisal. Motivation and Emotion 21, 211–235 (1997)
21. Schlosberg, H.: Three dimensions of emotion. Psychological Review 61(2), 81–88 (1954)
22. Schuller, B., Steidl, S., Batliner, A.: The interspeech 2009 emotion challenge. In: Interspeech, pp. 312–315 (2009)
23. Steidl, S.: Automatic Classification of Emotion-Related User States in Spontaneous Children's Speech, 1st edn. Logos Verlag (2009)
24. Vidrascu, L., Devillers, L.: Real-life emotions in naturalistic data recorded in a medical call center. In: LREC 2006 Workshop: Emotion (2006)
25. Warrens, M.: Inequalities between multi-rater kappas. Advances in Data Analysis and Classification 4(4), 271–286 (2010)
26. Witten, I.H., Frank, E.: Data Mining: Practical Machine Learning Tools and Techniques with Java Implementations, 1st edn. The Morgan Kaufmann Series in Data Management Systems. Morgan Kaufmann, San Francisco (1999)

"Should I Teach or Should I Learn?" - Group Learning Based on the Influence of Mood

César F. Pimentel

INESC-ID and Instituto Superior Técnico, Technical University of Lisbon
Av. Prof. Dr. Aníbal Cavaco Silva, 2744-016 Porto Salvo, Portugal
cesar.pimentel@ist.utl.pt

Abstract. One's mood influences one's inclination to either rely on one's current beliefs or search for different ones. Since mood may reflect one's failures and achievements from interacting with the environment, perhaps this influence is working to our advantage.

We propose a simple agent architecture, where the behaviors of learning from or teaching other agents are dependent on the agent's current mood. Using a particular multi-agent scenario, we demonstrate how this approach can lead an entire group of agents to learn a structured concept that was unknown to any of the agents.

1 Introduction

It is currently accepted that emotions and moods influence human reasoning, belief management, and decision making, in ways that are often advantageous to the individual (see, e.g. [4,7]). In the field of Affective Computing [10], researchers have been using this assumption to design systems and agents that are more successful in their interactions with users (see, e.g. [1,2]), or in the performance of specific tasks (see, e.g. [11,8]).

Note, however, that the advantageous nature of some affective phenomena is relatively faint or even questionable. One such phenomenon is how one's mood affects one's preference to either rely on one's current beliefs or search for different ones [5]. This may be advantageous if the current mood reflects the appropriateness of the beliefs at stake, but a person's mood may often reflect situations that are unrelated to the matter at hand, or situations that are not salient at the present moment [3].

Our hypothesis, in this paper, is that a simple model of the bias provided by the mood, in a multi-agent system, can be sufficient to lead the agents to learn the optimal way to perform a given task. From the verification of this hypothesis we can conclude that this influence of mood may indeed be advantageous for artificial agents.

The problem faced by the multi-agent system is to discover the optimal way to execute a given task. More concretely, every agent must learn how to execute the task in the way that maximizes the likelihood of achieving successful results, and there is no feedback informing the agent why an execution succeeds or fails.

S. D'Mello et al. (Eds.): ACII 2011, Part II, LNCS 6975, pp. 72–80, 2011.

Agents may decide to ask for advice from other agents who, in turn, may or may not give advice.

In Section 2 we review the influence of mood in behaviors of assimilation and accommodation. In Section 3 we describe the type of problem that we consider for a multi-agent system, and our approach to addressing it. Next, in Section 4, we discuss the results obtained from testing our approach in the "Doors and Keys" scenario. Finally, in Section 5, we present some concluding remarks.

2   Assimilation versus Accommodation

Clore and Gasper's *processing principle* [3] claims that, when one is engaged in solving a problem or accomplishing a given task, feelings can provide feedback on one's respective performance. Feelings of negative emotions, such as sadness, may be interpreted as failure feedback and one is lead to disbelieve one's beliefs and techniques used so far, and search for new information. On the other hand, feelings of positive emotions, such as happiness, may be interpreted as success feedback and one is lead to strengthen one's current beliefs and stereotypes. The authors refer to experimental research supporting this phenomenon.

In the work presented by Fiedler and Bless [5], the authors cite Piaget [9], who distinguishes two modes of cognitive behavior, that can be summarized as follows:

Assimilation. In this mode, one assimilates the stimuli into one's own structures. One actively elaborates, relying on one's knowledge. One is curious and not cautious and makes active inferences under uncertainty.
Accommodation. In this mode, one reacts reliably to external demands or threats. One "sticks to the stimulus facts" and updates one's own structures to accommodate external requirements.

Consistently with the processing principle, Fiedler and Bless claim that: Positive affective states (in particular, positive moods) facilitate active generation (input transformation, inference, productive thinking, creativity), and trigger assimilation; Negative affective states (in particular, negative moods) facilitate conservation (to keep record of input from outside or from memory), and trigger accommodation. The authors explain that these effects do not correspond to superficial response tendencies, but rather to genuine effects on memory and internal beliefs, and present extensive empirical evidence for their claims [5].

In consonance with these theories, Forgas [6] also explains that, while negative moods facilitate questioning and weakening of beliefs, positive moods facilitate reliance on existing beliefs.

We point out that, when the experienced moods are actually caused by failures and successes in the performance of tasks, this mechanism may sometimes be useful to the individual: One may become biased to prefer new beliefs when one's own beliefs have led to failure, and to rely on one's own beliefs when they have led to success. Thus, by transmitting more or less confidence, moods may sometimes serve as a guide to keeping beliefs that lead to more successful results.

In essence, while positive moods promote reliance and usage of current belief systems, negative moods promote updating, preventing the individual from losing reality. Fiedler and Bless consider the coordination of these two modes "an important aspect of affective-cognitive behavior regulation" [5, p. 165].

3   Problem and Approach

As discussed in Section 2, negative moods may reflect insecurity and conveniently promote belief change, while positive moods may reflect confidence and conveniently increase resistance to belief change. This convenience, however, is far from guaranteed because, even when one's mood is a fairly good indicator of one's confidence regarding the task at hand, it is not enough to identify precisely which beliefs are advantageous/disadvantageous with respect to that task. So the question arises:

Is this mechanism advantageous to human beings?

We do not make any claims regarding humans, but we hope to shed some light on this question, by addressing an analogous question with respect to artificial agents.

We consider the problem of a group of agents with the goal of learning the best way to execute a task or action (henceforth called target action). Every time an agent tries to execute the target action, the only feedback the agent receives is whether the action succeeded or failed. The failure or success of an attempt depends on the agent's beliefs, more specifically on how the agent believes the action should be executed. Note, however, that results are not deterministic, that is, executing the action the same way (i.e. using the same beliefs) does not guarantee the same result. Consequently, what an agent's beliefs determine is the likelihood of obtaining successful results, and the agent's aim is to adjust those beliefs in such way that maximizes that likelihood. What makes this problem challenging is the fact that, when an execution fails or succeeds, the agent does not know which beliefs are responsible for that failure or success.

Notice that this problem is not new, in AI. We can say that the multi-agent system is faced with the problem of learning a concept that is composed of several beliefs, and executing the target action corresponds to testing those beliefs, to some extent. We can also particularize it to the problem of classification in machine learning, where an agent's beliefs define the classifier, and executing the target action corresponds to testing that classifier with a given instance.

The approach we use, for this problem, is inspired by the influence of mood on behaviors of assimilation and accommodation. Next, we describe this approach in more detail.

Every agent has a variable representing its mood. The mood of an agent is affected by the results of executing the target action in the following way:

- A failure decreases the agent's mood;
- A success increases the agent's mood.

In turn, an agent's mood affects its behavior in the following way:

- The lower the mood, the higher the probability that the agent will ask for advice from another agent (when given the opportunity);
- When asked for advice, the higher the mood, the higher the probability that the agent will give advice.

When an agent asks for advice from another agent who, in turn, decides to give it, the first one changes one or more of its beliefs to accommodate one or more beliefs communicated by the second agent.

Thus, low mood leads to more learning and less teaching, while high mood leads to more teaching and less learning. This is obviously inspired by the phenomenon described in Section 2: Low mood leads to less confidence and more belief change (typical of accommodation), while high mood leads to more confidence and less belief change (typical of assimilation).

In essence, agents can play the roles of teachers and/or learners and, hopefully, those who teach are more likely to have more adequate beliefs than those who learn. Note, however, that the beliefs that are transmitted (from one agent to another) are chosen randomly, because an agent never knows which beliefs are adequate/inadequate.

When an agent's mood is considerably low, it is a good indicator that its beliefs are mostly inadequate, since they led to a large number of failures. Our approach, for these situations, is to apply a spontaneous change of beliefs, simulating a radical behavior of accommodation. More concretely, the agent changes its beliefs to new random beliefs, before even seeking advice. This may be helpful in two ways: a) It may cause an improvement in the agent's beliefs (since they were likely very inadequate); b) It may introduce variety of beliefs in the population, very important when one or more useful beliefs are not present in any of the agents.

Given the problem we consider, and the approach we propose (described above), the question we want to answer to is the following:

Can a group of agents guided only by these simple rules effectively learn and solve the problem?

We recall that solving the problem consists of learning the most adequate beliefs. By most adequate beliefs we mean the beliefs that maximize the likelihood of being successful in the execution of the target action.

We point out that we are not searching for the best or most effective approach in solving this problem. Nor do we claim that the approach we use is the best in any way. Our goal is only to show that, by mimicking a simple affective phenomenon (the influence of mood on behaviors of assimilation and accommodation), and using no other learning algorithms or techniques, we can make a group of agents learn, in the context of the described problem. Although out of the scope of our work, if results are positive, it is a fairly good indicator that the actual affective phenomenon can be advantageous to human beings.

4   A Testing Scenario: "Doors and Keys"

In the previous section we describe the problem that is considered and our approach to addressing it, inspired on an affective phenomenon. Our aim is to show that this approach is sufficient to allow a group of agents to effectively learn and solve the problem. In this section we present the results that we obtained when tested this approach in a concrete scenario: the "Doors and Keys" scenario.

In this scenario we have a two-dimensional rectangular space populated by two types of entities, all randomly placed at the start of the simulation:

Agents (represented by bugs). Each agent holds, as beliefs, a sequence of digits that form a key (i.e. a combination). Agents randomly move throughout the map and interact with other agents and doors as they meet them:
- An agent may ask for/give advice from/to another agent, depending on its mood, as dictated by our approach (see Section 3). Giving advice consists of changing one of the digits from the receiver's key, to match that digit in the sender's key.
- Agents repeatedly try their keys on the doors they meet. As prescribed by our approach (see Section 3), failure causes the agent's mood to decrease and success causes it to increase.

Doors (represented by houses). These are fixed entities where agents can try their keys. A key is successful on a door if and only if a certain digit has a required value. The specific digit and value depend only on the door in question, but the agents are unaware of this association (so that the problem conserves the uncertainty discussed in Section 3).

In the context of this scenario, we measure the adequacy/fitness of a key as the number of doors that key can open. A simulation ends successfully when all agents find the master key, that is, the key that can open all doors (in other words, the key with a fitness equal to the number of doors). We recall, however, that an agent never knows the fitness of its key.

We implemented this scenario using the NetLogo tool [12]. Figure 1 shows the area of the simulation in an arbitrary state of its execution. The color of an agent reflects its current mood (closer to green reflects a higher mood, closer to red reflects a lower mood), and the number beside it corresponds to the fitness of its key (unknown to the agents).

For the purposes of allowing the recreation of our experiments we now refer to their specific parameterizations. The mood of an agent is a value $m \in\ ]-1, 1[$. A success adds $0.3 \times (1 - m)$ to the mood, while a failure subtracts $0.3 \times (1 + m)$ from it. When the agent is given the opportunity, the probability of wanting advice is approx. $((1 - m)/2)^2$ and the probability of giving advice is approx. $((1 + m)/2)^2$. A spontaneous change of beliefs occurs whenever the agent's mood drops below -0.8. Notice that all these settings follow the approach described in Section 3.

We consider a population of 40 agents, and two difficulty levels. The low difficulty level has 5 doors and a key radix of 6 (i.e., keys have 5 digits, each ranging from 0 to 5, resulting in 7'776 possible combinations). The high difficulty

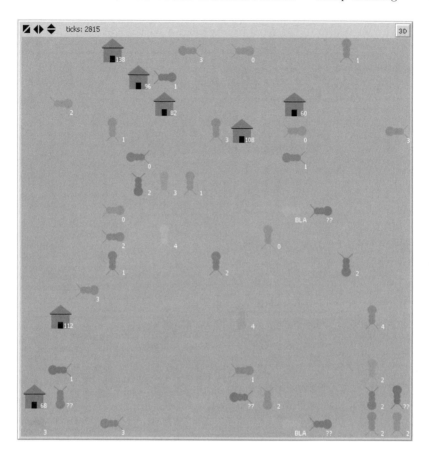

Fig. 1. Snapshot of the simulation area in the "Doors and Keys" scenario

level has 7 doors and a key radix of 10 (i.e., keys have 7 digits, each ranging from 0 to 9, resulting in 10'000'000 possible combinations).

After running the simulation 40 times, 20 for each difficulty level, we obtained the results shown in Table 1. This table shows, for each difficulty level, the average and standard deviation of the number of ticks required for all agents to learn the master key (the key that opens all doors). A tick corresponds to a step of the simulation, where every agents perform one single action (e.g., to turn, to move one step, to try one door, etc.).

Figure 2 shows the evolution of the fitness of the agents' keys, in a typical simulation at the high difficulty level. This particular simulation lasted 6366 ticks until all agents learned the master key (i.e. the key with fitness 7). The top graph shows the evolution of the best key and the average of the keys, in the population. The bottom graph shows the evolution of the percentage of agents that have keys with low, medium or high fitness.

Table 1. Number of ticks (steps) required for all agents to learn the master key

Difficulty	Average Ticks	Standard Deviation
Low	3577.4	775.3
High	7310.4	1930.9

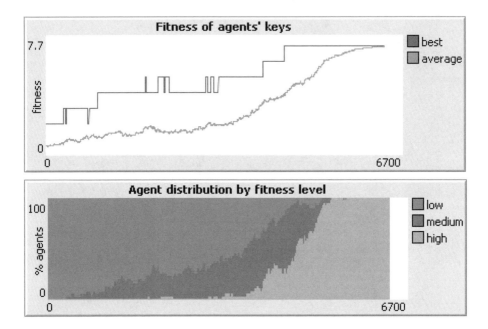

Fig. 2. Evolution of the keys' fitness, at the high difficulty level

It should be pointed out that, at the high difficulty level, sometimes the agents are not able to learn the master key. This happens when the group of agents rapidly learns a key that can open 6 of the doors (instead of all 7), before enough variety is introduced among the agents' beliefs. Because the agents have a high mood and none of them holds the missing digit, they will not make the necessary change of beliefs. This situation occurred in only about 2% of the times that the simulation was run at high difficulty, so we considered it negligible for the purposes of Table 1.

With the exception of the rare occurrences described in the previous paragraph, we observe that the entire group of agents is able to learn the most adequate beliefs, thus solving this instantiation of the problem described in Section 3. Even in the cases when the master key is not learnt, group learning occurs, to a considerable extent.

From the results obtained in this scenario, we validate our initial hypothesis, that a simple model of the affective phenomenon described in Section 2 may be sufficient to lead a group of agents to learn a given concept.

5   Conclusions

Humans can be led to behaviors of assimilation or accommodation as a consequence of their mood. We propose the use of simple rules, inspired by this affective phenomenon, in a multi-agent system that aims at solving a particular class of problems. A mood variable is used, that reflects the agent's failures and successes, and behaviors of learning or teaching are dependent on this variable. Using the "Doors and Keys" scenario, we have shown that this mechanism may be sufficient to allow the agents to learn and solve problems of this type.

The class of problems we consider includes several known problems in AI, such as the problem of classification in the field of machine learning. We do not claim to have found the most effective approach, to these problems, only an approach that works while capturing a human affective phenomenon with simplicity. In addition, since we are simulating a human tendency, we hope our results may shed some light regarding the possible advantageous nature of the actual tendency in human beings.

This work is still preliminary. We believe our results may contribute in motivating the conception of agent architectures to incorporate artificial affective phenomena. These phenomena may simultaneously help produce advantageous behavior and human-like behavior.

References

1. Burleson, W.: Affective Learning Companions: Strategies for Empathetic Agents with Real-Time Multimodal Affective Sensing to Foster Meta-Cognitive and Meta-Affective Approaches to Learning, Motivation, and Perseverance, PhD Thesis, MIT Media Lab (September 2006)
2. Burleson, W., Picard, R.W.: Evidence for Gender Specific Approaches to the Development of Emotionally Intelligent Learning Companions. IEEE Intelligent Systems, Special Issue on Intelligent Educational Systems 22(4), 62–69 (2007)
3. Clore, G.L., Gasper, K.: Feeling is Believing: Some Affective Influences on Belief. In: Frijda, N.H., Manstead, A.S.R., Bem, S. (eds.) Emotions and Beliefs - How Feelings Influence Thoughts, pp. 10–44. Cambridge University Press, Cambridge (2000)
4. Damásio, A.R.: Descartes' Error: Emotion, Reason and the Human Brain. Grosset/Putnam Press, New York (1994)
5. Fiedler, K., Bless, H.: The Formation of Beliefs at the Interface of Affective and Cognitive Processes. In: Frijda, N.H., Manstead, A.S.R., Bem, S. (eds.) Emotions and Beliefs - How Feelings Influence Thoughts, pp. 144–170. Cambridge University Press, Cambridge (2000)
6. Forgas, J.P.: Feeling is Believing? The Role of Processing Strategies in Mediating Affective Influences on Beliefs. In: Frijda, N.H., Manstead, A.S.R., Bem, S. (eds.) Emotions and Beliefs - How Feelings Influence Thoughts, pp. 108–143. Cambridge University Press, Cambridge (2000)
7. Frijda, N.H., Manstead, A.S.R., Bem, S. (eds.): Emotions and Beliefs - How Feelings Influence Thoughts. Cambridge University Press, Cambridge (2000)
8. Marreiros, G., Santos, R., Ramos, C., Neves, J.: Context-Aware Emotion-Based Model for Group Decision Making. IEEE Intelligent Systems 25(2), 31–39 (2010)

9. Piaget, J.: The Origins of Intelligence in Children. International University Press, New York (1952)
10. Picard, R.: Affective Computing. The MIT Press, Cambridge (1997)
11. Pimentel, C.F., Cravo, M.R.: 'Don't think too much!' - Artificial Somatic Markers for Action Selection. In: Cohn, J., Nijholt, A., Pantic, M. (eds.) Proceedings of the 2009 International Conference on Affective Computing & Intelligent Interaction, ACII 2009, vol. I, pp. 55–62. IEEE, Amsterdam (2009)
12. Wilensky, U.: NetLogo. Center for Connected Learning and Computer-Based Modeling. Northwestern University, Evanston, IL (1999),
http://ccl.northwestern.edu/netlogo/

How Low Level Observations Can Help to Reveal the User's State in HCI

Stefan Scherer[1,2], Martin Schels[1], and Günther Palm[1]

[1] Institute of Neural Information Processing, Ulm University, Germany
[2] Speech Communication Lab, Trinity College Dublin, Ireland
stefan.scherer@gmail.com

Abstract. For next generation human computer interaction (HCI), it is crucial to assess the affective state of a user. However, this respective user state is – even for human annotators – only indirectly inferable using background information and the observation of the interaction's progression as well as the social signals produced by the interlocutors. In this paper, coincidences of directly observable patterns and different user states are examined in order to relate the former to the latter. This evaluation motivates a hierarchical label system, where labels of latent user states are supported by low level observations. The dynamic patterns of occurrences of various social signals may in an integration step infer the latent user's state. Thus, we expect to advance the understanding of the recognition of affective user states as compositions of lower level observations for automatic classifiers in HCI.

Keywords: human computer interaction, annotation schemes, affective state, multiparty dialog.

1 Introduction

Current human machine interaction only takes place on a crude explicit question-answer level, whereas human human interaction is multifaceted, consisting of manifold interactive feedback loops between interlocutors, comprising social components, moods, feelings, personal goals, nonverbal and paralinguistic conversation channels and the like [1,5]. In order to close this gap it is crucial for a machine to perceive and understand the user's current interaction and affective state. Most of the research aiming towards recognizing the user's state focuses on the recognition of emotions [2], often the so called big six introduced by [3] and [4]. However, it is not entirely clear what is meant by the word emotion nor what types of emotion or states are relevant for human machine interaction. Further, as stated in [9], traditional theory on emotion includes extremes experienced throughout human lives that never occur in human computer interaction.

In this work, we elaborate on the set of labels, describing user dispositions in HCI as introduced in [13]. These labels comprise categories of different complexity: several are directly inferable (e.g. a subject is laughing), while others are only accessible, when provided with context of the interaction – even for

S. D´Mello et al. (Eds.): ACII 2011, Part II, LNCS 6975, pp. 81–90, 2011.

human annotators. In this context, the aim of this paper is to connect simpler observations to a higher level subject state by evaluating and revealing the pairwise coincidences of labels using t-tests. These coincidences and their dynamic patterns of occurrences in turn support the idea that social signals can serve as basic building blocks that help to infer the latent subjects' state within HCI.

The remainder of this paper is organized as follows: in Section 2, the data collection and the used annotation schemes are described. In Section 3, the interconnection between the labels are evaluated and the results are discussed. Finally, Section 4 concludes.

2   The PIT Corpus of German Multi-party Dialogs

The data collection used for the evaluation is is the "PIT corpus of German multi-party dialogs" [15,14], which is recorded using a WOZ approach. The scenario is a restaurant search, which is composed of three dialog participants: two human subjects (U1 and U2), discussing their choice of a restaurant, and one computer (S) assisting them. This supporting system acts as an independent dialog partner and only turns active when addressed by the main user U1. The system S itself acts as an independent dialog partner and becomes active as soon as the users start to speak about the specified domain.

In Figure 1, the utilized setup of the system and a typical scene of the interaction is shown. Each dialog involves two human participants, who interact with the system operated by the wizard. The system reacts to questions or gives hints about possible restrictions or search queries.

The acquired corpus consists of 36 dialogs with 72 participants, between 19 and 51 years of age (on average 24.4 years); 31 of them female. The shortest recorded dialog lasts 2:43 minutes, the longest lasted 18:24 minutes. For an exact distribution of dialogs and dialog duration please refer to [14].

One of the challenges, dealing with unscripted and naturalistic interactions, as available in the PIT corpus, is the lack of knowledge about the actual ground truth of the participant's affective states. In contrast to acted emotional data it is not possible to fully control the behavior. On the other hand, this lack of control provides naturalistic behavior of users while interacting with machines. The available labels, developed in this work, for the naturalistic interaction data are shown in Table 1. The annotations in this work are provided in different levels: subject state, talk style, events, focus of user, and dominant dialog role. These levels group similar categories used for the annotation: several of these labels are directly inferable from the data, e.g. laughter or the different talk styles. Others are more complex and require context of the conversation for the annotator, such as the subject state. Additionally, in all layers the annotations are temporal attributes and can be assigned with varying lengths and offsets. Using this annotation approach, 15 out of the previously mentioned 36 dialogs were annotated using the well known labeling tool ANVIL [6]. In order not to introduce any bias, the annotators had to annotate the subject state layers of the dialogs in first screenings before knowing about the objective layers. Each

Table 1. Extended list of label groups and organization in layers as introduced in [13]. The top and most abstract level is the subject state layer. Lower levels are more objective observations and comprise social signals (i.e. paralinguistic cues and nonverbal behavior). The rightmost column indicates a short version of the bullet points provided to the annotators.

Level	Label	Meaning
Subject state	Interested	listening (not active), showing interest, reading (silent/loud)
	Uninterested	distracted, uninterested, not paying attention
	Surprised reacting	surprised, facial expression, utterance of surprise
	Embarrassment	embarrassment, insecure, blushing, confused
	Impatient	commenting waiting, impatient movement
	Stressed	seeming stressed (work, appointments), hasty behavior
	negative accepting	may be compromising, disappointment
	positive accepting	pleased with outcome, neutral acceptance
	Disagreement	disagreeing with the outcome but not accepting yet
Talk style	Commanding	non-natural command style talk, imperative speech
	Off-Talk	non-related to topic or HCI
	Ironic	speaking ironically about something
	Explaining	pedagogical, arguing, giving facts
	Active Listening	nodding, back-channeling, non-verbal communication
	Question	posing a question go get information
	Thinking	loud thinking, pausing, hm... what shall we do?
Events	Laughs	loud laughters, silent ones, prominent smiles
	Silence	agreeing or disagreeing silences
	Exciting Moments	for the participants
	Topic Shifts	change of topic
	Waiting	waiting for a reply (mostly due to WOZ lags)
Focus of user U1	User U2	the focus lies on person B
	System	the focus lies on the system
	Others	the focus is something else
	Changing focus	there is a shift of focus (i.e. phase of head or eye movement)
Dominant dialog role	User U1/U2	one person is dominant (longer periods)
	Eq. Active	lively conversation, back and forth between participants
	Eq. Passive	slow and boring conversation

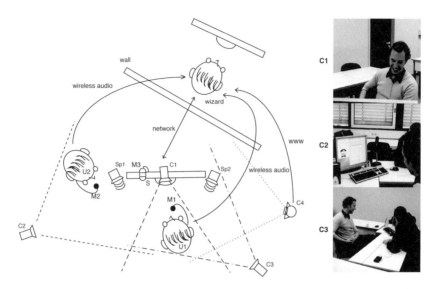

Fig. 1. Schematic view of the Wizard-of-Oz recording setup. The primary user marked as U1 interacts with the secondary user U2 and the System S. The wizard is located in another room and receives real time input from camera C4, and microphones M1 and M2. The subjects receive audiovisual output from the speakers Sp1-2 and from the screen of S. Camera C1 records the face of U1 directly and cameras C2-3 record the scenery. The figure is adapted from [15]. On the right side, a typical scene taken from a recording from all three different camera angles is shown.

lower level was then annotated separately in consecutive annotation runs. The distribution of labels over the dialogs and subject roles is listed in Table 2. Additionally, the average durations and the standard deviations are listed there. Further, alongside the listed labels, the focus of attention and the actual gaze direction of the primary subject was annotated and analyzed [16].

3   Evaluation and Discussion

In the following three labels, namely interested, positive accepting[1], and negative labels[2] are statistically analyzed in order to find significant correlates between the lower and higher levels.

In order to measure the coincidence of the simpler annotations with the subject state, the relative overlap of these lower level labels with the subject state was measured for all the annotated dialogs. The relative overlap r is calculated as the overlapping length o of the lower objective label with respect to the length of the subject state annotation l: $r = \frac{o}{l} \in [0, 1]$. The result is evaluated using

---

[1] An offer or suggestion of the system is perceived positively by the subject.
[2] All negative subject states combined, i.e. uninterested, embarrassed, impatient, stressed, negative accepting, disagreement.

Table 2. Number of occurrences and durations of labels for user U1 and U2. All four annotation layers are listed with their respective labels. The durations are listed in seconds.

Subject state	Avg. Length		Std. Deviation		Duration		Occurrences	
	U1	U2	U1	U2	U1	U2	U1	U2
Interested	13.1	13.5	11.0	11.5	4012.6	3599.2	306	266
Uninterested	11.4	11.9	4.5	8.1	91.2	261.7	8	22
Surprised reacting	6.6	4.7	7.6	2.4	159.1	32.9	24	7
Embarrassment	9.4	9.4	7.5	7.0	366.4	103.2	40	11
Impatient	7.6	5.6	6.5	4.5	175.2	90.2	23	16
Stressed	5.8	3.5	2.7	2.3	69.5	7.0	12	2
neg. accepting	4.9	5.1	4.0	3.3	173.0	111.5	35	22
pos. accepting	6.1	6.1	5.0	4.7	904.5	725.9	149	119
Disagreement	5.5	9.3	3.4	5.1	82.9	102.0	15	11
Talk style								
Commanding	4.1	4.8	2.5	4.2	252.8	124.6	61	26
Off-Talk	10.3	9.9	6.7	6.0	227.7	138.9	22	14
Ironic	5.4	4.0	4.9	2.8	75.2	56.0	14	14
Explaining	8.5	5.0	7.5	3.6	1296.7	474.9	153	95
Active Listening	9.1	14.2	5.7	15.6	2731.5	4071.9	299	287
Question	4.3	4.4	2.5	4.3	595.6	352.0	137	80
Thinking	4.5	4.6	3.2	2.4	90.7	68.4	20	15
Reading	9.6	n/a	5.3	n/a	105.2	n/a	11	n/a
Event								
Laughs	3.2	2.9	1.5	1.7	352.9	306.8	112	107
Silence	9.0	9.3	7.2	9.4	135.1	74.6	15	8
Exciting Moments	7.1	3.7	7.5	1.4	56.5	14.8	8	4
Topic Shifts	2.1	2.1	1.3	1.3	21.2	21.2	10	10
Waiting	4.8	8.0	3.5	5.1	135.7	88.4	28	11
Dom. dialog role	Average		Standard dev.		Duration		Occurrences	
User U1	10.9		11.2		1460.4		134	
User U2	7.7		5.0		271.2		35	
System S	10.5		4.8		1988.3		189	
Eq. Active	18.8		15.6		1765.2		94	
Eq. Passive	10.7		6.6		363.0		34	

box plots where brackets with * or ** indicate significant (p < .05) and highly significant (p < .01) differences in the overlaps calculated using paired t-tests. The boxes denote 50% of the data and the median value is shown as the middle line of the plot. Whiskers include 1.5 times the standard deviation of the data and outliers marked as crosses are further away from the median.

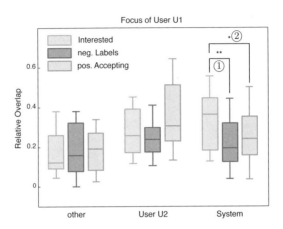

Fig. 2. Comparison of the relative overlaps for the subject states interested, positive accepting and negative labels of the users U1 with his focus towards the system, user U2, or elsewhere (other)

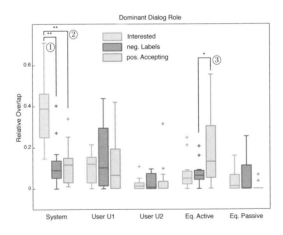

Fig. 3. Comparison of the relative overlaps for the subject states interested, positive accepting and negative labels of the users U1 with the dominant dialog role annotations

In Figure 2, it is seen that the focus of attention towards the system differs significantly over the three targeted subject states. In detail, U1 is labeled significantly (p = .003, ①) more as focusing on the system while he is labeled as interested contrary to negative labels. Further, he significantly (p = .031, ②) focuses the system more while interested in contrast to the label positive accepting.

In Figure 3, the dominant dialog role annotations are compared to U1's subject states: if the system takes over the dominant role in the conversation, highly significant support for the state interested is found (vs. positive accepting p = .001, ①; vs. negative labels p < .001, ②). It is also seen that if all participants are equally active in the dialog the state positive accepting is significantly (p = .043, ③) overlapped to a higher extent.

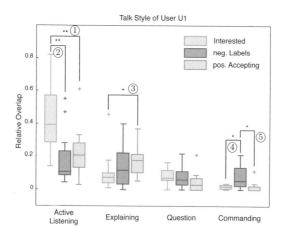

Fig. 4. Comparison of the relative overlaps for the subject states interested, positive accepting and negative labels of the users U1 with the talk style/utterances of user U1

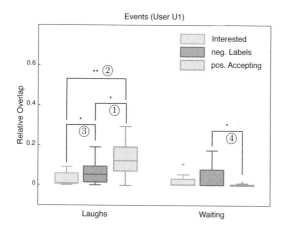

Fig. 5. Comparison of the relative overlaps for the subject states interested, positive accepting and negative labels of the users U1 with the two most frequent U1 related events (laughs and waiting)

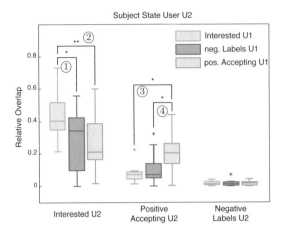

Fig. 6. Comparison of the relative overlaps for the subject states interested, positive accepting and negative labels of the users U1 and U2

Single turns, utterances or paralinguistic cues of subject U1 can be investigated in Figure 4. It is seen that the overlap for active listening, including many feedback and back-channeling utterances and paralinguistic cues, such as "um", or "hm", is highly significantly larger for the state of interested as opposed to the other two categories (vs. positive accepting p = .001 , ①; vs. negative labels p < .001, ②). Further, the amount of overlap with respect to the talk style explaining for positive accepting is significantly higher compared to interested (p = .028, ③). The overlap of questions posed is not significantly higher if the user is interested, whereas the annotations of commanding ares significantly overlapping more with the negative labels as with the two other categories (vs. interested p = .012, ④; vs. positive accepting p = .019, ⑤).

Additionally, Figure 5 allows the examination of the relevance of the labels subsumed in "events" for the identification of the user's state in the interaction. Laughter overlaps significantly more in the state of positive accepting as opposed to the negative annotations (p = .012, ①) and highly significantly more in contrary to interested (p < .001, ②). This finding supports the idea that U1 is commenting positively perceived suggestions with a surprised or pleased smile or laughter. Further, the overlap of laughs with the negative labels in comparison to interested is significant too (p = .018, ③). Figure 5 also shows that the relative amount of overlap of the annotation of waiting with negative subject state labels is significantly higher than the one for positive accepting (p = .046, ④).

In Figure 6, a comparison of the subject state of U1 to the one of U2 is shown. The labels interested and positive accepting correlate between both users forming some sort of common interactional state. The relative overlap of the interested state of U2 with the state of interested of U1 is significantly higher (p = .022, ①) than the negative label overlap and highly significant (p = .001, ②) for positive accepting. Further, if U1 is in the state of positive accepting we can observe significantly higher overlaps for the subject state positive accepting of U2 (vs.

interested: p = .017, ③; vs. negative labels p = .010, ④), which indicates some sort of mimicry behavior of U2.

4   Conclusions and Future Directions

This paper links the different categories of labels, first introduced in [13], in order to reveal the dynamics of patterns and correlations among them. These annotations are grouped in various sets combining labels of similar character, i.e. subjective user state labels, as well as coarse and fine grained observations, such as dialog roles or laughter (compare Table 1), arranged in a hierarchical structure. The analysis revealed several significant dependencies between the subjectively annotated user's state and the low level observations (i.e. social signals, etc.). These dependencies support the hierarchical approach that social signals and the patterns in which they can be observed can serve as basic building blocks that help infer the current users' interactional state.

These dynamic multimodal patterns could now in turn be used to automatically detect the user's state: Work, such as [10,12], have for example shown that it is possible to recognize laughter in naturalistic conversations, or in [8] head poses and the focus of a subject is recognized. These automatic detection for the lower level observations could now be integrated in hierarchical classification approaches. The inherent temporal structure of this application demands classifiers that are able to incorporate these dynamics, such as hidden Markov models or echo state networks. Further, such a hierarchical architecture needs to be robust with respect to uncertainty and possible sensory outage or failure.

The proposed annotation approach, however, is not exhaustive and extensions are straightforward. In [16] for instance it has been shown that voice quality can be used to infer the affective state of the speaker and [11] shows the capability to automatically recognize it. Additionally, the subject state layer comprising the so called conversational dispositions is not compulsory, but could in principal be exchanged by other schemes, such as dimensional affect annotations.

Acknowlegdements. The presented work was developed within the Transregional Collaborative Research Centre SFB/TRR 62 "Companion-Technology for Cognitive Technical Systems" funded by the German Research Foundation (DFG). The work of Martin Schels is supported by a scholarship of the Carl-Zeiss Foundation.

References

1. Campbell, W.N.: On the use of nonVerbal speech sounds in human communication. In: Esposito, A., Faundez-Zanuy, M., Keller, E., Marinaro, M. (eds.) COST Action 2102. LNCS (LNAI), vol. 4775, pp. 117–128. Springer, Heidelberg (2007)
2. Cowie, R., Douglas-Cowie, E., Tsapatsoulis, N., Votsis, G., Kollias, S., Fellenz, W., Taylor, J.G.: Emotion recognition in human-computer interaction. IEEE Signal Processing Magazine 18(1), 32–80 (2001)

3. Darwin, C.: The expression of emotion in man and animals, 3rd edn. HarperCollins, London (1978)
4. Ekman, P.: Facial expression and emotion. American Psychologist 48, 384–392 (1993)
5. Kendon, A. (ed.): Nonverbal Communication, Interaction, and Gesture. Selections from Semiotica Series, vol. 41. Walter de Gruyter, Berlin (1981)
6. Kipp, M.: Anvil - a generic annotation tool for multimodal dialogue. In: Proceedings of the European Conference on Speech Communication and Technology (Eurospeech), Aalborg, pp. 1367–1370. ISCA (2001)
7. Layher, G., Liebau, H., Niese, R., Al-Hamadi, A., Michaelis, B., Neumann, H.: Robust stereoscopic head pose estimation in human-computer interaction and a unified evaluation framework. To Appear in 16th International Conference on Image Analysis and Processing (ICIAP 2011). Springer, Heidelberg (2011)
8. Russell, J.A., Barrett, L.F.: Core affect, prototypical emotional episodes, and other things called emotion: dissecting the elephant. Journal of Personality and Social Psychology 76(5), 805–819 (1999)
9. Scherer, S., Glodek, M., Schwenker, F., Campbell, N., Palm, G.: Spotting laughter in naturalistic multiparty conversations: a comparison of automatic online and offline approaches using audiovisul data. ACM Transactions on Interactive Intelligent Systems: Special Issue on Affective Interaction in Natural Environments (accepted for publication)
10. Scherer, S., Kane, J., Gobl, C., Schwenker, F.: Investigating fuzzy-input fuzzy-output support vector machines for robust voice quality classification. IEEE Transactions on Audio, Speech and Language Processing (under review)
11. Scherer, S., Schwenker, F., Campbell, W.N., Palm, G.: Multimodal laughter detection in natural discourses. In: Ritter, H., Sagerer, G., Dillmann, R., Buss, M. (eds.) Proceedings of 3rd International Workshop on Human-Centered Robotic Systems (HCRS 2009). Cognitive Systems Monographs, pp. 111–121. Springer, Heidelberg (2009)
12. Scherer, S., Trentin, E., Schwenker, F., Palm, G.: Approaching emotion in human computer interaction. In: International Workshop on Spoken Dialogue Systems (IWSDS 2009), pp. 156–168 (2009)
13. Strauss, P.-M., Hoffmann, H., Minker, W., Neumann, H., Palm, G., Scherer, S., Traue, H.C., Weidenbacher, U.: The PIT corpus of german multi-party dialogues. In: Proceedings of the Sixth International Language Resources and Evaluation (LREC 2008), Marrakech, Morocco, pp. 2442–2445. ELRA (2008)
14. Strauss, P.-M., Hoffmann, H., Neumann, H., Minker, W., Palm, G., Scherer, S., Schwenker, F., Traue, H.C., Weidenbacher, U.: Wizard-of-oz data collection for perception and interaction in multi-user environments. In: Proceedings of the Fifth International Language Resources and Evaluation (LREC 2006), pp. 2014–2017. ELRA (2006)
15. Strauss, P.-M., Scherer, S., Layher, G., Hoffmann, H.: Evaluation of the PIT corpus or what a difference a face makes? In: Calzolari, N., Choukri, K., Maegaard, B., Mariani, J., Odjik, J., Piperidis, S., Rosner, M., Tapias, D. (eds.) Proceedings of the Seventh International Conference on Language Resources and Evaluation (LREC 2010), Valletta, Malta, pp. 3470–3474. ELRA (May 2010)
16. Yanushevskaya, I., Gobl, C., Chasaide, A.N.: Voice quality and loudness in affect perception. In: Proceedings of Speech Prosody 2008, Campinas, Brazil, pp. 29–32. ISCA (2008)

Investigating Acoustic Cues in Automatic Detection of Learners' Emotion from Auto Tutor

Rui Sun and Elliot Moore II

Georgia Institute of Technology
School of Electrical and Computer Engineering
210 Technology Circle, Savannah, GA, 31407
rsun7@gatech.edu, em80@mail.gatech.edu

Abstract. This study investigates the emotion-discriminant ability of acoustic cues from speech collected in the automatic computer tutoring system named as Auto Tutor. The purpose of this study is to examine the acoustic cues for emotion detection of the speech channel from the learning system, and to compare the emotion-discriminant performance of acoustic cues (in this study) with the conversational cues (available in previous work). Comparison between the classification performance obtained using acoustic cues and conversational cues shows that the emotions: flow and boredom are better captured in acoustics than conversational cues while conversational cues play a more important role in multiple-emotion classification.

Keywords: Speech, Emotion detection, Acoustic features, Human-computer interaction, Auto Tutor.

1 Introduction

The interest of researchers in the field of human-computer interaction (HCI) has been developed to build more effective, user-friendly, and intelligent applications [1,2,3,4,5,6,7]. Computer tutoring system with user emotion detection is one of the focuses. Researchers extracted multiple cues to recognize users' emotion. One of the computer tutoring systems is ITSPOKE[1]. The ITSPOKE group collected features including the acoustic-prosodic (pitch related, energy related, duration, speaking rate, pause-duration, and number of internal silence) and the lexical (i.e., manually transcribed or recognized speech) features to predict three emotion states (negative, neutral, and positive) of the users. Their result, in general, showed the lexical features yielded higher predictive utility than acoustic-prosodic features [1].

Another computer tutoring system, Auto Tutor, developed by the University of Memphis involved multiple channels [2] to detect the learners' emotion, such as facial expression, body gesture [5], and speech [6]. In the speech channel, the features they used were the conversational cues, which consist of five aspects of information: temporal, response, answer quality, tutor directness, and tutor feedback (more details in Section 4). However, no work has been reported involving

S. D'Mello et al. (Eds.): ACII 2011, Part II, LNCS 6975, pp. 91–100, 2011.

the features of acoustics from the speech channel. Acoustics have been reported to carry rich emotion information in speech and well studied for emotion recognition [1,4,8,9,10]. This motivated the study to investigate the performance of acoustic cues from speech in learner's emotion detection of Auto Tutor. In this paper, we use the same speech data and methodology as that in the work using conversational cues for emotion detection of Auto Tutor [6] and compare the performance of acoustic cues working in emotion detection with that of the conversational cues. In addition, Sequential Floating Forward Selection (SFFS) is applied as extra study on the acoustics for feature selection and the selected features was evaluated and examined to provide more detailed analysis of the acoustic features in emotion detection of Auto Tutor HCI.

2 Data

The speech data used for this study was provided by the Auto Tutor system from the University of Memphis [11] (UM data). The UM data contains the recordings of 30 users' (15 females and 15 males) dialog when they were learning with Auto Tutor. UM data covers seven emotions including 'neutral', 'boredom', 'confusion', 'flow', 'frustration', 'delight', and 'surprise'. 'Neutral' was defined as no emotion or feeling. 'Boredom' was defined as being weary or restless through lack of interest. 'Confusion' was defined as a noticeable lack of understanding. 'Flow' was a state of interest resulting from involvement in an activity. 'Frustration' was defined as dissatisfaction or annoyance. 'Delight' was a degree of satisfaction. And 'surprise' was wonder or amazement, especially from the unexpected [11]. These emotion categories were labeled by the user himself/herself (i.e., self-evaluation) through reviewing the recorded video of their learning interaction procedure after the learning session. The number of utterances with emotion labels is shown in Table 1.

Table 1. Number of samples of UM database

Emotion	neutral	boredom	confusion	flow	frustration	delight	surprise
No.samples	277	268	319	348	204	78	17

To make a balanced classification and equivalent comparison, this study excluded emotions 'delight' and 'surprise' in the analysis with the following reasons: 1) the number of samples in emotion categories 'delight' and 'surprise' is considerably smaller than that of other emotions, which could cause a bias in classification evaluation; 2) the comparable work in [6] excluded the two emotions for the same reason. Therefore, the dataset in this analysis consists of 1416 samples from 30 speakers in five emotion categories: 'neutral', 'boredom', 'confusion', 'flow', and 'frustration'.

3   Features

The acoustic cues used in this study consist of two features sets, glottal wave-form features and a feature set including the prosodic, spectral, and other voice related features (e.g., probability of voicing, jitter, and shimmer). The glottal waveform provides a representation of the shaping of the volume velocity of air-flow *through* the vocal folds during voiced speech. Research has shown that the glottal waveform dynamics can play an important role in voice characterization [9,10,12,13,14]. Fig. 1 shows an example of the glottal waveform (Fig. 1(b)) and glottal waveform derivative estimate (Fig. 1(c)) for one cycle of voiced speech (Fig. 1(a)). One total cycle (TC) consists of an open phase (O) and closed phase (C). The open phase is divided into an opening phase (OP) (i.e., abduction) and closing phase (CP) (i.e., adduction). The opening phase may sometimes be further divided into the length of the primary opening (T_{o1}, i.e. OP) and a secondary opening (T_{o2}). The distinction between T_{o1} and T_{o2} is marked by a an increase in the slope during the opening phase (i.e. smaller slope for (T_{o1}, larger slope for T_{o2}).

The extraction of the glottal features for each speech utterance was processed in four steps [10]: (1) each utterance was divided into frames four pitch periods long for feature extraction purposes (2) glottal closure instants (GCI's) were obtained using the DYPSA algorithm [15] on each frame (3) glottal waveform estimates were obtained for each frame using the Rank-Based Glottal Quality Assessment (RBGQA) algorithm [16], which iterates around approximate loca-tions of GCI's to find the optimal analysis window position for deconvolution

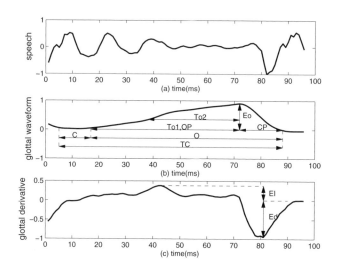

Fig. 1. Example of the time-based parameters extracted from the glottal waveform dur-ing a single speech cycle. (a) One-pitch cycle of speech (b) Glottal waveform estimate (c) Glottal waveform derivative.

Table 2. Time-based glottal features extracted from the glottal waveform estimations (see Fig. 1)

Abbr.	Explanation	Equation
OQ1	(open quotient, from primary glottal opening)	$OQ1 = \frac{T_{o1}+CP}{TC}$
OQ2	(open quotient, from secondary glottal opening)	$OQ2 = \frac{T_{o2}+CP}{TC}$
AQ	(amplitude quotient)	$AQ = \frac{E_o}{E_d}$
NAQ	(normalized amplitude quotient)	$NAQ = \frac{AQ}{TC}$
ClQ	(closing quotient)	$ClQ = \frac{CP}{TC}$
OQa	(open quotient based on Liljencrants-Fant model)	$OQa = \frac{E_o}{TC}(\frac{\pi}{2EI} + \frac{1}{E_d})$
SQ1	(speed quotient, from primary glottal opening)	$SQ_1 = \frac{T_{o1}}{TC}$
SQ2	(speech quotient, from secondary glottal opening)	$SQ_2 = \frac{T_{o2}}{TC}$
QOQ	(quasi-open quotient)	[18]

via the covariance method of linear predictive analysis (LPA) (for simplicity, an LPA order of 16 was used for all speakers) (4) for each frame, the 11 glottal features (the time-based nine features listed in Table 2 followed by two spectral-based features described below) were computed using version 0.3.1 of the APARAT toolbox [17]. All features were quantified using seven statistics (i.e, the mean, median, minimum, maximum, standard deviation, range, and inter-quartile) across all frames of an utterance to form the representation of this utterance. The feature extraction produced 77 glottal waveform features.

Spectral-based features calculated by APARAT on the glottal waveform included: *DH12* (the difference in the first and second glottal formants, in dB [19]) and *HRF* (the Harmonic Richness Factor, in dB [20]). These parameters were calculated as shown in Eq. 1 and Eq. 2, where *X(F0)* is the spectral amplitude at the fundamental frequency (*F0*), *X(2*F0)* is the amplitude at two times the fundamental frequency, and *X(f_i)* is the spectral amplitude in the ith harmonics (f_1 is the fundamental frequency *F0*).

$$DH12 = 10\log\frac{|X(F0)|^2}{|X(2*F0)|^2}, \tag{1}$$

$$HRF = 10\log\frac{\sum_{i>1}|X(f_i)|^2}{|X(f_1)|^2}. \tag{2}$$

Another set of energy related, spectral related, and other voice related features were extracted using the openSMILE toolkit [21]. The low-level descriptors (LLD) are listed in Table 3. Up to 39 functionals were applied to LLD to generate 4368 features [22].

Based on the above, a 4445-dimensional acoustic feature set was created for each utterance sample for all five emotion categories (excluding delight and surprise) as listed in Table 1.

Table 3. openSMILE low-level descriptors (LLD)[22]

Energy Related	Spectral Related	Other Voice Related
Sum of auditory spectrum	RASTA-style spectrum	F0
Sum of RASTA-style filtered spectrum	MFCC 1-12	Probability of voicing
RMS energy	Spectral energy	Jitter
Zero-crossing rate	Spectral roll off point	Shimmer
	Spectral statistics	

4 Methodology

In the comparison work [6], the emotion states of speech data (UM data) were labeled by four evaluators: the user himself/herself (i.e., self-evaluation), peer (other user), and two trained judges. Based on the evaluator, seven sets of emotion labels were generated: self-evaluation (the user evaluated himself/herself), peer-evaluation (another user's evaluation), two trained judges separately, agreement shared between the two trained judges, agreement shared between more than two evaluators (including self, peer, and the two trained judges), and agreement shared between more than three evaluators (including self, peer, and the two trained judges). Except for the self-evaluation label, other label sets are not available in this study, so the comparison will focus on the experiments using self-evaluation as the emotion label. The features used in the comparison work [6] are 17 conversational cues from five aspects: temporal (e.g., duration, number of topics, number of turns, etc.), response (number of words, number of chars, etc.), answer quality (similarity to an expectation, the change in the similarity, etc.), tutor directness (hint, prompt, correction, etc.), and tutor feedback (positive, neutral, negative, etc.). The 17 features was reduced in dimension using Principle Component Analysis (PCA). The reduced feature set were evaluated by a list of classifiers in the WEKA environment [23], among which Adaboost.M1 is the classifier yielded the highest accuracy rate for the self-evaluation label data. The classification was conducted in two sets of experiments: multiple-emotion classes and binary-emotion classes. The multiple-emotion classification including 5-classes (all five emotions) and 4-classes ('neutral' excluded); the binary classification is between two emotions: neutral and one from the other four emotions. For each classification task, the number of samples in each class was forced to be equal by randomly selecting N samples from every class (N is the smallest class's size). The classification for each experiment was repeated 10 times (trials) using the balanced samples. The averaged result over 10 trails was the representation of the classification experiment.

For the comparison purpose, this study adopted the methodology in [6]. Dimension reduction using PCA was conducted, followed by classification using Adaboost.M1. However, due to the large difference in the dimension of features (17 conversational cues vs. 4445 acoustic cues), additional feature selection (Sequential Floating Forward Selection - SFFS) was applied to the 4445-dimension acoustic feature set. The selected features were evaluated by classification tasks using Adaboost.M1 classifier as well. AdaBoost.M1 is a boosting algorithm. It improves the 'weak' learning algorithm by repeatedly applying it to different distributions or weighings of training samples and eventually forming a 'stronger' learning algorithm [24]. This classifier was chosen in this additional study because it was one of the classifiers yielded best classification result in D'Mello's work [6], and also it was evaluated in prior works to show more robust performance compared with other learning methods [1]. The software WEKA [23] was used for SFFS and Adaboost.M1 classification and MATLAB executed PCA to create new feature sets with the 95% variation represented.

It should be noticed that acoustic features are speaker-dependent because they capture the characteristics of speakers (e.g., gender and culture). To eliminate the acoustic difference from factors other than emotion, speaker normalization was applied to the data first. The equation for speaker normalization is shown in Equation (3):

$$\hat{f_{i,j}} = \frac{f_{i,j} - mean(f_{i,j})}{std(f_{i,j})}, \tag{3}$$

where $f_{i,j}$ is the i_{th} feature descriptor for speaker j across the samples of all emotions and std refers to the standard deviation.

5   Result

The classification result is shown in Table 4. The classification results using PCA (95% variation represented) are all approximately equal to the baseline (chance) as shown in the row of 'PCA95%variation'. While all classification accuracy rates using SFFS are above chance (i.e, the baseline). The higher accuracy rate using SFFS than PCA implies that feature selection is benefit for large dimension feature set. Therefore, the focus of result expression will be on comparing the results using SFFS (instead of PCA) with D'Mello's work [6]. From the multiple-emotion tasks shown in columns '5class' and '4class' of Table 4, the 5-class and 4-class ARs are lower than D'Mello's results using conversational cues. However, acoustic cues yielded higher (boredom and flow) or similar (confusion and frustration) accuracy rate in all binary-emotion classifications between neutral and emotional states (the rightmost four columns in Table 4).

Table 4. Comparison: Classification Accuracy Rate (AR) (%)

AR	5class	4class	neutral vs. boredom	neutral vs. confusion	neutral vs. flow	neutral vs. frustration
baseline (chance)	20.0	25.0	50.0	50.0	50.0	50.0
SFFS	24.9	31.6	69.1	61.8	66.6	64.6
PCA95%variation	20.1	24.9	47.3	54.2	50.5	52.6
D'Mello [6]	29.5	35.1	61.3	58.9	52.9	64.1

Following the analysis in [6], the F-measure scores in Table 5 were calculated by dividing the doubled number of correctly classified samples (i.e., true positive) belonging to one class by the total number of samples of false positive, false negative, and doubled true positive from the confusion matrix [25]. For multiple-emotion tasks (5-class and 4-class), Acoustic cues outperform conversational cues for flow, while conversational cues win in confusion and frustration for both 5/4-class tasks. Neutral and boredom are distinguished from other emotions with fairly similar scores using conversational cues and acoustics (26%, 25% for neutral, and 32%, 32% for boredom) for 5-class. In the 4-class case, acoustics yield higher score in boredom. Considering 4 and 5 classes together, flow exhibits the most acoustic separation, while the score using conversational cues is the lowest. This could be explained that among the five emotions (including neutral), flow (i.e., interest, engaged) is mostly an arousal related emotion [4]. Previous work showed that arousal degree (involvement) were captured more using acoustic cues comparing using the degree valence (pleasant of emotion) [26]. Therefore, the emotion flow, describing the involvement, has the largest separation using acoustic cues and is captured by acoustics better than the conversational cues in this study. The F-measure scores for binary classification (the rightmost four columns in Table 5) support the accuracy rate results (the rightmost four columns in Table 4). Acoustic cues yield higher (boredom and flow) or similar (confusion and frustration) scores than conversational cues. And the two scores in each binary classification is fairly balanced. The observation indicates the distinguishing capability of acoustic cues working in detecting 'flow' and 'boredom' of the computer tutoring system.

Table 5. Comparison: F-measure scores (D: the comparison work [6], P: the present work)(%)

F-measure	5class		4class		boredom		confusion		flow		frustration	
	D	P	D	P	D	P	D	P	D	P	D	P
neutral	26	25	na	na	57	71	63	63	59	66	66	63
boredom	32	32	35	51	67	68						
confusion	35	11	43	11			57	62				
flow	13	48	33	66					54	67		
frustration	35	6	41	0							63	66

To have a closer investigation on the performance of acoustic cues in distinguishing emotions, the binary classification between two emotional states was also conducted and the result is shown in Table 6. The best performance is from the pair of boredom and flow with the AR 71.4% while the lowest AR is 61.8% from the pair of confusion and frustration. This is possibly caused by the fact that the largest involvement separation is between the pair flow (i.e., interest) and boredom (i.e., lack of interest) and the involvement, as described above, is highly related with acoustics. The result in Table 6 shows that although confusion and frustration failed in multiple-emotions classification (i.e., all 5-class and

Table 6. Binary Classification Accuracy Rate (AR) between Emotional States (%)

AR	boredom	confusion	flow
confusion	67.7		
flow	71.4	65.8	
frustration	63.4	61.8	68.5

4-class), they can be recognized with a over 61.8% AR in pair-wise classification tasks. Confusion and frustration exhibit discriminant ability in acoustics.

Examining the selected acoustic features provides the details of which aspect of acoustics works for emotion recognition in this study. The features selected in all 10 trials for each experiment are listed in Table 7. Pitch (i.e., F0) related feature was selected in all experiments. Comparing emotions boredom and flow with the other two, more shimmer and spectral related features were selected. The larger number of features selected for boredom and flow (mostly from shimmer and spectral) can contribute to the better performance of the binary classification of the two emotions.

Table 7. Features Selected using SFFS in All 10 Trials

	5class	4class	boredom	confusion	flow	frustration
F0	1	1	1	1	1	1
jitter		1	1		1	
shimmer			5	1		
spectral			4	1	4	
mfcc			1	1	1	1
energy					2	
voicing			1	1		
total	1	2	13	5	9	2

6 Discussion and Conclusion

This paper examined the acoustic cues in detecting learner's emotion of Auto Tutor system and compare the results with available work using conversational cues [6] from the same dataset. The binary-emotion classification result is better (for emotion boredom and flow) or comparable (confusion and frustration) to the comparison work in [6]. This result reveals that the emotions: flow and boredom are better captured in acoustics than conversational cues while conversational cues play a more important role in multiple-emotion classification. These results are related with the results delivered by the ITSPOKE group mentioned in Section 1. Their group studied the acoustic-prosodic features (part of the acoustic cues in the present study) and lexical cues (part of the conversational cues in [6]) from the user's speech in the computer tutoring system ITSPOKE. Their results showed lexical cues outperformed acoustic-prosodic cues in distinguishing negative, neutral, and positive emotions of users [1]. The emotion states in their research are more distributed along the valence dimension (pleasant or unpleasant) than the arousal (active or passive). While in the present study, boredom and flow are emotions with extremely opposite degrees along the arousal dimension, for which the acoustic cues yield higher accuracy rate (AR).

The comparison work used Principle Component Analysis (PCA) for feature selection and extraction on their 17 conversational cues. However, the PCA did not work well on the 4445-dimension features set in this study (the AR was close to the rate by chance). This could be possibly explained that the new dimensions created by PCA representing the largest diversity of data, however, this diversity may come from the inner-class of emotion itself instead of between-classes. Also, the 95% variation PCA applied on 4445-dimension feature set still resulted in a large dimension of subset comparing with the size of sample, which is not suitable for classification. Therefore, the feature selection SFFS was required in this study and was the focus in the comparison result. What's more, the comparison between acoustic cues and conversational cues is available only using the self-judgement of emotion labels. More emotion-labeling strategies were employed in D'Mello's study and produced better recognition rate. This could be the improvement and future work of the emotion detection using acoustic cues.

References

1. Litman, D.J., Forbes-Riley, K.: Recognizing student emotions and attitudes on the basis of utterances in spoken tutoring dialogues with both human and computer tutors. Speech Communication 48, 559–590 (2006)
2. D'Mello, S., Graesser, A.: Multimodal semi-automated affect detection from conversational cues, gross body language, and facial features. User Modeling and User-Adapted Interaction 20, 147–187 (2010)
3. Fragopanagos, N., Taylor, J.G.: Emotion recognition in human-computer interaction. Neural Networks 18, 389–405 (2005)
4. Cowie, R., Douglas-Cowie, E., Tsapatsoulis, N., Votsis, G., Kollias, S., Fellenz, W., Taylor, J.G.: Emotion recognition in human-computer interaction. IEEE Signal Processing Magazine 18, 32–80 (2001)
5. D'Mello, S., Graesser, A.: Automatic detection of learners emotions from gross body language. Applied Artificial Intelligence 23, 123–150 (2009)
6. D'Mello, S., Craig, S.D., Witherspoon, A., McDaniel, B., Graesser, A.: Automatic detection of learners affect from conversational cues. User Modeling and User-Adapted Interaction 18, 45–80 (2008)
7. McKeown, G., Valstar, M.F., Cowie, R., Pantic, M.: The semaine corpus of emotionally coloured character interactions. In: 2010 IEEE International Conference on Multimedia and Expo. (ICME), pp. 1079–1084 (2010)
8. Busso, C., Sungbok, L., Narayanan, S.: Analysis of emotionally salient aspects of fundamental frequency for emotion detection. IEEE Transactions on Audio, Speech, and Language Processing 17, 582–596 (2009)
9. Moore, E., Clements, M.A., Peifer, J.W., Weisser, L.: Critical analysis of the impact of glottal features in the classification of clinical depression in speech. IEEE Transactions on Biomedical Engineering 55, 96–107 (2008)

10. Sun, R., Moore, E., Torres, J.: Investigating glottal parameters for differentiating emotional categories with similar prosodics. In: IEEE International Conference on Acoustics, Speech and Signal Processing, ICASSP 2009, Taipei, Taiwan (2009)

11. Graesser, A., D'Mello, S., Chipman, P., King, B., McDaniel, B.: Exploring relationship between affect and learning with autotutor. In: The 13th International Conference on Artificial Intelligence in Education, pp. 16–23 (2007)

12. Cummings, K.E., Clements, M.A.: Analysis of the glottal excitation of emotionally styled and stressed speech. The Journal of the Acoustical Society of America 98, 88–98 (1995)

13. Moore, E., Clements, M., Peifer, J., Weisser, L.: Investigating the role of glottal features in classifying clinical depression. In: Proceedings of the 25th Annual International Conference of the IEEE, Engineering in Medicine and Biology Society, vol. 3, pp. 2849–2852 (2003)

14. Moore, E., Torres, J.: A performance assessment of objective measures for evaluating the quality of glottal waveform estimates. In: Speech Communication (2007) (in press)

15. Patrick, A.N., Anastasis, K., Jon, G., Mike, B.: Estimation of glottal closure instants in voiced speech using the dypsa algorithm. IEEE Transactions on Audio, Speech, and Language Processing 15, 34–43 (2007)

16. Moore, E., Torres, J.: A performance assessment of objective measures for evaluating the quality of glottal waveform estimates. In: Speech Communication (2007) (in press)

17. Airas, M., Pulakka, H., Backstrom, T., Alku, P.: A toolkit for voice inverse filtering and parametrisation. In: Interspeech (2005)

18. Laukkanen, A.M., Vilkman, E., Alku, P., Oksanen, H.: Physical variations related to stress and emotional state: a preliminary study. Journal of Phonetics 24, 313–335 (1996)

19. Titze, I.R., Sundberg, J.: Vocal intensity in speakers and singers. The Journal of the Acoustical Society of America 91, 2936–2946 (1992)

20. Childers, D.G.: Vocal quality factors: Analysis, synthesis, and perception. The Journal of the Acoustical Society of America 90, 2394–2410 (1991)

21. Eyben, F., Wollmer, M., Schuller, B.: Openear - introducing the munich open-source emotion and affect recognition toolkit. In: 3rd International Conference on Affective Computing and Intelligent Interaction and Workshops, ACII 2009, pp. 1–6 (2009)

22. Schuller, B., Steidl, S., Batliner, A., Schiel, F., Krajewski, J.: The interspeech 2011 speaker state challenge. In: Interspeech, Italy (2011)

23. Hall, M., Frank, E., Holmes, G., Pfahringer, B., Reutemann, P., Witten, I.H.: The weka data mining software: An update. SIGKDD Explorations 11 (2009)

24. Freund, Y., Schapire, R.E.: Experiments with a new boosting algorithm. In: The Thirteenth Interantional Conference on Machine Learning (1996)

25. Witten, I.H., Freank, E.: Data Mining: Practical Machine Learning Tools and Techniques. Morgan Kaufmann, San Francisco (2005)

26. Hirschberg, J., Liscombe, J., Venditti, J.: Experiments in emotional speech. In: ISCA and IEEE Workshop on Spontanous Speech Processing and Recognition, Tokyo, Japan, pp. 119–125 (2003)

The Affective Triad: Stimuli, Questionnaires, and Measurements

Simone Tognetti, Maurizio Garbarino, Matteo Matteucci, and Andrea Bonarini

Politecnico di Milano, IIT Unit, Dipartimento di Elettronica ed Informazione,
Piazza Leonardo Da Vinci 32,20133 Milano, Italy
{tognetti,garbarino,matteucci,bonarini}@elet.polimi.it

Abstract. Affective Computing has always aimed to answer the question: which measurement is most suitable to predict the subject's affective state? Many experiments have been devised to evaluate the relationships among three types of variables (*the affective triad*): stimuli, self-reports, and measurements. Being the real affective state hidden, researchers have faced this question by looking for the measure most related either to the stimulus, or to self-reports. The first approach assumes that people receiving the same stimulus are feeling the same emotion; a condition difficult to match in practice. The second approach assumes that emotion is what people are saying to feel, and seems more likely.

We propose a novel method, which extends the mentioned ones by looking for the physiological measurement mostly correlated to the self-report due to emotion, not the stimulus. This guarantees to find a measure best related to subject's affective state.

Keywords: affective computing, emotion, emotion model, video game, stimuli, self report, physiology, affective triad.

1 Introduction

The problem of estimating the affective state of a subject raises the following doubt: which measurement is the most suitable to predict the subject's affective state? This problem is historically related to the Psychophysiology community that, since the 50's, investigated operationalization (i.e., the measurement of a certain phenomenon) of psychological states from physiological variables. Stern [1] defined Psychophysiology as: "*any research in which the dependent variable (the subject's response) is a physiological measure and the independent variable (the factor manipulated by the experimenter) a behavioral one*". Affective Computing has extended Psychophysiology works with new modalities (e.g., speech, posture, gesture, and facial expressions) to eestimate emotions. Moreover, Affective Computing leaked the experimentation outside the labs.

Researchers have coped with the afore mentioned problem by creating suitable experiments where three fundamental types of variables have been manipulated and/or measured: the stimulus received by the subject, the ground truth of emotion (e.g., a priori hypothesis based on stimuli/task, expert judgment annotation,

S. D´Mello et al. (Eds.): ACII 2011, Part II, LNCS 6975, pp. 101–110, 2011.

or self report assessment), and the measure obtained from one of the available modalities (e.g., physiology, posture, gesture, speech and facial expressions). We call these factors *the affective triad*. The concept of affective state (or emotion) has always been latent in the experiments since it is (and it will always be) a hidden state that could never be measured directly.

Being the affective state hidden, researchers in Affective Computing have adopted two main, conceptually different, approaches to find the measurement that is most suitable to predict the subject's affective state. The first approach (we call it *psychophysiology approach*) is widely used in the psychophysiology community and assumes that a given stimulus produces the same emotion for everyone. Unfortunately, this assumption is not always valid since emotions are individual mechanisms and different subjects might feel different emotions when exposed to the same stimulus. One example is the IAPS database [2] that has been quite criticized by the affective computing community due to its poor ability to induce specific emotions. Other works by Kim et al. [3] and Broek et al. [4] successfully adopted the *psychophysiology approach*. In all these examples, the answer to our question is given by looking at the measure that best relates to the stimulus. Self reports are used as a control mechanism.

A second approach is the one proposed by Yannakakis et al. [5] (we call it *preference learning approach*), which considers as ground truth the users' self-reported emotion between pairs of situations. Being emotion a subjective state [6], only the subject itself has the epistemic authority to express it. Under this assumption, the relationship between the observed measures and questionnaire answers is directly estimated, independently from the stimuli the subjects received. For the sake of completeness we observe that in literature we find also a third approach, proposed by Picard et al. [7] with guided imaginary experiments. This approach assumes that emotions are individualistic processes, like for preference learning. However, the solution proposed is to use only one subject in the experiments and leaving the choice of a stimulus (e.g., a picture) to the subject in order to target a specific personal emotion (e.g., through a guided imaginary procedure). These experiments aim at obtaining personalized models and the results cannot be easily averaged through the population of individuals.

We propose a novel framework to answer the question of which measurement is the most suitable to predict the subject's affective state. With our method, a new approach in between *preference learning approach* and *psychophysiology approach* can be defined. We call this approach *comprehensive approach*. In particular, our framework allows to find measures (e.g., physiological features or game metrics) that: (1) maximizes the dependence to the self report and (2) minimizes the dependence to the stimulus. The first criterion supports the preference learning assumption that emotion is an individual concept strongly related to what people state to feel. The second criterion tries to avoid that the measure depends directly from the stimulus that subjects is receiving.

The combination of these two criteria gives the possibility to obtain a measure that tends to be independent from the stimulus given the subject's affective state, which we assume to be strongly related to self reports (and, therefore to the actual emotions). In this way, it is possible to exclude those variables that are more related to the task itself rather than to the emotion. This is just what affective computing needs: to discriminate the user emotional state rather than the task that generates it.

We will introduce a model that allows: (1) to describe the affective process, (2) to describe in a computational form the criteria that we want to maximize. This model is an operative tool and it can be used to investigate different aspect of emotion estimation problem stated in terms of the question: which measurement is the most suitable to predict the subject's affective state?

The rest of this paper is organized as follows: in Section 2 we will introduce the working hypothesis of the model, and we will formalize the emotion estimation problem under the assumption made by the three approaches we mentioned: psychophysiology, preference learning and comprehensive. In Section 3 we will introduce the experimental setting under which this work has been done. In Section 4 we present the method that has been used to compare the different approaches and, finally, in Section 5, we compare the results and draw some conclusions.

2   The Working Hypothesis

In this paper, we propose a simple model of the affective interaction between a person and an artificial entity (e.g., computer, car, robot). The minimal structure of the model is depicted in Figure 1. Although being a simplified one, this model is general enough to represent many different applications as well as laboratory experiments that have been proposed in both Psychophysiology (e.g., Fridlund et al. [8], Cacioppo et al [9]) and Affective Computing (e.g., Picard et al. [7], Kim et al. [3] and Yannakakis et al. [5]) communities.

2.1   The Emotion and the Affective Triad

The majority of works proposed in literature makes use of three fundamental variables: stimulus, self report, and a measure obtained from one of the available modalities (e.g., physiology, posture, gesture, speech and facial expressions). The model we propose looks at these variables in terms of nodes in a Bayesian Network. In addition to these variables we add a fourth one representing the concept of affective state, or emotion (see Figure 1).

Emotion E represents the emotional state of subject. It has a given domain ranging on linguistic values, such as "excitation", "boredom", etc., or on continuous values, such as the Arousal-Valence plane. The emotion is also what psychophysiologists have called psychological construct [9]. Understanding its value is the goal of the investigation process typical of Affective Computing, so it is what we aim to infer from the measurement of other data. **E** is not directly accessible and it is considered to be a hidden variable: we assume that we cannot observe directly its value.

Stimulus I represents a (possibly multi-modal) stimulus that the artificial entity is able to produce, and that, hopefully, has some effect on the subject.

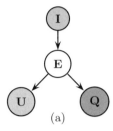

Fig. 1. A simple model of affective phenomena. Circles represent the variables and arrows represent statistical dependences among variables.

Many methods have been used to stimulate the subjects. In *mental workload* analysis researchers used tasks with an increasing level of difficulty [10]. The IAPS/IADS database has been widely used in *multimedia* scenarios [11]. In *videogames*, the typical stimulus is characterized by different versions of a game for which a parameter is set to modify speed, complexity, or challenge in the game [12,5,13,14].

Questionnaire Q represents the answers to one or more questions asked to the subject to obtain an affective self report, during or, more often, after the interaction. Emotion is a subjective state and only the subject has the epistemic authority to express it (e.g., [6]). The principal way we can use to know what emotion is felt by subjects is to ask them. Both absolute questionnaires (e.g., Likert [15] or SAM [16]), and relative ones (e.g., two alternative forced choice [5]) have been used in Psychophysiology and Affective Computing.

Measure U is the effect of (possibly multi-modal) unintentional interaction that is produced unconsciously by the subject and perceived by the artificial entity, and it should not be the direct effect of the stimuli, but the reflection of the emotional state on the subject. The Affective Computing community has proposed a large amount of modalities from which **U** is computed: physiology, posture, gesture, speech and facial expressions. See D'Mello et al.[17] for a detailed review.

A recent example applied to videogames field can be found in Yannakakis et al. [18], where the stimulus **I** is represented by controllable features, the measure **U** is represented by physiological responses, and the questionnaire **Q** is represented by differential questions about emotional states.

The model of Figure 1 is characterized by a set of conditional independences that are represented with arcs, according to the Bayesian Network formalism. The relationship **I** → **E** represents the influence of stimuli on the emotional state and it describes to what extent a particular stimulus can produce a specific emotion. The evidence of the existence of this relationship comes from cognitive studies [19]. The relationship **E** → **U** represents the influence of emotions on the measures; it is the subject of investigation in both Psychophysiology and Affective Computing. The relationship **E** → **Q** represents the influence of emotions on questionnaire answers. Self reports have always taken a relevant position in emo-

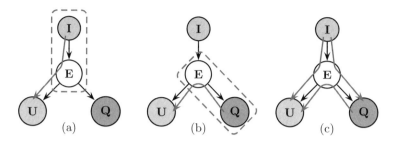

Fig. 2. The two possibilities of interpreting emotions to be related to stimuli (a) or to self reports (b). (c) represent the complete set of relationships in the affective triad.

tion estimation problems since they are supposed to be related to the emotional state **E** more than any other variable.

2.2 A Formal Definition

The model we are proposing can represent the two assumptions stated so far by the *psychophysiology* and *preference learning* approaches. The first assumes **U** to be strongly related to **I**, while the second assumes **U** to be strongly related to **Q**. These two situations are depicted on our model in Figure 2 (a) and (b) respectively. These assumptions lead to different answers to the question: which measurement **U** is the most suitable to predict the subject's affective state? Researchers that are following the psychophysiology approach, case (a), will look for a measure **U** that maximizes its dependence from **I** (Eqn. 1), while researchers that are following the preference learning approach, case (b), will look for a measure **U** that maximizes the dependence from **Q** (Eqn. 2):

$$\mathbf{U}^* = \arg\max_{\mathbf{U}} ||\mathbf{I} \to \mathbf{U}|| \quad (1) \qquad \mathbf{U}^* = \arg\max_{\mathbf{U}} ||\mathbf{Q} \to \mathbf{U}|| \quad (2)$$

where $||\mathbf{X} \to \mathbf{Y}||$ is a notation for the statistical dependence measure (e.g., represented by the correlation coefficient or χ^2 from the Pearson test of independence, or by the p of a Fisher's exact test if the number of samples is low). The comprehensive approach, Figure 2(c), combines these two criteria by looking for a measure **U** that minimizes the dependence from I while maximizing the dependence from **Q**:

$$\mathbf{U}^* = \arg\max_{\mathbf{U}} ||\mathbf{Q} \to \mathbf{U}|| - ||\mathbf{I} \to \mathbf{U}|| \quad (3)$$

In practice, **U** should be the measure that is more dependent from **Q** and at the same time less dependent from **I**.

The presented framework can be used in any affective computing experiment where stimulus **I**, measure **U**, and self report questionnaire **Q** are present. In the following sections, we present an example of a practical application of the proposed methodology.

3   Applying the Model: A Case Study on Videogame

The objective of our case study is to determine which is the best measure, either derived from physiological measurements or video game logs, to predict subjective preference among different gaming conditions by means of the criteria expressed by Eqn. 1, 2, and 3. We use the dataset from the experiment reported in [13] where the reader can find a thorough description of the experimental protocols. The experiment was originally devised to test the preference learning approach in the estimation of subject's preference while playing a car racing game (TORCS), thus preference learning is briefly described while presenting the experiment; interested readers could find a more detailed description in [5]. The rest of this section aims to explain how the proposed approach to the investigation of the model and its features is operational and enables, on real cases, quantitative evaluations.

The experiment is characterized by a binary stimulus $\mathbf{I}$, encoding two cognitively different aspects for the subject and universally identifiable: $\mathbf{I} = \{A, B\}$. On a simple oval track, each of the 75 subjects enrolled in the study raced against one player. As stimuli, we used two gaming conditions with different levels of challenge: a situation where the expertise of the opponent is the same as subject and another situation, where differences in ability are so high that we expect player get bored. In the last variant, the opponent is challenging and this resulted to be the most preferred situation.

Preference learning is based on differential measures obtained after the presentation of two stimuli $\mathbf{I}_1$ and $\mathbf{I}_2$ performed at subsequent times. Moreover, in order to avoid any ordering effect, we stimulated the subjects with all the possible stimulation sequences that, in this case, are two: AB or BA. Therefore, we can rewrite our stimulus as: $\mathbf{I} = \{AB, BA\}$, semantically related to the increase or the decrease of challenge.

At the end of a stimulation sequence we asked the subjects to report their emotional state in a differential way. We asked them whether the first stimulus in the sequence was preferred to the second one (this situation is represented as $\mathbf{I}_1 > \mathbf{I}_2$). The admissible answers are therefore two: $\mathbf{Q} \in \{1, 0\}$, where 1 means "yes", i.e., $\mathbf{I}_1 > \mathbf{I}_2$, and 0 means "no", i.e., $\mathbf{I}_1 < \mathbf{I}_2$. The "obvious" assumption is that subjects select one or the other answer according to which of the two stimuli in the sequence had produced the most appreciated affective reaction.

Finally, we extracted from game logs and physiological signals the measures upon which we would like to predict subject's preference. The physiological measures are some statistics (e.g., mean and variance) computed from blood volume pulse (BVP), galvanic skin response (GSR), respiration and skin temperature (see [13] for a detailed list). Game log features are derived from: actions (e.g., accelerator, brake, and steer commands), space (e.g., distance between opponents, angle between the car and the circuit route, and distance from the center of the roadway), and performance (e.g., number of overtakes, speed, and lap time) similarly to what reported in [20].

In order to keep the analysis simple, we use a linear preference learning model with only one feature at a time. It uses a differential measure $\Delta\mathbf{U} = \mathbf{U}_1 - \mathbf{U}_2$ by

Table 1. Variables in the affective triad and their values

Stimulus $\mathbf{I}$		Measure $\mathbf{U}$		Questionnaire $\mathbf{Q}$	
I	AB	U	$\Delta\mathbf{U} > 0$	Q	0
$\sim I$	BA	$\sim U$	$\Delta\mathbf{U} \leq 0$	$\sim Q$	1

considering the difference between the value of the measure of interest $\mathbf{U}$ during the first and the second stimuli of a sequence, respectively. Therefore, $\Delta\mathbf{U}$ can assume only two values $\Delta\mathbf{U} > 0$ or $\Delta\mathbf{U} \leq 0$.

Table 3 summarizes the variables characterizing the affective triad described in this section. We introduced the notation $\{I, \sim I\}$ to represent the increment or decrement of challenge, the notation $\{U, \sim U\}$ to represent the positive and negative value of the variable $\mathbf{U}$, and $\{Q, \sim Q\}$ to represent the values $\{0, 1\}$ of $\mathbf{Q}$. Please notice the different representation of the variable, e.g., $\mathbf{I}$, and its value, e.g., I. Moreover, the mapping between the symbols (e.g. I U and Q) and their semantics (e.g., AB $\Delta\mathbf{U} > 0$ and 0) does not influence the analysis: we could have chosen the opposite notation (e.g. $I = BA$ or $Q = 1$) for one or more the variables and the result would not have changed since we have *binary variables*.

4   Methods

Having defined the experimental settings in terms of stochastic variables, the method we used to compare the influence of each measure is represented by the correlation coefficients $||\mathbf{Q} \rightarrow \mathbf{U}|| = \chi^2_{\mathbf{QU}}$ and $||\mathbf{I} \rightarrow \mathbf{U}|| = \chi^2_{\mathbf{IU}}$. The goal is to identify the measure $\mathbf{U}^*$ among all the extracted measures that satisfies one of the criteria expressed by Eq. 1, 2, and 3.

In order to compute $\chi^2_{\mathbf{QU}}$ and $\chi^2_{\mathbf{IU}}$ we started by considering the joint distribution $P(\mathbf{I}, \mathbf{U}, \mathbf{Q})$, presented in Table 2 (a). Then, we considered the three contingency tables associated to $\mathbf{I} \rightarrow \mathbf{Q}$, $\mathbf{I} \rightarrow \mathbf{U}$ and $\mathbf{Q} \rightarrow \mathbf{U}$ presented in Table 2 (b), (c), and (d), respectively. The dependence $\mathbf{I} \rightarrow \mathbf{Q}$ does not change over different $\mathbf{U}$ and does not influence the criteria of Eq. 1, 2 and 3, however it is useful for control purposes.

The χ^2 values are obtained by considering: the degree of freedom of the test $DF = (R-1)*(C-1)$ where R is the number of levels for the first variable and C is the number of levels for the second variable (in our case $DF = (2-1)*(2-1) = 1$); the expected frequencies $E_{r,c} = (n_r * n_c)/N$, where n_r is the count for level r of first variable (i.e., count of row r), n_c is the count of level c of the second variable (i.e., count of column c) and N is the total number of samples; tests statistic $\chi^2 = \sum_{r,c}[(O_{r,c} - E_{r,c})^2/E_{r,c}]$; $p-value$ as the probability of observing the sample statistic as extreme as the test statistic.

If the number N of sample is low, it is better to use the Fisher's exact test instead of a Pearson χ^2 test of independence. Moreover, it is important to notice that we are using such analysis to numerically evaluate the strength of the statistical dependence between the considered variables and not to determine if such variables are independent.

Table 2. (a) represents $P(\mathbf{I}, \mathbf{U}, \mathbf{Q})$. Each cell n_i counts the samples that correspond to the values of the variables $\mathbf{I}$, $\mathbf{U}$, and $\mathbf{Q}$. N is the total number of samples. (b), (c), and (d) are the contingency tables of $\mathbf{I} \to \mathbf{Q}$, $\mathbf{I} \to \mathbf{U}$ and $\mathbf{U} \to \mathbf{Q}$. Each cell sums the coefficients reported in (a).

(a)

I	U	Q	
I	U	Q	n_1
I	U	$\sim Q$	n_2
I	$\sim U$	Q	n_3
I	$\sim U$	$\sim Q$	n_4
$\sim I$	U	Q	n_5
$\sim I$	U	$\sim Q$	n_6
$\sim I$	$\sim U$	Q	n_7
$\sim I$	$\sim U$	$\sim Q$	n_8
			N

(b)

I, Q	Q	$\sim Q$	
I	$n_1 + n_3$ $P(I, Q)$	$n_2 + n_4$ $P(U, \sim Q)$	$n_1 + n_2 + n_3 + n_4$ $P(I)$
$\sim I$	$n_5 + n_7$ $P(\sim U, Q)$	$n_6 + n_8$ $P(\sim U, \sim Q)$	$n_5 + n_6 + n_7 + n_8$ $P(\sim I)$
	$n_1 + n_3 + n_5 + n_7$ $P(Q)$	$n_2 + n_4 + n_6 + n_8$ $P(\sim Q)$	N

(c)

U, I	I	$\sim I$	
U	$n_1 + n_2$ $P(U, I)$	$n_5 + n_6$ $P(U, \sim I)$	$n_1 + n_2 + n_5 + n_6$ $P(U)$
$\sim U$	$n_3 + n_4$ $P(\sim U, I)$	$n_7 + n_8$ $P(\sim U, \sim I)$	$n_3 + n_4 + n_7 + n_8$ $P(\sim U)$
	$n_1 + n_2 + n_3 + n_4$ $P(I)$	$n_5 + n_6 + n_7 + n_8$ $P(\sim I)$	N

(d)

U, Q	Q	$\sim Q$	
U	$n_1 + n_5$ $P(U, Q)$	$n_2 + n_6$ $P(U, \sim Q)$	$n_1 + n_2 + n_5 + n_6$ $P(U)$
$\sim U$	$n_3 + n_7$ $P(\sim U, Q)$	$n_4 + n_8$ $P(\sim U, \sim Q)$	$n_3 + n_4 + n_7 + n_8$ $P(\sim U)$
	$n_1 + n_3 + n_5 + n_7$ $P(Q)$	$n_2 + n_4 + n_6 + n_8$ $P(\sim Q)$	N

Table 3. (a) Contingency table for $\mathbf{I} \to \mathbf{Q}$. Contingency tables for $\mathbf{I} \to \mathbf{U}$ and $\mathbf{Q} \to \mathbf{U}$ where $\mathbf{U}$ is (b) the number of overtakes, (c) $rrate_{max}$

(a)

I, Q	Q	$\sim Q$	
I	187 0.4156	38 0.0844	225 0.5000
$\sim I$	51 0.1133	174 0.3867	225 0.5000
	238 0.5289	212 0.4711	450

$\chi^2_{IQ} = 164.96$

(b)

U, I	I	$\sim I$	
U	225 0.5000	3 0.0067	228 0.5067
$\sim U$	0 0.0000	222 0.4933	222 0.4933
	225 0.5000	225 0.5000	450

$\chi^2_{IU} = 438.16 \; p-val = 0$

U, Q	Q	$\sim Q$	
U	188 0.4178	40 0.0889	228 0.5067
$\sim U$	50 0.1111	172 0.3822	222 0.4933
	238 0.5289	212 0.4711	450

$\chi^2_{QU} = 162.15 \; p-val = 0$

(c)

U, I	I	$\sim I$	
U	116 0.2578	130 0.2889	246 0.5467
$\sim U$	109 0.2422	95 0.2111	204 0.4533
	225 0.5000	225 0.5000	450

$\chi^2_{IU} = 1.76, \; p-val = 0.185$

U, Q	Q	$\sim Q$	
U	104 0.2311	142 0.3156	246 0.5467
$\sim U$	134 0.2978	70 0.1556	204 0.4533
	238 0.5289	212 0.4711	450

$\chi^2_{QU} = 24.53 \; p-val = 7.32 * 10^{-7}$

5   Results

In this section, we compare the measures selected as best predictors for user's affective state, according to 3 different criteria: (1) $\mathbf{U}^* = \arg\max_{\mathbf{U}} \chi^2_{\mathbf{IU}}$, from the psychophysiology approach, (2) $\mathbf{U}^* = \arg\max_{\mathbf{U}} \chi^2_{\mathbf{QU}}$, from the preference learning approach 3) $\mathbf{U}^* = \arg\max_{\mathbf{U}} \chi^2_{\mathbf{QU}} - \chi^2_{\mathbf{IU}}$, from the comprehensive approach.

Table 3(a) shows the relationship $\mathbf{I} \to \mathbf{Q}$, that is independent from the choice of $\mathbf{U}$. Stimulus is strongly dependent from the self report. $\mathbf{I}$ is related to the reported preference $\mathbf{Q}$ in approximately the 80% (sum of values on the main diagonal) of samples. This means that the induction mechanism was not *"perfect"* and a level of uncertainty has been introduced in $\mathbf{I} \to \mathbf{E} \to \mathbf{Q}$.

Both criterion (1) and (2) selected the same feature, that is *the number of overtakes* (called shortly *#o*) during the race; it belongs to the set of features extracted from the games log (similar to what reported in [20]). In Table 3(b) are represented the contingency tables for $\#o$; we can observe that there is a high correlation between $\#o$ and the self reports ($\chi^2_{\mathbf{QU}} = 162.15$), and an even higher correlation between $\#o$ and $\mathbf{I}$ ($\chi^2_{\mathbf{IU}} = 438.16$). This might be a symptom of the fact that $\#o$ is not really a measure of the affective state, but for the stimulus. Therefore, even if both criteria (1) and (2) will select the measure $\#o$, we might have doubts to say that the number of overtakes is a good feature to estimate the subject's affective state. An explanation comes from the comparison of Table 3(a) and 3(b): $\#o$ is in practice a function of $\mathbf{I}$, that in turns targets the emotion in a large portion of the population. We might say that a high number of overtakes tends to augment the player's preference challenge but, an increased preference does not necessary come from an increased number of overtakes.

The comprehensive approach (3), instead, selects *the maximum respiration rate* (called shortly $rrate_{max}$), a physiological measure that was reported as a good feature for this experiment also in [13], where only physiological features were considered. Table 3(c) presents the contingency tables for $rrate_{max}$. We could observe that $rrate_{max}$ is more related to $\mathbf{Q}$ than I: $\chi^2_{\mathbf{QU}} = 24.53 > \chi^2_{\mathbf{IU}} = 1.76$. So, differently to what happened for criteria (1) and (2), criterion (3) selects a feature that really brings information to predict $\mathbf{Q}$ that cannot be inferred from knowledge about $\mathbf{I}$. Such information is only due to the hidden variable $\mathbf{E}$, the one we are actually investigating in Affective Computing.

Considering the pure "self reports prediction", criterion (3) selects a feature $rrate_{max}$ ($\chi^2_{\mathbf{QU}} = 24.53$) having worse performance ($\#o$, $\chi^2_{\mathbf{QU}} = 162.15$); such a high performance is manly due to high $P(\mathbf{Q}|\mathbf{I}) = 0.802$ (see Table 3(a)).

In conclusion, our approach provides a mechanism to identify measures that are specifically correlated to the subject's emotional state $\mathbf{E}$ more than to the stimuli that have induced it. By being able to identify such a measurement, we expect to be able to design experiments that lead $P(\mathbf{Q}|\mathbf{I})$ and $P(\mathbf{U}|\mathbf{I})$ to be uniform over different values of $\mathbf{I}$. Formally stated, we would like to have both $\mathbf{Q}$ and $\mathbf{U}$ independent from $\mathbf{I}$ given $\mathbf{E}$. In such case, $\mathbf{E}$ gains the Markov property we base our affective model upon, and we might expect to have a $\mathbf{U}$ that answers the question introduced at the beginning.

Acknowledgments. This research has been partially supported by a grant by the Italian Institute of Technology (IIT). We would like to thank Luca Del Giudice that has partially performed the analysis presented in this paper during his master thesis.

References

1. Stern, J.: Toward a definition of Psychophysiology. Psychophysiology 1(1), 90 (1964)
2. Bradley, M.M., Lang, P.J.: The International Affective Picture System (IAPS) in the Study of Emotion and Attention. In: Coan, J.A., Allen, J.J.B (2007)
3. Kim, K., Bang, S., Kim, S.: Emotion recognition system using short-term monitoring of physiological signals. Medical and Biological Engineering and Computing 42(3), 419–427 (2004)

4. Van den Broek, E., Westerink, J.: Considerations for emotion-aware consumer products. Applied Ergonomics 40(6), 1055–1064 (2009)
5. Yannakakis, G., Hallam, J.: Entertainment modeling in physical play through physiology beyond heart-rate. In: Paiva, A.C.R., Prada, R., Picard, R.W. (eds.) ACII 2007. LNCS, vol. 4738, pp. 254–265. Springer, Heidelberg (2007)
6. Stanford encyclopedia of philosophy - emotion,
   http://plato.stanford.edu/entries/emotion/
7. Picard, R., Vyzas, E., Healey, J.: Toward machine emotional intelligence: Analysis of affective physiological state. IEEE Transactions on Pattern Analysis and Machine Intelligence, 1175–1191 (2001)
8. Fridlund, A., Schwartz, G., Fowler, S.: Pattern recognition of self-reported emotional state from multiple-site facial EMG activity during affective imagery. Psychophysiology 21(6), 622–637 (1984)
9. Cacioppo, J., Tassinary, L., Berntson, G.: Handbook of Psychophysiology, 3rd edn. Cambridge University Press, New York (2007)
10. Rowe, D., Sibert, J., Irwin, D.: Heart rate variability: indicator of user state as an aid to human-computer interaction. In: Proceedings of the SIGCHI Conference on Human Factors in Computing Systems, pp. 480–487. ACM Press/Addison-Wesley Publishing Co. (1998)
11. Tognetti, S., Alessandro, C., Bonarini, A., Matteucci, M.: Fundamental issues on the recognition of autonomic patterns produced by visual stimuli. In: Proceeding of the International Conference on Affective Computing and Intelligent Interaction, ACII 2009, IEEE, Amsterdam (2009)
12. Mandryk, R., Inkpen, K.: Physiological indicators for the evaluation of co-located collaborative play. In: Proceedings of the 2004 ACM Conference on Computer Supported Cooperative Work, p. 111. ACM, New York (2004)
13. Tognetti, S., Garbarino, M., Bonarini, A., Matteucci, M.: Modeling player enjoyment from physiological responses in a car racing game. In: 2010 IEEE Symposium on Computational Intelligence and Games (CIG), pp. 321–328. IEEE, Los Alamitos (2010)
14. Tognetti, S., Garbarino, M., Bonarini, A., Matteucci, M.: Enjoyment recognition from physiological data in a car racing game. In: Proceedings of the 3rd International Workshop on Affective Interaction in Natural Environments, AFFINE 2010, pp. 3–8. ACM, New York (2010)
15. Likert, R.: A technique for the measurement of attitudes. Archives of Psychology 140, 1–55 (1932)
16. Bradley, M., Lang, P.: Measuring emotion: the self-assessment manikin and the semantic differential. Journal of Behavior Therapy and Experimental Psychiatry 25(1), 49–59 (1994)
17. Calvo, R., D'Mello, S.: Affect detection: An interdisciplinary review of models, methods, and their applications. IEEE Transactions on Affective Computing, 18–37 (2010)
18. Yannakakis, G., Martínez, H., Jhala, A.: Towards affective camera control in games. User Modeling and User-Adapted Interaction 20(4), 313–340 (2010)
19. Ortony, A., Clore, G., Collins, A.: The cognitive structure of emotions. Cambridge Univ. Pr., Cambridge (1990)
20. Martınez, H., Hullett, K., Yannakakis, G.: Extending Neuro-evolutionary Preference Learning through Player Modeling. In: 2010 IEEE Symposium on Computational Intelligence and Games, CIG (2010)

Relevance Vector Machine
Based Speech Emotion Recognition

Fengna Wang[1], Werner Verhelst[1,2], and Hichem Sahli[1,3]

[1] Vrije Universiteit Brussel, AVSP, Department ETRO
VUB-ETRO, Pleinlaan 2, 1050 Brussels, Belgium
[2] Interdisciplinary Institute for Broadband Technology - IBBT
Gaston Crommenlaan 8, 9050 Ghent, Belgium
[3] Interuniversity Microelectronics Centre - IMEC
VUB-ETRO, Pleinlaan 2, 1050 Brussels, Belgium
{fwang,wverhels,hichem.sahli}@etro.vub.ac.be

Abstract. This work aims at investigating the use of relevance vector machine (RVM) for speech emotion recognition. The RVM technique is a Bayesian extension of the support vector machine (SVM) that is based on a Bayesian formulation of a linear model with an appropriate prior for each weight. Together with the introduction of RVM, aspects related to the use of SVM are also presented. From the comparison between the two classifiers, we find that RVM achieves comparable results to SVM, while using a sparser representation, such that it can be advantageously used for speech emotion recognition.

1 Introduction

Speech emotion recognition aims at recognizing the underlying emotional state of the speaker from his or her speech signal. Together with facial expression analysis, speech emotion recognition has gained increasing attention during the last decade. This is mainly motivated by intelligent Human - Machine Interaction required for different kinds of applications.

In the field of speech emotion recognition, a number of classification approaches have already been explored, which can be categorized in two types. The first type is considered as static modeling approach, which computes statistical measurements of relevant features over an appropriate *emotion unit*, e.g. a word or an utterance [1,2]. In these approaches, the temporal dynamics within the expression of emotions are largely lost. The second type, referred to as dynamic modeling approach, provides a better consideration of the temporal dynamics of emotions using frame unit based features. An example of such models is the Hidden Markov Model (HMM) [3,4].

As one kind of the static modeling approach, the support vector machine (SVM) became popular for speech emotion recognition since the last few years. Subsequently, comparison between SVM and other static approaches as well as HMM was explored extensively [3,5]. Although in some cases as indicated in [3,5], SVM performs worse, but it is proved to be an efficient classifier which can be

S. D'Mello et al. (Eds.): ACII 2011, Part II, LNCS 6975, pp. 111–120, 2011.

used in various situations. However, despite its success, there are still a number of significant and practical disadvantages of the SVM learning methodology [6]. In this work, we propose the relevance vector machine (RVM) as classifier for speech emotion recognition, and compare its performance to the SVM approach. RVM is a Bayesian extension of SVM that can achieve comparable performance to SVM while providing a sparser model.

The paper is organized as follows. In Sects. 2.1 and 2.2, we review the theory of the SVM and RVM techniques. In Sect. 3, we introduce the features used in our work, and in Sect. 4, we present the results of the considered classification techniques for speech emotion recognition tasks. Sect. 5 draws the conclusion and presents the future work.

2   Classifiers

2.1   Support Vector Machine

We begin our discussion of SVM with a two-class classification problem. Suppose we are given a set of input-target pairs $\{x_i, y_i\}_{i=1}^{N}$, where the feature vectors $x_i \in \mathbf{R}^n$ and the class label $y_i \in \{-1, +1\}$. Typically, we base our classification upon the function $f(x; \mathbf{w})$ defined over the transformed feature space $\phi(x)$, and learning is the process of inferring this function. A flexible and popular set of candidates for $f(x; \mathbf{w})$ is of the form:

$$f(x; \mathbf{w}) = \mathbf{w}^{\mathbf{T}} \phi(x) + b = \sum_{i=1}^{N} \omega_i \phi_i(x) + b , \qquad (1)$$

where the basis functions are parameterized by the training vectors using a *kernel function* $K(x, x_i)$: $\phi_i(x) \equiv K(x, x_i)$, $\mathbf{w} = (\omega_1, ..., \omega_N)$ is the weight vector, and $b \in \mathbf{R}$ is a bias parameter.

It is assumed that the training data set is linearly separable in the transformed feature space, so that by definition there exits at least one choice of the parameters $\mathbf{w}$ and b such that the function in (1) satisfies $f(x_i; \mathbf{w}) > 0$ for points having $y_i = +1$ and $f(x_i; \mathbf{w}) < 0$ for points having $y_i = -1$, so that $y_i f(x_i; \mathbf{w}) > 0$ for all training data points. For selecting the best parameters $\mathbf{w}$ and b, SVM uses the concept of the *margin*, which represents a measure of class separation efficiency, defined to be the smallest distance between the decision boundary $f(x_i; \mathbf{w}) = 0$ and any of the samples.

However, standard SVMs do not provide posterior probability to enable further post-processing, e.g. serving as the input of a pairwise coupling method. In the toolkit Weka [7], which is adopted in our experiments, a logistic regression model is fitted to the support vector machine output to obtain probability estimates. The logistic model for one class is defined as

$$p(y = 1|x) = \frac{1}{1 + e^{-f(x;\mathbf{w})}} \qquad (2)$$

2.2   Relevance Vector Machine

Tipping [6] introduced the Relevance Vector Machine (RVM) as a probabilistic sparse kernel model based on the support vector machine theory. Each of the model's weights has associated a prior that is characterized by a set of hyperparameters whose values are determined during the learning process.

Consider the two-class classification problem, where we are given a set of input-target pairs $\{x_i, y_i\}_{i=1}^{N}$, in which the feature vectors $x_i \in \mathbf{R}^n$ and the class label $y_i \in \{0, 1\}$. Similarly to the SVM, we have the decision function $f(x; \mathbf{w})$ in a new feature space defined by the *kernel function* $K(x, x_i)$, and learning is the process of inferring this function. A flexible and popular set of candidates for $f(x; \mathbf{w})$ is that of the form:

$$f(x; \mathbf{w}) = \sum_{i=1}^{N} \omega_i K(x, x_i) . \tag{3}$$

For the classification using RVM, the posterior probability of the membership of classes $p(y|x; \mathbf{w})$ is a logistic sigmoid link function, $p(y = 1|x; \mathbf{w}) = \sigma(f(x; \mathbf{w}))$, $p(y = 0|x; \mathbf{w}) = 1 - \sigma(f(x; \mathbf{w}))$, where $\sigma(f) = \frac{1}{(1+e^{-f})}$. Assuming independence of the input vectors $x_i, i = 1, ..., N$, the likelihood adopting the Bernoulli function is written as

$$p(\mathbf{y}|\mathbf{x}; \mathbf{w}) = \prod_{i=1}^{N} p(y_i|x_i; \mathbf{w}) \tag{4}$$

$$= \prod_{i=1}^{N} [\sigma(f(x_i; \mathbf{w}))]^{y_i} [1 - \sigma(f(x_i; \mathbf{w}))]^{1-y_i} . \tag{5}$$

In (3), a zero-mean Gaussian distribution is assigned for each weight parameter ω_i, and hence we have the weight prior distribution

$$p(\mathbf{w}|\alpha) = \prod_{i=1}^{N} \mathcal{N}(\omega_i|0, \alpha_i^{-1}) \tag{6}$$

where $\alpha = (\alpha_1, \alpha_2, ..., \alpha_N)$ is a vector of N additional variables, which are called *hyper-parameters*. They are associated independently with each weight, and are intended to moderate the strength of each weight prior. The parameters α_i and w_i of the model are computed through an iteration procedure until convergence is achieved [8].

For comparable recognition performances, the advantage of RVM is that it uses fewer kernel functions compared to SVM. This is illustrated in Sect. 4.3 by analyzing the number of relevance vectors in RVM and the number of support vectors in SVM. Less relevance vectors means less memory and less processing time during classification, which makes possible the usage of RVM as a 'real-time' classifier, since the training procedure can be performed off-line and in advance.

2.3   Multi-class Classification

In speech emotion recognition, more than two emotion classes are used. Each
SVM or RVM is a binary-class classifier, so, in order to classify more than two
classes, multi-class SVMs and multi-class RVMs are needed. There are two basic
strategies for solving K-class problems with SVMs or RVMs. The first one is the
one vs. all scheme that composes K binary-class SVMs/RVMs to separate one
class from all the other classes, and the second one is the *one vs. one* scheme
(pairwise coupling approach) that composes all pairs of classes for binary-class
SVMs/RVMs. In the *one vs. one* scheme, with K classes (emotions), $K(K-1)/2$
SVMs/RVMs are trained to separate two emotional classes. In this paper, the
one vs. one scheme proposed by Hastie and Tibshirani [9] is used, because of the
following reasons. First, the *one vs. one* scheme is easily constructed. Although
the one vs. one scheme has as a shortcoming its tendency to build many binary-
class SVMs/RVMs, this scheme is excellent at training cost compared to the *one
vs. all* scheme. Also, the *one vs. all* scheme can lead to an ambiguous classification
process.

3   Feature Extraction

In this work, the most commonly used feature measurements for speech emotions [5,10], which are related to pitch, intensity and Mel-frequency Cepstral
Coefficients (MFCC), are selected. The pitch, intensity, low-pass intensity, high-
pass intensity, and the norm of the absolute vector derivative of the first 10
MFCC components are firstly extracted from the speech signal. Next, four series
are further derived from each original series: the series of minima, the series of
maxima, the series of the durations between local extrema of the 10 Hz smoothed
curve, and the series itself. Then ten low-level statistical measures are calculated
from the $5 \times 4 = 20$ series, resulting in a 200 dimensional feature vector as shown
in Table 1.

Table 1. Feature sets used in our experiments

Acoustic features	Derived series	Statistics
• Intensity	•Minima	•Mean
• Lowpass intensity	•Maxima	•Maximum
• Highpass intensity	•Durations between local extrema	•Minimum
• Pitch	•The feature series itself	•Range
• Norm of absolute		•Variance
vector derivative of		•Median
the first 10 MFCC		•First quartile
components		•Third quartile
		•Inter-quartile range
		•Mean absolute value
		of the local derivative

4   Experimental Results and Analysis

4.1   Speech Database

For the assessment of the considered classifiers, we perform the speech emotion recognition experiments on four databases, namely, Berlin [11], Danish [12], Kismet [13], and BabyEars [14]. The breakdown of the emotional class distribution in the four databases is given in Table 2.

Table 2. Emotional classes in the four databases

Berlin		Danish		Kismet		BabyEars	
Anger	127	Anger	52	Approval	185	Approval	212
Sadness	52	Sadness	52	Attention	166	Attention	149
Happiness	64	Happiness	51	Prohibition	188	Prohibition	148
Neutral	78	Neutral	133	Soothing	143		
Fear	55	Surprise	52	Neutral	320		
Boredom	79						
Disgust	38						

4.2   Feature Selection

Feature selection, if correctly done, gives a number of simultaneous improvements: it eliminates irrelevant features that impair the recognition rates; it lowers the input dimensionality (and therefore improves generalization); it saves computational time and other resources. In this study we consider two feature selection approaches, correlation based feature selection (CFS) [15], and SVM based feature selection [16].

4.3   Results and Analysis

We first analyze the usage of the RVM on the binary class classification problem, then on the multi-class case. In both cases, the analysis is studied with feature selection and without feature selection. In all classification experiments, we use the 10-fold stratified cross validation training strategy, and adopt the accuracy as the test measurement, which is defined as the proportion of true results (both true positives and true negatives) in the population. Moreover, polynomial kernels (P) with orders from 1 to 3 and radial basis function kernels (R) are also considered.

Binary Class Classification.   For these experiments a polynomial kernel of order 2 is adopted. Table 3 gives the overall results. The emotion categories are represented by their first two letters, the number of training sample for each class is given between parenthesis. The obtained accuracy and the required number of vectors (support or relevance) are averaged over a number of repetitions.

From the comparison between the two classifiers, as shown in Table 3, one can notice that RVM achieves comparable results to SVM, while using a sparser

Table 3. Binary classification results

Berlin

	vectors		accuracy (%)			vectors		accuracy (%)	
	RVM	SVM	RVM	SVM		RVM	SVM	RVM	SVM
An/Sa(179)	2	18	100	100	Ha/Ne(142)	5.4	34	90.1	97.2
An/Ha(191)	9.8	92	77.0	76.4	Ha/Fe(119)	7.5	40	86.6	89.9
An/Ne(205)	4	29	98.1	98.5	Ha/Bo(143)	4.4	31	95.8	94.4
An/Fe(182)	6.2	41	93.4	91.8	Ha/Di(102)	5.9	35	90.2	93.1
An/Bo(206)	4.7	27	94.7	99.5	Ne/Fe(133)	7.2	44	90.2	90.2
An/Di(165)	5.7	35	94.6	95.8	Ne/Bo(157)	7.1	48	93.6	91.1
Sa/Ha(116)	2.1	19	99.1	100	Ne/Di(116)	6	37	89.7	94.0
Sa/Ne(130)	4.4	26	96.9	95.4	Fe/Bo(134)	4.8	33	94.0	98.5
Sa/Fe(107)	3.9	29	93.5	94.4	Fe/Di(93)	4.9	31	91.4	91.4
Sa/Bo(131)	5.7	39	90.1	93.9	Bo/Di(117)	8.1	46	90.6	94.9
Sa/Di(90)	3.7	22	93.3	94.4					

Danish

	vectors		accuracy (%)			vectors		accuracy (%)	
	RVM	SVM	RVM	SVM		RVM	SVM	RVM	SVM
An/Sa(104)	1	37	50.0	87.5	Sa/Ne(185)	7.1	73	83.8	77.8
An/Ha(103)	1	63	48.5	58.2	Sa/Su(104)	1	34	50.0	95.2
An/Ne(185)	9.3	63	81.6	84.3	Ha/Ne(184)	9.6	55	88.0	88.6
An/Su(104)	1	54	50.0	76.0	Ha/Su(103)	1	73	49.5	60.2
Sa/Ha(103)	1.4	41	54.4	84.5	Ne/Su(185)	9	44	95.1	96.8

Kismet

	vectors		accuracy (%)			vectors		accuracy (%)	
	RVM	SVM	RVM	SVM		RVM	SVM	RVM	SVM
Ap/At(351)	12.7	116	83.7	84.3	At/So(309)	5.9	32	98.1	98.4
Ap/Pr(373)	9.3	57	95.4	96.8	At/Ne(486)	7.8	44	96.9	97.7
Ap/So(328)	8.2	58	94.5	96.3	Pr/So(331)	8.3	47	97.9	99.4
Ap/Ne(505)	8.9	66	92.9	96.2	Pr/Ne(508)	11.6	123	87.8	90.0
At/Pr(354)	2.9	29	99.4	100	So/Ne(463)	13.2	75	92.9	97.0

BabyEars

	vectors		accuracy (%)			vectors		accuracy (%)	
	RVM	SVM	RVM	SVM		RVM	SVM	RVM	SVM
Ap/At(361)	11.4	138	78.4	79.8	At/Pr(297)	10.8	124	76.8	76.8
Ap/Pr(360)	11.4	149	76.1	75.8					

representation. Indeed, in the case of SVM, the number of support vectors is high compared to the number of relevance vectors of RVM. In the case of SVM, support vectors are those laying either on the margin or on the 'wrong' side of the decision boundary, they are a kind of boundary located vectors. So to some degree, their number gives a general idea about how much two classes are overlapping in the feature space. However, in the case of RVM, the relevance vectors give an idea about how the features are distributed.

The low classification accuracy obtained by RVM on the Danish database could be explained by the small number of relevance vectors, which means that

Table 4. Classification accuracy (%) after CFS feature selection on Danish database

	vectors		accuracy (%)			vectors		accuracy (%)	
	RVM	SVM	RVM	SVM		RVM	SVM	RVM	SVM
An/Sa(47)	8.8	24	90.4(P)	89.4(P)	Sa/Ha(58)	10	31	92.2(P)	88.3(P)
An/Ha(10)	3	73	68.9(R)	65.0(P)	Sa/Su(57)	8.4	23	94.2(P)	95.2(R)
An/Su(9)	5.2	57	83.7(R)	85.6(P)	Ha/Su(9)	2.1	83	64.1(R)	56.3(P)

most classes are located at the same place in the feature space. This could be due to the large dimensionality of the feature vector and to the possible dependence between its elements. Hence, to eliminate irrelevant features that impair the recognition accuracy, feature selection has been made. The correlation based feature selection (CFS) is used to select the most relevant features for those 6 pairwise classes on which RVM has weak performances. The obtained classification accuracies are shown in Table 4, in which the number of the selected features is indicated between the parenthesis, and the accuracy is the best result of RVM and SVM using both polynomial kernel (P) and radial basis function kernel (R).

As can be seen from Table 4, RVM achieves better results when using more discriminative features. Like most other classifiers, RVM requires more discriminative feature attributes for increasing its classification accuracy. But on the other hand, SVM is again shown to be immune to the detrimental effects of a large number and possibly noisy feature attributes. However, from a practical perspective, RVM still has more advantages than SVM, since irrelevant feature attributes could be largely excluded using feature selection techniques.

Multi-class Classification.   For the multi-class classification we used both polynomial kernels with orders from 1 to 3 and RBF kernels. Table 5 summarizes the obtained best classification accuracy using the full 200 feature attributes, where 'H' represents the human perception accuracy. As it can be seen, the RVM classification performance is comparable to that of SVM on Kismet and BabyEars, as well as to the literature results.

Table 5. Classification accuracy (%) without feature selection

	Berlin	Danish	Kismet	BabyEars
RVM	73	56	88	69
SVM	77	63	87	68
Literature	79 [17] H: 85 [11]	54 [18] H: 67 [19]	82 [13]	67 [14]

We further applied CFS feature selection approach and obtained better classification accuracy for all the databases, as indicated in Table 6, where the number of selected features are indicated between parenthesis. Nevertheless, the SVM still gives better accuracy on the Berlin and Danish database.

Table 6. Classification accuracy (%) with CFS feature selection technique

	Berlin(55)	Danish(48)	Kismet(86)	BabyEars(73)
RVM-Poly	74	59	84	69
RVM-RBF	72	56	89	61
SVM-Poly	75	65	86	70
SVM-RBF	75	59	84	69

Finally, to further analyze the classification accuracy on the Berlin and Danish database, we performed the SVM based feature selection technique. Since on the one hand, this technique gives a ranking order while CFS only gives the relative best feature subsets. On the other hand, as indicated in paper [16], SVM based feature selection approach can eliminate the redundancy automatically and yields better and more compact feature subsets. The obtained results are illustrated in Fig. 1, depicting the classification accuracy for different kernel types, versus the number of best features used for the classification. Table 7 gives the obtained best classification accuracies, corresponding to the maximum of the curves of Fig. 1.

For the Berlin database, Fig. 1 shows 70% recognition accuracy is already achieved when using only 5 selected features. However, the RVM performance is still a bit lower than that of SVM. In addition, for Berlin database, both RVM

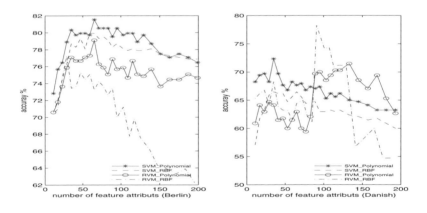

Fig. 1. Number of selected features v.s. accuracy

Table 7. Classification accuracy (%) with SVM feature selection technique

	Berlin	Danish
RVM-Poly	79	71
RVM-RBF	77	78
SVM-Poly	82	72
SVM-RBF	80	67

and SVM results are all lower than the human performance (see Table 5). For the Danish database, a sharp increase of RVM's performance can be observed from the graph of Fig.1, and when there are more than 100 feature attributes, RVM tends to give better results.

5   Conclusion

The goal of the current paper is to highlight the potential of the relevance vector machine (RVM) as a speech emotion classifier. RVM is a relatively new classification method and this work is, to our knowledge, the first one that uses it as a recognition engine for speech emotion recognition. Experiments show that RVM can achieve comparable results to the SVM. Moreover RVM results in a sparser model, which requires less time and less memory in the recognition phase, therefore it can be advantageously used for speech emotion recognition as a real-time classifier, since the training phase can be performed off-line and in advance.

Further research will aim at combining RVM with other kinds of classifiers to get better results, as well as investigating other affective features and analyzing cross corpus classification.

Acknowledgements. The research reported in this paper was supported in part by the CSC-VUB scholarship grant [2009] 3012, and the EU FP7 project ALIZ-E grant 248116.

References

1. Vogt, T., André, E.: Comparing feature sets for acted and spontaneous speech in view of automatic emotion recognition. In: 2005 IEEE International Conference on Multimedia and Expo., pp. 474–477 (2005)
2. Batliner, A., Steidl, S., Schuller, B., Seppi, D., et al.: Combing efforts for improving automatic classification of emotional user states. In: Language Technologies, IS-LTC, pp. 240–245 (2006)
3. Wagner, J., Vogt, T., André, E.: A systematic comparison of different HMM designs for emotion recognition from acted and spontaneous speech. In: Paiva, A.C.R., Prada, R., Picard, R.W. (eds.) ACII 2007. LNCS, vol. 4738, pp. 114–125. Springer, Heidelberg (2007)
4. Schuller, B., Rigoll, G., Lang, M.: Hidden markov model-based speech emotion recognition. In: IEEE International Conference on Acoustics, Speech, and Signal Processing, vol. 2 (2003)
5. Shami, M., Verhelst, W.: An evaluation of the robustness of existing supervised machine learning approaches to the classification of emotions in speech. Speech Communication 49, 201–212 (2007)
6. Tipping, M.E.: Sparse bayesian learning and the relevance vector machine. The Journal of Machine Learning Research 1, 211–244 (2001)
7. Witten, I.H., Frank, E.: Data mining: practical machine learning tools and techniques with java implementations. Morgan Kaufmann, San Francisco (2000)
8. Tipping, M.E., Faul, A.C.: Fast marginal likelihood maximisation for sparse bayesian models. In: Proceedings of the Ninth International Workshop on Artificial Intelligence and Statistics, vol. 1 (2003)

9. Hastie, T., Tibshirani, R.: Classification by pairwise coupling. Annals of Statistics 26, 451–471 (1998)
10. Rong, J., Li, G., Chen, Y.P.P.: Acoustic feature selection for automatic emotion recognition from speech. Information Processing and Management 45, 315–328 (2009)
11. Paeschke, A., Sendlmeier, W.F.: Prosodic characteristics of emotional speech: measurements of fundamental frequency movements. In: SpeechEmotion (2000)
12. Engberg, I.S., Hansen, A.V.: Documentation of the danish emotional speech database DES. Interal AAU report, Center for Person Kommunikation, Denmark (1996)
13. Breazeal, C., Aryananda, L.: Recognition of affective communicative intent in robot-directed speech. Autonomous Robots 12, 83–104 (2002)
14. Slaney, M., McRoberts, G.: BabyEars: a recognition system for affective vocalization. Speech Communication 39, 367–384 (2003)
15. Hall, M.A.: Correlation-based feature selection for machine learning. Methodology (1999)
16. Guyon, I., Weston, J., Barnhill, S., Vapnik, V.: Gene selection for cancer classification using support vector machine. Machine Learning 46, 389–422 (2002)
17. Chandrakala, S., Sekhar, C.C.: Classification of multi-variate varying length time series using descriptive statistical features. Pattern Recognition and Machine Intelligence, 13–18 (2009)
18. Hammal, Z., Bozkurt, B., Couvreur, L., Unay, D., Caplier, A., Dutoit, T.: Passive versus active: vocal classification system. In: Proc. Eusipco, Turkey (2005)
19. Ververidis, D., Kotropoulos, C.: Automatic speech classification to five emotional states based on gender information. In: Proc. Eusipco, Vienna, pp. 341–344 (2004)

A Regression Approach to Affective Rating of Chinese Words from ANEW

Wen-Li Wei, Chung-Hsien Wu, and Jen-Chun Lin

Department of Computer Science and Information Engineering,
National Cheng Kung University, Tainan, Taiwan, R.O.C.
{lilijinjin,chunghsienwu,jenchunlin}@gmail.com

Abstract. Affective norms for the words is an important issue in textual emotion recognition application. One problem with existing research is that several studies were rated with a large number of participants, making it difficult to apply to different languages. Moreover, difference in culture across different ethnic groups makes the language/culture-specific affective norms not directly translatable to the applications using different languages. To overcome these problems, in this paper, a new approach to semi-automatic labeling of Chinese affective norms for the 1,034 words included in the affective norms for English words (ANEW) is proposed which use a rating of small number of Chinese words from ontology concept clusters with a regression-based approach for transforming the 1,034 English words' ratings to the corresponding Chinese words' ratings. The experimental result demonstrated that the proposed approach can be practically implemented and provide adequate results.

Keywords: affective norm, ANEW, ontology, regression.

1 Introduction

The aim of affective computing, introduced by Picard in 1997 [1], is to give computers the ability to recognize, express, and in some cases, "have" emotions. Recently, affective computing has many fields of applications in computer science such as human robot interaction and dialogue systems. In terms of emotion representation, in psychologist's definition, the dimensional model is an important way of representing affect. For instance, Thayer [2] proposed a model for emotion description, as shown in Fig. 1. The two-dimensional emotion space was divided into four quadrants in terms of valence and arousal. "Valence" stands for the degree of pleasantness of the emotion, which is typically characterized as a continuous range of affective responses extending from "unpleasant (negative)" to "pleasant (positive)." "Arousal" stands for the level of activation of the emotion, and it is characterized as a range of affective responses extending from "calm" to "excited." Hence, a growing number of emotion recognition studies are using the two-dimensional plane to be a better emotion representation.

S. D'Mello et al. (Eds.): ACII 2011, Part II, LNCS 6975, pp. 121–131, 2011.
© Springer-Verlag Berlin Heidelberg 2011

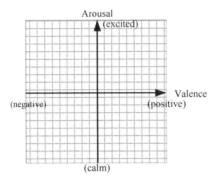

Fig. 1. Thayer's two-dimensional emotion model

Mehrabian [3] and Ambady [4] noted that the affective state can be transmitted by various channels and levels of message including face, voice, and semantic content for communication. In addition to audio or visual emotion recognition [5], [6], text sentimental recognition [7], [8] also plays an important role in many applications of human computer interaction. With the increasing usage of Web blog, the text sentimental analysis has been widely investigated and the word is fundamental for text-based emotion recognition [9]. Hence, this paper will focus on affective norms for the words through the two-dimensional emotion plane.

In text-based emotion recognition, there have been several studies in the literature focusing on how to assess each word in the affective dimensions. For example, the affective norms for English words (ANEW) introduced by Bradley and Lang in 1999 [10] contains a set of normative emotional ratings for 1,034 English words. The ANEW is developed and distributed by national institute of mental health center for the study of emotion and attention in order to provide standardized materials available to researchers in the study of emotion and attention. The goal is to use the self-assessment manikin (SAM), which was originally devised by Lang in 1980 [11] for rating affective words. Based on SAM, subjects rated the words in the ANEW on the dimensions of pleasure, arousal, and dominance. The subjects introduced to participate in the experiment were the students with psychology major. Since the experimental procedure will spend a lot of time and manpower on labeling all words, the rating method and result are difficult to apply to other languages in practice.

Based on the ANEW, Redondo [12] constructed the Spanish version of the ANEW using an adaptation approach. It is similar to the ANEW discussed above, in which the evaluations were also done in the dimensions of valence, arousal and dominance using SAM. In addition, the assessments are based on 720 participants' rating of the 1,034 Spanish words translated from the words included in the ANEW. The purpose of the study is to find if cultural difference exists between the American and the Spanish populations in the ratings of the words included in the ANEW. The findings suggest that the existence of statistical differences between the mean values of the Spanish and American ratings in the three emotional dimensions is remarkable. For example, regarding the arousal dimension, the ANEW words were rated as more activating by Spanish subjects than those by American ones. One explanation for this is that the Spanish subjects interpreted the ratings of the words in terms of a higher emotional reactivity. Although the findings will be useful to analyze the result of subjects' rating in the different languages, the assessments of 1,034 words were also done manually. The experimental procedure on labeling all the words is time-consuming and labor-intensive and the rating results are thus difficult to apply to other languages in practice.

As shown in the above literature review, existing research in affective rating still needs to label all the words. This tedious procedure limits the application on different languages. For this reason, in light of these concerns, the purpose of this paper is to present a new approach to obtain the affective rating results of 1,034 Chinese words which were translated from the words included in the ANEW based on a small set of Chinese words labeling. In detail, the primary methods that we propose are described as follows: (see Fig. 2) (a) divide the 1,034 words included in the ANEW into four quadrants based on the values of arousal and valence to keep the affective dimensional characteristic; (b) cluster the English words in each quadrants through a suggested upper merged ontology (SUMO) concept [13]; (c) randomly select a small set of English words from each SUMO cluster; (d) translate the selected small set of English words into Chinese words according to the mapped WordNet sense; (e) label the valence and arousal of the selected small set of Chinese words (162 Chinese words) through the SAM; (f) generate a regression model for affective norm transformation from each SUMO cluster; and (g) transform the 1,034 English words' ratings into the 1,034 Chinese words' ratings through the trained regression model.

We have organized the rest of this paper as follows: Section 2 describes the purpose of SUMO-based clustering algorithm and provides a thorough description to the proposed affective norms regression. Section 3 presents and discusses the results for a number of analyses. Finally, Section 4 draws the conclusions.

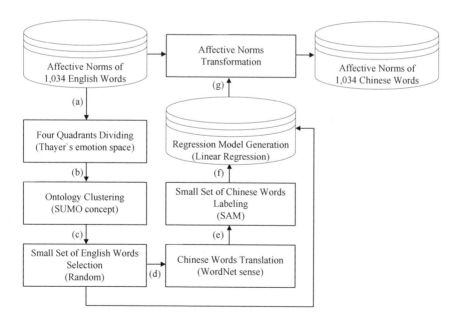

Fig. 2. The flow chart of the proposed method

2   Method

2.1   A SUMO-Based Clustering Algorithm

SUMO, developed by the IEEE standard upper ontology working group and now having a variety of applications in search, linguistics and reasoning, is adopted for word clustering in this work. SUMO is the formal ontology that has been mapped to the entire WordNet lexicons [14]. The concept of SUMO is to link the conceptual hierarchy through the way of an inheritance tree shown in Fig. 3.

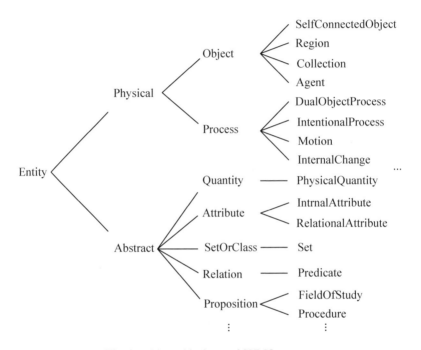

Fig. 3. A hierarchical tree of SUMO concept

The connection structure of the SUMO and WordNet is illustrated in Fig. 4. As shown in Fig. 4, the solid line nodes indicate the SUMO concept; the dotted line nodes represent the WordNet synset; the solid lines denote the SUMO concept relation; and the dotted lines represent the SUMO-WordNet connection. Hence, the relation between SUMO and WordNet enriches WordNet database files by tagging each synset with the corresponding SUMO concept. Using Table 1 as an example, the results reflected in Table 1 indicate that "bouquet" and "chocolate" map to the same "SelfConnectedObject" concept; "delight" and "happy" also map to the same "InternalAttribute" concept. However, in order to keep the unique characteristic for each quadrant, the same SUMO concepts may be used in four quadrants respectively.

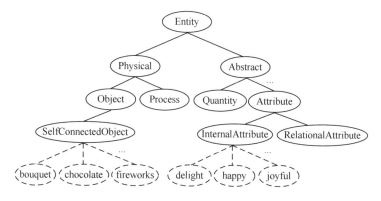

Fig. 4. The relation between SUMO and WordNet

Table 1. The examples illustrate the relation between words and the SUMO concepts

English	Chinese	Quadrant	SUMO Concept	English	Chinese	Quadrant	SUMO concept
bouquet	花束	I	SelfConnectedObject	delight	欣喜	I	InternalAttribute
chocolate	巧克力	I	SelfConnectedObject	happy	高興的	I	InternalAttribute
fireworks	煙火	I	SelfConnectedObject	joyful	快樂的	I	InternalAttribute
bomb	炸彈	II	SelfConnectedObject	angry	生氣的	II	InternalAttribute
gun	槍	II	SelfConnectedObject	insane	發狂的	II	InternalAttribute
poison	毒物	II	SelfConnectedObject	rage	盛怒	II	InternalAttribute
crutch	拐杖	III	SelfConnectedObject	gloom	憂鬱	III	InternalAttribute
pus	膿	III	SelfConnectedObject	sad	悲傷	III	InternalAttribute
scar	傷痕	III	SelfConnectedObject	shy	膽小的	III	InternalAttribute
book	書	IV	SelfConnectedObject	kindness	仁慈	IV	InternalAttribute
clothing	衣服	IV	SelfConnectedObject	relaxed	輕鬆	IV	InternalAttribute
pillow	枕頭	IV	SelfConnectedObject	thankful	感激的	IV	InternalAttribute

In this paper, a SUMO-based clustering algorithm was proposed to help select a small set of words for labeling. We employed the SUMO concept to cluster the 1,034 English words. First, we have divided the 1,034 English words into four quadrants according to the original valence and arousal from ANEW. Next, we assumed that the WordNet synsets with the same SUMO concept has similar valence and arousal values. Hence, we used SUMO to partition the words in each quadrant into several concept groups. In practice, in order to reduce the total number of clusters (i.e. to keep a small set of words for labeling), we partition the words in each quadrant into the number of clusters at the fourth level of the hierarchical tree based on SUMO concept. The fourth level of the hierarchical tree has a total of 39 clusters. However, not all the SUMO concepts have mapping words. For example, in the first quadrant, the "Set" concept has no mapping word. Following SUMO clustering, the first quadrant contains 16 clusters; the second quadrant contains 16 clusters; the third quadrant contains 14 clusters; and the forth quadrant contains 20 clusters. Based on the proposed SUMO-based clustering, we then randomly select at most three words from each SUMO cluster. Hence, we have a total of 162 words selected for labeling.

2.2   Affective Norms Linear Regression

The linear regression has been widely used for regression analysis for its easy performance analysis and reliable prediction performance [15]. There is no need for temporal information or geometric operation. In general, linear regression has been widely used for modeling the relationship between two variables. Hence, in this paper we employ a linear regression function f to transform the source language words' affective ratings x to the target language words' affective ratings y. It can be described mathematically as:

$$y = f(x) \tag{1}$$

where x is the valence or arousal values of the source word and y is the valence or arousal values of the target word. For example, as shown in Fig. 5, we hope to transform each English word's rating to the corresponding Chinese word's rating. That is, the valence and arousal of "vandal" is 2.71 and 6.40 in English, respectively and the transformed valence and arousal of the corresponding Chinese word "摧殘者" is 2.00 and 7.50, respectively.

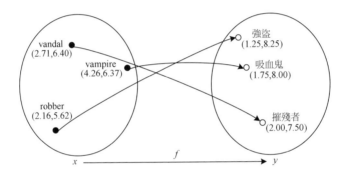

Fig. 5. The idea of regression approach to transform English words' affective ratings to Chinese words' affective ratings

Let f be a linear function, defined by

$$f(x) = \beta_0 + \beta_1 x \tag{2}$$

Equation (2) can be written as a linear regression model

$$y = \beta_0 + \beta_1 x \tag{3}$$

where β_0 and β_1 are the regression coefficients.

Suppose there are n data point pairs (x_i, y_i) in each SUMO cluster, where $i=1,\dots,n$. The goal is to calculate the point estimates of β_0 and β_1. The least squares method finds its optimum when the sum of squares, S, is a minimum [16].

$$S = \sum_{i=1}^{n} \left[y_i - \left(\beta_0 + \beta_1 x_i \right) \right]^2 \tag{4}$$

The minimum of the sum of squares is found by setting the gradient to zero.

$$\begin{cases} \dfrac{\partial S}{\partial \beta_0} = -2 \sum_{i=1}^{n} \left[y_i - \left(\beta_0 + \beta_1 x_i \right) \right] = 0 \\[3mm] \dfrac{\partial S}{\partial \beta_1} = -2 \sum_{i=1}^{n} \left[y_i - \left(\beta_0 + \beta_1 x_i \right) \right] x_i = 0 \end{cases} \tag{5}$$

Thus, we get

$$\begin{cases} \displaystyle\sum_{i=1}^{n} y_i = n \cdot \beta_0 + \left(\sum_{i=1}^{n} x_i \right) \beta_1 \\[3mm] \displaystyle\sum_{i=1}^{n} x_i y_i = \left(\sum_{i=1}^{n} x_i \right) \beta_0 + \left(\sum_{i=1}^{n} x_i^2 \right) \beta_1 \end{cases} \tag{6}$$

We can then see that β_0 and β_1 are given by

$$\hat{\beta}_1 = \frac{\displaystyle\sum_{i=1}^{n} x_i y_i - \sum_{i=1}^{n} x_i \sum_{i=1}^{n} y_i / n}{\displaystyle\sum_{i=1}^{n} x_i^2 - \left(\sum_{i=1}^{n} x_i \right)^2 / n} = \frac{\displaystyle\sum_{i=1}^{n} \left(x_i - \bar{x} \right) \left(y_i - \bar{y} \right)}{\displaystyle\sum_{i=1}^{n} \left(x_i - \bar{x} \right)^2} \tag{7}$$

$$\hat{\beta}_0 = \bar{y} - \hat{\beta}_1 \bar{x}$$

Finally, substitute $\hat{\beta}_0$ and $\hat{\beta}_1$ into equation (3) yields

$$y = \hat{\beta}_0 + \hat{\beta}_1 x \tag{8}$$

Hence, we can transform the source language words' affective ratings x (i.e. valence or arousal of English words) to the target language words' affective ratings y (i.e. valence or arousal of Spanish or Chinese words) through a linear regression model for each SUMO cluster in each quadrant.

3   Experiment

3.1   Experiment Design

Our database consists of two parts. Part I contains valence and arousal rating results of 1,034 words in the original ANEW [10] and Part II contains valence and arousal rating results of 1,034 words in Spanish [12]. Based on the proposed regression model, the experimental results of transformation have two results: English ratings transformed to Spanish ratings (E → S) and English ratings transformed to Chinese ratings (E → C).

The rating procedure was implemented according to a paper-and-pencil version of the SAM. The participants were four native Chinese speakers: two females and two males, ranging in age from 28 to 30 years old. Following the word selection process, in this experiment, 162 words were selected. Before rating, the instructions provided in [10] were provided to each subject. In order to avoid fatigue, the rating procedure was divided into three sessions during one week. The procedure took approximately half an hour for each subject.

3.2   Experiment Results

To evaluate the proposed SUMO-based clustering algorithm, in this paper, we compare the proposed method with traditional k-means clustering algorithm on the $E \rightarrow S$. Following the $E \rightarrow S$ transformation results, the mean value of Euclidean distance (MED) was used to investigate the difference between the transformed 1,034 Spanish words' ratings and the original 1,034 rated Spanish words' ratings. Suppose there are m clusters in each quadrant and n rating point pairs $(y_{i,j}^v, y_{i,j}^a)$ in each cluster, where $i=1,\ldots,m$ and $j=1,\ldots,n$. The MED of each quadrant is estimated as

$$MED = \frac{\sum_{i=1}^{m}\left(\sum_{j=1}^{n}\sqrt{(y_{i,j}^v - \hat{y}_{i,j}^v)^2 + (y_{i,j}^a - \hat{y}_{i,j}^a)^2}\right)}{m \times n} \tag{9}$$

where $y_{i,j}^v$ and $y_{i,j}^a$ are the valence and arousal of the original rating for the j-th word in the i-th cluster, respectively. Similarly, $\hat{y}_{i,j}^v$ and $\hat{y}_{i,j}^a$ are the valence and arousal of the transformed rating for the j-th word in the i-th cluster, respectively.

Table 2 presents the MED between k-means and the proposed method in four quadrants and the average of four quadrants. The results indicate that the proposed method outperformed the k-means in each quadrant. We also demonstrate the above results in Fig. 6. In Fig. 6 cluster #3 obtained from the k-means algorithm and the SUMO concept "InternalChange" in quadrant IV was compared. The x-axis and y-axis represent valence and arousal of 9-point rating scale, respectively; the black cross indicates the original English words' rating; the red cross represents the original Spanish words' rating; the blue mark means the predicted rating from $E \rightarrow S$; and the three circles show the small set of words selected. The result shows the data distribution of the English words in the k-means cluster has high compactness based on the distance measure. However, the English words mapped to Spanish words have significant variation. A reasonable explanation is that the k-means clustering does not consider the sense of the words. Hence, the result of k-means cluster may contain various senses of the words, and will be significantly influenced by the impact of cultural difference. Contrast to the k-means method, the English words in the SUMO-based clusters has close sense. Hence the mapping from English words to Spanish words is more consistent and the transformation result MED was smaller than that using k-means method. Consequently, the result indicated that the proposed SUMO-based clustering algorithm was useful to affective norms clustering.

Based on the above analysis, we perform E → C with the ratings from a small set of Chinese words according to the SUMO-based clustering algorithm. The purpose of selecting three Chinese words for labeling from each SUMO clustering was to evaluate the performance of the proposed regression approach (i.e. two for regression model training and another one for evaluation). The effect of the proposed regression approach reflected in Table 3 shows that the norm differences between the original Chinese ratings and the transformed Chinese ratings are smaller than that between the original English ratings and the corresponding Chinese ratings. The reason is that the difference in culture across different ethnic groups or different languages is an important factor for affective interpretation. In addition, this finding also confirms that the proposed regression approach can be adopted to transform the ratings in one language to another language.

Table 2. MED between k-means and the proposed SUMO-based clustering algorithm

Quadrant Clustering method	I	II	III	IV	Avg.
k-means	0.956	0.765	0.805	0.727	0.813
SUMO-based (proposed method)	0.870	0.590	0.735	0.705	0.725

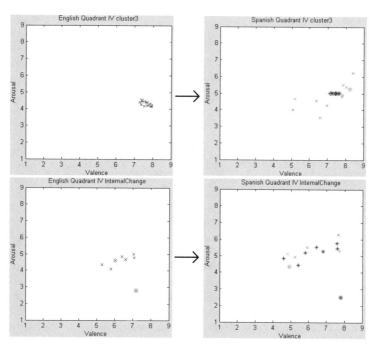

Fig. 6. Examples of results from E → S for k-means (top) and SUMO-based approach (bottom)

Table 3. Transformation results for different norms

Norm difference ⟍ Quadrant	I	II	III	IV	Avg.
Rated English ⟺ Rated Chinese	1.260	1.218	1.712	1.605	1.449
Rated Chinese ⟺ Transformed Chinese	0.912	0.893	1.185	0.991	0.995

4 Conclusion

In this paper, we propose a new approach to obtain affective ratings of a large set of Chinese words based on the ratings from a small set of Chinese words using a linear regression model. The experimental result have demonstrated that the proposed approach can be practically implemented and obtain adequate results. Hopefully, it can be applied to affective rating in different languages efficiently and serve as a basis for further study in textual emotion recognition.

References

1. Picard, R.W.: Affective Computing. MIT Press, Cambridge (1997)
2. Thayer, R.E.: The Biopsychology of Mood and Arousal. Oxford University Press, Oxford (1989)
3. Mehrabian, A.: Communication Without Words. Psychol. Today 2(4), 53–56 (1968)
4. Ambady, N., Rosenthal, R.: Thin Slices of Expressive Behavior as Predictors of Interpersonal Consequences: A Meta-Analysis. Psychol. Bull. 111, 256–274 (1992)
5. Wu, C.H., Yeh, J.F., Chuang, Z.J.: Emotion Perception and Recognition from Speech. In: Affective Information Processing, ch. 6, pp. 93–110 (2009)
6. Zeng, Z., Pantic, M., Roisman, G.I., Huang, T.S.: A Survey of Affect Recognition Methods: Audio, Visual, and Spontaneous Expressions. IEEE Transactions on Pattern Analysis and Machine Intelligence 31, 39–58 (2009)
7. Wu, C.H., Chuang, Z.J., Lin, Y.C.: Emotion Recognition from Text Using Semantic Labels and Separable Mixture Models. In: ACM Transactions on Asian Language Information Processing, vol. 5, pp. 165–182. ACM, New York (2006)
8. Wu, C.H., Liang, W.B.: Emotion Recognition of Affective Speech Based on Multiple Classifiers Using Acoustic-Prosodic Information and Semantic Labels. IEEE Transactions on Affective Computing 2(1), 1–12 (2011)
9. Yang, C.H., Lin, K.H.Y., Chen, H.H.: Building Emotion Lexicon from Weblog Corpora. In: Proceedings of 45th Annual Meeting of Association for Computational Linguistics, pp. 133–136. Czech Republic, Prague (2007)
10. Bradley, M.M., Lang, P.J.: Affective Norms for English Words (ANEW): Instruction Manual and Affective Ratings. Technical Report, The Center for Research in Psychophysiology, University of Florida (1999)
11. Lang, P.J.: Behavioral Treatment and Bio-Behavioral Assessment: Computer Applications: Technology in Mental Health Care Delivery Systems. In: Sidowski, J.B., Johnson, J.H., Williams, T.A. (eds.) pp. 119–137. Ablex Publishing, Norwood (1980)
12. Redondo, J., Fraga, I., Padrón, I., Comesaña, M.: The Spanish Adaptation of ANEW (Affective Norms for English Words). J. Behavior Research Methods 39, 600–605 (2007)

13. The Academia Sinica Bilingual Ontological Wordnet (BOW) - Ontology, http://bow.sinica.edu.tw/ont/
14. Niles, I., Pease, A.: Linking Lexicons and Ontologies: Mapping WordNet to the Suggested Upper Merged Ontology. In: Proceedings of the IEEE Conference on Information and Knowledge Engineering, Las Vegas, Nevada, pp. 412–416 (2003)
15. Yang, Y.H., Lin, Y.C., Su, Y.F., Chen, H.H.: A Regression approach to Music Emotion Recognition. IEEE Transactions on Audio, Speech and Language Processing 16(2), 448–457 (2008)
16. Sen, A., Srivastava, M.: Regression Analysis: Theory, Methods, and Applications. Springer, New York (1990)

Active Class Selection for Arousal Classification

Dongrui Wu[1] and Thomas D. Parsons[2]

[1] Machine Learning Laboratory, GE Global Research Center
One Research Circle, Niskayuna, NY 12309 USA
wud@ge.com
[2] Institute for Creative Technologies, University of Southern California
12015 Waterfront Drive, Playa Vista, CA 90094 USA
tparsons@ict.usc.edu

Abstract. Active class selection (ACS) studies how to optimally select the classes to obtain training examples so that a good classifier can be constructed from a small number of training examples. It is very useful in situations where the class labels need to be determined before the training examples and features can be obtained. For example, in many emotion classification problems, the emotion (class label) needs to be specified before the corresponding responses can be generated and recorded. However, there has been very limited research on ACS, and to the best knowledge of the authors, ACS has not been introduced to the affective computing community. In this paper, we compare two ACS approaches in an arousal classification application. Experimental results using a kNN classifier show that one of them almost always results in higher classification accuracy than a uniform sampling approach. We expect that ACS, together with transfer learning, will greatly reduce the data acquisition effort to customize an affective computing system.

Keywords: Active class selection, active learning, affective computing, arousal classification, nearest neighbors classification, transfer learning.

1 Introduction

Active learning [11, 13, 21] has been attracting a great deal of research interest recently. It addresses the following problem: Suppose that we have lots of unlabeled training examples and the labels are very difficult, time-consuming, or expensive to obtain; then, which training examples should be selected for labeling so that the maximum learning (classification or prediction) performance can be obtained from the minimum labeling effort? For example, in speech emotion estimation [30, 6], the utterances and their features can be easily obtained; however, it is difficult to evaluate the emotions they express. In this case, active learning can be used to select the most informative utterances to label so that a good classifier or predictor can be trained based on them. Many different approaches have been proposed for active learning [21] so far, e.g., uncertainty sampling [9], query-by-committee [22, 12], expected model change [20], expected error reduction [18], variance reduction [2], and density-weighted methods [32].

S. D'Mello et al. (Eds.): ACII 2011, Part II, LNCS 6975, pp. 132–141, 2011.
© Springer-Verlag Berlin Heidelberg 2011

One fundamental assumption in active learning is that the training examples can be obtained without knowing the classes (i.e., features can be obtained without knowing the labels). However, in practice there may be situations that the class label needs to be determined first before the training examples can be obtained. For example, in the arousal classification experiment reported in [28], where a Virtual Reality Stroop Test (VRST) was used to obtain training examples, one needs to select a level of arousal (which is the class label) first, and then displays the appropriate test to elicit the corresponding physiological responses, from which the features can be extracted [16]. A classifier is then constructed to estimate a subject's arousal level from physiological responses. So, the problem becomes how to optimally select the classes to obtain training examples so that a good classifier can be constructed from a small number of training examples.

Unlike the rich literature on active learning, there has been limited research on active class selection (ACS). Weiss and Provost [27] studied a closely-related problem: if only n training examples can be selected, in what proportion should the classes be represented? However, as suggested and verified by Lomasky et al. [10], if one can control the classes from which training examples are generated, then utilizing feedback during learning to guide the generation of new training data may yield better performance than learning from any *a priori* fixed class distributions. They proposed several ACS approaches to iteratively select classes for new training instances based on the existing performance of the classifier, and showed that ACS may result in better classification accuracy.

In this paper we apply ACS to the arousal classification problem [28], where three arousal levels need to be distinguished using physiological responses. We implement two of Lomasky et al.'s ACS approaches and perform extensive experiments to compare their performance. To the authors' best knowledge, this is the first time that ACS has been introduced to the affective computing community.

The remainder of this paper is organized as follows: Section 2 introduces the ACS algorithms. Section 3 presents the experimental results of ACS in arousal classification. Section 4 draws conclusions and points out some future research directions.

2   Active Class Selection (ACS)

This section introduces two iterative ACS algorithms. For simplicity we use the k-nearest neighbors (kNN) classifier; however, the algorithms can also be extended to more advanced classifiers like the support vector machine (SVM) [25].

We assume that there are C classes and no limits on generating instances of a particular class. All methods begin with a small set of l_0 labeled training examples, where l_i is the number of instances to generate in Iteration i. ACS is used to determine p_i^c ($0 \leq p_i^c \leq 1$), the portion of the l_i instances that should be generated from Class c. We compare the following three approaches, of which the first is our baseline and the latter two are ACS schemes proposed in [10]:

1. *Uniform*: All classes are uniformly sampled, i.e., $p_i^c = \frac{1}{C}$. This is also the baseline method used in [10]. Uniform sampling is the most intuitive and

frequently used method if there is no *a priori* knowledge on how the sampling should be better done.

2. *Inverse* (ACS$_1$): This method relies on the assumption that poor class accuracy is due to not having observed enough training examples. It requires internal cross-validation to evaluate the performance of the current classifier so that the poor class can be identified. Leave-one-out cross-validation was used in this paper. In Iteration i, we record the classification accuracy (in the leave-one-out cross-validation) for each class, a_i^c, $c = 1, 2, ..., C$. Then, the probability of generating a new instance from Class c is proportional to the inverse of a_i^c, i.e.,

$$p_i^c = \frac{\frac{1}{a_i^c}}{\sum_{c=1}^{C} \frac{1}{a_i^c}} \tag{1}$$

3. *Accuracy Improvement* (ACS$_2$): This method is based on the intuition that the accuracy of classes that have been well learned will not change with the addition of new data and thus we should focus on classes that can be improved. Again, it requires internal cross-validation to evaluate the performance of the classifier in the current iteration so that its accuracy can be compared with the classifier in the previous iteration. Leave-one-out cross-validation was used in this paper. In Iteration i, we record the classification accuracy (in the leave-one-out cross-validation) for each class, a_i^c, $c = 1, 2, ..., C$. Then, the probability of generating a new instance from Class c is

$$p_i^c = \max\left(0, \frac{a_i^c - a_{i-1}^c}{\sum_{c=1}^{C}(a_i^c - a_{i-1}^c)}\right) \tag{2}$$

The detailed algorithms for ACS$_1$ and ACS$_2$ are given below.

Algorithm 1. The algorithm for ACS$_1$

Input: $N = \sum_{i=0}^{i-1} l_i$ initial training examples in Iteration i; l_i, the number of new instances to generate in Iteration i; k, the size of the neighborhood in the kNN classifier

Output: The l_i new instances generated in Iteration i

foreach j *in* $[1, N]$ **do**
| Compute the kNN classification result using the jth training example in
| validation and the rest $N - 1$ examples in training;
end
Compute the per-class classification accuracy in the internal leave-one-out cross-validation a_i^c, $c = 1, 2, ..., C$;
Generate l_i new training examples according to (1)

Algorithm 2. The algorithm for ACS$_2$

Input: $N = \sum_{i=0}^{i-1} l_i$ initial training examples in Iteration i; l_i, the number of new instances to generate in Iteration i; a_{i-1}^c, $c = 1, 2, ..., C$, the per-class classification accuracy in the internal leave-one-out cross-validation from Iteration $i - 1$; k, the size of the neighborhood in the kNN classifier;

Output: The l_i new instances generated in Iteration i

foreach j in $[1, N]$ **do**

    Compute the kNN classification result using the jth training example in validation and the rest $N - 1$ examples in training;

end

Compute the per-class classification accuracy in the internal leave-one-out cross-validation a_i^c, $c = 1, 2, ..., C$;

Generate l_i training examples according to (2)

3 Experiment

This section presents our experimental results on comparing the three sampling approaches, with application to the arousal classification problem introduced in [28].

3.1 Data Acquisition

The use of psychophysiological measures in studies of persons immersed in high-fidelity virtual environment scenarios offers the potential to develop current physiological computing approaches [1] into affective computing [17] scenarios. Affective computing has been gaining popularity rapidly in the last decade because it has great potential in the next generation of human-computer interfaces [17, 24, 26]. An important task in implementing an affective computing system is affect recognition, which recognizes the user's affect from various signals, e.g., speech [5, 8, 19, 30], facial expressions [15, 4], physiological signals [3, 7, 28], etc.

The Virtual Reality Stroop Task (VRST) [16, 28] utilized in this paper involves the subject being immersed into a virtual Humvee as it travels down the center of a road, during which Stroop stimuli [23] appear on the windshield, as shown in Fig. 1. The VRST stimuli are presented within both "safe" (low threat) and "ambush" (high threat) settings. Low threat zones consist of little activity aside from driving down a desert road, while the more stressful high threat zones include gunfire, explosions, and shouting amongst other stressors. Psychophysiological measures of skin conductance level (SCL), respiration (RSP), vertical electrooculograph (VEOG), electrocardiographic activity (ECG), and electroencephalographic activity (EEG) are recorded continuously throughout exposure to the virtual environment.

There are many different scenarios eliciting different levels of arousal in VRST. In this study we chose the following three of them to affect different arousal levels, which had been used in [28]: 1) Scenario I: Low threat, color naming; 2) Scenario II: High threat, color naming; and, 3) Scenario III: High threat,

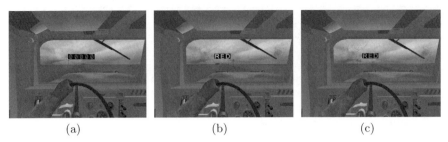

Fig. 1. The Humvee Stroop Scenarios. (a) Color Naming; (b) Word Reading; and, (c) Interference.

interference. Each scenario consisted of 50 tests. Three colors (Blue, Green, and Red) were used, and they were displayed with equal probability. In Scenario I, 50 colored numbers were displayed at random locations on the windshield one by one while the subject was driving through a safe zone. Scenario II was similar to Scenario I, except that the subject was driving through an ambush zone. Scenario III was similar to Scenario II, except that Stroop tests instead of color naming tests were used. In terms of arousal, the three scenarios are in the order of I < II < III.

A total of 19 college aged students participated in this experiment. Strict exclusion criteria were enforced so as to minimize the possible confounding effects of additional factors known to adversely impact a person's ability to process information, including psychiatric (e.g., mental retardation, psychotic disorders, diagnosed learning disabilities, Attention-Deficit/Hyperactivity Disorder, and Bipolar Disorders, as well as substance-related disorders within two years of evaluation) and neurologic (e.g., seizure disorders, closed head injuries with loss of consciousness greater than 15 minutes, and neoplastic diseases) conditions. The University of Southern California's Institutional Review Board approved the study. After informed consent was obtained, basic demographic information was obtained.

3.2   Comparative Study

One of the 19 subjects did not respond at all in one of the three scenarios, and was excluded as an outlier. Only the remaining 18 subjects were studied. Each subject had 150 responses (50 for each arousal level). The same 29 features as those in [28] were used. In the comparative study $k = \{1, 2, 3, 4\}$, since we want to examine whether the performance of ACS is consistent for different k. We studied each subject separately, and for each subject $l_0 = k + 1$ (so that we can run leave-one-out cross-validation using the kNN classifier). Only one new instance was generated in each iteration. After Iteration i, the kNN classification performance was evaluated using the rest $150 - (k + i + 1)$ responses from the same subject. We repeated the experiment 100 times (each time the l_0 initial training examples were chosen randomly) for each subject and k and then report the average performance of the three class-selection approaches. It is necessary to repeat the experiment many times to make the results statistically meaningful because there are two forms of randomness: 1) a subject generally had different responses at the same arousal level (class label), so for the same sequence of class labels the training examples were different; and, 2) the new class label was generated according to a probability distribution instead of deterministically.

Experimental results for $k = \{1, 2, 3, 4\}$ are shown in Fig. 2. Each of the first 18 sub-figures in (a)-(d) represents a different subject, and the last sub-figure shows the average performance of the three class-selection approaches over the 18 subjects. Observe that:

1. Generally ACS_1 (Inverse) always outperformed the uniform sampling approach. To show that the performance difference is statistically significant, we performed paired t-tests to compare the average performances of ACS_1 and the uniform sampling approach for $k = \{1, 2, 3, 4\}$ and $\alpha = 0.05$. When $k = 1$, $t(17) = 4.66$, $p = 0.0002$. When $k = 2$, $t(17) = 9.06$, $p < 0.0001$. When $k = 3$, $t(16) = 8.27$, $p < 0.0001$. When $k = 4$, $t(15) = 7.97$, $p < 0.0001$. Clearly, the performance difference is always statistically significant.

   Interestingly, in [10] Lomasky et al. pointed out that the inverse method did not work well. We think this is because the performance of an ACS approach is highly application-dependent, and the inverse approach is particularly suitable for the arousal classification problem. This was partially supported by the fact that Lomasky et al. compared five different sampling approaches in [10] on two datasets, and none of them seemed to be universally better than others. However, more experiments and analysis are needed to better understand the underlying reasons and also the stability of the inverse method.

2. ACS_2 (Accuracy improvement) always had the worst performance among the three sampling approaches. This is because in each iteration only one new instance is generated (assume it belongs to Class c'), and hence very probably in the next iteration only the classification accuracy of Class c' is improved; as a result, ACS_2 keeps generating new instances from Class c' and makes the class distribution very imbalanced. Some typical trajectories of selected training example classes for Subject 1 are shown in Fig. 3. Clearly, ACS_2 tends to stick to a particular class.

3. The overall classification performance decreased as k increased. The exact reason is still under investigation. However, the performance downgrade of ACS_1 was smaller than the uniform sampling approach. This suggests that ACS_1 is less sensitive to k, which is good when it is difficult to determine the optimal k.

In summary, we have demonstrated through a simple kNN classifier the advantages of ACS, which include higher classification accuracy and more robustness to parameter selection.

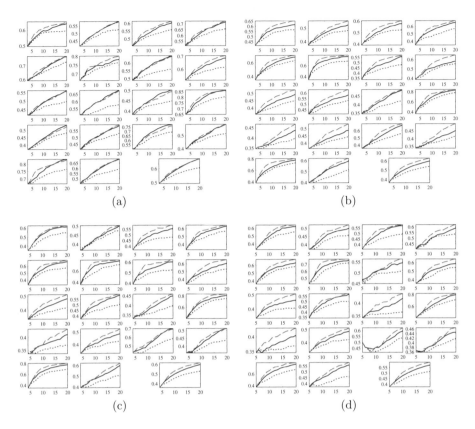

Fig. 2. Performance comparison of the three class-selection approaches on the 18 subjects. (a) $k = 1$; (b) $k = 2$; (c) $k = 3$; (d) $k = 4$. The horizontal axis shows the number of training examples, and the vertical axis shows the testing accuracy on the remaining examples from the same subject. —: Uniform; – – –: ACS_1 (Inverse); - - -: ACS_2 (Accuracy Improvement).

We need to point out that ACS has more computational cost than the uniform sampling approach, because before acquiring each new training example it needs to compute the leave-one-out cross-validation performance and then to determine which class to sample. However, since a person's physiological responses or affective states cannot change very quickly (usually on the order of seconds), and the extra computational cost only occurs during the training process, it does not hinder the applicability of ACS.

Finally, note that the purpose of the experiments is not to show how good a kNN classifier can be in arousal classification; instead, we aim to demonstrate how ACS can improve the performance of an existing classifier. Also, as we have shown in this section, not necessarily all ACS algorithms can always improve the classification performance. For each particular application, a small dataset may be needed to identify the ACS approach.

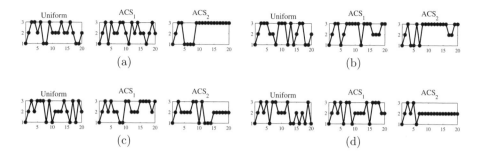

Fig. 3. Typical trajectories of selected training example classes for Subject 1. (a) $k = 1$; (b) $k = 2$; (c) $k = 3$; (d) $k = 4$. The horizontal axis shows the index of training examples, and the vertical axis shows the corresponding class index.

4   Conclusions and Future Research

Active class selection studies how to optimally select the classes to obtain training examples so that a good classifier can be constructed from a small number of training examples. In this paper, we have compared two ACS approaches in an arousal classification application. Experimental results using a kNN classifier showed that the inverse ACS approach generally resulted in higher classification accuracy and more robustness than the uniform sampling approach. To the best knowledge of the authors, this is the first time that ACS has been applied to affective computing problems.

Our future research includes:

1. To compare ACS approaches using more advanced classifiers like SVM, logistic regression, etc, and also on more affective computing datasets, to study whether the performance improvement is consistent and universal.
2. To integrate ACS with feature selection. As it has been shown in [28], many of the 29 features are not useful. However, the useful features are subject-dependent. As the features directly affect the NNs, it is necessary to integrate ACS with feature selection for further performance improvement.
3. To integrate ACS with classifier parameter optimization, e.g., k in the kNN classifier, and C, ϵ and the kernel parameters in the SVM [25].
4. To combine ACS with transfer learning [14,31] in affective computing. A major assumption in many classification and prediction algorithms is that the training and test data are in the same feature space and have the same distribution. However, this does not hold in many real-world applications. For example, in the arousal classification experiment introduced in this paper, a subject's physiological responses at a certain arousal level are generally quite different from another's. This makes it difficult to make use of other subjects' responses. In this paper we ignored other subjects' responses completely in classifying an individual subject's arousal level. However, all subjects' responses should still be similar at some extent, and hence other subjects'

responses may also be useful in classifying an individual subject's arousal levels. Transfer learning is a framework to address this kind of problems by making use of auxiliary training examples. We [29] have applied inductive transfer learning to the above arousal classification problem and showed that the auxiliary training examples can indeed improve the classification performance. We expect that further performance improvement can be obtained by combining transfer learning and ACS, i.e., very few user-specific training examples are needed to obtain satisfactory classification accuracy if ACS and transfer learning are integrated properly. This would make it much easier to customize an affective computing system for individual use.

References

1. Allanson, J., Fairclough, S.: A research agenda for physiological computing. Interacting With Computers 16, 858–878 (2004)
2. Cohn, D.: Neural network exploration using optimal experiment design. In: Proc. Advances in Neural Information Processing Systems (NIPS), Denver, CO, vol. 6, pp. 679–686 (1994)
3. Fairclough, S.H.: Fundamentals of physiological computing. Interacting with Computers 21, 133–145 (2009)
4. Fasel, B., Luettin, J.: Automatic facial expression analysis: A survey. Pattern Recognition 36(1), 259–275 (2003)
5. Grimm, M., Kroschel, K., Mower, E., Narayanan, S.S.: Primitives-based evaluation and estimation of emotions in speech. Speech Communication 49, 787–800 (2007)
6. Grimm, M., Kroschel, K., Narayanan, S.S.: The Vera Am Mittag German audiovisual emotional speech database. In: Proc. Int'l Conf. on Multimedia & Expo. (ICME), Hannover, German, pp. 865–868 (2008)
7. Kim, J., Andre, E.: Fusion of multichannel biosignals towards automatic emotion recognition. In: Lee, S., Ko, H., Hahn, H. (eds.) Multisensor Fusion and Integration for Intelligent Systems. LNEE, vol. 35, pp. 55–68. Springer, Heidelberg (2009)
8. Lee, C.M., Narayanan, S.S.: Toward detecting emotions in spoken dialogs. IEEE Trans. on Speech and Audio Processing 13(2), 293–303 (2005)
9. Lewis, D., Catlett, J.: Heterogeneous uncertainty sampling for supervised learning. In: Proc. Int'l. Conf. on Machine Learning (ICML), New Brunswick, NJ, pp. 148–156 (July 1994)
10. Lomasky, R., Brodley, C.E., Aernecke, M., Walt, D., Friedl, M.: Active class selection. In: Proc. 18th European Conference on Machine Learning, Warsaw, Poland, pp. 640–647 (September 2007)
11. MacKay, D.J.C.: Information-based objective functions for active data selection. Neural Computation 4, 589–603 (1992)
12. McCallum, A., Nigam, K.: Employing EM in pool-based active learning for text classification. In: Proc. Int'l. Conf. on Machine Learning (ICML), Madison, WI, pp. 359–367 (July 1998)
13. Muslea, I., Minton, S., Knoblock, C.A.: Active learning with multiple views. Journal of Artificial Intelligence Research 27, 203–233 (2006)
14. Pan, S.J., Yang, Q.: A survey on transfer learning. IEEE Trans. on Knowledge and Data Engineering 22(10), 1345–1359 (2010)

15. Pantic, M., Rothkrantz, L.: Automatic analysis of facial expressions: The state of the art. IEEE Trans. on Pattern Analysis and Machine Intelligence 22(12), 1424–1445 (2000)
16. Parsons, T., Courtney, C., Arizmendi, B., Dawson, M.: Virtual reality Stroop task for neurocognitive assessment. Studies in Health Technology and Informatics 143, 433–439 (2011)
17. Picard, R.: Affective Computing. The MIT Press, Cambridge (1997)
18. Roy, N., McCallum, A.: Toward optimal active learning through sampling estimation of error reduction. In: Prof. Int'l. Conf. on Machine Learning (ICML), Williamstown, MA, pp. 441–448 (2001)
19. Schuller, B., Lang, M., Rigoll, G.: Recognition of spontaneous emotions by speech within automotive environment. In: Proc. German Annual Conf. on Acoustics, Braunschweig, Germany, pp. 57–58 (March 2006)
20. Settles, B., Craven, M., Ray, S.: Multiple-instance active learning. In: Advances in Neural Information Processing Systems (NIPS), Vancouver, BC, Canada, pp. 1289–1296 (December 2008)
21. Settles, B.: Active learning literature survey. Computer Sciences Technical Report 1648, University of Wisconsin–Madison (2009)
22. Seung, H., Opper, M., Sompolinsky, H.: Query by committee. In: Proc. ACM Workshop on Computational Learning Theory, Pittsburgh, PA, pp. 287–294 (July 1992)
23. Stroop, J.: Studies of interference in serial verbal reactions. Journal of Experimental Psychology 18, 643–661 (1935)
24. Tao, J., Tan, T.: Affective computing: A review. In: Tao, J., Tan, T., Picard, R.W. (eds.) ACII 2005. LNCS, vol. 3784, pp. 981–995. Springer, Heidelberg (2005)
25. Vapnik, V.: The Nature of Statistical Learning Theory. Springer, Berlin (1995)
26. Vesterinen, E.: Affective computing. In: Digital Media Research Seminar, Finland (2001)
27. Weiss, G.M., Provost, F.: Learning when training data are costly: The effect of class distribution on tree induction. Journal of Artificial Intelligence Research 19, 315–354 (2003)
28. Wu, D., Courtney, C.G., Lance, B.J., Narayanan, S.S., Dawson, M.E., Oie, K.S., Parsons, T.D.: Optimal arousal identification and classification for affective computing: Virtual Reality Stroop Task. IEEE Trans. on Affective Computing 1(2), 109–118 (2010)
29. Wu, D., Parsons, T.D.: Inductive transfer learning for handling individual differences in affective computing. In: D´Mello, S., et al. (eds.) Affective Computing and Intelligent Interaction, Part II, vol. 6975, pp. 142–151. Springer, Heidelberg (2011)
30. Wu, D., Parsons, T.D., Mower, E., Narayanan, S.S.: Speech emotion estimation in 3D space. In: Proc. IEEE Int'l Conf. on Multimedia & Expo. (ICME), Singapore, pp. 737–742 (July 2010)
31. Wu, P., Dieterich, T.G.: Improving SVM accuracy by training on auxiliary data sources. In: Proc. Int'l Conf. on Machine Learning, Banff, Alberta, Canada, pp. 871–878 (July 2004)
32. Xu, Z., Akella, R., Zhang, Y.: Incorporating diversity and density in active learning for relevance feedback. In: Proc. European Conference on Information Retrieval (ECIR), Rome, Italy, pp. 246–257 (April 2007)

Inductive Transfer Learning for Handling Individual Differences in Affective Computing

Dongrui Wu[1] and Thomas D. Parsons[2]

[1] Machine Learning Laboratory, GE Global Research Center
One Research Circle, Niskayuna, NY 12309 USA
wud@ge.com
[2] Institute for Creative Technologies, University of Southern California
12015 Waterfront Drive, Playa Vista, CA 90094 USA
tparsons@ict.usc.edu

Abstract. Although psychophysiological and affective computing approaches may increase facility for development of the next generation of human-computer systems, the data resulting from research studies in affective computing include large individual differences. As a result, it is important that the data gleaned from an affective computing system be tailored for each individual user by re-tuning it using user-specific training examples. Given the often time-consuming and/or expensive nature of efforts to obtain such training examples, there is a need to either 1) minimize the number of user-specific training examples required; or 2) to maximize the learning performance through the incorporation of auxiliary training examples from other subjects. In [11] we have demonstrated an active class selection approach for the first purpose. Herein we use transfer learning to improve the learning performance by combining user-specific training examples with auxiliary training examples from other subjects, which are similar but not exactly the same as the user-specific training examples. We report results from an arousal classification application to demonstrate the effectiveness of transfer learning in a Virtual Reality Stroop Task designed to elicit varying levels of arousal.

Keywords: Affective computing, arousal classification, individual differences, nearest neighbors classification, transfer learning.

1 Introduction

The use of psychophysiological measures in studies of persons immersed in high-fidelity virtual environment scenarios offers the potential to develop current physiological computing approaches [1] into affective computing [7] scenarios. An important task in implementing an affective computing system is affect recognition, which recognizes the user's affect from various signals, e.g., speech [12], facial expressions [5], physiological signals [10], and multimodal combination [15]. In [10,6] we introduced an adaptive virtual environment for assessment and rehabilitation of neurocognitive and affective functioning. The Virtual Reality Stroop Task (VRST) [6], utilized also in this paper, involves the subject being immersed

S. D'Mello et al. (Eds.): ACII 2011, Part II, LNCS 6975, pp. 142–151, 2011.

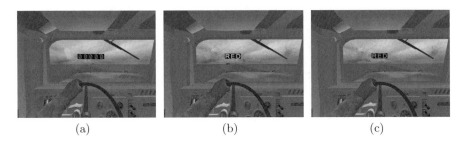

(a)   (b)   (c)

Fig. 1. The Humvee Stroop scenarios. (a) Color Naming; (b) Word Reading; and, (c) Interference.

into a virtual Humvee as it travels down the center of a road, during which Stroop stimuli [8] appear on the windshield, as shown in Fig. 1. The VRST stimuli are presented within both "safe" (low threat) and "ambush" (high threat) settings. Low threat zones consist of little activity aside from driving down a desert road, while the more stressful high threat zones include gunfire, explosions, and shouting amongst other stressors. Psychophysiological measures of skin conductance level, respiration, vertical electrooculograph, electrocardiographic activity, and electroencephalographic activity are recorded continuously throughout exposure to the virtual environment.

In [10] we used a support vector machine (SVM) to classify the three arousal levels in the VRST, and showed that when each subject is considered separately, an average classification rate of 96.5% can be obtained; however, the average classification rate was much lower (36.9%, close to random guess) when a subject's arousal level was predicted from other subjects' arousal levels.

We believe this reflects research into psychophysiology and individual differences. Results from a study conducted by Ito and Cacioppo [2] revealed that individuals respond with positivity offset and negativity bias. Positivity offset means that persons respond more strongly to mildly pleasant than to mildly unpleasant stimuli. Negativity bias means that a person responds more strongly to very unpleasant stimuli than to very pleasant stimuli. Individual differences were quite obvious in our previous experiments as we also performed feature selection in constructing the individual classifiers, and the features for different subjects were significantly different from each other.

Given the large individual differences, it is difficult to accurately classify a subject's arousal levels using a classifier trained from only responses from other subjects. However, the responses from other subjects still contain some useful information, as people exhibit similar (though usually not exactly the same) behaviors at the same affect state (otherwise we cannot recognize others' affects in social activities). So, increased classification accuracy may be obtained by combining the responses from other subjects and a small number of training examples from the subject. This is the idea of transfer learning [4], which is elaborated in the next section. If this hypothesis is veridical, then only a very small number of user-specific training examples are needed to individualize an affective computing system, which will greatly increase its usability and popularity. This paper presents some experimental results on transfer learning for handling individual differences in arousal classification and proposes several future research directions. To the best of the authors' knowledge, this is the first time that transfer learning has been introduced to the affective computing community.

The remainder of this paper is organized as follows: Section 2 introduces the concept of transfer learning. Section 3 presents some experimental results on transfer learning for handling individual differences in arousal classification. Section 4 draws conclusions and proposes some future research directions.

2   Transfer Learning

A major assumption in many classification and prediction algorithms is that the training and future (test) data are in the same feature space and have the same distribution [4]. However, it does not hold in many real-world applications. For example, in the arousal level classification experiment introduced above, a subject's physiological responses at a certain arousal level are generally quite different from another's, and their perceptions of arousal are also different. In such cases, knowledge transfer, if done successfully, would greatly improve the learning performance by eliminating much training example acquisition efforts. Transfer learning [4, 13] is a framework for addressing this problem.

Definition 1 *(Transfer Learning).* *[4] Given a source domain $\mathcal{D}_S$ and learning task $\mathcal{T}_S$, a target domain $\mathcal{D}_T$ and learning task $\mathcal{T}_T$, transfer learning aims to help improve the learning of the target predictive function $f_T(\cdot)$ in $\mathcal{D}_T$ using the knowledge in $\mathcal{D}_S$ and $\mathcal{T}_S$, where $\mathcal{D}_S \neq \mathcal{D}_T$, or $\mathcal{T}_S \neq \mathcal{T}_T$.*

In the above definition, a domain is a pair $\mathcal{D} = \{\mathcal{X}, P(X)\}$, where $\mathcal{X}$ is a feature space and $P(X)$ is a marginal probability distribution, in which $X = \{x_1, ..., x_n\} \in \mathcal{X}$. $\mathcal{D}_s \neq \mathcal{D}_T$ means that either $\mathcal{X}_s \neq \mathcal{X}_T$ or $P_S(X) \neq P_T(X)$, i.e., either the features in the source domain and the target domain are different, or their marginal probability distributions are different. Similarly, a task is a pair $\mathcal{T} = \{\mathcal{Y}, P(Y|X)\}$, where $\mathcal{Y}$ is a label space and $P(Y|X)$ is a conditional probability distribution. $\mathcal{T}_S \neq \mathcal{T}_T$ means that either $\mathcal{Y}_S \neq \mathcal{Y}_T$ or $P(Y_S|X_S) \neq P(Y_T|X_T)$, i.e., either the label spaces between the source and target domains are different, or the conditional probability distributions between the source and target domains are different.

Particularly, in this paper we are interested in *inductive transfer learning* [4], where $\mathcal{T}_S \neq \mathcal{T}_T$ but there is no requirement on whether $\mathcal{D}_S$ should be the same as $\mathcal{D}_T$ or not. As a result, a few labeled data in the target domain are required as training data to induce the target predictive function.

In the transfer learning literature the data in the source domain is usually called *auxiliary data* and the data in the target domain *primary data*. For the arousal level classification application introduced in the Introduction, primary data are user-specific training examples, and auxiliary data can be training examples from other subjects. In [13] it has been shown that when the primary training dataset is very small, training with auxiliary data can significantly improve classification accuracy, even when the auxiliary data is significantly different from the primary data. This result can be understood through a bias/variance analysis. When the number of primary training data is very small, a learned classifier will have large variance and hence large error. Incorporating auxiliary data, which increases the number of training examples, can effectively reduce this variance, but possibly increase the bias, because the auxiliary and primary training data have different distributions. This also suggests that as the amount of primary training data increases, the utility of auxiliary data should decrease [13].

3   Experiment

In this section we present some experimental results on transfer learning for handling individual differences in arousal classification. Data for this experiment was drawn from the VRST. Psychophysiological measures were used to predict levels of threat and cognitive workload. Herein primary data are user-specific training examples, and auxiliary data are training examples from other subjects. For simplicity, we use the k-nearest neighbors (kNN) classifier.

3.1   Method

Suppose there are N^p training examples $\{\mathbf{x}_i^p, y_i^p\}_{i=1,2,...,N^p}$ for the primary supervised learning problem (user-specific training examples), where $\mathbf{x}_i^p$ is the feature vector of the ith training example and y_i^p is its corresponding class label. The superscript p indicates the *primary* learning task. Additionally, there are N^a auxiliary training examples (training examples from other subjects) $\{\mathbf{x}_i^a, y_i^a\}_{i=1,2,...,N^a}$, whose distribution is somehow similar to the primary training examples but not exactly the same. So, the auxiliary training examples should be treated as weaker evidence in designing a classifier.

   In kNN we need to optimize the number of NNs, k. This must be done through internal I-fold cross-validation [9, 13]. The most important parameter in determining the optimal k is the *internal I-fold cross-validation accuracy*, i.e., the number of the internal cross-validation examples that are correctly classified, n_v. However, because N^p is very small, different k may easily result in the same n_v. For example, when $N^p = 3$ and $I = 3$, there are a total of three examples in the internal 3-fold cross-validation (one in each fold, and the process is repeated three times); so, n_v can only be $\{0, 1, 2, 3\}$, and several different k may result in $n_v = 3$. The *classification margin in internal cross-validation*, m_v, is then used to break the ties: when two ks give the same number of n_v, the one with a larger m_v is preferred. This idea was motivated by the concept of error margin in [13]. In this paper m_v is computed as the number of votes for the correct class minus the number of votes for the predicted class, summed over all instances in the internal I-fold cross-validation. So, m_v is a non-positive number, and the larger the better. Once the optimal ks are identified for different kNN classifiers, their performances can be compared using the testing accuracy.

As pointed out in [13], in many learning algorithms, the training data play two separate roles. One is to help define the objective function, and the other is to help define the hypothesis. Particularly, in kNN one role of the auxiliary data is to help define the objective function and the other is to serve as potential neighbors. In this paper we investigate these two roles separately. The following three kNN classifiers were implemented and compared:

1. kNN_1, which is a baseline kNN classifier without using the auxiliary data, i.e., it uses only the N^p primary training examples in the internal I-fold cross-validation algorithm.
2. kNN_2, which also uses the N^a auxiliary examples in the training part of the internal I-fold cross-validation algorithm, i.e., in each iteration of the internal cross-validation it combines the $I-1$ folds of the N^p primary training examples with the N^a auxiliary examples in training and uses the rest fold of the N^p primary training examples in validation.
3. kNN_3, which also uses the N^a auxiliary examples in the validation part of the internal I-fold cross-validation algorithm, i.e., in each iteration it uses the $I-1$ folds of the N^p primary training examples in training and combines the rest fold of the N^p primary training examples with the N^a auxiliary examples in validation.

The pseudo-codes for training kNN_2 and kNN_3 are given below. The pseudo-code for training kNN_1 is the same as that for kNN_2, except that the N^a auxiliary data are not used at all. Note that in testing kNN_1 and kNN_3 use their optimal k and the N^p primary training examples, whereas kNN_2 uses its optimal k and the N^p primary training examples plus the N^a auxiliary training examples, to be consistent with how its k is trained.

3.2   Results

A total of 19 college-aged subjects participated in the study. Presentation of the VRST version of the Stroop was counterbalanced. While experiencing the VRST, participant psychophysiological responses were recorded using the Biopac MP150 system. The University of Southern California's Institutional Review Board approved the study.

We classify three arousal levels in this paper, which are the same as those in [10]. One of the 19 subjects did not respond at all in one of the three scenarios, and was excluded as an outlier. Only the remaining 18 subjects were studied. The features were the same as those 29 features in [10].

In the experiments $I = 3$ and $K = 5$. Because each subject had 150 responses (50 for each arousal level), $N^a = 150 \times 17 = 2550$. We performed experiments for each subject separately, and for each subject we increased N^p from 3 (one response at each arousal level) to 15 (5 responses at each arousal level) in internal cross-validation, and used the resulting optimal k for testing on the remaining $150 - N^p$ primary examples. We repeated the experiment 100 times (each time the N^p primary training examples were chosen randomly) for each subject and report the average performance of the three kNN algorithms, as shown in Fig. 2. Observe that:

Algorithm 1. The algorithm for training kNN_2

Input: N^p primary training examples; K, the maximum number of NNs in I-fold internal cross-validation

Output: k_o, the optimal number of NNs in the kNN classifier

Initialize: The maximum number of correct classifications in internal cross-validation $\overline{n}_v = 0$; The maximum classification margin in internal cross-validation $\overline{m}_v = -10^{10}$;

Partition the N^p primary training examples into I folds;

foreach k *in* $[1, K]$ **do**
$\quad$ $n_v = 0$, $m_v = 0$;
$\quad$ **foreach** i *in* $[1, I]$ **do**
$\quad\quad$ Compute the kNN classification results using the ith fold of the primary training examples in validation, the rest $I - 1$ folds *plus the N^a auxiliary data* in training, and k as the number of NNs;
$\quad\quad$ $n_v = n_v + n_v^i$ and $m_v = m_v + m_v^i$, where n_v^i is the number of correct classifications in the ith validation, and m_v^i is the total classification margin in the ith validation;
$\quad$ **end**
$\quad$ **if** $n_v > \overline{n}_v$ **then**
$\quad\quad$ $\overline{n}_v = n_v$, $\overline{m}_v = m_v$, $k_o = k$;
$\quad$ **else if** $n_v = \overline{n}_v$ *and* $m_v > \overline{m}_v$ **then**
$\quad\quad$ $\overline{m}_v = m_v$, $k_o = k$;
$\quad$ **end**
end

---

1. For all three kNN classifiers, generally as N^p increases, the testing performance also increases, which is intuitive.
2. Sometimes kNN_2 significantly outperforms kNN_1 and kNN_3, but its overall performance is the worst. Recall that in kNN_2 for each iteration of the internal I-fold cross-validation the $(I - 1)N^p/I$ primary training examples were combined with the $N^a = 17N^p$ auxiliary examples in training. As the number of auxiliary examples is significantly larger than that of the primary examples, most of the neighbors are from the auxiliary data. So, the performance of kNN_2 is highly dependent on the amount of individual differences. We conjecture that for subjects that kNN_2 performs very well (e.g., Subject 14), at least one of the rest 17 subjects must have very similar profile. This also suggests that significant performance improvement may be obtained if we can identify the most similar subjects and only use them in kNN_2. This will be one of our future research directions.
3. kNN_3 always outperforms kNN_1, especially when N^p is very small. This is because when N^p is small, several different ks may give the same validation accuracy (i.e., a very small number of training examples do not have enough discriminative power), and hence the information in the N^a auxiliary training examples is very useful in helping determine the optimal k. To show that the difference between kNN_1 and kNN_3 is statistically significant, we performed paired t-tests, as shown in Table 1. Observe that except for Subject 6, all differences are significant.

Algorithm 2. The algorithm for training kNN$_3$

Input: N^p primary training examples; K, the maximum number of NNs in I-fold internal cross-validation

Output: k_o, the optimal number of NNs in the kNN classifier

Initialize: The maximum number of correct classifications in internal cross-validation $\overline{n}_v = 0$; The maximum classification margin in internal cross-validation $\overline{m}_v = -10^{10}$;

Partition the N^p primary training examples into I folds;

foreach k *in* $[1, K]$ **do**

  $n_v^p = 0$, $m_v^p = 0$, $n_v^a = 0$, $m_v^a = 0$;

  foreach i *in* $[1, I]$ **do**

    Compute the kNN classification results using the ith fold of the primary training examples *plus the* N^a *auxiliary data* in validation, the rest $I - 1$ folds in training, and k as the number of NNs;

    $n_v^p = n_v^p + n_v^{i,p}$, and $m_v^p = m_v^p + m_v^{i,p}$, where $n_v^{i,p}$ is the number of correct classifications in the ith fold of the primary data, and $m_v^{i,p}$ is the total classification margin in the ith fold of the primary data;

    $n_v^a = n_v^a + n_v^{i,a}$, and $m_v^a = m_v^a + m_v^{i,a}$, where $n_v^{i,a}$ is the number of correct classifications in the auxiliary data, and $m_v^{i,p}$ is the total classification margin in the auxiliary data;

  end

  if $n_v^p > \overline{n}_v^p$ **then**

    $\overline{n}_v^p = n_v^p$, $\overline{m}_v^p = m_v^p$, $\overline{n}_v^a = n_v^a$, $\overline{m}_v^a = m_v^a$, $k_o = k$;

  else if $n_v^p = \overline{n}_v^p$ *and* $n_v^a > \overline{n}_v^a$ **then**

    $\overline{m}_v^p = m_v^p$, $\overline{n}_v^a = n_v^a$, $\overline{m}_v^a = m_v^a$, $k_o = k$;

  else if $n_v^p = \overline{n}_v^p$ *and* $n_v^a = \overline{n}_v^a$ *and* $m_v^p > \overline{m}_v^p$ **then**

    $\overline{n}_v^a = n_v^a$, $\overline{m}_v^a = m_v^a$, $k_o = k$;

  else if $n_v^p = \overline{n}_v^p$ *and* $n_v^a = \overline{n}_v^a$ *and* $m_v^p = \overline{m}_v^p$ *and* $m_v^a > \overline{m}_v^a$ **then**

    $\overline{m}_v^a = m_v^a$, $k_o = k$;

  end

end

---

4. When N^p increases, the performances of kNN$_3$ and kNN$_1$ converge. This is because for large N^p, the validation accuracy in the internal cross-validation on the primary training examples only is enough to distinguish among different ks, and hence the effect of the auxiliary data is reduced, i.e., the *"else if"* loops in Algorithm 2 are rarely used.

In summary, the accuracy of a kNN classifier can be improved with the help of auxiliary training examples from other subjects, especially when the number of primary training examples is very small. As a result, fewer user-specific training examples may be needed to tailor an affective computing system for individual use.

Finally, note that the purpose of the experiments is not to show how good a kNN classifier can be in arousal classification; instead, we aim to demonstrate how transfer learning can improve the performance of an existing classifier. Also, as we have shown in this section, not necessarily all transfer learning algorithms

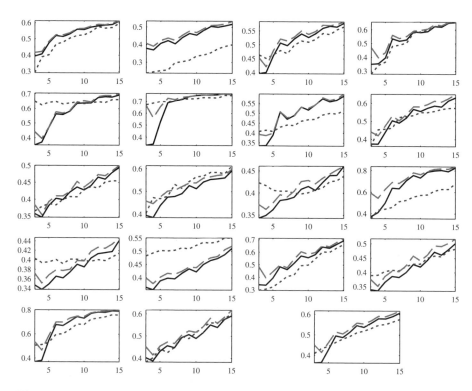

Fig. 2. Performance comparison of the three kNN classifiers on the 18 subjects. Each of the first 18 sub-figures represents a different subject. The last sub-figure shows the average performance of the three kNN classifiers over the 18 subjects. The horizontal axis shows N^p, and the vertical axis shows the testing accuracy on the $150 - N^p$ examples from the same subject. —: kNN_1; - - -: kNN_2; – – –: kNN_3.

Table 1. Paired t-test results on kNN_1 and kNN_3. $\alpha = 0.05$ and $df = 12$.

Subj.	1	2	3	4	5	6	7	8	9	10	11	12	13	14	15	16	17	18
t	5.5	9.9	4.0	3.1	2.6	2.0	2.3	6.4	5.8	5.3	6.1	3.1	8.9	6.8	3.5	14.0	2.6	8.3
p	<.01	<.01	<.01	<.01	.02	**.07**	.04	<.01	<.01	<.01	<.01	<.01	<.01	<.01	<.01	<.01	.02	<.01

can always improve the classification performance. For each particular application, a small dataset may be needed to identify the best transfer learning approach.

4   Conclusions and Future Research Directions

In this paper we have introduced the concept of transfer learning and demonstrated how it can be used to handle individual differences in affective computing through an arousal level classification example. Experiments on 18 subjects showed that a kNN classifier which made use of the auxiliary data in cross-validation can always achieve better performance than the one using the primary data only. Especially, the performance improvement was significant when the number of primary training examples is very small. The results suggest that transfer learning is a very promising technique for handling individual differences in affective computing, and it can help tailor an affective computing system for individual users with very few user-specific training examples. To the best knowledge of the authors, this is the first time that transfer learning has been applied to affective computing problems.

This paper represents our first attempt on using transfer learning in affective computing. We plan to further pursue this interesting research in the following directions:

1. To integrate transfer learning with feature selection. As it has been shown in [10], many of the 29 features are not useful. However, the useful features are subject-dependent. As the features directly affect the NNs, it is necessary to integrate transfer learning with feature selection for further performance improvement.

2. We will consider removing outliers from the auxiliary data to make them more consistent, because we believe that the data for each subject in the auxiliary data should be consistent by themselves: If a subject's arousal levels cannot be classified reliably based on his/her own previous responses, how can that subject's profile be used to help classify another subject's arousal level? In other words, if a subject cannot reliably classify his/her own arousal level, then unlikely he/she can give good suggestions on another subject's arousal level. One possible approach is that for each subject in the auxiliary data, we remove a minimum number of outliers so that a 100% accurate kNN classifier can be obtained for him/her. The remaining data from all subjects can then be combined to form the auxiliary dataset.

3. It may be beneficial to not mix the responses from all subjects in the auxiliary data, e.g., we can treat each of the remaining 17 subjects' responses as a separate auxiliary dataset, perform transfer learning on each auxiliary dataset, and then fuse the outcome.

4. We will carefully design the primary training examples to further minimize the number of training examples needed to tailor an affective computing system for individual use. Active class selection [3] is one such approach. In [11] we have shown that it can achieve better performance than learning from random training examples by using feedback during learning to guide the generation of new training data.

5. We will apply transfer learning to affective computing problems beyond classification, e.g., regression [12], and preference learning [14], where the users' affects are expressed as preferences instead of classes or numbers.

References

1. Allanson, A., Fairclough, J.: A research agenda for physiological computing. Interacting With Computers 16, 858–878 (2004)

2. Ito, T., Cacioppo, J.: Variations on a human universal: Individual differences in positivity offset and negativity bias. Cognition & Emotion 19, 1–26 (2005)
3. Lomasky, R., Brodley, C.E., Aernecke, M., Walt, D., Friedl, M.: Active class selection. In: Proc. 18th European Conference on Machine Learning, Warsaw, Poland, pp. 640–647 (September 2007)
4. Pan, S.J., Yang, Q.: A survey on transfer learning. IEEE Trans. on Knowledge and Data Engineering 22(10), 1345–1359 (2010)
5. Pantic, M., Rothkrantz, L.: Automatic analysis of facial expressions: The state of the art. IEEE Trans. on Pattern Analysis and Machine Intelligence 22(12), 1424–1445 (2000)
6. Parsons, T., Courtney, C., Arizmendi, B., Dawson, M.: Virtual reality Stroop task for neurocognitive assessment. Studies in Health Technology and Informatics 143, 433–439 (2011)
7. Picard, R.: Affective Computing. The MIT Press, Cambridge (1997)
8. Stroop, J.: Studies of interference in serial verbal reactions. Journal of Experimental Psychology 18, 643–661 (1935)
9. Varma, S., Simon, R.: Bias in error estimation when using cross-validation for model selection. BMC Bioinformatics 7(91) (2006)
10. Wu, D., Courtney, C.G., Lance, B.J., Narayanan, S.S., Dawson, M.E., Oie, K.S., Parsons, T.D.: Optimal arousal identification and classification for affective computing: Virtual Reality Stroop Task. IEEE Trans. on Affective Computing 1(2), 109–118 (2010)
11. Wu, D., Parsons, T.D.: Active class selection for arousal classification. In: D′Mello, S., et al. (eds.) Affective Computing and Intelligent Interaction, Part II, vol. 6975, pp. 132–141. Springer, Heidelberg (2011)
12. Wu, D., Parsons, T.D., Mower, E., Narayanan, S.S.: Speech emotion estimation in 3D space. In: Proc. IEEE Int'l. Conf. on Multimedia & Expo. (ICME), Singapore, pp. 737–742 (July 2010)
13. Wu, P., Dietterich, T.G.: Improving SVM accuracy by training on auxiliary data sources. In: Proc. Int'l. Conf. on Machine Learning, Banff, Alberta, Canada, pp. 871–878 (July 2004)
14. Yannakakis, G.N., Maragoudakis, M., Hallam, J.: Preference learning for cognitive modeling: A case study on entertainment preferences. IEEE Systems, Man and Cybernetics – A 39(6), 1165–1175 (2009)
15. Zeng, Z., Pantic, M., Roisman, G.I., Huang, T.S.: A survey of affect recognition methods: Audio, visual, and spontaneous expressions. IEEE Trans. on Pattern Analysis and Machine Intelligence 31(1), 39–58 (2009)

The Machine Knows What You Are Hiding: An Automatic Micro-expression Recognition System

Qi Wu[1,2], Xunbing Shen[1,2], and Xiaolan Fu[1,*]

[1] State Key Laboratory of Brain and Cognitive Science, Institute of Psychology,
Chinese Academy of Sciences, Beijing, China
fuxl@psych.ac.cn
[2] Graduate University of Chinese Academy of Sciences, Beijing, China

Abstract. Micro-expressions are one of the most important behavioral clues for lie and dangerous demeanor detections. However, it is difficult for humans to detect micro-expressions. In this paper, a new approach for automatic micro-expression recognition is presented. The system is fully automatic and operates in frame by frame manner. It automatically locates the face and extracts the features by using Gabor filters. GentleSVM is then employed to identify micro-expressions. As for spotting, the system obtained 95.83% accuracy. As for recognition, the system showed 85.42% accuracy which was higher than the performance of trained human subjects. To further improve the performance, a more representative training set, a more sophisticated testing bed, and an accurate image alignment method should be focused in future research.

Keywords: Micro-expression, Mutual information, Dynamical weight trimming, GentleSVM, Gabor filters.

1 Introduction

The frequency of violent and extreme actions around the world is increasing. Scientists and engineers are forced to develop new techniques to detect those actions. Psychologists have made some progress within this domain. In 1969, Ekman and Friesen discovered the existence of micro-expressions [1]. A micro-expression is an extremely quick facial expression of emotion that lasts for 1/25s to 1/5s. It is an involuntary expression shown on the face when humans are trying to conceal or repress their emotions, and it is expressed in the form of seven universal facial expressions [2] [3] [4] [6] [7] [8]. Micro-expressions reveal human's real intent. Therefore, they can be essential behavioral clues for lie and dangerous demeanor detections [2] [4]. The USA government even has already employed this technique in its counter-terrorism practice [5].

However, micro-expressions are barely perceptible to humans [1]. To solve this problem, Ekman developed the Micro Expression Training Tool (METT) [6]. Frank et al. reported that it was still difficult for human to detect real-life micro-expressions

---

* Corresponding author.

S. D´Mello et al. (Eds.): ACII 2011, Part II, LNCS 6975, pp. 152–162, 2011.

even after the training of METT (about 40% correct) [7]. Due to this incompetence, researchers and practitioners have to analyze the videos frame by frame, which is very time-consuming. Efficient technical adjuncts are in great need within this domain.

The combination of computer science and psychology research fields can satisfy these needs. Two independent groups of computer scientists have already addressed this issue. In [8], Polikovsy et al. used the 3D gradients orientation histogram descriptor to represent the motion information. Results show that this method can recognize action units with good precision at some facial regions and it also can analyze the expressions' phases. Shreve et al. proposed novel expression segmentation methods in [9] and [10]. Utilizing the optical strains caused by non-rigid motions, their algorithms can automatically spot macro- and micro-expressions.

These studies have some shortcomings. The method proposed by Polikovsy et al. [8] cannot directly measure the durations of expressions. In addition, their algorithm was evaluated on an artificial dataset in which subjects were asked to simulate micro-expressions with low facial muscle intensity. However, micro-expressions can hardly be falsified and it is the duration but not the intensity that defines micro- and macro-expressions (expressions with durations that are longer than the micros' are called macro-expressions) [1] [4]. The main dataset used by Shreve et al. [9] [10] is also artificial and the false alarm rate of their method for micro-expressions is too high.

One of the challenges faced by researchers is that there is no large enough standard micro-expression database to train an accurate system by utilizing the dynamical features like in [25]. In fact, no researchers have ever investigated the dynamics of micro-expressions. However, the appearance of micro-expression completely resembles the seven basic expressions [3] [4] [6] [8], so it is possible for researchers to train a system based on existing facial expression databases by utilizing only the appearance-based features while ignoring the dynamical information. In this paper, we propose a new approach for automatic micro-expression recognition. The system ignores the dynamical information and analyzes the videos frame by frame. The structure of the paper is as follows. In section 2, an algorithm for facial expression recognition is described and its performance is evaluated, providing the foundation for micro-expression recognition. In Section 3, we modify and apply the algorithm to micro-expressions. We conclude the paper in Section 4.

2   An Algorithm for Facial Expression Recognition

2.1   Dataset, Face Detection, and Preprocessing

The algorithm was evaluated for its facial expression recognition performance on Cohn and Kanade's dataset (CK) [11]. The neutral and one or two different peak frames of 374 sequences from 97 subjects were employed, resulting in 518 images. For each selected subject, only one neutral frame was chosen. Algorithms were trained to recognize the six basic and the neutral expressions.

Images are first converted to grayscale with 8-bit precision. Then the faces are automatically detected by using the algorithm developed by Kienzle et al. [12]. Detected faces are rescaled to 48×48 pixels.

2.2 Feature Extraction

Gabor filters are employed to extract features from detected faces. The two-dimensional Gabor filters are defined as follows:

$$\Psi_{u,v}(z) = \frac{\| k_{u,v} \|^2}{\sigma^2} e^{(-\| k_{u,v} \|^2 \| z \|^2 / 2\sigma^2)} (e^{i k_{u,v} z} - e^{-\sigma^2/2}) . \tag{1}$$

where $k_{u,v} = k_v e^{i\phi_u}$, $k_v = \frac{k_{max}}{f^v}$, $\phi_u = \frac{u\pi}{8}, \phi_u \in [0, \pi)$, and $z = (x, y)$.

$e^{i k_{u,v} z}$ is the oscillatory wave function.

In our proposed algorithm, we use the Gabor filters with 9 scales and 8 orientations, while $\sigma = 2\pi, k_{max} = \pi/2$, and $f = \sqrt{2}$.

2.3 Improved Gentleboost

Adaboost has been applied successfully to a variety of problems (e.g. [14]). In contrast to Adaboost, Gentleboost converges faster, and performs better for object detection problems [15]. Considering its excellent performance [16], we initially chose Gentleboost as the classifier.

Mutual Information and Dynamical Weight Trimming. The weak classifier selection and combination methods determine the efficiency of boosting algorithm [17]. Here we incorporate mutual information (MI) [14] to eliminate non-effective weak classifiers for Gentleboost to improve its performance.

Before a weak classifier is selected, the MI between the new and selected classifiers is examined to make sure the information carried by the new classifier has not been captured by the selected ones. At stage $T+1$ when T weak classifiers $\{h_{v(1)}, h_{v(2)}, ... h_{v(T)}\}$ have been selected, the function for measuring the maximum MI of the candidate classifier h_j and the selected classifiers can be defined as follows:

$$R(h_j) = \max_{t=1,2,...,T} MI(h_j, h_{v(t)}) . \tag{2}$$

where $MI(h_j, h_{v(t)}) = H(h_j) + H(h_{v(t)}) - H(h_j, h_{v(t)})$, $H(x)$ is the entropy of random variable x, and $H(x, y)$ is the joint entropy of random variable x and y. Each weak classifier is considered as a random variable, so $MI(h_j, h_{v(t)})$ represents the mutual information between the two random variables h_j and $h_{v(t)}$. For a weak classifier with discrete values like the regression stump which is employed in this study, the probability values required by MI calculation could be estimated by simply counting the number of possible cases and dividing that number with the total number of training samples. To determine whether the new classifier is effective or not, $R(h_j)$ is compared with a pre-defined threshold of mutual information (TMI). If it is larger than TMI, the classifier is considered as non-effective and a new one is selected from the candidate classifiers.

Because the training of Gentleboost is time-consuming, researchers are forced to train and evaluate this algorithm on low dimensional small data sets. However, due to the extra computation required by MI, the training of Gentleboost even would become longer [14]. Here we extend the idea of dynamical weight trimming (DWT) [18] for Gentleboost to compensate for this problem. This implementation is still called DWT.

At each round, training samples are filtered according to a threshold $t(\beta)$ which is the βth percentile of the weight distribution over training data at the corresponding iteration. Training samples with weight less than the threshold are not used for training. Since the weak classifier is not trained on the whole training samples and is selected according to MI, the weighted error of selected classifier may even be more than or equal to 0.5. To exclude such non-effective classifiers, $t(\beta)$ is dynamically changed according to the classification error. Details are shown in Fig. 1.

For multiclass classification, the one-against-all method is implemented. The expression category decision is implemented by choosing the classifier with the maximum decision function value for the test example. Details are shown in Fig. 1.

---

1) Input: for class l, input N training samples $(x_i, y_i), i = 1, 2, ..., N$ with m positive $(y_i = 1)$ and l negative $(y_i = -1)$ samples

2) Initialization: weights $w_{1,i} = \begin{cases} 1/2m, \text{if } i \text{ is a positive sample} \\ 1/2l, \text{if } i \text{ is a negative sample} \end{cases}$, $\beta = \beta_0$

3) For $t = 1, 2, ..., T$

   a) Filter training samples based on parameter $t(\beta)$

   b) Train candidate classifiers based on the filtered training samples. For each candidate classifier h_j,

   record the weighted squared error: $\varepsilon_j = \sum_i w_{t,i}(h_j(x_i) - y_i)^2$

   For (;;)

   Choose h_u with the lowest ε_u from the candidate classifiers

   Calculate $R(h_u)$ according to Eq. (2)

   If $R(h_u) < TMI$

   The classifier is chosen, $h_t = h_u$, calculate the weighted error $E_t = \sum_t \frac{1}{2} w_{t,i} |y_i - sign(h_t(x))|$

   Goto c)

   Else

   Remove h_u from the candidate list, if all candidates are removed, stop training.

   End Loop

   c) If $E_t \geq 0.5$ and not all training samples are employed, then $\beta = \beta / 2$, goto a). If $E_t \geq 0.5$ and all training samples are used, then stop training. Else goto d)

   d) Update the weights $w_{t+1,i} = w_{t,i} e^{-y_i h_t(x_i)}$ and renormalize, $\beta = \beta_0$.

4) Output the final decision function: $H(x,l) = \sum_{t=1}^{T} h_t(x)$.

Fig. 1. The improved Gentleboost algorithm for binary classifier

Experimental Results and Discussions. The proposed algorithm was implemented in Matlab and tested on a Core i5 650 system with 4GB memory. The 10-fold cross validation was used as the testing paradigm that subjects were randomly separated into 10 groups of roughly equal size and did 'leave one group out' cross validation.TMI and β were set to 0.1^{1}. The best results were obtained when 120 features were employed by each binary classifier.

Table 1. Performance of imroved Gentleboost

Classifier	Accuracy	Training time[2]
Gentleboost, MI+DWT	88.61%	85019.71s
Gentleboost, DWT	85.33%	84644.05s
Gentleboost,MI	87.83%	122817.91s
Original Gentleboost	86.48%	122364.53s

As shown in Table 1, the MI+DWT combination improved Gentleboost's accuracy. Although this combination has the highest accuracy score, the 88.61% accuracy obtained by our algorithm is still not satisfactory enough.

Results also showed that the training speed of Gentleboost was improved by the MI+DWT combination (1.44 times faster than original). This effect is brought by the DWT implementation. It should be noted that, for most problems, $\beta = 0.1$ should be able to bring acceptable results because the data used for training carries 90 percent of the total weight. As shown in Table 1, the accuracy of Gentleboost with DWT was only slightly lower than the original Gentleboost. The larger value of β can bring faster training speed, but it will also introduce more errors [18]. A trade-off between speed and accuracy must be considered.

2.4 GentleSVM

It has been shown that SVMs can provide state-of-the-art accuracy for the facial expression recognition problem [13] [16]. To further improve the performance of our proposed algorithm, we chose to use the Gentleboost algorithm as a feature selector preceding the SVM classifiers. This combination is called GentleSVM.

In feature selection by Gentleboost, each Gabor filter is treated as a weak classifier. Gentleboost picks the best of those classifiers, and then adjusts the weight according to the classification results. The next filter is selected as the one that gives the best performance on the errors of the previous filter. All the selected features are then united to form a new representation. Then the 1-norm soft margin linear SVMs are trained on the selected Gabor features. For multiclass classification, the one-against-all method is implemented. The expression category decision is implemented by choosing the classifier with the maximum geometric margin for the test example.

---

[1] For all the experiments described in this paper, the mutual information was measured in bans.
[2] The time required for 10 times trainings.

Experimental Results and Discussions. The proposed algorithm was implemented and tested on same platform as in Section 2.3. Testing paradigm was the same to Section 2.3. TMI and β were set to 0.1. The best results were obtained when 200 features were selected for each expression category.

Table 2. Performance of GentleSVM

Classifier	Accuracy	Training time[3]
Original SVM	88.03%	883.62s
GentleSVM, MI+DWT	92.66%	18.85s
GentleSVM, DWT	90.93%	19.31s
GentleSVM, MI	92.47%	17.79s
Original GentleSVM	90.35%	19.00s

Table 3. Accuracy for each expression category

Classifier	Sadness	Surprise	Anger	Disgust	Fear	Happiness	Neutral
Original SVM	82.43%	93.06%	84.13%	93.75%	75.41%	92.55%	91.11%
GentleSVM, MI+DWT	85.14%	98.61%	87.03%	96.86%	86.89%	96.81%	94.44%
GentleSVM, DWT	85.14%	98.61%	87.03%	96.88%	80.33%	94.68%	91.11%
GentleSVM, MI	85.13%	100%	85.71%	96.88%	86.89%	96.81%	93.33%
Original GentleSVM	82.43%	98.61%	88.89%	95.31%	83.61%	96.81%	85.56%

As shown in Table 2, all GentleSVM variants outperformed the original SVM and our improved Gentleboost, and all GentleSVM variants completed the 10 times trainings within 20s, which means that after the training of Gentleboost the system can be further improved with only a little cost of time. Within these GentleSVM variants, the best result was obtained by the MI+DWT combination (92.66%). Taken all results together, we can safely conclude that the MI+DWT combination improves the performance of Gentleboost both for classification and feature selection.

As shown in Table 3, all GentleSVM variants and original SVM recognized surprise, disgust, happiness, and neutral expressions with good precisions. As for sadness, anger, and fear, the performance of all the classifiers were lower. However, all these accuracy scores for GentleSVM variants were still above 80%.

Bartlett et al. [13] have conducted similar experiments by using the Computer Expression Recognition Toolbox on CK. They reported 93% correct for an alternative forced choice of the six basic expressions plus neutral [13]. To the best of our knowledge, this is the highest performance obtained by appearance based approach on CK. Their results are not directly comparable to us due to different protocols,

---

[3] The time required for 10 times trainings.

preprocessing methods, and so on, but we can see from the results that the best accuracy score obtained by us (92.66%) is very similar to theirs. Such accuracy is encouraging for an automatic system without complicated preprocessing procedures. It establishes a firm foundation for micro-expression recognition.

3   An Automatic Micro-expression Recognition System

To recognize micro-expressions, the algorithm described above is applied to videos to determine the expression label for each video frame. Then the label outputs are scanned. Durations of expressions are measured according to the transition points and the video's frame-rate. For example, if a video's frame-rate is 30 fps, and its label output is 111222, then the transition points are the first frame, the point where $1 \rightarrow 2$, and the last frame. So the durations of expression 1 and 2 are both 1/10s. Then the micro-expression and its expression label are extracted according to its definition. Expressions that last for 1/25s to 1/5s are considered as micro-expressions, whereas expressions with durations that are longer than 1/5s are considered as macro-expressions and are ignored [1] [3] [4]. Considering contempt is not universal as the other six basic expressions [7], presently the system is only trained to recognize micro-expressions from the six prototypic categories. Fig. 2 illustrates its framework.

Fig. 2. Overview of the proposed automatic micro-expression recognition system

3.1   A New Training Set, the Test Set, and the Extra Preprocessing Procedure

A new training set was collected to promote the system's generalization ability. To be more specific, 1109 images were collected from facial expression databases [11] [19] [20] [21] [22] [23] and 26 images were downloaded from the Internet.

Micro-expression videos from METT [6] were employed as the test set. Forty-eight micro-expression videos from the six basic expression categories were all employed. In each video, there was a flash of frontal view micro-expression, preceded and followed by about 2s of frontal view neutral expressions. The system's performance was evaluated by two indexes. As for spotting, the system had to identify the hidden expressions as micro-expressions. No false alarms were accepted. As for recognition, the system had to correctly label the micro-expressions.

To compensate for the illumination differences between facial expression databases, an extra preprocessing procedure is performed that the grayscale values of each rescaled face are normalized to zero mean and one unit variance.

3.2   Experimental Results and Discussions

The system was implemented and tested in the same environment as in Section 2. TMI and β were set to 0.1. Two hundred features were selected for each expression.

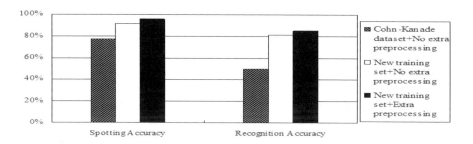

Fig. 3. The performance of the automatic micro-expression recognition system on METT

Table 4. The performances for Caucasians and Asians

Race	Recognition accuracy	Sample size[4]
Caucasian	95.8%	904
Asian	75%	160

As shown in Fig. 3, if the training set was changed to CK and the extra preprocessing was not performed, the system's recognition accuracy on METT was only 50% which was even lower than the performance of naive human subjects on the pretest phrase of METT [7] [24]. However, when the system was trained on the new training set, its spotting accuracy reached 91.67% and the recognition accuracy was 81.25%. When the extra preprocessing procedure was added, the spotting accuracy reached 95.83%, and the recognition accuracy was 85.42%. This recognition accuracy was even higher than the performance of trained human subjects (70%–80%) on the posttest phrase of METT [7] [24]. This result highlights the need for large training set in practice and the necessity of the extra preprocessing procedure. Considering the contribution of the extra preprocessing was only about 4% when the training set was large, this result suggests that researchers should focus more on the training set than the preprocessing method.

---

[4] The number of examples in the new training set.

A detailed analysis indicates that our new training set is still not representative enough. In our test set, one half of the subjects are Caucasians, while the other half is Asian. Results showed that the final system performed differently for these two different races (as shown in Table 4). Compared with the large sample size of Caucasians in the new training set, the sample size of Asians in this training set is small, thus limiting the performance of our final system for Asians. A more representative training set should be collected in the future.

The results obtained above are still preliminary. The micro-expressions in METT are in their simplest forms that the micro-expressions are in frontal-view and there are no large head rotations and speech related expressions in the video. The micro-expressions in real-life situations are more complicated than in METT. Therefore, it is necessary to collect a more comprehensive testing bed in order to evaluate the system in more realistic situations or to investigate the dynamics of micro-expressions.

It should be noted that no image alignments are performed in our system. Inaccurate image alignments may impair the performance of the system in real-life applications [16]. Therefore, future improvements should focus on the image alignment method in order to handle head rotations and image shifts.

It also should be noted that intelligent systems like the one described above must be applied cautiously in practice. Although the micro-expression hypothesis is widely accepted among psychologists, some empirical studies suggest that over-reliance on micro-expressions as an indicator of deception is likely to be ineffective. It is necessary for the researchers to take other behavioral clues into consideration [3] [5].

4   Conclusions

In this paper, we presented a new approach for facial micro-expression recognition. The system ignores the dynamical information and analyzes the videos frame by frame. Results showed that the performance of our final system on METT test was better than the performance of trained human subjects.

Acknowledgments. This research was supported in part by grants from 973 Program (2011CB302201) and the National Natural Science Foundation of China (61075042).

References

1. Ekman, P., Friesen, W.V.: Nonverbal Leakage and Clues to Deception. Psychiatry 32, 88–97 (1969)
2. Ekman, P.: Lie Catching and Microexpressions. In: Martin, C. (ed.) The Philosophy of Deception, pp. 118–133. Oxford University Press, Oxford (2009)
3. ten Brinke, L., MacDonald, S., Porter, S., O' Conner, B.: Crocodile Tears: Facial, Verbal and Body Language Behaviors Associated with Genuine and Fabricated Remorse. Law. Hum. Behav., 1–11 (2011)

4. Ekman, P.: Telling Lies, 2nd edn. Norton, New York (2009)
5. Weinberger, S.: Intent to Deceive: Can the Science of Deception Detection Help to Catch Terrorists? Nature 465, 412–415 (2010)
6. Ekman, P.: Micro Expression Training Tool. University of California, San Francisco (2003)
7. Frank, M.G., Herbasz, M., Sinuk, K., Keller, A., Nolan, C.: I See How You Feel: Training Laypeople and Professionals to Recognize Fleeting Emotions. In: The Annual Meeting of the International Communication Association. Sheraton New York, New York City (2009), http://www.allacademic.com/meta/p15018_index.html
8. Polisovsky, S., Kameda, Y., Ohta, Y.: Facial Micro-Expressions Recognition Using High Speed Camera and 3D-Gradients Descriptor. In: The Proceedings of 3rd International Conference on Imaging for Crime Detection and Prevention, pp. 1–6 (2009)
9. Shreve, M., Godavarthy, S., Manohar, V., Goldgof, D., Sarkar, S.: Towards Macro- and Micro-Expression Spotting in Videos using Strain Patterns. In: The Proceeding of IEEE Workshop on Applications of Computer Vision, pp. 1–6 (2009)
10. Shreve, M., Godavarthy, S., Goldgof, D., Sarkar, S.: Macro- and Micro- Expression Spotting using Spatio-temporal Strain. To appear in Face and Gesture, Santa Barbara (March 2011), http://www.cse.usf.edu/~mshreve/publications/FG11.pdf
11. Kanade, T., Cohn, J.F., Tian, Y.: Comprehensive Database for Facial Expression Analysis. In: Proceedings of the 4th IEEE International Conference on Automatic Face and Gesture Recognition, pp. 46–53 (2000)
12. Kienzle, W., Bakir, G., Franz, B., Scholkopf, M.: Face Detection - Efficient and Rank Deficient. In: Advances in Neural Information Processing Systems, vol. 17, pp. 673–680 (2005)
13. Bartlett, M., Whitehill, J.: Automated Facial Expression Measurement: Recent Applications to Basic Research in Human Behavior, Learning, and Education. In: Calder, A., Rhodes, G., Haxby, J.V., Johnson, M.H. (eds.) Handbook of Face Perception. Oxford University Press, USA (2010), http://mplab.ucsd.edu/~marni/pubs/Bartlett_FaceHandbook_2010.pdf
14. Shen, L., Bai, L.: Mutualboost Learning for Selecting Gabor Features for Face Recognition. Pattern. Recogn. Lett. 27, 1758–1767 (2006)
15. Torralba, A., Murphy, K.P., Freeman, W.T.: Sharing Features: Efficient Boosting Procedures for Multiclass Object Detection. In: Proceedings of 2004 IEEE Computer Society Conference on Computer Vision and Pattern Recognition, pp. 762–769 (2004)
16. Whitehill, J., Littlewort, G., Fasel, I., Bartlett, M., Movellan, J.: Toward Practical Smile Detection. IEEE Trans. Pattern. Anal. Mach. Intell. 31, 2106–2111 (2009)
17. Gao, N., Tang, Q.: On Selection and Combination of Weak Learners in AdaBoost. Pattern. Recogn. Lett. 31, 991–1001 (2010)
18. Jia, H., Zhang, Y.: Fast Adaboost Training Algorithm by Dynamic Weight Trimming. Chinese. J. Comput 32, 336–341 (2009)
19. Pantic, M., Valstar, M.F., Rademaker, R., Maat, L.: Web-Based Database for Facial Expression Analysis. In: Proceedings of IEEE International Conference on Multimedia and Expo., pp. 317–321 (2005)
20. Wallhoff, F.: Facial Expressions and Emotion Database. Technische Universität München (2006), http://www.mmk.ei.tum.de/~waf/fgnet/feedtum.html

21. Lyons, M.J., Akamatsu, S., Kamachi, M., Gyoba, J.: Coding Facial Expressions with Gabor Wavelets. In: Proceedings of the Third IEEE International Conference on Automatic Face and Gesture Recognition, pp. 200–205 (1998)

22. Roy, S., Roy, C., Fortin, I., Either-Majcher, C., Belin, P., Gosselin, F.: A Dynamic Facial Expression Database. J. Vis. 7, 944a (2007)

23. Ekman, P., Friesen, W.V.: Pictures of Facial Affect. Consulting Psychologists Press, California (1976)

24. Russell, T.A., Elvina, C., Mary, L.P.: A Pilot Study to Investigate the Effectiveness of Emotion Recognition Remediation in Schizophrenia Using the Micro-Expression Training Tool. Brit. J. Clin. Psychol. 45, 579–583 (2006)

25. Koelstra, S., Pantic, M., Patras, I.: A Dynamic Texture-Based Approach to Recognition of Facial Actions and Their Temporal Models. IEEE Trans. Pattern Anal. Mach. Intell. 32(11), 1940–1954 (2010)

EMOGIB: Emotional Gibberish Speech Database for Affective Human-Robot Interaction

Selma Yilmazyildiz, David Henderickx, Bram Vanderborght,
Werner Verhelst, Eric Soetens, and Dirk Lefeber

Interdisciplinary Institute for Broadband Technology (IBBT), Belgium,
Dept. of Electronics and Informatics (ETRO - DSSP),
Vrije Universiteit Brussel, Belgium
Dept. of Cognitive Psychology, Vrije Universiteit Brussel, Belgium
Dept. of Mechanical Engineering (MECH - RMM), Vrije Universiteit Brussel, Belgium
{syilmazy,david.henderickx,bram.vanderborght,
wverhels,eric.soetens,dlefeber}@vub.ac.be,
http://www.ibbt.be/,http://www.vub.ac.be/

Abstract. Gibberish speech consists of vocalizations of meaningless strings of speech sounds. It is sometimes used by performing artists or by cartoon animations (e.g.: Teletubbies) to express intended emotions, without pronouncing any actually understandable word. The facts that no understandable text has to be pronounced and that only affect is conveyed create the advantage of gibberish in affective computing. In our study, we intend to experiment the communication between a robot and hospitalized children using affective gibberish. In this study, a new emotional database consisting of 4 distinct corpuses has been recorded for the purpose of affective child-robot interaction. The database comprises speech recordings of one actress simulating a neutral state and the big six emotions: anger, disgust, fear, happiness, sadness and surprise. The database has been evaluated through a perceptual test for all subsets of the database by adults and one subset of the database with children, achieving recognition scores up to 81%.

Keywords: emotional speech database, emotional speech corpus, affective speech, gibberish speech, human-computer interaction.

1   Introduction

Everyone would have heard a small baby communicating with his or her mother. But most likely not many would have paid attention to how smoothly they communicate their emotions without saying any single meaningful word. Although it is common knowledge that small children are able to do this, this effect is hard to replicate technically.

Like in the communication of babies with their mothers, a nonsense language like gibberish can be a successful carrier to express emotions and affect. Moreover, since there is no meaningful content and the focus of the listener is entirely on the conveyed affect, gibberish might even be more effective than meaningful

S. D´Mello et al. (Eds.): ACII 2011, Part II, LNCS 6975, pp. 163–172, 2011.

speech. This is the main motivation to use affective gibberish speech for communication between robots and children in our study.

In our previous study [4], the experiments concluded that gibberish speech can convey the emotions as effectively as semantically neutral speech. This supports our intention to use gibberish speech to express the emotions of the robots. In that study [4], to produce gibberish speech, we developed a program that replaces the vowel nuclei in a text with other vowel nuclei of the same language such that the text loses its meaning. We then used the generated gibberish text as input for TTS engines to produce the gibberish speech. But there are two drawbacks of this method. The final expressive speech strongly depends on the TTS engine quality and the voice quality of the emotions in the database is lost. To overcome these drawbacks, we decided to use a data-driven method that starts with a gibberish emotional database.

The lack of databases with genuine interaction is a key challenge in the studies of emotion expression. Observational or post hoc analyses of human interaction data is a method that could be used but it is a fairly impractical route to choose. As a result in most of the currently available databases acting has been used [1]. Busso and Narayanan argue that the methodologies and materials used to record the existing corpora are the main problem with the existing databases and not the use of actors itself. Some of the important requirements that need to be carefully considered in the design of the database are the speaker selection, contextualization and social setting, utilization of acting styles, usage of trained actors and the definition of the emotional descriptors [2].

However, the usage of affective gibberish speech and targeting the primary usage of the database in communication between robots (such as Probo[12] and NAO) and children help to simplify some of these requirements. First of all, there is no context in the gibberish speech. Secondly, Moris theory of the uncanny valley suggests that when robots look and act almost like actual humans, it causes a response of revulsion among human observers. The "valley" in the uncanny valley hypothesis represents a dip in the positivity of human reaction as a function of a robot's lifelikeness [3]. We can deduce from the uncanny valley theory that when the children notice a certain level of acting or unnaturalness in the synthesized speech of the robot will not necessarily negatively affect their overall communication experience with these robots.

2   EMOGIB-Emotional Gibberish Speech Database

EMOGIB is an expressive gibberish speech database that contains approximately 15 minutes of speech ($\sim$1800 words) for each big six emotions (anger, disgust, fear, happiness, sadness, surprise) and 25 minutes of speech ($\sim$4100 words) for neutral state. It has 4 different gibberish corpuses: C1 & C3 - generated by using the whole consonant and vowel space of Dutch and English, C2 & C4 - generated by using the whole vowel space and voiceless consonant space of Dutch and English. The reason of generating C2 & C4 comes from the ease of using voiceless consonants for automatic segmentation and manipulation.

2.1 Speaker Selection

Many of the requirements that effects the quality of the final database are influenced by the acting qualities of the selected speaker. Even though it is possible to improve the performance of the speaker by carefully designing the recording conditions[2], the speaker selection is still a key factor.

A call for speakers was distributed to the theater/drama schools in the country. Six of the candidates were invited for a phone interview. The candidates were all informed before the interview that they would be asked to voice-act in the interview. We sent them four sentences (one in English, one in Dutch and two nonsense sentences) that might be used as scripts to voice-act.

The interview started with a friendly talk where we asked their personal information such as their name, age, study program, languages spoken, experience in voice acting, experience in communication with children. The questions in the second part were structured in a way that we could evaluate the candidates on the following criteria: the ability to easily switch the voice to another type, the ability to act emotions, the ability to act nonsense sentences, the flexibility of the voice, the duration of the recording session, the capability of maintaining the voice quality during the recording session and the ability to act as fitting the required characteristics. We described them certain characteristics of an imaginary robot (such as *humor, pleasure, funny, stupid, emotional, sympathetic*) and asked them to speak spontaneously as if being one of those robots. This was to evaluate their ability to easily switch the voice to another type and their ability to act as fitting the required characteristics. To judge their ability to act emotions and their ability to act nonsense sentences, we instructed them to act the scripts that we sent them in six basic emotions (*happiness, sadness, fear, surprise, anger, and disgust*). Finally, to assess the flexibility/limits of their voice, we requested them to act in certain ages and genders such as *male, female, child, old man, old lady*. All the interview sessions were conducted through an Alcatel-Lucent 4019 phone in hands-free mode and the sessions were recorded to be able to listen to them later for evaluation.

Based on the above criteria, a 20 year old female drama student was selected as the speaker for the actual recordings.

2.2 Text Corpus

Languages consist of ruled combinations of words and words consist of specially ordered combinations of syllables. Syllables are often considered the phonological "building blocks" of the words of a particular language. The syllables usually contain an onset, a nucleus and a coda. "Nucleus" is usually a vowel-like sound where 'onset' and 'coda' are consonant clusters.

We created 4 sets of corpuses for the recordings, each set containing 7 different script sets (one for each emotion category and one for the neutral category). The first corpus set was generated by replacing the entire vowel nuclei and consonant clusters in the selected Dutch texts using a weighted swapping mechanism in accordance with the natural probability distribution of the *vowel nuclei* and the *consonant clusters* of Dutch. For the generation of the second corpus set, the entire consonant clusters in a Dutch text were replaced in accordance with the natural probability distribution of *voiceless consonant clusters* of Dutch while the vowel nuclei were replaced in accordance with the natural probability distribution of the *vowel nuclei* of Dutch. The third and the fourth corpuses were created accordingly but this time using English texts and the corresponding probability distributions of *vowel nuclei, consonant clusters* and *voiceless consonant clusters* of English. The structure of the four corpuses are summarized in Table 1.

The probabilities of occurrence in English and Dutch are calculated for each vowel nucleus (as explained in [4]) and for each consonant cluster. For consonant clusters begin (onset), middle and end (coda) consonant cluster probabilities were calculated separately. Similarly, the same calculations are performed for the voiceless consonant clusters (begin, middle, end). The probabilities were calculated using texts of approximately 27000 words from a large online text corpus - Project Gutenberg [5].

Table 1. The summary of the corpus structures

Corpuses			
NAME	LANGUAGE	CONSONANT DISTRIBUTION	VOWEL DISTRIBUTION
C1	Dutch	Whole consonant space	Whole vowel space
C2	Dutch	Voiceless consonant space	Whole vowel space
C3	English	Whole consonant space	Whole vowel space
C4	English	Voiceless consonant space	Whole vowel space

The texts were categorized in a way that we would have controlled variation in the sentences. These sentences contained different number of words, starting from one word up to ten words. In each emotion category the proportion of the number of words was the same.

The sentences were organized in paragraph structure to provide a dialogue impression. This is the kind of structure similar to dialogues used in theatre/film scripts.

2.3   Actual Recordings

Setup. The recordings took place in our recording lab [6] where the proper acoustic absorption was provided. The speaker was sitting on a stool chair with a proper headphone. The microphone (Neumann U87) was at a fixed position from the mouth of the speaker. Reading pane was put at a position where the speaker felt comfortable. Fig. 1 shows the recording set up.

The control room was outside the recording chamber and there was a window connecting the rooms visually.

Fig. 1. The recording setup

Recording Procedure. The recordings started with voice tuning practices. The voice type should have suited the robotic character communicating with children. On the other hand, as the speaker would use the same type of the voice for a long period of time, it was important to find the voice type that the speaker felt comfortable with. We let the speaker improvise a few different voice types and recorded all of them. Considering the above two criteria, we chose one of the voice types in consultation with the speaker. During the recordings, we periodically played back the recorded sample of the voice type in order to keep the voice type stable during the entire recording session.

We repeated the same reference building procedure before each emotion recording as well. Taking the recorded base voice as a reference, the speaker improvised each emotion with that voice type. Then we kept the final sample as a reference for that emotion and let the actress train for a while. At the beginning of each script paragraph, we played the reference and the speaker continued acting in the same voice quality of the emotion. Also during the recordings, whenever a difference in the level/quality of emotion or voice type was noticed, that part was compared with the reference and re-recorded if needed.

A stuffed prototype of Probo was put in the recording room. This helped the speaker to act as being the robot. The photographic facial expressions of the robot were pinned on the face of the stuffed prototype to visualize the robot's emotions. The speaker found that method very helpful for getting back in the mood.

Before the recordings, a short discussion was held with the speaker about how to get in the mood for the different emotions. The speaker was also a drama trainer for children. She told us that in their acting trainings, they let the trainees close their eyes and relive some scenes from their lives that had the particular moods/emotions. We let her use the same method that she was used to to put herself in the mood. Only when she could not bring any scene from her life, we told her a short story in that particular emotion about Probo.

The speaker chose the emotion as well as the text corpus to start with. We planned 5-10 minutes of breaks hourly but the speaker could also take a break whenever she felt tired.

The recordings were done with Pro-Tools 8 and the pre-amplifier used was Earthworks 1021. All the data is recorded with 48 kHz sampling rate and 24 bits.

3   Evaluations

3.1   Experiments

We performed a series of two experiments; one with adult listeners and one with children listeners. While more subjects participated to the children experiment, the audio part of the children experiment was structured as a subset of the adults experiment. Only one database subset (C1) was used in the children experiment. Aside from the audio section, the children experiment has also included visual and audiovisual sections. The children experiment is analyzed and discussed in detail in [7].

Ten subjects participated to the adult experiment. The age of the subjects varied between 27 and 32.

Random samples were selected from each database subset (C1, C2, C3, C4) for each emotion category. The length of the samples had to be long enough so that the subjects could evaluate effectively. On the other hand, the length should not be too long not to lose the attention of the participants. So we decided to use 10 seconds of samples. Four different samples of 10 seconds are created for each emotion.

We instructed the subjects to listen to a number of samples of which they might not understand the meaning. The order of the samples were distributed randomly across emotions and we only used a single presentation order for all the subjects. The subjects were requested to choose which one of the possible emotions *anger*, *disgust*, *fear*, *happiness*, *sadness*, *surprise* or *neutral* matched the speech sample they heard. Subjects were allowed to listen to the samples as often as they desired.

As the final goal is to create a *natural sounding* gibberish language that can be used in building expressively interacting computing devices, the naturalness of the database had to be evaluated. Thus, in a second question, the subjects were asked to pay attention to the naturalness of the samples. They were instructed that the sample was considered as natural when it sounded rather like an unrecognized real language and not as an unnatural or random combination of sounds. Subjects were asked to assess their perception of the naturalness of the samples using Mean Opinion Scores (MOS) in a scale from 1 to 5. We also asked them to write down the language if the sample sounded like a language they knew to investigate if it is still possible to recognize the original language of the corpuses after consonant and vowel swapping.

3.2   Results

Fig. 2 shows the emotion recognition results for all 4 experimental corpuses (C1, C2, C3, C4). "Correct" stands for the emotion that was perceived as the intended

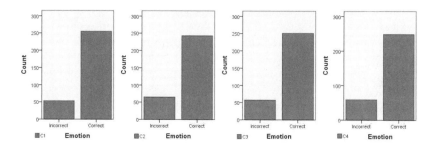

Fig. 2. Emotion recognition results for all 4 experimental corpuses (C1, C2, C3, C4, from left to right)

emotion and "incorrect" stands for the emotion that was perceived as one of the other emotions and not the intended one. As can be seen from the graphs, there is not a big difference in the recognition results which was also confirmed by the Kruskal-Wallis test.

When we analyzed the results emotion-by-emotion, a statistical significant difference is found only with *happiness* among the different corpuses. The recognition result of *happiness* was significantly lower in C2 than the other corpuses.

Overall/combined emotions versus recognized emotions are shown in the confusion matrix of Table 2. *Sadness* was recognized by most of the participants (94%). The recognition rate of *sadness* was followed by *neutral* with 88%, *surprise* with 87%, *happiness* with 84%, *disgust* with 74%, *fear* with 73% and *anger* with 66%. *Fear* was usually confused with *surprise* and *anger* was usually confused with *neutral* or *surprise*.

In the children experiment in which only C1 was used,*sadness* was recognized the best (100%). This was followed by *surprise* with 86%, *fear* with 71% and *disgust* with 57%. *Happiness* was often confused with *anger* and vice-versa which resulted in a lower recognition (29% and 46%, respectively). Much better results were achieved in the adult experiment for the same corpus C1 (91% and 64% for *happiness* and *anger*, respectively). This difference can be an indication that children and adults might have a different interpretation of, especially, *happiness*. For the other emotions, the recognition rates for C1 in the adult experiment were as following: 100% for *sadness* and *surprise*, 91% for *fear*, 55% for *disgust*.

Table 3 shows the average MOS scores for each corpus. As can be seen, the overall mean score is 3.6. This implies that the gibberish speech is perceived as natural by most of the subjects. The MOS results of corpus C1 was slightly higher than the other corpuses but a Kruskal-Wallis did not show a significant difference.

In the children experiment, the participants were provided with the question requesting a Mean Opinion Score (MOS) for the voice. The average MOS score for if the subjects liked the voice was 7.03 (out of 10).

Fig. 3 shows to what extent the subjects were able to identify the original language in C1 and C3. It was seen that, for most of the subjects both of the

Table 2. Overall confusion matrix (expressed in %)

	Neutral	Anger	Disgust	Fear	Happiness	Sadness	Surprise
Neutral	**87.5**	1.1	0.0	0.0	9.7	0.6	1.1
Anger	13.1	**66.5**	3.4	1.1	5.7	0.6	9.7
Disgust	4.5	8.0	**75.0**	0.6	2.3	8.0	1.7
Fear	0.0	6.3	0.0	**73.3**	1.1	7.4	11.9
Happiness	1.7	0.6	0.6	2.8	**84.1**	5.7	4.5
Sadness	0.6	1.1	0.0	4.0	0.6	**93.8**	0.0
Surprise	2.3	3.4	0.6	1.7	1.1	4.0	**86.9**

Table 3. Experimental results for MOS scores

Corpus	Mean MOS
C1	3.7
C2	3.6
C3	3.6
C4	3.5
General Mean	**3.6**

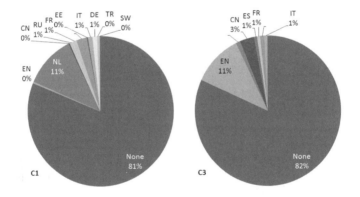

Fig. 3. Percentages of language recognition for C1 and C3 corpuses

corpuses did not sound as any language they knew. For the samples that the subjects thought they had recognized an existing language, the majority of them suspected these to be Dutch or English, for C1 and C3 respectively.

4   Conclusions and Further Work

In this paper, we described our emotional gibberish database with its primary aim of affective communication between robots and their children users.

The perception experiments showed respectable emotion recognition results of up to 81% overall (and even up to 94% for certain emotions). No statistically significant difference is found in the overall recognition results and emotion-wise (only with an exception of *happiness*) between all the four unique corpuses. This means that our methodology of recording induced emotions from an actor gave stable recognition results. We believe that the main driving reason for this stability was mostly our utilization of the control/reference sentence which was described in Section 2.3.

Between the children and the adult experiments, a remarkable difference was noticed with *happiness*(29% and 91%). This might be an indication that children and adults might have a different interpretation of *happiness* but further research is needed to check this hypothesis.

It is seen that the gibberish language we created resembles a natural language for most of the subjects (with an overall mean score of 3.6 on a scale of 1 to 5). That is important since our goal is to create a meaningless language that sounds like a real language.

In general, the gibberish language we created does not sound as any other languages known by the subjects. For the corpuses where a natural distribution of consonants and vowels was used (C1 and C3), the gibberish speech still sounded slightly like the languages of the texts that were used to create the gibberish texts.

As no statistically significant difference is found between the four different corpuses, for both emotion recognition results as well as for the naturalness, we can use all the four corpuses for emotional speech communication studies.

Combining the results from adult experiment that the gibberish speech resembled a natural language with an average MOS of 3.6 (out of 5) with the results of the children experiment that they liked the voice with an average MOS of 7.0, we can conclude that this database can be used in further studies focusing the children aged 10 to 14.

Apart from the described usage, our database could also be used as a segmental evaluation method for synthetic speech [8] or to test the effectiveness of affective prosodic strategies [9], and it can also be applied in actual systems [10], [11]. With the data recorded we also have a large interest to study the turn taking process of a conversation. As the text corpus was structured in a paragraph manner, start and stop sentences exist in the database. We envision that by analyzing the data recorded we will be able to develop a two-way conversation utterance structure for human robot interaction.

Acknowledgments. The research reported in this paper was supported in part by the Research counsel of the Vrije Universiteit Brussel with horizontale onderzoeksactie HOA16 and by the European Commission (EU-FP7 project ALIZ-E, ICT-248116). Special thanks to Mr Ronny Van Heue, the principal and the students of Koninklijk Atheneum Beveren for their help and support in the experiments with the children.

References

1. Douglas-Cowie, E., Campbell, N., Cowie, R., Roach, P.: Emotional speech:Towards a new generation of databases. Speech Communication 40, 33–60 (2003)
2. Busso, C., Narayanan, S.: Recording audio-visual emotional databases from actors: a closer look. In: Second International Workshop on Emotion: Corpora for Research on Emotion and Affect, International Conference on Language Resources and Evaluation - LREC (2008)
3. Wilson, D.E., Reeder, D.A.M.: Mammal Species of the World: A Taxonomic and Geographic Reference. Johns Hopkins University Press, Baltimore (2005)
4. Yilmazyildiz, S., Latacz, L., Mattheyses, W., Verhelst, W.: Expressive Gibberish Speech Synthesis for Affective Human-Computer Interaction. In: Sojka, P., Horák, A., Kopeček, I., Pala, K. (eds.) TSD 2010. LNCS, vol. 6231, pp. 584–590. Springer, Heidelberg (2010)
5. Hart, M.: Project Gutenberg (2003), http://www.gutenberg.org
6. ETRO Audio-Visual Lab, http://www.etro.vub.ac.be/Research/Nosey_Elephant_Studios/
7. Yilmazyildiz, S., Henderickx, D., Vanderborght, B., Verhelst, W., Soetens, E., Lefeber, D.: Multi-Modal Emotion Expression for Affective Human-Robot Interaction (paper submitted)
8. Carlson, R., Granström, B., Nord, I.: Segmental Evaluation Using the Esprit/SAM Test Procedures and Mono-syllabic Words. In: Bailly, G., Benont, C. (eds.) Talking Machines, pp. 443–453 (1990)
9. Yilmazyildiz, S., Mattheyses, W., Patsis, Y., Verhelst, W.: Expressive Speech Recognition and Synthesis as Enabling Technologies for Affective Robot-Child Communication. In: Zhuang, Y., Yang, S., Rui, Y., He, Q. (eds.) PCM 2006. LNCS, vol. 4261, pp. 1–8. Springer, Heidelberg (2006)
10. Oudeyer, P.Y.: The Synthesis of Cartoon Emotional Speech. In: International Conference on Prosody, pp. 551–554. Aix-en-Provence, France (2002)
11. Breazeal, C.: Sociable Machines: Expressive Social Exchanges Between Humans and Robots. PhD thesis, MIT AI Lab (2000)
12. Saldien, J., Goris, K., Yilmazyildiz, S., Verhelst, W., Lefeber, D.: On the design of the huggable robot Probo. Journal of Physical Agents, Special Issue on Human Interaction with Domestic Robots 2 (2008)

Context-Sensitive Affect Sensing and Metaphor Identification in Virtual Drama

Li Zhang[1] and John Barnden[2]

[1] School of Computing, Teesside University, UK
[2] School of Computer Science, University of Birmingham, UK
{l.zhang}@tees.ac.uk

Abstract. Affect interpretation from story/dialogue context and metaphorical expressions is challenging but essential for the development of emotion inspired intelligent user interfaces. In order to achieve this research goal, we previously developed an AI actor with the integration of an affect detection component on detecting 25 emotions from literal text-based improvisational input. In this paper, we report updated development on metaphorical affect interpretation especially for sensory & cooking metaphors. Contextual affect detection with the integration of emotion modeling is also explored. Evaluation results for the new developments are provided. Our work benefits systems with intention to employ emotions embedded in the scenarios/characters and open-ended input for visual representation without detracting users from learning situations.

Keywords: affect detection/sensing, metaphor, emotion modeling and context.

1 Introduction

Recognition of complex emotions from open-ended multi-threading dialogue and diverse metaphorical expressions is a challenging but inspiring research topic. In order to explore this line of research, previously we developed an affect inspired AI agent embedded in an improvisational virtual environment interacting with human users. The human players are encouraged to be creative at their role-play under the improvisation of loose scenarios. The AI agent is capable of detecting 25 affective states from users' open-ended improvisational input and proposing appropriate responses to stimulate the improvisation[1] [1, 2].

We notice in the collected transcripts, metaphors and similes are used extensively to convey emotions such as "mum rocks", "u r an old waiter with a smelly attitude", "I was flamed on a message board", "a teenage acts like a 4 year old" etc. Such figurative expressions describe emotions vividly. Fainsilber and Ortony [3] commented that "an important function of metaphorical language is to permit the expression of that which is difficult to express using literal language alone". There is also study on general linguistic cues on affect implication in figurative expressions as theoretical inspiration to our

---

[1] The previous work was supported by grant RES-328-25-0009 from the ESRC under the ESRC/EPSRC/DTI 'PACCIT' programme. It was also partially supported by EPSRC grant EP/C538943/1.

S. D´Mello et al. (Eds.): ACII 2011, Part II, LNCS 6975, pp. 173–182, 2011.

research [4]. Thus affect detection from metaphorical phenomena draws our research attention. In this paper, we particularly focus on affect interpretation of a few metaphors including cooking and sensory metaphors.

Moreover, our previous affect sensing is conducted purely based on the analysis of each turn-taking input itself without using any contextual inference. However, most relevant contextual information may produce a shared cognitive environment between speakers and audience to help inference affect embedded in emotionally ambiguous input and facilitate effective communication. As Sperber & Wilson [5] stated in *Relevance* theory "communication aims at maximizing relevance and speakers presume that their communicative acts are indeed relevant". Such relevant contextual profiles have also been employed in our present work to model cognitive aspect of personal and social emotion and assist affect sensing from literal and figurative input. In our previous user testing, we used several scenarios including the Crohn's disease scenario[2]. The AI agent played a minor role in this scenario. In this paper, we mainly employ the collected transcripts of this scenario for the illustration of metaphor phenomena recognition and contextual affect detection.

2 Related Work

Much research has been done on creating affective agents. Indeed, emotion theories, particularly that of Ortony et al. [6] (OCC), are used widely in such research. Gratch and Marsella [7] presented an integrated emotion model of appraisal and coping, in order to reason about emotions and to provide social intelligence for virtual agents. Aylett et al. [8] also focused on the development of affective behaviour planning. Mason [9] discussed the construction of an agent with compassionate intelligence and suggested an irrational new form of affective inference.

Text-based affect detection becomes a rising research branch recently. Façade [10] included shallow natural language processing for characters' open-ended input. But the detection of major emotions, rudeness and value judgements was not mentioned. Zhe and Boucouvalas [11] demonstrated an emotion extraction module embedded in an Internet chatting environment. However the emotion detection focused only on emotional adjectives, and did not address deep issues such as figurative expression of emotion. Also, the concentration purely on first-person emotions is narrow. Ptaszynski et al. [12] developed an affect detection component with the integration of a web-mining technique to detect affect from users' input and verify the contextual appropriateness of the detected emotions. However, their system targeted conversations only between an AI agent and one human user in non-role-playing situations, which reduced the complexity of the modeling of the interaction context.

3 Metaphorical Affect Detection

Metaphorical language can be used to convey emotions implicitly and explicitly, which also inspires cognitive semanticists [4]. Examples such as, "he is boiling mad"

---

[2] Peter has Crohn's disease and has the option to undergo a life-changing but dangerous surgery. He needs to discuss the pros and cons with friends and family. Janet (Mum) wants Peter to have the operation. Matthew (younger brother) is against it. Arnold (Dad) is not able to face the situation. Dave (the best friend) mediates the discussion.

and "joy ran through me", describe emotional states in a relatively explicit way. There are also cooking metaphors implying emotions implicitly, such as "he is grilled by the teacher". Especially we notice some cooking and sensory metaphors with affective implication share similar linguistic syntactical cues. The sensory metaphor we focus on includes temperature, smell, taste, and light metaphors. We gather the following examples for the study of semantic and syntactical structures of such metaphorical expressions, including cooking metaphor: "he dishes out more criticism than one can take", "she was burned by a shady deal"; light metaphor: "you lit up my life"; temperature metaphor: "they are kindling a new romance"; taste metaphor: "bittersweet memories" and smell metaphor: "love stinks".

In the above cooking metaphor examples, the cooking actions are performed on cognitive abstract entities ('temper', 'criticism') or human agents ('she') [physical cooking actions + abstract entities/human agents]. Sometimes, human agents are the objects of cooking actions performed by abstract subject entities. Similarly in the sensory metaphor examples, the light and temperature metaphors show similar syntactical structures with actions conducted respectively on existence ('my life') or relationship abstract entities ('romance') [physical actions + abstract entities]. Emotion abstract entities are also used as subjects that are capable of performing actions such as love in smell metaphors [abstract subject entities + physical actions]. Overall, the above cooking and sensory metaphors indicate that: abstract entities are able to perform physical actions while they can also be the objects of physical actions. We use such analysis to sense these metaphor phenomena and their affective states.

First, we use Rasp [13] to identify each subject, verb phrase and object in each sentence. Then we particularly send the main terms in these three components to WordNet [14] to recover their hypernyms. If the inputs indicate structures of 'abstract subject entities + actions' or 'physical actions + abstract object entities', then the inputs are recognized as metaphorical expressions. For example, the AI agent carries out the following processing to process the metaphorical expression "the teacher dishes out more criticism than one can take".

1. Rasp: the input -> 'subject NN1 (teacher) + VVZ (dish+es) + RP (out) + DAR (more) + object NN1 (criticism)'
2. WordNet: 'teacher' -> person; 'dish' -> hypernym: 'provide', 'supply'; 'criticism' -> disapproval -> communication -> abstract entity;
3. An evaluation profile (Esuli & Sebastiani [15]) determines: 'provide'-> positive; 'criticism' and 'disapproval' -> negative.
4. The input indicates -> 'the human subject performs a 'positive' promoting action towards the 'negative' object abstract entity (criticism) -> recognized as metaphor.
5. Thus the speaker (i.e. the writer) may experience a 'negative' emotion.

Although the above metaphor recognition is at its initial stage, the system makes attempts to recognize cooking and sensory metaphors using such analysis. It can also recognize other metaphorical input such as "she is burnt by a shady deal", "deep, dark thoughts", "he stirred up all kinds of emotion" etc.

4   Exploitation in Contextual Affect Sensing

Since our previous detection was performed solely based on the analysis of individual input, contextual information was ignored. However, research work of Hareli and Rafaeli [16] discussed emotion evolution within individuals and in social context given various stimuli and focused on emotion cycle study of how emotions of an individual influence the emotions, thoughts and behaviors of others and vice versa. Therefore in this section, we discuss cognitive emotion simulation for personal and social context, and our approach developed based on these aspects to interpret affect from emotionally ambiguous input, especially affect justification of the previously detected 'neutral' expressions based on the analysis of individual turn-taking input.

Hareli and Rafaeli also suggested that context profiles for affect detection included social and personal contexts. In our study, personal context may be regarded as one's improvisational mood in communication context. We believe that one's own emotional states have a chain effect, i.e. the previous emotional status may influence later emotional experience. We make attempts to include such effects into emotion modeling. Bayesian networks are used to simulate such personal causal emotion context. In the Bayesian example shown in Figure 1, we regard the first, second and third emotions experienced by one user respectively as A, B and C. We assume that the second emotion B, relies on the first emotion A. Further, we assume that the third emotion C, relies on both the first and second emotions A and B. In our application, given two or more most recent emotions a user experiences, we predict the most probable emotion this user implies in the current input using a Bayesian network.

Briefly, a Bayesian network employs a probabilistic graphical model to represent causality relationship and conditional (in)dependencies between domain variables. It has a set of directed arcs linking pairs of nodes: an arc from a node X to a node Y means that X (parent emotion) has a direct influence on Y (successive child emotion). Such causal modeling between variables reflects the chain effect of emotional experience. It uses the conditional probabilities (e.g. P[B|A], P[C|A,B]) to reflect such influence between prior emotional experiences to successive emotional expression. The network topology shown in Figure 1 is used to model personal emotional context.

In Figure 1, conditional probabilities are needed to be calculated for the emotional state C given any combination of the emotional states A and B. Theoretically, emotional states A and B could be any combination of potential emotional states. In our application, we mainly consider the following 10 most frequently used emotional states for contextual affect analysis including 'neutral', 'happy', 'approval', 'grateful', 'caring', 'disapproval', 'sad', 'scared', 'threatening', and 'angry'. Any combination of the above emotional states could be used as prior emotional experience of the user thus we have overall 100 (10 * 10) combinations for the two preceding emotions. Also each conditional probability for each potential emotional state given two prior emotional experiences (such as P[happy |A,B], P[approval |A,B] etc) will be calculated. The emotional state with the highest conditional probability is selected as the most probable emotion the user conveys in the current turn-taking. We construct a Bayesian network for each character to sense his/her improvisational mood.

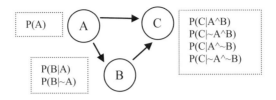

Fig. 1. An emotion Bayesian network

At the training stage, two human judges (not involved in any development) marked up 3 example transcripts of the Crohn's disease scenario. 450 turn-taking inputs with agreed annotations were used for the training of Bayesian networks with 35% positive expressions, 39% negative and 26% neutral inputs. For each character, we extract three sequences of emotions from the improvisation of the 3 example transcripts to produce prior conditional probabilities. We take a frequency approach to determine the conditional probabilities for each Bayesian network. When an affect is annotated for a turn-taking input, we increment a counter for that expressed emotion given the two preceding emotions. For each character, a conditional probability table is produced based on the training data. An example is presented in Table 1.

Table 1. An example conditional probability table for emotions expressed by one character

		Probability of the predicted emotional state C being:			
Emotion A	Emotion B	Happy	Approval	...	Angry
Happy	Neutral	P00	P01	...	P09
Neutral	Angry	P10	P11	...	P19
Disapproval	Disapproval	P20	P21	...	P29
Angry	Angry	P30	P31	...	P39

In the above table, the predicted emotional state C could be any of the most frequently used 10 emotions. At the training stage, the frequencies of emotion combinations in a 100 * 10 ((A*B)*C) matrix are produced dynamically. This matrix represents counters (N_{CAB}) for all outcomes of C given all the combinations of A and B. A one-hundred-element array is also needed to store counters (N_{AB}) for all the combinations of two prior emotions, A and B. Such a conditional probability matrix is constructed at run-time for each human-controlled character in the Crohn's disease scenario based on the training emotional sequences.

For the prediction of an emotion state mostly likely implied in the current input by a particular character at the testing stage, the two prior recent emotional states are used to determine which row to consider in the conditional probability matrix, and select the column with the highest conditional probability as the final output. The emotional sequences used for testing expressed by each character have also been used to further update and enrich the training samples so that these testing emotional states may also help the system to cope with any new emotional inclination because of each character's creative improvisation. Example conditional probability calculations are shown in the following, where N represents the total number of emotions shown so far by one character and N with a subscript indicates the number of a specific emotion shown given previously expressed emotions. E.g., $N_{happy\_neutral\_approval}$ indicates the occurrences that two prior emotions A and B are respectively happy & neutral and the subsequent emotional state C is approval.

$$P(A = happy) = N_{happy}/N; P(B = neutral| A = happy) = N_{happy\_neutral}/N$$
$$P(C = approval| A = happy, B = neutral) = N_{happy\_neutral\_approval}/N_{AB}$$

An example algorithm of the Bayesian affect sensing is provided in the following. For the initial run of the algorithm, A, B and C are initialized with the most recent affects detected for each character purely based on the analysis of individual input.

Pseudo-code for affect prediction using a Bayesian network

```
Function Bayesian_Affect_Prediction {
1. Verify the contextual appropriateness of the affect C
   predicted by the Bayesian reasoning;
2. Produce the row index, i, for any given combination of the
   two preceding emotional states A & B in the matrix;
3. Indicate the column index, j, for the recommended affect C;
4. Increment N_AB[i] and N_CAB[i][j];
5. Update two preceding emotions by:
   Emotion A = Emotion B; Emotion B = The newly recommended
   affect C;
6. Produce the new row index, k, for any given combination of
   the updated two preceding emotional states A & B;
7. Calculate probabilities (i.e. P[C|A,B] = N_CAB
   [k][column]/N_AB[k]) for the predicted emotional state C
   being any of the 10 emotions;
8. Select and return the affect with highest probability as the
   predicted affect C; }
```

At the testing stage, when an affect is predicted for a user's input using the Bayesian network, the contextual appropriateness of the detected affect will be further justified. The verification processing using neural network-based reasoning, which will be introduced at a later stage, results in a final recommended affect. Then the conditional probability table obtained from the training stage is updated with the newly recommended affect and its two preceding emotions. The above processing is iterative to predict affect throughout an improvisation for a particular character based on his/her personal emotional profiles. We extract the following example interaction from the Crohn's disease scenario and use the sequence of emotions expressed by Janet to illustrate how the contextual affect sensing using the Bayesian algorithm performs. Based on the affect detection purely from the analysis of each individual input, we assigned an emotional label for each input in the following as the first step.

1. Arnold: son, lets not think about the operation now. What's for dinner love. [disapproval]
2. Janet: no no peter needs to know what's goin to happen to him darling. [disapproval]
3. Peter: dad, I cannot leav it for later. [disapproval]
4. Dave: what's ur symptoms. [neutral]

5.   Janet: peter cannot eat too much. Don't be so rude, dave. [disapproval]
6.   Arnold: sweetheart, please I don't want to talk about it now. [disapproval]
7.   Janet: How u think peter feels HUH!!! [angry]
8.   Matthew: yeah, peter is more important   [approval]
9.   Janet: Arnold, u just think about urself! [neutral] -> [angry]

Affect annotation based on the analysis of individual turn-taking input has derived 'disapproval', 'disapproval' and 'angry' respectively for Janet's 2nd, 5th and 7th inputs. 'Neutral' has been detected for Janet's very last input, the 9th input.

In our application, the context-based affect sensing will run as a backstage processing to monitor the affect interpretation from the analysis of each individual input and it will especially make a prediction when 'neutral' is detected based on the analysis of the users' input itself. I.e. it has two running modes: monitoring and active prediction. If the affect detection based on the analysis of individual input itself derives a non-neutral emotional state X, then the Bayesian inference is running in the monitoring mode and its prediction is ignored. This detected affect X is also used for the updating of the conditional probability table (i.e. the increment of the frequency of the emotion X given two preceding emotions). Otherwise if 'neutral' is interpreted from the analysis of the input itself (such as the 9th input), then the Bayesian network is switched to active prediction mode and its output is verified of its contextual appropriateness and used to justify the previously detected 'neutral' annotation.

Therefore in the above example, since the 9th input is interpreted as 'neutral', the contextual Bayesian affect inference is activated. As mentioned earlier, the algorithm uses the most recent three emotions experienced by Janet to initialize emotions A, B & C. Thus the two preceding emotions A & B are respectively 'disapproval' and 'disapproval', while the subsequent emotion C is 'angry'. We increment both of the counters: $N_{disapproval\_disapproval}$ and $N_{disapproval\_disapproval\_angry}$. Then the system updates the two preceding emotions by shifting B to A and replacing the emotion B with C, i.e. the updated preceding emotions A & B are respectively 'disapproval' and 'angry'. Then conditional probabilities, P[C| disapproval, angry], are calculated for the predicted emotional state C based on the frequencies obtained from the training data. The emotion 'angry' with the highest output probability is regarded as the most probable emotion (the writer's emotion) implied in the 9th input from Janet.

Since our processing is iterative, the contextual appropriateness of the detected affect 'angry' is further verified by the social context inference using neural networks. The counter of $N_{disapproval\_angry}$ is also incremented. If the inference of the communication context further strengthens the prediction, we also increment the counter for the emotion 'angry' given two preceding emotions as 'disapproval' and 'angry', i.e. $N_{disapproval\_angry\_angry}$. Otherwise, the counter for any recommended other affect supported by the social context inference given the same two preceding emotions is incremented. Thus the testing emotional profiles are used to update the frequencies obtained from the training set to improve the algorithm's generalization abilities for future prediction. In this way, the AI agent is capable of predicting the improvisational mood of each character throughout the improvisation. Detailed evaluation results of the Bayesian inference are provided in the evaluation section.

However, since the Bayesian approach gathers frequencies of emotional sequences throughout improvisations and learns emotional inclination in a global manner for each character, it relies heavily on the probability table produced based on such frequencies for future prediction. It tends to give higher prediction for emotions with high occurrences than those with comparatively low frequencies following any two given preceding emotions even though the local interaction context's strong disapproval. Thus it may lead to affect sensing errors.

Therefore another effective channel is needed to sense affect implication in the most related social interaction context to complement the Bayesian inference. Since there are 5 human-controlled characters involved in one session, we use the most recent emotional implications contributed by these 5 characters in their recent inputs as the direct related context. We employ a neural network-based inference to provide another justification channel for contextual affect analysis. A supervised Backpropagation learning is used to sense the positive, neutral and negative implication embedded in the most related context. The network employs three (1 input, 1 hidden and 1 output) layers with 5 nodes in the input layer and 3 nodes respectively in the hidden and output layers. The 5 nodes in the input layer indicate the most recent emotional implications expressed by the 5 characters. The 3 outputs represent the predicted positive, neutral and negative implication in this interaction context. If in the most related context, one character has more than 1 emotional input, then the average emotional implication is calculated and employed as the input to the neural nets. At the training and test stages, we assign each emotion with a value between 0 and 1 as input to the neural nets, e.g. according to their distance to 'neutral', happy = 0.1, grateful = 0.2, caring = 0.3, approving = 0.4, neutral = 0.5, disapproving = 0.6, sad = 0.7, scared = 0.8, threatening = 0.85, and angry/rude = 0.9. Other ways of assigning values to emotion inputs are also attempted, which produce exactly the same prediction. We used 110 emotional interaction contexts extracted from 4 transcripts for training and employed 112 new contexts for testing.

For the above example, in order to further justify the contextual appropriateness of the detected affect 'angry' for the 9th input, first of all, we retrieve the most recent emotional contribution from each character: Peter ('disapproval': 3rd), Dave ('neutral': 4th), Janet ('disapproval': 5th & 'angry': 7th), Arnold ('disapproval': 6th); and Matthew ('approval': 8th). Then the test emotional input sequence is generated as: Peter [0.6], Janet [(0.6+0.9)/2 = 0.75], Arnold [0.6]; Matthew [0.4] and Dave [0.5]. The neural network outputs this interaction context is likely to be 'negative' with prediction probabilities 0.499, 0.30 and 0.29 respectively for negative, neutral and positive implications. Thus the 'anger' emotion predicted for the 9th input is verified as the appropriate emotion embedded in a consistent 'negative' interaction context.

5   Evaluations

We previously carried out user testing with 220 secondary school students in the UK schools and transcripts were also recorded to allow further evaluation. Generally, our previous results based on the collected questionnaires indicate that the AI character has usefully stimulated the improvisation under different circumstances. We also produce a new set of results for the evaluation of the updated affect detection component with contextual and metaphorical interpretation based on the analysis of some previously recorded transcripts of the Crohn's disease scenario. Generally two human judges marked up the affect of 400 turn-taking user inputs from the recorded 4 transcripts of this scenario (different from those used for the training of Bayesian and neural nets) using the three emotion labels: positive, negative and neutral. We obtain the Cohen's Kappa inter-agreement between the human annotators is 0.83. Then 360 inputs with agreed annotations are used as gold standards with 32% positive, 46% negative and 22% neutral expressions. Then the 360 agreed annotations are used to measure the performance of the improvisational mood modeling in personal emotion context using Bayesian networks. The achieved affect annotations are converted into purely positive, negative and neutral. The evaluation results are provided in Table 2.

Table 2. Detailed measurement of improvisational mood modeling using Bayesian networks

	Precision	Recall	F-measure
Positive	58.7%	71.1%	64.3%
Negative	84.5%	65.2%	73.6%
Neutral	39.5%	53.6%	45.5%

The overall accuracy rate for the Bayesian network based emotion prediction is 65.1%. Briefly, precision indicates the exactness of a classifier. A higher precision implies less false positives. Recall measures the completeness with a higher recall indicating less false negatives. In Table 2, generally negative emotions are well detected across testing subjects with better precision. However, there were cases that other positive and neutral expressions were also predicted with negative indications, which leads to less precision for positive and neutral expressions and lower recall for negative expressions. One most obvious reason is that the Bayesian inference tends to give high prediction for emotions with high occurrences given any two preceding emotions. Because of the nature of the scenario, improvisations tend to be filled with negative expressions such as worrying, arguing etc. Thus the prediction sometimes failed to sense the positive or neutral emotion evolution in local context immediately and led to recognition errors. However, although positive and neutral expressions are recognized less well, due to their comparatively low frequencies, the performances of affect sensing from such expressions are promising at this stage. Articles of personal emotional experience from the Experience Project website (www.experienceproject.com) will also be used to improve performances.

Moreover, we also provide Cohen's Kappa for the performance of the affect sensing in social interaction context using neural networks. The inter-agreement between human judges is approximately 0.91 for the annotation of the 112 testing contexts from the selected 4 transcripts, while the inter-agreements between human judges and the neural network inference are respectively 0.71 and 0.70. The results indicate that evaluation implication embedded in the related context is well recovered. We also aim to extend the evaluation of the context-based affect detection using transcripts from other scenarios. Moreover, using a metaphorical resource (http://knowgramming.com), our approach for disease, cooking and sensory metaphor recognition obtains 48% average accuracy rate. Also, we intend to use other resources (e.g. Wallstreet Journal) to further evaluate the metaphorical affect sensing.

Overall, we made initial developments of an AI agent with emotion and social intelligence, which employs context profiles for affect interpretation using Bayesian and neural networks and performs metaphor recognition. Although the AI agent could be challenged by the rich diverse variations of the language phenomena and other improvisational complex context situations, we believe these areas are very crucial for development of effective intelligent user interfaces and our processing has made promising initial steps towards these areas. Our research could also be used as a testbed and inspiration of theoretical study on how affect is conveyed metaphorically.

References

1. Zhang, L.: Exploitation on Contextual Affect Sensing and Dynamic Relationship Interpretation. ACM Computers in Entertainment 8(3) (2010)
2. Zhang, L., Gillies, M., Dhaliwal, K., Gower, A., Robertson, D., Crabtree, B.: E-drama: Facilitating Online Role-play using an AI Actor and Emotionally Expressive Characters. International Journal of Artificial Intelligence in Education 19(1), 5–38 (2009)
3. Fainsilber, L., Ortony, A.: Metaphorical uses of language in the expression of emotions. Metaphor and Symbolic Activity 2(4), 239–250 (1987)
4. Kövecses, Z.: Are There Any Emotion-Specific Metaphors? In: Athanasiadou, A., Tabakowska, E. (eds.) Speaking of Emotions: Conceptualization and Expression, pp. 127–151. Mouton de Gruyter, Berlin (1998)
5. Sperber, D., Wilson, D.: Relevance: Communication and cognition, 2nd edn. Blackwell, Oxford (1995)
6. Ortony, A., Clore, G.L., Collins, A.: The Cognitive Structure of Emotions. Cambridge U. Press, Cambridge (1998)
7. Gratch, J., Marsella, S.: A Domain-Independent Framework for Modeling Emotion. Journal of Cognitive Systems Research 5(4), 269–306 (2004)
8. Aylett, A., Louchart, S., Dias, J., Paiva, A., Vala, M., Woods, S., Hall, L.E.: Unscripted Narrative for Affectively Driven Characters. IEEE Computer Graphics and Applications 26(3), 42–52 (2006)
9. Mason, C.: The Logical Road to Human Level AI Leads to a Dead End. In: Proceedings of Fourth IEEE International Conference on Self-Adaptive and Self-Organizing Systems Workshop, Hungary, pp. 312–316 (2010)
10. Mateas, M.: Interactive Drama, Art and Artificial Intelligence. Ph.D. Thesis. School of Computer Science, Carnegie Mellon University (2002)
11. Zhe, X., Boucouvalas, A.C.: Text-to-Emotion Engine for Real Time Internet Communication. In: Proceedings of International Symposium on Communication Systems, Networks and DSPs, pp. 164–168. Staffordshire University, UK (2002)
12. Ptaszynski, M., Dybala, P., Shi, W., Rzepka, R., Araki, K.: Towards Context Aware Emotional Intelligence in Machines: Computing Contextual Appropriateness of Affective States. In: Proceeding of IJCAI 2009 (2009)
13. Briscoe, E., Carroll, J.: Robust Accurate Statistical Annotation of General Text. In: Proceedings of the 3rd International Conference on Language Resources and Evaluation, Las Palmas, Gran Canaria, pp. 1499–1504 (2002)
14. Fellbaum, C.: WordNet, an Electronic Lexical Database. The MIT press, Cambridge (1998)
15. Esuli, A., Sebastiani, F.: Determining Term Subjectivity and Term Orientation for Opinion Mining. In: Proceedings of EACL 2006, Trento, IT, pp. 193–200 (2006)
16. Hareli, S., Rafaeli, A.: Emotion cycles: On the social influence of emotion in organizations. Research in Organizational Behavior 28, 35–59 (2008)

An Android Head for Social-Emotional Intervention for Children with Autism Spectrum Conditions

Andra Adams and Peter Robinson

University of Cambridge Computer Laboratory
{Andra.Adams,Peter.Robinson}@cl.cam.ac.uk

Abstract. Many children with autism spectrum conditions (ASC) have difficulties recognizing emotions from facial expressions. Behavioural interventions have attempted to address this issue but their drawbacks have prompted the exploration of new intervention strategies. Robots have proven to be an engaging and effective possibility. Our work will investigate the use of a facially-expressive android head as a social partner for children with ASC. The main goal of this research is to improve the emotion recognition capabilities of the children through observation, imitation and control of facial expressions on the android.

1 Introduction

Autism spectrum conditions (ASC) are characterized by difficulties in social interaction and communication, as well as repetitive behaviour and narrow interests [20]. The prevalence of diagnosed ASC has shown a steady increase over the past 40 years [6]. New technologies offer interesting possibilities for intervention techniques for children with ASC. In particular, this work investigates the use of a facially-expressive android head in an intervention to improve emotion recognition capabilities in children with ASC. Over a series of sessions, the children will both observe, imitate and control the facial expressions of the robot to enact various emotions.

2 Background

This interdisciplinary work builds on research in three main areas: autism spectrum conditions, human-robot interaction, and affective computing.

2.1 Autism Spectrum Conditions

Difficulties with facial expressions in ASC. Of particular interest to this work are the findings that children with ASC have difficulties with face processing tasks, as usefully summarized by Tanaka et al [28]. As a result, children with ASC do not become "face experts" in the same way that neurotypical children do, particularly since facial expressions are fleeting and unpredictable in

S. D´Mello et al. (Eds.): ACII 2011, Part II, LNCS 6975, pp. 183–190, 2011.

real-time social scenarios. We attempt to address this issue by providing children with ASC an opportunity to practise facial expression recognition in a more predictable setting than typical social environments.

The value of imitation as an intervention strategy. Even in individuals without ASC, imitation plays an important role in cognitive development [19]. Infants mimic their parents and others as a means of developing their social and communication skills. Not surprisingly, intervention techniques that employ reflection, imitation and synchronicity have been successful in improving the social behaviour of children with ASC [17,11].

Our research will use imitation in two ways. Firstly, the child is asked to imitate the facial expressions of a particular emotion that it has observed on the robot's face. This encourages the development of the child's own imitation capabilities. Secondly, as the child attempts to mimic what he/she has previously seen on the robot, the robot itself will be mimicking the facial expressions of the child. This serves both to show the child what his/her facial expressions look like and to encourage further social interaction.

Emotion recognition intervention strategies for children with ASC. Emotion recognition plays a crucial role in effective social interaction. Our ability to attribute emotions to others from their outward appearance (facial, gestural, vocal) is often referred to as "mind-reading" [3], an ability which allows us to discern the mental states of others to better predict their beliefs, values, emotions and intentions. In particular, research has suggested that facial expressions are likely the most important source of affective information in humans [2].

Behavioural interventions targeting emotion recognition are common. These interventions typically consist of a few hours of training every week over a period of several months, and usually employ a teacher, therapist or parent that is familiar to the child [8]. But behavioural interventions are socially exhausting and often focus only on basic emotions since time constraints prevent further exploration [16]. New computer-based technologies can help to solve both of these issues without compromising the interactivity of a therapy session. Furthermore, computer-based technologies are often inherently motivating to children with ASC [4] and allow them to work at their own pace with as much or as little repetition as desired. Examples include the interactive emotional taxonomy of the Mind Reading DVD [5], the social scenarios of The Transporters series [12] and many others [27,15].

One of the important goals of any emotion recognition intervention is to ensure that the recognition of facial expressions and emotions is generalizable to unfamiliar scenarios. In this respect, there is an important difference between explicitly-taught and implicitly-taught interventions. Explicitly-taught interventions, like the Mind Reading DVD, are devoid of social context and confine the recognition of emotions to simplified scenarios. Implicitly-taught interventions, like The Transporters series, situate emotions in a relevant social context and are therefore more likely to generalize to real-world social scenarios.

2.2   Human-Robot Interaction

Robots for children with ASC. Human-robot interaction is a promising area for autism therapy. Robots are simplified, more predictable versions of human beings and research suggests that for many children with ASC, robots are more appealing and engaging than their human counterparts [26].

It is the fine balance between predictability and autonomy that makes robots promising social partners for children with ASC. Inanimate toys lack the ability to prompt children with ASC to break out of their repetitive behaviours and engage socially. On the opposite end of the spectrum, human peers behave far too unpredictably for a child with ASC, inducing stress and anxiety during social interaction. The controllable autonomy of robots offers the best of both worlds. Slowly increasing the autonomy of the robot challenges the child with ASC to engage in a variety of social interaction scenarios without pushing the child too far out of his/her comfort zone.

Robots vs software avatars. The fact that robots have a physical representation yet still have the controllable autonomy of software avatars make them ideal as learning tools for children with ASC. The physical representation of the robot provides engagement in physical space that cannot be achieved easily by a software avatar (e.g. physical proximity, touch, viewing angle) [9].

Androids vs simplistic robots. Simplistic robots, such as robot trucks and rolling spheres, have been successfully used in social interaction scenarios with children with ASC including basic motor imitation and "tag"-like games [18,10]. These simple robots often take the form of common toys to increase familiarity and mitigate adverse reactions from the children. The simple animism that is added to these formerly inanimate objects has been used to help with turn-taking, eye gaze, self-initiated behaviour, imitation and shared attention [10].

However, robots with simplistic forms do not have the features required to teach more complex social interactions. For example, teaching emotion recognition from facial expressions requires the robot to have basic facial features. These facial features can either be highly realistic or abstracted and cartoon-like. Research has suggested that children with ASC tend to be more comfortable with non-humanoid feature-less robots [23], which encourages the use of simple cartoon-like facial features. Yet the difficulty with generalization experienced by children with ASC suggests to us that more realistic human-like facial features will result in greater transferability of recognition rates to real human faces.

The FACE project at the University of Pisa is currently the only autism therapy project using a realistic android head [21]. Its aim is to improve the social and emotive capabilities of children with autism by using the android as an interface between the therapist and the child with ASC. To date, FACE is able to express and recognize Ekman's six basic emotions at various levels of intensity, and is controlled by both the therapist and the child via a traditional

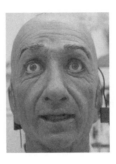

Fig. 1. Various facial expressions displayed on our android head from Hanson Robotics

screen-keyboard-mouse interface. Preliminary studies suggest that children with ASC are interested in interacting socially with the android, including sponta- neous imitation of its head and facial movements. This successful social interac- tion with FACE suggests that realistic androids have an important role to play in autism intervention techniques. Our realistic android is shown in Figure 1.

2.3 Affective Computing

Selecting a corpus of emotionally-expressive data. There are many factors to consider when selecting a corpus of emotionally-expressive facial data. Natu- ralistic data is preferred to acted data since the timings and motions differ be- tween the two and hence naturalistic data is more representative of the real-world [30]. However naturalistic data is extremely difficult to collect and label [1]. Cor- pora that include complex emotions are more desirable than those that contain only Ekman's six basic emotions [24]. Furthermore, moving images are preferred to still images since humans are best able to recognize emotions through facial movement [7]. Lastly, facial appearance (age, sex, ethnicity) has been shown to shape the perception of emotional expressions [14], and therefore databases that feature multiple subjects are preferred to single-subject databases.

For our proposed work, the videos from the Mind Reading DVD have been selected as a reasonable corpus of emotional expression. The Mind Reading col- lection consists of more than 2400 videos depicting 412 different emotions with at least six different actors portraying each emotion. The 412 emotions are pre- sented in a hierarchical taxonomy and have been validated by a panel of in- dependent judges [13]. Although the emotional expressions in these videos are acted and not naturalistic, the wide variety of emotions and the use of multiple actors make this corpus an attractive choice.

Creating realistic expressions on the robot. It is essential that the robot accurately mimics the facial expressions in the Mind Reading videos. We use the FaceTracker software [25] to locate 66 feature points on the face which are then converted into motor movements for the robot, as shown in Figure 2.

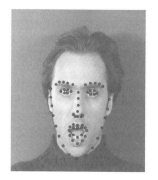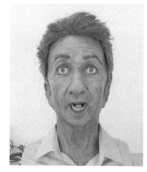

Fig. 2. Video images (left) are analyzed to track facial feature points (centre) which are converted to motor movements on the robot (right)

3   Methodology

We designed an intervention to assess the effect of an android head on the emotion recognition capabilities of children with ASC. Intended to span several months, the intervention begins with an initial familiarization period where the child is introduced to the robot in a comfortable, non-threatening manner. A therapist, teacher or parent is present to demonstrate the capabilities of the robot. Next, the child begins the two phases of the intervention: playback and imitation of the Mind Reading videos, and social interaction during a card game.

3.1   Playback and Imitation of the Mind Reading Videos

The first phase of the intervention is intended to expose the child to a wide variety of emotional facial expressions. An emotion is selected from the 412 emotions from the Mind Reading DVD and one of the six videos for that emotion is "acted out" by the robot while the child observes. The child is then asked to recreate the facial expressions of that emotion on the robot. To control the motion of the robot, the child's own facial actions are used. A video camera pointed at the child's face captures his/her facial expressions and this information is in turn fed back into the robot to control its facial movements.

This type of control is useful in three major ways. Firstly, it transforms the child from passive to active learner by engaging the child in an interactive exchange with the robot. Secondly, it encourages the child to look at all parts of the robot's face rather than only the mouth region, as many children with ASC are prone to do [22]. Thirdly and most importantly, in order to control the robot, the child must first learn to imitate the facial expressions of the robot on his/her own face. As previously discussed, this use of imitation has great value in improving social interaction for children with ASC.

The child's imitation is captured and evaluated based on accuracy (correctness of facial actions) and timeliness (ordering and timing between facial actions).

Feedback is given to the child both from the teacher/parent/therapist and from the algorithmic assessment of the captured video.

3.2   Social Interaction during a Card Game

Given the relative success of The Transporters series over the Mind Reading DVD [4], it is evident that situating facial expressions within a social context is an important factor for emotion recognition. Therefore in the second phase of the intervention, the child will play a card game such as "War" with the robot and the social context of the game will dictate the robot's facial responses. Frustration, confusion, happiness, thinking, interest, sadness and many other emotions will be elicited by the card game and the robot will respond with appropriate facial expressions. The teacher/parent/therapist can interrupt the game at any point to encourage the child to consider the current mental state of the robot.

3.3   Evaluation of Intervention

The intervention will be evaluated through performance tasks completed by the children before and after the intervention with the robot. The children will be asked to label the emotions observed in videos from three sources:

- **Mind Reading DVD:** videos of acted emotions (some previously seen in the intervention and some unfamiliar), each portrayed by either a human actor or the robot
- **Recordings from the card game:** videos of the game, each showing either a child or the robot with surrounding social context
- **The Transporters series:** video clips of novel social situations with unfamiliar characters

As with the evaluation of The Transporters series [12], each video will be accompanied by three possible labels: the correct emotion, an emotion of opposite valence, and an emotion of the same valence. Our selection of performance tasks allows us to evaluate the children's emotion recognition skills as well as their ability to generalize these skills to unfamiliar situations.

Furthermore, five groups of children will participate in the study to control for other factors and to compare against similar intervention strategies: an ASC robot intervention group, an ASC software avatar intervention group, an ASC Mind Reading intervention group, an ASC control group and a neurotypical control group. The ASC robot intervention group will participate in the intervention as described above, the ASC cartoon avatar intervention group will participate in the intervention described above but a software avatar will substitute for the robot, the ASC Mind Reading intervention group will use the Mind Reading DVD, and the two control groups will not participate in any intervention.

4   Conclusion

Our work will investigate the use of a facially-expressive android head in improving emotion recognition capabilities in children with ASC. We have designed an intervention in which children are encouraged to observe, interact with and imitate the android, giving them valuable practice in attributing emotions to facial expressions. We have proposed detailed performance tasks for evaluating the success of this intervention technique, particularly concerning generalization of emotion recognition skills to real-world social situations.

The proposed work with the robot could be extended to other possible interventions, including addressing non-verbal social cues such as gaze-direction and turn-taking, or providing practice with social context via emotion elicitation activities.

Acknowledgements. This work is generously supported by the Gates Cambridge Trust. The sample video frame in Figure 2 uses the MMI-Facial Expression Database [29].

References

1. Afzal, S., Robinson, P.: Natural affect data - collection & annotation in a learning context. In: ACII 2009, pp. 1–7. IEEE, Los Alamitos (2009)
2. Ambady, N., Rosenthal, R.: Thin slices of expressive behavior as predictors of interpersonal consequences: A meta-analysis. Psychological Bulletin 111(2) (1992)
3. Baron-Cohen, S.: Mindblindness: an essay on autism and theory of mind. MIT Press, Cambridge (2001)
4. Baron-Cohen, S., Golan, O., Ashwin, E.: Can emotion recognition be taught to children with autism spectrum conditions? Philosophical Transactions of the Royal Society B: Biological Sciences 364(1535), 3567 (2009)
5. Baron-Cohen, S., Golan, O., Wheelwright, S., Hill, J.J.: Mind reading: the interactive guide to emotions (2004)
6. Baron-Cohen, S., Scott, F.J., Allison, C., Williams, J., Bolton, P., Matthews, F.E., Brayne, C.: Prevalence of autism-spectrum conditions: UK school-based population study. The British Journal of Psychiatry 194(6), 500 (2009)
7. Bassili, J.N.: Facial motion in the perception of faces and of emotional expression. Journal of Experimental Psychology: Human Perception and Performance 4(3), 373 (1978)
8. Bauminger, N.: The facilitation of social-emotional understanding and social interaction in high-functioning children with autism: Intervention outcomes. Journal of Autism and Developmental Disorders 32(4), 283–298 (2002)
9. Breazeal, C., Brooks, R.: Robot emotion: A functional perspective. Who Needs Emotions, 271–210 (2005)
10. Dautenhahn, K., Werry, I.: Towards interactive robots in autism therapy: Background, motivation and challenges. Pragmatics & Cognition 12(1), 1–35 (2004)
11. Dawson, G., Adams, A.: Imitation and social responsiveness in autistic children. Journal of Abnormal Child Psychology 12(2), 209–226 (1984)
12. Golan, O., Ashwin, E., Granader, Y., McClintock, S., Day, K., Leggett, V., Baron-Cohen, S.: Enhancing emotion recognition in children with autism spectrum conditions: an intervention using animated vehicles with real emotional faces. Journal of Autism and Developmental Disorders 40(3), 269–279 (2010)
13. Golan, O., Baron-Cohen, S.: Systemizing empathy: Teaching adults with asperger syndrome or high-functioning autism to recognize complex emotions using interactive multimedia. Development and Psychopathology 18(02), 591–617 (2006)

14. Hess, U., Adams, R.B., Kleck, R.E.: The face is not an empty canvas: how facial expressions interact with facial appearance. Philosophical Transactions of the Royal Society B: Biological Sciences 364(1535), 3497 (2009)
15. Hopkins, I.M., Gower, M.W., Perez, T.A., Smith, D.S., Amthor, F.R., Casey Wimsatt, F., Biasini, F.J.: Avatar assistant: Improving social skills in students with an ASD through a computer-based intervention. Journal of Autism and Developmental Disorders, 1–13 (2011)
16. Howlin, P., Baron-Cohen, S., Hadwin, J.: Teaching children with autism to mindread: A practical guide for teachers and parents. J. Wiley & Sons, Chichester (1999)
17. Ingersoll, B., Gergans, S.: The effect of a parent-implemented imitation intervention on spontaneous imitation skills in young children with autism. Research in Developmental Disabilities 28(2), 163–175 (2007)
18. Michaud, F., Théberge-Turmel, C.: Mobile robotic toys and autism. Socially Intelligent Agents, pp. 125–132 (2002)
19. Nadel, J., Guérini, C., Pezé, A., Rivet, C.: The evolving nature of imitation as a format for communication (1999)
20. American Psychiatric Association Task Force on DSM-IV. In: Diagnostic and Statistical Manual of Mental Disorders: DSM-IV-TR. Amer. Psychiatric Pub. Inc., Washington (2000)
21. Pioggia, G., Sica, M.L., Ferro, M., Igliozzi, R., Muratori, F., Ahluwalia, A., De Rossi, D.: Human-robot interaction in autism: FACE, an android-based social therapy. In: The 16th IEEE International Symposium on Robot and Human Interactive Communication, pp. 605–612. IEEE, Los Alamitos (2007)
22. Riby, D.M., Doherty-Sneddon, G., Bruce, V.: The eyes or the mouth? Feature salience and unfamiliar face processing in williams syndrome and autism. The Quarterly Journal of Experimental Psychology 62(1), 189–203 (2009)
23. Robins, B., Dautenhahn, K., Dubowski, J.: Does appearance matter in the interaction of children with autism with a humanoid robot? Interaction Studies 7(3), 509–542 (2006)
24. Rozin, P., Cohen, A.B.: High frequency of facial expressions corresponding to confusion, concentration, and worry in an analysis of naturally occurring facial expressions of americans. Emotion 3(1), 68 (2003)
25. Saragih, J.M., Lucey, S., Cohn, J.F.: Face alignment through subspace constrained mean-shifts. In: 2009 IEEE 12th International Conference on Computer Vision, pp. 1034–1041. IEEE, Los Alamitos (2009)
26. Scassellati, B.: How social robots will help us to diagnose, treat, and understand autism. Robotics Research, 552–563 (2007)
27. Silver, M., Oakes, P.: Evaluation of a new computer intervention to teach people with autism or asperger syndrome to recognize and predict emotions in others. Autism 5(3), 299 (2001)
28. Tanaka, J.W., Wolf, J.M., Klaiman, C., Koenig, K., Cockburn, J., Herlihy, L., Brown, C., Stahl, S., Kaiser, M.D., Schultz, R.T.: Using computerized games to teach face recognition skills to children with autism spectrum disorder: the Let's Face It! program. Journal of Child Psychology and Psychiatry 51(8), 944–952 (2010)
29. Valstar, M.F., Pantic, M.: Induced disgust, happiness and surprise: an addition to the MMI facial expression database. In: International Language Resources and Evaluation Conference (May 2010)
30. Valstar, M.F., Pantic, M., Ambadar, Z., Cohn, J.F.: Spontaneous vs. posed facial behavior: automatic analysis of brow actions. In: Proceedings of the 8th International Conference on Multimodal Interfaces, ICMI 2006, pp. 162–170. ACM, New York (2006)

Automatic Emotion Recognition from Speech
A PhD Research Proposal

Yazid Attabi and Pierre Dumouchel

École de technologie supérieure, Montréal, Canada
Centre de recherche informatique de Montréal, Montréal, Canada
{Yazid.attabi,pierre.dumouchel}@crim.ca

Abstract. This paper contains a PhD research proposal related to the domain of automatic emotion recognition from speech signal. We started by identifying our research problem, namely the acute confusion problem between emotion classes and we have cited different sources of this ambiguity. In the methodology section, we presented a method based on simililarity concept between a class and an instance patterns. We dubbed this method as Weighted Ordered classes – Nearest Neighbors. The first result obtained exceeds in performance the best result of the state-of-the art. Finally, as future work, we have made a proposition to improve the performance of the proposed system.

Keywords: Emotion recognition, simililarity concept, speech signal.

1 Problem

The automatic emotion recognition (AER) from speech is subject of increasing interest in the recent years given the broad field of applications that can benefit from this technology. For example, a speaker emotional state recognition system can be used to develop natural and effective human-machine interaction system and more sensitive interface to the user behaviour. Used in a distance learning context, a tutoring system could detect bored users and allows a change of style and level of the material provided, or provides a compensation and emotional encouragement [1].

AER may also be used to: (1) support the driving experience and encourage better driving, given that driver emotion and driving performance are often intrinsically linked [2]; (2) detect the presence of extreme emotions, especially fear, in the context of surveillance in public places [3]; (3) automatically prioritize messages accumulated in the mailbox with different criterions such as emotional urgency, valence (happy vs. sad) and arousal (calm vs. excited). This can be used to alert the voicemail account owner and enables him to listen first to the important messages [4]; (4) use the special features carried by emotions in the development of more robust and accurate systems for automatic speaker verification [5]; (5) assess the urgency of a call and therefore helps to take a decision in the context of a medical call center offering medical advice to patients [6]; (6) improve customer service when the AER system is integrated into interactive voice response system in commercial call centers [7].

S. D´Mello et al. (Eds.): ACII 2011, Part II, LNCS 6975, pp. 191–199, 2011.

Despite all the research efforts, the performances of AER systems designed remain relatively low compared to related fields such as speaker verification. The low recognition rate is reflected through the high level of confusion between emotion classes.

1.1 Confusion Sources

The confusion between classes can have several sources. The first raison can be related to the uncertainty that characterize the definition of emotion in the psychology domain, namely which theory to use categorical or dimensional, and in the case of categorical theory how many categories exists and what are these classes? This uncertainty can lead to an overlap between defined classes at their acoustic information spaces because of the lack of clear boundaries between different categories of emotion that marks the transition from one emotion to another. On the other hand, the overlap in the acoustic space is not limited to the neighboring classes but also between some emotions in a symmetrical position with respect to the active / passive axis of the dimensional model shown in Figure 2. The joy and anger classes are an example of ambiguity case confirmed by several studies [8, 9].

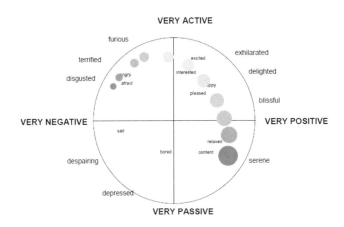

Fig. 1. Emotions mapped in Activation-Evaluation space with FEELTRACE (Cowie et al.)

Another important factor which increases the ambiguity is the significant variability between different individuals in the expression of same emotion class. This wide range of variability can have several origins such as the culture, the age, the gender of the speaker and its spoken language.

Finally, the noise contained in the emotion corpus increases the confusion. This noise can be induced by annotators during the labelling operation. This is particularly true for blended emotions such as fear and anger felt, for instance by a parent to his son when the latter crosses the road running at a red light.

2 Objectives

In this research project, our goal is to improve the performance of AER systems by mitigating the problem of ambiguity between emotion classes. We are particularly interested to recognize emotions of the categorical model or of the dimensional model converted to binary labels (e.g. active vs. passive or positive vs. negative). These AER systems are primarily intended to be deployed in a call center context, so we will focus on the use of speech signal as input data for the system.

3 Emotions and Related Works

3.1 Theoretical Models of Emotion

According to Scherer in [10], there are three theories which influence the research:

Discrete theory, which states that a small number of basic emotions exist. These emotions are recognized through very specific response patterns in physiology, and in facial and vocal expression.

Dimensional Theory, where the emotional states are mapped in two or three-dimensional space such as valence, activity and control dimensions.

Componential models of emotion, often based on appraisal theory, has the advantage to be more open with respect to the kind of emotional states. These models emphasize the variability of different emotional states as produced by different types of appraisal patterns [10].

3.2 Types of Emotional Speech

As reported in [10], there are three methods to constitute an emotional corpus:

Natural emotions are recordings of spontaneous emotional states naturally occurred. It is characterized by a high ecological validity but suffers from the limited number of available speakers and presents difficulties for the annotation.

Simulated emotions are emotional states portrayed by professional or lay actors according to emotion labels or typical scenarios. Although this method permits easily to constitute an emotion corpus however it has been criticized that this kind of emotion are more exaggerated than natural or induced emotion.

Induced emotions are specific emotional states experimentally induced in groups of speakers.

3.3 Related Work

In the literature, several systems have been experimented to address the issue of emotion recognition from speech signal. In this section we will present these systems with respect to four criteria: type of feature information, 2) the temporal scope of features, 3) speech unit used in the analysis of an utterance, 4) and the type of approaches chosen to design the classifier.

Unit of Analysis

The analysis unit is the smallest segment of speech used as input to the classifier to get a partial or complete decision. The tested units are:

Utterance: The utterance is most used unit in studies [4, 11, 12].

Phoneme: A study in [13] where a modeling is based on phoneme class shows that vowels are more emotionally salient than other classes.

Syllable: In [14], the authors show that performances based on whole turn outperform those based on syllabic unit.

Word: According to the results of [15], the word unit is preferable to the utterance if an effective word segmentation system is available.

Chunk: The turn is automatically segmented into fragments, depending on the acoustic properties of the turn [14]. The results show that the system performance based on the chunk unit is better than syllable unit but lower than turn unit.

Pseudo-syllable: Unit which length is guided by the valleys of the energy contour [16].

Temporal Feature Scope

The temporal scope of features can be either short-term or long-term information.

Short-term information (STI): Short-term information represents the local information which extends over an interval of time called frame. We distinguish two types of STI: the spectral information conveyed by the spectral coefficients such as Mel-Frequency Cepstral Coefficients (MFCC), or the prosodic information [11, 17].

Long-term information (LTI): It characterizes the utterance as a whole. The most commonly LTI features used are the prosody, as well as voice quality (e.g. shimmer and jitter) [4, 12, 14], or can be combined with spectral coefficients [15].

Note that some authors have introduced linguistic information, e.g. information on lexical and discourse levels, in combination with paralinguistic information [6, 18].

Models of Classifiers

Several models of classifier were experimented and most of the models fall into one of these three approaches:

Static approach: In the static approach, models such as GMM, support vector machines (SVM) are used [1, 14].

Dynamic approach: In this approach, the hidden Markov model (HMM) is largely used as classifier. The advantage of HMM models is that they allow to model the temporal structure of utterances [4, 13, 17].

Fuzzy logic approach: This approach is based on the fuzzy logic inference system. This choice is motivated by the uncertainties that characterize emotions, particularly the problem of the lack of clear boundaries between different emotions [7, 19].

4 Methodology

In this section, we present the proposed methodology to address the problem of confusion between emotion classes.

4.1 Data Description

The designed AER systems will be experimented using three different emotion corpora, two spontaneous and one simulated:

Bell Canada (Bell) dataset
This corpus is composed of spontaneous emotions recorded from customer calls of Bell Canada automated call center. Annotated into two classes (positive vs. negative), it contains approximately 5000 dialogues for each language (French and English).

FAU AIBO (AIBO) dataset
This corpus consists of spontaneous recordings of German children interacting with a pet robot. The corpus is composed of 18216 chunks and labelled into five categories: Anger, Emphatic, Neutral, Positive and Rest.

LDC Emotional Prosody dataset
This corpus contains English audio recordings of emotions simulated in 15 categories selected according to the study of Banse & Scherer [8].

4.2 Modeling

Weighted Ordered classes – Nearest Neighbors (WOC-NN)
The methodology presented in this section, dubbed "Weighted Ordered classes – Nearest Neighbors" (WOC-NN), is basically inspired from the dimensional theory model of figure 2 where we observe the absence of any clear boundary between emotions except that each categorical emotion is characterized by neighbourhood of other emotion classes which are more or less closer to it. We will use this concept of closeness or similarity / dissimilarity between classes of the dimensional model in order to attenuate the confusion problem of categorical emotions.

The concept of weighted ordered class pattern
The decision rule in WOC-NN is based on pattern matching between test data and target class pattern. Each emotion class E_i is characterized by a neighborhood pattern which represents the set of all emotion classes ordered with respect to their closeness to the class E_i. The order of class reflects the degree of similarity with the class E_i relatively to other classes. In the test phase, the neighborhood pattern of the test data is generated and compared to each neighborhood pattern of each class. The distance metric used in the comparison is the sum of differences between the rank classes of the two neighborhood patterns, known as Hamming distance. The target class of the test data corresponds to the class whose neighborhood pattern gets the minimum distance, i.e., the class which has the higher number of similar neighbor classes with the test data. Since not all class ranks in the neighborhood pattern have the same power of discrimination, each rank class in the pattern is weighted by a coefficient value proportional to the degree of its discrimination.

Neighborhood Pattern Feature Space
In the front-end system, The *Mel*-Frequency Cepstral Coefficients (MFCC) are extracted and used as input features used to learn the model of each emotion class. The Gaussian Mixture Model (GMM), a generative model, is used as function of probability density estimation to compute likelihood scores of the data. These likelihood

scores are then used to generate the ranked neighborhood classes of each emotion class with respect to their proximity. The degree of proximity is based on the likelihood values of each model class. More the likelihood scores of two models are close to each other more the classes associated with the two models are considered as tightly adjacent classes and vice-versa.

Let $E_1, E_2,..., E_C$ be C emotion classes and λ_i is the GMM model of class E_i. Let $\mathbf{X}$ represent a set of cepstral vectors of speech data and $\hat{\mathbf{X}}$ represents the likelihood vector for $\mathbf{X}$ over the C models.

Each emotion class is represented by a vector of emotion classes ordered from the nearest closed one to most far one. These ranks are obtained by sorting the likelihood scores l_i of the vector $\hat{\mathbf{X}}$, where $l_i = P(X|\lambda_i)$, in descending order:

$$l_{r_1} \geq l_{r_2} \geq \cdots \geq l_{r_C} \tag{1}$$

The rank vector r of equation (2) constitutes the neighborhood pattern.

$$\mathbf{r} = [r_1\, r_2 \cdots r_C]^T \tag{2}$$

CLASSIFICATION SYSTEM

Let $\mathbf{r}$ and $\mathbf{r}'$ denote the neighborhood patterns of a test utterance $\mathbf{X}$ and a class emotion E_i respectively. The distance between $\mathbf{r}$ and $\mathbf{r}'$ is computed using *Hamming* distance. We introduce a C-dimensional vector $\mathbf{v}$, with indicator element $v_j = 1$ if $r_j \neq r'_j$ and $v_j = 0$ otherwise. We will refer to $\mathbf{v}$ as a *distance pattern*.

The direct use of *Hamming* distance as metric for the classification supposes that each class rank of a neighborhood pattern has the same power of discrimination as other ranks. This is misleading particularly for the first rank. For this reason we introduce a vector of coefficients, $\mathbf{w}_i = [w_{i1}\, w_{i2} \cdots w_{iC}]^T$, to weight each rank of the neighborhood pattern, where w_{ij} represents the weight coefficient of rank j of the ith class neighborhood pattern. The new metric, is expressed as :

$$\mathcal{D}_{wH}(\mathbf{r},\mathbf{r}') = \mathbf{w}_i^T\, \mathbf{v} \tag{3}$$

The weights ranks are obtained by measuring the importance of each rank for each neighborhood pattern separately. Thus each neighborhood pattern of an emotion class E_i has his distinct weight vector $\mathbf{w}_i$. In order to estimate these weights, the C-class problem is transformed to a two-class problem: discrimination between correct and wrong distance patterns using logistic regression function.

For empirical raisons, e.g. when the data are sparse, some classes in the neighborhood pattern may not be enough representative of dissimilarity between neighborhood patterns and should be discarded. For *WOC-NN* system, we selected ranks of classes associated with positive weight coefficients obtained with the logistic regression. This is feasible because of the type of the output class (which represents correct or incorrect pattern) of the logistic regression problem.

EXPERIMENTAL RESULTS

WOC-NN is experimented using the FAU AIBO [20] emotional speech corpus and its performance is compared with GMM system and the state-of-the art.

Table 1. Experiments results on FAU AIBO data

Systems	Unweighted average
GMM-Bayes	41.05
WOC-NN	**42.47**
Lee et al. [21]	41.3
Kockmann et al. (fusion of 2 systems) [22]	41.7

The results of Table 1 show that WOC-NN has better performance than GMM-Bayes system with a relative gain of 3.46%. Also, when compared to the best single system performance [21] and to the best combined systems performance [22] of Interspeech 2009 Emotion Challenge, WOC-NN method exceeds relatively their performances by 2.83% and 1.85% respectively. For more details about this method see [23].

Future Work

In the proposed framework, we computed the neighbourhood patterns in the likelihood score space. As future work, we will use the feature space level instead. An interesting feature vector space candidate is the *i-vector* space. The *i-vector* representation, used first in speaker verification [24], is a low dimensional vector of a given high dimensional *supervector* (a vector obtained by a concatenation of mean vector of each component of a GMM model). The space dimensionality reduction can be performed using a Factor Analysis model (FA) or a Probabilistic Principal Component Analysis (PPCA). This feature space will provide us more flexibility to deal with the variability in the expression of emotions between individuals and therefore reducing the overlap between classes.

5 The Main Contribution

In this proposal, we started by identifying our research problem, namely the acute confusion problem between emotion classes that characterizes the AER Systems. We also identified the different sources of this ambiguity. As a main contribution, we presented our methodology to improve the AER systems performances, namely *WOC-NN,* to make them closer for future deployment.

References

1. Li, W., Zhang, Y., Fu, Y.: Speech emotion recognition in E-learning system based on affective computing. In: Proceedings - Third International Conference on Natural Computation, ICNC, Hainan, China, pp. 809–813 (2007)

2. Jones, C.M., Jonsson, I.-M.: Performance analysis of acoustic emotion recognition for in-car conversational interfaces. In: Stephanidis, C. (ed.) UAHCI 2007 (Part II). LNCS, vol. 4555, pp. 411–420. Springer, Heidelberg (2007)

3. Clavel, C., et al.: De la construction du corpus émotionnel au système de détection le point de vue applicatif de la surveillance dans les lieux publics. Revue d'Intelligence Artificielle 20(4-5), 529–551 (2006)

4. Inanoglu, Z., Caneel, R.: Emotive alert: HMM-based emotion detection in voicemail messages. In: International Conference on Intelligent User Interfaces, Proceedings IUI, San Diego, CA, United States, pp. 251–253 (2005)

5. Panat, A.R., Ingole, V.T.: Affective state analysis of speech for speaker verification: Experimental study, design and development. In: Proceedings - International Conference on Computational Intelligence and Multimedia Applications, India, pp. 255–261 (2007)

6. Devillers, L., Vidrascu, L.: Real-life emotion recognition in speech. In: Müller, C. (ed.) Speaker Classifcation II. LNCS (LNAI), vol. 4441, pp. 34–42. Springer, Heidelberg (2007)

7. Lee, C.M., Narayanan, S.: Emotion Recognition Using a Data-Driven Fuzzy Inference System. In: Eurospeech, Geneva (2003)

8. Banse, R., Scherer, K.R.: Acoustic Profiles in Vocal Emotion Expression. Journal of Personality and Social Psychology, 614–636 (1996)

9. Ververidis, D., Kotropolos, C.: Automatic speech classification to five emotional states based on gender information. In: Proc. of Eusipco, pp. 341–344 (2004)

10. Scherer, K.R.: Vocal communication of emotion: A review of research paradigms. Speech Communication 40(1-2), 227–256 (2003)

11. Sethu, V., Ambikairajah, E., Epps, J.: Speaker normalisation for speech-based emotion detection. In: 15th International Conference on Digital Signal Processing, Cardiff, UK, pp. 611–614 (2007)

12. Grimm, M., Kroschel, K.: Rule-based emotion classification using acoustic features. In Proc. 3rd Internat. Conf. on Telemedicine and Multimedia Communication. Kajetany, Poland (2005)

13. Lee, C.M., et al.: Emotion Recognition based on Phoneme Classes. In: ICSLP, Korea (2004)

14. Schuller, B., et al.: Comparing one and two-stage acoustic modeling in the recognition of emotion in speech. In: IEEE Workshop on Automatic Speech Recognition and Understanding, Japan (2007)

15. Schuller, B., et al.: Towards more reality in the recognition of emotional. In: IEEE International Conference on Acoustics, Speech, and Signal Processing, Honolulu, HI, USA, pp. 941–944 (2007)

16. Attabi, Y.: Reconnaissance automatique des émotions à partir du signal acoustique, Master Thesis, École de technologie supérieure (ÉTS), Montréal (2009)

17. Huang, R., Ma, C.: Toward a speaker-independent real-time affect detection system. In: 18th International Conference on Pattern Recognition, Hong Kong, China (2006)

18. Chen, C., You, M., Song, M., Bu, J., Liu, J.: An enhanced speech emotion recognition system based on discourse information. In: Alexandrov, V.N., van Albada, G.D., Sloot, P.M.A., Dongarra, J. (eds.) ICCS 2006. LNCS, vol. 3991, pp. 449–456. Springer, Heidelberg (2006)

19. Lee, C.M., Narayanan, S.: Emotion Recognition Using a Data-Driven Fuzzy Inference System. In: Eurospeech, Geneva (2003)

20. Schuller, B., Steidl, S., Batliner, A.: The Interspeech 2009 Emotion Challenge. In: Interspeech. ISCA, Brighton (2009)

21. Lee, C., Mower, E., Busso, C., Lee, S., Narayanan, S.: Emotion Recognition Using a Hierarchical Binary Decision Tree Approach. In: Interspeech, ISCA, Brighton (2009)
22. Kockmann, M., Burget, L., Černocký, J.: Brno University of Technology System for Interspeech 2009 Emotion Challenge. In: Interspeech. ISCA, Brighton (2009)
23. Attabi, Y., Dumouchel, P.: Weighted Ordered Classes - Nearest Neighbors: A New Framework for Automatic Emotion Recognition From Speech. In: Interspeech. ISCA, Florence (2011)
24. Dehak, N., Kenny, et al.: Front-End Factor Analysis for Speaker Verification Submitted to IEEE Transactions on Audio, Speech and Language Processing (2009)

Multimodal Affect Recognition in Intelligent Tutoring Systems

Ntombikayise Banda and Peter Robinson

Computer Laboratory, University of Cambridge
15 JJ Thompson Avenue, Cambridge, CB3 0FD, UK

Abstract. This paper concerns the multimodal inference of complex mental states in the intelligent tutoring domain. The research aim is to provide intervention strategies in response to a detected mental state, with the goal being to keep the student in a positive affect realm to maximize learning potential. The research follows an ethnographic approach in the determination of affective states that naturally occur between students and computers. The multimodal inference component will be evaluated from video and audio recordings taken during classroom sessions. Further experiments will be conducted to evaluate the affect component and educational impact of the intelligent tutor.

Keywords: Affective Computing, Multimodal Analysis, Intelligent Tutoring Systems.

1 Introduction

In human-interaction, 55% of affective information is carried by the body whilst 38% by the voice tone and volume, and only 7% person by the words spoken [1]. Ekman [2] further suggests that non-verbal behaviours are the primary vehicles for expressing emotion. With the availability of computational power, and great advances in the fields of computer vision and speech recognition, it is now possible to create systems that can detect facial expressions, gestures and body postures from video and audio feed. Furthermore, systems that can integrate different modalities can offer powerful and much more pleasant computer experiences as they would be embracing users' natural behaviour.

The research is directed towards equipping intelligent tutoring systems with the ability to infer complex mental states from multiple modalities. Until recently, emotion has been a neglected dynamic in the design of intelligent tutors. Ingleton [3] argues that emotion is not merely the affective product of learning but is rather a constitutive of the activity of learning. She further states that emotions shape learning and teaching experiences for both students and teachers as they play a key role in the development of identity and self-esteem. The work therefore seeks to allow the tutoring system to maximize the learning potential of a student by detecting mental states such as frustration, interest and confusion from facial expressions, head gestures and speech prosody.

S. D'Mello et al. (Eds.): ACII 2011, Part II, LNCS 6975, pp. 200–207, 2011.
© Springer-Verlag Berlin Heidelberg 2011

The core component of the research is related to the *affective response* of the intelligent tutor upon detection of a mental state. The aim of the system is to keep the student in a motivated state throughout the learning session. This requires the system to determine strategies that will trigger an *affect transition* from a negative to a positive state in an efficient and appropriate manner. We will therefore seek to answer questions such as "which affective states are conducive to learning and which ones are not?", "which interventions are effective?", "when should the tutor intervene?" and "how often should the tutor intervene?".

2 Background

2.1 Affect-Sensitive Intelligent Tutors

Human tutors have been shown to be effective due to their ability to provide students with constant, timely and appropriate feedback, and the interactive manner in which they guide the student towards a solution. This in turn prevents the student from disengaging from the studies when they are unable to find solutions. According to Wolcott [4] teachers rely on nonverbal means such as eye contact, facial expressions and body language to determine the cognitive states of students, which indicate the degree of success in the instructional transaction. Embedding an affect-recognition component in an intelligent tutoring system will enhance its ability to provide the necessary guidance, and make the tutoring sessions more interactive and thus effective.

2.2 Intervention Strategies

Prior to the expansion of research in affective computing, feedback-oriented intelligent tutors used various cognitive and expert models which would trigger a response when the student behaviour diverges from that of the expert or cognitive model [5]. To take into account the difference in cognitive skills of learners, Ohlosson's study emphasized the need to model student patterns and learn their academic weaknesses and strengths, and consider this information when deciding on the appropriate teaching strategy. He further suggested that intelligent tutors have internal representation of the subject matter so that it can generate appropriate material specifically adapted for the learner. For example, it should be able to offer a definition, an explanation or a practise problem when the student responses indicate that the material has not been grasped [6]. Adding affect to the tutoring system builds on Ohlosson's ideas in that by tailoring material based on the emotion detected and other cognitive variables, the student will be at a better position to learn.

The critical questions in the tutoring system's teaching strategy relates to the *timing*, *frequency* and the *nature* of the intervention. The help policy adopted by Project LISTEN's Reading Tutor [7] is a great example of timing of the tutor's intervention. In their work, help is offered when a student skips a word, misreads a word, gets stuck or clicks for help. Beck et al. [8] explored the possibility of offering pre-emptive assistance by letting the tutor pronounce a difficult word before an attempt by the student. The system was however found to be biased towards long words and a student's past mistakes. One could argue that students should be allowed to attempt to pronounce the word first, and the tutor can then confirm or correct the pronunciation. Allowing students to make mistakes leads them into a correction cycle which increases the time exposure to material, which may yield better recall rates (a theory supported by Herrington et al [9]).

The affective content of an intervention is another important factor when formulating strategies. Jennifer Robison [10] conducted a study on the application of parallel and reactive feedback, where the former relates to identifying with the student's emotion, and the latter concerns the display of emotions that aim to alter or enhance the observed affect. Her preliminary study suggests that the nature of affective feedback given could lead to either positive or negative consequences, and that due consideration should be given to the current affect state of the learner when selecting affective responses.

2.3 Evaluating Intelligent Tutoring Systems

The common goal of intelligent tutors is to impart knowledge as effectively and efficiently as possible. We will be focusing on the achievement and affect measures related to the educational impact of the system. Many studies perform pre- and post-tests to determine if the learning objectives were met. Since affective computing is a relatively new field, measures to evaluate the impact of affective feedback are still in their early stages of design. One measure that seems to be widely used is the L measure introduced by D'Mello [11] which is a probability function that analyses and maps out transitions between affective states making it possible to extrapolate the success or failure of the strategies employed.

2.4 Related Work

The recent focus towards emotionally-sensitive intelligent tutors has led to studies exploring the inference of academic-related emotions from various channels such as facial expressions, speech prosody and physiological signals. These tutors have the ultimate goal of keeping the student motivated or interested in their work by adapting their tutoring strategies based on the observed behaviour of the student. Amongst these are the ITSPOKE and AutoTutor intelligent tutoring systems.

The ITSPOKE (Intelligent Tutoring SPOKEn) dialogue system [12] guides a student through an essay-type qualitative physics problem by eliciting complete explanations and correcting misconceptions. It uses acoustic and prosodic features extracted from student speech to recognize three affect categories, namely, *positive* (encompassing affect states such as confidence and interest), *neutral* and *negative* (a blanket category for emotions such as uncertainty, confusion, boredom, frustration) states. It achieves an accuracy of 80.53% for the three-way classification.

While this is a great start towards adapting to students' emotional states, intelligent tutors need to have a more granular understanding of emotions as mental states such as boredom and confusion have distinct causes and should be addressed appropriately.

The AutoTutor [13] addresses this problem by detecting more affective states, namely, boredom, confusion, flow, frustration and neutral. It infers emotion from conversational cues, body posture and facial features and uses an embodied pedagogical agent to synthesize affective responses through animated facial expressions and modulated speech. The authors are still however investigating the fusion of these channels. The proposed work differs from the current approaches in that it explores the fusion of visual and audio cues to infer academic mental states (which according to our knowledge has not been addressed in the learning domain). Other research works in audio-visual emotion recognition systems have been centred on basic emotions which have distinct signatures thus making such systems easier to model. The various ways that one can express mental states such as thinking, compounded by the task of working with unrestricted natural behaviour of students, makes this a challenging problem.

3 Work to Date

We propose the framework depicted in Figure 1 for the recognition of emotion in an intelligent tutoring system. The emotion recognition components (which were developed in-house) provide automatic analysis of facial expressions, head gestures and speech prosody. The first research task was to adapt and re-train these two subsystems to meet the specifications of the project. This includes identifying new features and incorporating them into the system.

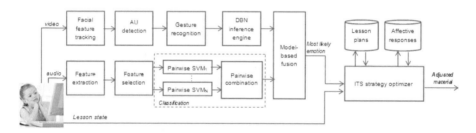

Fig. 1. A multimodal framework for the affect-sensitive intelligent tutor

3.1 Data

The initial system tests were based on the MindReading DVD due to the lack of audio-visual databases enacting discrete complex mental states [14]. The audio analysis section is evaluated on the extended MindReading audio DVD as the number of training files in the original DVD is insufficient to characterize emotional speech.

3.2 Facial Expression Analysis

The recognition of affect from the face remains a challenging task due to the variability of an expression amongst different people, and even within the same person as it is time and context-dependent. The first task in facial expression analysis is representing the face as abstract components for measurement. The most commonly used system for the coding and measurement of the face is the Facial Action Coding System developed by Ekman and Friesen [15]. FACS is an anatomically-based system which uses minimal units (called action units) to describe visible muscle activities that occur for all types of facial movements. The 44 defined action units include eye and head positions and movements.

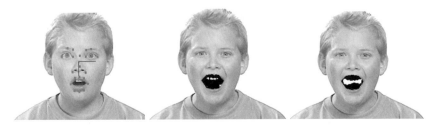

Fig. 2. Three image frames from the MindReading DVD of a child actor expressing the affective state of '*impressed*' within the *interest* mental state group at different time instances, with (a) showing the 22 feature points from the NevenVision tracker, (b) tracking of teeth to represent the *teeth present* gesture, (c) aperture tracking gesture indicating the *mouth open* gesture

The research builds on an in-house real-time complex mental state recognition system developed by el Kaliouby and Robinson [16]. The system abstracts the recognition process into three levels, namely, action unit detection, gesture recognition and mental state inference. The first level involves the tracking of the face from a video sequence using the FaceTracker[1] which outputs 22 feature points (see Figure 2(a)) and head orientation measures (pitch, yaw, roll). The FaceTacker uses Gabor wavelet image transformation and neural networks for its tracking. Action units are detected from the displacement of the features and through appearance-based features.

The second level encodes the detected action units into gestures to allow for complex movements such as head nods and head shakes to be represented. The sequence of action units representing a gesture are modelled using hidden Markov models (HMM) to capture the temporal nature of the gestures. During executing time, the HMMs output quantized probabilities of whether or not a gesture was observed from the sequence of detected action units. The system was extended to recognize gestures such as the presence of teeth and the tracking of an open mouth as seen in Figures 2(b) and 2(c), and to detect furrows.

The final level uses dynamic Bayesian networks (DBNs) to model the unfolding emotion based on the quantized probabilities from the gesture recognition component. Inference is carried out in real time with each emotion modelled as a separate DBN. The inference engine employs a sliding window technique which allows it to predict an emotion based on the history of six gesture observations. The probability scores from the DBNs are integrated over a time period (video length or turn basis) and the emotion with the highest score is selected.

3.3 Audio Analysis

Emotion recognition from audio is concerned with *how* speech is conveyed. The audio analysis component used in the research is an adaptation of the framework introduced by Sobol-Shikler [17] and enhanced by Pfister [18]. The OpenSMILE library extracts 6555 features which represent pitch, spectral envelope, and energy feature groups (amongst others); delta and acceleration information; and their

---

[1] FaceTracker is part of the NevenVision SDK licensed from Google Inc.

functionals (e.g. min, max, mean, percentiles and peaks). A correlation-based feature selection method is applied to reduce dimensionality. The selected features are used in the training and classification of emotions using pairwise support vector machines with radial basis function kernels. Table 1 shows the performance of the pairwise support vector machines.

Table 1. Pairwise classification results of eight complex mental states using RBF SVMs. The number in brackets refers to the number of features selected for each pairwise class.

	excited	interested	joyful	opposed	stressed	sure	thinking	unsure
absorbed	84.2 [80]	86.3 [62]	86.5 [107]	81.7 [82]	83.3 [85]	83.2 [70]	80.7 [66]	78.2 [43]
excited		82.4 [76]	78.5 [38]	83.8 [40]	75.8 [22]	75.9 [68]	86.1 [134]	79.2 [102]
interested			86.8 [89]	85.0 [61]	87.0 [80]	91.2 [79]	80.1 [77]	75.0 [43]
joyful				81.8 [51]	79.7 [65]	85.3 [113]	84.7 [139]	83.1 [109]
opposed					85.3 [82]	76.6 [43]	88.2 [97]	86.9 [54]
stressed						85.0 [89]	86.2 [124]	76.4 [83]
sure							87.0 [115]	87.5 [78]
thinking								72.2 [75]

The pairwise comparisons are combined to calculate the average output probabilities and the count of pairwise wins for each emotion.

3.4 Multimodal Fusion

In Sharma's extensive introduction to fusion of multiple sensors [19], three distinct levels of integrating data are highlighted, namely, data, feature and decision fusion methods. Data fusion is automatically excluded from the consideration as it applies to observations of the same type (for example, two video camera recordings taken at different angles). Feature fusion is applied when the raw observations have been transformed into feature representations and is ideal for synchronized feeds. Decision fusion, also called late fusion, deals with the fusion of decisions computed independently by the respective components. Synchronizing the video and audio channels and aligning emotional segments is a challenging task, especially with the complexity of mental states investigated which need temporal and spatial information to be captured. We have chosen decision fusion given its robust architecture and resistance to sensor failure. The approach however loses information of mutual correlation between the audio and video modalities [20].

The probability scores from the facial expression and audio analysis subsystems are fed into an SVM for training and classification. Due to lack of corresponding training and test data, the multimodal component could not be reliably evaluated. This will however be remedied by a data collection exercise discussed in the next section.

4 Future Work

4.1 Ethnography Study and Data Collection

The next step involves spending time in primary schools with learners between the ages of ten and twelve to conduct a behavioural analysis to determine conditions that trigger negative affect, the immediate impact the affect has on the student's task and strategies that tutors and teachers employ to reverse the negative affect. This will involve recording students in their interactions with computers and tutors, and during traditional class sessions. Such a study will allow us to identify the common mental states experienced in a variety of learning activities, and to decide upon the mental states that our refined recognition system will detect. This will also serve as a great opportunity to collect recordings of natural (and elicited) data that will be used for training and testing the multimodal system. A crowdsourcing approach for the affect annotation of video and audio recordings will be followed.

4.2 Multimodal Recognition for Natural Data

Once the data has been collected, the multimodal recognition system will be configured to work with natural data. We will investigate the use of other sensors, such as an eye tracker for gaze detection, to increase the accuracy of the system.

4.3 Intervention Strategies

The main contribution of the research will stem from the task of developing computer-based affect-related intervention strategies to maintain interest and an overall positive affect during learning sessions. A study will be conducted to determine which emotions can provide the transition from a negative mental state to a positive one. The study will involve inducing positive affect in students, then subsequently inducing a negative affect and applying a random selection to reverse the affect transition. The findings of the study will be formulated into strategies and incorporated into the tutoring system. We will also investigate the timing and frequency of the interventions.

4.4 Evaluation

The multimodal recognition system will be evaluated on the natural emotions collected from the ethnographic study. The intervention component of the intelligent tutor will be evaluated through simulations and self-report, and the results will be analysed using the L probability function for successful affective transitions. The educational impact of the system will be evaluated through a control experiment involving two groups of students. One group will be subjected to learn unfamiliar material through self-study whilst the other through the intelligent tutor. Pre- and post-tests will be conducted to determine knowledge gained, and a subsequent test at a later date to test retention of information.

Acknowledgements. The financial assistance of the South African National Research Fund (NRF), Bradlow Foundation Scholarship and Google Anita Borg Memorial Scholarship towards this research is hereby acknowledged.

References

1. Paleari, M., Lisetti, C.: Toward Multimodal Fusion of Affective Cues. In: Proceedings of the1st ACM International Workshop on Human-Centered Multimedia (2006)
2. Ekman, P., Friesen, W.: Nonverbal behaviour in pschotherapy research. Research in Pschotherapy 3, 179–216 (1968)
3. Ingleton, C.: Emotion in learning: a neglected dynamic. Cornerstones of Higher Education 22, 86–99 (2000)
4. Wolcott, L.: The distance teacher as reflective practitioner. Educational Technology 1, 39–43 (1995)
5. Murray, T.: Authoring Intelligent Tutoring Systems: An Analysis of the State of the Art. Internal Journal of Artificial Intelligence in Education 10, 98–129 (1999)
6. Ohlsson, S.: Some Principles of Intelligent Tutoring. Instructional Science 14, 293–326 (1986)
7. Mostow, J., Aist, G.: Giving help and praise in a reading tutor with imperfect listening - because automated speech recognition means never being able to say you're certain. CALICO Journal 16, 407–424 (1999)
8. Beck, J.E., Jia, P., Sison, J., Mostow, J.: Predicting student help-request behavior in an intelligent tutor for reading. In: Proceedings of the 9th International Conference on User Modeling (2003)
9. Herrington, J., Oliver, R., Reeves, T.C.: Patterns of engagement in authentic online learning environments. Australian Journal of Educational Technology 19, 59–71 (2003)
10. Robison, J., McQuiggan, S., Lester, J.: Evaluating the consequences of affective feedback in intelligent tutoring systems, pp. 1–6 (2009)
11. D'Mello, S., Taylor, R.S., Graesser, A.: Monitoring Affective Trajectories during Complex Learning. In: Proceedings of the 29th Annual Meeting of the Cognitive Science Society, Austin, TX, pp. 203–208 (2007)
12. Litman, D., Forbes, K.: Recognizing Emotions from Student Speech in Tutoring Dialogues. In: Proceedings of the ASRU 2003 (2003)
13. D'Mello, S., Jackson, T., Craig, S., Morgan, B., Chipman, P., White, H., Person, N., Kort, B., el Kaliouby, R., Picard, R.W., Graesser, A.: AutoTutor Detects and Responds to Learners Affective and Cognitive States. In: Workshop on Emotional and Cognitive Issues at the International Conference of Intelligent Tutoring Systems (2008)
14. Baron-Cohen, S., Golan, O., Wheelwright, S., Hill, J.J.: Mind Reading: The Interactive Guide to Emotions. Jessica Kingsley Publishers, London (2004)
15. Ekman, P., Friesen, W.V.: Facial Action Coding System: a technique for the measurement of facial movement. Consulting Psychologists Press, Palo Alto (1978)
16. el Kaliouby, R., Robinson, P.: Real-time Inference of Complex Mental States from Facial Expressions and Head Gestures. In: Real-Time Vision for Human-Computer Interaction, pp. 181–200. Springer, Heidelberg (2005)
17. Sobol-Shikler, T., Robinson, P.: Classification of complex information: inference of co-occurring affective states from their expressions in speech. IEEE Transactions on Pattern Analysis and Machine Intelligence 32, 1284–1297 (2010)
18. Pfister, T., Robinson, P.: Speech emotion classification and public speaking skill assessment. In: Salah, A.A., Gevers, T., Sebe, N., Vinciarelli, A. (eds.) HBU 2010. LNCS, vol. 6219, pp. 151–162. Springer, Heidelberg (2010)
19. Sharma, R., Pavlovic, V.I., Huang, T.S.: Toward a multi- modal human computer interface. In: Beun, R.-J. (ed.) Multimodal Cooperative Communication, pp. 89–112. Springer, Heidelberg (2001)
20. Zeng, Z., Pantic, M., Huang, T.S.: Emotion Recognition Based on Multimodal Information. In: Affective Information Processing (2008)

Candidacy of Physiological Measurements for Implicit Control of Emotional Speech Synthesis

Shannon Hennig

Italian Institute of Technology, Genoa, Italy
shannon.hennig@iit.it

Abstract. There is a need for speech synthesis to be more emotionally expressive. Implicit control of a subset of affective vocal effects could be advantageous for some applications. Physiological measures associated with autonomic nervous system (ANS) activity are potential candidates for such input. This paper describes a pilot study investigating physiological sensor readings as potential input signals for modulating the speech synthesis of affective utterances composed by human users. A small corpus of audio, heart rate, and skin conductance data has been collected from eight doctoral student oral defenses. Planned analysis and research phases are outlined.

Keywords: emotionally expressive speech, speech acoustics, physiological measures, heart rate, skin conductance, speech synthesis.

1 Introduction

Humans have a remarkable capacity for conveying affective information through speech, however current speech synthesis technology is unable to fully approximate the subtle affective details of how people speak. Information about a speaker's intent, attitude, affect and emotional state can be conveyed through variations in the speaker's pitch, loudness, rhythm and voice quality [1–4]. While it is known that speech carries more than linguistic information, there is variability in how the terms extra-linguistic, non-linguistic and paralinguistic are used to talk about this information [5, 6].

For the purposes of this article, the term *paralinguistic* will refer to all non-linguistic information. In contrast with those who use the term paralinguistic primarily to refer to intentional vocal effects, this article will use Lyons' categorization of paralinguistic information as having both a communicative and informative component [7]. In this paper, *communicative cues* refer to those used intentionally by speakers, such as emphatic stress and rising intonation, whereas *informative cues* convey affective information regardless of whether the speaker intends to express it. Informative cues, the focus of this study, include organic information related to a person's health as well as expressive information related to momentary changes in a speaker's emotional state [8]. To complicate matters, many suprasegmental vocal effects convey multiple types of paralinguistic information.

S. D´Mello et al. (Eds.): ACII 2011, Part II, LNCS 6975, pp. 208–215, 2011.
© Springer-Verlag Berlin Heidelberg 2011

1.1   Paralinguistic Information and Speech Synthesis

One challenge in affective computing is how to make synthetic speech approximate the affective capabilities of human speech [9]. Speech synthesis technology has sufficiently evolved to the point that, within its limits, it has many useful applications [10, 11]. There are many advances to celebrate, particularly in the areas of intelligibility and in creating natural-sounding voices, but open questions remain regarding the affective capabilities of speech synthesis [9, 12]. Many speech synthesis systems are capable, to varying degrees, of producing the first two of Monrad-Kron's types of prosody [13], *intrinsic prosody* (e.g., difference between interrogative and declarative utterances) and *intellectual prosody* (e.g., contrastive stress, emphatic stress, etc.), however less progress has been made with regards to *emotional prosody* and the grunts, sighs and hesitations of *inarticulate prosody* [14].

1.2   Open Questions for Affective Speech Synthesis

Schröder has identified two key challenges for affective speech synthesis: improving the ability to synthesize various vocal effects and to identify appropriate contexts for using them [12] as illustrated in Figure 1 by the shaded boxes 3 and 1 respectively. This author expands upon these two challenges, and considers the selection of the linguistic and paralinguistic content to be synthesized as an additional specific challenge. Although this could be considered part of Schröder's two challenges, this author believes that breaking down the challenges more specifically better illustrates the different realities that exist when there is a human in the loop. Specifically, in contrast to machine, computer and robot users, the first two columns in Figure 1 are partially solved for human users. Typically people can identify context and experience natural emotional reactions and given an input method, such as typing, can create relevant linguistic and communicative paralinguistic content. In contrast, selecting the informative cues normally produced without conscious awareness during natural speech production (box 2b in Figure 1) is difficult for people and all aspects are difficult for non-human users.

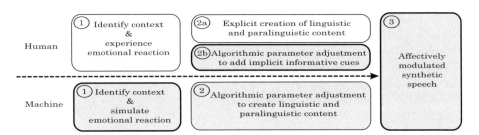

Fig. 1. Challenges highlighted in gray of producing emotionally expressive synthesized speech for humans and nonhuman entitites

1.3   Production of Emotional Speech Synthesis

Humans need a means of modulating the affective information in synthesized messages without exceeding their cognitive, linguistic and motor abilities. This is particularly true in the context of assistive technology in which people with motor impairments use synthetic speech for face-to-face communication [10].

Implicit control options may be useful for aspects of emotional speech synthesis. Pfeifer, Bongard and Grand's concept of morphological computation in particular might be relevant, which they defined as processes that are "performed by the body that otherwise would have to be performed by the brain" thereby allowing a person to offload some processing demands to the body or environment ([15], p 96). During natural human speech production, various body systems, including the autonomous nervous system, can be simultaneously reacting to fluctuations in a speaker's internal mood, affect or emotion [16]. These measurable changes in muscle tension, blood flow, and electrodermal activity [17] can cause momentary changes in the vocal tract configuration which could modify the speech signal. This collection of reactions and events could implicitly alter natural speech production with little or no conscious speaker involvement. Schrerer and colleagues outlined such a possibility in great detail [2, 18]. In other words, theoretically, the human body has automatic and semi-automatic mechanisms for conveying a speaker's affective reactions.

1.4   Relationship between ANS Measures and Speech Acoustics

Compared to the extensive literature linking speech and emotion [1, 2, 18, 19] and the literature relating emotions to physiological measures [16], relatively fewer studies have directly explored the relationships between physiological activity and speech acoustics. Until recently, the technologies to record physiological signals were invasive, limited to lab settings, and not conducive to studying naturally occurring communication and interaction [17]. Motor behaviors, including speech and gestures, are also known to confound the recording of ANS signals, and thus many experiments of ANS activity and emotions have strictly controlled a subject's movements, including speech. The exact nature of how the fluctuations in ANS activity relate to speech and subsequent listener judgments is unknown, but it is increasingly possible to investigate such questions in ecologically valid ways as recording technology becomes less invasive [20, 21].

Given that speech acoustics and emotions are correlated and that emotions and psychophysiological measures are thought to be related, there could be a useful link between affective information coded in ANS activity and the listener through the speech signal, as illustrated in Figure 2.

2   Research Scope

The scope of this pilot study is to consider whether physiological signals could be a source of information to facilitate the synthesis of informative vocal cues.

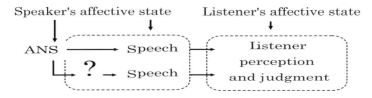

Fig. 2. Possible links between a speaker's ANS activity and listener response, contingent on the speaker's and listener's affective states, in which speech varies with ANS activity or a possible unknown co-associated mechanism (question mark)

This could be of immediate benefit for people with disabilities who desire more affectively rich text to speech on speech generating devices (SGD) and may also have research applications when using people, and their emotional intelligence, to test new speech synthesis technology.

The first step is to determine whether there is a relationship between ANS activity and listener judgment. This could be thought of as a system identification problem with measurements of ANS activity as inputs and listener reactions as outputs of a black box. A public speaking situation has been selected as a starting point to sample physiological activity and speech simultaneously to be later judged by listeners.

Specifically, this pilot study aims to answer the following questions:

1. Is there evidence of correlations between fluctuations in physiological measures of ANS activity (e.g., heart rate, skin conductance, etc.) and listener judgments during spontaneously occurring human speech?
2. Are there any potential mappings between specific observable ANS measures and speech acoustics that might be utilized for implicit control of informative paralingusitic cues during speech synthesis?

3   Work to Date

In order to address these questions, a pilot study has been initiated using a public speaking methodology. At this stage, physiological and speech data have been collected during eight doctoral student defenses at the Italian Institute of Technology. Due to technical malfunctions, one data set is missing heart rate data and another data set has only low quality audio recorded from a webcam. Listener judgment data remains to be collected and subsequent data analysis is planned.

3.1   Methodology

Doctoral oral defenses were selected as the initial context for simultaneously sampling physiological measurements and speech acoustics. Speakers are anticipated to attempt to minimize the production of intentional communicative cues, but still inadvertently produce informational cues related to changes in internal affective arousal evoked by the demands of the situation. It is hypothesized that the doctoral defenses will be a conservative initial sample. A higher portion of informative cues to communicative cues are expected, facilitating the study of the cues in question. Additionally, this controlled setting was considered a good starting point because contextual factors such as the location, audience, and purpose considered important for affective speech production [14] would be relatively consistent between speakers and similar speaking situations will occur in the future allowing any findings to be replicated with additional speakers.

Participants. Eight doctoral students provided informed consent (4 males, 4 females, ages 28-32). All practiced wearing the sensors one week before the talk. Before data collection, participants were told that the study was about stress levels during public speaking, not emotions and speech acoustics. The participants' native languages were Italian (5 students), Arabic (2 students), and French (1 student). Each person ranked his or her own English skills with the Common European Framework of Reference [22] as independent (B1 or B2) or higher, with the exception of one student who ranked oral production at a basic (A2) level.

The group of students who agreed to participate were highly variable with respect to cultural and linguistic background. Although this may introduce confounding factors, we chose to continue with the study given that informative cues are anticipated to be more culturally and linguistically universal than other paralinguistic cues and because further research with more homogeneous groups and speakers speaking in their first language are planned to confirm this assumption.

Procedure and Equipment. Each talk consisted of a 20 minute prepared slide presentation, applause, question and answer session by a committee of professors and then final applause.

Electrodermal Responses were recorded from speakers' wrists with Q sensors (Affectiva, www.affectiva.com) with a sample rate of 32 Hz. The sensors were put on at least 20 minutes before the talk to ensure adequate moisture between the skin and sensor for recording purposes. The Q sensors also measured skin temperature and three degrees of acceleration.

Heart Rate. A mass-market heart rate monitor (Polar Wind chest strap transmitter and CS600 receiver, www.polar.fi) recorded R-R time intervals.

Speech. Audio was recorded with a wireless lapel microphone. The signal was received by a wireless Mipro ACT-51 UHR diversity receiver connected to a Jedia JDM MA-1410 preamplifier. An usb analog to digital converter was connected to a laptop dedicated to the task. Speech was recorded and later exported as a WAV file using Audacity open-source software (http://audacity.sourceforge.net) set to a 44100Hz sample rate and 32 floating bit sample format.

Video. In order to capture contextual information regarding the slide transitions, speakers' movements, and other events during the talks, a webcam was used to non-obtrusively record video of the presentations.

3.2   Preliminary Results of Doctoral Studies

Changes in both skin conductance and heart rate were observed at the key transition points including the start of the talk, the transition to the question and answer section, and final applause at the end. Raw skin conductance tonic levels were highly variable between the eight speakers as was skin conductance responses.

4   Work in Progress

4.1   Listener Judgments

After synchronizing all data streams, short audio samples will be extracted from spoken segments of each recorded talk and played for two groups of non-English speaking listeners. In this manner, each talk's linguistic content will be masked without altering the speech signal.

The first listener group will subjectively rank the audio regarding how confident, easy to listen to, and believable each speaker seems from the audio recordings. The second group will be divided into subgroups to continuously rank, using a slider mechanism, either the speakers' affective valence, arousal, or dominance depending on group assignment. In other words, each listener will be told to either indicate how positive or negative, how emotional, or how in control the speaker sounds.

4.2   Planned Analyses

For the skin conductance data, phasic measures are being calculated regarding the mean intensity and the 1st and 2nd derivatives of skin conductance level. For tonic aspects, rate of responses and length of time between responses will be calculated. For the cardiac data, HRV and LF to HF ratios are being calculated.

The two sets of listener judgments will then be compared to skin conductance and heart rate variables to determine whether there is any relationship between physiological measurements and listener judgments.

If listener judgments do appear to vary with ANS activity, a more detailed analysis of the speech acoustics fluctuations and specific cardiac and/or skin conductance measures and specific speech acoustic features will be conducted. For the audio samples, mean, range, standard deviation, and jitter/shimmer respectively will be calculated for f0 and intensity. Additionally, syllable per minute calculations are planned. Speaker hand movement, as measured by the accelerometer in the Q sensor, and general body movement, as captured by the video, can be used to investigate possible effect of movements.

5   Planned Future Work

Based on the literature, we believe that it is theoretically possible that a speaker's measurable ANS activity could be related to the subsection of speech that conveys informative paralinguistic cues to a listener. If this proves true, wearable physiological sensors may be able to improve the implicit expression of vocal affect through informative cues while allowing human users to focus their cognitive and motor resources on explicitly controlling the communicative aspects of their synthesized messages. The current pilot study is only a first step.

The technological capability to effectively synthesize a full range of vocal effects does not yet exist and it is beyond the scope of this research project to tackle this challenging open question. That said, depending on the potential mappings found between physiological signals and acoustic measurements it may be possible to develop a speech synthesizer prototype using existing technology.

Such a prototype could test whether any benefit can be seen at this early stage, within the limitations of existing TTS technology, of using ANS signals as implicit input for algorithms that modulate the synthesis of the informative subset of paralinguistic cues. An encoder-decoder testing paradigm [19] would be used to validate these mapping by measuring the effect on listeners during interactive tasks, such as giving spatial directions and word guessing parlor games, using an instant messaging format in which encoders type messages to an unseen communication partner, while wearing physiological sensors, that will be read by the speech synthesizer to the decoder/listener. Outcome measures would include observed performance and ratings of the experience of using a speech synthesizer with and without ANS-based modulation.

The development of this speech synthesis prototype will require collaboration with people with expertise in speech synthesis. Decisions will also need to be made regarding the type of synthesis to be used (e.g., HMM based, nonuniform selection, etc.) which will depend on which vocal effects are revealed in the planned analyses given that existing TTS technologies vary in their capacity to adjust acoustic parameters without sacrificing intelligibility or naturalness.

Additionally given the small sample of culturally and linguistically heterogeneous speakers, any findings would be need to be treated with caution. Additional speech samples will be gathered to determine whether any observed relationships between physiological signals, listener judgments, and speech acoustics are also observed in a larger sample of speakers, from speakers in more informal interactions, and from speakers speaking in their first language.

References

1. Juslin, P.N., Laukka, P.: Communication of emotions in vocal expression and music performance: Different channels, same code? Psychol. Bull. 129(5), 770–814 (2003)
2. Banse, R., Scherer, K.R.: Acoustic profiles in vocal emotion expression. J. Pers. Soc. Psychol. 70(3), 614–636 (1996)
3. Campbell, N., Mokhtari, P.: Voice quality: The 4th prosodic dimension. In: 15th ICPhS, pp. 2417–2420 (2003)

4. Murray, I.R., Arnott, J.L.: Toward the simulation of emotion in synthetic speech: A review of the literature on human vocal emotion. J. Acoust. Soc. Am. 93(2), 1097–1108 (1993)
5. Fernandez, R.: A Computational Model for the Automatic Recognition of Affect in Speech. Phd thesis, Massachusetts Institute of Technology, Cambridge, MA (2004)
6. Schötz, S.: Linguistic & paralinguistic phonetic variation in speaker recognition & text-to-speech synthesis. Term paper, Department of Linguistic and Phonetics. Lund University (2002)
7. Lyons, J.: Semantics. Cambridge University Press, Cambridge (1977)
8. Traunmüller, H.: Evidence for demodulation in speech perception. In: Proceedings of the 6th ICSLP, vol. 3, pp. 790–793 (2000)
9. Burkhardt, F., Stegmann, J.: Emotional speech synthesis: Applications, history and possible future. In: Proc. ESSV 2009, Dresden (2009)
10. Mirenda, P., Beukelman, D.R.: Augmentative & Alternative Communication: Supporting Children & Adults With Complex Communication Needs, 3rd edn. Paul H Brookes Pub. Co. (2005)
11. Lai, J., Karat, C.-M., Yankelovich, N.: Conversational speech interfaces and technologies. In: Sears, A., Jacko, J.A. (eds.) The Human-Computer Interaction Handbook, 2nd edn., pp. 381–391. CRC Press, Taylor & Francis (2008)
12. Schröder, M.: Expressive speech synthesis: Past, present, and possible futures. In: Tao, J., Tan, T. (eds.) Affective Information Processing, pp. 111–126. Springer, London (2009)
13. Monrad-Krohn, G.H.: Dysprosody or altered "melody of language". Brain 70(4), 405–415 (1947)
14. Campbell, N.: Developments in corpus-based speech synthesis: Approaching natural conversational speech. IEICE T. Inf. Syst. 88(3), 376–383 (2005)
15. Pfeifer, R., Bongard, J., Grand, S.: How the Body Shapes the Way We Think: A New View of Intelligence. The MIT Press, Cambridge (2007)
16. Cacioppo, J.T., Tassinary, L.G., Berntson, G.G.: Handbook of Psychophysiology, 3rd edn. Cambridge Univ. Pr., New York (2007)
17. Peter, C., Ebert, E., Beikirch, H.: Physiological sensing for affective computing. In: Tao, J., Tan, T. (eds.) Affective Information Processing, pp. 293–310. Springer, London (2009)
18. Scherer, K.R.: Vocal correlates of emotional arousal and affective disturbance. In: Wagner, H.L., Manstead, A.S.R. (eds.) Handbook of Social Psychophysiology, pp. 165–197. Wiley, New York (1989)
19. Juslin, P.N., Scherer, K.R.: Vocal expression of affect. In: Harrigan, J.A., Rosenthal, R., Scherer, K.R. (eds.) The New Handbook of Methods in Nonverbal Behavior Research. Series in Affective Science, pp. 65–135. Oxford Univeristy Press, New York (2008)
20. Lisetti, C.L., Nasoz, F.: Using noninvasive wearable computers to recognize human emotions from physiological signals. EURASIP Journal on Applied Signal Processing 11, 1672–1687 (2004)
21. Poh, M.Z., Swenson, N.C., Picard, R.W.: A wearable sensor for unobtrusive, Long-Term assessment of electrodermal activity. IEEE Transactions on Biomedical Engineering 57(5), 1243–1252 (2010)
22. Council of Europe: Common European Framework of Reference for Languages: Learning, Teaching, Assessment. Cambridge Univ. Press (2001)

Toward a Computational Approach for Natural Language Description of Emotions

Abe Kazemzadeh

University of Southern California

Abstract. This is a précis of the author's dissertation proposal about natural language description of emotions. The proposal seeks to explain how humans describe emotions using natural language. The focus of the proposal is on words and phrases that refer to emotions, rather than the more general phenomena of emotional language. The main problem is that if descriptions of emotions refer to abstract concepts that are local to a particular human (or agent), then how do these concepts vary from person to person and how can shared meaning be established between people. The thesis of the proposal is that natural language emotion descriptions refer to theoretical objects, which provide a logical framework for dealing with this phenomenon in scientific experiments and engineering solutions. An experiment, *Emotion Twenty Questions* (EMO20Q), was devised to study the social natural language behavior of humans, who must use descriptions of emotions to play the familiar game of twenty questions when the unknown word is an emotion. The idea of a theory based on natural language propositions is developed and used to formalize the knowledge of a sign-using organism. Based on this pilot data, it was seen that approximately 25% of the emotion descriptions referred to emotions as objects with dimensional attributes. This motivated the author to use interval type-2 fuzzy sets as a computational model for the meaning of this dimensional subset of emotion descriptions. This model introduces a definition of a variable that ranges over emotions and allows for both inter- and intra- subject variability. A second set of experiments used interval surveys and translation tasks to assess this model. Finally, the use of spectral graph theory is proposed to represent emotional knowledge that has been acquired from the EMO20Q game.

1 Background and Motivation

The dissertation proposal begins by claiming that natural language communication and emotional empathy are two distinguishing characteristics of human beings and that these together make it possible for emotional information to be transmitted to and understood by people who were not necessarily first-hand observers of the original emotional information being communicated. It is claimed that modeling this phenomenon will be the basis of both scientific insights and engineering solutions. In particular, description of abstract phenomena like emotions can carry over to other types of behavior description, which currently rely on categorical labels or Likert scales as a description methodology. These labels and scales explicitly refer to the data they describe, but the author claims that

S. D'Mello et al. (Eds.): ACII 2011, Part II, LNCS 6975, pp. 216–223, 2011.

they implicitly refer to theoretical objects that are at a conceptual level once removed from observational data. The notion of a definite description and a theoretical object are attributed to Russell and Carnap, respectively [1,2]. Regarding natural language descriptions of emotions as definite descriptions and theoretical entities allows the author to propose the formulation of an algebraic framework for dealing with these. The conceptual meaning of emotion words are interpreted as a region of an emotional space, and natural language descriptions of emotions further refine this space.

The author gives two engineering applications that such a model could be applied to. First, it would enable computers to understand natural language descriptions of emotions and use these to describe emotional data to a users. Currently there is much research being done on emotional user interfaces, but these often aim to recognize the user's emotional state. However, there are times when a user may want to convey emotional information that is not his or her current state, such as in an after-the-fact emotional self-report, or for social purposes of telling a story or gossip.

Another application is new-media technologies that expand the notion of *presence*, which allows a user to broadcast their status to others. Current approaches to processing emotional language are derived from processing longer documents, while recent trends in electronic communication tend toward very short documents. Also, current approaches rely on models of emotion that are limited to a specific theory or set of emotion labels, while current technologies tend toward allowing user to use any emotional description they choose. The proposed approach addresses these issues by focusing on shorter word or utterance level descriptions and explicitly aiming to understand a potentially unlimited variety of emotion descriptions.

The author makes the distinction between what he calls scientific descriptions and natural language descriptions of emotions. Scientific descriptions seek to precisely define emotions for people who study them. Natural language descriptions are how ordinary people describe emotions. Scientific descriptions can be seen as a linguistic division of labor for those whose study emotions as an occupation or avocation, but this division of labor is problematic because its terminology often overlaps with the common, natural language terms. Mindfulness of this distinction is important when the object of study is natural language and naturalistic emotions that do not fit into precise categories.

2   Thesis and Approach

The author's proposed thesis is that while natural language descriptions of emotions *can* be referentially grounded in specific human behavior and situations in the world, *in general* there is an intermediate conceptual representation, in lieu of the physical reference, that is referred to in cases when emotional information is communicated among those who are not first-hand witnesses of the observed emotional behavior and situation. Because this conceptual representation is not directly tied to physical observations, and because it cannot be directly shared with other agents, this representation is vague and varies from person to person.

However, this vagueness and variability does not hinder the ability of people to communicate and reason about such data. It is hypothesized that such a conceptual representation contains information that helps humans reason about emotions abstractly by the use of logical relations between emotions, such as similarity and subsethood, and by association of certain sets of behaviors and situations with particular emotion concepts. Although all the attributes of these concepts are not shared among each agent, it is possible for agents to arrive at shared meaning through natural language communication.

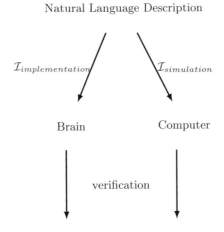

Fig. 1. Interpretation of descriptions in a model: implementation vs. simulation

The author proposes an approach which considers two types of models for interpretation ($\mathcal{I}$) of natural language descriptions of emotions, implementations and simulations, which correspond to answering scientific and engineering questions, respectively, as seen in Fig. 1. It is hypothesized that human understanding of natural language descriptions of emotions that refer to conceptual scales [5,6] are *implemented* by structures of the brain that are specialized in spacialization and wayfinding, such as the hippocampus, and subject to the effects of lateralization that have been observed for emotional words in patients with aphasia [3,4]. The conceptual representation of emotions can be computationally *simulated* using abstract scales in a conceptual space using interval type-2 fuzzy sets which capture inter- and intra-subject uncertainty and a computational implementation called *perceptual computing* [7].

To computationally model emotional concepts, the author uses an algebraic representation where emotions are fuzzy sets in an emotional space. An *emotional variable* ε represents an arbitrary region in this emotional space, i.e. $\varepsilon \subset E$, with the subset symbol $\subset$ used instead of set membership ($\in$) to represent regions in this emotion space in addition to single points. The conceptual meaning of

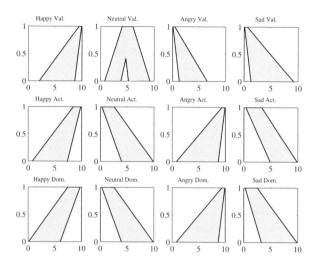

Fig. 2. Example of emotional variables as interval type-2 fuzzy sets that range over valence, activation, and dominance

an emotion word can be represented an by emotional variable that is associated with that word. An *emotion codebook* $V = (W_V, eval_V)$ is a set of words W_V and a function $eval_V$ that maps words of W_V to their corresponding region in the emotional space, $eval_V : W_V \rightarrow E$. Thus, an emotional vocabulary can be seen as a dictionary for looking up the meaning of an emotion word, which is represented as an interval type-2 fuzzy set to represent that these sets have fuzzy boundaries (e.g. Fig. 2). Similarity and subsethood are functions $E \times E \rightarrow [0, 1]$, where similarity is a measure of the similarity of two emotions and subsethood is a fuzzy logic interpretation of subsethood that allows for partial subsethood values.

The author uses mathematical logic to relate the model of emotion concepts with natural language descriptions. The definition of *theory* from mathematical logic states that a theory Γ is simply a set of sentences in some language $\mathcal{L}$ that is true of a model M [8,9]. In the case of the author's formulation, Γ is the set of natural language statements that are true with respect to particular emotions and negations of the statements that are false for a given emotion, $\mathcal{L}$ is the language of propositional logic, and M is a model of emotion concepts, which is is only accessible through observation of communicative behavior. In this view, the theory of a set of emotions can be seen as an matrix Γ indexed by the emotions in one dimension and the natural language statements in the other dimension. If the theory Γ refers to emotions ε_m for $1 \leq m \leq |E|$ and propositions p_n for $1 \leq n \leq |P|$, then Γ will be an $|E| \times |P|$ matrix.

Ordinarily, Boolean algebra would dictate that this matrix would consist of ones and zeros. Such a representation of general concepts has been explored under the aegis of *formal concept analysis* [10]. However, as the matrix is sparse one must represent the fact that not all of the combinations of questions and emotions have been encountered and that there may be some contradiction among subjects. To this end, we propose that the matrix be a $(1, 0, -1)$-matrix, i.e., a *signed matrix/graph* [11], where 1 indicates that the proposition of column-m is true for the emotion of row-n, -1 indicates that it is false, and 0 indicates that it has not been seen or that a contradiction has been encountered. This representation can be interpreted as an adjacency matrix by which the connectivity of various propositions with various emotions can be assessed using spectral graph theory.

3   Methodology and Experimental Results

The proposed thesis is supported by two main experiments. The first is a game called Emotion Twenty Questions (EMO20Q), which is used to construct a theory of emotions (where a theory is defined as above). The second experiment involved surveys that collected user responses to emotion words on interval-valued slider scales, which were used to construct a fuzzy logic model of emotion words that could account for both inter- and intra-subject variability.

The EMO20Q game is played like the ordinary game of twenty questions, but the object to be guessed in 20 or fewer turns is limited to emotion words. Furthermore, the game was played on an XMPP chat server so that games could be recorded and paralinguistic effects minimized. The questions asked are used to generate propositions about emotions and the answers to the questions determine whether the propositions are true or false of the emotion word. The fact that the emotion word is guessed by the other player demonstrates how shared meaning is established even though both players may have different concepts and different ways of describing emotions. Also, as an experimental methodology, it benefits from not limiting the emotions the players can pick nor the questions they ask. Therefore, it is not biased toward any particular scientific theory of emotions.

Pilot studies of EMO20Q were carried out with 12 players who played 26 matches. All except three matches were successfully completed, and they had a mean and median length of 12 and 15.5 turns, respectively, when unsuccessful games were considered to be 20 turns. This experiment yielded descriptive statistics about how the players used natural language to ask about emotions, which can be seen in Table 1.

When taken as simple text strings, the questions used in the game form a very sparse space of propositions. When the underlying meaning of the questions are represented as a logical formula (by manual annotation), the space becomes less sparse because superficial differences in the same logical proposition are ignored. This annotation process was termed *standardization*.

Although standardization reduced the sparsity of the data, it was still an open question whether the reduction of sparsity was sufficient to provide a coherent knowledge base. The criteria used to determine whether the knowledge was coherent was connectivity of the adjacency graph of the signed-matrix described above.

Table 1. Examples of question categories

Question Categories	Examples
identity (42%)	*is it angry?*
	guilt?
attribute (13%)	*is it something one feels for long periods of time?*
	is it a strong emotion?
similarity/	*is the emotion a type of or related to content or zen contentment (is that a*
subsethood (10%)	*word?_)*
	so it's similar to excited?
situational (14%)	*is the emotion more likely to occur when you are tired?*
	would i feel this if my dog died?
behavior (3%)	*you can express it in an obvious way by sighing?*
	do adults usually try to discourage children from feeling this?
causal (7%)	*yes. mynext question is can it harm anyone besides the feeler?*
	I think I know, but I'll ask one more question...does it ever cause children to
	wake up and cry?
social (8%)	*are you less likely to experience the emotion when around good firiends?*
	13)would you feel that towards someone who is superior to you?
miscelaneous (3%)	*i dont' know if this is a valid question, but does it start with the letter D?*
	or an aspirational emotion?
	does the word function or can be conjugated as anything eles? i.e. can it be a
	verb too?

The connectivity was determined through two spectral graph methods: finding the eigenvalues of the graph Laplacian of the absolute-value of the adjacency graph and computing the power series of this graph. To make the matrix Γ above into square, symmetric adjacency matrix, we define the adjacency matrix of Γ, $A = A(\Gamma)$ to be an $M + N \times M + N$ matrix as follows:

$$A(\Gamma) = \begin{bmatrix} zeros(M) & \Gamma^T \\ \Gamma & zeros(N) \end{bmatrix}$$

The absolute value $|A|$ of A describes whether questions have been asked of objects, regardless of whether the answer was yes or no. It is this graph $|A|$ that is used as and indicator about the connectivity of an agent's knowledge. The Laplacian L of a signed graph is calculated by subtracting the absolute adjacency matrix $|A|$ from the diagonal absolute degree matrix $\bar{D}_{ii} = \sum_j |A_{ij}|$, $L = \bar{D} - |A|$. From the matrix L one can tell the number of connected components of A by counting the number of zero eigenvalues. Thus, if there are three eigenvalues that equal zero, the graph is composed of three separate connected components. A graph Laplacian with one zero eigenvalue is a single connected graph. To determine the exact emotion-question pairs that are disconnected, the power series of A is used to count the number of walks between the two nodes. The value of $(A^l)_{ij}$ determines how many walks of length l exist between nodes i and j. If l is greater than the total number of nodes (the combined number of emotions and questions) and the value of $(A^l)_{ij}$ is zero, then there is no path between the nodes. This indicates for an automated agent playing EMO20Q a question that can be asked to improve its knowledge. From this spectral graph analysis, it was determined that overall, the graph was a single connected component except for questions that did not receive a clear yes or no answer.

The second experiment presented in the proposal was a web survey to present subjects with an emotion word and collect their responses in terms of valence, activation, and dominance values. The first experiment showed that, together, dimensional descriptions of emotions and similarity/subsethood descriptions accounted for nearly a fourth of the observed data. Valence, activation, and dominance are also one of the common ways of representing emotions. Similarity and subsethood judgments were not explicitly queried, but rather they were derived from the fuzzy membership functions of the valence, activation, and dominance values, as seen in Fig. 2. The novel aspect of this methodology, known as the *interval approach* and first described in [12], is that instead of giving a response as a value on Likert scale, subjects respond with an interval on the scale, which allows them to indicate their uncertainty so that intra-subject uncertainty to be measured. The interval approach then aggregates the individual intervals from each subject to make a membership function, like those in Fig. 2, for each emotion.

Several sub-experiments were carried out, all with the same methodology, but different emotion vocabularies. One vocabulary was a set of seven emotion words that are commonly used as labels for emotional corpora and the second vocabulary was derived from the first by adding "very" and "sort of" to the first. Another vocabulary was a list of 40 colloquial emotion words from a blogging site that allowed users to indicate their moods [13]. Finally, the fourth vocabulary was a Spanish vocabulary of 30 words that was taken from a mental health promotion.

The accuracy of the resulting fuzzy sets was assessed using a translation task that involved mapping from one vocabulary to another using similarity and subsethood measures. The translation accuracy was thus a proxy for the accuracy of the fuzzy sets themselves. Translation between emotion vocabularies is a need that can arise when different researchers use different categorizations to label emotional data. The accuracy was determined by comparing the model's translations with human translations. The author found that mapping from one vocabulary to another resulted in performance of up to 86% when a small output vocabulary was used (chance accuracy of $1/7$) and approaching 50% when a large output vocabulary was used (chance accuracy of $1/40$).

4   Conclusion

The author based his thesis on the following papers, both published and under review. In [14,15,16] attempts at user modeling of human-computer dialogs was undertaken. In particular, [16] examined a scale of user activation level that was obtained by a machine learning technique known as model trees. [17] explored the natural language expressions of common sense psychology concepts, such as concepts like "planning", "execution", "causation", "belief", etc., as they were expressed in text corpora. In [18,19] the first interval type-2 fuzzy logic model of emotions were created and the formal description of this model will be found in [20]. The EMO20Q game was proposed in [21] and the spectral graph analysis is introduced in [22].

References

1. Russell, B.: On denoting. Mind 14, 479–493 (1905)
2. Carnap, R.: The methodological character of theoretical concepts. Minnesota Studies in the Philosophy of Science I, 39–76 (1956)

3. Richardson, J.T.E.: The effect of word imageability in acquired dyslexia. Neuropsychologia 13, 281–288 (1975)
4. Landis, T.: Emotional words: What's so different from just words. Cortex 42, 823–830 (2006)
5. Lakoff, G., Johnson, M.: Metaphors We Live By. University of Chicago Press, Chicago (1980)
6. Gardenfors, P.: Conceptual Spaces: The Geometry of Thought. MIT Press, Cambridge (2000)
7. Mendel, J.M., Wu, D.: Perceptual Computing: Aiding People in Making Subjective Judgements. IEEE Press and John Wiley and Sons, Inc. (2010)
8. Enderton, H.B.: A Mathematical Introduction to Logic, 2nd edn. Academic Press, London (2001)
9. Forster, T.: Logic, Induction, and Sets. Cambridge University Press, Cambridge (2003)
10. Ganter, B., Wille, G.S.R. (eds.): Formal Concept Analysis: foundation and applications. Springer, Berlin (2005)
11. Kunegis, J., Lommatzsch, A., Bauckhage, C.: The slashdot zoo: Mining a social network with negative costs. In: World Wide Web Conference (WWW 2009), Madrid, pp. 741–750 (April 2009)
12. Liu, F., Mendel, J.M.: An interval approach to fuzzistics for interval type-2 fuzzy sets. In: Proceedings of Fuzzy Systems Conference, FUZZ-IEEE (2007)
13. Mishne, G.: Applied Text Analytics for Blogs. PhD thesis, University of Amsterdam (2007)
14. Shin, J., Narayanan, S., Gerber, L., Kazemzadeh, A., Byrd, D.: Analysis of user behavior under error conditions in spoken dialogues. In: ICSLP, Denver (2002)
15. Kazemzadeh, A., Lee, S., Narayanan, S.: Acoustic correlates of user response to errors in human-computer dialogues. In: ASRU, St. Thomas, U.S. Virgin, Islands (2003)
16. Kazemzadeh, A., Lee, S., Narayanan, S.: Using model trees for evaluating dialog error conditions based on acoustic information. In: Proceedings of the 1st ACM International Workshop on Human-Centered Multimedia, Santa Barbara, California, USA, pp. 109–114 (2006)
17. Gordon, A., Kazemzadeh, A., Nair, A., Petrova, M.: Recognizing expressions of commonsense psychology in english text. In: Proceedings of the 41st Annual Meeting on Association for Computational Linguistics, ACL 2003 (2003)
18. Kazemzadeh, A., Lee, S., Narayanan, S.: An interval type-2 fuzzy logic system to translate between emotion-related vocabularies. In: Proceedings of Interspeech, Brisbane, Australia (September 2008)
19. Kazemzadeh, A.: Using interval type-2 fuzzy logic to translate emotion words from spanish to english. In: IEEE World Conference on Computational Intelligence (WCCI) FUZZ-IEEE Workshop (2010)
20. Kazemzadeh, A., Lee, S., Narayanan, S.: An interval type-2 fuzzy logic model for the meaning of words in an emotional vocabulary (2011) (under review)
21. Kazemzadeh, A., Georgiou, P.G., Lee, S., Narayanan, S.: Emotion twenty questions: Toward a crowd-sourced theory of emotions. In: D'Mello, S., et al. (eds.) Proceedings of ACII 2011, Part II, vol. 6975, pp. 1–10. Springer, Heidelberg (2011)
22. Kazemzadeh, A., Lee, S., Georgiou, P.G., Narayanan, S.: Determining what questions to ask, with the help of spectral graph theory. In: Proceedings of Interspeech (2011)

Expressive Gesture Model for Humanoid Robot

Le Quoc Anh and Catherine Pelachaud

CNRS, LTCI Telecom ParisTech, France
{quoc-anh.le,catherine.pelachaud}@telecom-paristech.fr

Abstract. This paper presents an expressive gesture model that generates communicative gestures accompanying speech for the humanoid robot Nao. The research work focuses mainly on the expressivity of robot gestures being coordinated with speech. To reach this objective, we have extended and developed our existing virtual agent platform GRETA to be adapted to the robot. Gestural prototypes are described symbolically and stored in a gestural database, called lexicon. Given a set of intentions and emotional states to communicate the system selects from the robot lexicon corresponding gestures. After that the selected gestures are planned to synchronize speech and then instantiated in robot joint values while taking into account parameters of gestural expressivity such as temporal extension, spatial extension, fluidity, power and repetitivity. In this paper, we will provide a detailed overview of our proposed model.

Keywords: expressive gesture, lexicon, BML, GRETA, NAO.

1 Objectives

Many studies have shown the importance of the expressive gestures in communicating messages as well as in expressing emotions in conversation. They are necessary for speaker to formulate his thoughts [12]. They are also crucial for listeners. For instance they convey complementary, supplementary or even contradictory information to the one indicated by speech [9].

The objective of this thesis is to equip a physical humanoid robot with capability of producing expressive gestures while talking. This research is conducted within the frame of a project of the French Nation Agency for Research, ANR GVLEX that has started since 2009 and lasts for 3 years. The project aims to model a humanoid robot, NAO, developed by Aldebaran [4], able to read a story in an expressive manner to children for several minutes without boring them. In this project, a proposed system takes as input a text to be said by the agent. The text has been enriched with information on the manner the text ought to be said (i.e. with which communicative acts it should be said). The behavioral engine selects the multimodal behaviors to display and synchronizes the verbal and nonverbal behaviors of the agent. While other partners of the GVLEX project deal with expressive voice, our work focuses on expressive behaviors, especially on gestures.

The expressive gesture model is based at first on an existing virtual agent system, the GRETA system [1]. However, using a virtual agent framework for a

S. D´Mello et al. (Eds.): ACII 2011, Part II, LNCS 6975, pp. 224–231, 2011.

physical robot raises several issues to be addressed. Both agent systems, virtual and physical, have different degrees of freedom. Additionally, the robot is a physical entity with a body mass and physical joints which have a limit in movement speed. This is not the case of the virtual agent. Our proposed solution is to use the same representation language to control the virtual agent and the physical agent, here the robot Nao. This allows using the same algorithms for selecting and planning gestures, but different algorithms for creating the animation.

The primary goal of our research is to build an expressive robot able to display communicative gestures with different behavior qualities. In our model, the communicative gestures are ensured to be tightly tied with the speech uttered by the robot. Concerning the gestural expressivity, we have designed and implemented a set of quality dimensions such as the amplitude (SPC), fluidity (FLD), power (PWR) or speed of gestures (TMP) that has been previously developed for the virtual agent Greta [6]. Our model takes into account the physical characteristics of the robot.

2   Methodology

We have extended and developed the GRETA system to be used to control both, virtual and physical, agents. The existing behavior planner module of the GRETA system remains unchanged. On the other hand, a new behavior realizer module and a gestural database have been built to compute and realize the animation of the robot and of the virtual agent respectively. The detail of the developed system is described in the Section 4.

As a whole, the system calculates nonverbal behavior that the robot must show to communicate a text in a certain way. The selection and planning of gestures are based on information that enriches the input text. Once selected, the gestures are planned to be expressive and to synchronize with speech, then they are realized by the robot. To calculate their animation, gestures are transformed into key poses. Each key pose contains joint values of the robot and the timing of its movement. The animation module is script-based. That means the animation is specified and described with the multimodal representation markup language BML [11]. As the robot has some physical constraints, the scripts are calculated making it feasible for the robot.

Gestures of the robot are stored in a library of behaviors, called Lexicon, and described symbolically with an extension of the language BML [11]. These gestures are elaborated using gestural annotations extracted from a storytelling video corpus [14]. Each gesture in robot lexicon should be verified to make it executable for the robot (e.g. avoid collision or singular positions). When gestures are selected and realized, their expressivity is increased by considering a set of six parameters of gestural dimensions [6].

3   State of the Art

Several expressive robots are being developed. Behavior expressivity is often driven using puppeteer technique [13,22]. For example, Xing and co-authors propose to compute robot's expressive gestures by combining a set of primitive movements. The four movement primitives include: walking involving legs movement, swing-arm for keeping the balance in particular while walking, move-arm to reach a point in space and collision-avoid to avoid colliding with wires. A repertoire of gestures is built by combining primitives sequentially or additionally. However this approach is difficult to apply to humanoid robots with a serial motor-linkage structure.

Imitation is also used to drive a robot's expressive behaviors [3,8]. Hiraiwa et al [8] uses EMG signals extracted from a human to drive a robot's arm and hand gesture. The robot replicates the gestures of the human in a quite precise manner. This technique allows communication via the network. Accordingly, the robot can act as an avatar of the human. Another example is Kaspar [3]. Contrary to work aiming at simulating highly realistic human-like robot, the authors are looking for salient behaviors in communication. They define a set of minimal expressive parameters that ensures a rich human-robot interaction. The robot can imitate some of the human's behaviors. It is used in various projects related to developmental studies and interaction games.

In the domain of virtual agents, existing expressivity models either act as filters over an animation or modulate the gesture specification ahead of time. EMOTE implements the effort and shape components of the Laban Movement Analysis [2]. These parameters affect the wrist location of the humanoid. They act as a filter on the overall animation of the virtual humanoid. On the other hand, a model of nonverbal behavior expressivity has been defined that acts on the synthesis computation of a behavior [5]. It is based on perceptual studies conducted by Wallbott [21]. Among a large set of variables that are considered in the perceptual studies, six parameters [6] are retained and implemented in the Greta ECA system. Other works are based on motion capture to acquire the expressivity of behaviors during a physical action, a walk or a run [16].

Recent works have tendency to develop a common architecture to drive gestures of both virtual and physical agent systems. For instance, Salem et al. [20] develop the gesture engine of the virtual agent Max to control the humanoid robot ASIMO through a representation language, namely MURML. Nozawa et al. [18] use a single MPML program to generate pointing gestures for both animated character on 2D screen and humanoid robot in 3D space.

Similarly to the approaches of Salem and Nozawa, we have developed a common BML realizer to control the Greta agent and the NAO robot. Compared to other works, our system focus on implementing the gestural expressivity parameters [6] while taking into account the robot's physical constraints.

4   System Overview

The approach proposed in this thesis relies on the system of the conversational agent Greta following the architecture of SAIBA (cf. Figure 1). It consists of three separated modules [11]: (i) The first module, Intent Planning, defines communicative intents to be conveyed; (ii) The second, Behavior Planning, plans corresponding multimodal behaviors to be realized; (iii) and the third module, Behavior Realizer, synchronizes and realizes the planned behaviors. The results of the first module is the input of the second module through an interface described with a representation markup language, named FML (Function Markup Language). The output of the second module is encoded with another representation language, named BML [11]] and then sent to the third module. Both languages FML and BML are XML-based and do not refer to specific animation parameters of the agent (e.g. wrist joint).

Fig. 1. SAIBA framework for multimodal behavior generation [11]

Aiming at being able to use the same system to control both agents (i.e. the virtual one and the physique one), however, the robot and the agent do not have the same behavior capacities (e.g. the robot can move its legs and torso but does not have facial expression and has very limited arm movements). Therefore the nonverbal behaviors to be displayed by the robot should be different from those of the virtual agent. For instance, the robot has only 2 hand configurations, open and closed; it cannot extend one finger only. Thus, to do a deictic gesture it can make use of its whole right arm to point at a target rather than using an extended index finger as done by the virtual agent. To control communicative behaviors of the robot and the virtual agent, while taking into account the physical constraint of both, two lexicons are taken into consideration, one for the robot and one for the agent. The Behavior Planning module of the GRETA framework remains the same. From the BML file outputted by the Behavior Planner, we instantiate the BML tags from either gestural repertoires. That is, given a set of intentions and emotions to convey, GRETA computes, through the Behavior Planning, the corresponding sequence of behaviors specified with BML. At the Behavior Realizer layer, some extensions are added to be able to generate animation specific to different embodiments (i.e. Nao and Greta). Firstly, the BML message received from Behavior Planner is interpreted and scheduled by a sub-layer called Animations Computation. This module is common for both agents. Then, an embodiment dependent sub-layer, namely Animation Production, generates and executes the animation corresponding to the specific implementation of agent. Figure 2 presents an overview of our system.

To ensure that both the robot and the virtual agent convey similar information, their gestural repertoires should have entries for the same list of communicative intentions. The elaboration of repertoires encompasses the notion of gestural family with variants proposed by Calbris [9]. Gestures from the same

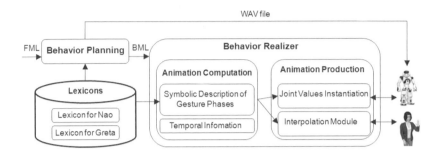

Fig. 2. An overview of the proposed system

family convey similar meanings but may differ in their shape (i.e. the element deictic exists in both lexicons; it corresponds to an extended finger or to an arm extension).

5   Gestural Lexicon

Symbolic gestures are stored in a repertoire of gestures (i.e. gestural lexicon) using an extension of the BML language. We rely on the description of gestures of McNeill [15], the gestural hierarchy of Kendon [10] and some notions from the HamNoSys system [19] to specify a gesture. As a result, a gestural action may be divided into several phases of wrist movement, in which the obligatory phase is called *stroke* transmitting the meaning of the gesture. The stroke may be preceded by a preparatory phase which puts the hand(s) of agent to the position ready for the stroke phase. After that it may be followed by a retraction phase that returns the hand(s) of agent to relax position or a position initialized by the next gesture.

In the lexicon, only the description of stroke phase is specified for each gesture. Other phases will be generated automatically by the system. A stroke phase is represented through a sequence of key poses, each of which is described with the information of hand shape, wrist position, palm orientation, etc.

The elaboration of gestures is based on gestural annotations extracted from a Storytelling Video Corpus [14]. All gestural lexicon are tested to guarantee its realizability on the robot.

6   Behavior Realizer

The main task of Behavior Realizer (BR) is to generate an animation of the agent (virtual or physical) from a BML message. This message contains descriptions of signals, their temporal information and values of expressivity parameters as illustrated in the Figure 3. The process is divided into two main stages. The first stage, called Animation Computation can be used in common for both agents while the second, Animation Production is specific to a given agent. This

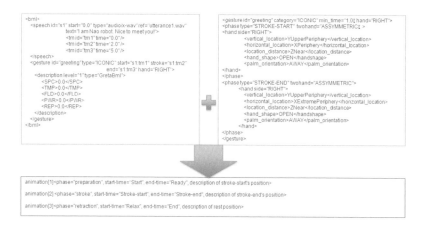

Fig. 3. An example of data processing in Behavior Realizer

architecture is similar to the system proposed by the Heloir et al. [7]. However our solution is different that it aims at different embodiments [17].

6.1   Synchronization of Gestures with Speech

The synchronization is obtained by adapting gestures to the speech structure. The temporal information of gestures in BML tags are relative to the speech by time markers (see Figure 3). The time of each gestural phase is indicated with several sync points (start, ready, stroke-start, stroke, stroke-end, relax, end). Following an observation of McNeill [15], the stroke phase coincides or precedes emphasized words of the speech. Hence the timing of the stroke phase should be indicated in the BML description. Meanwhile the timing of other phases is supposed to be based on the timing of the stroke phase.

6.2   Animation Computation

This module analyses a BML message received from Behavior Planner and loads corresponding gestures from the lexicon. Based on available and necessary time, the module checks if a gesture is executable. Then it calculates symbolic values and timing for each gesture phase while taking into account gestural expressivity parameters (e.g. the duration of gestural stroke phase is decreased when the temporal extension (TMP) is increased and vice-versa).

6.3   Animation Production

In this stage, the system generates the animation by instantiating the symbolic description of the planned gesture phases into joint values thanks to the Joint Values Instantiation module. One symbolic position will be translated into concrete values of six robot joints (ShoulderPitch, ShoulderRoll, ElbowYaw, ElbowRoll, WristYaw, Hand) [17]. Then the animation is obtained by interpolating between joint values with robot built-in proprietary procedures [4].

7   Conclusion and Future Work

We have presented an expressive gesture model that is designed and implemented for the humanoid robot Nao. The model focuses not only on the coordination of gestures and speech but also on the signification and the expressivity of gestures conveyed by the robot. While the gestural signication is studied carefully when elaborating a repertoire of robot gestures (i.e. lexicon), the gestural expressivity is increased by adding the gestural dimension parameters specified by the GRETA system. A procedure creating a gestural lexicon overcoming physical constraints of the robot has been defined.

In the future, we propose to implement all of the expressivity parameters and to valid the model through perceptive evaluations. As well the implementation of gesture animation and expressivity should be evaluated. An objective evaluation will be set to measure the capability of the implementation. A subjective evaluation will be made to test how expressive the gesture animation is perceived on the robot when reading a story.

Acknowledgment. This work has been funded by the GVLEX project (http://www.gvlex.com).

References

1. Pelachaud, C., Gelin, R., Martin, J.-C., Le, Q.A.: Expressive Gestures Displayed by a Humanoid Robot during a Storytelling Application. In: New Frontiers in Human-Robot Interaction (AISB), Leicester, GB (2010)
2. Chi, D., Costa, M., Zhao, L., Badler, N.: The EMOTE model for effort and shape. In: Proceedings of the 27th Annual Conference on Computer Graphics and Interactive Techniques, pp. 173–182 (2000)
3. Dautenhahn, K., Nehaniv, C., Walters, M., Robins, B., Kose-Bagci, H., Mirza, N., Blow, M.: Kaspar–a minimally expressive humanoid robot for human–robot interaction research. Applied Bionics and Biomechanics 6(3), 369–397 (2009)
4. Gouaillier, D., Hugel, V., Blazevic, P., Kilner, C., Monceaux, J., Lafourcade, P., Marnier, B., Serre, J., Maisonnier, B.: Mechatronic design of NAO humanoid. In: Robotics and Automation, ICRA 2009, pp. 769–774. IEEE, Los Alamitos (2009)
5. Hartmann, B., Mancini, M., Pelachaud, C.: Towards affective agent action: Modelling expressive ECA gestures. In: International Conference on Intelligent User Interfaces-Workshop on Affective Interaction, San Diego, CA (2005)
6. Hartmann, B., Mancini, M., Pelachaud, C.: Implementing expressive gesture synthesis for embodied conversational agents. In: Gibet, S., Courty, N., Kamp, J.-F. (eds.) GW 2005. LNCS (LNAI), vol. 3881, pp. 188–199. Springer, Heidelberg (2006)
7. Heloir, A., Kipp, M.: EMBR – A realtime animation engine for interactive embodied agents. In: Ruttkay, Z., Kipp, M., Nijholt, A., Vilhjálmsson, H.H. (eds.) IVA 2009. LNCS, vol. 5773, pp. 393–404. Springer, Heidelberg (2009)

8. Hiraiwa, A., Hayashi, K., Manabe, H., Sugimura, T.: Life size humanoid robot that reproduces gestures as a communication terminal: appearance considerations. In: Computational Intelligence in Robotics and Automation, vol. 1, pp. 207–210. IEEE, Los Alamitos (2003)

9. Iverson, J., Goldin-Meadow, S.: Why people gesture when they speak. Nature 396(6708), 228–228 (1998)

10. Kendon, A.: Gesture: Visible action as utterance. Cambridge University Press, Cambridge (2004)

11. Kopp, S., Krenn, B., Marsella, S., Marshall, A., Pelachaud, C., Pirker, H., Thórisson, K., Vilhjálmsson, H.: Towards a common framework for multimodal generation: The behavior markup language. In: Gratch, J., Young, M., Aylett, R.S., Ballin, D., Olivier, P. (eds.) IVA 2006. LNCS (LNAI), vol. 4133, pp. 205–217. Springer, Heidelberg (2006)

12. Krauss, R.: Why do we gesture when we speak? Current Directions in Psychological Science 7(2), 54–60 (1998)

13. Lee, J., Toscano, R., Stiehl, W., Breazeal, C.: The design of a semi-autonomous robot avatar for family communication and education. In: Robot and Human Interactive Communication (ROMAN 2008), pp. 166–173. IEEE, Los Alamitos (2008)

14. Martin, J.C.: The contact video corpus (2009)

15. McNeill, D.: Hand and mind: What gestures reveal about thought. University of Chicago Press, Chicago (1992)

16. Neff, M., Fiume, E.: Methods for exploring expressive stance. Graphical Models 68(2), 133–157 (2006)

17. Niewiadomski, R., Bevacqua, E., Le, Q., Obaid, M., Looser, J., Pelachaud, C.: Cross-media agent platform. In: 16th International Conference on 3D Web Technology (2011)

18. Nozawa, Y., Dohi, H., Iba, H., Ishizuka, M.: Humanoid robot presentation controlled by multimodal presentation markup language mpml. In: Robot and Human Interactive Communication (ROMAN 2004), pp. 153–158. IEEE, Los Alamitos (2004)

19. Prillwitz, S.: HamNoSys Version 2.0: Hamburg notation system for sign languages: An introductory guide. Signum (1989)

20. Salem, M., Kopp, S., Wachsmuth, I., Joublin, F.: Generating robot gesture using a virtual agent framework. In: Intelligent Robots and Systems (IROS 2010), pp. 3592–3597. IEEE, Los Alamitos (2010)

21. Wallbott, H.: Bodily expression of emotion. European Journal of Social Psychology 28(6), 879–896 (1998)

22. Xing, S., Chen, I.: Design expressive behaviors for robotic puppet. In: Control, Automation, Robotics and Vision (ICARCV 2002), vol. 1, pp. 378–383. IEEE, Los Alamitos (2002)

Emotion Generation Integration into Cognitive Architecture

Jerry Lin

Information Sciences Institute
4676 Admiralty Way, Suite 1001
Marina del Rey, CA 90292
jerrylin@isi.edu

Abstract. Emotions play an important role in human intelligence and human behavior. It has become important to model emotions, especially in the context of cognitive architecture. Current models of emotion are greatly underdetermined by experimental data from psychology, cognitive science, and neuroscience literature. I raise the hypothesis that deeper integration between emotion and cognition will produce models with much greater explanatory power. The thesis is that the use of a semantic associative network as a memory model will serve to both deepen and broaden integration between emotion and cognition. To test this, an affective cognitive architecture will be built with a semantic associative network at its heart, and will be compared to existing models as well as tested against existing experimental data.

1 Introduction

Emotions are an integral part of human existence. The study of emotions has taken place for centuries now. Since the early days of philosophy, emotion was often regarded as only being able to cloud the mind from rational thought.

Modern research by those such as Bechara and Damasio showed that the human mind fails to make normal decisions in the absence of emotions in cognitive processing. These findings contradicted traditional opinions of emotion, and Bechara and Damasio asserted that emotions contain important information to aid cognitive processes, particularly in optimizing benefit of decisions [2].

Interest in computational emotion has emerged in hopes of achieving several goals: improve artificial intelligence to near human level intelligence, improve models of human behavior, improve human computer interaction, and aid in the development of cognitive scientific, psychological, and neuroscientific understanding of emotions. Recently, there has been a resurgence of research activity in the study of emotions.

The fields of cognitive science, psychology, and neuroscience have had a long tradition of emotion theory [24], and this research established that emotion and cognition are intimately connected. This plethora of theory is often self-contradictory and lacks the level of detail about underlying data and processes to be implemented on a computer.

S. D'Mello et al. (Eds.): ACII 2011, Part II, LNCS 6975, pp. 232–239, 2011.
© Springer-Verlag Berlin Heidelberg 2011

Many computational models of emotion have been developed [21, 3, 20, 11, 12]. Nearly all of these models focus on addressing the question of the processes that underlie appraisal and are also subject to the early criticism of AI research by Allen Newell that they are so focused on specifics (i.e. studying just one part of cognition in isolation) that they lose sight of the big picture necessary to understand the human mind [22]. Emotions, unlike other AI cognitive processes, are dependent on all other aspects of cognition, and arguably must be studied in context [6, 5, 8–10, 21] for us to establish a comprehensive computational model. Moreover, neurological study has shown that emotions developed before higher cognitive processes in the human brain, forming a foundation on which the modern mind now acts [23].

The significant computational models all acknowledge the importance of emotion's integration with previous work in cognitive architecture [15]; however, they either avoid addressing the problem entirely or do so in a very limited fashion.

The open questions in interaction between emotion and cognition can be viewed in two areas:

1. Emotional effects - how emotional signals affect cognitive processes such as learning or planning
2. Emotion generation - how cognitive processes play a role in the generation and decay of emotions

This thesis will focus on the latter. Another thesis within the same research group is being worked on in parallel on the former.

2   Problem Statement

Current models of emotion are greatly underdetermined by experimental data from psychology, cognitive science, and neuroscience literature. A computational model of emotion which contains the power to explain the experimental data will require greater integration with existing cognitive architecture research. There has not yet been a set of algorithms, mechanisms, and data structures proposed to allow complete integration of cognitive architectures with emotion generation (or emotion effect), despite the consensus of emotional-cognitive interdependence.

3   Aims and Objectives

The aim of this research is to create a modern cognitive architecture that embodies recent research regarding human intelligence (both rational and irrational behavior) by implementing a set of algorithms, mechanisms, and data structures underlying the architecture which will allow deeper and/or broader integration between well-established theories of emotion and cognition. With deeper integration, a model should predict human behavior with higher accuracy, and with breadth, the model would be able to explain a greater set of phenomena. This set of algorithms, mechanisms, and data structures will be proposed and experimented with within this cognitive architecture. My hypothesis is that techniques can be developed to facilitate better integration of emotion and cognition which will lead to computational models with greater explanatory power than existing models.

The objective of this achievement is to contribute to the original goals of emotions research: improve artificial intelligence to near human level intelligence, improve models of human behavior, improve human computer interaction, and aid in the development of cognitive scientific, psychological, and neuroscientific understanding of emotions.

It is also a hope that the cognitive architecture yielded from this research will provide a state-of-the-art framework for collaborative cognitive systems and AI research.

4   Research Method

The aim of this thesis is to propose a set of algorithms, mechanisms, and data structures which allow well established theories of emotion to be integrated with approaches in cognitive architecture, namely in relation to the semantic associative network. This is based on my hypothesis that techniques can be developed to facilitate better integration of emotion and cognition which will lead to models with greater explanatory power than existing models.

To achieve the proposed contributions, the following landmark activities are planned in the following order:

1. Complete survey on the area of computational emotion generation
2. Study and discuss the necessary components for emotional integration into a cognitive architecture
3. Design a system with these components (EmoCog)
4. Implement EmoCog
5. Empirically evaluate EmoCog's explanatory power in comparison with other models of computational emotion by testing for complex emotional-cognitive phenomena coverage
6. Empirically evaluate EmoCog's predictive power with respect to rigorously reviewed experimental data by testing if EmoCog can reproduce observed data
7. Deploy EmoCog to a problem domain then observe and report results, post evaluation

5   Proposed Approach

The approach was developed with two main bodies of work laying the groundwork. Those works being work done on emotions and memory by Bower [7, 6] where he developed the associative network theory of emotion [5] and work done on computational models of emotion, namely EMA [21] the idea of appraisal frames were clearly and usefully modeled. Bower's student, J. Anderson later used similar ideas to develop a model of memory which worked well with a complete cognitive architecture (ACT-R) [1], though void of emotions. Other major works in cognitive architecture have also influenced the choices made in this approach, namely Soar [13], ICARUS [14], and CLARION [25], and their use of associative memory variants as well as choice of cognitive components.

The blackboard approach has been the dominant method for interaction between heterogeneous cognitive processes in most cognitive architectures, which leads to the conjecture that the memory substrate that serves as the blackboard, is the foundation to integration between components. Appraisal theory poses emotions arising from a series of cognitive processes, namely appraisal. This led to the choice to study a blackboard memory structure that would better serve the generation and use of complex emotional data. Since both affective and cognitive processes have been demonstrated with associative networks, they served as a firm starting point.

The representation of appraisals is non-trivial within associative networks. This is why the novel idea of using semantic links and valence and arousal on individual nodes within the associative network was introduced. Instead of keeping an appraisal frame associated with a specific concept or schemata, various semantic links can be built to represent appraisals. For an example, in the case of a causal agent of an event, a causal semantic link is created between the event and the agent schemata.

With this semantic associative network are a set of algorithms and mechanisms which are all non-trivial tasks in one or more other models. These algorithms and mechanisms are the second novel propositions which will serve to broaden the emotional-cognitive phenomena coverage of the overall architecture.

This finally leads to the construction of various hypotheses and experiments which will serve as the body of my thesis and series of upcoming publications.

6   Progress to Date

Currently items 1 - 3 have been completed but require continuous updating. The survey is always evolving to include new work since this is a very active area of research and many disciplines are relevant.

A paper with the initial arguments and discussion for the components for emotional integration has been produced, addressing item 2 [18]. To do this, we cited a set of four normative emotional phenomena and the experimental data associated with it. An example of this is incidental emotion or emotion which is unrelated to the task or decision at hand. Studies have shown that if sad music plays while a customer shops, the customer will spend more money and be less discriminating with purchases [16]. We identified the theoretical constructs appraisal, emotional arousal and decay, associative memory, emotional

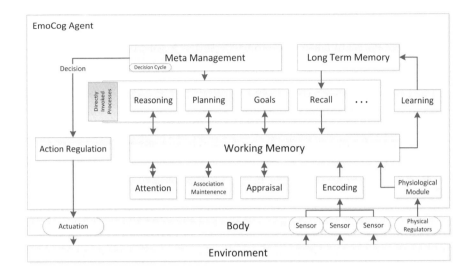

Fig. 1. EmoCog Cognitive Architecture

memory, expectation and alternate possibility generation, and mood as central to emotional integration. We raised the hypothesis that these theoretical constructs are sufficient to address all the phenomena and any architecture includes a strict subset of these ideas would lack the power to explain the entire set of phenomena.

An initial system design (item 3) has been proposed and submitted for discussion and has been published in the FLAIRS-24 conference affective computing track [19]. A high level architectural is shown as figure 1. Here is where many of EmoCog's technical details have been presented, identifying some of the mechanisms and data underlying the computation. Of special note is our decision cycle, currently conceived as part of a metacognitive process which deliberates on the time spent acting as well as cognitively elaborating. This design is also naturally a continuously evolving artifact. It will evolve with the selection and function of components from item 2 with a scope likely adjusted constantly depending on resources.

The implementation of our system, EmoCog, has begun and we currently have a very basic agent running. Most of the vital pieces for emotional competency are not yet in place. Some version which should be capable for use in early experiments addressing items 5 - 7 is expected early next year. Figure 2 shows the current implementation structure with the modules which are currently operating shaded.

We also have an interesting problem domain which we have spent time studying which will aid in addressing item 7. That is modeling human behaviors, including the various imperfections we are perceived to have, in a security simulation test range. Discussion of the greater impact of this approach as well as some of our experiences have been reported [17, 4].

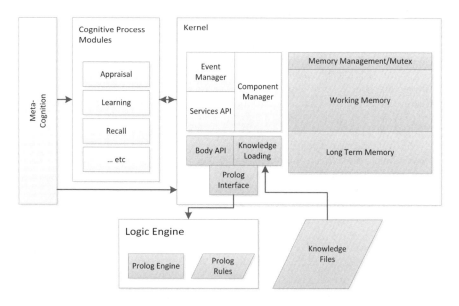

Fig. 2. EmoCog Implementation Structure Block Diagram

7 Contributions to Affective Computing

The main contributions of this research can be summarized in the following list:

1. An architectural framework, built to allow flexible and open-ended experimentation of interplay between emotional and cognitive processes.
2. Computational model of emotion built from the ground up, where emotion is integrated at every level of cognitive architecture.
3. Improve explanatory and predictive power of modern computational models of emotion.

References

1. Anderson, J.R., Bothell, D., Byrne, M.D., Douglass, S., Lebiere, C., Qin, Y.: An Integrated Theory of the Mind. Psychological Review 111(4), 1036–1060 (2004), http://www.ncbi.nlm.nih.gov/pubmed/15482072
2. Bechara, A., Damasio, H., Damasio, A.: Emotion, decision making and the orbitofrontal cortex. Cerebral Cortex (2000), http://cercor.oxfordjournals.org/cgi/content/abstract/10/3/295
3. Becker-Asano, C., Wachsmuth, I.: Affective computing with primary and secondary emotions in a virtual human. Autonomous Agents and Multi-Agent Systems 20(1), 32–49 (2009), http://www.springerlink.com/index/10.1007/s10458-009-9094-9
4. Botello, A., Lin, J., Mozzacco, D., Sutton, J.E., Spraragen, M., Blythe, J., Zyda, M.: An Agent Architecture for Large-scale Security Simulation. Tech. rep. Information Sciences Institute, Marina del Rey, CA (2011)

5. Bower, G.: Mood and Memory. American Psychologist (1981),
   http://psycnet.apa.org/
   ?fa=main.doiLanding&fuseaction=showUIDAbstract
6. Bower, G.: Affect and Cognition. Philosophical Transactions of the Royal Society of London B(302), 387–402 (1983)
7. Bower, G.: How might emotions affect learning (1992)
8. Cosmides, L., Tooby, J.: Evolutionary Psychology and the Emotions (2000),
   http://www.psych.ucsb.edu/research/cep/emotion.html
9. D'Mello, S., Person, N., Lehman, B.: Antecedent-Consequent Relationships and Cyclical Patterns between Affective States and Problem Solving Outcomes. In: Proceedings of 14th International Conference on Artificial Intelligence In Education, pp. 57–64. IOS Press, Amsterdam (2009),
   http://emotion.autotutor.org/files/dmello-aps-aied09.pdf
10. Finucane, M.L., Alhakami, A., Slovic, P., Johnson, S.M.: The affect heuristic in judgments of risks and benefits. Journal of Behavioral Decision Making 13(1), 1–17 (2000),
    http://doi.wiley.com/10.1002/%28SICI%291099-0771%28200001/03
    %2913%3A1%3C1%3A%3AAID-BDM333%3E3.0.CO%3B2-S
11. Fum, D., Stocco, A.: Memory, emotion, and rationality: An ACT-R interpretation for Gambling Task results. In: Proceedings of the Sixth International Conference on Cognitive Modelling, Lawrence Erlbaum, Citeseer, Mahwah, NJ (2004),
    http://citeseerx.ist.psu.edu/viewdoc/download?doi=10.1.1.139.9815
    &rep=rep1&type=pdf
12. Hudlicka, E.: Reasons for Emotions: Modeling Emotions in Integrated Cognitive Systems, pp. 1–37 (2007)
13. Laird, J.: Extending the Soar Cognitive Architecture. In: Proceeding of the 2008 Conference on Artificial General Intelligence 2008: Proceedings of the First AGI Conference, Amsterdam, pp. 224–235 (2008),
    http://portal.acm.org/citation.cfm?id=1566174.1566195
14. Langley, P., Choi, D.: A Unified Cognitive Architecture for Physical Agents. In: Proceedings of the Twenty-First National Conference on Artificial Intelligence, vol. 21. AAAI Press, Boston (2006),
    http://www.aaai.org/Papers/AAAI/2006/AAAI06-231.pdf
15. Langley, P., Laird, J., Rogers, S.: Cognitive architectures: Research issues and challenges. Cognitive Systems Research 10(2), 141–160 (2009),
    http://linkinghub.elsevier.com/retrieve/pii/S1389041708000557
16. Lerner, J.S., Small, D.A., Loewenstein, G.: Heart Strings and Purse Strings: Carryover Effects of Emotions on Economic Decisions. Psychological Science 15(5), 337–341 (2004), http://www.ncbi.nlm.nih.gov/pubmed/15102144
17. Lin, J., Blythe, J., Clark, S., Davarpanah, N., Hughston, R., Zyda, M.: Unbelievable Agents for Large Scale Security Simulation. In: Working Notes for the 2010 AAAI Workshop on Intelligent Security, Atlanta, Georgia, pp. 20–25 (2010),
    http://ncr.isi.edu/papers/SecArt10.pdf
18. Lin, J., Blythe, J., Zyda, M.: Foundation for Emotion Capable Cognitive Architectures. In: Under Review (2011)
19. Lin, J., Spraragen, M., Blythe, J., Zyda, M.: EmoCog: Computational Integration of Emotion and Cognitive Architecture. In: Proceedings of the Twenty-Fourth FLAIRS Conference (2011)
20. Marinier, R., Laird, J., Lewis, R.: A computational unification of cognitive behavior and emotion. Cognitive Systems Research (2009),
    http://linkinghub.elsevier.com/retrieve/pii/S1389041708000302

21. Marsella, S., Gratch, J.: EMA: A process model of appraisal dynamics. Cognitive Systems Research (2009),
    http://linkinghub.elsevier.com/retrieve/pii/S1389041708000314
22. Newell, A.: Unified Theories of Cognition. Harvard University Press, Cambridge (1990),
    http://scholar.google.com/scholar?hl=en&q=newell+unified+theories+of +cognition&btnG=Search&as_sdt=2000&as_ylo=&as_vis=0#7
23. Panksepp, J.: The Neuro-Evolutionary Cusp Between Emotions and Cognitions Emergence of a Unified Mind Science 1. Evolution and Cognition 7(2), 141–163 (2001)
24. Schorr, A.: Appraisal: The evolution of an idea, pp. 20–33 (2001),
    http://scholar.google.com/scholar?q=Appraisal:+The+evolution+of+an+idea &hl=en&btnG=Search&as_sdt=2001&as_sdtp=on#0
25. Sun, R.: The CLARION cognitive architecture: Extending cognitive modeling to social simulation. Cognition and Multi-Agent Interaction: From Cognitive… (2006),
    http://books.google.com/books?hl=en&lr=&id=V1RyhTamPkgC&oi=fnd &pg=PA79&dq=clarion+cognitive+architecture &ots=ilG2lKwCzV&sig=iHZYBIWKeaAUDQLoOIq_8Lwrq5o

Emotion Recognition Using Hidden Markov Models from Facial Temperature Sequence

Zhilei Liu and Shangfei Wang*

Key Lab of Computing and Communicating Software of AnHui Province
School of Computer Science and Technology
University of Science and Technology of China
HeFei, AnHui, P.R. China
leivo@mail.ustc.edu.cn, sfwang@ustc.edu.cn

Abstract. In this paper, an emotion recognition from facial temporal sequence has been proposed. Firstly, the temperature difference histogram features and five statistical features are extracted from the facial temperature difference matrix of each difference frame in the data sequences. Then the discrete Hidden Markov Models are used as the classifier for each feature. In which, a feature selection strategy based on the recognition results in the training set is introduced. Finally, the results of the experiments on the samples of the USTC-NVIE database demonstrate the effectiveness of our method. Besides, the experiment results also demonstrate that the temperature information of the forehead is more useful than that of the other regions in emotion recognition and understanding, which is consistent with some related research results.

Keywords: emotion recognition, facial temporal sequence, Hidden Markov Models.

1 Introduction

As the development of Human-Computer Interaction (HCI) in the domain of health care, service robotic, security industry, gaming and so on, emotional HCI has attracted more and more attentions in the past few years, in which, proper understanding of human emotions is a key problem to be solved first.

Human's emotions could be manifested in various ways, including both the external signals, such as facial expressions, body gestures, speech and so on, and some internal signals, such as blood flow, heart rate, EEG, body temperature and so on [7]. Compared to the emotion recognition using other signals, the emotion recognition based on the temperature information reflected through the infrared thermal images may be more practical because of its non-invasive and non-verbal characteristics [5], [7], [8], [13]. Generally speaking, two kinds of features extracted from the infrared thermal data are considered in most of existing researches, the first one is the imaging features extracted from the infrared thermal images, for instance: Benjamín Hernández, Gustavo Olague et al. selected

---

* This author is the corresponding author.

S. D´Mello et al. (Eds.): ACII 2011, Part II, LNCS 6975, pp. 240–247, 2011.

the Gray Level Co-occurrence Matrix (GLCM) to compute region descriptors of the infrared images and used them to distinguish the expressions of surprise, happiness and anger [14], Guotai Jiang et al. conducted the facial expression recognition through drawing and analyzing the whole geometry characteristics and some geometry characteristics of the ROI in infrared images by using mathematics morphology [15], Yasunari Yoshitomi et al. extracted the features by using a two-dimensional discrete cosine transformation (2D-DCT) to transform the gray scale values of each block in the face portion of an infrared image into frequency components, and these features were used in their expression recognition systems [9]; the other feature is the temperature feature recorded by infrared cameras, such as: Masood Mehmood Khan et al. have tried to use the variances in the thermal intensity values recorded at thermally significant locations on human faces as the features to discern some pretended expressions as well as the pretended and the evoked emotional expressions [10], [11], Brain R. Nhan and Tom Chau have extracted the time, frequency and time-frequency features derived from 12 adults' thermal infrared data to classify the natural responses of subject-indicated levels of arousal and valence stimulated by the International Affective Picture System [6], A. Merla and G. L. Romani have studied the facial thermal signatures of 10 healthy volunteers' three fundamental emotional conditions: stress, fear and pleasure arousal [12]. All these works have shown that the human's emotion states or expressions are relevant to the properties of the facial temperature. However, to our best knowledge, most researches extracted the features from a single apex or onset and apex infrared thermal data or images, only a few features are extracted from the emotional data sequences, which may lose some useful information contained in the sequences [16].

In this paper, an emotion recognition method using the temporal information of the facial temperature data is provided. Firstly, the temperature data of the facial region are extracted and segmented into some facial sub regions. Secondly, the temperature difference histogram features (TDHFs) and five statistic features (StaFs) are extracted from each facial sub region's temperature difference matrix obtained from two consecutive frames in the sequences. Thirdly, a feature selection strategy based on each feature's recognition ability on the training data is used, and these selected features are used in some discrete Hidden Markov Models (HMMs) to recognize the emotion states. Experiments performed on the samples selected from the USTC-NVIE database [1] are implemented to verify the effectiveness of this method. Compared with other researches, the contribution of this paper is that the temporal information of the human facial temperature data in different emotion states is fully considered, and our research is one of the first concerted attempts at emotion recognition using the temporal information of human's facial temperature data sequences.

The remainder of the paper is organized as follows. The details of our approach are explained in Section 2, experiments and results conducted on the USTC-NVIE database are given in Section 3, finally, some conclusions and future works are described in Section 4.

2   Methodology

The schematic representation of our approach is shown as Fig. 1, which could be divided into four modules, named data preprocessing and feature extraction, feature selection and classification. The details are provided as follows.

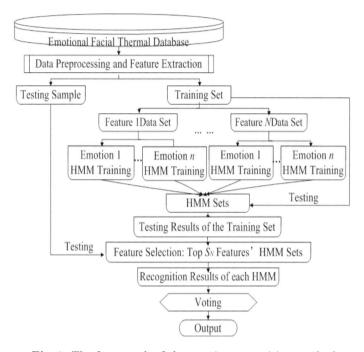

Fig. 1. The framework of the emotion recognition method

2.1   Data Preprocessing and Feature Extraction

The temperature variations of the objects could be detected by an infrared thermal camera based on the objects' infrared radiations and the black body radiation law. Firstly, the temperature data of each frame is converted into a gray-scale image, which is used to obtain the facial region's temperature data. Secondly, it is difficult to achieve automatic location of the feature points in the infrared image due to its low resolution and low contrast, for this reason, three points P_l, P_r and P_n are marked manually in our approach, which are the centers of the both eyes and the nose tip. After that, the facial region's temperature

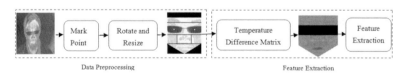

Fig. 2. The procedure of data preprocessing and feature extraction

is determined and marked out based on these three points. Thirdly, the facial region's temperature data matrix is rotated based on the angle of the P_l and P_r in the horizontal direction and resized based on the distance of P_l and P_r and the distance between the P_n and the connection line of P_l and P_r. Finally, this facial mask's temperature matrix is obtained as shown in Fig. 2, and this facial mask is divided into five regions, named forehead, eye, nose, mouth and cheek.

For each facial sub-region, the temperature difference matrix (DMat) between two consecutive frames could be obtained, from which some features are extracted. In this paper, two kinds of features are extracted, named temperature difference histogram features (TDHFs) and statistical features (StaFs). TDHF describes the data distribution of the DMat, which is similar to the gray level histogram of a gray image. Suppose the size of DMat is $M \times N$, the lower limit and the upper limit of the DMat data are L and U separately, and the dimension of the TDHF is D, then the TDHF of DMat could be defined as formula (1).

$$TDHF(i) = \frac{\sum_{m=1}^{M} \sum_{n=1}^{N} [T(i-1)) < DMat(m,n) \leq T(i)]}{M \times N} \tag{1}$$

In which, $i = 1, 2, ..., D$, $T(i) = L + \frac{(U-L) \times i}{D}$ is the endpoint of the i-th interval and $TDHF(i)$ is the frequency of data points between the interval of $(T(i-1), T(i)]$ in DMat.

Besides, five StaFs are also extracted from each DMat, which are: VAR, which is the variance of the DMat; MEAN, which is the mean of DMat; ADDP and ADDN, which represent the mean of positive and negative values of DMat; ABS which is the mean of absolute values of DMat.

Thus, D-dimensional TDHFs and 5-dimensional StaFs are extracted from each DMat of each facial sub region in the recording temperature sequence.

2.2   Feature Selection Strategy

In our method, a feature selection strategy based on each feature's recognition results in the training set is considered. Suppose N-dimensional features have been extracted and the classifier of each feature could be trained by using the training set at first. Next, for each feature, the recognition results of the samples in the training set could be obtained through these well trained classifiers. After that, these features are sorted based on their average recognition rates in the training set. Finally, the classifiers of S_N best selected features with the highest S_N average recognition rates are selected and used in the testing phase.

2.3   Emotion Recognition Using HMMs

HMM is a statistical Markov model in which the system being modeled is assumed to be a Markov process with unobserved states, which could be well applied in the classification problem based on sequence features, especially known for its application in temporal pattern recognition such as speech, handwriting, gesture recognition and so on [2], [4]. In this paper, the discrete HMM is adopted as the classifier for each feature by using the HMM toolbox for Matlab [3].

Before the classification, the feature data quantization of each dimension is performed. Take the i-th dimension feature data $F(i)$ of all the samples as the example, these data are normalized into the interval of $[0, 1]$ and the probability distribution between 0 and 1 is calculated at first. Suppose the feature data are quantified to 1,2,...,N, which is the same as the number of the state variable in the HMMs, then the data within the probability distribution interval of $[\frac{(m-1)}{N}, \frac{(m)}{N})$ are quantified as m, in which $m = 1, 2, ..., N$.

Next, for the feature of each dimension in each facial sub region, n different HMMs are established for n-different specific emotion states respectively in the model training phase. Thus, $(D + 5) \times 5 \times n$ HMMs are constructed in our method. In the model testing phase, a test sample's recognition result of i-th feature is determined based on the category of the HMM with the maximum log-likelihood value of these n specific HMMs, and this sample's final emotion state is determined by the voting strategy based on these recognition results of $(D + 5) \times 5$ features.

3   Experiments and Results

3.1   Experimental Conditions

The samples in our experiment are selected from the USTC-NVIE database [1], which contains both spontaneous and posed expressional images of more than 100 subjects, recorded simultaneously by a visible and an infrared thermal camera, with illumination provided from three different directions. In each experiment, subject's emotions are elicited by watching some emotional videos and reported in the self-reported data including the evaluation value of the six basic emotions, named happiness, disgust, fear, sad, surprise and anger, on 5-point scale. This self-reported data are used to determine the emotion label of this subject when watching this emotional video. Based on the analysis results in [1], three emotions are considered in this paper, that is happiness, disgust and fear, which have the greatest impact to the facial temperature among these six emotions, and 176 samples' temperature data sequences are selected and used in the following experiments, including 69 happiness, 42 disgust and 65 fear. All these samples' self-report data about the primary emotion category are larger than 1.

The size of the facial mask is 80×84. As most of the subjects wore glasses, thereby masking the thermal features of the eye region, then eye regions is not taken into account in our experiment. The lower and upper limits of the DMat are -10 and 10, and the dimension of the TDHF is 20. Thus, for each facial sub region, 20 TDHFs and 5 StaFs are extracted.

In these discrete HMMs, the feature data are quantified into 1,2,...,12, which is the same as the number of state variable in our paper, the number of the observed variable is 12. In the training phase, the Baum-Welch estimation method is used, and the initial probability vector P, state transition matrix A and observation

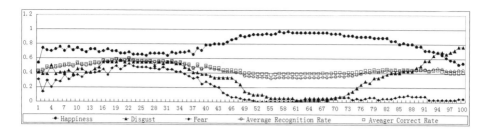

Fig. 3. The recognition rates with different number of selected features

probabilities matrix B are all random initialized. The leave-one-sample-out cross-validation is adopted in the following experiments.

3.2   Results and Analysis

Experiments with different number of the selected features are conducted, the results are shown as Fig. 3, in which, the recognition rate of each emotion state, the average recognition rate and average correct rate are described.

From Fig. 3, we could find that when the number of the selected feature is 22 the best overall recognition results are achieved, that is, the recognition rates of happiness, disgust and fear are 0.68116, 0.57143 and 0.52308 respectively, the average recognition rate and average correct rate are 0.59189 and 0.59660 respectively. When the classification is conducted without feature selection, in other words, the selected feature number is 100, the recognition rates of happiness, disgust and fear are 0.53623, 0.76191 and 0.04615 respectively, the average recognition rate and average correct rate are 0.44810 and 0.40910, which verifies the effectiveness of the feature selection strategy in our method.

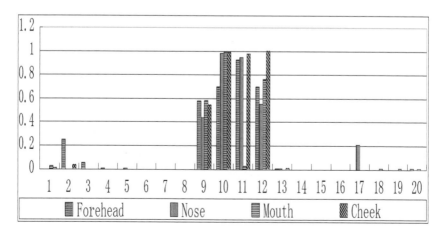

Fig. 4. The probability distribution of the TDHF features in each facial sub-region

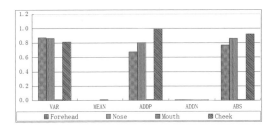

Fig. 5. The probability distribution of the StaFs features in each facial sub-region

Table 1. The distribution the best selected features

	Forehead	Nose	Mouth	Cheek
TDHF	9,10,11,12	10,11,12	9,10,12	9,10,11,12
StaF	VAR,ADDP,MEAN	VAR,ADDP,MEAN	NULL	VAR,ADDP,MEAN

Next, the distributions of all the features in each facial sub region of all the samples are analyzed as follows when the number of the selected features is set to 22. The probability distribution of the 20-TDHFs and five StaFs in four facial sub region are described in Fig. 4 and Fig. 5, and the distributions of these 22 best selected features with the highest recognition rates in each facial region are shown in Table 1, from which we conclude that:

1) From Fig. 4 and Fig. 5, we could find that the most used HDTFs are in 9-12 dimensions, and the most used StaFs are VAR, ADDP and ABS;

2) Most of the best selected features are belong to the forehead region, which indicates that forehead's temperature features are more useful than the other regions', however, the mouth region's features are the least, especially for the StaFs, no one is included, which means that these StaFs of temperature data in the mouth are inadequate to represent these emotion states, all these results are consistent with the analysis in [1], [17].

4   Conclusion and Future Work

In this paper, an emotion recognition method based on the temporal information of the human facial temperature data and discrete HMMs is introduced, in which, a feature selection strategy based on the recognition result of the training set is adopted to improve the overall recognition rate. Finally, experiments on the samples selected from the USTC-NVIE database are implemented to verify the effectiveness of our method.

Some additional works are necessary to improve the accuracy of the recognition before the practical applications can be realized, for example, the automatic facial location and feature extraction, parameter optimization in the classifiers, the decision strategy of the final results and so on, all these works will be completed in the future.

Acknowledgments. The authors would like to thank all the subjects who participated in the experiments. This work is supported by National Program 863 (2008AA01Z122), Youth Creative Project of USTC and SRF for ROCS, SEM.

References

1. Wang, S., Liu, Z., Lv, S., Lv, Y., Wu, G., Peng, P., Chen, F., Wang, X.: A Natural Visible and Infrared Facial Expression Database for Expression Recognition and Emotion Inference. IEEE Transactions on Multimedia, 682–691 (2010)
2. Cohen, I., Garg, A., Huang, T.S.: Emotion recognition from facial expressions using multilevel HMM. In: NIPS (2000)
3. Hidden Markov Model Toolbox for Matlab,
   http://www.cs.ubc.ca/~murphyk/Software/HMM/hmm.html
4. Nefian, A.V., Liang, L., Pi, X., Xiaoxiang, L., Mao, C., Murphy, K.: A coupled HMM for audio-visual speech recognition. In: International Conference on Acoustics, Speech and Signal Processing CASSP 2002, pp. 2013–2016 (2002)
5. Puri, C., Olson, L., Pavlidis, I., Levine, J., Starren, J.: StressCam: non-contact measurement of users' emotional states through thermal imaging. In: CHI Extended Abstracts, pp. 1725–1728 (2005)
6. Nhan, B.R., Chau, T.: Classifying affective states using thermal infrared imaging of the human face. IEEE Transaction on Biomedical Engineering 57(4), 979–987 (2010)
7. Gunes, H., Pantic, M.: Automatic, Dimensional and Continuous Emotion Recognition. International Journal of Synthetic Emotions 1(1), 68–99 (2010)
8. Pavlidis, I., Levine, J.: Thermal image analysis for polygraph testing. IEEE Engineering in Medicine and Biology Magazine 21(6), 56–64 (2002)
9. Yoshitomi, Y.: Facial Expression Recognition for Speaker Using Thermal Image Processing and Speech Recognition System. In: Proc. of 10th WSEAS International Conference on Applied Computer Science, pp. 182–186 (2010)
10. Khan, M.M.: Cluster-analytic classification of facial expressions using infrared measurements of facial thermal features. Ph.D. Thesis, Department of Computing and Engineering, University of Huddersfield, Huddersfield, UK (2008)
11. Khan, M.M., Ward, R.D., Ingleby, M.: Classifying pretended and evoked facial expressions of positive and negative affective states using infrared measurement of skin temperature. Trans. Appl. Percept. 6, 1 (2009)
12. Merla, A., Romani, G.L.: Thermal signatures of emotional arousal: A functional infrared imaging study. In: IEEE 29th Annu. Int. Conf., pp. 247–249 (2007)
13. Calvo, R.A., D'Mello, S.: Affect Detection: An Interdisciplinary Review of Models, Methods, and Their Applications. IEEE Transactions on Affective Computing 1(1), 18–37 (2010)
14. Hernández, B., Olague, G., Hammoud, R., Trujillo, L., Romero, E.: Visual learning of texture descriptors for facial expression recognition in thermal imagery. Computer Vision and Image Understanding 106(2-3), 258–269 (2007)
15. Jiang, G., Song, X., Zheng, F., Wang, P., Omer, A.M.: Facial Expression Recognition Using Thermal Image. In: 27th Annual International Conference of the Engineering in Medicine and Biology Society, IEEE-EMBS 2005, pp. 631–633, 17–18 (2006)
16. Bassili, J.N.: Emotion recognition: The role of facial movement and the relative importance of upper and lower areas of the face. J. Personality Social Psychology 37, 2049–2058 (1979)
17. Merla, A., Romani, G.L.: Thermal signatures of emotional arousal: A functional infrared imaging study. In: Proc. IEEE 29th Annu. Int. Conf., pp. 247–249 (2007)

Interpreting Hand-Over-Face Gestures

Marwa Mahmoud and Peter Robinson

University of Cambridge

Abstract. People often hold their hands near their faces as a gesture in natural conversation, which can interfere with affective inference from facial expressions. However, these gestures are valuable as an additional channel for multi-modal inference. We analyse hand-over-face gestures in a corpus of naturalistic labelled expressions and propose the use of those gestures as a novel affect cue for automatic inference of cognitive mental states. We define three hand cues for encoding hand-over-face gestures, namely hand shape, hand action and facial region occluded, serving as a first step in automating the interpretation process.

1   Introduction

Nonverbal communication plays a central role in how humans communicate and empathize with each other. The ability to read nonverbal cues is essential to understanding, analyzing, and predicting the actions and intentions of others. As technology becomes more ubiquitous and ambient, machines will need to sense and respond to natural human behaviour. Over the past few years, there has been an increased interest in machine understanding and recognition of people's affective and cognitive states, especially based on facial analysis. One of the main factors that limit the accuracy of facial analysis systems is hand occlusion.

Hand-over-face gestures, a subset of emotional body language, are overlooked by automatic affect inferencing systems. Many facial analysis systems are based on geometric or appearance facial feature extraction or tracking. As the face becomes occluded, facial features are either lost, corrupted or erroneously detected, resulting in an incorrect analysis of the person's facial expression. Figure 1 shows a feature point tracker in an affect inference system [11] failing to detect the mouth borders in the presence of hand occlusion. Only a few systems recognise facial expressions in the presence of partial face occlusion, either by estimation of lost facial points [2,17] or by excluding the occluded face area from the classification process [6]. In all these systems, face occlusions are a nuisance and are treated as noise, even though they carry useful information.

This research proposes an alternative facial processing framework, where face occlusions instead of being removed, are combined with facial expressions and head gestures to help in machine understanding and interpretation of different mental states. We present an analysis of hand-over-face gestures in a naturalistic video corpus of complex mental states. We define three hand cues for encoding hand-over-face gestures, namely hand shape, hand action and facial region occluded and provide a preliminary assessment of the use of depth data in detecting hand shape and action on the face.

S. D´Mello et al. (Eds.): ACII 2011, Part II, LNCS 6975, pp. 248–255, 2011.
© Springer-Verlag Berlin Heidelberg 2011

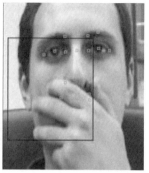

Fig. 1. In existing facial expression recognition systems hand-over-face occlusions are treated as noise

2   Why Hands?

From kinesics, the study and interpretation of non-verbal behaviour related to movement, the movement of the body, or separate parts, conveys many specific meanings. Ekman and Friesen [7] developed a classification system identifying five types of body movements; in most of them, hand gestures constitute an important factor and they contribute to how emotions are expressed and interpreted by others. Human interpretation of different social interactions in a variety of situations is most accurate when people are able to observe both the face and the body. Ambady and Rosenthal [1] have observed that ratings of human understanding of a communication based on the face and the body are 35% more accurate than the ratings based on the face alone.

Although researchers focus on facial expressions as the main channel for social emotional communication, de Gelder [4] suggests that there are similarities between how the brain reacts to emotional body language signals and how facial expressions are recognized. Hand-over-face gestures are not redundant information; they can emphasize the affective cues communicated through facial expressions and speech and give additional information to a communication. De Gelder's studies reveal substantial overlap between the face and the hand conditions, with other areas involved besides the face area in the brain. When the observed hand gesture was performed with emotion, additional regions in the brain were seen to be active emphasizing and adding meaning to the affective cue interpreted. In situations where face and body expressions do not provide the same meaning, experiments showed that recognition of the facial expression was biased towards the emotion expressed by the body language [5].

There is ample evidence that the spontaneous gestures we produce when we talk reflect our thoughts - often thoughts not conveyed in our speech [9]. Moreover, gesture goes well beyond reflecting our thoughts, to playing a role in shaping them. In teaching contexts, for example, children are more likely to profit from instruction when the instruction includes gesture - whether from the student or

Fig. 2. The meaning conveyed by different hand-over-face gestures according to Pease and Pease [15]

the teacher - than when it does not. Teachers who use gestures as they explain a concept are more successful at getting their ideas across, and students who spontaneously gesture as they work through new ideas tend to remember them longer than those who do not move their hands [3]. Gesture during instruction encourages children to produce gestures of their own, which, in turn, leads to learning.

3   Hand-Over-Face Gestures in Natural Expressions

In *The Definitive Book of Body Language*, Pease and Pease [15] attempt to identify the meaning conveyed by different hand-over-face gestures, as shown in Figure 2. Although they suggest that different positions and actions of the hand occluding the face can imply different affective states, no quantitative analysis has been carried out.

Studying hand-over-face gestures in natural expressions is a challenging task since most available video corpora lacked one or more factors that are crucial for our analysis. For instance, MMI [14] and CK+ [12] don't have upper body videos or hand gestures, while BU-4DEF [16] and FABO [10] datasets contain only posed non-naturalistic data. That was one of the motivations for building Cam3D, which is a 3D multi-modal corpus of natural complex mental states. The corpus includes labelled videos of spontaneous facial expressions and hand gestures of 12 participants. Data collection tasks were designed to elicit natural expressions. Participants were from diverse ethnic backgrounds and with varied

| Bored | Happy | Thinking | Thinking | Unsure |

| Thinking | Thinking | Thinking | Thinking |

Fig. 3. Different hand shape, action and face region occluded are affective cues in interpreting different mental states

fields of work and study. For more details on Cam3D, refer to Mahmoud et al. [13].

We have analysed hand-over-face gestures and their possible meaning in spontaneous expressions. By studying the videos in Cam3D, we argue that hand-over-face gestures occur frequently and can also serve as affective cues. Figure 3 presents sample frames from the labelled segments of hand-over-face gestures.

Hand-over-face gestures appeared in 21% of the video segments (94 segments), with 16% in the computer-based session and 25% in the dyadic interaction session. Participants varied in how much they gestured, some exhibited a lot of gestures while others only had a few. Looking at the place of the hand on the face in this subset of the 94 hand-over-face segments, the hand covered upper face regions in 13% of the segments and lower face regions in 89% of them, with some videos having the hand overlapping both upper and lower face regions. This indicates that in naturalistic interactions hand-over-face gestures are very common and that hands usually cover lower face regions, especially chin, mouth and lower cheeks, more than upper face regions.

3.1   Coding of Hand Gestures

Looking for possible affective meaning in those gestures, we introduced a preliminary coding of hand gestures. we encoded hand-over-face gestures in terms of three cues: hand shape, hand action and facial region occluded by the hand. These three cues can differentiate and define different meaningful gestures. Moreover, coding of hand-over-face gestures serves as a first step in automating the process of interpreting those gestures.

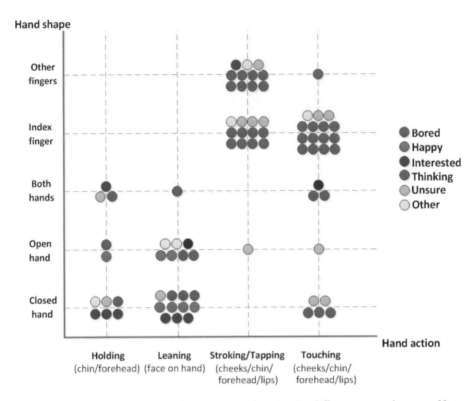

Fig. 4. Encoding of hand-over-face shape and action in different mental states. Note the significance of the index finger actions in cognitive mental states.

Figure 4 shows the distribution of the mental states in each category of the encoded hand-over-face gestures. For example, index finger touching face appeared in 12 *thinking* segments and 2 *unsure* segments out of a total of 15 segments in this category. The mental states distribution indicates that passive hand-over-face gestures, like leaning on the closed or open hand, appear in different mental states, but they are rare in cognitive mental states. This might be because those gestures are associated with a relaxed mood. On the other hand, actions like stroking, tapping and touching facial regions - especially with index finger - are all associated with cognitive mental states, namely *thinking* and *unsure*. Thus, we propose the use of hand shape and action on different face regions as a novel cue in interpreting cognitive mental states.

3.2   Hand Detection Using 3D Data

Automatic detection of the hand when occluding the face is challenging because the face and the hand usually have the same colour and texture and the hand can take different possible shapes. The recent availability of affordable depth sensors (such as the Microsoft Kinect) is giving easy access to 3D data. 3D

Fig. 5. Simple background subtraction based on depth threshold shows that depth images provide details of hand shape that can be utilised in automatic recognition defining different hand cues

information can be used to improve the results of expression and gesture tracking and analysis. Cam3D provides a depth image for each frame in the labelled video segments, which enabled us to investigate the potential use of depth information in automatic detection of hand over face.

We used simple thresholding technique on the depth images in order to visualise how the hand can be segmented over the face using depth. Figure 5 presents preliminary results of this simple manual thresholding of the depth image. First, we define the depth value of the face in the depth image, using major facial points like the mouth and the nose. Then, we perform background subtraction based on the depth value of the face. Finally, we add the colour values for the segmented pixels to differentiate between hands or other objects in front of the face.

Initial results show that depth images provide details of hand shape that can be utilised in automatic recognition defining different hand cues. We are currently working in combining depth information with computer vision techniques for automatic detection of hand-over-face cues.

4   Conclusion and Future Work

We have presented an alternative facial processing framework, where face occlusions instead of being removed, are studied to be combined with facial expressions and head gestures to help in machine understanding and interpretation of different mental states. We analysed hand-over-face gestures in naturalistic video corpus of complex mental states and defined a preliminary coding system for hand cues, namely hand shape, hand action and facial region occluded. Looking at the depth images, we noticed the potential of using depth information in automatic detection of hand shape and action over the face. Our future work can be summarised in the following sections.

4.1   Analysis of More Hand-Over-Face Gestures

The lack of available multi-modal datasets slows down our work in analysing the meaning of hand-over-face gestures. Cam3D currently has 94 video segments of labelled hand gestures, which is not enough for studying all possible meaning of hand gestures. More than one category in our coding matrix had less than two videos, which might not be representative of the whole category. Future work includes collecting more data and adding more videos to the corpus. Studying hand-over-face gestures in more videos of natural expressions, we expect to enhance our coding schema and discover more encoded mental states associated with other hand-over-face gestures.

4.2   Automatic Detection of Hand Cues

Automatic detection of hand shape, action and facial region occluded will include exploring computer vision techniques in hand detection that are robust to occlusion, as well as further analysis of Cam3D depth images. Automatic detection of hand cues is a step towards automatic inference of their corresponding mental states.

4.3   Automatic Coding of Hand Gestures

One of the possible applications of this research is to provide tools for developmental psychologists who study gesture, and language in child development and social interactions to be able to objectively measure the use of gestures in speech and in communication instead of manual watching and coding, such as in the work done by Goldin-Meadow [8]

4.4   Multimodal Inference System

Ultimately, our vision is to to implement a multi-modal affect inference framework that combines facial expressions, head gestures as well as hand-over-face gestures. This includes looking at integration techniques, such as: early integration or feature fusion versus late integration or decision fusion. Moreover, we aim at answering questions like: how the face and gesture combine to convey affective states? When do they complement each other and when do they communicate different messages?

Acknowledgment. We would like to thank Yousef Jameel Scholarship for generously funding this research. We would like also to thank Tadas Baltrušaitis for his help in the analysis of Cam3D corpus.

References

1. Ambady, N., Rosenthal, R.: Thin slices of expressive behavior as predictors of interpersonal consequences: A meta-analysis. Psychological Bulletin 111(2), 256 (1992)

2. Bourel, F., Chibelushi, C., Low, A.: Robust facial expression recognition using a state-based model of spatially-localised facial dynamics. In: IEEE Automatic Face and Gesture Recognition (2002)

3. Cook, S., Goldin-Meadow, S.: The role of gesture in learning: do children use their hands to change their minds? Journal of Cognition and Development 7(2), 211–232 (2006)

4. De Gelder, B.: Towards the neurobiology of emotional body language. Nature Reviews Neuroscience 7(3), 242–249 (2006)

5. De Gelder, B.: Why bodies? Twelve reasons for including bodily expressions in affective neuroscience. Phil. Trans. of the Royal Society B 364(1535), 3475 (2009)

6. Ekenel, H., Stiefelhagen, R.: Block selection in the local appearance-based face recognition scheme. In: Computer Vision and Pattern Recognition Workshop, pp. 43–43. IEEE, Los Alamitos (2006)

7. Ekman, P., Friesen, W.: The repertoire of nonverbal behavior: Categories, origins, usage, and coding. Semiotica 1(1), 49–98 (1969)

8. Goldin-Meadow, S.: Hearing gesture: How our hands help us think. Belknap Press (2005)

9. Goldin-Meadow, S., Wagner, S.: How our hands help us learn. Trends in Cognitive Sciences 9(5), 234–241 (2005)

10. Gunes, H., Piccardi, M.: A bimodal face and body gesture database for automatic analysis of human nonverbal affective behavior. In: International Conference on Pattern Recognition, vol. 1, pp. 1148–1153. IEEE, Los Alamitos (2006)

11. el Kaliouby, R., Robinson, P.: Real-Time Inference of Complex Mental States from Facial Expressions and Head Gestures. In: Real-Time Vision for Human Computer Interaction, pp. 181–200. Springer, Heidelberg (2005)

12. Lucey, P., Cohn, J., Kanade, T., Saragih, J., Ambadar, Z., Matthews, I.: The extended Cohn-Kanade dataset (CK+): A complete dataset for action unit and emotion-specified expression. In: Computer Vision and Pattern Recognition Workshop, pp. 94–101. IEEE, Los Alamitos (2010)

13. Mahmoud, M., Baltrusaitis, T., Robinson, P., Reik, L.: 3D corpus of spontaneous complex mental states. In: D′Mello, S., et al. (eds.) ACII 2011, Part I. LNCS, vol. 6974, pp. 205–214. Springer, Heidelberg (2011)

14. Pantic, M., Valstar, M., Rademaker, R., Maat, L.: Web-based database for facial expression analysis. In: IEEE Conf. Multimedia and Expo., p. 5. IEEE, Los Alamitos (2005)

15. Pease, A., Pease, B.: The definitive book of body language. Bantam (2006)

16. Sun, Y., Yin, L.: Facial expression recognition based on 3D dynamic range model sequences. In: Forsyth, D., Torr, P., Zisserman, A. (eds.) ECCV 2008, Part II. LNCS, vol. 5303, pp. 58–71. Springer, Heidelberg (2008)

17. Tong, Y., Liao, W., Ji, Q.: Facial action unit recognition by exploiting their dynamic and semantic relationships. IEEE Transactions on Pattern Analysis and Machine Intelligence, 1683–1699 (2007)

Toward a Computational Model of Affective Responses to Stories for Augmenting Narrative Generation

Brian O'Neill

School of Interactive Computing, Georgia Institute of Technology
boneill@cc.gatech.edu

Abstract. Current approaches to story generation do not utilize models of human affect to create stories with dramatic arc, suspense, and surprise. This paper describes current and future work towards computational models of affective responses to stories for the purpose of augmenting computational story generators. I propose two cognitively plausible models of suspense and surprise responses to stories. I also propose methods for evaluating these models by comparing them to actual human responses to stories. Finally, I propose the implementation of these models as a heuristic in a search-based story generation system. By using these models as a heuristic, the story generation system will favor stories that are more likely to produce affective responses from human readers.

Keywords: Affective computing, narrative cognition, computational models, dramatic arc, suspense, surprise.

1 Introduction

Narrative as entertainment, in the form of oral, written, or visual storytelling, plays a central role in many forms of entertainment media, including novels, movies, television, and theatre. One of the reasons for the prevalence of storytelling in human culture may be due to the way in which narrative is a cognitive tool for situated understanding [1, 2]. This narrative intelligence is central in the cognitive processes that we employ across a range of experiences, from entertainment contexts to active learning. Expert storytellers who craft narratives for entertainment – films, novels, games, etc. – often structure their narratives to elicit an emotional response from the viewer, reader, or player. The concept of the dramatic arc, identified by Aristotle [3], is one common pattern of emotional impact on an audience.

The construction of novel quality stories is a challenging task, even for humans. For more than 30 years, computer scientists have been trying to answer the question of whether, and how, intelligent computational systems can create stories from scratch. To date, story generation systems have been unreliable when it comes to creating novel and aesthetically pleasing stories with dramatic structure. Zagalo et al. [4] argue for the use of dramatic arc and intelligent emotion detection in story generation and storytelling systems. However, we are not aware of any systems that have adequately adopted this approach to story generation. Simply put, story generation systems do not have sufficient understanding of story aesthetics nor how story structure affects emotional change in an audience.

S. D'Mello et al. (Eds.): ACII 2011, Part II, LNCS 6975, pp. 256–263, 2011.

The primary objective of my research is to develop an intelligent system that incorporates models of dramatic arc and human affective responses to suspense and surprise for the purpose of story generation. There are many ways to produce dramatic arc in a story [5]. Two related approaches to producing dramatic arc are to make stories suspenseful or surprising; Abbott describes suspense and surprise as the two things that "give narrative its life" [6]. Despite the importance and prevalence of suspense as a storytelling tool, there has been little investigation of computational techniques for generating or understanding suspense. This paper describes work towards a computational model of affective responses to stories, focusing on suspense and surprise, and a story generation system that makes use of those models. The following sections describe related work and the objectives of this research. Sections 4-5 describe current progress on this work and planned future work, respectively.

2 Related Work

Suspense occurs in an audience – the reader or watcher of a narrative – when the audience perceives that a protagonist is faced with the possibility of an undesirable outcome. Gerrig and Bernardo suggest that one method used by authors to make readers feel suspense is to reduce the quantity and/or quality of plans available to the protagonist for avoiding an undesirable outcome [7]. They suggest that readers act as problem-solvers on behalf of the protagonist and when readers can only devise low-quality plans, or struggle to come up with any plans for a hero to escape the predicament, the perception of suspense will increase. In these studies, they found that readers reported higher suspense levels when story excerpts suggested potential escapes and then quickly eliminated them, thus reducing the quantity of available plans for the protagonist.

Branigan [5] suggests that suspense and surprise are the result of knowledge disparities between the audience and the characters. An author creates suspense by providing the audience with more knowledge than the characters, particularly about the possibility of undesirable outcomes. Conversely, surprise is created when the characters possess more knowledge than the audience. Suspense has also been described as a lack of closure within a narrative [6]; authors manipulate readers by appearing to satisfy the need for closure, only to take it away. Abbott describes successful narratives as chains of suspense and surprise.

To this point, story generation systems have been unreliable at creating novel stories with dramatic arc. However, there has been progress at generating surprising and suspenseful discourses for existing stories. Suspenser [8] computationally attempts to find a suspenseful telling of an existing story. Suspenser tries excluding different sets of events from the discourse to maximize a suspense rating. The level of suspense of any telling of a story is measured by generating all possible plans a protagonist might have and taking the ratio of failed plans to successful plans. Prevoyant [9] uses a computational model of flashback and foreshadowing to produce a reordered version of a story intended to elicit feelings of surprise in human readers. Prevoyant rearranges the events of a given story in order to produce surprise from outcomes that are unexpected by readers. Prevoyant does not measure the level of unexpectedness; rather, unexpectedness is defined as the reader's inability to find a plan explaining the outcome without the events of the flashback. Each of these systems receives the complete story as input and modifies the discourse of those stories – which events of the story are told, and in what order – to produce a suspenseful or surprising ordering of events. In my research, I do not seek to modify the discourse of existing stories; rather, I want to read the story incrementally, and identify the aspects of the story that produce suspense or surprise responses. These will be used to create a model of suspense and surprise that can then be applied as a heuristic for the generation of stories that produce affective responses.

Story generation systems solve the problem of finding a sequence of events that can be told to a human audience as a story. Some story generation systems use non-emotional aesthetic qualities, such as novelty [10] or character believability [11]. A number of story generation and interactive narrative systems apply tension ratings; however these ratings are hard-coded into discrete events as absolute ratings. None of these tension ratings are based on models of affective response. The MEXICA story generation system [10] models reader tension as a measure of how satisfactory the state of the story is. Certain events in MEXICA define an increase or decrease in tension as an effect of the event. The amount of the change in tension for a given event is defined in advance by the user of the system. MEXICA tracks the tension over the course of the story and compares the changes in tension to other stories that it knows. Porteous et al. [12] describe an interactive storytelling system that allows users to control the level of tension in the story. The system produces a pacing and ordering of events that best fits the curve representing the provided tension levels. The interactive drama, Façade [13], tracks tension as a factor in managing the interactive narrative. The Façade drama manager has an ideal tension curve and probabilistically changes the tension in the narrative to try to match the ideal curve. Each event in the story has a number of possible presentations based on character affinity and the tension level. The drama manager selects a presentation based on how well it fits the scene so far and the ideal tension level at that point of the story. Rather than hard-coding tension ratings, I argue that a better approach would be to base these ratings on models of affective response.

3   Research Objectives

The objective of this research is to address two primary questions related to computational modeling of aesthetics and affect in narrative:

- How do we computationally model affective response to stories?
- How can we utilize computational models of affective response to stories to automatically generate more suspenseful or more surprising stories?

As described above, current approaches to story generation do not use affective response as a means of creating new stories. Many of these story generation systems also lack a model of dramatic arc. It is my belief that we can generate better stories by incorporating each of these elements into the story generation process. In my efforts to address these research questions, I plan to implement two models of affective response to stories, emphasizing surprise and suspense. I will then incorporate these models into a story generation system – effectively using them as a heuristic to guide the story generation process. Evaluation of the story generation system will involve asking readers to compare stories produced by this system to a comparable story generator that lacks models of dramatic arc and affective response.

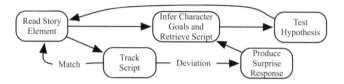

Fig. 1. This flowchart represents the process used by the Surprise Model to read a story, infer character goals, and track scripts in order to recognize surprise responses

4   Current Progress

My current progress towards the development of a model of affective response is made up of two cognitively-plausible computational models, one each for the generation of surprise and suspense responses to narratives. At this stage, neither model has been fully implemented. The Surprise Model is based on the construction of a possible reader model as the story is being read, focusing on the superordinate goals of the characters in the story [14]. The Suspense Model tracks the goals and plans of the protagonist, identifies possible failures in each, and assesses the likelihood of escape from failure states [15].

4.1   Surprise Model

The Surprise Model, based on an earlier model of computational narrative comprehension [14], constructs one possible reader mental model of the story incrementally, as it is being read. Authors and directors can achieve audience surprise in several ways. One such approach is by providing the audience with less information that the characters in the story have [5]. Using this observation, I focus on surprise that originates from a character doing something unexpected. The Surprise Model focuses on character goals because (a) they are easily inferred by readers, and (b) actions in stories are typically driven by character goals. Readers feel surprise when the predictions they make about the story, such as inferring characters' superordinate goals, are incorrect. Figure 1 shows the process used by the Surprise Model to identify surprise responses.

A story is provided to the Surprise Model as input, and story elements are read one at a time. I do not address any aspect of natural language understanding or computer vision necessary to literally read or view a creative artifact such as a story or film. Rather it reads an annotated version of the story or film script, where an annotation contains relevant information about the scene, characters, and non-diegetic information that may be used to elicit an affective response from the audience.

The search for superordinate character goals drives the process because of the importance of goals in story comprehension and sense-making [16]. The Surprise

Model, acting as a surrogate for a human audience, uses several strategies to hypothesize the superordinate goal for each character that is actively engaged in the current event. These strategies prefer goals that have been explicitly stated in the story or were inferred in previous iterations. In the process of inferring character goals, the Surprise Model may also retrieve a script that expresses likely future actions. The Surprise Model tests the hypothesized goal and script using a narrative planner, which creates a narrative that links the events of the story with the hypothesized character goals. If the planner cannot form a narrative that links the events and hypothesized goals, then the Surprise Model uses a different strategy to identify a goal.

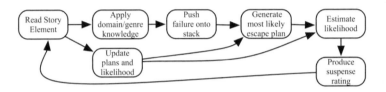

Fig. 2. This flowchart represents the process used by the Suspense Model to move from reading part of a story to producing a suspense rating

Once a goal and script have been retrieved, the Surprise Model tracks that script as the story continues. When a character deviates from the hypothesized goal or the retrieved script, the Surprise Model re-tests the goal and script using the narrative planner. Surprise responses can occur when the inferred goal was incorrect or when characters deviate from the expected plan to carry out the inferred goals. When this occurs, the Surprise Model infers a new goal based on the new information in the story and retrieves a new script to predict the characters' actions.

4.2 Suspense Model

The Suspense Model, proposed in [15], is based on the correlation between the perceived likelihood of a protagonist's failure and the amount of suspense reported by the audience. The Suspense Model reads the story incrementally, attempting to predict failures in the protagonist's goals and plans. The likelihood of averting the predicted failures is used to compute a suspense rating. The flowchart in Figure 2 shows the complete suspense process. The key points of the model are highlighted below.

The Suspense Model reads an annotated story, one element at a time. After reading an element, the next step is the application of domain and genre knowledge. The Suspense Model contains scripts and schemas pertaining to common stories and genre techniques in order to simulate the domain and genre knowledge that authors and directors regularly expect their audiences to have. These scripts and schemas are also used to identify the goals and/or plans of the protagonist. Once the protagonist's plan has been identified, the system searches for a potential failure in that plan.

The Suspense Model uses its knowledge of the story, the protagonist's goals and plans, and the potential failure to find an *escape plan*, a plan that allows the protagonist to avoid the undesirable outcome while still completing his original plan.

We generate an escape plan for the purpose of identifying the likelihood of the protagonist's escape, which is correlated with the suspense felt by a human audience. As events that are more easily retrieved from memory are perceived by humans to be more likely [17], the system presumes that the first escape-plan is the most likely to succeed. The likelihood of the plan is calculated as a function of the state of the world, the costs of the actions in the plan, and the time available before the failure can no longer be averted.

Finally, the Suspense Model uses this likelihood to calculate a suspense rating. Recall that Gerrig and Bernardo [7] found that reducing the quantity or quality of plans available to the protagonist led to readers reporting higher levels of suspense. Plans with lower likelihoods of succeeding can be seen as being of poorer quality. Thus, as likelihood of escape increases, the suspense rating is expected to decrease. The calculation of suspense rating also factors in the severity (negative utility) of the failures and the audience's affinity for the characters in question.

Once the Suspense Model has calculated a suspense rating, it continues to the next event in the story. As events are added, the model (a) updates the suspense rating, (b) finds a new escape-plan and recalculates suspense, or (c) notes the aversion of the potential failure and moves on to identifying or resolving other potential failures.

5 Future Work

The remaining work on the Surprise and Suspense Models is implementation and evaluation. I plan to (a) assist in the knowledge engineering problem for each model, (b) evaluate the ratings provided by the models with ratings provided by a human audience by correlating with the suspense and surprise levels reported by actual human audiences, and (c) demonstrate the effective use of these models as heuristics for generating stories with dramatic arc.

5.1 Knowledge Engineering

The Surprise and Suspense Models both require a library of scripts and schemas representing domain and genre knowledge. To avoid researcher bias, I plan to acquire these scripts through experimental procedures. Participants will be asked to provide fragments of stories, delineating the events that occur in these fragments and identifying the superordinate goals of the characters in these situations. These responses will be compiled into script-like structures, based on the plan networks described by Orkin [18]. Compiling the responses into scripts will be automated if possible, but may not be necessary for small-scale experimentation with the models.

5.2 Evaluation of Models

Once the Surprise and Suspense Models have been implemented, I will conduct evaluations of the ratings that these systems produce, in order to be certain that the ratings produced by the models reflect actual human affective responses. In this study, I plan to ask human subjects to watch a movie and have them provide ratings of their suspense and surprise levels as they watch. These ratings will be compared to the ratings produced by the Surprise and Suspense Models. It is not necessary for the numerical ratings to match precisely between humans and the affective response models. Rather, the evaluation will look to see that the relative increase and decrease in suspense levels are comparable between humans and these models, and that the relative suspense levels at different points of the movies are also comparable.

5.3 Applying Affective Models to Story Generation

Current attempts at story generation have not been able to reliably produce aesthetically pleasing stories with dramatic structure without manual, ad-hoc encoding of tension values for states and actions. I argue that this is the result of story generation systems not using cognitively plausible models of affective response as part of the generation process. I propose to integrate the Surprise and Suspense Models into a search-based narrative generation system to show that the models can improve the aesthetic quality of computer-generated stories. Search-based narrative generation has been a popular approach, in part, because of the many correlations between AI plans and narrative structures [11]. A search-based story generator solves the problem of finding a sequence of story events that achieves a set of causal, structural, and aesthetic requirements. The search process is guided by a heuristic function that may be based on a number of factors, possibly including length, believability, and a number of ad-hoc rules about the story. By incorporating the Surprise and Suspense Models into the heuristic, a search-based narrative generator will, in a principled manner, favor narrative structures that lead the reader to affective responses.

To evaluate the narrative generation system, I aim to show that the inclusion of the Surprise and Suspense Models can result in greater affective responses and quality judgments in human readers than in an equivalent narrative generation system that does not use my models. I propose the following experimental design. Two story generators will be developed; the control and experimental systems will be identical except for the inclusion of the affective response models in the experimental system. Both story generators will be provided with the first half of a story. This story will be handcrafted and empirically evaluated to trigger concern for a protagonist. By holding the first half of the story constant, we can avoid unfair comparisons on the variables that we care about. Each system will complete the story and human study participants will be asked to rate stories generated by both systems, indicating affective response levels as well as subjective indications of overall story quality. We hypothesize that the stories generated by the experimental system, implementing the affective response models, will receive higher ratings from the study participants. If the within-subjects ratings of stories produced by the model-guided story generator are better than those created by the control system, then this work will represent a valuable contribution to a number of fields, including affective computing, particularly in the context of stories, as well as computational creativity and aesthetics.

References

1. Bruner, J.: The Narrative Construction of Reality. Critical Inquiry 18, 1–21 (1991)
2. Gerrig, R.J.: Experiencing Narrative Worlds: On the Psychological Activities of Reading. Yale University Press, New Haven (1993)

3. Aristotle: The Poetics (T. Buckley trans.). Prometheus Books, Buffalo (1992) (Original work published 350 B.C.E.)
4. Zagalo, N., Barker, A., Branco, V.: Story reaction structures to emotion detection. In: Proceedings of the 1st ACM Workshop of Story Representation, Mechanism, and Context, pp. 33–38. ACM Press, New York (2004)
5. Branigan, E.: Narrative Comprehension and Film. Routledge, New York (1992)
6. Abbott, H.P.: The Cambridge Introduction to Narrative. Cambridge University Press, Cambridge (2008)
7. Gerrig, R.J., Bernardo, A.B.I.: Readers as Problem-Solvers in the Experience of Suspense. Poetics 22, 459–472 (1994)
8. Cheong, Y.-G.: A Computational Model of Narrative Generation for Suspense. Doctoral dissertation, North Carolina State University (2007)
9. Bae, B.-C., Young, R.M.: A Use of Flashback and Foreshadowing for Surprise Arousal in Narrative Using a Plan-Based Approach. In: Spierling, U., Szilas, N. (eds.) ICIDS 2008. LNCS, vol. 5334, pp. 156–167. Springer, Heidelberg (2008)
10. Pérez y Pérez, R., Sharples, M.: MEXICA: A Computational Model of a Cognitive Account of Creative Writing. Journal of Experimental and Theoretical Artificial Intelligence 13, 119–139 (2001)
11. Riedl, M.O., Young, R.M.: Narrative Planning: Balancing Plot and Character. Journal of Artificial Intelligence Research 39, 217–268 (2010)
12. Porteous, J., Teutenberg, J., Pizzi, D., Cavazza, M.: Visual Programming of Plan Dynamics using Constraints and Landmarks. In: Proceedings of the 21st International Conference on Automated Planning and Scheduling, pp. 186–193. AAAI Press, Freiburg (2011)
13. Mateas, M.: Interactive Drama, Art and Artificial Intelligence. Doctoral dissertation, Carnegie Mellon University (2002)
14. O'Neill, B., Riedl, M.: Simulating the Everyday Creativity of Readers. In: Proceedings of the Second International Conference on Computational Creativity, pp. 153–158. AAAI Press, Mexico City (2011)
15. O'Neill, B., Riedl, M.: Toward a Computational Framework of Suspense and Dramatic Arc. In: D'Mello, S., et al. (eds.) ACII 2011, Part I. LNCS, vol. 6974, pp. 246–255. Springer, Heidelberg (2011)
16. Graesser, A.C., Singer, M., Trabasso, T.: Constructing Inferences During Narrative Text Comprehension. Psychological Review 101, 371–395 (1994)
17. MacLeod, C., Campbell, L.: Memory Accessibility and Probability Judgments: An Experimental Evaluation of the Availability Heuristic. Journal of Personality and Social Psychology 63, 890–902 (1992)
18. Orkin, J.D.: Learning Plan Networks in Conversational Video Games. Masters of Science thesis, Massachusetts Institute of Technology (2007)

Recognizing Bodily Expression of Affect in User Tests

Marco Pasch and Monica Landoni

University of Lugano,
Via Buffi 13, 6900 Lugano, Switzerland
{marco.pasch,monica.landoni}@usi.ch

Abstract. We describe our planned research in using affective feedback from body movement and posture to recognize affective states of users. Bodily expression of affect has received far less attention in research than facial expression. The aim of our research is to further investigate how affective states are communicated through bodily expression and to develop an evaluation method for assessing affective states of video gamers based on this knowledge. Current motion capture systems are often intrusive to the user and restricted to lab environments, which results in biasing user experience. We propose a non-intrusive recognition system for bodily expression of affect in a video game context, which can be deployed in the wild.

Keywords: affect, expression, recognition, user test, body, posture, movement.

1 Introduction

With interactive devices becoming ever more ubiquitous, the field of human-computer interaction has seen a turn from investigating business environments and how to make task-related interaction more effective and efficient towards finding out how interaction can happen in a more joyous and satisfying way in all facets of everyday life. In use scenarios where task completion is not central anymore, but replaced by maybe more difficult to define criteria such as providing users with a good experience, we find ourselves in need of tools to assess these experiences.

A tricky part in evaluations is to capture how users feel during the interaction with an interactive application. Often they have difficulties expressing their feelings towards a new tool or application. Self-report methods, e.g. questionnaires, focus groups, "think aloud" walkthroughs; also rely on participants having good linguistic skills. This and the ability to provide objective feedback are desirable features when selecting participants in user-centered evaluation experiments, even more so when looking at usability issues known to have a strong subjective component. Emotions and the ability to keep track of them explicitly play a critical role in this context even if traditionally there have not been any specific instruments for gathering this type of feedback so that it could be used as a filter when interpreting feedback data.

In recent years, the field of affective computing has come up with a number of approaches that provide more objective data. Typically, these approaches detect one or several modes of affective feedback. Intentionally or not, we continuously express affect. This can happen verbally, through the tone of our voice and our choice of

S. D´Mello et al. (Eds.): ACII 2011, Part II, LNCS 6975, pp. 264–271, 2011.

words, as well as non-verbally, through our facial expressions, posture, gestures, amongst others [1]. Also physiological data like heart rate or skin conductance have been used to infer the affective state of the user. As social beings, it comes natural to us to also read the affective states of the people around us. Automatically recognizing a person's affective state is still one of the big challenges in affective computing.

Of the non-verbal channels, facial expressions have received the most attention in research. We now have a good knowledge of how individual facial muscles work together to form an expression and how others perceive expressions. Less is known on how affect is communicated through postures and bodily movements.

2 Background

The research described here mainly touches on two research areas. One is user experience research, in particular methods for assessing the user experience. The other is non-verbal expression of affect, a sub-field of affective computing.

2.1 Assessing User Experience

There is no consensus on the definition of user experience. Instead, it appears more useful to see it as an umbrella term for a variety of different needs [2] and a number of different sets of needs have been proposed [3, 4, 5, 6, 7].

McCarthy and Wright [3] argue that user experience should consider the emotional, intellectual, and sensual aspects of our interactions with technology. Technology is more than just a means to an end in that we do not just use technology; we live with it. They also see an interdependence between a technology and the experience that it co-shapes. An experience has no final state, there are continuously sense-making processes happening like anticipating, connecting, interpreting, reflecting, appropriating, and recounting.

Jordan [4] distinguishes a different set of needs, which he labels pleasures: Physical pleasure refers to the body and senses; social pleasure represents relationships with family, friends, co-workers, etc. Psychological pleasure refers to emotional and cognitive processes in the mind, e.g. doing something engaging. Ideological pleasure represents tastes and values. Jordan states that some of the pleasures are universal, while some are specific to culture and context.

As definitions of user experience and its constituents vary significantly, it is useful to look at how empirical studies of user experience interpret and operationalize it. In a recent review of such empirical studies, Bargas-Avila and Hornbæk [8] find that the most frequently investigated dimensions within user experience are emotions, enjoyment and aesthetics.

Methods for assessing the user experience can be first and foremost distinguished by whether they are based on subjective self-report of users or obtained from objective measurements of users engaging with an interactive application.

The subjective user experience can be obtained through verbal and non-verbal methods. In practice, most evaluations rely on verbal methods, such as post-experimental interviews and questionnaires. A more recent development are non-verbal methods. One example is the use of a slider [9] used as a physical manifestation of a Likert scale ranging from very positive to very negative. Users are instructed to continuously use it to express their emotional state during interaction. Another approach aims at improving affective feedback from children. As part of an evaluation children are asked to prepare drawings in which they express their experience [10]. Afterwards experts review the drawings.

Objective measurements include data from observations of the users' behavior, physiological data, facial and bodily expressions, and voice. Behavior can be assessed by e.g. measuring the performance of the user in terms of speed required for task-solving, measuring how often and with how much force the user clicks the mouse or punches keys, or by measuring the eye gaze of the user. In particular eye gaze is a popular measure for getting an idea which of the items on screen catch the attention of the user. Physiological data from measuring heart rate, skin conductance, and others allows inferences on arousal states of users and whether their valence is positive or negative. Often several measures are combined and data fusion algorithms are applied to get a more stable assessment of users' affective states. Yet to date, such objective measurements are not used widely in practice.

2.2 Bodily Expression of Affect

When we look into research on non-verbal expression of affect, the vast majority of studies focus on facial expressions. We now have a fair understanding of how individual facial muscles contribute to an expression [11] and how expressions are perceived in terms of affect [12]. De Gelder [13] estimates that over 95 per cent of studies have used faces as stimuli for the assessment of emotional states. The remaining 5 per cent are split between human voice, other auditory signals, and the smallest number has looked into the body as a source for human communication of affect.

De Gelder then asks why researchers have not shown more interest in the body. It is by no means a new area of research and dates at least back to James' study of expression of body posture from 1932 [14]. One difficulty that arises from using the body as stimulus to study the expression of emotions is the fact that the human body is complex. The complexity stems from a big number of joints and all possible rotations around these joints that result in a large number of degrees of freedom. It can be argued that the complexity of the body is the reason why there exist no formal models for body postures as there are for facial expressions (e.g., the facial action coding system [15]).

Yet, studies into bodily expression of affect have shown that changes in affective states can be observed in changes in posture [16]. It has also been put forward that facial expressions can be deliberately manipulated for deceptive purposes. Bodily expressions are thought of providing a more honest image of a person's affective state, as we are not as aware of our bodily display as of our facial expressions. Also, the relationship between affective state and posture appears to be bidirectional. Riskind and Gotay [17] present evidence that the sheer posture of a person has influence on the mental state. In their study, subjects put in a hunched and threatened posture report greater stress than subjects put in a relaxed posture.

In our own research, we investigated the movements of video-gamers playing Nintendo Wii Sports games [18]. We found movement patterns, which correspond to the strategies players used, based on their motivation for playing in the first place. Interviews revealed that some gamers are aware of changes in the way they move, depending on their current mood while playing.

Bianchi-Berthouze [19] investigated which types of body movements can be observed in the context of video games. In her model she distinguishes task-related movements (i.e. task-control, task-facilitating, and otherwise task-related), expression of affect, and gesturing for social interaction.

An issue within research on non-verbal expression of affect lies in the differences in methodology used in studies. This starts with the choice of emotion model. Calvo and D'Mello [20] note that even as researchers in affective computing try to remain agnostic to the different theories that have been put forward in emotion research their output is "rife with theoretical assumptions that impact their effectiveness." Some studies use Ekman's [21] model of basic emotions [22, 23] or a variation of it in that they either apply more [16, 24, 25] or fewer [26, 27] emotion labels. Other studies use dimensional models of affect or a component process model of emotion [28].

Most studies present observers with static body postures in form of images. As mentioned earlier, the human body is complex. A practical consequence of the complexity is that studies employ various techniques to limit the complexity and operate with small subsets of all physically possible postures. Postures can be chosen without a specific emotion in mind [14], participants can be asked to describe everyday situations [24] or to spontaneously perform postures after inducing emotional states [22], or participants' self-report can be measured [25]. Other studies use prototypical postures, depicting clearly defined emotions, either performed by actors [26, 27] or defined manually [23].

Also the type of stimulus is of importance. The DANVAS-POS set [29] shows people in various sitting and standing postures, with their faces painted over with a black marker so that facial expressions cannot be seen. James [14] used photographs of a mannequin. Most of the more recent studies use computer-generated stimuli, which comes with the big advantage that parameters such as visual appearance, posture, viewpoint, detail, and lighting, can be controlled.

Knowing how the different approaches influence outcomes (e.g., the agreement rates of observers on the emotion depicted in an image) could help us in assessing individual approaches and compare the outcomes. In one of our own studies [30], we investigated how the type of stimulus influences agreement rates and found that agreement rates varied for different levels of realism of the stimulus (a mannequin vs. a virtual human). Even if consolidation is not a central aim of the research presented here, outlining the variations in methodology raises awareness to be cautious when making decisions concerning the underlying emotion model, type of stimulus, and experiment design in general.

3   Research Aims and Approach

The main hypothesis of this research is that **affect can be recognized from static body posture and body movement for assessing the user experience.**

A first step in proving the hypothesis is to build a recognition system that fulfills the following requirement: First, it must provide accurate information on posture and movements of the user. In the past, motion capture suits were used for this. These were either suits based on sensors placed on an exoskeleton or camera-based systems with visual markers that are placed on the user. Having worked with an exoskeleton type suit in a previous study investigating motivation and movement patterns of video gamers playing Nintendo Wii games [18], we have first hand experience on how intrusive exoskeleton suits are. Wearing such a suit heavily influences the affective experience of a user, which is certainly a thing one wants to avoid in a study on measuring affect. But also camera-based systems (e.g., Vicon) come with a disadvantage in that they are carefully calibrated into a room and moving them to a different location is labor-intensive. As a result, the use of camera-based system is limited to a lab environment. This is certainly a disadvantage when studying user experience and many researchers advocate the evaluation of systems that are meant to be used in everyday life should also be evaluated there and not in an (to the user alien) lab environment [31, 32]. We can conclude from this our requirements two and three: The recognition system has to be non-intrusive in order not to influence the user experience and it should be mobile and able to operate in a number of different settings.

The system we are currently building is based on the recently introduced Microsoft Kinect movement sensor. The Kinect sensor is a camera-based movement sensor, emitting an infrared grid and aggregating the reflected light into a skeleton representation of the body. It is fairly robust in terms of ability to function in changing (indoor) environments and totally non-intrusive for the user. As it is an optical system users do not have to wear specific clothes.

With this system we want to build a database of affective movements and postures. Most studies to date have only looked at static postures. With our recognition system we are able to also look at movements. As other studies have done before, we start with acted displays of affect. Exaggerated as they are, they facilitate recognition at an early stage. As the system matures we plan to move to more subtle displays of affect, which stem from test participants not instructed to display anything in particular, but simply asked to engage in a movement-based or active video game such as Nintendo Wii games, XBOX games including a Kinect sensor, or others. We believe that active video games allow us to observe a bigger variety of movements than in sedentary use scenarios.

A special focus of attention is to observe the interaction between two and possible more gamers. In her model on movement types, Bianchi-Berthouze [19] stresses that affect expression facilitates social interaction. The Kinect sensor and its analytical software are able to track several people at a time. This gives us the opportunity to study in detail what kind of affective expressions we can observe and how they influence and regulate the social interaction of gamers in various scenarios (e.g., collaborative vs. opposed).

4   Contribution and Relevance

The research presented in this paper envisages two main contributions:

The first contribution is the **investigation of human expression of affect through the body**. While it is established that we express our affective states through posture and the way we move, the knowledge of how affect is communicated, perceived and interpreted is limited. Also, consolidating the results of existing studies is difficult as the studies often differ heavily in methodology and investigate different scenarios, e.g. dance or rehabilitation. The research presented here contributes specifically a deeper investigation on how users of active video games express affect through the body. We also aim at shedding more light on what types of movements we can observe and how in multi-gamer scenarios the bodily expression of affect influences the interaction between gamers.

The second contribution is to present **a new method for assessing the affective user experience**, again in the context of active video games. A robust version of the system described earlier could assist researchers as well as practitioners in evaluations of interactive products. Fusing readings from bodily expression of affect with readings from other modes, such as facial expressions, voice, or others will result in more robust multi-modal affect recognition systems.

The immediate application of the research described here lie in the evaluation of active video games. A next step could be to integrate affect recognition based on a number of channels including posture and movement directly into such games. A game able to sense the emotion of its users could then adapt gameplay, e.g. become easier when detecting frustration of more difficult when detecting boredom. This could ensure a continuous positive user experience.

The envisaged outcome of the research presented here appears also relevant for other domains. Also in the area of embodied conversational agents and social robots, it appears beneficial if the agent or robot receives information on the affective state of its human interlocutor in order to adapt it. In human-human interaction we continuously do so and providing agents and robots with this capability would make them more realistic, i.e. more human-like. Also in the area of physical rehabilitation, a system that can recognize and analyze posture and movement could assist therapists in identifying problematic areas and aid in monitoring therapy. In educational scenarios, detecting boredom, frustration or fear can be valuable for ensuring continued motivation of students.

5 Conclusions

We described our planned research in using affective feedback from body movement and posture to recognize affective states of video gamers. The recognition system we propose is non-intrusive and can be deployed in various environments allowing us to study the user "in the wild".

We outlined a number of issues both in user experience research as well as affective computing. As this is work-in-progress at an early stage we certainly raise more questions than we can currently answer.

Yet, we believe that the work we present here can help us to get a deeper understanding of how affect is expressed through the body and to study social aspects of non-verbal communication of affect in multi-gamer scenarios. We are also positive that our work can result in a new tool to assess emotions in the evaluation of games and interactive products in general.

References

1. Zeng, Z., Pantic, M., Roisman, G.I., Huang, T.S.: A Survey of Affect Recognition Methods: Audio, Visual, and Spontaneous Expressions. IEEE Transactions on Pattern Analysis and Machine Intelligence 31(1), 39–58 (2009)
2. Hassenzahl, M., Tractinsky, N.: User experience – a research agenda. Behaviour & Information Technology 25(2), 91–97 (2006)
3. McCarthy, J., Wright, P.: Technology as Experience. MIT Press, Cambridge (2004)
4. Jordan, P.: Designing Pleasurable Products. Taylor & Francis, Abington (2002)
5. Gaver, W.W., Martin, H.: Alternatives. Exploring information appliances through conceptual design proposals. In: Proceedings of the CHI 2000 Conference on Human Factors in Computing, pp. 209–216. ACM Press, New York (2000)
6. Hassenzahl, M.: Emotions can be quite ephemeral. We cannot design them. Interactions 11, 46–48 (2004)
7. Norman, D.A.: Emotional Design. Why we love or hate everyday things. Basic Books, New York (2004)
8. Bargas-Avila, J.A., Hornbaek, K.: Old Wine in New Bottles or Novel Challenges? A Critical Analysis of Empirical Studies of User Experience. In: Proceedings of the 2011 Annual Conference on Human Factors in Computing Systems (CHI 2011), pp. 2689–2698 (2011)
9. Lottridge, D.: Evaluating human computer interaction through self-rated emotion. In: Gross, T., Gulliksen, J., Kotzé, P., Oestreicher, L., Palanque, P., Prates, R.O., Winckler, M. (eds.) INTERACT 2009. LNCS, vol. 5727, pp. 860–863. Springer, Heidelberg (2009)
10. Xu, D., Read, J.C., Sim, G., McManus, B.: Experience it, draw it, rate it: capture children's experiences with their drawings. In: IDC 2009: Proceedings of the 8th International Conference on Interaction Design and Children, pp. 266–270. ACM Press, New York (2009)
11. Rinn, W.E.: The neuropsychology of facial expression: a review of the neurological and psychological mechanisms for producing facial expression. Psychological Bulletin 95(1), 52–77 (1984)
12. Ekman, P., Friesen, W.V.: Head and body cues in the judgment of emotion: a reformulation. Perceptual and Motor Skills 24(3), 711–724 (1967)
13. De Gelder, B.: Why bodies? Twelve reasons for including bodily expressions in affective neuroscience. Phil. Trans. R. Soc. B 364, 3475–3484 (2009)
14. James, W.T.: A study of expression of body posture. Journal of General Psychology 7, 405–437 (1932)
15. Ekman, P., Friesen, W.: Manual for the facial action coding system. Consulting Psychology Press, Palo Alto (1978)
16. Wallbott, H.G.: Bodily expression of emotion. European Journal of Social Psychology 28(6), 879–896 (1998)
17. Riskind, J.H., Gotay, C.C.: Physical Posture: Could It Have Regulatory or Feedback Effects on Motivation and Emotion? Motivation and Emotion 6(3), 273–298 (1982)
18. Pasch, M., Bianchi-Berthouze, N., van Dijk, B., Nijholt, A.: Movement-based sports video games: Investigating motivation and gaming experience. Entertainment Computing 1(2), 49–61 (2009)
19. Bianchi-Berthouze, N.: Does body movement affect the player engagement experience? In: Proc. of KEER 2010 - International Conference on Kansei Engineering and Emotion Research, pp. 1953–1963 (2010)

20. Calvo, R.A., D'Mello, S.: Affect Detection: An Interdisciplinary Review of Models, Methods, and Their Applications. IEEE Trans. o. Aff. Computing 1(1), 18–37 (2010)
21. Ekman, P.: Basic emotions. In: Dalgleish, T., Power, M. (eds.) Handbook of Cognition and Emotion. John Wiley & Sons, Sussex (1999)
22. Ekman, P., Friesen, W.V.: Head and body cues in the judgment of emotion: a reformulation. Perceptual and Motor Skills 24(3), 711–724 (1967)
23. Coulson, M.: Attributing emotion to static body postures: recognition, accuracy, confusions, and viewpoint dependence. Journal of Nonverbal Behaviour 28(2), 117–139 (2004)
24. Kudoh, T., Matsumoto, D.: Crosscultural examination of the semantic dimensions of body posture. Journal of Personality and Social Psychology 48(6), 1440–1446 (1985)
25. Grammer, K., Fink, B., Oberzaucher, E., Atzmüller, M., Blantar, I., Mitteroecker, P.: The representation of self reported affect in body posture and body posture simulation. Collegium Antropologicum 28(suppl. 2), 159–173 (2004)
26. Kleinsmith, A., De Silva, P.R., Bianchi-Berthouze, N.: Cross-cultural differences in recognizing affect from body posture. Interacting w. Computers 18(6), 1371–1389 (2006)
27. De Silva, P.R., Bianchi-Berthouze, N.: Modeling human affective postures: an information theoretic characterization of posture features. Computer Animation and Virtual Worlds 15(3-4), 269–276 (2004)
28. Clay, A., Real, M., Wijdenes, P., Andre, J.M., Lespinet-Najib, V.:: Movement transcriptions of SECs in componential process model. Presented at the CHI 2011, Workshop on Embodied Interaction: Theory and Practice in HCI (2011)
29. Pitterman, H., Nowicki Jr., S.: A test of the ability to identify emotion in human standing and sitting postures. Genetic, Social, and General Psychology Monographs 130(2), 146–162 (2004)
30. Pasch, M., Poppe, R.: Person or Puppet? The Role of Stimulus Realism in Attributing Emotion to Static Body Postures. In: Paiva, A.C.R., Prada, R., Picard, R.W. (eds.) ACII 2007. LNCS, vol. 4738, pp. 83–94. Springer, Heidelberg (2007)
31. Höök, K.: Mobile life – innovation in the wild. In: Gross, T., Gulliksen, J., Kotzé, P., Oestreicher, L., Palanque, P., Prates, R.O., Winckler, M. (eds.) INTERACT 2009. LNCS, vol. 5726, pp. 1–2. Springer, Heidelberg (2009)
32. Harper, R., Rodden, T., Rogers, Y., Sellen, A. (eds.): Being human: Human-Computer Interaction in the year 2020. Microsoft Research, Cambridge (2008)

An Integrative Computational Model of Emotions

Luis-Felipe Rodríguez[1], Félix Ramos[1], and Gregorio García[2]

[1] Department of Computer Science, Cinvestav Guadalajara, México
{lrodrigue,framos}@gdl.cinvestav.mx
[2] Department of Neuropsychology, Benemérita Universidad Autónoma de Puebla
{gregorio.garcia}@correo.buap.mx

Abstract. In this paper we propose a computational model of emotions designed to provide autonomous agents with mechanisms for affective processing. We present an integrative framework as the underlying architecture of this computational model, which enables the unification of theories explaining the different facets of the human emotion process and promotes the interaction between cognitive and affective functions. This proposal is inspired by recent advances in the study of human emotions in disciplines such as psychology and neuroscience.

Keywords: Computational Models of Emotions, Integrative Frameworks, Cognitive and Affective Functions, Autonomous Agents.

1 Introduction

Computational Models of Emotions (CMEs) are software systems designed to synthesize the operations and architectures of the components that constitute the process of human emotions. These models include mechanisms for the evaluation of stimuli, elicitation of emotions, and generation of emotional responses [13]. CMEs are useful in several areas. In disciplines such as psychology and neuroscience they serve as testbed for the evaluation, completion, and improvement of theoretical models [1]. In the field of artificial intelligence, CMEs are usually incorporated into agent architectures, enabling autonomous agents (AAs) to recognize and simulate emotions and execute emotionally-driven responses [6].

The development of CMEs has been primarily driven by advances in the study of human emotions. In particular, most CMEs are inspired by psychological theories [2, 7, 12–14, 28], which explain the process of emotions from a functional perspective, investigating the inputs, outputs, and behaviors of the components that constitute this process. Similarly, disciplines such as cognitive and affective neuroscience have recently reported significant progress in explaining the internal mechanisms underlying human emotions [4, 25]. The theories originated in these fields investigate emotions in terms of brain functions, brain structures, and neural pathways, providing a deeper understanding of the components involved in the processing of emotions. Unfortunately, related literature reports few CMEs whose development is based on this type of evidence [2, 28].

S. D´Mello et al. (Eds.): ACII 2011, Part II, LNCS 6975, pp. 272–279, 2011.

Regardless of the theoretical approach taken into account in the development of CMEs, most theories have constraints that cause variabilities in the internal design of these computational models. For example, due to the complexity in the study of human emotions, theoretical models focus on particular facets of the emotion process, which are explained at various levels of abstraction and from different perspectives. Furthermore, the number and type of the components that constitute the emotion process and the definitions of concepts used to describe affective processes widely differ among theories. Nevertheless, theoretical models complement each other to allow the development of functional CMEs [24].

These and other issues discussed below have to be addressed in the development of CMEs. The architectures of such computational models should provide proper environments for the unification of heterogeneous theories that explain the different facets of human emotions. In this paper, we propose a CME that incorporates *an integrative* and *scalable architecture* which *promotes the interaction between affective and cognitive functions*. This proposal is mainly inspired by Newell's ideas on *unified theories of cognition* [17] as well as by theoretical advances in the field of neuroscience.

2   Related Work

In general, CMEs summarize the emotion process in three phases: stimuli evaluation, emotion elicitation, and emotional responses. In the first phase, CMEs evaluate the emotional significance of perceived stimuli using a series of criteria. For example, MAMID [8] performs an assessment of stimuli in terms of their valence using appraisal variables such as expectation and novelty. In the second phase, this type of information is used to elicit particular emotions and determine their associated intensity. For example, WASABI [2] uses a three-dimensional space to decide which emotions will be elicited. In the last phase, emotions influence processes such as decision making [8], conversational skills [7], and facial expressions [2]. However, despite this general and well accepted abstract cycle, CMEs address each of this phases in very different ways.

One aspect that causes a marked difference among CMEs is the number and type of affective functions they take into account for the processing of emotions. Marsella and Gratch [14] consider mood as the unique affective modulator for the elicitation of emotions. Marinier et al. [12] implement a mechanism that includes emotions, mood, and feeling to determine the affective experience of AAs. Gebhard [7] integrates emotions, mood, and personality to achieve affective processing in conversational AAs. However, the operational and architectural roles that such affective factors play in each model also differs.

Regardless of how CMEs address the phases described above and the number and type of affective processes they involve, their implementation is primarily inspired by psychological theories. The most implemented approach is the *appraisal theory* [7, 12, 14], which explains the elicitation and differentiation of emotions based on the relationship between individuals and their environment [19, 21]. However, most psychological theories lack the detail needed to fully meet the requirements of a computational model, forcing developers to include additional "working assumptions" to achieve functional systems.

Regarding the labeling of emotions, while some CMEs are not interested in providing specific models for this procedure [12, 14], others focus on the elicitation of categorical emotions [5, 7]. The CMEs included in the first class argue that the labeling of emotions depends on diverse factors such as culture and personality, which may or may not be considered in CMEs. Nevertheless, nearly all CMEs use the emotional labels included in the groups of basic and non-basic emotions.

There are several case studies in which CMEs have proven useful. In each case emotions modulate the verbal and non-verbal behavior of AAs differently. Moreover, although it is recognized that such behavior is carried out by cognitive functions in humans, CMEs are not fully committed with building coherent systems that integrate both affective and cognitive processing.

In summary, the operational and architectural variability in CMEs may be explained as follows. First, there is not a universal and well-accepted theory explaining human emotions, consequently, CMEs are implemented according to the theories in which they are based. Second, they are mainly inspired by psychological theories, which lack the detail needed to fully implement a computational system and force the inclusion of a variety of subjective assumptions. Finally, since each CME is designed for a specific purpose, they must meet different requirements which restrict the elements to be included in their design. Furthermore, the design of CMEs has been restricted by two conditions. First, as many of them have been integrated in cognitive frameworks [2, 12], they are required to meet specific constraints imposed by these models. Second, although other stand-alone CMEs have been proposed, they are developed to process affective information to modulate specific cognitive functions [5, 7], limiting thus the development of more comprehensive models of emotion. See table 1 for a concise analysis of the issues discussed here.

3   Proposed Model

This section covers the two concepts that comprise our proposal, which aim to address the issues identified previously. We first introduce an integrative framework intended to unify affective and cognitive models, and then present the main characteristics and properties of the proposed CME.

3.1   Fundamentals for an Integrative Framework

Based on the previous review and advances in the study of human emotions, we identify two issues that must be considered in the development of CMEs:

1. *Integrative and scalable architecture*: CMEs must incorporate frameworks that consistently allow the unification of theories and models that explain the diverse components of human emotions. Although most CMEs can be

Table 1. Some major differences among CMEs

Model	Foundations	Affective Processes	Emotions Labels	Effects of Emotions	Case Studies
EMA [14]	Appraisal theory by Smith and Lazarus [27]	Emotions and mood	Surprise, Hope, Joy, Fear, Sadness, Anger, and Guilt	Agent's expressions, attentional processes, beliefs, desires, and intentions	Decision-making in Virtual Humans developed for training purposes
Flame [5]	Appraisal theory by Ortony et al. [19] and Roseman et al. [21]	Emotions, motivational states, and mood	Joy, Sad, Disappointment, Relief, Hope, Fear, Pride, Shame, Reproach, and Admiration. *Complex emotions*: Anger (sad + reproach), Gratification (joy + admiration), Gratitude (joy + pride), and Remorse (sad + shame)	Action selection	Decision-making in virtual pets showing believable behavior
Marmid [8]	Diverse appraisal theories [26, 27] and psychological personality models [15]	Emotions and personality	Anxiety/fear, Anger/aggression, Negative affect (sadness, distress), and positive affect (joy, happiness)	Goal and action selection	Virtual humans for training and psychotherapy environments [9]
Alma [7]	Appraisal model by Ortony et al. [19], the Five Factor Model of personality [15], and the PAD Temperament space by Mehrabian [16]	Emotions, mood, and personality	Admiration, Anger, Disliking, Disappointment, Distress, Fear, Fears Confirmed, Gloating, Gratification, Gratitude, Happy For, Hate, Hope, Joy, Liking, Love, Pity, Pride, Relief, Remorse, Reproach, Resentment, Satisfaction, Shame	*Verbal and Non-verbal Expressions* such as wording, length of phrases, and facial expressions. *Cognitive Processes* such as Decision-Making	Embodied Conversational Agents
Cathexis [28]	Diverse psychological [21] and neuropsychological [4] theories	Emotions, drives, mood, and personality	*Primary emotions*: Anger, Fear, Sadness/Distress, Enjoyment/Happiness, Disgust, and Surprise. This model handles *secondary emotions* but does not provides an explicit model for the labeling of them	*Agent's Expressivity* such as facial expressions and body postures. *Cognitive Processes* such as perception, memory, and action selection	Decision-making in virtual and physical agents
PEACTIDM [12]	Appraisal theory by Scherer [23] and physiological concepts of feelings by Damasio [4]	Emotions, mood, and feelings	This model implements the model by Scherer [23] for the mapping of appraisal dimension values to specific modal emotions	General cognitive behavior	Goal-directed Autonomous Agents
WASABI [2]	Appraisal theory by Scherer [23], PAD space by Mehrabian [16], and physiological concepts by Damasio [4]	Emotions and mood	*Primary emotions*: Angry, Annoyed, Bored, Concentrated, Depressed, Fearful, Happy, Sad, Surprised. *Secondary emotions*: Hope, Fears-confirmed, Relief	Facial expressions, involuntary behaviors such as breathing, and voluntary behaviors such as verbal expressions	Emotional expressions and responses in virtual players

seen as integrative frameworks, they usually include only those aspects that allow them to meet their design objectives. Moreover, they are not committed to the construction of suitable environments for the steady incorporation of new findings about this human function, which is an essential requirement since the brain mechanisms underlying emotions begin to be revealed [3].

2. *Consistent model for the interaction between affective and cognitive functions*: although nearly all CMEs are aware of the antecedents and consequents of emotions (i.e., perception and motor-action), in most cases they are not committed with establishing proper interfaces for the interaction between various affective and cognitive processes. In this sense, CMEs should be developed so that they properly handle both affective and cognitive data.

A coherent framework addressing these issues will undoubtedly change the way in which CMEs are developed, leading to significant advances in the field of affective computing. In addition, these two aspects encourage the creation of CMEs that not only present certain differences with respect to their operational and architectural assumptions, but that incorporate frameworks which allow the proper integration of the various components of the human emotions process.

We consider evidence from psychology and neuroscience to create an integrative framework that addresses these two issues, which represents the underlying architecture of the CME that we propose in section 3.2. Such integrative framework is designed on the basis of a multiprocess and multilevel perspective as shown in figure 1 [18]. It considers several brain functions, areas, and nuclei for the processing of emotions [11, 20]. In figure 1, the level two consists of a series of abstract models of cognitive and affective functions, such as mood and personality, which interact in order to achieve the dynamics of emotions [22]. These abstract models comprise various architectural components (at level three) whose collaborative work produce their corresponding behavior. While the modules in the level two take the role of brain functions, the modules in level three simulate the operations and architectures of brain structures.

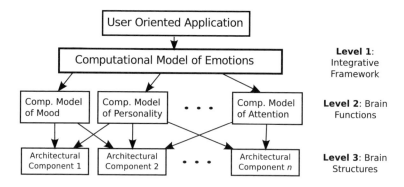

Fig. 1. Integrative framework for a CME

In this manner, we can establish the following hypotheses. The proposed CME will incorporate an *integrative and scalable architecture*, since traditional and modern theories explaining the diverse facets of human emotions can be implemented in this framework by using the structural and operational basis within it. Similarly, *cognitive models* explained in terms of these two levels can be implemented using the same structural and operational constraints used for implementing affective processes. This approach allows reducing and validating the "working assumptions" in CMEs used to achieve functional systems and induced by psychological theories. Finally, neuroscience is increasingly able to explain many processes that are common to all individuals [25], allowing us to address the emotion process by implementing the core mechanisms from which emotional behavior emerges [10].

3.2   Design of the CME

In this section we describe the characteristics and properties of the CME we are proposing, which is based on the integrative framework described above. The following list sets out the requirements for the construction of a functional model of emotions, which is composed of modules that simulate brain functions according to the level two in figure 1. This functional model, in a top-down approach, will serve as the starting point for the design and implementation of the architectural components in level three.

- *Dynamics of Emotion*: the emotion process follows a cycle in which all emotionally charged stimuli impact the agent's emotional state.
- *Emotion Regulation*: emotions are re-evaluated when the contextual conditions in which they were first generated have changed or are no longer appropriate to implement the corresponding emotional responses.
- *Environment Adaptability*: an element in the environment is always appreciated by the agent differently at different times.
- *Affective and Cognitive Processes*: emotions have to do with a dynamic influence between diverse cognitive and affective phenomena.
- *Internal and External Emotion Elicitors*: the dynamic of emotions is driven by the assessment of external and internal stimuli.
- *Labeling of Emotions*: it is needed a correlation between the emotional state of the agent and an emotional label.
- *Emotions Intensity*: emotions are generated with an associated intensity, which is necessary to modulate the agent's responses induced by emotions.
- *Emotional Reactions*: emotions always generate verbal/non-verbal behavior.

4   Conclusions and Future Work

Computational models of emotion are highly influenced by theoretical models that investigate the actual process of emotions. These theories address particular facets of this human function and explain them using different levels of abstraction and from different perspectives. Most CMEs are based on psychological approaches, which lack the detail needed to fully develop computational models. On this basis, we proposed an integrative framework for unifying theories explaining emotions in terms of brain functions, brain structures, and neural pathways. Which provides a convenient environment for the steady inclusion of evidence about the functioning of human emotions, and allows the proper interaction between cognitions and emotions. We also presented the main characteristics of a CME to be implemented in this integrative framework.

Future research focuses on the following tasks:

- Identification of the cognitive–affective processes that meet the characteristics and properties of the proposed CME (functional model at level two).
- Identification of the brain structures and interactions that underlie the processes in the functional model (architectural model at level three).
- Formalization of the internal operations of the CME.
- Analysis of computational techniques for implementing each process in the CME.
- Implementation of the CME.
- Development of case studies and evaluations.

Acknowledgments. The authors would like to acknowledge the PhD scholarship (CONACYT grant No. 229386) sponsored by the Mexican Government for their partial support to this work. We would like to thank the anonymous reviewers for their valuable comments and suggestions.

References

1. Armony, J.L., Servan-Schreiber, D., Cohen, J.D., LeDoux, J.E.: Computational modeling of emotion: explorations through the anatomy and physiology of fear conditioning. Trends in Cognitive Sciences 1(1), 28–34 (1997)
2. Becker-Asano, C.W., Wachsmuth, I.: Affective computing with primary and secondary emotions in a virtual human. Autonomous Agents and Multi-Agent Systems 20(1), 32–49 (2010)
3. Dalgleish, T., Dunn, B.D., Mobbs, D.: Affective neuroscience: Past, present, and future. Emotion Review 1(4), 355–368 (2009)
4. Damasio, A.R.: Descartes' error: Emotion, Reason, and the Human Brain, 1st edn. Putnam Grosset Books, New York (1994)
5. El-Nasr, M.S., Yen, J., Ioerger, T.R.: Flame–fuzzy logic adaptive model of emotions. Autonomous Agents and Multi-Agent Systems 3(3), 219–257 (2000)
6. Fellous, J.-M., Arbib, M.A.: Who needs emotions?: the brain meets the robot. Oxford University Press, Oxford (2005)
7. Gebhard, P.: Alma: a layered model of affect. In: Proceedings of the International Conference on Autonomous Agents And Multiagent Systems, pp. 29–36 (2005)
8. Hudlicka, E.: This time with feeling: Integrated model of trait and state effects on cognition and behavior. Applied Artificial Intelligence: An International Journal 16(7-8), 611–641 (2002)
9. Hudlicka, E.: A computational model of emotion and personality: Applications to psychotherapy research and practice. In: Proceedings of the 10th Annual CyberTherapy Conference: A Decade of Virtual Reality (2005)

10. Lane, R.D., Nadel, L., Allen, J.J.B., Kaszniak, A.W.: The study of emotion from the perspective of cognitive neuroscience. In: Lane, R.D., Nadel, L. (eds.) Cognitive Neuroscience of Emotion. Oxford University Press, New York (2000)
11. LeDoux, J.E., Phelps, E.A.: Emotion networks in the brain. In: Lewis, M., Haviland-Jones, J.M. (eds.) Handbook of Emotions, pp. 159–179. Guilford Press, New York (2000)
12. Marinier, R.P., Laird, J.E., Lewis, R.L.: A computational unification of cognitive behavior and emotion. Cognitive Systems Research 10(1), 48–69 (2009)
13. Marsella, S., Gratch, J., Petta, P.: Computational models of emotion. In: Scherer, K.R., Bänziger, T., Roesch, E.B. (eds.) Blueprint for Affective Computing: A Source Book, 1st edn. Oxford University Press, Oxford (2010)
14. Marsella, S.C., Gratch, J.: Ema: A process model of appraisal dynamics. Cognitive Systems Research 10(1), 70–90 (2009)
15. McCrae, R.R., John, O.P.: An introduction to the five-factor model and its applications. Journal of Personality 60(2), 175–215 (1992)
16. Mehrabian, A.: Pleasure-arousal-dominance: A general framework for describing and measuring individual differences in temperament. Current Psychology 14(4), 261–292 (1996)
17. Newell, A.: Unified theories of cognition. Harvard University Press, Cambridge (1990)
18. Ochsner, K.N., Barrett, L.F.: A multiprocess perspective on the neuroscience of emotion. In: Mayne, T.J., Bonanno, G.A. (eds.) Emotions: Currrent Issues and Future Directions, pp. 38–81. Guilford Press, New York (2001)
19. Ortony, A., Clore, G.L., Collins, A.: The cognitive structure of emotions. Cambridge University Press, Cambridge (1990)
20. Phan, K.L., Wager, T.D., Taylor, S.F., Liberzon, I.: Functional neuroimaging studies of human emotions. CNS Spectrums 9(4), 258–266 (2004)
21. Roseman, I.J., Spindel, M.S., Jose, P.E.: Appraisals of emotion-eliciting events: Testing a theory of discrete emotions. Journal of Personality and Social Psychology 59(5), 899–915 (1990)
22. Rusting, C.L.: Personality, mood, and cognitive processing of emotional information: Three conceptual frameworks. Psychological Bulletin 124(2), 165–196 (1998)
23. Scherer, K.R.: Appraisal considered as a process of multi-level sequential checking. In: Scherer, K.R., Schorr, A., Johnstone, T. (eds.) Appraisal Processes in Emotion: Theory, Methods, Research, pp. 92–120. Oxford University Press, New York (2001)
24. Scherer, K.R.: Emotion and emotional competence: conceptual and theoretical issues for modelling agents. In: Scherer, K.R., Bänziger, T., Roesch, E.B. (eds.) Blueprint for Affective Computing: A Source Book. Oxford University Press, Oxford (2010)
25. Shepherd, G.M.: Creating modern neuroscience: the revolutionary 1950s. Oxford University Press, Oxford (2009)
26. Smith, C.A., Kirby, L.D.: Toward delivering on the promise of appraisal theory. In: Scherer, K.R., Schorr, A., Johnstone, T. (eds.) Appraisal Processes in Emotion, Oxford, NY (2001)
27. Smith, C.A., Lazarus, R.S.: Emotion and adaptation. In: Pervin, L.A. (ed.) Handbook of Personality: Theory and Research, pp. 609–637. Guilford Press, New York (1990)
28. Velásquez, J.D.: Modeling emotions and other motivations in synthetic agents. In: Proceedings of the Fourteenth National Conference on Artificial Intelligence and Ninth Conference on Innovative Applications of Artificial Intelligence, pp. 10–15 (1997)

Affective Support in Narrative-Centered Learning Environments

Jennifer Sabourin

Department of Computer Science, North Carolina State University, Raleigh NC 27695
jlrobiso@ncsu.edu

Abstract. The link between affect and student learning has been the subject of increasing attention in recent years. Affective states such as flow and curiosity tend to have positive correlations with learning while negative states such as boredom and frustration have the opposite effect. Consequently, it is a goal of many intelligent tutoring systems to guide students toward emotional states that are conducive to learning through affective interventions. While much work has gone into understanding the relation between student learning and affective experiences, it is not clear how these relationships manifest themselves in narrative-centered learning environments. These environments embed learning within the context of an engaging narrative that can benefit from "affective scaffolding." However, in order to provide an optimal level of support for students, the following research questions must be answered: 1) What is the nature of affective experiences in interactive learning environments? 2) How is affect impacted by personal traits, beliefs and learning strategies, and what role does affect have in shaping traits, beliefs, and learning strategies? 3) What strategies can be used to successfully create an optimal affective learning experience?

Keywords: Affective interfaces, applications in education.

1 Introduction

Affect has begun to play an increasingly important role in intelligent tutoring systems. The intelligent tutoring system community has seen the emergence of work on affective student modeling [1], detecting frustration and stress [2,3], detecting student motivation [4], and diagnosing and adapting to student self-efficacy [5]. All of this work seeks to increase the fidelity with which affective and motivational processes are understood and utilized in intelligent tutoring systems in an effort to increase the effectiveness of tutorial interactions and, ultimately, learning. This level of emphasis on affect is not surprising given the impact it has been shown to have on learning outcomes. Student affective states influence problem-solving strategies, the level of engagement exhibited by the student, and the degree to which he or she is motivated to continue with the learning process [6,7]. All of these factors have the potential to influence both how students learn immediately and their learning behaviors in the future. Consequently, developing techniques for keeping students in an affective state that is conducive to learning has been a focus of recent work [8,9,10].

S. D´Mello et al. (Eds.): ACII 2011, Part II, LNCS 6975, pp. 280–288, 2011.
© Springer-Verlag Berlin Heidelberg 2011

Unfortunately, there is not yet a clear understanding of how emotions occur during learning and, in particular, how individual learning environments impact the emotional experience. It is also unclear which emotional states are optimal for individual students. This is likely to vary based on student needs and experience. Affective experiences may also have interesting immediate and long term effects on how students perceive learning and their levels of confidence and motivation moving forward. Finally, current research on how best to respond to student affect has yielded varying and often conflicting conclusions [5,11]. For these reasons, it is challenging to design affective support systems for learning environments.

The goal of this research is to examine these issues within narrative-centered learning environments. These environments embed the educational process within a story with the objective of leveraging narrative's motivating features such as compelling plots, engaging characters, and fantastical settings [12]. These environments also offer the potential for affective experiences that are supplementary to those experienced in more typical interactive learning environments [13]. The ability to understand and control the emotional experiences of students in narrative-centered learning environments could lead to significant gains for student learning and motivation. The proposed research aims to achieve this goal by answering the following three research questions: (1) What is the nature of affective experiences in interactive learning environments? (2) How is affect impacted by personal traits, beliefs and learning strategies and what role does affect have in shaping these qualities? (3) What strategies can be used to successfully create an optimal affective experience?

2   Research Questions

The overarching goal of the proposed research is to *characterize* and *facilitate* affective experiences in narrative-centered learning environments in order to achieve *optimal* immediate learning gains and future long-term outcomes. This goal can be achieved through exploration of three lines of investigation. The first relates to the *characterization* of affective experiences. In particular it is important to understand the types of emotions that are experienced in narrative-centered learning environments as well as the antecedents and consequences associated with each. While the precise cognitive and affective mechanisms underlying learning experiences is not yet well understood, there has been significant progress in attempting to identify the emotions that students are likely to experience and how these may affect the learning process. For instance, Kort *et al.* [6] present a model of learning emotions which can be represented as a cycle that occurs throughout the learning process. Other studies have investigated how emotional experiences transpire in computational environments. Both D'Mello *et al.* and Baker *et al.* have shown that students are most likely to remain in the same state through time and that certain emotional transitions are more likely than others [14,15]. These results, and their replication in subsequent studies, suggest that there is an underlying model modulating the likelihood of students experiencing particular affective states.

The second research question relates to defining *optimal* experiences. Students' emotional states can strongly impact how the student learns [7] and interacts with learning environments [15,16]. Students with highly negative experiences such as frustration and boredom are expected to persist in these negative states and may disengage from the learning task [16]. Bored students are particularly likely to engage in harmful behaviors such as gaming the system. There is also evidence that there may be some students who are better at regulating their affective experiences during learning [17]. For example, students who are focused on learning rather than objective measures of performance are more likely to recover from set-backs and states of confusion [13]. Understanding the interrelation between these personal traits, learning and student affect will contribute to a clearer understanding of optimal outcomes.

Finally, the third research question builds directly on the second by attempting to *facilitate* affective experiences. These efforts are intended to yield a variety of strategies that can be shown to induce optimal affective experiences. To date, a broad range of strategies has been suggested for improving student affect. Chaffar and Frasson [8] propose an Emotional Intelligent Agent which utilizes guided imagery, music and presented images in an attempt to induce optimal emotional states for each student. D'Mello *et al.* [9] have also proposed methods for responding to student affect using empathetic and tutorial dialogue acts accompanied by visual facial expressions and emotionally synthesized speech. Alternatively, Murray and VanLehn provide affective support without directly encouraging or displaying emotional states [18]. Instead, they use a decision theoretic approach to determine when the delivery of hints may hinder or improve student morale and independence.

3   Methodology

Work has begun on each of the research directions outlined above. These efforts have centered on empirical studies of the affective experiences of students interacting with the narrative-centered learning environment, CRYSTAL ISLAND (Figure 1). This environment is being created in the domains of microbiology and genetics for middle school students. It features a science mystery set on a recently discovered volcanic island where a research station has been established to study the unique flora and fauna. Students play the role of the protagonist, Alex, who is attempting to discover the identity and source of an unidentified disease plaguing a newly established research station. Most previous work on affect in CRYSTAL ISLAND has been conducted in small-scale studies outside of the target demographic (e.g. [13]) while the work presented here represents the first large-scale investigation into the proposed research questions with the target demographic of eighth grade students.

Analysis of affective experiences in narrative-centered learning environments utilizes data collected from a study involving eighth grade students from two rural North Carolina middle schools. From the first school, data from 296 students was collected. After removing instances with incomplete data or logging errors, there were 260 students remaining. From the second school, data was collected from 154 students with 140 students remaining after cleaning the data.

Students' affect data was collected during the learning interactions through regular self-report prompts. Students were prompted every seven minutes to self-report their current mood and "status" through an in-game smartphone device (Figure 2). Students selected one emotion from a set of seven options, which included: *anxious, bored, confused, curious, excited, focused,* and *frustrated*. Each emotion label was accompanied by an emoticon to help illustrate the mood to students. After selecting an emotion,

Fig. 1. CRYSTAL ISLAND environment   **Fig. 2.** Self-report device

students were instructed to briefly type a few words about their current status in the game, similarly to how they might update their status in an online social network. The seven minute intervals between self-reports was selected to balance a desire for a rich picture of affective experience and to avoid irritating the students. Future work may investigate the use of other techniques of affect detection to avoid issues with self-report such as honesty of the student and interruption from the learning environment.

4   Initial Results

Initial work at characterizing the affective experiences of students in CRYSTAL ISLAND has shown some interesting similarities and differences from the results found in other learning environments. For instance, positive, learning-focused emotions such as *focused* (23%) and *curious* (19%) accounted for the majority of student's self-reported emotions. *Confusion* (16%) and *frustration* (16%) were the next most frequent emotional states. These emotional states are expected to result from the open-ended nature of the CRYSTAL ISLAND environment. The environment does not tell students specifically what they should be doing at any given time which may be different from their classroom learning experiences. The somewhat high levels of these emotional states suggest that there may be some students who may need

Table 1. Frequency and proportion of emotion self-reports

Emotion	School 1		School 2		Total	
	Freq	Per	Freq	Per	Freq	Per
anxious	86	4.6%	41	4.0%	127	4.4%
bored	159	8.5%	84	8.2%	243	8.4%
confused	300	16.1%	167	16.3%	467	16.2%
curious	347	18.6%	203	19.8%	550	19.1%
excited	251	13.5%	126	12.3%	377	13.1%
focused	417	22.4%	252	24.6%	669	23.2%
frustrated	303	16.3%	150	14.7%	453	15.7%
Total	**1863**	-	**1023**	-	**2886**	-

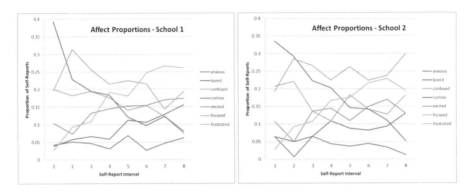

Fig. 3. Graphs of the proportion of affect self-reports across time

increased levels of guidance, though other students may benefit from exploring the environment on their own.

While it is interesting to examine the occurrence of emotional states in the environment, this analysis is only worthwhile if it is expected to extend to future populations. Therefore, it was important to compare the relative frequency of emotional states for each school. The frequency for each school is presented in (Table 1). The relative frequencies appear very similar for each emotional state and a chi- squared analysis indicates that there are not significant differences in the frequencies, $\chi 2$ (6, N=400) = 4.368, p=0.627.

Perhaps even more interesting than the similarity in the frequencies of emotional states is how these frequencies change over time. Since each student was prompted at routine intervals, we can measure students' states at approximately the same times across studies. The two graphs of Figure 3 show the change in proportion of self-reports at each time interval. It is interesting to examine the striking similarities between the two graphs. For instance, for both populations *curiosity* is the most frequent report in the first interval and drops rapidly and steadily from there. While students are initially *curious* at the beginning of the interaction, this curiosity wanes over time, being replaced by other emotions. Interestingly, both *frustration* and *excitement* increase over time.

5 Future Directions

Initial results suggest that there is a broad range of affective experiences across students. Students have different goals, varying levels of prior knowledge, and different levels of achievement in the environment. However, while there are likely as many different experiences as there are students interacting with the game, early investigations in the self-report data suggest that there may be regularities in the emotional patterns that are occurring. In particular, students' "status" messages that were entered at the time of the affect self-report help to provide additional insight into these patterns over what can be determined only from the self-reported emotional

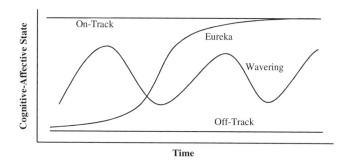

Fig. 4. Graphical representation of four proposed student categories

states. Based on a preliminary investigation of students' reports and affective states, four common patterns of behavior emerged. A graphical representation of these student patterns is depicted in Figure 4.

On-track students begin the interaction with an idea of the goals they wish to accomplish. They proceed through the game generally having a plan and while they may experience some confusion or frustration in executing their plan, they rarely flounder or become overwhelmed. These students generally report more positive affect and likely have a greater success in completing the mystery.

Eureka students, on the other hand, begin the experience confused over what goals they should be seeking. They may be initially overwhelmed by the open-ended environment and be unsure of how to proceed. However, after some initial exploration these students get a feel for their objectives in solving the mystery and are able to set further goals. Towards the end of their interaction they resemble the high knowledge students, reporting a higher frequency of positive emotions.

Wavering students demonstrate a pattern of constant alternation between confusion and finding their way. These students do not experience the 'eureka' moment of the other students in which they gain insight into how to proceed through the rest of the interaction. Instead these students seem to be focusing on one problem at a time and once a solution is discovered they again experience a sense of confusion over what they should be doing next. These students have mixed affective experiences and may perhaps be the most difficult to identify since there is not a strong pattern of behavior.

Off-track students have a very different experience. These students are not able to overcome their confusion and sense of being overwhelmed like the *Eureka students*. These students spend the entire interaction confused or frustrated. They are more likely to disengage from the learning activity and report boredom and a desire for the interaction to be over. These students seem like they may need to be the primary focus of affective or hint-based intervention strategies.

Table 2 provides sample self-reports from students that fit into each category. From reading through the student's descriptions of their status, it is clear which category the student likely belongs to. However, automatic detection of these categories from affective reports is likely difficult given the complexity of the statements and emotional experiences. Additionally, since it is expected that these students would likely benefit from different types of affective scaffolding and feedback, early detection of their category would be highly important. It would not be beneficial to classify a student as floundering after he or she has been left overwhelmed for the majority of the interaction and may have already given up. An important direction for future work is to use human experts to categorize students based on their statements. Given these categories, analyses can be conducted to determine if a particular profile of personalities or in-game behaviors can be used to identify each category of students. These categories can be used to guide affective feedback and scaffolding for students providing higher levels of support to the students who are more likely to be feeling overwhelmed.

Table 2. Sample affect and statements indicating student categories

Student 54 – On-Track	*Student 52 - Eureka*
confused: I think I'm trying to find the something that caused the disease that's spreading.	**confused:** can't really find something to do
focused: I am trying to find the stuff that could have caused the disease.	**confused:** still can't find what to do
focused: I think I know what one of these people has as their disease	**frustrated:** I can't find something to do
focused: I am trying to find the food or drink that caused these people to get sick.	**focused:** I have found a way to test things
frustrated: I am trying to find the eggs. I think that is what caused these people to get sick.	**excited:** I have found out how to talk to the people
focused: I found the source of the illness	**excited:** I have found a contaminated food
	focused: close to finding the illness
Student 99 - Wavering	*Student 81 – Off-Track*
confused: looking for clues	**confused:** I don't understand this game
focused: trying to find out	**frustrated:** I'm getting more and more confused every time
frustrated: hard to find the cure	**frustrated:** I'm not getting any of this
focused: I think I found something	**frustrated:** I'm not understanding where I'm supposed to find out all the information to cure these people!?!
confused: I don't know what to do	
focused: I think I'm close	**frustrated:** I just want to stop playing
frustrated: I don't get it	**frustrated:** when does this game end?
	frustrated: I don't get it

6 Conclusions

The types of emotions we associate with learning influence how likely we are to actively engage in learning activities and perceive learning as a positive experience. Because of this significant impact on learning, it is important to develop an understanding of students' emotional states during learning experiences. The objective of the research agenda presented in this paper is to provide affective support for students in narrative-centered learning environments. Initial work in characterizing the affective experiences of students in the CRYSTAL ISLAND environment suggests that affective phenomena are generalizable across populations but that individual students have very different experiences. This lends support to the importance of characterizing the different types of experiences that typically occur so that these patterns may be identified early in the interactions. In this way, customized affective scaffolding may be provided to students who are at-risk for highly negative experiences in order to improve overall affect before too much negativity occurs.

Acknowledgments. The authors wish to thank members of the IntelliMedia lab for their assistance, Omer Sturlovich and Pavel Turzo for use of their 3D model libraries, and Valve Software for access to the Source™ engine and SDK. This research was supported by the National Science Foundation under Grants REC-0632450, DRL-0822200, and IIS-0812291. This material is based upon work supported under a National Science Foundation Graduate Research Fellowship.

References

1. Conati, C., Maclaren, H.: Empirically building and evaluating a probabilistic model of user affect. User Modeling and User-Adapted Interaction 19, 267–303 (2009)
2. Burleson, W., Picard, R.W.: Affective Learning Companions: strategies for empathetic agents with real-time multimodal affective sensing to foster meta-cognitive and meta-affective approaches to learning, motivation, and perseverance by Affective Learning Companions (2006)
3. McQuiggan, S., Lee, S., Lester, J.: Early prediction of student frustration. In: Paiva, A.C.R., Prada, R., Picard, R.W. (eds.) ACII 2007. LNCS, vol. 4738, pp. 698–709. Springer, Heidelberg (2007)
4. de Vicente, A., Pain, H.: Informing the detection of the students' motivational state: An empirical study. In: Cerri, S.A., Gouardéres, G., Paraguaçu, F. (eds.) ITS 2002. LNCS, vol. 2363, pp. 933–943. Springer, Heidelberg (2002)
5. Beal, C., Lee, H.: Creating a pedagogical model that uses student self reports of motivation and mood to adapt ITS instruction. In: Workshop on Motivation and Affect in Educational Software, in Conjunction with the 12th Intl. Conf. on Artificial Intelligence in Education
6. Kort, B., Reilly, R., Picard, R.W.: An affective model of interplay between emotions and learning: reengineering educational pedagogy-building a learning companion. In: Proc. of the IEEE Intl. Conf. on Advanced Learning Technologies, pp. 43–46
7. Picard, R.W., Papert, S., Bender, W., Blumberg, B., Breazeal, C., Cavallo, D., Machover, T., Resnick, M., Roy, D., Strohecker, C.: Affective Learning — A Manifesto. BT Technology Journal 22, 253–269 (2004)
8. Chaffar, S., Frasson, C.: Using an emotional intelligent agent to improve the learner's performance. In: Workshop on Emotional and Social Intelligence in Learning Environments in Conjuction with Intl. Conf. of Intelligent Tutoring Systems, Citeseer (2004)
9. D'Mello, S., Jackson, T., Craig, S., Morgan, B., Chipman, P., White, H., Person, N., Kort, B., el Kaliouby, R., Picard, R., Graesser, A.C.: AutoTutor detects and responds to learners affective and cognitive states. In: Proc. of the Workshop on Emotional and Cognitive Issues in ITS in Conjunction with the 9th Intl. Conf. on Intelligent Tutoring Systems, pp. 31–43
10. Forbes-Riley, K., Litman, D.: Adapting to student uncertainty improves tutoring dialogues. In: Proc. of the 14th Intl. Conf. on Artificial Intelligence in Education (2009)
11. Shute, V.J.: Focus on Formative Feedback. ETS, Princeton (2007)
12. Malone, T., Lepper, M.: Making learning fun: A taxonomy of intrinsic motivations for learning. In: Snow, R.E., Far, M.J. (eds.) Aptitude, Learning, and Instruction: III. Cognitive and Affective Process Analyses, pp. 223–253 (1987)
13. McQuiggan, S., Robison, J., Lester, J.: Affective transitions in narrative-centered learning environments. Educational Technology and Society 13, 40–53 (2010)
14. Mello, S.D., Taylor, R.S., Graesser, A.: Monitoring Affective Trajectories during Complex Learning. Methods (2004)

15. Baker, R.S.J.d., D'Mello, S.K., Rodrigo, M.M.T., Graesser, A.C.: Better to be frustrated than bored: The incidence, persistence, and impact of learners' cognitive–affective states during interactions with three different computer-based learning environments. Intl. Journal of Human-Computer Studies 68, 223–241 (2010)

16. Sabourin, J., Rowe, J., Mott, B., Lester, J.: When Off-Task is On-Task: The Affective Role of Off-Task Behavior in Narrative-Centered Learning Environments. In: Proc. of the 15th Intl. Conf. on Artificial Intelligence in Education, Auckland, New Zealand (2011)

17. Meyer, D.K., Turner, J.C.: Re-conceptualizing Emotion and Motivation to Learn in Classroom Contexts. Educational Psychology Review 18, 377–390 (2006)

18. Murray, R.C., VanLehn, K.: DT tutor: A decision-theoretic, dynamic approach for optimal selection of tutorial actions. In: Gauthier, G., VanLehn, K., Frasson, C. (eds.) ITS 2000. LNCS, vol. 1839, pp. 153–162. Springer, Heidelberg (2000)

Automatic Understanding of Affective and Social Signals by Multimodal Mimicry Recognition

Xiaofan Sun[1], Anton Nijholt[1], Khiet P. Truong[1], and Maja Pantic[1,2]

[1] Human Media Interaction, University of Twente
PO Box 217, 7500 AE Enschede, The Netherlands
[2] Department of Computing, Imperial College
180 Queen's Gate, London SW7 2AZ, UK
{x.f.sun,k.p.truong,a.nijholt}@ewi.utwente.nl,
m.pantic@imperial.ac.uk

Abstract. Human mimicry is one of the important behavioral cues displayed during social interaction that inform us about the interlocutors' interpersonal states and attitudes. For example, the absence of mimicry is usually associated with negative attitudes. A system capable of analyzing and understanding mimicry behavior could enhance social interaction, both in human-human and human-machine interaction, by informing the interlocutors about each other's interpersonal attitudes and feelings of affiliation. Hence, our research focus is the investigation of mimicry in social human-human and human-machine interactions with the aim to help improve the quality of these interactions. In particular, we aim to develop automatic multimodal mimicry analyzers, to enhance affect recognition and social signal understanding systems through mimicry analysis, and to implement mimicry behavior in Embodied Conversational Agents. This paper surveys and discusses the recent work we have carried out regarding these aims. It is meant to serve as an ultimate goal and a guide for determining recommendations for the development of automatic mimicry analyzers to facilitate affective computing and social signal processing.

Keywords: Mimicry detection, mimicry expression information extraction, mimicry behavior encoding, mimicry expression classification, affective computing, social signal processing, embodied conversational agent.

1   Introduction

People's behaviors show diversity in personality, culture, growing-up background, social norms and expectations. Due to these differences, sometimes, a harmonious communication does not last long between two or more persons, especially when they support different opinions or when they are in competition. Socially intelligent systems are capable of sensing or detecting information relevant to human social interaction and are able to make this information readily available to people, these systems have the potential to improve interactions between different people in a manner that will increase feelings of rapport, affiliation and harmony. It is considered

S. D'Mello et al. (Eds.): ACII 2011, Part II, LNCS 6975, pp. 289–296, 2011.
© Springer-Verlag Berlin Heidelberg 2011

that, among other behavioral cues, mimicry behavior (mirroring, e.g. person A nods or smiles following person B who has nodded or smiled too) provide important clues for the analysis and investigations of human interactions, mainly in two ways. Firstly, mimicry serves as an important indicator of cooperativeness and empathy during conversation. The second is its application as a means to enriching communication. The impact of a practical technology to mediate human interactions in real time would be enormous both for society as a whole (improving business relations, cultural understanding, communication relationship, etc) and personal daily social interactions. Hence, we propose to investigate mimicry behavior in human-human interaction with the aim to build automatic mimicry analyzers and mimicry-enabled Embodied Conversational Agents (ECAs).

In the following sections, we firstly discuss mimicry and related work in social psychology. In section 3 we present our aims and objects in our research on mimicry analysis in machine understanding approach. In section 4.1, we explain how our data was collected and what visual and vocal features we analyzed. In section 4.2 we present our methods and technique to automatically recognize mimicry and analyze the concepts learned by models. Finally, in section 5, we conclude the main contribution of our research to affective computing.

2   Related Work/Background

Mimicry-related research in experimental psychology has been driven by two primary objectives. The first objective concerns collecting and detecting various types of the mimicry or synchrony behaviors by establishing the emergence of mimicry by aggregating instances of to-be-imitated behavior (e.g., face touching) during social interactions [1]. The second objective aims to examine the relationship between coordinated behavior and perceptions of social connectedness [2], that is, to find out whether there is a relationship between those behaviors and social interactions. And if so, what is the exact relationship and in which situations do what types of those behaviors occur?

Building on these two primary objectives, recent research explored whether people, without intention or awareness, "use" mimicry to their advantage [3]. People can consciously or automatically mimic the behaviors of others because their goals activate behavioral strategies and plans of action that help them pursue those goals [4], [5], [6]. Individuals can mimic many different aspects of their interaction partners, including speech patterns, facial expressions, emotions, moods, postures, gestures, mannerisms, and idiosyncratic movements [1], [3], [7], [8]. In short, previous studies in social psychology report that the more mimicry is observed, the more smoothly the interaction is perceived: mimicry enhances resonance, creates rapport and affiliation suggesting that it serves to strengthen social bonds.

Given the huge advances in computer vision and algorithmic gesture detection [9], coupled with the propensity for more and more computers to utilize high-bandwidth connections and embedded video cameras, the potential for computer agents to detect, mimic, and implement human gestures [10] and other behaviors (such as vocal cues) is quite boundless and promising. The current findings suggest that non-verbal behavior could easily be added to computer agents to improve the user's experience unobtrusively; moreover, we propose that mimicry behaviors should be added to conversational agents to make them more social. In the following sections, we explain our plans for mimicry research in the context of affective computing and social signal understanding.

3   Aims and Objectives

We have recently witnessed significant advances not only in the machine analysis of nonverbal cues, but also in the field of affective computing and social signal understanding [11]. However, only few works have so far attempted to identify social attitudes such as interest, liking, or agreement through automatic means. In moving towards more naturalistic human-computer interactions, it is necessary to have machines that are capable of detecting and understanding social attitudes, and subsequently, are able to react adequately considering the current situation and the communicative goals. Since mimicry is one of the important behavioral indicators of social and affective attitudes in social interaction, the aims of our research include 1) the automatic recognition and understanding of nonverbal mimicry (both visual and vocal), 2) the enhancement of automatic affect recognition and social signal understanding by the use of mimicry behavior information, and 3) the generation of mimicry behavior in ECAs to improve ECA-human interaction.

4   Methodology

We present our methods to reach the goals as described earlier. For each goal, we shortly describe what we already have done to reach this goal and/or what we are planning to do.

4.1   Automatic Recognition of Nonverbal Mimicry

Our first goal is to develop a system capable of recognizing and understanding nonverbal mimicry. We first need to develop 1) a multimodal database suitable for automatic visual and vocal mimicry analysis and 2) feature extraction methods to represent mimicry in detectable visual and vocal cues. We report on our work carried out to analyze mimicry automatically.

4.1.1   Database Setup
Recent work that we have carried out concerns setting up a multimodal database of mimicry occurring in interpersonal social interactions which allows us to (1) explore and understand how astute people are in detecting mimicry in social interactions, (2) examine and annotate the implications of explicit mimicry occurrences in terms of social perceptions of the mimickers, (3) classify various mimicry and mimicry behavior forms for emotion recognition (positive and negative). The most significant distinction from current affective databases is that it contains natural dyadic behavior, including mimicry. Moreover, the experiments recorded are designed to explore the relationship between the occurrence of mimicry and human affect. The corpus is recorded using a wide range of devices including face-to-face-talking and individual

close-talk fixed microphones, individual and room-view video cameras from different views, all of which produce output signals that are synchronized with each other (Fig. 1). We are planning to make manual annotations for many different phenomena, including dialogue acts, turn-taking, affect, and some head, hand gestures, body movement and facial expression (Fig. 2). The dataset consists of 54 recordings of dyadic face-to-face interactions: 34 are discussions on a political topic, and 20 are conversations situated in a role-playing game. The subjects, 40 participants and 3 confederates, were recruited from Imperial College London; all of the participants self-reported their felt experiences. The recordings and ratings are stored in a database. Later, the corpus will be made available to the scientific community through a web-accessible database. For a more detailed description of the database, readers are referred to [12].

Fig. 1. Simultaneous views from all cameras

Fig. 2. Annotation tool interface includes labels

4.1.2   Multimodal Mimicry Cues Analysis

One of the most important sub-goals in our research is to extract and detect the visual and auditory features that specify temporal changes in expressions in order to measure mimicry from audio and video modalities. There have been a considerable number of studies on feature extraction for speech analysis. However, especially for prosody analysis, these features are still not well defined; for each feature there are multiple definitions and different analysis methods. Recent research has aimed at identifying the most significant speech and visual features for affective computing but the specific contribution of each feature to affect analysis is still unclear. However, for our research goal it is not necessary to find out the contribution of each feature to specific human affect. Instead, the focus is on changes and similarities of visual and vocal behavior. For visual cues, we presented a way to detect visual mimicry in a machine understanding approach [13], [14] in which we demonstrated that in face-to-face interaction, after a while, a confederate has the tendency to take over body postures, head movements, and hand gestures of the participants with whom he/she is interacting. Specifically, we find that participants or confederates who are being mimicked are more willing to alter the way in which they interact with others to share similar affect or attitudes in order to obtain more agreement and to express understanding or similar attitudes. They did not only mimic postures, mannerisms, moods or emotions, but they also mimicked several speech related behaviors. We also demonstrated how vocal behavioural information expressed between two interlocutors can be used to detect and identify vocal mimicry [15]. As future work, we plan to investigate other visual and vocal feature representations of mimicry. The method and extracted features used in the current study are not enough to represent visual mimicry in a machine learning approach. Because the correlation of a motion intensity histogram is not reliable and stabile for recognizing visual-based mimicry, we can only say, to a certain degree, that participants are moving the same body parts with a similar intensity. No details about temporal and specific expressions of various human actions can be given which are needed to represent visual mimicry.

Hence, in future work, for automatic visual-based mimicry detection, more kinematic-based features are needed such that analyses similar to those carried out for non-verbal vocal mimicry can be performed. Focus on the optical flow fields in motion parts of a body, computation of kinematic features (e.g., divergence, vorticity, symmetric flow fields etc.) and the classification of these features for recognizing mimicry will be our primary research goal to achieve the ultimate goal to assess human affect in terms of automatic mimicry analysis. With respect to non-verbal vocal mimicry, we have not looked yet at other non-verbal vocal variables such as utterance lengths and switching pause durations which are known to converge between speakers. Furthermore, in addition to prosodic vocal behavior, people may also mimic the quality of voice which can be measured through voice quality and spectral features. We will investigate the commonly used spectral features Mel-Frequency Cepstrum Components (MFCCs) in combination with speaker recognition modeling techniques to evaluate the similarity between two voices. Further, it is interesting to find out whether the repetition of vocal events such as laughter can be used as a measure for mimicry. We will also look at methods to determine the presence of non-verbal vocal mimicry more locally (rather than globally). How to combine information from various modalities, e.g., facial expressions, vocal expressions, and body movement expressions, for multimodal mimicry recognition is another interesting future research topic. The most challenging problems of multimodal mimicry recognition lies in feature extraction and the use of probabilistic graphical models when fusing the various modalities. As mimicry recognition is closely related to the field of affective computing and shares similar difficult issues, we will also put effort in solving these issues such as obtaining reliable affective data, obtaining ground truth labels, and the use of unlabeled data. Finally, we want to understand how variables, such as personality and emotion, regulate mimicry in interaction so that automatic mimicry detection algorithms can take these into account. To that end, we will take a closer look at our data, and analyze mimicry taking into account the willingness of the participants to mimic in certain situations.

4.2   Use of Mimicry Information to Understand Affective and Social Behavior

Our second goal is to investigate the interrelationships among mimicry and various affects, attitudes, or mental states in interaction. We propose to employ a machine learning approach to model these interrelationships. In further research, we attempt to classify automatic mimicry behaviors based only on nonverbal multimodal cues. We attempt to demonstrate that it is possible to classify various mimicry behaviors (e.g. head movements, body postures, and hand gestures) according to the findings from social psychology which mimicry behaviors are relative to creating rapport, affiliation, and smoother communication. We could propose to explicitly model the complex hidden dynamics of the multimodal cues using the Hidden Conditional Random Field (HCRF), HMM, and DBN. Firstly we will show that those models are able to capture what kinds of mimicry are used in backchannel, are used for conveying social attitudes (e.g. expressing similar attitudes, acceptance, interest), giving response (e.g. listening, understanding,) or other (e.g. unsure). We could present an approach to analyze the concepts learned by the HCRF model and show that these coincide with the findings from social psychology regarding mimicry conveys similar attitudes, understanding, interest, and acceptance. We also could prepare which model performs better and which model can be automatically analyzed to identify what sets of features are the most discriminative in each class. Then we could demonstrate that what kinds of mimicry cues are the most discriminative (important) cues for identifying different classes. In those models, the parameters level (lower level) in the top of the model only contains various variables/parameters which represent the general features; all the features which are used to model the object domain can be estimated by those parameters. The structure level (higher level) of the model is constructed by the structure nodes so that more than one layers' network can be used for representing the different object domains. Finally, all the layers will be connected in the suitable structure to represent our final domain problem. In our domain problem, the highest layer in the structure level is the most abstract layer and specifies what the mental state is (agree/disagree, uncertain, like/dislike, concentrating etc.). The intermediate level (hidden states) layers describe whether and what kind of interactional mimicry exists. The lower level layers describe how to recognize the human behaviors defined in social interactions by parameter estimations and combinations or learning algorithms.

4.3   Mimicry in Embodied Conversational Agents

For our third goal, we will first explore methods and results presented in experimental social psychology that can be used to embody mimicry in agents. The role mimicry plays in social interaction will be embodied in human-agent conversation to make the agent more social and intelligent. The key to facilitate social and intelligent interaction in context between an agent and a human is to build an accurate model of supporting communication for various individuals. A model based on knowledge about the other's group affiliation (from non-verbal behaviour, cultural display rules and so on) and based on the individual's own unique behavioural habits and tendencies (by observation and learning) will form expectations about potential meanings and intentions. The most challenging problem in generating mimicry behavior for agents is to determine in what situation and to what extent the mimicking behavior should occur.

5   Contribution

Our proposed mimicry research serves to identify, "feeling", and "understanding" behaviors of interactants in human and agent interaction with the help of mimicry behavioral information. By instantiating and manipulating psychological theories, through the use of nonverbal cues, we can endow agents with the ability to evolve in and engage in social interactions and to enhance face-to-face communication. From the automatic understanding of social signals and prediction of how these signals affect social situations, immediate applications can be derived to help people with less confidence, to train people for improved social interaction tasks, in general or specifically such as in negotiation. Hence, in sum, our contributions to affective computing and human-machine interaction contain (1) the understanding of how human mimicry works and subsequently, the development of automatic mimicry analyzers for ECAs, (2) the improvement of the recognition of social and affective attitudes such as (dis-)agreeing and (dis-)liking through mimicry information, and (3) knowledge about the timing and the extent to which mimicry should occur in human-machine interaction by generating mimicry behavior in agents. This technology would also strongly influence science and technology by, for example, providing a powerful new class of research tools for social science and anthropology. While the primary goal of such an effort would be to facilitate direct mediated communication between people, advances here will also facilitate interactions between humans and machines.

References

1. Chartrand, T.L., Bargh, J.A.: The chameleon effect: The perception-behavior link and social interaction. Journal of Personality and Social Psychology 76, 893–910 (1999)
2. Bernieri, F.J.: Coordinated movement and rapport in teacher-student interactions. Journal of Nonverbal Behavior 12, 120–138 (1988)
3. Chartrand, T.L., Jefferis, V.E.: Consequences of automatic goal pursuit and the case of nonconscious mimicry. In: Forgas, J.P., Williams, K.D., von Hippel, W. (eds.) Responding to the Social World: Implicit and Explicit Processes in Social Judgments and Decisions, pp. 290–305. Psychology Press, Philadelphia (2003)
4. Dijksterhuis, A.: Automatic social influence: The perception-behavior link as an explanatory mechanism for behavior matching. In: Forgas, J.P., Williams, K.D. (eds.) Social Influence: Direct and Indirect Processes, pp. 95–108. Psychology Press, Philadelphia (2001)
5. Dijksterhuis, A., Bargh, J.A.: The perception-behavior expressway: Automatic effects of social perception on social behavior. In: Zanna, M. (ed.) Advances in Experimental Social Psychology, pp. 1–40. Academic Press, San Diego (2001)

6. Gueguen, N., Jacob, C., Martin, A.: Mimicry in social interaction: Its effect on human judgment and behavior. European Journal of Sociences 8 (2009)
7. Lakin, J.L., Chartrand, T.L.: Using nonconscious behavioral mimicry to create affiliation and rapport. Psychological Science 14, 334–339 (2003)
8. Lakin, J.L., Jefferis, V.E., Cheng, C.M., Chartrand, T.L.: The Chameleon Effect as social glue: Evidence for the evolutionary significance of nonconscious mimicry. Journal of Nonverbal Behavior 27, 145–162 (2003)
9. Huang, H.H., Cerekovic, A., Tarasenko, K., Levacic, V., Zoric, G., Pandzic, I.S., Nakano, Y., Nishida, Y.: Integration embodied conversational agent components with generic framework. Multiagent and Grid Systems-An Interational Journal 4, 371–386 (2008)
10. Kopp, S.: Social resonance and embodied coordination in face-to- face conversation with artificial interlocutors. Speech Communication 52(6), 587–597 (2010)
11. Pantic, M., Nijholt, A., Plentland, A., Huang, T.S.: Human-Centred Intelligent Human-Computer Interaction (HCI^2)): how far are we from attaining it? Journal of Autonomous and Adaptive Communications Systems 1(2), 168–187 (2008)
12. Sun, X.F., Lichtenauer, J., Valstar, M., Nijholt, A., Pantic, M.: A Multimodal Database for Mimicry Analysis. In: D´Mello, S., et al. (eds.) ACII 2011, Part I, vol. 6974, pp. 367–376. Springer, Heidelberg (2011)
13. Sun, X.F., Truong, K., Nijholt, A., Pantic, M.: Automatic Visual Mimicry Expression Analysis in Interpersonal Interaction. In: Fourth IEEE Workshop on CVPR for Human Communicative Behavior Analysis, Held in Conjunction with CVPR 2011, Colorado Springs, USA (to appear, 2011)
14. Sun, X.F., Nijholt, A., Pantic, M.: Towards Mimicry Recognition during Human Interactions: Automatic Feature Selection and Representation. In: Proceedings 4th International ICST Conference on Intelligent Technologies for Interactive Entertainment (INTETAIN 2011), Genoa, Italy, May 25-27 (to appear, 2011)
15. Sun, X.F., Truong, K.P., Pantic, M., Nijholt, A.: Towards Visual and Vocal Mimicry Recognition in Human-Human Interactions. In: Proceedings 2011 IEEE International Conference on Systems, Man, and Cybernetics (IEEE SMC 2011), Special Session on Social Signal Processing, Anchorage, Alaska, October 9-12 (to appear, 2011)

Using Facial Emotional Signals for Communication between Emotionally Expressive Avatars in Virtual Worlds

Yuqiong Wang and Joe Geigel

Rochester Institute of Technology
102 Lomb Memorial Dr
Rochester NY 14623 USA

Abstract. In this paper we explore the applications of facial expression analysis and eye tracking in driving emotionally expressive avatars. We propose a system that transfers facial emotional signals including facial expressions and eye movements from the real world into a virtual world. The proposed system enables us to address the questions: How significant are eye movements in emotion expression? Can facial emotional signals be transferred effectively, from the real world into virtual worlds? We design an experiment to address the questions. There are two major contributions of our work: 1) We propose a system that incorporates eye movements for transferring facial emotions; 2) We design an experiment to evaluate the effectiveness of the facial emotional signals.

Keywords: facial expression analysis, facial emotional signal, eye gaze, avatar expression, virtual world.

1 Introduction

In recent decades, there has seen a growing interest in performance-driven avatars, and their presence in virtual environments such films, computer games, virtual classrooms, etc. In the film industry, where expressiveness is being emphasized, high resolution models and significant amount of offline editing are utilized to achieve the goal [17]. With sufficient time and effort, an almost identical face model can be created to accurately replicate the facial motions of a real person [1]. It seems that avatars can be as expressive as their human counterparts, if there is no much constrain (e.g. time, hardware cost, etc). On the other end of the spectrum are systems to be used in realtime applications such as gaming and videoconferencing, where user-friendliness, affordability, automation and realtime performance is the priority. These systems usually utilize less complex model and simpler animation scheme. Many existing systems are based on avatars that are compliant with Action Units (AUs) [6], Facial Animation Parameters (FAPs) [16], or the six basic expressions proposed by Ekman [7]. In one recent work [22], where a realtime performance-driven facial animation system was implemented using a video camera and a depth sensor, the facial expressions of the avatars are produced via a combination of predefined blendshapes.

S. D'Mello et al. (Eds.): ACII 2011, Part II, LNCS 6975, pp. 297–304, 2011.

If avatars in the film industry seem to have achieved realism, how effective can fully-automated, realtime-animated avatars be?

Another observation is most existing realtime systems have omitted eye movements. Avatars animated by these system either have empty eyes, or static eyes. Being an important channel of communication in the real world, how do eye movements - such as gaze direction, fixation, and blinking - impact emotion expression in virtual worlds? With the incorporation of eye movements, can facial expressions be more effectively transferred from a real person to an avatar?

In this study we propose a realtime system for transferring facial emotional signals, including facial expressions and eye movements, from the real world into virtual worlds, followed by an experiment to address the two questions:

a. Can facial emotional signals be transfered effectively from the real world to virtual worlds in realtime?

b. How significant are eye movements as emotional signals in virtual worlds?

2   Aim and Objective

2.1   Facial Expression Analysis

Facial expression analysis is the problem of classifying facial motion and facial feature deformation into abstract classes [8]. The state-of-art is posed (deliberate) facial expressions in controlled environment can be recognized with high accuracy [23]. Open research issues in this area include: 1) Designing algorithms that are less sensitive to head pose, illumination, and partial occlusion. 2) Analyzing genuine facial expressions, i.e. spontaneous expressions that are short-lived, accompanied by on-set and off-set, some of which may not fit into any semantically described category. 3) Expanding the output categories from basic expressions to more nonbasic emotional states. 4) Fusing information from the face with head and body gestures for human behavior analysis. For detailed reviews on existing systems please refer to [8] [20] [23].

Recently, some newly emerged systems have successfully classified a real person's facial expressions and animated an avatar's face accordingly in realtime, with the help of a depth sensor [22]. We aim at further exploring the application of depth sensors in this area, and developing a realtime system that transfers facial expressions along with eye movements.

2.2   Eye Movements

Eye movements mainly refer to fixation or gaze durations, saccadic velocities, saccadic amplitudes, and various transition-based parameters between fixations and/or regions of interest [18]. There has been some research work analyzing the impact of eye gaze in conversations. Gaze is found to play several important roles in conversational context, including 1) monitoring, 2) regulatory, and 3) expressive functionalities, as summarized in [12]; or 1) paying attention, 2) signaling attention, 3) regulation, and 4) intimacy as stated in [10].

What is the impact of eye gaze and other eye movements in emotion expression? Some researchers have discovered that eye gaze can affect the perception of certain facial expressions. For instance, direct eye gaze increases the perception of anger, while averted eye gaze enhances the fearfulness [15]. Similarly, the experiment described in [19] indicated that eye gaze is associated with neutral and anger: direct gaze is related to anger and joy, while averted gaze could indicate fear and sadness [11] [5]. Overall, for threatening expressions, the eye region could even be as informative as the whole face [21]. It was further proposed in [13] that length of eye contact is used to maintain a comfortable level of intimacy. And continuous gaze was highly rated in the impression measures of "liking/evaluation" and "activity/potency" [2]. Another group of researchers established connections between eye movements and activities such as surfing the web, writing emails, etc [4].

While there still exist arguments that eye gaze's effects on expressions are uncertain [3], we hypothesize that eye movement is part of the facial expression, and facial expressions can be more effectively transferred with incorporation of eye movements.

2.3   Research Objectives

Our objectives are: 1) Investigating the role of eye movements in emotion expression in virtual worlds, emphasizing its importance, and providing insight for systems that utilizes emotionally expressive avatars. 2) Evaluating the effectiveness of transfered facial expressions, and how the effectiveness is influenced by eye movements.

3   Methodology

3.1   System Design

To achieve our goals, we propose a realtime system that transfers facial emotional signals, including both facial expressions and eye movements from a real person to an avatar. There are three major components in the system, as shown in Fig. 1. First, the subject's facial emotional signals are captured via three channels: a video camera captures the image, a depth sensor (e.g. Kinect) detects the scene depth, and an eye tracker tracks the eyes.

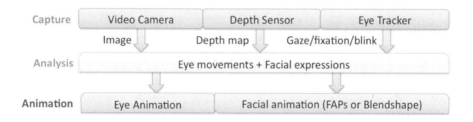

Fig. 1. System Diagram

Next, the facial expression analysis module combines the three channels and classifies the expression. Facial expressions are either classified as Facial Animation Parameters (FAPs) [16], which are elementary expressions, or Blendshapes, which describe full-face expressions. An algorithm which is similar to [22] is used. On the other hand, eye movements are represented by gaze vector, fixation, and blinking pattern.

The system can accordingly utilize a female avatar or a male avatar on the screen, depending on the gender of the user. While there are some questions such as 1) How realistic should the avatars be, given the 'uncanny valley observation' [14]; 2) How does the likeliness between the avatar and the real performer impact the virtual communication. Given the goal of the system, we use one semi-realistic female avatar for all the female subjects, and one semi-realistic male avatar for all the male subjects. We are interested in exploring the above questions in future study.

Finally, the facial animation modules drives the avatar according to the classification output. the avatar may either move individual muscles (FAPs), or pose one of the Blendshapes. The eyes are animated separately. For each frame, the location of eyeballs is calculated using the gaze vector, whereas fixation and blinking patterns are applied directly.

3.2   Experiment Design

Data Capture. The subjects of the experiment are randomly sampled population from both genders, various ethnic groups, and a diversity of educational background. The subjects are divided into three groups: performers, audiences, and judges. Performers and audiences contribute to the data capture process, whereas judges participate in the evaluation process.Performers and audiences are paired, forming groups of two. For each group, the performer and the audience are placed in two separate rooms, each equipped with a camera, an eye tracker, and a display. The camera and eye tracker function in conjunction to capture the facial emotional signals, including facial muscle movements as well as eye movements (gaze, fixation, and blinking). The performer and the audience can see each other's avatar via the displays placed in front of them.

It should be noted that in order to cope with the disparity issue [9] in the context of video conferencing (i.e. when one party looks into the other's eyes in the video, the latter wouldn't perceive the gaze because the former is not looking into the camera), the camera is placed near the center of the display, right between the avatar's eyes on the screen. The display is large enough to allow sufficient room between the two eyes for placing the camera. The camera is suspended and fixed using thin cables. Fig. 2 shows an illustration of the system. Then the performer is given 5-10 minutes to either present a topic, tell a story, or start a conversation which evokes a wide range of emotions. Under the premise that all movements are genuine (not fabricated or posed), the performers are encouraged to be as visually expressive as possible. The audience plays the role of a responsive listener - maintaining eye contact with the performer, acknowledging the reception of the message, giving responses whenever necessary, etc.

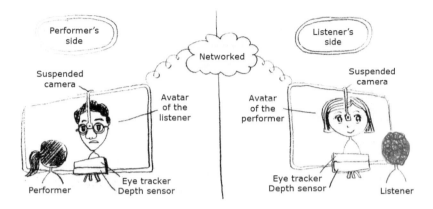

Fig. 2. Data Capture

Facial Emotional Signal Transfer. The facial emotional signal transferring system described in Section 3.1 is used to transfer the signals from the performer's face to an avatar's. In order to analyze the role of eye movements in the context of communication in virtual worlds, the system can transfer facial emotional signals in three different levels:

  a. Facial expressions are transferred but not eye movements, the avatar has static eyes;

  b. Facial expressions are transferred, eye movements are not transfered but noise-based eye animation is applied to the avatar;

  c. Both facial expressions and eye movements are transferred.

Data Preparation. The avatar will be animated in all three levels. All animations will be recorded. Therefore in total we have four video clips:

1) The video recording of the real performer;
2) The avatar animation, with facial expressions, but static eyes;
3) The avatar animation, with transferred facial expressions, and noised-based eye animation;
4) The avatar animation, with transferred facial expressions and eye animation.

Next, all four video clips are segmented and filtered by an expert, with each segment containing the onset, apex, and offset of one emotion expression (the emotion is segmented as long as it is distinguishable; it does not need to fall into any established category. As a matter of fact the occurrence of prototypic expressions or AUs/FAPs will be relatively rare in real-world scenarios than in laboratory settings). The segments are labelled so that there is a correspondence between the original expression and the transferred expression, however the labels are hidden from the participants. The labelled segments are then shuffled.

Evaluation. In this stage the judges are presented with shuffled video segments. The judges evaluate the effectiveness of the transferred facial emotional signals via two measurements:

First, they score each individual video segment. Four criterions are provided, each can be assigned any value between -1 and 1, with -1 meaning complete mismatch and 1 for complete match. The four criterions are:

    a. *Positiveness (Is the subject delivering any enlightening signals?)*
    b. *Engagement (Is the subject interested/focused?)*
    c. *Approachability (Does the subject look open/friendly?)*
    d. *Expectability (Does the subject not look surprised?)*

After they complete the first measurement, they are shown the video clip of real performer, followed by the corresponding avatar animations. They rate the avatar animations based on the following criterion: Overall, how effective are the transferred facial emotional signals? They can use any number between 0 and 5, with 0 meaning totally ineffective, and 5 meaning totally effective.

3.3   Data Analysis

Finally, the results are collected and analyzed. We conduct the standard Analysis of Variance (ANOVA) and compare the results between the original video and each of the avatar animations. The mean scores with their variances will indicate the overall effectiveness of the transferred emotions. By analyzing the differences across the three avatar animations with different level of eye movements, we can conclude the significance of eye movements in avatar emotion expression.

4   Conclusion

The major contributions of our work to the field of affective computing can be found in two aspects:

1) Eye Movements as Emotional Signals. Given the observation that eye movements are omitted from current facial expression analysis, we hypothesis that eye movements are one crucial channel for expressing emotions in the context of communication in virtual worlds. We attempt to integrate eye movements with facial expression analysis, and we evaluate the importance of eye movements as emotional signal. Our system serves as an early effort to incorporate eye movements along with facial expression analysis, which calls for succeeding systems to investigate the problem.

2) The Effectiveness of Transferred Emotions. While there are numerous systems that map facial expressions from a real person to an avatar, we found few studies in literature to evaluate the effectiveness of the transferred emotions. We have observed the need of emotionally expressive avatars that can be animated and rendered in realtime, and we carry out an experiment to access their effectiveness, in the hope of encouraging more real-world aware systems.

We also plan on making all the video clips from experiment available to the research community. These include the original videos of the performers, avatar animations under three different levels of eye movements, as well as all the labeled video segments. These video clips will serve as a video database of real-world spontaneous expressions with eye movements.

Acknowledgements. This work is based on research supported by the US National Science Foundation under Award IIS-0713201. The authors would also like to thank the anonymous reviewers for their valuable feedback.

References

1. Alexander, O., Rogers, M., Lambeth, W., Chiang, M., Debevec, P.: The digital emily project: photoreal facial modeling and animation. In: ACM SIGGRAPH 2009 Courses, SIGGRAPH 2009, pp. 12:1–12:15. ACM, New York (2009), http://doi.acm.org/10.1145/1667239.1667251
2. Argyle, M., Lefebvre, L., Cook, M.: The meaning of five patterns of gaze. European Journal of Social Psychology 4(2), 125–136 (1974), http://dx.doi.org/10.1002/ejsp.2420040202
3. Banse, R., Scherer, K.R.: Acoustic profiles in vocal emotion expression, vol. 70, pp. 614–636 (1996)
4. Bulling, A., Ward, J., Gellersen, H., Troster, G.: Eye movement analysis for activity recognition using electrooculography. IEEE Transactions on Pattern Analysis and Machine Intelligence PP(99), 1 (2011)
5. Cowie, R., Douglas-Cowie, E.: Automatic statistical analysis of the signal and prosodic signs of emotion in speech. In: Proceedings of the Fourth International Conference on Spoken Language, ICSLP 1996, vol. 3, pp. 1989–1992 (1996)
6. Ekman, P., Friesen, W.V.: Facial action coding system. Consulting Psychologists Press (1978)
7. Ekman, P., Friesen, W.V., O'Sullivan, M., Chan, A., Diacoyanni-Tarlatzis, I., Heider, K., Krause, R., LeCompte, W.A., Pitcairn, T., Ricci-Bitti, P.E., Scherer, K., Tomita, M., Tzavaras, A.: Universals and cultural differences in the judgments of facial expressions of emotion. Journal of Personality and Social Psychology 53(4), 712–717 (1987)
8. Fasel, B., Luettin, J.: Automatic facial expression analysis: a survey. Pattern Recognition 36, 259–275 (2003)
9. Gemmell, J., Toyama, K., Zitnick, C., Kang, T., Seitz, S.: Gaze awareness for video-conferencing: a software approach. IEEE Multimedia 7(4), 26–35 (2000)
10. Heylen, D.K.J.: A closer look at gaze. In: Pelachaud, C., André, E., Kopp, S., Ruttkay, Z.M. (eds.) Creating Bonds with Embodied Conversational Agents, pp. 3–9. University of Utrecht (2005)
11. Russell, J.A.: The psychology of facial expression. Cambridge University Press, Cambridge (1997)
12. Kendon, A.: Some functions of gaze-direction in social interaction. Acta Psychologica 26(1), 22–63 (1967), http://www.ncbi.nlm.nih.gov/pubmed/6043092
13. Argyle, M., Eye-contact, D.J., Argyle, M.: Citation index (sci)and the social sciences citation index (ssci) indicate (1978)

14. MacDorman, K.F.: Subjective ratings of robot video clips for human likeness, familiarity, and eeriness: An exploration of the uncanny valley. In: ICCSCogSci 2006 Long Symposium Toward Social Mechanisms of Android Science, p. 4 (2005)

15. NDiaye, K., Sander, D., Vuilleumier, P.: Self-relevance processing in the human amygdala: Gaze direction, facial expression, and emotion intensity. Emotion 9(6), 798–806 (2009)

16. Pakstas, A.: MPEG-4 Facial Animation: The Standard,Implementation and Applications. John Wiley & Sons, Inc., New York (2002)

17. Sagar, M.: Facial performance capture and expressive translation for king kong. In: SIGGRAPH 2006: ACM SIGGRAPH 2006 Sketches, p. 26. ACM, New York (2006)

18. Salvucci, D.D., Goldberg, J.H.: Identifying fixations and saccades in eye-tracking protocols. In: Proceedings of the 2000 Symposium on Eye Tracking Research & Applications, ETRA 2000, pp. 71–78. ACM, New York (2000), http://doi.acm.org/10.1145/355017.355028

19. Shang, J., Liu, Y., Fu, X.: Dominance modulates the effects of eye gaze on the perception of threatening facial expressions. In: 8th IEEE International Conference on Automatic Face Gesture Recognition, FG 2008, pp. 1–6 (2008)

20. Tian, Y.L., Kanade, T., Cohn, J.: Facial expression analysis. In: Li, S., Jain, A. (eds.) Handbook of Face Recognition. Springer, Heidelberg (2003)

21. Walker, M.A., Cahn, J.E., Whittaker, S.J.: Improvising linguistic style: Social and affective bases for agent personality, pp. 96–105. ACM Press, New York (1997)

22. Weise, T., Bouaziz, S., Li, H., Pauly, M.: Realtime performance-based facial animation. ACM Transactions on Graphics (Proceedings SIGGRAPH 2011) (August 2011)

23. Zeng, Z., Pantic, M., Roisman, G., Huang, T.: A survey of affect recognition methods: Audio, visual, and spontaneous expressions. IEEE Transactions on Pattern Analysis and Machine Intelligence 31(1), 39–58 (2009)

Building Rapport with a 3D Conversational Agent

Whitney L. Cade, Andrew Olney, Patrick Hays, and Julia Lovel

Institute for Intelligent Systems, University of Memphis, 365 Innovation Dr.,
Memphis, TN, USA
{wlcade,aolney,dphays,jcmnrslv}@memphis.edu

Abstract. While embodied conversational agents improve a user's experience
with a system, systems meant for repeated use may need agents that build a
relationship with the user. Anita is a low-cost 3D agent capable of talking,
displaying emotions, gesturing, and postural mimicry, all of which may increase
the rapport between agent and user. Motion capture and pressure sensors were
used to create an agent capable of realistic, responsive motions.

1 Introduction

Embodied conversational agents have been used in task-oriented computer applications
to improve task performance and user experience. By talking, gesturing, and displaying
affective facial expressions in a humanlike way, embodied agents may increase the
rapport between the user and the agent [1]. Rapport improves conversational
coordination between speakers and eventually allows disagreements to be an acceptable
part of the conversation [2]. Therefore, a rapport-building agent could improve a user's
experience with the system.

Rapport is often built nonverbally. For instance, humans naturally mimic the
posture of their conversational partner in order to induce liking in the partner [3].
Gestures, another nonverbal mode of communication, create a common ground
necessary for communication and understanding [4]. Facial expressions can not only
signal the emotions being felt, but can also mark a lack of rapport, e.g. disgust [5].

We have created a low-cost embodied agent capable of speech, affective facial
expression, gesture, and postural mirroring. While many agents have a subset of these
rapport-building capabilities, we have united all of these aspects in one responsive
embodied agent capable of realistic human motion. We believe this may increase
attention, motivation, liking, and persistent use of the system over time.

2 Anita, the Reactive Conversational Agent

One of the major objectives in creating a multi-capable agent was to make a flexible
3D model on limited budget. Our conversational agent, Anita, was created using 3D
Studio Max, a versatile 3D modeling software offered freely for educational purposes,
and operates within the runtime environment Microsoft XNA. This gives the creator
the freedom to control the agent in a world space so that any motion is possible, and
the motion can be reactive to the user's input.

S. D'Mello et al. (Eds.): ACII 2011, Part II, LNCS 6975, pp. 305–306, 2011.

The agent is capable of gestures and expressions using morphing and skeletal animation. To create human-like movements, we built a motion capture system using four Sony Playstation Eye cameras and a low-cost motion capture program called iPi. The motion capture system was used to map a human actor's gestures and movements into a set of skeletal animations. We selected typical conversational gestures such as head nodding and an arm gesture that suggests that it is the user's turn to speak. These gestures can be dynamically or statically placed into the dialogue of the agent.

The agent also receives posture information from the user so that the agent can mirror the user's posture using Wii Fit Balance Boards to measure posterior body pressure [6]. Center of mass posture information is translated into dynamic, responsive agent leaning. Thus a user leaning heavily to the left would see this posture mirrored by the agent on screen, where the amount of lean is weighted by the posture information received from the Wii Fit.

Visible speech, emotion, and facial expressions are created using morph targets generated using Facegen, which creates high resolution heads. These morphs include visemes (phonemic mouth shapes), which give the agent the ability to lipsync with a text-to-speech voice, facial expressions such as sad, angry, happy, neutral, raised eyebrow, etc. Each morph target may be blended with the others to create composite expressions, such as happy surprise while speaking.

Anita represents both an effort to bring about a high quality agent using low cost equipment, and also the marriage of several avenues shown to create rapport between interlocutors (Demo video: http://www.youtube.com/watch?v=1gS3HLjgB7U).

Acknowledgments. This research was supported by a grant awarded by the Institute of Education Sciences (Grant R305A080594). Any opinions, findings and conclusions, or recommendations expressed in this paper are those of the authors and do not necessarily reflect the views of the funding agencies.

References

1. Cassell, J., Gill, A.J., Tepper, P.A.: Coordination in Conversation and Rapport. In: Proceedings of the ACL Workshop on Embodied Language Processing, pp. 40–50. Omnipress, Madison (2007)
2. Tickle-Degnan, L., Rosenthal, R.: The Nature of Rapport and its Nonverbal Correlates. Psychol. Inq. 1(4), 285–293 (1990)
3. Chartrand, T.L., Bargh, J.A.: The Chameleon Effects: The Perception Behavior Link and Social Interaction. J. Pers. Soc. Psychol. 76(6), 893–910 (1999)
4. Clark, H., Brennan, S.: Grounding in Communication. In: Resnick, L.B., Levine, J.M., Teasley, J.S.D. (eds.) Perspectives on Socially Shared Cognition, pp. 127–149. American Psychological Association, Washington (1991)
5. Wang, N., Gratch, J.: Rapport and Facial Expression. In: Proceedings of International Conference on Affective Computing and Intelligent Interaction. IEEE Computer Society Press, Los Alamitos (2009)
6. Olney, A., D'Mello, S.K.: A DIY Pressure Sensitive Chair for Intelligent Tutoring Systems. In: Aleven, V., Kay, J., Mostow, J. (eds.) ITS 2010. LNCS, vol. 6095, pp. 456–456. Springer, Heidelberg (2010)

Siento: An Experimental Platform for Behavior and Psychophysiology in HCI

Rafael A. Calvo, Md. Sazzad Hussain, Payam Aghaei Pour, and Omar Alzoubi

School of Electrical and Information Engineering, University of Sydney, Australia
{Rafael.Calvo,Sazzad.Hussain,
Payam.Aghaeipour,Omar.Alzoubi}@sydney.edu.au

Abstract. We describe Siento, a system to perform different types of affective computing studies. The platform allows for dimensional or categorical models of emotions, self-reported vs. third party reporting and can record and process multiple types of modalities including video, physiology and text. It has been used already in a number of studies. This type of systems can improve the repeatability of experiments. The system is also used for data acquisition, feature extraction and data analysis applying machine learning techniques.

Keywords: Affective computing, psychophysiology, machine learning, HCI.

1   Introduction

Affective computing (AC) experiments need to be repeatable across subjects, experimental setting and locations (e.g. research labs). Many experimental factors can be taken into account. Studies can vary in their underlying emotion model, their annotation process and other particulars of each experiment. Some experiments are implemented in controlled environments using stimuli and measuring responses. Others aim to study interactions (i.e. with computers) in naturalistic scenarios. Different modalities can be evaluated in different scenarios, each with different requirements. Systems need to be built so they can adapt to the different possible experimental conditions. AC tools have generally been designed ad hoc for each experiment or application domain. This ad hoc approach often leads to low reusability of code and design, leading to poorer quality and higher cost for each study.

We describe Siento[1], a system that aims to address this issue and has been used in a number of studies collecting data from physiological sensors, webcams and screen-cams that record the screen with the user interaction. The description aims to provide insights to those considering building their own systems. Siento will be freely available for research use.

1.1   Siento

Recording video can be done with any webcam supported by Matlab, and we recently experimented with a range camera (Microsoft Kinect). For physiological recording,

---

[1] http://sydney.edu.au/engineering/latte/projects/siento.shtml

S. D'Mello et al. (Eds.): ACII 2011, Part II, LNCS 6975, pp. 307–308, 2011.

Siento integrates in-house and commercial systems. We generally use the BIOPAC MP150 system with AcqKnowledge software to capture data. Biopac's Matlab API can also be used for real-time data acquisition. The Biopac system can be used to record a variety of physiological signals (ECG, GSR, EMG, EEG etc).

A design principle in Siento is to use other available libraries and tools. We have integrated Weka that has a collection of machine learning algorithms for data analysis. We also found it faster for evaluating different techniques and algorithms. Siento uses machine learning libraries in Matlab including PRTools for feature selection and classification and AuBT for extracting statistical features from physiological signals. As for other modalities, tools like eMotion by Visual Recognition are used for extracting facial features. The interaction with the participants is recorded by saving a screen-cam using Snagit. The applications for running experiments (e.g. logs, protocols), presenting stimulus (e.g. IAPS images) and self reports (e.g. video annotations) are implemented in-house with Matlab.

The experimental protocols can be highly controlled as when we used it for studies involving images from the International Affective Picture System (IAPS) [1]. In this scenario the images were used as stimulus where behavioral and physiological data from participants are recorded. Our studies following this approach have improved our understanding of how physiological signals can be used for detecting affective states and how fusion of these channels can improve accuracy [2].

Another type of study is less structured and aims at recording users' interactions with a system in a natural setting. We have studied how students' affective states change during the interactions wit AutoTutor an Intelligent Tutoring system [3].

The toolkit can be used for these two type of protocols (controlled and natural interaction) and for combinations of the two, as in a study where we are evaluating how normative databases can be used to train a user model aimed at making a user independent system.

1.2 Web Presentation

Following is the link to a web-viewable presentation of Siento:
http://www.youtube.com/watch?v=IwaqhVz9tss&feature=player_embedded

References

1. Lang, P.J., Bradley, M.M., Cuthbert, B.N.: International affective picture system (IAPS): Technical manual and affective ratings. The Center for Research in Psychophysiology, University of Florida, Gainesville, FL (1997)
2. Hussain, M.S., Calvo, R.A., Aghaei Pour, P.: Hybrid Fusion Approach for Detecting Affects from Multichannel Physiology. In: D'Mello, S., et al. (eds.) ACII 2011, Part I. LNCS, vol. 6974, pp. 568–577. Springer, Heidelberg (2011)
3. Aghaei Pour, P., Hussain, M.S., AlZoubi, O., D'Mello, S., Calvo, R.: The Impact of System Feedback on Learners' Affective and Physiological States. In: Aleven, V., Kay, J., Mostow, J. (eds.) ITS 2010. LNCS, vol. 6094, pp. 264–273. Springer, Heidelberg (2010)

A Gesture-Based Interface and Active Cinema

Mark J. Chavez and Aung Sithu Kyaw

Nanyang Technological University, School of Art, Design & Media,
81 Nanyang Drive, Level 4, Room 18, Singapore 637458
{mchavez,skaung}@ntu.edu.sg

Abstract. Visual design affects the viewer with various meanings depending upon how it is presented. Our research optimizes visual design in a short animated movie format whose plot is a fixed linear narrative. Designed and functioning in a simulation environment we manipulate the visual design of this short movie according to feedback detected from the viewer. Our goal is to explore the film-maker's ability to refine and optimize a movie experience in a real-time environment working toward a system that dynamically optimizes the visual and auditory impact of a narrative. In this paper, we describe a prototype system that explores and demonstrates these ideas.

Keywords: animation, design, movie, storytelling, archetype, simulation.

1 Introduction

Over the past three years at our Active Cinema (adaptive movie) system research conducted at School of Art, Design and Media (ADM), Nanyang Technological University (NTU), Singapore, has been working on creating a movie system that derives data from an audience retrieving gestural activity and assuming emotional meaning from those gestures, then feeding back that data to the movie by tweaking and fine-tuning the visual design of an animated movie in real-time. This done to provide an optimize experience for a given target audience.

In traditional animated film production, creating a highly optimized movie to give a unique movie screening experience is a tough challenge. Animators have to carefully stage character performance as per the narrative of the story. Directors give feedback and the animators redraw, refine and re-animate based on the comments, a very time consuming and labor intensive process. We attempt to streamline this process by creating a movie system which takes the emotive feedback from a small audience or director and refining the design of the movie in real-time.

2 Our Approach

We use the Unreal Development Kit (UDK) as the real-time rendering engine for our movie system and Microsoft Kinect to detect the audience motions and gestures. We've implemented our own middleware system that works as an interface between UDK and Microsoft Kinect sensor.

S. D'Mello et al. (Eds.): ACII 2011, Part II, LNCS 6975, pp. 309–310, 2011.
© Springer-Verlag Berlin Heidelberg 2011

Fig. 1. Screenshots from our short film in extreme, standard and cute design

We have created a repository of character designs in 3 different styles: Cute, Standard and Extreme. Cute style uses soft and cartoonish colors, more rounded, simple shapes and forms. The mood designed to reflect design states in popular media would be the best to describe the look we wanted. For extreme style, we tend to present it in a more violence, gore features in textures. A low-key black and white and contrast in tones. It is a film noir style. Standard style is basically the in-between of Cute and Extreme. Though closer to a realistic use of light, color and form. We use different camera movement techniques to further distinguish these states.

Currently only the motion of audience is used as a trigger to decide which visual design to render. In particular, we are using the agitation in the audience as a value to determine the style value. We've set up our movie to changes in style if there is significant degree of motion detected in the audience; changing to another style set when less motion is detected. **Fig. 1** shows the renderings of different styles in the actual movie, triggered in real-time. It is the same movie narrative but based on audience interaction, they see a different visual design.

3   Appendix

This research is formed as collaboration among the School of Art, Design and Media, the School of Computer Engineering, the School of Electrical and Electronic Engineering and the Wee Kim Wee School of Communications and Information at Nanyang Technological University, Singapore. And it is funded and supported by the National Research Foundation and the Media Development Authority, Singapore.

- CaN Research, http://vimeo.com/19064100, http://visual-analysis.com/
- School of Art, Design and Media - http://www.adm.ntu.edu.sg/Pages/Home.aspx
- School of Computer Engineering - http://sce.ntu.edu.sg/Pages/Home.aspx

OperationARIES!: Aliens, Spies and Research Methods

Carol M. Forsyth[1], Arthur C. Graesser[1], Keith Millis[2],
Zhiqiang Cai[1], and Diane Halpern[3]

[1] Institute for Intelligent Systems, The University of Memphis, Innovation Drive,
Memphis,TN 38152
[2] Northern Illinois University, Psychology Department, DeKalb, Illinois 60115
[3] Claremont McKenna College, Psychology Department, 500 E.
9th Street Claremont, CA 91711
{cmfrsyth,a-graesser}@memphis.edu, kmillis@niu.edu,
zcai@memphis.edu, diane.halpern@cmc.edu

Abstract. *Operation ARIES!* is an Intelligent Tutoring System that teaches research methodology in a game-like atmosphere. There is a dramatic storyline that engages and motivates students as they acquire both declarative knowledge and critical reasoning skills. ARIES has three modules in which students maintain mixed-initiative dialogue with multiple artificial agents. The internal architecture is similar to that of AutoTutor which uses natural language interaction in the tutorial dialogues. Learning as well as the engaging and motivating factors of ARIES are currently being investigated.

Keywords: Intelligent Tutoring System, engagement, serious game, natural language processing, artificial agent.

Science fiction novels and video games have often incorporated an alien invasion theme in order to engage a wide variety of audiences. *Operation ARIES!* (Acquiring Research Investigative and Evaluative Skills, https://sites.google.com/site/ariestutor/) is an Intelligent Tutoring System that employs the alien theme in order to motivate students while teaching them research methodology. Scientific literacy is at a dangerously low level in the United States [1] leaving students academically unprepared as well as susceptible to many false claims in the media. ARIES addresses this problem by teaching students how to understand, evaluate, and critique research studies while engaging them in a dramatic storyline presented via artificial agents' speech, e-mails, and videos across three distinct modules (i.e., the Training Module, the Case-Study Module, and the Interrogation Module).

In the Training Module, students adaptively learn topics of research methodology through an E-Text, multiple-choice questions, and conversations with two pedagogical agents. In the Case Study module, an element of competition is introduced when the human must play against an artificial agent in order to accrue points. The student who correctly identifies the most flaws in presented research studies is awarded the most points and wins the game. In the Interrogation Module, the plot thickens as the alien threat becomes more imminent. The human student must interrogate suspects who are accused of presenting problematic research in order to

S. D'Mello et al. (Eds.): ACII 2011, Part II, LNCS 6975, pp. 311–312, 2011.
© Springer-Verlag Berlin Heidelberg 2011

brainwash the public. The student must uncover the true identity of the suspect (alien or human) by generating specific questions about the presented research study.

Operation ARIES! utilizes a similar internal architecture to that of AutoTutor [2], a system that has produced considerable learning gains compared to reading a textbook for an equivalent amount of time [3]. Specifically, both Autotutor and ARIES use natural language processing in order to facilitate mixed-initiative dialogue between the human student and the artificial agent. The human input is processed with Latent Semantic Analysis (LSA, a statistical method for representing the conceptual meaning of a word based on its relationship to other words [4]) and a matching algorithm which compares the human input to regular expressions embedded within curriculum scripts. These curriculum scripts also contain the agent's conversational contributions that incorporate scaffolding techniques such as feedback, hints, prompts to elicit specific words, and misconception correction.

Investigators are evaluating both the learning and game-like aspects of *OperationARIES!* Preliminary analysis suggests that the Training Module is successful in teaching students research methodology[5].Currently, we are investigating the engaging and motivating factors within ARIES as well as how cognitive and affective individual differences play a role in this distinction.

Acknowledgement. This research was supported by the Institute of Education Sciences(R305B070349). The opinions expressed are those of the authors and do not represent views of the U.S. Department of Education.

References

1. National Science Board. Science and Engineer Indicators 2006. Arlington, VA, NSB 06-01 (2006)
2. Graesser, A.C., Lu, S., Jackson, G.T., Mitchell, H., Ventura, M., Olney, A., Louwerse, M.M.: AutoTutor: A Tutor with Dialogue in Natural Language. Beh. Research Meth., Inst., and Comps. 36, 180–193 (2004)
3. Graesser, A.C., Chipman, P., Haynes, B.C., Olney, A.: AutoTutor: An Intelligent Tutoring System with Mixed-Initiative Dialogue. IEEE Trans. In Ed. 48, 612–618 (2005)
4. Landauer, T., McNamara, D.S., Dennis, S., Kintsch, W. (eds.): Handbook of Latent Semantic Analysis. Erlbaum, Mahwah (2007)
5. Millis, K., Forsyth, C., Butler, H., Wallace, P., Graesser, A., Halpern, D.: Operation ARIES! A Serious Game for Teaching Scientific Inquiry. In: Oikonomou, J., Ma, M., Lakhmi, J. (eds.) Serious Games and Edutainment Applications. Springer, Heidelberg (in press)

EMO20Q Questioner Agent

Abe Kazemzadeh, James Gibson,
Panayiotis Georgiou, Sungbok Lee, and Shrikanth S. Narayanan⋆

Signal Analysis and Interpretation Lab,
University of Southern California
http://sail.usc.edu

Abstract. In this demonstration, we present an implementation of an emotion twenty questions (EMO20Q) questioner agent. The ubiquitous twenty questions game is a suitable format to study how people describe emotions and designing a computer agent to learn and reason about abstract emotion concepts can provide further theoretical insights. While natural language poses many challenges for the computer in human-computer interaction, the accessibility of natural language has made it possible to acquire data of many players reasoning about emotions in human-human games. These data are used to automate a computer questioner agent that asks the user questions and, based on that user's answers, attempts to guess the emotion that the user has in mind.

Keywords: dialog agents, emotions.

1 Proposed System

Emotion Twenty Questions (EMO20Q) is a variation on the traditional twenty questions game where emotions are the objects that must be guessed, instead of any arbitrary objects. It is an asymmetrical game whose players take one of two roles, questioner or answerer. For a complete discussion of the rules and intricacies of the *Emotion Twenty Questions* game please see [1], also presented at ACII. Although, with respect to the general twenty questions game, the search space of objects in EMO20Q is limited, emotions add a level of subjectivity to the game that makes it challenging for human and computer players alike.

Our objective is to study the human capabilities of describing emotions using natural language. EMO20Q provides an experimental method to observe this in a loosely controlled way [1]. We view computational modeling and simulation as an extention of our observational analysis. To this end, we use observational data derived from human-human EMO20Q games to inform the abilities of an automated agent which, in this case, plays the questioner role. The key issues that we aim to observe and model are: natural language descriptions of emotions, cooperative and competitive dialog interaction, intersubjectivity, inference with incomplete knowledge, and representations of uncertainty.

⋆ This work was supported in part by the NSF, DARPA, and the USC Annenberg Graduate Fellowship Program.

S. D′Mello et al. (Eds.): ACII 2011, Part II, LNCS 6975, pp. 313–314, 2011.

2 Technical Content

The natural language data obtained from human-human emotion twenty question games can be viewed as a bipartite graph in which questions and answers are connected by positive and negative edges, where +1 corresponds to a "yes" answer, −1 to a "no" answer, and 0 for indefinite or unseen answers to question/emotion pairs. In this formulation there are a number of possible ways that an agent could ask the questions and consequently attempt to guess the contemplated emotion.

Firstly, appropriate questions must be asked. In terms of an agent, this requires that the observed questions are ranked in some way such that they are able to help traverse the graph and discover the desired emotion. There are many way the problem of choosing appropriate questions could be approached: choosing at random, using spectral graph theory, using an information theoretic approach (e.g., choose the questions that provide maximal mutual information). Clearly a reasonable automated agent should do better than choosing at random. Of the latter two options mentioned, maximizing the mutual information between question was chosen in order to rank the questions such that the ones asked by the agent provide valuable information about the most emotions while also not offering redundant information.

Secondly, when information is obtained from the human user, in the form of answers to the questions the agent must use this information to ascertain the concealed emotion. Because of the sparse nature of this dataset (currently we have 42 emotions, 431 question types, and 644 question asking events), it is crucial that the agent is able to do some inference based upon the answers it receives and it's prior knowledge.

3 Evaluation

We are in the process of collecting data that will help characterize the agent's performance. Our initial experiments show that such an agent is feasible. The method we employ to choose the questions uses actual user input, so individual questions are very realistic, but the ordering of the questions is less natural. Our next efforts will be to try graph-based models of inference, which we think may be more human-like.

4 Resources

Our demo can be accessed at http://sail.usc.edu/emo20q/questioner/questioner.cgi. We endeavor to make our data and methodologies accessible to the community. These can be found at http://sail.usc.edu/emo20q/repos.html.

Reference

1. Kazemzadeh, A., Georgiou, P.G., Lee, S., Narayanan, S.: Emotion twenty questions: Toward a crowd-sourced theory of emotions. In: D'Mello, S., et al. (eds.) Proceedings of ACII 2011, Part II, vol. 6975, pp. 1–10. Springer, Heidelberg (2011)

A Game Prototype with Emotional Contagion

Gonçalo Pereira, Joana Dimas, Rui Prada, Pedro A. Santos, and Ana Paiva

INESC-ID and Instituto Superior Técnico, Technical University of Lisbon
Porto Salvo, Portugal
{goncalo.pereira,joana.dimas,rui.prada}@gaips.inesc-id.pt,
pasantos@math.ist.utl.pt, ana.paiva@inesc-id.pt

Abstract. Emotional contagion (EC) in games may provide players with an unique experience. We have developed a turn-based role playing prototype game which incorporates a model based on the EC process. While playing, users have the opportunity to observe the effects of emotional events on individual characters and on the group through simulated emotional contagion dynamics.

Keywords: emotional contagion, agents, videogame.

1 Description of the System

Over the years, virtual agents have proved to play a major role in the context of games. In fact, they improve the gaming experience by increasing fun, while immersing players in a more engaging and often emotional manner. Actually, providing artificial agents with emotional behavior increases their perceived realism, and consequently, their believability.

Despite the aforementioned potential of providing games with virtual agents capable of displaying emotion, little research has been devoted to the emotional contagion (EC) process. One of the most insightful works [3] defines EC as: *"the tendency to automatically mimic and synchronize expressions [...] to converge emotionally"*. This process has been known to influence group dynamics on both the individual and group level [3,1]. As such, EC may be especially relevant in a gaming context, and in fact, provide users with an unique game experience.

We have developed a turn-based role playing prototype game which incorporates a model that relies on the underlying principles of the EC process. While playing, users will have the opportunity to observe the effects of emotional events on individual characters and on the group through simulated EC dynamics.

The game is based on a story which describes the journey of three characters that have taken the quest to protect dragons from monsters. The user controls these characters and is initially placed on a map with several challenges. To finish the game he must navigate through the challenges and defeat all the monsters. Challenges range from fighting monsters or finding precious items, to finding a dead dragon, among others. These may have different emotional impacts on characters. In order to represent EC effects in groups and emphasize its game impact, our prototype also displays modifiers to player stats (health, attack and defense), depending on the characters' emotional state.

S. D'Mello et al. (Eds.): ACII 2011, Part II, LNCS 6975, pp. 315–316, 2011.

2   Technical Content

Our game prototype's EC processes are based on a model which follows the EC paradigm, published in this conference "A Generic Emotional Contagion Computer Model". While focusing on the individual level, the EC behavior emerges from individual interactions among agents.

The agent's emotional state is based on the set of emotions defined in the Emotional Contagion Scale (ECS) [2]: love, happiness, fear, anger and sadness. By using the ECS we are able to parameterize our agents according to measurements done with the ECS scale. Besides this essential feature, the EC process also depends on both relationships among agents and their extroversion.

The EC processes occur at the agent's level and consist of three modules:

Contagion Filter. This module filters other agents' emotional expressions based on the current features of one particular agent. The susceptibility of an agent being affected by a particular emotion is given by both the agent's ECS score regarding that emotion and the agent's relationship with the agent that expresses it, in terms of intimacy and power distance.

Mood Updater. This module updates the agent's emotional state. Every emotion is subject to a natural decay towards the agent's natural mood, except when a particular emotion is retained by the agent's Contagion Filter. In this case, the intensity of the retained emotion is added to the agent's current value regarding the corresponding emotion.

Expression Filter. This module allows the agent to create an emotional expression. The decision of whether to express a particular emotion or not depends on both the agent's extroversion and its power position within the agents' group it belongs to.

3   Links

The web-viewable presentation illustrating the system:
http://web.ist.utl.pt/gdgp/CA/presentation.pptx

Acknowledgments. This work was supported by FCT (INESC-ID multiannual funding) through the PIDDAC Program funds and also by FCT scholarship SFRH / BD / 66663 / 2009 .

References

1. Barsade, S.: The Ripple Effect: Emotional Contagion and Its Influence on Group Behavior. Administrative Science Quarterly 47(4), 644–677 (2002)
2. Doherty, R.: The emotional contagion scale: A measure of individual differences. Journal of Nonverbal Behavior 21(2), 131–154 (1997)
3. Hatfield, E., Cacioppo, J., Rapson, R.: Primitive emotional contagion. Review of Personality and Social Psychology 14, 151–177 (1992)

A Smartphone Interface for a Wireless EEG Headset with Real-Time 3D Reconstruction

Arkadiusz Stopczynski, Jakob Eg Larsen, Carsten Stahlhut,
Michael Kai Petersen, and Lars Kai Hansen

DTU Informatics, Cognitive Systems
Technical University of Denmark, Building 321, DK-2800 Kgs. Lyngby, Denmark
{arks,jel,cs,mkp,lkh}@imm.dtu.dk

Abstract. We demonstrate a fully functional handheld brain scanner consisting of a low-cost 14-channel EEG headset with a wireless connection to a smartphone, enabling minimally invasive EEG monitoring in naturalistic settings. The smartphone provides a touch-based interface with real-time brain state decoding and 3D reconstruction.

1 Introduction

Functional brain imaging techniques including fMRI and PET provide moving picture access to the living human brain, however, relying on complex, heavy hardware they offer limited comfort for the user, and thus can not be used under naturalistic conditions. This induces largely unknown biases into the current state of the art brain scanning, thought to be particularly problematic for studies of emotion and social cognition [1]. While cap-based EEG systems are less constraining, their wiring typically limits comfort and movement. There are obvious advantages of brain monitoring under naturalistic conditions, to study how we perceive our surroundings in mobile real-life settings [1]. Here, we demonstrate a minimally invasive and mobile brain monitoring system (see Fig. 1) offering real-time brain state decoding and 3D cortical activity visualization within a low-cost highly mobile smartphone environment. The system can quantify brain states, e.g. emotional responses, and the 3D visualization can be used for bio-feedback. Such feedback can have significant behavioral effects including improvements in reaction times, emotional responses, and musical performance, while clinical applications include attention deficit, hyperactivity disorder, and epilepsy [2]. Such applications will benefit from a low-cost and easy-to-use personal brain monitor.

2 System Architecture

Our system constitutes a fully portable EEG based real-time functional brain scanner including stimulus delivery, data acquisition, logging, brain state decoding and 3D activity visualization. The raw EEG data is acquired with a wireless Emotiv 14 channel 'Neuroheadset' with a sampling rate of 128Hz and electrodes positioned at AF3, F7, F3, FC5, T7, P7, O1, O2, P8, T8, FC6, F4, F8, AF4 (the

S. D'Mello et al. (Eds.): ACII 2011, Part II, LNCS 6975, pp. 317–318, 2011.

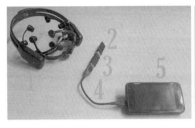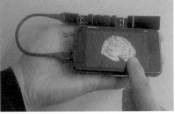

Fig. 1. (left) The system with Emotiv EPOC wireless EEG headset (1), Receiver module with USB connector (2), USB connector and adapter (3+4), and Nokia N900 (5). (right) Touch-based interaction with a 3D model of the brain using the smartphone.

international 10-20 system). The headset transmits the EEG data to a receiver module connected to a Nokia N900 smartphone. Custom-made software for the phone transmits the EEG data to a server or processes it locally, enabling real-time brain state decoding and a rich bio-feedback signal for the user in the form of a 3D rendering of the active cortical EEG sources. The user can interact with the 3D brain model by touch gestures (see Fig. 1).

3   Evaluation

A major concern in mobile real-time systems is the power consumption, hence battery life. Our experiments with local logging of EEG data allowed 7.5 hours continuous usage, whereas remote logging allowed 3.5 hours. The 3D brain model contains 1028 vertices and 2048 triangles and is stored in the mobile application. Brain activity is reflected by changing colors, allowing rendering performance of approximately 30 fps and fluent touch-based interaction with the 3D model. The current design of the system has a delay of approximately 150 ms. between the signal emerging in the brain and being visualized on the smartphone. We have performed brain state decoding experiments including simple finger tapping and more complex affective stimuli (IAPS picture viewing). In both cases we have found that the system decodes at error rates significantly less than a random baseline model. In conclusion, our early tests of the system indicate the potential of minimally invasive and low-cost EEG monitoring in naturalistic settings.

Supporting Material. http://milab.imm.dtu.dk/eeg

Acknowledgments. This work is supported in part by the Danish Lundbeck Foundation through CIMBI Center for Integrated Molecular Brain Imaging.

References

1. Makeig, S., Gramann, K., Jung, T.P., Sejnowski, T.J., Poizner, H.: Linking brain, mind and behavior. Int. J. Psychophysiol. 73(2), 95–100 (2009)
2. Weiskopf, N., Scharnowski, F., Veit, R., Goebel, R., Birbaumer, N., Mathiak, K.: Self-regulation of local brain activity using real-time functional magnetic resonance imaging (fmri). J. Physiol. Paris (2005)

Prediction of Affective States through Non-invasive Thermal Camera and EMG Recordings

Didem Gokcay, Serdar Baltaci, Cagri Karahan, and Kemal Dogus Turkay

Middle East Technical University, Informatics Institute
didem@ii.metu.edu.tr

Abstract. We propose utilization of thermal camera recordings along with simultaneous EMG recordings to monitor the dynamically changing affective state of a human. Affective state is depicted along the valence and arousal dimensions, such that readings from EMG are mapped onto the valence axis and readings from the thermal camera are mapped onto the arousal axis. The combined system increases the accuracy in prediction of affective states due to a larger palette of extracted features.

Keywords: Valence, Arousal, EMG, Thermal Camera, Movie.

1 Introduction

Subjective experience, emotional expression, and physical sensation are complementary components of emotions. While subjective experience of current emotions is hard to investigate, emotional expression is easy to study especially through facial expressions. The third component, physical sensation is manifested through the autonomous nervous system, which in turn modifies physiological arousal. Currently, changes in facial expressions are quantifiable through either optical cameras or facial EMG recordings [3,5]. Changes in physiological arousal are also quantifiable through skin conductance [4] or thermal camera recordings [6,7].

Once captured, emotions can be categorized or quantized in two different ways [2]:

1. Using distinct emotional classes such as happy, angry, fearful, surprised (Circumplex model)
2. Through continuous values along two orthogonal axes, valence and arousal (Dimensional model)

In order to account for emotional states, most recently, the dimensional model has gained impetus. According to this model, emotions consist of 2 measures: valence and arousal. While valence can be predicted from facial expressions or gestures, arousal can be predicted from physiological features such as perspiration or blood flow.

In the literature, measurement of valence and arousal from facial attributes have been either inaccurate or invasive. For valence, facial expressions can be measured by FACs [1] from optical camera recordings, but some hidden cues such as clenching of teeth can not be detected this way. EMG recordings are best to capture such hidden facial expressions, however the current practice of wiring people with electrodes for this purpose is prohibiting [3,5]. For arousal, detecting physiological arousal from

S. D´Mello et al. (Eds.): ACII 2011, Part II, LNCS 6975, pp. 319–321, 2011.

skin conductance have been a widely accepted procedure, but it requires electrode placement so it is not practical. Recently thermal cameras are introduced to predict arousal from increased blood flow in the face [6,7].

In our demonstration, we will present a non-invasive system for collecting facial valence and arousal information from subjects on the fly, while subjects view a movie with emotional content, or alternatively participate in an interactive computer game. This system consists of a wireless eeg cap from EMOTIV and a thermal camera. The scientific contribution of our demostration involves merging features from both EMG and thermal recordings for better prediction of a dynamically changing affective state. The originality is due to the use of the EMOTIV cap, which embodies innovative wireless technology for capturing EMG. This system has potential for widespread use because it is non-invasive and robust to environmental noise.

2 Setup and Results

We use an EMOTIV eeg cap and Pelco thermal camera to measure valence and arousal from the face of a subject who is passively viewing movie strips. We extracted the car-chase scene from Blues Brothers (21'50''-28'25'') and ballet practice scene from Black Swan (75'30''-90'30'') to elicit pleasant versus negatively arousing emotions respectively. Based on the first movie, we observed that we can predict pleasant emotions through the 'smile' (zygomatic) motion with great success. Furthermore, there is subtle negative correlation (-0.11) with arousal read-out from between the eyes. This replicates findings from the literature regarding low-level interaction between valence and arousal. Based on the second movie, we observed that negatively arousing emotions can be predicted by the 'furrow' (corrugator) reflex successfully. Furthermore, there is significant correlation (0.46) between the arousal reported by thermal camera and arousal reported by self-evaluation of subjects.

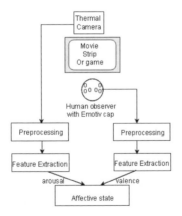

Fig. 1. Sketch of the proposed system for non-invasive affect prediction

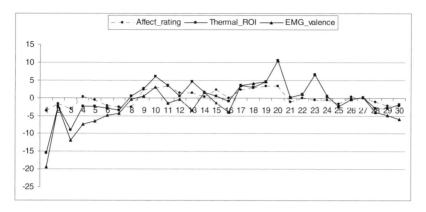

Fig. 2. Self-evaluated arousal, thermal camera mean intensities and 'furrow' EMG for a strip from the Black Swan movie (data is downsampled to 30 sec)

References

1. Ekman, P., Friesen, W.V.: Facial action coding system: A technique for the measurement of facial movement. Consulting Psychologists Press, Palo Alto (1978)
2. Gökçay, D.: Emotional Axes: Psychology, Psychophysiology and Neuroanatomical Correlates. In: Gökçay, D.,Yıldırım, G. (eds.) Affective Computing and Interaction: Psychological, Cognitive and Neuroscientific Perspectives. IGI Global (2011)
3. Gruebler, A., Suzuki, K.: Measurement of distal EMG Signals using a Wearable Device for Reading Facial Expressions. In: Proceedings of the IEEE EMBS, pp. 4594–4597 (2010)
4. Lang, P.J., Reenwald, M.K.C., Bradley, M., Hamni, A.O.: Looking at pictures: Affective, facial, visceral and behavioral reactions. Psychophysiology 30, 261–273 (1993)
5. Lapatki, B.G., Oostenveld, R., Van Dijk, J.P., Jonas, I., Zwarts, M.J., Stegeman, D.F.: Optimal placement of bipolar surface EMG electrodes in the face based on single motor unit analysis. Psychophysiology 47, 299–314 (2010)
6. Shastri, D., Merla, A., Tsiamyrtzis, P., Pavlidis, I.: Imaging Facial Signs of Neurophysiological Responses. IEEE Transactions on Biomedical Engineering 56(2), 477–484 (2009)
7. Yun, C., Shastri, D., Pavlidis, I., Deng, Z.O.: Game, Can You Feel My Frustration?: Improving User's Gaming Experience via StressCam. In: Proceedings CHI, pp. 2195–2204 (2009)

The First Audio/Visual Emotion Challenge
and Workshop – An Introduction

Björn Schuller[1], Michel Valstar[2], Roddy Cowie[3], and Maja Pantic[2,4]

[1] Technische Universität München,
Institute for Human-Machine Communication, Munich, Germany
schuller@tum.de
[2] Imperial College London, Intelligent Behaviour Understanding Group, London, UK
michel.valstar@imperial.ac.uk
[3] Queen's University, School of Psychology, Belfast, BT7 1NN, UK
r.cowie@qub.ac.uk
[4] Twente University, EEMCS, Twente, The Netherlands
m.pantic@imperial.ac.uk

Abstract. The *Audio/Visual Emotion Challenge and Workshop* (http://sspnet.eu/avec2011) is the first competition event aimed at comparison of automatic audio, visual, *and* audiovisual emotion analysis. The goal of the challenge is to provide a common benchmark test set for individual multimodal information processing and to bring together the audio and video emotion recognition communities, to compare the relative merits of the two approaches to emotion recognition under well-defined and strictly comparable conditions, and establish to what extent fusion of the approaches is possible and beneficial. A second motivation is the need to advance emotion recognition systems to be able to deal with naturalistic behavior in large volumes of un-segmented, non-prototypical and non-preselected data as this is exactly the type of data that real systems have to face in the real world. Three emotion detection sub-challenges were addressed: emotion detection from audio, from video, or from audiovisual information. As benchmarking database the SEMAINE database of naturalistic dialogues was used. Emotion needed to be recognized in terms of positive/negative valence, and high and low activation (arousal), expectancy, and power.

In total, 41 research teams registered for the challenge. The data turned out to be challenging indeed: The dataset consists of over 4 hours of audio and video recordings, 3,838 words uttered by the subject of interest, and over 1.3 million video frames in total, making it not only a challenge to detect more complex affective states, but also to deal with the sheer amount of data.

Besides participation in the Challenge, papers were invited addressing in particular the differences between audio and video processing of emotive data, and the issues concerning combined audio-visual emotion recognition.

We would like to particularly thank our sponsors – the Social Signal Processing Network (SSPNet), and the HUMAINE Association, all 22 members of the Technical Program Committee for their timely and insightful reviews of the submissions: Anton Batliner, Felix Burkhardt, Rama Chellappa, Mohamed Chetouani, Fernando De la Torre, Laurence Devillers, Julien Epps, Raul Fernandez, Hatice Gunes, Julia Hirschberg, Aleix Martinez, Marc Mehu, Marcello Mortillaro, Matti Pietikäinen, Ioannis Pitas, Peter Robinson, Stefan Steidl, Jianhua Tao, Mohan Trivedi, Matthew Turk, Alessandro Vinciarelli, and Stefanos Zafeiriou, and of course all participants.

S. D´Mello et al. (Eds.): ACII 2011, Part II, LNCS 6975, p. 322, 2011.
© Springer-Verlag Berlin Heidelberg 2011

Dimensionality Reduction and Classification Analysis on the Audio Section of the SEMAINE Database

Ricardo A. Calix[*], Mehdi A. Khazaeli, Leili Javadpour, and Gerald M. Knapp

Louisiana State University, Industrial Engineering, 3128 Patrick F. Taylor Hall, Baton Rouge, LA, U.S.A.
{rcalix1,marabk2,sjavad1,gknapp}@lsu.edu

Abstract. This paper presents an analysis of the audio section of the SEMAINE database for affect detection. Chi-square and principal component analysis techniques are used to reduce the dimensionality of the audio datasets. After dimensionality reduction, different classification techniques are used to perform emotion classification at the word level. Additionally, for unbalanced training sets, class re-sampling is performed to improve the model's classification results. Overall, the final results indicate that Support Vector Machines (SVM) performed best for all data sets. Results show promise for the SEMAINE database as an interesting corpus to study affect detection.

Keywords: speech processing, dimensionality reduction, affect detection.

1 Introduction

Human robot interactions and automatic understanding of multimedia information will require methods that can detect and interpret emotion. In the area of information retrieval, for instance, there are many text and audio collections on the web that may contain what a user needs but that do not contain the metadata necessary to find it. As a result, there is a gap between semantic meaning in content and low level speech features. Therefore, developing efficient technologies that can detect these semantic concepts, especially as they relate to emotions, retrieve them, and make them available in an enriched way could improve communication and overall user satisfaction.

Many corpora have been developed for emotion detection. The SEMAINE affect database [1] is one such corpus. The SEMAINE corpus was made to study natural conversations between artificial intelligence agents and humans. The audio section of the corpus contains 1941 features per sample which is defined as a word. The training partition has 20,183 samples, the development set includes 16,311 samples, and the test section includes 13,856 samples for a total of 50,350 samples per the entire corpus. The SEMAINE corpus can be useful because it uses well established affective dimensions such as activation, expectation, power, and valence. It also provides the already extracted features per sample (per word) for use in affective machine learning approaches.

---

[*] AVEC 2011.

S. D´Mello et al. (Eds.): ACII 2011, Part II, LNCS 6975, pp. 323–331, 2011.

This paper presents an analysis of the audio section of the SEMAINE Affect database for affect detection. The focus is on dimensionality reduction and class re-sampling of the audio feature set provided for the First International Audio/Visual Challenge (AVEC 2011). After dimensionality reduction, the dataset was employed in training and testing several machine learning approaches, of which Support Vector Machines (SVM) had the best results. Results of the classification and feature analysis performed on the training, development and testing sections of the audio dataset are presented and discussed.

2   Literature Review

Many studies have been conducted in affect detection in speech. Authors such as Luengo et al. [6] and Busso et al. [2] have analyzed different types of methodologies and speech features for use in emotion detection in speech. Busso et al. [2] simplified the analysis to a binary problem instead of studying the pitch contour in terms of finer grained emotional categories. The approach used by Busso et al. [2] has the advantage of being independent of the emotional descriptors and can be used as a first step in more sophisticated multiclass emotion recognition systems. Luengo et al. [6] used a blind unsupervised clustering method using the k-means algorithm [6]. Their approach was focused on the use of classification for detecting coarse grained or fine grained emotion classes. Linear discriminant analysis (LDA) has also been used in speech emotion recognition applications [14, 20, 21]. The usage limitation of LDA is that the reduced dimensionality must be less than the number of classes [22]. LDA and MDS (Multidimensional Scaling) also help to reduce the feature dimensionality for emotion recognition [16].

Although important, the methods presented in these studies are difficult to compare because there is currently no gold standard affect corpus that can be used to evaluate multimodal affect detection methodologies. AVEC 2011 proposes to address this issue by introducing the SEMAINE corpus and promoting an affect analysis challenge to compare methods and results. The format and features of the SEMAINE database are described in [1].

There are many different corpora for emotion detection but each corpus has differences in the labels and annotation scheme based on the application domain. Additionally, determining how to accurately develop the ground truth scores for a corpus is difficult since inter-annotator agreement is low for subjective tasks like emotion detection. In general, two types of features have been used: the "big six" (happy, sad, etc.) and the primitives of valence, expectation, power, and activation as in [9] and [1].

Furthermore, dimensionality reduction is an important aspect that needs to be addressed when using large feature sets such as the ones used in emotion detection. For a given dataset size, the performance of a classifier will eventually start to decrease with increased dimensionality. Dimensionality reduction is applied to decrease the complexity of the model development. Using dimensionality reduction techniques in speech emotion recognition applications also reduces storage and computational requirements, and gives insights about the features that are most useful for the classification task [11].

Standard approaches for dimensionality reduction include feature selection (e.g. chi-square ranking) or feature transformation (e.g. Principal Component Analysis). In feature selection, the main objective is finding the feature subset that achieves the best classification between classes, and in understanding insights of the feature contributions. In contrast, in feature transformation the objective is finding a suitable mapping from the original feature space to another space with reduced dimensionality while preserving as much of the variability in the data as possible for effective classification.

Feature selection methods like Sequential Forward Search [23, 15] and Sequential Floating Forward Search (SFFS) [24, 25, 17] need heavy computation to evaluate all the feature subsets. And only part of the classification information remains. The SFFS algorithm finds an optimum subset of features by insertions (i.e. by appending a new feature to the subset of previously selected features) and deletions (i.e. by discarding a feature from the subset of already selected features) of the original features based on meeting a given condition [26].

Feature selection with chi-square keeps some of the original features without transformation. This allows for insights into the types of features that help for a particular prediction task. Additionally, feature selection techniques like chi-square ranking are less computationally expensive than other approaches such as Principal Component Analysis (PCA) and can therefore be performed quickly. The chi-square metric used to determine the feature contribution is calculated [10] as follows:

$$\chi^2(t,c) = \frac{(AD-CB)^2}{(A+C)\times(B+D)\times(A+B)\times(C+D)} \tag{1}$$

where t is a feature, c is the class, A represents the number of times that c and t co-occur, B represents the number of times that t occurs without c, C represents the number of times that c occurs without t, and D represents the number of times neither t nor c occur.

In contrast, feature extraction methods like PCA (Principal Component Analysis) transform the data to a new feature set. PCA has the advantage that it can significantly reduce the dimensionality of the dataset and address issues of multi-collinearity or correlation between the features. The downside, however, is that the original features are transformed to new features so insights are missed and that the process is computationally intensive and also expensive.

The main objective of PCA is to determine the main components e_1, e_2, e_3,...,e_i that can explain a percentage "v" of the variance in the data. The e_i values are a linear combination of the original features in the data. The concept of PCA is simple. First, the d-dimensional mean vector μ and d x d covariance matrix S are computed for the dataset. Next, the eigenvectors and eigenvalues are computed and sorted according to decreasing eigenvalue. The data is then projected onto the first M principal components that capture "v" variability.

The cost function for PCA [19] is formulated as follows:

$$J = \sum_{n=1}^{N} \sum_{i=M+1}^{d} (X_n^T e_i - \overline{X}^T e_i)^2 = \sum_{i=M+1}^{d} e_i^T S e_i \tag{2}$$

To find M, the general solution to the minimization of J is obtained by selecting the $\{e_i\}$ to be eigenvectors of the covariance matrix which are given by

$$Se_i = \lambda_i e_i \tag{3}$$

where i = 1,..., D, D is the dimensionality, and the eigenvectors $\{e_i\}$ are chosen to be orthonormal [19].

The PCA feature extraction method has been used extensively in the context of speech emotion recognition [15, 16]. You et al [14] used Linear Discriminant Analysis (LDA), PCA and feature selection by Sequential Forward Selection (SFS) (in which features are sequentially added to an empty candidate set until adding more features doesn't decrease the criterion [13]) for reducing the acoustic features before classifying the speech data [12]. They have also used PCA, LDA and a combination of PCA+LDA method for feature dimensionality reduction. However, for different emotions, different methods achieved the best recognition results [14].

Finally, to perform classification, there are many approaches. Important methods used in the literature for classification include Naïve Bayes, Multilayer perceptron, K-nearest neighbor, random forests, and Support Vector Machines. In fact there has been no agreement on which classifier is the most suitable for emotion classification and each classifier has its own advantages and disadvantages [11]. In order to combine the advantages of several classifiers, researchers have been working on combining a group of classifiers together [17, 18].

Generally speaking, kernel based methods perform better than other methods because they have the capability through the kernel trick of mapping the data to higher dimensional spaces. This technique may make data that is not linearly separable in a lower dimensional space to be separable in higher dimensional space. A popular example of kernel based methods in most studies is Support Vector Machines (SVM). In this work, Support Vector Machines achieved the best results.

Support Vector Machines are a binary classifier based on statistical learning theory. The main objective of support vector machines is to find the maximum margin that separates samples from two classes. Since errors usually occur in practice, the SVM approach also tries to minimize the sum of these errors. Formally, the objective function subject to constraints is formulated [3] as follows:

Min $$\frac{1}{2}\|W\|^2 + C\sum \varepsilon_i \tag{4}$$

S.T. $$Y_i(W \cdot X_i + b) \geq 1 - \varepsilon_i \tag{5}$$

where W is the weight vector perpendicular to the separating hyper plane, C is the cost of the errors, E_i are the errors, Y_i is the class per sample i, Xi is the feature vector for sample i, and b is the bias.

3 Methodology

To perform the analysis of the audio section of the SEMAINE database, different feature reduction, re-sampling, and classification techniques were applied and tested. Only the 1941 speech features that were provided for the challenge were used for the analysis. No new or additional features were used.

The work presented in this paper was performed on two regular laptop computers with maximum capacity of 6 GB of RAM memory and Pentium i3 core processor. Therefore, computational speed and memory usage were essential parts of the methodology and analysis. To deal with the large size of the data in the audio section of the SEMAINE corpus, several dimensionality reduction techniques had to be applied. Hence, the issue of computational performance influenced some of the decisions regarding parameter selection to perform feature reduction and classification analysis.

First, the dimensionality of the data set was reduced from 1941 speech features to less than 400 for each emotion class (activation, expectation, power, and valence) using chi-square feature selection. The chi-square feature selection technique removes all samples with a chi-square metric of zero or less. Chi-square ranking processes the data faster than PCA and therefore served as an initial filter to reduce the dimensionality.

Second, after chi-square feature selection, the remaining features are mapped to a new feature set using Principal Component Analysis (PCA). PCA analysis is based on the variance-covariance matrix, and the one-to-one correspondence between the original vectors is lost in this matrix. In dimensionality reduction enough eigenvectors should be chosen to account for a percentage of the variance in the original data. There is a trade-off when selecting the cut-off. In general, the objective is to select a high value of the variability tolerance so that a lot of the variability is captured while reducing the dimensionality of the feature space. However, as the SEMAINE audio dataset is large, retaining 95% of the variability means that the dimensionality is still very large and computation times are long.

To perform a proper significance test to evaluate the different classifiers, multiple runs must be made. This means that the processing will be long. To reduce processing time, therefore, the cutoff was reduced to 70%. This reduction produces a smaller dimensional feature sets which helps to evaluate classifiers. The downside, of course, is that the lower variability cutoff may have caused some information to be lost.

Five classification methodologies were analyzed to determine the one that performed the best. A paired T-test with a significance level of 0.05 was used to determine if the difference between classifiers was significant. The significance testing is performed with WEKA's experimenter using 10-fold cross validation with 10-iterations. This comparison is performed using the training subset only. For the significance testing, PCA was used with a cut-off variance of 70% to make the analysis more computational tractable. The five classifier used for the analysis are Naïve Bayes, Multilayer perceptron, K-nearest neighbor, random forests and Support Vector Machines (SVM).

For imbalanced training datasets, a re-sampling approach based on Chawla's SMOTE oversampling [5] technique is applied. The valence, power, and expectation training datasets were re-sampled by increasing the lowest class by 20%, 23%, and 32%, respectively. The activation (arousal) training dataset was balanced and therefore did not require re-sampling. The LibSVM implementation [4] of the Support Vector Machines classifier was used to perform the classification analysis. The RBF kernel used a cost of 4 and gamma of 0.1. The data was normalized.

4 Analysis and Results

The initial dimensionality of the audio dataset is reduced using Chi-square feature selection and PCA. The corpus being used here consists of training, development and testing partitions. The training set is used for tuning the parameters of the implemented model. The challenge of this competition is measuring the classification and calculating the accuracy on the testing partition. But the labels of the testing data are unknown. Therefore, for selecting the optimal parameters and estimating the performance of the model, the training and development datasets were used. Classification accuracy for the development data set is measured using Recall and F-measure accuracy scores. Results of the test set are measured using WA and UA as defined by the AVEC 2011 challenge.

After chi-square feature ranking and removing all features equal to or below zero, the feature sets were reduced to 1273, 363, 652, and 714 for activation, expectation, power, and valence, respectively. The complete list of ranked features from chi-square feature analysis can be obtained from LSU-NLP [27]. This dimensionality reduction was followed by PCA dimensionality reduction. After PCA (95%), the activation (arousal) dataset was reduced to 385 features, the expectation dataset was reduced to 98 features, the power dataset was reduced to 196 features, and the valence dataset was reduced to 197 features.

From the feature ranking it seems that activation appears to have the features with the highest chi-square correlation metrics (1930-1740 chi measurement for the 15 highest ranked features). In contrast, expectation and valence have the lowest chi-square metrics (264-141 for expectation and 272-199 for valence). For the activation class, features related to spectral flux appear in the 15 highest ranked features. For the expectation class, features related to F0 final (sma) appear in the 15 highest ranked features. For the power category, features related to F0 final (sma) and spectral roll-off appear in the 15 highest ranked features, and , finally, for the valence category, features related to spectral roll-off appear in the 15 highest ranked features.

With regards to the lowest ranked features, the results also varied per class. For the activation class, features related to MFCCs are ranked the lowest. For the expectation class, features related to shimmer are ranked the lowest. For the power category, features related to harmonicity and MFCCs are ranked the lowest and, finally, for the valence category, features related to voicing and jitter appear to be ranked lowest. It is interesting to note that each class has its own set of best and worst ranked features and that the correlations as indicated by the chi-square metric are also different.

Table 1 shows the results of significance testing to compare classification approaches. As can be seen in Table 1, SVM performs best overall. The SVM method was found to be statistically better than all the other methods. The only two exceptions were for expectation where the multilayer perceptron did slightly better than SVM, and for Valence where Naïve Bayes was one percentage point higher than SVM. The test base method was SVM and the comparison field was the percent correct [8].

Table 1. Significance testing for classifier comparison

	Activation	Expectation	Power	Valence
SVM	66	59	63	56
Naïve Bayes	61*	58*	60*	57v
Random Forest	62*	59	58*	54*
Multilayer Perceptron	62*	61v	61*	56
Nearest Neighbour	58*	55*	56*	54*

Legend: v = statistically better   * = statistically worst

Table 2 and Table 3 present the results of the classification task using the development and test sets of the audio section of the SEMAINE corpus. The results on Tables 2 and 3 are presented using the metrics of F-measure and recall as these are the most common metrics in the literature. However, these values can be used to calculate the metrics of WA and UA which are used in the challenge. WA is the average recall and UA is formulated as follows:

$$UA = \frac{Recall_0 + Recall_1}{2} \tag{6}$$

From Table 2, it can be seen that the results are consistent with the AVEC 2011 baseline paper [7]. Tables 2 and 3 include the results of the classification accuracy using Support Vector Machines (SVM) on the development and test sets of the audio section of SEMAINE.

Table 2. Classification Results on the development Audio Section of the SEMAINE Database

			Activation		Expectation		Power		Valence	
			F	Recall	F	Recall	F	Recall	F	Recall
SVM	Dev.	0	61.6	69.4	75.5	84.4	36.7	30.8	41.8	44.5
		1	65.7	59.7	28.5	21.8	75.8	81.9	65.9	63.6
		Av.	64	63.8	59.8	63.5	62.9	65	57.6	57
				UA		UA		UA		UA
				64.5		53.1		56.3		54

For the development section (Table 2), results on each of the 2 classes, and overall performance are presented. On Table 2, "0" and "1" are the two classes used in the challenge of below and above 50% for the given primitive (e.g. valence, etc.). Avg. is the accuracy score for the given task per class. Dev. is the development set and test is the test set. Results from the analysis in Table 3 indicate that activation and expectation appear to be easier to classify than power and valence.

Table 3. Classification Results on the testing Audio Section of the SEMAINE Database

			Activation		Expectation		Power		Valence	
			WA	UA	WA	UA	WA	UA	WA	UA
SVM	Test		59.3	59.2	52.5	53.9	34.1	48.6	41.4	42.0

5 Conclusions

Results of the significance testing performed on the training set indicate that Support Vector Machines performs best over most of the classes in the training set. The use of dimensionality reduction considerably helps to reduce the size of the datasets and does not appear to decrease the classification accuracy of the methods when compared to the baseline paper [7]. The complete list of ranked features using the chi-square feature ranking method for each of the four emotion classes can be downloaded for additional analysis from LSU-NLP [27]. Results show promise for the SEMAINE database as an interesting corpus for affect detection analysis because the corpus appears to be well annotated, with appropriate classes, and a measure of annotator agreement.

Additionally, the corpus has many standard features already extracted and the complexity seems non-trivial which may be useful to a better understanding of emotions in multimedia data. Additionally, results from the analysis indicate that activation and expectation appear to be easier to classify than power and valence. Furthermore, the provided feature set helps with the classification task but does not perform as well as it could. Therefore, future work may incorporate the use of the words spoken in the audio recordings so that more semantic content is captured. Finally, future work can also consider combining the words and corresponding features into complete sentences so as to perform the analysis at the sentence level.

References

1. McKeown, G., Valstar, M., Pantic, M., Cowie, R.: The SEMAINE Corpus of Emotionally Coloured Character Interactions. In: Proceedings International Conference Multimedia & Expo., pp. 1–6 (2010)
2. Busso, C., Lee, S., Narayanan, S.: Analysis of Emotionally Salient Aspects of Fundamental Frequency for Emotion Detection. IEEE Transactions on Audio, Speech, and Language Processing 17(4), 582–596 (2009)
3. Burges, C.: A Tutorial on Support Vector Machines for Pattern Recognition. Data Mining and Knowledge Discovery 2, 121–167 (1998)
4. Chang, C., Lin, C.: LIBSVM: A Library for Support Vector Machines (2001), http://www.csie.ntu.edu.tw/~cjlin/libsvm
5. Chawla, N., Bowyer, K., Hall, L., Kegelmeyer, W.: SMOTE: Synthetic Minority Over-sampling Technique. Journal of Artificial Intelligence Research 16, 341–378 (2002)
6. Luengo, I., Navas, E., Hernaez, I.: Feature Analysis and Evaluation for Automatic Emotion identification in Speech. IEEE Transactions on Multimedia 12(6), 490–501 (2010)
7. Schuller, B., Valstar, M., Eyben, F., McKeown, G., Cowie, R., Pantic, M.: AVEC 2011 – The First International Audio/Visual Emotion Challenge. In: D´Mello, S., et al. (eds.) ACII 2011, Part II, vol. 6975, pp. 415–424. Springer, Heidelberg (2011)

8. Witten, I., Frank, E.: Data mining: Practical Machine Learning Tools and Techniques, 2nd edn. Morgan Kaufmann Publishers Inc., San Francisco

9. Grimm, M., Kroschel, K., Mower, E., Narayanan, S.: Primitives based evaluation and estimation of emotions in speech. Elsevier Speech Communication 49, 787–800 (2007)

10. Yang, Y., Pedersen, J.: A Comparative Study on Feature Selection in Text Categorization. In: Proceedings of the 14th International Conference on Machine Learning, pp. 412–420 (1997)

11. El Ayadi, M., Kamel, M., Karray, F.: Survey on speech emotion recognition: Features, classification schemes, and databases. Pattern Recognition 44, 572–587 (2011)

12. You, M., Chen, C., Bu, J., Liu, J., Tao, J.: Emotion recognition from noisy speech. In: IEEE International Conference on Multimedia and Expo., pp. 1653–1656 (2006)

13. Marcano-Cedeño, A., Quintanilla-Domínguez, J., Cortina-Januchs, M.G., Andina, D.: Feature selection using Sequential Forward Selection and classification applying Artificial Metaplasticity Neural Network. In: 36th Annual Conference on IEEE Industrial Electronics Society, pp. 2845–2850 (2010)

14. You, M., Chen, C., Bu, J., Liu, J., Tao, J.: A hierarchical framework for speech emotion recognition. In: IEEE International Symposium on Industrial Electronics, vol. 1, pp. 515–519 (2006)

15. Ververidis, D., Kotropoulos, C., Pitas, I.: Automatic emotional speech classification. In: Proceedings of IEEE International Conference on Acoustics, Speech, and Signal Processing (ICASSP 2004), vol. 1, pp. I-593–I-596 (2004)

16. Go, H., Kwak, K., Lee, D., Chun, M.: Emotion recognition from the facial image and speech signal. In: Proceedings of the IEEE SICE 2003, vol. 3, pp. 2890–2895 (2003)

17. Schuller, B., Lang, M., Rigoll, G.: Robust acoustic speech emotion recognition by ensembles of classifiers. In: Proceedings of the DAGA 2005, 31, Deutsche Jahrestagung für Akustik, DEGA, pp. 329–330 (2005)

18. Lugger, M., Yang, B.: Combining classifiers with diverse feature sets for robust speaker independent emotion recognition. In: Proceedings of EUSIPCO (2009)

19. Bishop, C.: Pattern Recognition and Machine Learning. Springer, Heidelberg (2006)

20. Xie, B., Chen, L., Chen, G.-C., Chen, C.: Statistical feature selection for mandarin speech emotion recognition. In: Huang, D.-S., Zhang, X.-P., Huang, G.-B. (eds.) ICIC 2005. LNCS, vol. 3644, pp. 591–600. Springer, Heidelberg (2005)

21. Schuller, B., Rigoll, G., Lang, M.: Speech emotion recognition combining acoustic features and linguistic information in a hybrid support vector machine-belief network architecture. In: Proceedings of the ICASSP 2004, vol. 1, pp. 577–580 (2004)

22. Duda, R., Hart, P., Stork, D.: Pattern Recognition. John Wiley and Sons, Chichester (2001)

23. Grimm, M., Kroschel, K., Narayanan, S.: Support Vector Regression for Automatic Recognition of Spontaneous Emotions in Speech. In: Proceeding of IEEE International Conference on Acoustics, Speech and Signal Processing, vol. 4, pp. 1085–1088 (April 2007)

24. Lugger, M., Yang, B.: The Relevance of Voice Quality Features in Speaker Independent emotion recognition. In: Proceeding of IEEE International Conference on Acoustics, Speech and Signal Processing, vol. 4, pp. 17–20 (April 2007)

25. Ververidis, D., Kotropoulos, C.: Fast sequential floating forward selection applied to emotional speech features estimated on DES and SUSAS data collections. In: Proceedings of the European Signal Processing Conference, EUSIPCO (2006)

26. Ververidis, D., Kotropoulos, C.: Fast and accurate sequential floating forward feature selection with the Bayes classifier applied to speech emotion recognition. Signal Processing 88(12), 2956–2970 (2008)

27. LSU-NLP, http://nlp.lsu.edu

Speech Emotion Recognition System Based on L1 Regularized Linear Regression and Decision Fusion

Ling Cen[1], Zhu Liang Yu[2], and Ming Hui Dong[1]

[1] Institute for Infocomm Research (I2R), A*STAR,
1 Fusionopolis Way, Singapore 138632
[2] The College of Automation Science and Engineering,
South China University of Technology, China

Abstract. This paper describes a speech emotion recognition system that is built for Audio Sub-Challenge of Audio/Visual Emotion Challenge (AVEC 2011). In this system, feature selection is conducted via L1 regularized linear regression in which the L1 norm of regression weights is minimized to find a sparse weight vector. The features with approximately zero weights are removed to create a well-selected small feature set. A fusion scheme by combining the strength from linear regression and Extreme learning machine (EML) based feedforward neural networks (NN) is proposed for classification. The experiment results conducted on the SEMAINE database of naturalistic dialogues distributed through AVEC 2011 are presented.

Keywords: feature selection, classification, linear regression, convex optimization.

1 Introduction

The technology for human-computer interaction has advanced rapidly over the recent decade. The ability of computers to recognize, understand and response to human speech is necessary to realize communications between human and computers. In human speech, both linguistic information and paralinguistic information that refers to the implicit messages such as emotional states of the speaker, are conveyed. Human emotions are associated with the feelings, thoughts and behaviors of humans. They carry important information on the speaker such as his/her desire, intent and response to the outside world. The phonologically identical utterances, for example, can be expressed in various emotions and convey different meanings. To realize natural and smooth interaction between human and computers, as such, it is important that a computer is able to recognize not only the linguistic contents but also the emotional states conveyed in human speech so that personalized responses can be delivered accordingly in human-computer interaction applications.

In the literature, a large number of studied have been reported. Many classification methods have been applied in speech emotion recognition, for example,

S. D´Mello et al. (Eds.): ACII 2011, Part II, LNCS 6975, pp. 332–340, 2011.

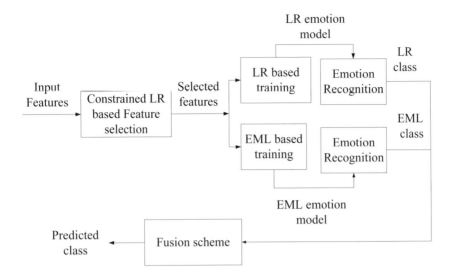

Fig. 1. Structure of the proposed speech emotion recognition system

k-nearest neighbor (kNN) classifier [1], Neural network (NN) [2–5], Linear Discriminant Classifiers with Gaussian class-conditional probability and kNN [6], Gaussian Mixture Model (GMM) [5], Support Vector Machines (SVMs) [7–9]. Several feature selection methods have been published as well, such as the combination of decision tree and random forest ensemble learning [10], forward selection [6], genetic algorithm [11], and Canonical Correlation Analysis [4]. The results are, however, far from being realistic in practical applications. Automatic recognition of speech emotion is a very challenging task because of the complexity of the emotions and lack of precise definition and modelling.

In this contribution to the Audio Sub-Challenge of AVEC 2011, a linear regression (LR) based feature selection method and a hybrid classification method are presented. Fig. 1 shows the basic diagram of our speech emotion recognition system. It can be broken down into 3 modules, namely, feature selection, model training, classification. The improvements achieved by our system are briefly concluded below.

1. In order to reduce the dimension of the baseline feature set that consists of 1941 features, a constrained linear regression based feature selection method is applied. During the optimization of regression weights, ℓ_1 norm of weights is minimized to find a sparse weight vector. The features with approximately zero weights are removed to create a well-selected small feature set. Unlike the feature selection methods presented in [10, 6, 11], this method does not need to repeatedly validate various selection forms via classification and evaluation during selection procedure. With a well-selected small feature set,

the irrelevant information can be removed in the original feature set. The calculation complexity is reduced with a decreased dimensionality too.

2. Convex optimization is employed to solve the optimization problems incurred in feature selection and emotion classification. It is an excellent tradeoff in efficiency between the analytical methods and the numerical techniques, in which a local minimum of the problem is also the global minimum.

3. Emotion models are trained independently using two base classifiers, i.e. Extreme learning machine (EML) based feedforward neural networks and LR method. Compared to the popular algorithms of feedforward neural networks like the conventional back-propagation (BP) algorithm and SVMs, EML has much faster learning speed and higher or similar generalization performance[12].

4. To improve the classification accuracy, a hybrid scheme is proposed to effectively combine the strength from LR and EML at the decision level.

The remaining part of this paper is organized as follows. In Section 2, feature selection based on LR and convex optimization is presented. Following that, a fusion scheme for emotion classification that combining LR and EML is described. The experiment results are shown in Section 4 and the concluding remarks are given in Section 5.

2   Feature Selection

Acoustic features that are correlated to emotions have been investigated in many studies. The pitch, intensity and the rate of speech as well as voiced and unvoiced segments have been commonly used in speech emotion recognition [13, 6, 1, 14, 15]. Besides these features directly extracted from speech signals, the features derived from mathematical transformation of basic acoustic features, e.g.Mel-Frequency Cepstral Coefficients (MFCC) [16, 17, 4, 5, 9], Linear Prediction-based Cepstral Coefficients (LPCC) [16, 5, 9], and Perceptual Linear Prediction (PLP) Cepstral Coefficients [5, 9] have also been used for detecting emotions from speech.

The studies on the behavior of the acoustic features in various emotions [18–22, 13] have shown that anger is associated with the highest energy and pitch level among anger, disgust, fear, joy and sadness. Disgust has a lower mean pitch level, a lower intensity level and a slower speech rate than the neutral state. Low levels of the mean intensity and mean pitch are measured with sadness. A high pitch level and a raised intensity level are found in speech expressed with fear. The pitch contour trend separates fear from joy. A downwards slope in the pitch contour can be observed in speech expressed with fear and sadness, while the speech with joy shows a rising slope. Observable variance on speech rate is found in different emotions.

However, there is still no conclusive evidence to show which set of features can provide the best recognition accuracy [8]. The baseline feature set provided in the audio sub-challenge of AVEC 2011 consists of 1941 features [23]. The features extracted for the purpose of emotion recognition are, however, not of equal importance. Working with a well-selected small feature set can not only remove the irrelevant information in the original feature set but also reduce computational load with a decreased dimensionality.

For this purpose, a LR based feature selection method is proposed in this section. Two advantages can be achieved by our method compared to other selection methods. First, it eliminates the need to repeatedly perform classification and evaluation during selection procedure, which consequently reduces computation cost incurred in selection. Second, by formulating selection of features as a convex optimization problem, it can be solved using very efficient numerical methods, like the Interior-Point Method (IPM) [24].

Let multidimensional variable $\mathbf{x} \in R^m$ be the input feature vector and binary variable y be the target output, i.e. $y = [1, 0]$, in a binary classification problem. We assume that y depends linearly on $\mathbf{x}$ and a set of weights $\mathbf{w}$, which can be expressed as

$$y = f(\mathbf{x}; \mathbf{w}) + \epsilon, \tag{1}$$

where ϵ is the regression error and $f(\mathbf{x}; \mathbf{w})$ is a linear function defined as

$$f(\mathbf{x}; \mathbf{w}) = w_0 + w_1 x_1 + ... + w_m x_m = [1 \ \mathbf{x}^T] \mathbf{w}. \tag{2}$$

The weights vector $\mathbf{w} = [w_0 \ w_1 \ \cdots \ w_m]^T$ can be estimated by fitting using the training data to minimize the least square error $J_n(\mathbf{w})$

$$J_n(\mathbf{w}) = \frac{1}{N} \sum_{i=1}^{N} (y_i - f(\mathbf{x}_i; \mathbf{w}))^2. \tag{3}$$

The objective of feature selection is to find a sparse weight vector $\mathbf{w}$. The features with approximately zero weights are then removed from the original feature set. By minimizing the ℓ_0 norm of $\mathbf{w}$, i.e. $\|\mathbf{w}\|_0$, we can find a sparse weight vector. The ℓ_0 norm $\|\mathbf{w}\|_0$ is the measure of the sparsity of $\mathbf{w}$, which is defined as the number of non-zero components in $\mathbf{w}$. However, $\|\mathbf{w}\|_0$ is non-convex over $\mathbf{w}$. In order to solve it efficiently, ℓ_0 norm is replaced with the ℓ_1 norm, i.e. minimizing $\|\mathbf{w}\|_1$ to control the sparsity of a vector. The equivalence of the ℓ_0 norm and the ℓ_1 norm has been well studied in [25–27]. Feature selection problem is then formulated as

$$\min_{\mathbf{w}} \ J_n(\mathbf{w}) + \alpha \|\mathbf{w}\|_1, \tag{4}$$

where α is a positive scalar weighting factor used to balance the tradeoff between the contribution of different terms. The objective function in (4) preserves the convexity of the problem and can be efficiently solved using convex optimization techniques. The obtained sparse weight vector can be used for feature selection.

3   Hybrid Classification Scheme

In order to improve the accuracy of classification, a hybrid classification scheme is proposed by combining two base classifiers, i.e. LR based classifier and EML based feedforward NN.

3.1 Base Classifiers

LR based classifier. A classification problem can be solved via linear regression by solving the following least squares optimization problem

$$\min_{\mathbf{W}} \quad \left\| y - [1 \ \mathbf{x}^T]\mathbf{w} \right\|_2 . \tag{5}$$

This can be solved using convex optimization as described before.

After the regression model has been trained, the regression function, $f(\mathbf{x}; \hat{\mathbf{w}})$ can be used to classify new samples as

$$\begin{aligned} y = 1, \quad &\text{if } f(\mathbf{x}; \mathbf{w}) \geq 0.5, \\ y = 0, \quad &\text{if } f(\mathbf{x}; \mathbf{w}) < 0.5. \end{aligned} \tag{6}$$

EML based feedforward NN. Tradition feedforward neural networks extensively use slow gradient-based learning algorithms to train neural networks and tunes the parameters iteratively, which makes their learning speed rather slow. To overcome these drawbacks, Huang and his colleagues have proposed a new learning algorithm called Extreme Learning Machine, which randomly chooses hidden nodes and analytically determines the output weights of the network [12]. Compared to other computational intelligence methods such as the conventional back-propagation (BP) algorithm and SVMs, ELM has much faster learning speed, ease of implementation, least human intervene, and high generalization performance. It has been reported by Huang et al. from the experimental results that ELM can produce better generalization performance and can learn thousands of times faster than traditional learning algorithms for feedforward neural networks.

3.2 Decision Fusion

In our system, EML feedforward NN is combined with LR based classification method to form a hybrid classification scheme. Let the output of two base classifiers be d_{lr} and d_{eml} and the final decision be y_f. Assuming y_f linearly depends on d_{lr} and d_{eml} and is expressed as

$$y_f = w_0 + w_{lr}d_{lr} + w_{eml}d_{eml} + \epsilon = [1 \ d_{lr} \ d_{eml}]\mathbf{w}_f + \epsilon \tag{7}$$

where $\mathbf{w}_f = [w_0, w_{lr}, w_{eml}]$ are weighting coefficients for fusion. $\mathbf{w}_f$ can be estimated based on the training dataset by solving the least-squares problem shown as

$$\min_{\mathbf{W}_f} \quad \left\| y_r - [1 \ d_{lr} \ d_{eml}]\mathbf{w}_f \right\|_2 , \tag{8}$$

where y_r is the target label.

4   Evaluation Results

To evaluate the effectiveness of the proposed system, some numerical experiments have been conducted on the Solid-SAL part of the SEMAINE database of naturalistic dialogues that are distributed through the AVEC 2011 Emotion Challenge. The information about the database can be found in [23] and [28]. There are 24 recordings in total, each of which has approximately 4 character conversation sessions. They were split into 3 partitions, i.e. a training, develop, and test partition each consisting of 8 recordings. There are 31, 32, and 32 sessions in training, develop, and test partitions, respectively. Four affective dimensions, i.e. Activation (Arousal), Expectation, Power, and Valence, are classified based on above or below average on word level. The baseline audio features [23] are used in classification. To reduce the variation across different sessions, speech normalization is performed on a session level by subtracting the mean of corresponding features. A reduced feature set having around 1000 features is selected for each dimension. In the EML based feedforward NN, sigmoidal function is used as the activation function.

Table 1. Classification accuracies for the Audio Sub-Challenge. WA stands for weighted accuracy, and UA for unweighted accuracy.

Activation	Proposed (develop)	Baseline (develop)	Proposed (test)	Baseline (test)
WA	58.74	63.7	50.78	55.0
UA	51.89	64.0	55.07	57.0
Expectation	Proposed (develop)	Baseline (develop)	Proposed (test)	Baseline (test)
WA	66.52	63.2	50.10	52.9
UA	50.24	52.7	51.08	54.5
Power	Proposed (develop)	Baseline (develop)	Proposed (test)	Baseline (test)
WA	65.91	65.6	26.03	28.0
UA	50.23	55.8	47.48	49.1
Valence	Proposed (develop)	Baseline (develop)	Proposed (test)	Baseline (test)
WA	62.93	58.1	45.26	44.3
UA	50.11	52.9	48.82	47.2

Tables 1 and 2 show the comparisons between our results and baseline results for training on the training partition and testing on the develop and test partitions in the Audio Sub-challenge and Audiovisual Sub-challenge, respectively. For the Audiovisual Sub-challenge, the results are calculated using audio features only. It can be seen from this table that our system perform better than baseline on develop partition for Audio Sub-Challenge and on test partition for Audiovisual Sub-Challenge, while only the accuracy of Valence dimension on test partition for Audio Sub-Challenge is higher than baseline results. It can be stated by the suitability of the method and the different characteristic of the database. It is also found that the difference between the accuracies of 2 classes is large in some cases. It seems to be caused by the unbalance of the training

Table 2. Classification accuracies for the Audiovisual Sub-Challenge using audio features only. (a) denotes the results using only the audio baseline classifiers [23].

Activation	Proposed (test)	Baseline (test-a)
WA	52.02	51.2
UA	52.25	51.2
Expectation	Proposed (test)	Baseline (test-a)
WA	63.73	59.2
UA	50.11	49.5
Power	Proposed (test)	Baseline (test-a)
WA	62.15	52.7
UA	50.72	45.9
Valence	Proposed (test)	Baseline (test-a)
WA	69.13	55.8
UA	49.97	46.5

data and overfitting occurred. Future work will be carried out to reduce the sensibility of the system and improve classification performance as well.

5   Conclusions

In this paper, a LR feature selection method and a hybrid classification scheme by combining LR and EML are presented, which work together to form an emotion classification system. The proposed system is evaluated using the SEMAINE database of naturalistic dialogues for Audio Sub-Challenge of AVEC 2011. In this system, features selection is realized by minimizing ℓ_1 norm of regression weights to get a sparse vector of regression weights. By combining the strength from LR and EML based classification methods, an efficient hybrid classification method is proposed for emotion classification.

References

1. Dellaert, F., Polzin, T., Waibel, A.: Recognizing emotion in speech. In: Proc. 4th International Conference on Spoken Language Processing, vol. 3, pp. 1970–1973 (October 1996)
2. Nicholson, J., Takahashi, K., Nakatsu, R.: Emotion recognition in speech using neural networks. In: Proceedings of 6th International Conference on Neural Information Processing, Stockholm, Sweden, vol. 2, pp. 495–501 (1999)
3. Petrushin, V.A.: Emotion in speech: recognition and application to call centers. In: Proceedings of Artificial Neural Networks in Engineering, pp. 7–10 (November 1999)
4. Cen, L., Ser, W., Yu, Z.L.: Speech emotion recognition using canonical correlation analysis and probabilistic neural network. In: Proc. 7th Int. Conf. Machine Learning and Application (ICMLA), San Diego, California, USA (December 2008)
5. Cen, L., Ser, W., Yu, Z.L., Cen, W.: Automatic Recognition of Emotional States from Human Speechs. In: Pattern Recognition Recent Advances, IN-TECH, pp. 431–449 (February 2010)

6. Lee, C., Narayanan, S.: Toward detecting emotions in spoken dialogs. IEEE Trans. on Speech and Audio Processing 13(2), 293–303 (2005)

7. Yu, F., Chang, E., Xu, Y.Q., Shum, H.Y.: Emotion detection from speech to enrich multimedia content. In: Proc. 2th IEEE Pacific-Rim Conf. Multimedia Int., Beijing, China (October 2001)

8. Zhou, J., Wang, G.Y., Yang, Y., Chen, P.J.: Speech emotion recognition based on rough set and svm. In: Proc. 5th IEEE Int. Conf. Cognitive Informatics, Beijing, China, vol. 1, pp. 53–61 (July 2006)

9. Cen, L., Dong, M.H., Li, H.Z., Yu, Z.L., Chan, P.: Machine Learning Methods in the Application of Speech Emotion Recognition. In: Application of Machine Learning, IN-TECH, pp. 1–19 (February 2010)

10. Rong, J., Chen, Y.-P.P., Chowdhury, M., Li, G.: Acoustic features extraction for emotion recognition. In: Proc. IEEE/ACIS International Conference on Computer and Information Science, vol. 11(13), pp. 419–424 (July 2007)

11. Oudeyer, P.Y.: The production and recognition of emotions in speech: features and algorithms. Proc. International Journal of Human-Computer Studies 59, 157–183 (2003)

12. Huang, G.B., Zhu, Q.Y., Siew, C.K.: Extreme learning machine: Theory and applications. Neurocomputing 70, 489–501 (2006)

13. Ververidis, D., Kotropoulos, C.: Emotional speech recognition: resources, features, and methods. Speech Communication 48(9), 1163–1181 (2006)

14. Petrushin, V.A.: Emotion recognition in speech signal: experimental study, development, and application. In: Proc. 6th International Conference on Spoken Language Processing, Beijing, China (2000)

15. Amir, N.: Classifying emotions in speech: A comparison of methods. In: Proc. Eurospeech (2001)

16. Specht, D.F.: Probabilistic neural networks for classification, mapping or associative memory. In: Proc. IEEE Int. Conf. Neural Network, vol. 1, pp. 525–532 (July 1988)

17. Reynolds, D.A., Quatieri, T.F., Dunn, R.B.: Speaker verification using adapted gaussian mixture model. Digital Signal Processing 10(1), 19–41 (2000)

18. Davitz, J.R. (ed.): The Communication of Emotional Meaning. McGraw-Hill, New York (1964)

19. Huttar, G.L.: Relations between prosodic variables and emotions in normal american english utterances. Journal of Speech Hearing Res. 11, 481–487 (1968)

20. Fonagy, I.: A new method of investigating the perception of prosodic features. Language and Speech 21, 34–49 (1978)

21. Havrdova, Z., Moravek, M.: Changes of the voice expression during suggestively influenced states of experiencing. Activitas Nervosa Superior 21, 33–35 (1979)

22. McGilloway, S., Cowie, R., Douglas-Cowie, E.: Prosodic signs of emotion in speech: preliminary results from a new technique for automatic statistical analysis. In: Proceedings of Int. Congr. Phonetic Sciences, Stockholm, Sweden, vol. 1, pp. 250–253 (1995)

23. Schuller, B., Valstar, M., Eyben, F., McKeown, G., Cowie, R., PanticCen, M.: AVEC 2011 - the first international audio/visual emotion challenge. In: D'Mello, S., et al. (eds.) ACII 2011, Part II., vol. 6975, pp. 415–424. Springer, Heidelberg (2011)

24. Boyd, S., Vandenberghe, L.: Convex optimization. Cambridge University Press, Cambridge (2004)

25. Donoho, D.: Compressed sensing. IEEE Trans. Inf. Theory 52(4), 1289–1306 (2006)

26. Li, Y.Q., Cichocki, A., Amari, S., Ho, D.W.C., Xie, S.L.: Underdetermined blind source separation based on sparse representation. IEEE Trans. Signal Processing 54(2), 423–437 (2006)
27. Li, Y.Q., Amari, S., Cichocki, A., Guan, C.T.: Probability estimation for recoverability analysis of blind source separation based on sparse representation. IEEE Trans. Inf. Theory 52(7), 3139–3152 (2006)
28. McKeown, G., Valstar, M., Pantic, M., Cowie, R.: The semaine corpus of emotionally coloured character interactions. In: Proc. Int. Conf. Multimedia and Expo., Stockholm, Sweden, pp. 1–6 (2010)

A Psychologically-Inspired Match-Score Fusion Model for Video-Based Facial Expression Recognition

Albert Cruz, Bir Bhanu, and Songfan Yang

Center for Research in Intelligent Systems
University of California, Riverside, California 92521-0425, USA
{acruz,syang}@ee.ucr.edu, bhanu@cris.ucr.edu

Abstract. Communication between humans is complex and is not limited to verbal signals; emotions are conveyed with gesture, pose and facial expression. Facial Emotion Recognition and Analysis (FERA), the techniques by which non-verbal communication is quantified, is an exemplar case where humans consistently outperform computer methods. While the field of FERA has seen many advances, no system has been proposed which scales well to very large data sets. The challenge for computer vision is how to automatically and non-heuristically *downsample* the data while maintaining the maximum representational power that does not sacrifice accuracy. In this paper, we propose a method inspired by human vision and attention theory [2]. Video is segmented into temporal partitions with a dynamic sampling rate based on the frequency of visual information. Regions are homogenized by a match-score fusion technique. The approach is shown to provide classification rates higher than the baseline on the AVEC 2011 video-subchallenge dataset [15].

Keywords: vision and attention theory; avatar image registration; local phase quantization.

1 Introduction

The field of video-based emotion recognition has been an active area of work [13, 14] and has progressed with the help of standardized data sets such as JAFFE [10], among the earliest, and state-of-the-art data sets such as Cohn-Kanade+ [9] and the MMI Database [19]. However, despite the existence of these standards, many papers select subsets of data or do not detail how training and testing sets are generated [18]. The challenge data sets such as FERA Challenge 2011 [18] and the Audio/Visual Emotion Challenge (AVEC 2011) [15] provide benchmarks to compare different emotion recognition systems on a common ground.

Facial Expression Recognition and Analysis (FERA) approaches typically extract frontal face images and compute either appearance features (such as Gabor wavelets [22] and the family of local binary patterns (LBP) type features [7]) or geometry related features (such as AAM based features [9]). Facial expression is commonly detected in terms of Facial Action Units, a minimal set of facial muscle actions, or the "big six" emotion labels. Fontaine *et al.* [3] assert that basic emotions can be described along the four dimensions: activation, expectancy, power and valence. AVEC 2011 [15] uniquely requires detection of emotion along these four axes.

S. D´Mello et al. (Eds.): ACII 2011, Part II, LNCS 6975, pp. 341–350, 2011.
© Springer-Verlag Berlin Heidelberg 2011

Current approaches routinely assume that video sequences are pre-cut such that a subject expresses a single emotion over the sequence. They take advantage of labeling the time point where emotion is the most intense, known as the apex. While knowledge of apex location positively affects performance, the labeling of a video sequence requires an expert. In uncut interview footage such as in Solid-SAL [11]—the data used in AVEC 2011—subjects express multiple apex maxima in a single video. In this paper an automatic approach for uncut and unlabeled video that does not require apex labeling is proposed.

1.1 Vision and Attention Theory Inspiration

Humans can suddenly change emotion state. This requires high frame-rates for the precise detection of changes. However, a constantly high frame-rate may not be necessary for the whole video. A subject is not likely to change emotion state while idle. High frame rates unnecessarily increase sample size. Intuitively, a recognition system should devote fewer resources when the subject in video is idle and more resources when there is action in the video, e.g., a high frame rate is required to properly describe an animated or speaking subject to represent changes in visual information whereas only a few frames are needed to describe a subject when idle with little change in visual information. In the human visual system, steady state visual information is processed at a rate of < 1 Hz [2]. This rate increases proportionally with the frequency of visual stimulus [5]. In this paper, we use this concept as inspiration for partitioning videos into temporal segments of varying sampling rates which changes proportionally with the frequency of visual information. Visual stimulus is quantified using a Discrete-Time Fourier-Transform (DTFT) of motion features and the dominant frequency controls the sampling rate locally for each time-segment.

Contribution. A psychologically-inspired perceptual model for segmenting video into time partitions with a dynamic, minimal frame rate needed to meaningfully represent each local volume is proposed. We propose homogenizing dynamic time partitions with a combination-based match-score level fusion technique which is experimentally selected based on the performance on the development set [15]. This approach is robust in that it does not require apex labeling and does not make any assumptions that would not scale to real world data. This approach directly addresses the sample dimensionality problem in AVEC 2011 while reducing a loss in the precision of emotion state changes.

2 Technical Approach

We propose the following recognition pipeline given in Fig. 1: (A) Frontal face region of interest are detected with a Viola-Jones framework [20]. (B) Faces are registered using Avatar Image Registration (AIR) [21] (C) Local Phase Quantization features (LPQ) [12] features are extracted and (D) each frame is classified using a linear Support Vector Machine (SVM). (E) Video data is segmented into time partitions of varying sampling rate from 1 Hz to the maximum video frame rate, controlled by the dominant frequency of the DTFT of motion features. (F) Test results are fused at the combination match-score level [6] using multiple matchers locally for each partition.

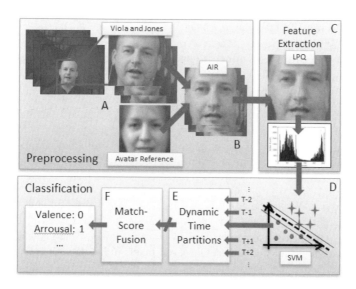

Fig. 1. System overview

2.1   Face Detection and Registration

Viola and Jones Face Detection. A Viola-Jones detector [20] is trained to detect frontal faces in order to extract regions of interest. In the Solid-SAL data set [11], pose may be extreme such that a frontal face is obscured, or a face may not be in a frame completely. For training, frames where the detector does not detect a frontal face are treated as bad samples and are withheld from model training. For testing, when the detector fails, it is not possible to properly classify the result using a model trained on frontal face features, as the image is not a frontal face and the result would be incorrect. In testing cases where features are not available, we assign the label with the highest *a priori* probability from training, for that emotion.

Avatar Image Registration. Images are aligned with Avatar Image Registration [21] which aligns face images at the scene-level with SIFT Flow [8]. Each frame is spatially warped to a single reference frame, called the Avatar Reference; enforcing global alignment. This powerful but simple approach will hallucinate a frontal, non-posed face image by aligning facial structures across individuals and emotions while maintaining internal-structure information.

SIFT Flow. SIFT Flow addresses the problem of image registration by aligning a query image to a target image at the scene level by spatially warping the query image to match the target image. The alignment task is formulated as an optical flow problem using dense SIFT descriptors. The objective function for SIFT Flow is formulated as:

$$E(w) = \sum_p \min(\|s_A(p) - s_i(p+w)\|_1) + \sum_p u^2(p) + v^2(p)/\sigma^2$$
$$+ \sum_{(p,q)\in N_q} (\min(\alpha|u(p) - u(q)|) + \min(\alpha|v(p) - v(q)|)) \tag{1}$$

where $p = (x, y)$ is a pixel in the image, $w(p)$ is the motion vector at pixel p between the query and target images where $w(p) = (u(p), v(p))$, s_A and s_i are the dense SIFT descriptors of the target image and the query image i respectively, ε is the 4-member neighborhood about p and α is the weighting parameter constraining displacement. One of the expressed purposes of this algorithm is to counteract object motion between two scenes. This makes SIFT Flow well suited to correcting facial plane motion.

Avatar Reference. While the SIFT Flow algorithm is powerful enough to align two images, a target image must be automatically generated for each frame to be registered to. There exists some veridical frontal face image $\hat{A}$, the Avatar Reference, that consists of deterministic values. Observed pixels in the data set are samples from the Avatar Reference that are corrupted by a zero-mean noise as a result of extraction errors, facial motion, skin tone, etc. Let f_i be an image. A pixel is observed as:

$$f_i(p) = \hat{A}(p) + \eta \tag{2}$$

where η is zero-mean noise. The minimum variance unbiased solution to Eq. (2) is:

$$\tilde{A}(p) = \frac{1}{N} \sum_i f_i(p) \tag{3}$$

where f_i is the ith image in data and N is the total number of frames in the data.

2.2 Feature Extraction

LPQ was originally introduced by Ojansivu and Heikkila [12] as a blur-invariant texture descriptor. In this paper, LPQ is preferred over LBP because the averaging from Eq. (3) causes some loss of high-frequency information. This is supported by performance in previous work [21]. Images are reduced to 8×8 regions and LPQ features are generated for each region.

Local Phase Quantization. In step one of LPQ, the 2-D DFT is computed locally. Let f be a sample image, and u be the image frequency coefficient. LPQ computes the local Fourier transform as:

$$F(u, x) = \sum_{y \in N_x} f(x - y)e^{-j2\pi u^t y} \tag{4}$$

where N_x is the neighborhood about x. F can be rewritten in terms of matrixes: $F = w_u^t f(x)$, where w_u is the basis vector for a given frequency u. LPQ computes the four complex frequencies: $u = \{[\gamma, 0]^t, [0, \gamma]^t, [\gamma, \gamma]^t, [\gamma, -\gamma]^t\}$. In step two, F is decorrelated with a whitening transform. Let G be the SVD of F, and $\langle G \rangle_x$ be the x-th component of G corresponding to the decorrelated 2-D DFT of neighborhood N_x from Eq. (4). In step three, the values are quantized. $\langle G \rangle_x$ is quantized with:

$$\langle G \rangle_x = \begin{cases} 1 & \text{if } \langle G \rangle_x \geq 0 \\ 0 & \text{otherwise} \end{cases} \tag{5}$$

$\langle G \rangle_x$ is encoded to an 8-bit scalar—each bit corresponding to one of the neighbors of x— with the following equation:

$$b(x) = \sum_{i=1}^{8} \langle G \rangle_x 2^{i-1} \tag{6}$$

Finally, a 256-bin histogram of $b(x)$ is generated and this is taken to be the feature vector for the image region.

2.3 Psychologically-Inspired Dynamic Temporal Volumes

Three conclusions can be drawn from inspection of the data sets: (A) The frame rate is too high to use all frames for training and testing. Video data in SolidSAL has a frame rate of ~50 FPS resulting in roughly 500,000 frames for the development set. Loading a feature vector of double precision numbers with that many samples and the feature cardinality from Sec. 2.2 requires more than 65GB of memory. (B) SolidSAL videos are interview footage, and there are times where the subject in frame is idle. It is not necessary to have such a high frame rate for these times. (C) States of emotion form homogenous regions. While a subject may change emotion suddenly, changes of emotion state are consistently low frequency, not erratic. From these observations, we propose using vision and attention theory to generate partitions with sampling rate defined dynamically per volume, and fusing the information in each partition with match-score fusion to resist high frequency changes of emotion state.

Algorithm 1. Dynamic assignment of β using dominant frequency of $V(\omega)$

```
procedure computebeta ({F¹ₚ, F²ₚ, ..., Fⁿₚ}, ℓ)
Input:    Sequence {F¹ₚ, F²ₚ, ..., Fⁿₚ} where p is a pixel and n is the
          number of frames; spacing parameter ℓ selected s.t. i
          iterates 1/s over video sequence.
Output:   Sampling rate vector β of length n/ℓ.
   Gₚ₁ = 0
   for i = 2...n :
      Gₚᵢ = optical_flow(Fᵢ⁻¹ₚ, Fᵢₚ)
   c = 1
   for j = 1:ℓ:n :
      for k = max({1, (j- ℓ/2)})...min({(j+ ℓ/2), n}) :
         v(k) = L¹{‖Gₚₖ‖}
      V = F{v - μᵥ}
      β(c) = ⌈argmax(V(ω))/2⌉
      c = c + 1
   return β
```

Intelligent Sampling with Vision and Attention Theory. An immediate solution to the size complexity problem is to sample the data at a constant rate. However, sampling the data too sparsely results in a weak model; too densely, the model is too expensive. It may not be necessary to sample the data at such a high frame rate during the time points when a subject is not active. However, subjects can suddenly change their emotional state. This merits a minimum sampling rate in order to precisely detect change in emotional state. A method is needed for automatically partitioning the data into meaningful segments that capture sudden changes, while weighing idle sequences less. We propose an approach which is perceptual psychology-inspired, where the local sampling rate changes in proportion to the frequency of visual information, see Sec. 1.1.

In this paper, we segment the data into temporal regions of 1 Hz. This is inspired by the minimum bound of the HVS [2]. Let τ define the domain of data with which classification is performed for a given temporal volume:

$$\tau = \{t : (t - \beta) < t < (t + \beta)\} \tag{7}$$

where β is the range with of data about t, controlling the sampling rate. When a person is active, the windows size β should be small; a person is idle, β should be large. A problem is posed where β must be selected dynamically. This must be done automatically per frame, without any knowledge of emotion labels. Visual information must be quantified in a way where frequency increases proportionally with activity in the image. SIFT Flow computes motion spatially, not temporally, and is unsuitable for this task. In this paper, we compute motion features as the magnitude of phase based optical flow [4]. Let $v(t)$ be the visual feature content signal computed as:

$$v(t) = \sum_{p} \|g(f_t(\boldsymbol{p}), f_{t-1}(\boldsymbol{p}))\| \tag{8}$$

where $\|g(f_1, f_2)\|$ is the magnitude of optical flow between frames f_1 and f_2. An assumption is made that the frequency of $v(t)$ increases when the subject is active. For these sequences, $v(t)$ is a signal of fluctuating frequency, see Fig. 2. However, when the subject is idle, the signal is a constant level. The dominant frequency of V defines the sampling rate β with the following equation:

$$\beta = \left\lceil \frac{1}{2} \mathrm{argmax}_\omega \left(V(\omega)\right)\right\rceil \tag{9}$$

where $V = \mathcal{F}\{v\}$ is computed with the FFT. Psuedo-code for computing $\boldsymbol{\beta}$ is provided in Algorithm 1. $\boldsymbol{\beta}$ is computed once for each temporal partition. For testing, frames which are not sampled are assigned the label given to the partition from the sampled frames.

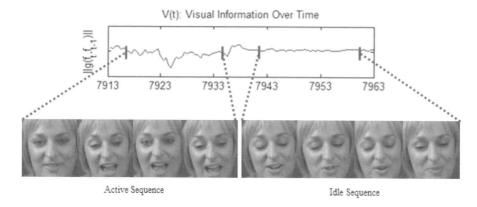

Fig. 2. $\|g(f_t(p), f_{t-1}(p))\|$ for development video 26 about frame 7938

Local Partition Match-Score Fusion. Observation (3) motivates combining match scores locally in each partition to enforce homologous label assignment. In this paper, we propose multiple snapshots, taken from the sampled frames of a local partition, to provide a more robust classification scheme. Fusion is performed at the combination based match-score level [16]. In combination based match-score fusion, the scores, or posterior probabilities from different match-scores are weighted and combined to give a final, scalar match-score. Let $\boldsymbol{X}_\tau$ be the sample feature vector of a local time partition τ; let $\tilde{w}$ be the assigned label from one of the classes $\{w_1, ..., w_m\}$; let $p_\tau(w_j|\langle \boldsymbol{X}_\tau \rangle_i)$ be the output of matcher given data at time i. The classification rule in a match-score combination approach is:

$$\tilde{w} = \text{argmax}_j \, K\left(P_1(w_j|\langle \boldsymbol{X}_\tau \rangle_{t-\beta}), ..., P_n(w_j|\langle \boldsymbol{X}_\tau \rangle_{t+\beta})\right) \qquad (10)$$

$K(.)$ is an aggregator that can implemented with the following rules:

Sum and Product Rules. The aggregators for the sum and product rules are as follows:

$$K\left(P_1(w_j|\langle \boldsymbol{X}_\tau \rangle_{t-\beta}), ..., P_n(w_j|\langle \boldsymbol{X}_\tau \rangle_{t+\beta})\right) = \frac{1}{Z} \sum_i P(w_j|\langle \boldsymbol{X}_\tau \rangle_i) \qquad (11)$$

$$K\left(P_1(w_j|\langle \boldsymbol{X}_\tau \rangle_{t-\beta}), ..., P_n(w_j|\langle \boldsymbol{X}_\tau \rangle_{t+\beta})\right) = \prod_i P(w_j|\langle \boldsymbol{X}_\tau \rangle_i) \qquad (12)$$

where (11) and (12) are the weighted sum and product rules, respectively. Z is a normalization s.t. Eq. (11) $\in [0,1]$.

Extrema Rules. In extrema rules, the class label w is assigned using a min or a max operator:

$$K\left(P_1\left(w_j|\langle \boldsymbol{X}_\tau\rangle_{t-\beta}\right), \dots, P_n\left(w_j|\langle \boldsymbol{X}_\tau\rangle_{t+\beta}\right)\right) = \min_i\left(P_1\left(w_j|\langle \boldsymbol{X}_\tau\rangle_i\right)\right) \qquad (13)$$

$$K\left(P_1\left(w_j|\langle \boldsymbol{X}_\tau\rangle_{t-\beta}\right), \dots, P_n\left(w_j|\langle \boldsymbol{X}_\tau\rangle_{t+\beta}\right)\right) = \max_i\left(P_1\left(w_j|\langle \boldsymbol{X}_\tau\rangle_i\right)\right) \qquad (14)$$

3   Results

Matchers are Support Vector Machines with a linear kernel from the LibSVM toolbox [1]. Feature is vector normalized to $[-1,1]$. For a detailed explanation of the data, and the development, training and testing sets, please refer to the Schuller *et al.* [15]. In this paper, we consider only the video sub-challenge. Results on the development set are given in Table 1. Match-score fusion rule used for testing is determined experimentally using 4-fold random cross-validation with a 75/25 split on development data. Similarly to baseline, expectancy and power features are more difficult to detect versus activation and valence. The max rule gives a better average versus other rules and is used for testing.

Results on the video-subchallenge are given in Table 2. WA stands for weighted accuracy, and is the classification rate. UA stands for unweighted accuracy, and is the average recall over the two classes. Proposed approach differs greatly from the baseline in three ways. In the event of Viola and Jones failure the method defaults to *a priori* probabilities—some videos in training and testing folds had a majority of irretrievable faces, making it a more difficult problem than the development set. The sampling rate is assigned dynamically, and reduces the amount of samples when the subject is not active. This allows training of a model on a larger number of samples without entering the domain of being too computationally expensive. Whereas approaches similar to the baseline approach might treat each frame in a video independently, in our model a video is comprised of dynamically sized partitions where a label consensus is reached with fusion.

Table 1. Development Classification Rates on the Video-Subchallenge for Different Match-score Rules

Accuracy (%)	Activation	Expectancy	Power	Valence	Average
Min Rule	64.48±5.4	65.22±7.9	58.55±6.0	64.21±6.7	63.12
Max Rule	69.30±3.0	65.58±5.5	59.87±6.0	67.79±4.9	65.64
Product Rule	64.15±3.5	67.02±4.8	58.27±5.2	64.71±4.8	63.53
Sum Rule	66.10±2.6	63.70±4.7	59.65±5.1	64.38±5.5	63.45

Table 2. Video-Subchallenge Testing Classification Rates

Accuracy (%)	Activation		Expectancy		Power		Valence	
	WA	UA	WA	UA	WA	UA	WA	UA
Testing	**56.51**	56.87	**59.67**	55.11	**48.52**	49.36	**59.24**	56.72

4 Conclusion

The concept of partitioning emotion video into dynamically sampled segments is explored. A model is proposed for controlling sampling rate in each local partition which was inspired by perceptual psychology where a partition was sampled according to the frequency of visual content. Then, posterior probabilities are combined for each local partition using a combination-based match-score fusion technique. Match-score rule was selected from 4-fold cross validation on the Development set. Performance on testing data is improved via intelligently selecting frames without unnecessarily increasing sample size. In the future, a comparison could be made between this method and with human judgments of expression changes in complex videos.

Acknowledgment. This work was supported in part by NSF grants 0727129 and 0903667. The contents and information do not reflect the position or policy of the U.S. Government.

References

1. Chang, C., Lin, C.: LibSVM: A Library for Support Vector Machines, http://www.csie.ntu.edu.tw/~cjlin/libsvm
2. Findlay, J., Gilchrist, I.: Active Vision: The Psychology of Looking and Seeing. Oxford University Press, Oxford (2003)
3. Fontaine, J., Scherer, K., Roesch, B., Ellsworth, P.E.: The World of Emotions is Not Two-dimensional. Psychological Science 18(2), 1050–1057 (2007)
4. Gautama, T., Van Hulle, M.: A Phase-Based Approach to the Estimation of the Optical Flow Field Using Spatial Filtering. IEEE Trans. on. Neural Nets 13(5), 1127–1136 (2002)
5. Haber, R., Hershenson, M.: The Psychology of Visual Perception. Holt, Rinehart & Winston, Oxford (1973)
6. Jain, A.K., Nandakumar, K., Ross, A.: Score Normalization in Multimodal Biometric Systems. Pattern Recognition 38(12), 2270–2285 (2005)
7. Jiang, B., Valstar, M., Pantic, M.: Action Unit Detection Using Sparse Appearance Descriptors in Space-time Video Volumes. In: IEEE Intl. Conf. on Automatic Face and Gesture Recognition (2011)
8. Liu, C., Yuen, J., Torralba, A.: SIFT Flow: Dense Correspondence across Scenes and Its Applications. IEEE Trans. on Pattern Analysis and Machine Intelligence 33(5), 978–994 (2011)
9. Lucey, P., Cohn, J.F., Kanade, T., Saragih, J., Ambadar, Z., Matthews, I.: The Extended Cohn-Kande Dataset (CK+): A complete facial expression dataset for action unit and emotion-specified expression. In: Human Communicative Behavior Analysis, Workshop of CVPR (2010)
10. Lyons, M., Akamatsu, S., Kamachi, M., Gyoba, J.: Coding Facial Expressions with Gabor Wavelets. In: Proc. IEEE Intl. Conf. on Automatic Face and Gesture Recognition (1998)
11. Mckeown, G., Valstar, M.F., Cowie, R., Pantic, M.: The Semaine Corpus of Emotionally Coloured Character Interactions. In: IEEE Intl. Conf. on Multimedia and Expo. (2010)
12. Ojansivu, V., Heikkila, J.: Blur Insensitive Texture Classification Using Local Phase Quantization. In: IEEE Intl. Conf. on Image and Signal Processing (2008)

13. Pantic, M., Rothkrantz, L.: Automatic analysis of facial expressions: the state of the art. IEEE Trans. on Pattern Analysis and Machine Intelligence 22(12), 1424–1445 (2000)
14. Samal, A., Iyengar, P.A.: Automatic recognition and analysis of human faces and facial expressions: a survey. Pattern Recognition 22(1) (1992)
15. Schuller, B., Valstar, M., Eyben, F., McKeown, G., Cowie, R., Pantic, M.: AVEC 2011 – The First Int'l. Audio/Visual Emotion Challenge. In: D´Mello, S., et al. (eds.) ACII 2011, Part II. LNCS, vol. 6975, pp. 415–424. Springer, Heidelberg (2011)
16. Snelick, R., Uludag, U., Mink, A., Indovina, M., Jain, A.K.: Large Scale Evaluation of Multimodal Biometric Authentication Using State-of-the-Art Systems. IEEE Trans. on Pattern Analysis and Machine Intelligence 27(3), 450–455 (2005)
17. Szeliski, R., Zabih, R., Scharstein, D., Veksler, O., Kolmogorov, V., Agarwala, A., et al.: A comparative study of energy minimization methods for Markov random fields with smoothness-based priors. IEEE Trans. on Pattern Analysis and Machine Intelligence 30(6), 1068–1080 (2008)
18. Valstar, M.F., Jiang, B., Mehu, M., Pantic, M., Scherer, K.: The First Facial Expression Recognition and Analysis Challenge. In: Proc. of IEEE Intl. Conf. on Face and Gesture Recognition (2011)
19. Valstar, M., Pantic, M.: Induced disgust, happiness and surprise: an addition to the MMI facial expression database. In: Proc. 3rd Intern. Workshop on EMOTION (satellite of LREC): Corpora for Research on Emotion and Affect (2010)
20. Viola, P., Jones, M.: Robust Real-Time Face Detection. Intl. J. on Computer Vision (2002)
21. Yang, S., Bhanu, B.: Facial expression recognition using emotion avatar image. The First Facial Expression Recognition and Analysis Challenge. In: IEEE Intl. Conf. on Face and Gesture Recognition (2011)
22. Yu, J., Bhanu, B.: Evolutionary feature synthesis for facial expression recognition. Pattern Recognition Letters 27 (2006)

Continuous Emotion Recognition Using Gabor Energy Filters

Mohamed Dahmane and Jean Meunier

DIRO, University of Montreal, CP 6128, Succursale Centre-Ville,
2920 Chemin de la tour, Montreal, Canada, H3C 3J7
{dahmanem,meunier}@iro.umontreal.ca

Abstract. Automatic facial expression analysis systems try to build a
mapping between the continuous emotion space and a set of discrete expression categories (e.g. happiness, sadness). In this paper, we present a
method to recognize emotions in terms of latent dimensions (e.g. arousal,
valence, power). The method we applied uses Gabor energy texture descriptors to model the facial appearance deformations, and a multiclass
SVM as base learner of emotions. To deal with more naturalistic behavior, the SEMAINE database of naturalistic dialogues was used.

1 Introduction

Within the affective computing research field, researchers are still facing a big
challenge to establish automated systems to recognize human emotions from
video sequences, since human affective behavior is subtle and multimodal. Recently, efforts have been oriented on how to modelize affective emotions in
terms of continuous dimensions (e.g. activation, expectation power, and valence),
rather than resolving the most known classification problems (e.g. happiness,
sadness, surprise, disgust, fear, anger, and neutral). Prior works on human facial
emotion recognition have focused on both images and video sequences. Different approaches were investigated including feature-based and appearance-based
techniques [3,10]. Most of these techniques use databases that were collected
under non realistic conditions [16]. An advance emotion recognition system
needs to deal with more natural behaviors in large volumes of un-segmented,
un-prototypical, and natural data [12]. The challenge data were collected from
the SEMAINE database [9] which consists of natural dialogue video sequences
that are more challenging and more realistic.

1.1 Overview of the Database

The dataset is based on the first part of the SEMAINE database called the
solid-SAL part. This part consists of 24 recordings, which were splitted into
three partitions: training (31 sessions: 501277 frames), development (32 sessions:
449074 frames), and test partition (32 sessions: 407772 frames). Each partition
consists of 8 recordings. Videos were recorded at 50 f/s and at a resolution of
780×580 pixels.

S. D′Mello et al. (Eds.): ACII 2011, Part II, LNCS 6975, pp. 351–358, 2011.

2   Overview of the Baseline Method

The challenge organizers method for the video feature sub-challenge is based on dense appearance descriptors. They used Uniform Local Binary Pattern (Uniform LBP). For each frame a preprocessing stage permits to extract the face region using the OpenCV face detector. Then a registration stage is performed by finding the two eye positions which were used, first, to remove any in-plane rotation of the face, and second the distance between these two locations was used to normalize for scale. The face was translated so that the subject's right eye centre is always at the coordinates $x = 80$, $y = 60$. The registered image was cropped to 200×200 pixels face region.

2.1   Challenge Baselines

For the emotion analysis problem, four classification sub-problems need to be solved: the originally continuous dimensions: *arousal, expectancy, power*, and *valence*, which were redefined as binary classification tasks by checking at every frame whether they were above or below average.

The cropped face area was divided into 100 squares with side of 20 pixels. Uniform LBP was applied and histograms of all 100 blocks were concatenated into a relatively high (5900) dimensional feature vector. Besides, as the video sequences were very large, the authors chose to sample periodically the data by selecting 1000 frames from the training partition and 1000 frames from the development partition. The extracted frame descriptors were used to train a Support Vector Machine (SVM) using Radial Basis Function (RBF) kernels.

No further details were given about possible preprocessing failure, for instance, if the face detector failed or if the eye detection was off.

The classification rate for every dimension is given in Table 1. It shows the accuracy for training on the training partition and testing on the development partition, as well as for training on the unification of the training and the development partitions and testing on the test partition sub-set.

Table 1. Baseline Results (WA stands for weighted accuracy, and UA for unweighted)

Accuracy	ACTIVATION		EXPECTATION		POWER		VALENCE	
	WA	UA	WA	UA	WA	UA	WA	UA
Devel	60.2	57.9	58.3	56.7	56.0	52.8	63.6	60.9
Test	42.2	52.5	53.6	49.3	36.4	37.0	52.5	51.2

3   Technical Approach

Our method uses dense facial appearance descriptors. We applied Gabor energy to extract the facial appearance features by calculating the responses to a set of filters. A multiclass Support Vector Machine with polynomial kernels was used as base learner of the affective dimensions.

3.1   Gabor Filtering

In the literature, one can find several attempts at designing feature–based methods using Gabor wavelets [13,6,14,7,15,16,2,8], due to their interesting and desirable properties including spatial locality, self similar hierarchical representation, optimal joint uncertainty in space and frequency as well as biological plausibility [4].

Gabor filtering permits to describe via image convolution, with Gabor wavelet (Eq. 1), the spatial frequency structure around the pixel $\mathbf{x}$.

$$\Psi_{\lambda,\theta,\varphi,\sigma,\gamma}\left(\mathbf{x}\right) \;=\; \exp\left(-\frac{x'^2 + \gamma^2\,y'^2}{2\sigma^2}\right)\cos\left(2\pi\,\frac{x'}{\lambda} + \varphi\right) \tag{1}$$

with

$$x' = x\,\cos\theta + y\,\sin\theta$$
$$y' = -x\,\sin\theta + y\,\cos\theta$$

and where $\lambda, \theta, \varphi, \sigma$, and γ stand, respectively, for wavelength, orientation, phase offset, aspect ratio, and the bandwidth.

3.2   Gabor Energy Filter

Relative to the simple linear Gabor filtering, the energy filter gives a smoother response to an edge or a line of appropriate width with a local maximum exactly at the edge or in the center of the line [11,5] (see figure 1).

The energy filter response is obtained by combining the convolutions obtained from two different phase offsets ($\varphi_0 = 0$) and ($\varphi_1 = \pi/2$) using the L_2-norm. Figure 1 shows the outputs of the Gabor energy filter vs. the standard Gabor filter applied on facial images with certain emotions, using 5 different orientations ($\theta \in [0:\pi/4:\pi]$) with $\lambda = 8$, $\varphi \in \{0, \pi/2\}$, $\gamma = 0.5$, and $b = 1$.

3.3   Data Processing

First, we used the OpenCV face detection to extract the face region in each frame, which is scaled to 200 by 200 pixels. We did not use eye positions to normalize for scale, as the OpenCV eye detector is too inaccurate to do this, particularly for oriented head or closed eyes. The Gabor energy filter output of the cropped face region was divided into 10×10 cells then, 25 blocks were defined by gathering 2×2 neighboring cells . For each cell, a local histogram was

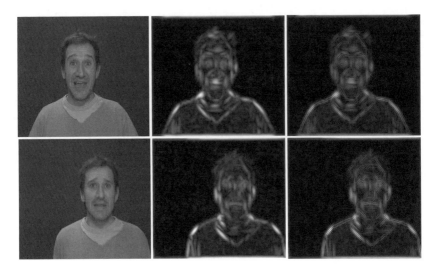

Fig. 1. Left column: facial images with a given emotion. **Middle** : Energy filter output. **Right**: Standard Gabor filter output.

processed in which each bin represented a frequency at a selected orientation. The parameters were set as follows $\lambda \in \{5, 10, 15\}$ and $\theta \in [0 : \pi/8 : 7\pi/8]$. So each histogram had 24 bins (3 frequencies×8 orientations). After that, for each block, the 4 local histograms were concatenated to generate a block-histogram that was locally normalized using the L_2-*norm*. Thus the local values were not affected by the extreme values in other blocks.

The 25 block-histograms were then concatenated into a region-histogram giving a single 2400 dimensional feature vector which remained relatively small compared to the baseline feature vector.

3.4   The Experimental Protocols

⋄ The protocol to decide which affective dimension label should be assigned to every frame consisted of a majority voting. In case of a tie, the class that occurred first in the alphabetical order was chosen. This does not introduce a bias in the results; since in this case by default, SVM assigns labels considering the class label order.

⋄ Because of the large amount of data (over 1.3 million frames) and relatively high feature dimensionality (2400 features per frame) we decided to sample frames from the videos sequences at interval of 10 frames. However, if a new class label appeared in the video, we decreased the sampling rate to 4 frames, after a while the rate was again increased to 10 frames. Thus, we reduced the risk of missing transitions in the affective continuous dimensions over the stream.

◇ If during preprocessing, the face detector failed, we decided in the case of training to simply discard the frame. Whereas, for the testing stage, the code label of the preceding frame was used to label the current frame.

◇ For practical considerations, we used a 4-bit binary code for class labeling. A '1' in the leftmost bit position indicated that the affective element "*valence*" was above average.

The SVM kernel that we used in this work, is given by equation (2). The penalty parameter for outliers was fixed to $C = 10$.

$$K(x, x_i^*) = (8. \ (x \cdot x_i^*) + 1.)^{10.} \tag{2}$$

The classification accuracies of the video sub-challenge over the different affective dimensions are shown in Table 2. The τ values indicate the different thresholds we used to translate the SVM hyperplane.

Two tests were performed, on two different partitions: development and test subsets. For the test set, the scores were computed by the organizers from the results that we emailed to them.

Table 2. The Results of our proposed method (WA stands for weighted accuracy, and UA for unweighted)

Accuracy(%)		ACTIVATION		EXPECTATION		POWER		VALENCE	
		WA	UA	WA	UA	WA	UA	WA	UA
Devel ($\tau = 0.0$)		54.9	55.0	51.8	51.2	53.2	52.8	56.6	55.5
Test	$\tau = 0.0$	63.4	63.7	35.9	36.6	41.4	41.1	53.4	53.6
	$\tau = -.2$	58.0	58.4	41.0	41.0	50.5	49.7	48.6	50.5
	$\tau = -.3$	55.1	55.7	46.7	43.0	50.4	49.5	48.6	51.0
	$\tau = -.4$	53.2	53.9	54.8	46.6	50.7	49.7	47.7	50.4

Table (2), shows that, on the development partition, all the different affective dimensions were recognized at approximately the same rates (Fig. 2). All obtained rates are better than chance but somewhat lower than the ones obtained by the baseline method probably due the RBF kernel that this method used.

Figure (3) shows that our method performs better than the baseline method for the *arousal, expectation,* and *power* classes. The three dimension accuracies are above 50%. *Power* was the most difficult affective class to recognize for the baseline method with only 36%. The lowest score we obtained was for *valence* with 48%.

The overall classification performance of the proposed approach reached 51.6% with almost equally distributed classification errors with a mean absolute deviation of 1 %. That is better than the 46.2% achieved by the baseline method with a higher MAD of 7 % (Fig. 4).

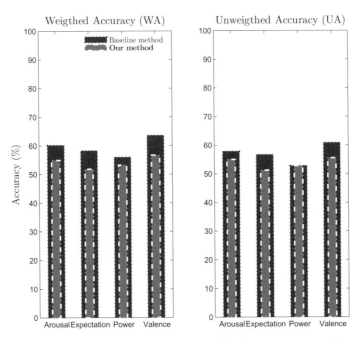

Fig. 2. Comparison of results: Test on the development partition

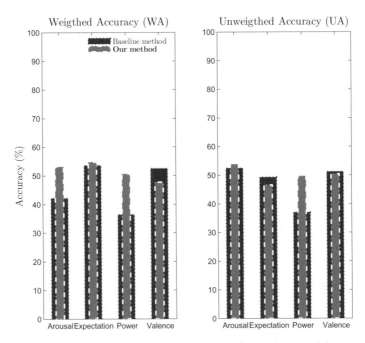

Fig. 3. Comparison of results: Test on the testing partition

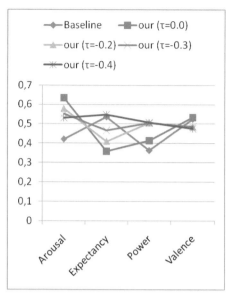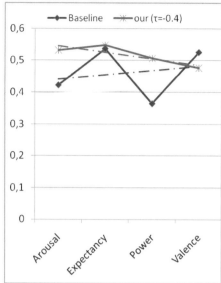

Fig. 4. Comparison of results: Test on the test partition at different SVM hyperplane

4   Conclusions

In this paper, we presented a method to recognize different emotions explained in terms of latent dimensions. We considered Gabor energy filters for image representation. For each face region, we used a uniform grid to integrate the filter response in one histogram by cell. The concatenated histogram represented the emotion descriptor. We used one multiclass polynomial-SVM to classify the extracted emotion descriptors.

The experiment evaluation on both development and test partitions, showed promising results on the challenging AVEC 2011 dataset. The overall classification performance of the affective dimensions classification reached 51.6% with the Gabor energy filters, and 46.1% with the LBP feature set.

In future, we intend to study the performance of radial-basis-function kernel SVM type, where the optimal parameters will be fixed by using what we called "epoch" based strategy [1]. Also, we will investigate the use of a threshold adjusting procedure that relaxes the SVM threshold from zero.

Acknowledgment. We gratefully acknowledge the support of the National Sciences and Engineering Research Council (NSERC) of Canada.

References

1. Dahmane, M., Meunier, J.: Emotion recognition using dynamic grid-based hog features. In: 2011 IEEE International Conference on Automatic Face Gesture Recognition and Workshops (FG 2011), pp. 884–888 (March 2011)

2. Donato, G., Bartlett, M.S., Hager, J.C., Ekman, P., Sejnowski, T.J.: Classifying facial actions. IEEE Transactions on Pattern Analysis and Machine Intelligence 21(10), 974–989 (1999)
3. Fasel, B., Luettin, J.: Automatic facial expression analysis: a survey. Pattern Recognition 36(1), 259–275 (2003)
4. Flaton, K., Toborg, S.: An approach to image recognition using sparse filter graphs. In: International Joint Conference on Neural Networks, vol. (1), pp. 313–320 (1989)
5. Grigorescu, C., Petkov, N., Westenberg, M.A.: Contour detection based on non-classical receptive field inhibition. IEEE Transactions on Image Processing 12(7), 729–739 (2003)
6. Lades, M., Vorbrüggen, J.C., Buhmann, J., Lange, J., von der Malsburg, C., Würtz, R.P., Konen, W.: Distortion invariant object recognition in the dynamic link architecture. IEEE Transactions on Computers 3(42), 300–311 (1993)
7. Liu, C., Wechsler, H.: Independent component analysis of gabor features for face recognition. IEEE Trans. on Neural Networks 4(14), 919–928 (2003)
8. Lyons, M., Akamatsu, S., Kamachi, M., Gyoba, J.: Coding facial expressions with gabor wavelets. In: Proceedings of the 3rd International Conference on Face & Gesture Recognition, FG 1998, p. 200. IEEE Computer Society, Washington, DC, USA (1998)
9. McKeown, G., Valstar, M., Pantic, M., Cowie, R.: The semaine corpus of emotionnally coloured character interactions. In: Proc. Int'l Conf. Mutlimedia & Expo., pp. 1–6 (2010)
10. Pantic, M., Rothkrantz, L.: Automatic Analysis of Facial Expressions: The State of the Art. IEEE Transactions on Pattern Analysis and Machine Intelligence 22(12), 1424–1445 (2000)
11. Petkov, N., Westenberg, M.A.: Suppression of contour perception by band-limited noise and its relation to non-classical receptive field inhibition. Biological Cybernetics 88(10), 236–246 (2003)
12. Schuller, B., Valstar, M., Eyben, F., McKeown, G., Cowie, R., Pantic, M.: Avec 2011 - the First International Audio/Visual Emotion Challenge. In: D'Mello, S., et al. (eds.) ACII 2011, Part II. LNCS, vol. 6975, pp. 415–424. Springer, Heidelberg (2011)
13. Shen, L., Bai, L.: A review on gabor wavelets for face recognition. Pattern Analysis and Applications 2(9), 273–292 (2006)
14. Tian, Y., Kanade, T., Cohn, J.: Evaluation of gabor wavelet–based facial action unit recognition in image sequences of increasing complexity. In: Proc. of the 5th IEEE Int. Conf. on Automatic Face and Gesture Recognition (2002)
15. Valstar, M., Pantic, M.: Fully automatic facial action unit detection and temporal analysis. In: CVPRW, p. 149 (2006)
16. Whitehill, J., Littlewort, G., Fasel, I., Bartlett, M., Movellan, J.: Toward Practical Smile Detection. IEEE Transactions on Pattern Analysis and Machine Intelligence 31(11), 2106–2111 (2009)

Multiple Classifier Systems for the Classification of Audio-Visual Emotional States

Michael Glodek, Stephan Tschechne, Georg Layher, Martin Schels,
Tobias Brosch, Stefan Scherer, Markus Kächele, Miriam Schmidt,
Heiko Neumann, Günther Palm, and Friedhelm Schwenker

Ulm University, Institute of Neural Information Processing, 89081 Ulm, Germany

Abstract. Research activities in the field of human-computer interaction increasingly addressed the aspect of integrating some type of
emotional intelligence. Human emotions are expressed through different modalities such as speech, facial expressions, hand or body gestures,
and therefore the classification of human emotions should be considered
as a multimodal pattern recognition problem. The aim of our paper is to
investigate multiple classifier systems utilizing audio and visual features
to classify human emotional states. For that a variety of features have
been derived. From the audio signal the fundamental frequency, LPC-
and MFCC coefficients, and RASTA-PLP have been used. In addition to
that two types of visual features have been computed, namely form and
motion features of intermediate complexity. The numerical evaluation
has been performed on the four emotional labels *Arousal, Expectancy,
Power, Valence* as defined in the AVEC data set. As classifier architectures multiple classifier systems are applied, these have been proven to
be accurate and robust against missing and noisy data.

1   Introduction

Research in affective computing aim to provide simpler and more natural interfaces for human-computer interaction applications. In this kind of applications detecting and recognizing the emotional status of an user is important
in order to develop efficient and productive human-computer interaction interfaces [3]. Analysis of human emotions and processing recorded data, for instance
the speech, facial expressions, hand gestures, body movements, etc. is a multi-
disciplinary field that has been emerging as a rich area of research in recent
times [5,11,20,24,21,27]. In this paper multiple classifier systems for the classification of audio-visual features have been investigated, the numerical evaluation
of the proposed emotion recognition systems has been carried out on the data
sets of the AVEC challenge [23]. Combining classifiers is a promising approach
to improve the overall classifier performance [25,19]. Such a team of classifiers
should be accurate and diverse [9]. While the requirement to the classifiers to be
as accurate as possible is obvious, diversity roughly means that classifiers should
not agree on the set of misclassified data. Various feature views on the audio and
visual data are utilized to achieve such a set of diverse and accurate classifiers.

S. D´Mello et al. (Eds.): ACII 2011, Part II, LNCS 6975, pp. 359–368, 2011.

2   Features

In the following section we briefly describe the features we extracted within the audio and visual channel, that served as input for the successive classification architecture.

2.1   Audio Features

For the audio analysis we extracted a variety of standard features:

Fundamental Frequency (f_0) and Energy. From each speech segments the f_0 values are extracted, using the f_0 tracker available in the ESPS/*waves+*[1] software package. This f_0 track as well as the energy of the plain wave signal is extracted from 32 ms frames with an offset of 16 ms. Both one dimensional signals are combined with the eight dimensional LPC signal to form a ten dimensional feature vector.

Linear Predictive Coding Coefficients (LPC). Linear predictive coding (LPC) is a popular method to represent the spectral envelope, which corresponds to a curve fitting tightly around the peaks of the short time log magnitude spectrum of a signal, in a highly compressed manner. As described in [14] the main reasons for the popularity of LPC are, that especially for steady state voiced regions of speech, such as vowels with constant vocal source pressure and tract, LPC provides a good approximation of the spectral envelope of the signal. However, the main flaws of LPC are in the representation of unvoiced regions of an utterance. Furthermore, the straightforward and computationally cheap method to extract the LPC coefficients outperforms most of the other methods to approximate the spectral envelope.

Mel Frequency Cepstral Coefficients (MFCC). The Mel frequency cepstral coefficient (MFCC) representation is motivated by biological factors, as the known perceptual variations in the human ear are modeled using a filter bank with filters linearly spaced in lower frequencies and logarithmically in higher frequencies in order to capture the phonetically important characteristics of speech [4]. The MFCC are extracted, following [28]:

1. The speech signal is divided into windowed frames of 25 ms in size with an offset of 10 ms. A Hamming window is applied to reduce discontinuities in the spectrum at the end of the frame.
2. For each frame calculate amplitude spectrum using short-term fast Fourier transform (FFT).
3. Apply a filter bank of triangular filters that are equally spaced in the Mel scale.
4. Take the log energy of every filter output.
5. Take discrete cosine transform (DCT) yielding de-correlated cepstral coefficients for each frame.

---

[1] http://www.speech.kth.se/software/

MFCC are quite commonly used features based on short-time spectrum in speech recognition tasks, since they are compact representations of the speech and its spectral envelope with the characteristic to retain most of the phonetically significant acoustic information [4]. As mentioned in [4] the key features of the MFCC include the following important points:

- Parameters such as MFCC derived from the short-term Fourier spectrum preserve acoustic information to a larger extent than those relying on LPC.
- MFCC allow an improved suppression of higher frequencies that are less relevant parts of the spectrum for speech applications.
- MFCC allow a very compact representation of the acoustic signal since only a few coefficients suffice for the most relevant data (mostly 8-24 coefficients).

Relative Spectral Perceptual Linear Predictive Coding (RASTA-PLP). The perceptual linear predictive (PLP) analysis is based on two perceptually and biologically motivated concepts, namely the critical bands, and the equal loudness curves [6,17]. Frequencies below 1 kHz need higher sound pressure levels than the reference, and sounds between 2 - 5 kHz need less pressure, following the human perception.

The critical band filtering is analogous to the MFCC triangular filtering, apart from the fact, that the filters are equally spaced in the Bark scale (not the Mel scale) and the shape of the filters is not triangular, but rather trapezoidal.

After the critical band analysis and equal loudness conversion, the subsequent steps required for the relative spectral (RASTA) processing extension, follow the implementation recommendations in [8]. After transforming the spectrum to the logarithmic domain and the application of RASTA filtering, the signal is transformed back using the exponential function.

The last steps are according to the estimation of the LPC coefficients. The LPC coefficients are calculated over the critical band energies of a single frame, which is followed by the transformation of the LPC coefficients to cepstral values. In [7], PLP speech analysis was first introduced as a method to represent speech signals with respect to the human perception and with as few parameters as possible. However, PLP was, as most of the other analysis techniques, sensitive towards steady-state spectral factors caused by transmission channels, such as telephone recordings or the usage of different microphones [8]. Therefore, [8] introduced the RASTA methodology for PLP rendering it more robust towards these channel distortions and reducing error rates in several speech recognition experiments with only a slightly more computationally expensive extraction method. In this study 21 critical bands are analyzed in frames of 25 ms in length and with a 10 ms offset.

2.2   Visual Features

Initial processing is organized along two mainly independent pathways, each specialized for the processing of form and shape as well as the processing of motion, respectively. The organization of both pathways is hierarchical, i.e. along a series of processing stages with increasingly larger scales of interaction [18]. Form processing is mainly orientation selective and combines activities to build representations of localized features and shape configurations. Motion processing, on the other hand, is direction selective and combines activities to build representations of flow discontinuities as well as motion patterns. We assume that the hierarchical processing in both pathways is organized in a similar fashion and, thus, make use of a generic processing architecture for neural feature extraction as shown in Figure 1. The architecture is a modified variant of the object-recognition model proposed by [10,16,26].

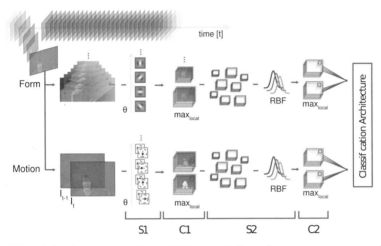

Fig. 1. Visual feature extraction. Motion and form features are processed along two separate pathways, composed of alternating layers of filtering (S) and non-linear pooling (C) stages. In layer S1, different scale representations of the input image are convolved with 2D Gabor filters of different orientations (form path) and a spatio-temporal correlation detector is used to build a discrete velocity space representation (motion path). Layer C1 cells pool the activities of S1 cells of the same orientation (direction) over a small local neighborhood and two neighboring scales and speeds, respectively. The layer S2 is created by a simple template matching of patches of C1 activities against a number of prototype patches. These prototypes are randomly selected during the learning stage (for details, see [10]). In the final layer C2, the S2 prototype responses are again pooled over a limited neighborhood and combined into a single feature vector which serves as input to the successive classification stage.

Initial Feature Detection for Form and Motion Processing. The model architecture consists of a series of stages consisting of alternating levels of filtering and pooling steps (S- and C-layers, respectively). These stages operate at different scales of spatial neighborhood.

- Oriented contrast detection. For the generation of initial contrast representation, an input image is transformed into a pyramid of 9 different spatial scales, with a downscaling factor of $2^{\frac{1}{4}}$ (using bicubic interpolation). Each scale is convolved with a bank of 2D Gabor filters given by

$$G(x, y) = \exp\left(-\frac{(X^2 + \gamma^2 Y^2)}{2\sigma^2}\right) \cdot \cos\left(\frac{2\pi}{\lambda} X\right), \tag{1}$$

where $X = x\cos\theta - y\sin\theta$ and $Y = x\sin\theta + y\cos\theta$ (for performance reasons only the even part is used). The variables x and y range from -5 to 5 and θ varies between 0 and π in steps of $\pi/6$. The aspect ratio γ, the effective width σ, and the wavelength λ are set to 0.3, 4.5, and 5.6, respectively (in accordance with [10]. This results in six orientation maps at each scale.

- Directional motion detection. The initial motion representation is generated by utilizing a spatio-temporal correlation detector which is quantized into 12 movement directions and two different speeds to build a discrete velocity space representation [1].

These maps represent the initial S1 layer for the form and motion path.

The activations are subsequently pooled over a small 10×10 spatial neighborhood and integrated over two neighboring scales by a local maximum operation. This operation forms the C1 layer representations in the form and motion pathway. The non-linear pooling operation by max-selection achieves an input pattern invariance against variations in position and size. The distributed activity maps are subsequently pruned by a combined thresholding and normalization step. Minimum and maximum activities, R_{min} and R_{max}, are determined at each location of S1 or C1 responses. Responses R of an S1/C1-unit are set to zero if $R < R_{min} + h(R_{max} - R_{min})$ where $h = 0.5$ denotes the inhibition level.

Intermediate-Level Feature Processing. In the successive processing stage, intermediate level features are learned by selecting the most descriptive and discriminative prototypes among an exhaustive number of response patches. This is achieved by randomly sampling the C1 responses. The resulting S2-prototype patterns P denote filters with complex feature selectivities topographically organized around the spatial locations of their most likely spacial occurrence. The response of an $n \times n$ patch of C1 units X to a particular S2-prototype P is calculated by

$$R(X, P) = \exp\left(-\frac{\|X - P\|^2}{2\sigma^2\alpha}\right), \tag{2}$$

implementing a Gaussian radial basis function to weight the allowed degree of dis-similarity w.r.t. prototypical patterns in the shape or motion domain, respectively. To further increase generalization, only the dominant activities at each spatial location of a patch P is taken into account. The standard deviation of the Gaussian σ is set to 1. A patch of C1 units X as well as the S2-prototype P have dimensions $n \times n \times 6$ in the form path, while $n \times n \times 12$ in the motion path ($n \in \{4, 8, 12, 16\}$). To obtain a larger degree of similarity in higher dimensional space. The normalization constant is set to $\alpha = (n/4)^2$ in the case of $n > 4$.

At the final stage, responses from all prototypical complex filters as generated in the S2 representation are again pooled over a limited spatial neighborhood. This process selectively operates on the different spatial scales. The responses are combined into a single C2 feature vector which serves as input to the classification architecture described in Section 3. For the implementation of the visual feature extraction architecture, we used the *CNS: Cortical Network Simulator* as described in [13].

3   Classifier Architectures

In this section the proposed multi classifier systems for the different sub-challenges are described.

3.1   Audio Sub-Challenge

For each label dimension and and for each audio feature a bag of hidden Markov models (HMM) have been trained [2,15]. The hidden states and the number of mixture components of the HMM have been optimized using a parameter search resulting in the selection of three hidden states and two mixture components in the Gaussian mixture model (GMM) having full covariance matrices.

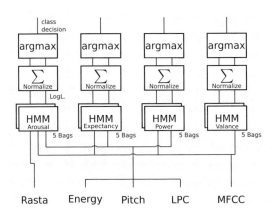

Fig. 2. Audio classifier system. For each label a bag of HMM have been trained on selected features sets.

The evaluation of the optimization process further inferred that some features appear to be inappropriate to detect certain labels. It turned out, that only the label *Arousal* can draw information from all features, *Expectancy* and *Power* performed better using only the energy, fundamental frequency and the MFCC features. The label *Valance* favored only the MFCC features. For each label the log likelihoods of every HMM trained on the features are summed. To obtain more robust models, we decided to additionally use five times as many models per class and summed the outcome as well.

Furthermore, the assumption was made that the labels are changing only slowly over time. We therefore conducted the classification on turn basis by collecting the detections within one turn and multiplied the likelihoods to obtain more robust detections. A schema visualizing the applied fusion architecture is shown in Figure 2. The results of this approach are reported in Table 1.

3.2   Video Sub-Challenge

Within the video challenge the ν-SVM^2 was employed as the central classifier [22]. We concatenated 300 form and 300 motion feature and used them to train a ν-SVM having a linear kernel and probabilistic outputs according to Platt [12]. Due to memory constraints only 10.000 randomly drawn samples were used. Again a parameter search was applied to obtain suitable parameters,

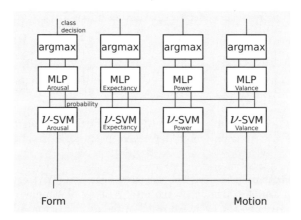

Fig. 3. Video classifier system. The form and motion features are concatenated and used to train ν-SVM for each label dimension. The outputs of the classifiers are used to train a intermediate fusion layer realized by multi layer perceptrons.

resulting in setting ν to 0.3 for *Arousal* and *Power* and 0.7 for *Expectancy* and *Valence*. Based on the results of all label dimensions an intermediate fusion was conducted using a multi layer perceptron (MLP) to obtain the final prediction. A schema illustrating the architecture used is shown in Figure 3. The results are reported in Table 1.

3.3   Audio-Visual Sub-Challenge

Considering the audio-visual challenge, we used the same approach for each modality as described in the earlier sections but omitted the last layer in which the class decision was performed. The probabilistic outputs of the video stream are collected using averaging and multiplication with a subsequent normalization such that the decision are on word level. The HMM log likelihood of the label

---

^{2} The implementation was taken from the well-known *libsvm* repository.

dimensions are transformed and normalized such that they are ranging between zero and one. By concatenating the results of all label dimensions, a new 12 dimensional feature vector is obtained. The new features are then used to train an intermediate fusion layer based on a MLP. Like in the audio challenge, the final decision is done on a turn basis by collecting the outputs within one turn and fusing them using multiplication. Figure 4 shows the audio-visual classifier system, while the results are given in Table 1.

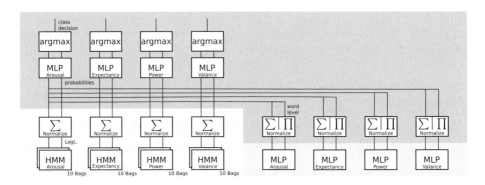

Fig. 4. Audio-visual classifier system. The output of all modalities are collected on word level and used to train a multi layer perceptron for each label dimension.

Table 1. Classification results. The weighted accuracy (WA) corresponds to the correctly detected samples divided by the total number of samples. The unweighted accuracy (UA) is given by the averaged recall of the two classes of a label dimension.

	Arousal		Expectancy		Power		Valence	
Data set	WA	UA	WA	UA	WA	UA	WA	UA
Audio sub-challenge								
Develop	66.9	67.5	62.9	58.5	63.2	58.4	65.7	63.3
Test	63.5	65.7	41.1	41.4	43.3	29.9	65.4	65.4
Video sub-challenge								
Develop	58.2	53.5	53.5	53.2	53.7	53.8	53.2	49.8
Test	56.9	57.2	47.5	47.8	47.3	47.2	55.5	55.5
Audiovisual sub-challenge								
Devel	69.3	70.6	61.7	60.1	61.3	59.1	68.8	66.4
Test	54.2	54.3	58.5	57.8	42.7	40.0	44.8	35.9

4   Discussion

The results presented in Table 1 are preliminary and must be evaluated in several directions: 1) Feature extraction techniques as described in the previous sections have been successfully applied to the recognition of Ekman's six basic emotions for benchmark data sets consisting of acted emotional data. In these data sets emotions shown by the actors are usually over-expressed and different from the emotional states that can be observed in the AVEC data set. 2) The classifier architecture is based on the so-called late fusion paradigm. This is a widely used fusion scheme that can be implemented easily just by integrating results of the pre-trained classifier ensemble by fixed or trainable fusion mappings, but more complex spatio-temporal patterns on an intermediate feature level can not be modeled by such decision level fusion scheme. 3) Emotional states of the AVEC data set are encode by crisp binary labels that difficult to get from human annotators. They have usually problems to assign a confident crisp label to an emotional scene (e.g. single spoken word or a few video frames), and thus dealing with fuzzy labels or labels together with a confidence value during annotation and classifier training phase could improve the overall recognition performance.

Acknowledgments. This work was been supported by a grant from the Transregional Collaborative Research Center SFB/TRR62 "Companion Technology for Cognitive Technical Systems" funded by the German Research Foundation (DFG).

References

1. Bayerl, P., Neumann, H.: A fast biologically inspired algorithm for recurrent motion estimation. IEEE Transactions on Pattern Analysis and Machine Intelligence 29(2), 246–260 (2007)
2. Breiman, L.: Bagging predictors. Machine learning 24(2), 123–140 (1996)
3. Cowie, R., Douglas-Cowie, E., Tsapatsoulis, N., Votsis, G., Kollias, S., Fellenz, W., Taylor, J.: Emotion recognition in human-computer interaction. Signal Processing Magazine 18(1), 32–80 (2001)
4. Davis, S., Mermelstein, P.: Comparison of parametric representations for monosyllabic word recognition in continuously spoken sentences. Transactions on Acoustics, Speech and Signal Processing 28(4), 357–366 (1980)
5. Devillers, L., Vidrascu, L., Lamel, L.: Challenges in real-life emotion annotation and machine learning based detection. Neural Networks 18(4), 407–422 (2005)
6. Hermansky, H.: Perceptual linear predictive (PLP) analysis of speech. Journal of the Acoustical Society of America 87(4), 1738–1752 (1990)
7. Hermansky, H., Hanson, B., Wakita, H.: Perceptually based linear predictive analysis of speech. In: International Conference on Acoustics, Speech, and Signal Processing (ICASSP), vol. 10, pp. 509–512. IEEE, Los Alamitos (1985)
8. Hermansky, H., Morgan, N., Bayya, A., Kohn, P.: RASTA-PLP speech analysis technique. In: International Conference on Acoustics, Speech, and Signal Processing (ICASSP), vol. 1, pp. 121–124. IEEE, Los Alamitos (1992)
9. Kuncheva, L., Whitaker, C.: Measures of diversity in classifier ensembles and their relationship with the ensemble accuracy. Machine Learning 51(2), 181–207 (2003)
10. Mutch, J., Lowe, D.: Object class recognition and localization using sparse features with limited receptive fields. International Journal of Computer Vision 80(1), 45–57 (2008)
11. Oudeyer, P.: The production and recognition of emotions in speech: features and algorithms. International Journal of Human-Computer Studies 59(1-2), 157–183 (2003)

12. Platt, J.: Probabilistic outputs for support vector machines and comparisons to regularized likelihood methods. In: Advances in Large Margin Classifiers, pp. 61–74 (1999)
13. Poggio, T., Knoblich, U., Mutch, J.: CNS: a GPU-based framework for simulating cortically-organized networks. MIT-CSAIL-TR-2010-013/CBCL-286 (2010)
14. Rabiner, L., Juang, B.: Fundamentals of speech recognition. Prentice-Hall Signal Processing Series (1993)
15. Rabiner, L.R.: A tutorial on hidden Markov models and selected applications in speech recognition. IEEE 77(2), 257–286 (1989)
16. Riesenhuber, M., Poggio, T.: Hierarchical models of object recognition in cortex. Nature Neuroscience 2, 1019–1025 (1999)
17. Robinson, D.W., Dadson, R.: A re-determination of the equal-loudness relations for pure tones. British Journal of Applied Physics 7, 166–181 (1956)
18. Rolls, E.: Brain mechanisms for invariant visual recognition and learning. Behavioural Processes 33(1-2), 113–138 (1994)
19. Schels, M., Schwenker, F.: A multiple classifier system approach for facial expressions in image sequences utilizing GMM supervectors. In: International Conference on Pattern Recognition (ICPR), pp. 4251–4254 (2010)
20. Scherer, S., Schwenker, F., Palm, G.: Classifier fusion for emotion recognition from speech. In: Advanced Intelligent Environments, pp. 95–117 (2009)
21. Schmidt, M., Schels, M., Schwenker, F.: A hidden markov model based approach for facial expression recognition in image sequences. In: Schwenker, F., El Gayar, N. (eds.) ANNPR 2010. LNCS(LNAI), vol. 5998, pp. 149–160. Springer, Heidelberg (2010)
22. Schölkopf, B., Smola, A.J., Williamson, R., Bartlett, P.: New support vector algorithms. Neural Computation 12(5), 1207–1245 (2000)
23. Schuller, B., Valsta, M., Eyben, F., McKeown, G., Cowie, R., Pantic, M.: The first international audio/visual emotion challenge and workshop (AVEC 2011). In: D'Mello, S., et al. (eds.) ACII 2011, Part II. LNCS, vol. 6975, pp. 415–424. Springer, Heidelberg (2011)
24. Schwenker, F., Scherer, S., Magdi, Y.M., Palm, G.: The GMM-SVM supervector approach for the recognition of the emotional status from speech. In: Alippi, C., Polycarpou, M., Panayiotou, C., Ellinas, G. (eds.) ICANN 2009, Part I. LNCS, vol. 5768, pp. 894–903. Springer, Heidelberg (2009)
25. Schwenker, F., Scherer, S., Schmidt, M., Schels, M., Glodek, M.: Multiple classifier systems for the recogonition of human emotions. In: El Gayar, N., Kittler, J., Roli, F. (eds.) MCS 2010. LNCS, vol. 5997, pp. 315–324. Springer, Heidelberg (2010)
26. Serre, T., Wolf, L., Poggio, T.: Object recognition with features inspired by visual cortex. In: IEEE Computer Society Conference on Computer Vision and Pattern Recognition (CVPR), vol. 2, pp. 994–1000 (2005)
27. Walter, S., Scherer, S., Schels, M., Glodek, M., Hrabal, D., Schmidt, M., Böck, R., Limbrecht, K., Traue, H.C., Schwenker, F.: Multimodal emotion classification in naturalistic user behavior. In: Jacko, J.A. (ed.) HCI International 2011, Part III. LNCS, vol. 6763, pp. 603–611. Springer, Heidelberg (2011)
28. Zheng, F., Zhang, G., Song, Z.: Comparison of different implementations of MFCC. Journal of Computer Science and Technology 16(6), 582–589 (2001)

Investigating the Use of Formant Based Features for Detection of Affective Dimensions in Speech

Jonathan C. Kim*, Hrishikesh Rao*, and Mark A. Clements*

School of Electrical and Computer Engineering,
Georgia Institute of Technology, Atlanta GA 30332, USA
{jon.kim,hrishikesh}@gatech.edu, clements@ece.gatech.edu

Abstract. The ability of a machine to discern various categories of emotion is of great interest in many applications. This paper attempts to explore the use of baseline features consisting of prosodic and spectral features along with formant based features for the purpose of classification of emotion along the dimensions of *arousal, valence, expectancy*, and *power*. Using three feature selection criteria namely maximum average recall, maximal relevance, and minimal-redundancy-maximal-relevance, the paper intends to find the criterion that gives the highest unweighted accuracy. Using a Gaussian Mixture Model classifier, the results indicate that the formant based features show a statistically significant improvement on the accuracy of the classification system.

Keywords: emotion, formants, feature selection.

1 Introduction

Human communication includes verbal communication and various forms of non-verbal communication such as vision, gesture, and expression. Strictly speaking, communication is defined as the mutual exchange of information or ideas. In the realm of human communication, affect or emotion adds an element of intrigue to the discussion of how information is conveyed and processed by humans. Whether it is the baby talk that a parent uses to communicate with a child in a higher pitch [1] or an angry customer talking to a customer service representative over the phone, affect in speech plays a key role in the development of humans. Training machines to discern emotions in speech is a problem in which a considerable amount of study has been carried out. There have been instances where it is possible to identify sadness and anger with a considerably high level of accuracy [2]. Our study focuses on finding the optimal feature sets for word level detection of the four affective dimensions, namely arousal, valence, power, and expectancy, using the SEMAINE database [3].

Section 2 discusses the usage of formant based features along with the baseline features provided, and it gives a description about the methodology of extracting the formant based features and the statistical measures.

---
* Supported by NSF grant No. CCF-1029679.

S. D′Mello et al. (Eds.): ACII 2011, Part II, LNCS 6975, pp. 369–377, 2011.
© Springer-Verlag Berlin Heidelberg 2011

Section 3 gives a description of the feature selection criteria used i.e. maximum relevancy, minimum-redundancy-maximum-relevancy, and maximum average recall. This section deals with how different criteria give the optimal set of features for the affective dimensions. This section also discusses about how the formant based features help in improving the accuracy of the classification model.

Section 4 deals with evaluating the improvement in the performance of the classification system due to the addition of formant based features along with the baseline features.

Section 5 describes the Gaussian Mixture Model (GMM) classification scheme used in this study and the results obtained using the three feature selection criteria.

Section 6 summarizes the important findings of this study.

2 Feature Extraction

The baseline feature set [4] primarily consists of prosodic, spectral, and energy; their statistic, regression, and local minima/maxima related functionals produce the total number of the 1941 features in the set. As an extension of the spectral features in the baseline set, the formant related features are extracted, and used in this study.

2.1 Formant Based Features

The shape of the vocal tract contains much useful information, and its representation has been widely used in speech recognition, speaker identification, gender classification, and in many other speech related applications. It also has been shown that the shape of the vocal tract is modified by the emotional states of the speaker [5]. Many algorithms[6] have been introduced to describe its resonances and cross-section areas during emotional speech production. The formants, a representation of the vocal tract resonances, can be modeled with linear prediction (LPC); spectral tilt, which is the difference in the amplitudes of the first and the third formants, was found to be useful for discriminating emotion along the dimension of valence [7]. In our method, the first three formants were found using LPC, and the coefficients were used to extract features that describe their amplitudes, frequencies, and the bandwidths.

To find the formant based features, the speech signal was downsampled to 8kHz, and filtered with a pre-emphasis filter as in (1). We used $\alpha = 0.97$ to boost the energy of the high frequency components of the signal.

$$H(z) = 1 - \alpha z^{-1} \tag{1}$$

The filtered signal, with sampling frequency *fs*, was divided into frames using 30 ms Hamming windows with a 15 ms overlap. A 10-pole LPC analysis was performed on each frame, and the complex root pairs of the LPC polynomial were calculated. The angle ω_k and radius r_k of the pole correspond to the frequency and amplitude of the kth formant. For $r \approx 1$, the radius of the pole is also related to the formant bandwidth BW_k as shown in (2) [8].

$$BW_k = g \left(\frac{1 - |r|}{\sqrt{|r|}} \right) \frac{fs}{2\pi} \qquad \text{,where } g = 2 \qquad (2)$$

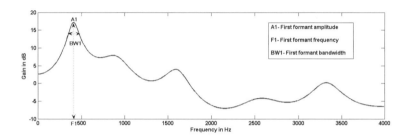

Fig. 1. 10-pole LPC response of the vowel /o/

Table 1. Description of formant based features

Feature	Description
A1-3	Formant amplitude
F1-3	Formant frequency
BW1-3	Formant bandwidth
A1-A2	Difference between A1 and A2
A2-A3	Difference between A2 andd A3
A1-A3	Difference between A1 and A3
F1-F2	Difference between F1 and F2
F2-F3	Difference between F2 and F3
F1-F3	Difference between F1 and F3
BW1/BW2	Ratio of BW1 to BW2
BW2/BW3	Ratio of BW2 to BW3
BW1/BW3	Ratio of BW1 to BW3

After obtaining the first three formant frequencies, amplitudes, and bandwidths, their interrelations were described by the differences and the ratios as shown in Table 1. The time series of these 18 features were then represented with 14 statistical measures and 4 regressional measures as shown in Table 2. This produces 324 formant-related features.

Table 2. List of statistical and regressional measures

Type	Measure
Statistical measure	Maximum, minimum, mean, standard deviation, kurtosis, skewness, flatness 1st, 2nd & 3rd quartiles, interquartile range, 1st & 99th percentiles and root mean square value
Regressional measure	Slope of linear regression, approximation error of linear regression, quadratic regression coefficient, and approximation error of quadratic regression

3   Feature Selection

With the novel formant based features, the total of 2265 features was obtained. In general a larger number of the features does not always result in better classification. It is important to reduce the dimensionality of the feature set, not only to speed up the detection process, but also to optimize detection performance. For this purpose, three algorithms were compared. Two feature selection algorithms explored are based on the criteria of maximal relevance (MaxRel) and minimum-redundancy-maximal-relevancy (mRMR) [9]. The third algorithm was based on maximal average recall (MaxARC). The feature selections for all three algorithms are done in two stages. The first stage was to rank the features according to each algorithm's criterion, and the second stage was to wrap the optimal feature set using sequential forward selection.

3.1   Maximal Relevance

The maximal-relevance method computes the set of features S, consisting of m features. The features are ranked from 1 to m by computing the mutual information between the solitary feature x_i and class c. The resulting set of features S has the largest dependency on the target class c as shown in (3).

$$\max \; D(S, c), \qquad D = \frac{1}{|S|} \sum_{x_i \in S} I(x_i; c) \qquad (3)$$

The mutual information between two random variables x_i and c is defined as,

$$I(x_i; c) = \sum \sum p(x_i, c) log \frac{p(x_i, c)}{p(x_i)p(c)} \qquad (4)$$

where $p(x_i, c)$ is the joint probability distribution function of x_i and c. The probability distribution functions of x_i and c are $p(x_i)$ and c respectively.

3.2   Minimal-Redundancy-Maximal-Relevance

The minimal-redundancy-maximal-relevance method is a two-pronged approach to select the optimal set of features. The maximal-relevance in (3) is first computed and followed by the minimal-redundancy. The redundancy is computed by finding the mutual information between features as in (5).

$$\min\ R(S),\qquad R = \frac{1}{|S|^2}\sum_{x_i,x_j\in S} I(x_i;x_j)\tag{5}$$

The mRMR criterion optimizes the difference between D and R, and the features are ranked by the values of ϕ.

$$\max\ \phi(D,R),\ \ \phi = D - R\tag{6}$$

It was shown that MaxRel and mRMR tend to perform better on the discrete features than the continuous ones [10], and it was recommended to discretize the features based on their mean values and standard deviations. Using two thresholds, mean $\pm$ one standard deviation, our continuous features were discretized into 3 states.

3.3 Maximum Average Recall

In the maximum average recall method, the features are ranked according to the average recall rate as defined in (7).

$$AverageRecall = \frac{1}{2}\left(\frac{TP}{TP+FP} + \frac{TN}{TN+FN}\right)\tag{7}$$

In (7), TP stands for true positive, FP for false positive, TN for true negative and FN for false negative. Since the data set for this study was highly unbalanced, the average recall criterion was chosen as an alternative. The average recall of each individual feature was calculated over 10-fold cross-validation using a GMM classifier with 32 mixtures. Unlike the other two methods, this method is classifier dependent.

3.4 Sequential Forward Selection

Using only the training set of the corpus, the features were ranked from 1 to 1000 by the three algorithms described above. Since the m best features are not the best m features [9], it is necessary to find the optimal subset of the features. Given the subset of ranked 1000 features, a sequential forward selection algorithm was used to wrap the features by adding features one-by-one in rank order [11]. Starting with first ranked feature, the feature x_i was added to the subset and tested for the reduction in the error rate. The feature x_i that did not result in an improvement in the error rate was discarded, and the feature resulted in the error rate reduction was kept in the subset. The error rate was tested with a 10-fold cross-validation using the GMM classifier.

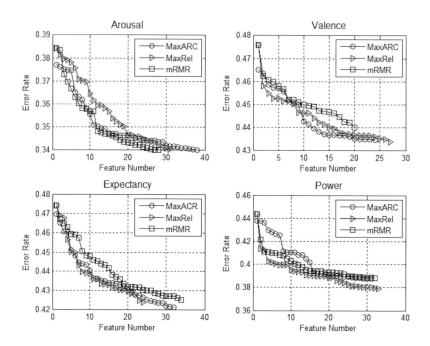

Fig. 2. Error rate vs. number of features for MaxRel, mRMR, and MaxArc using a 10-fold cross-validation method on the training set

3.5   Evaluation

The three feature selection criteria were used for the four models developed for the affective dimensions as shown in Fig. 2. It can be observed that the $MaxARC$ criterion's result for arousal is comparable to that of $mRMR$ for most of the features with both of them performing better than $MaxRel$. $MaxARC$ has the lowest error rate in expectation with more number of features. In power, there is a steep descent in the error rate in the first few iterations for $MaxRel$ and $mRMR$. After the 16th feature, $MaxARC$ converges with $mRMR$ while $MaxRel$ reaches to the lowest error rate for power. In valence, $MaxRel$ gives the lowest error rate. Thus, feature subsets selected by $MaxRel$ give the lowest error rates for valence and power, and the selections of $MaxARC$ give the lowest error rates for arousal and expectancy. There is no single winner for all four affective dimensions.

4   Evaluation on Formant Based Features

The effect of formant based features was investigated in two ways. First, the results from the feature selection criteria were used to study how a single formant feature improved the error rate when added in the subset. Second, 10-fold cross-validation was performed to compare before and after the formant based features.

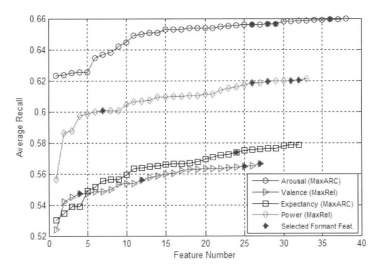

Fig. 3. Average recall (unweighted accuracy) vs. number of features to indicate the formant based features selected by the feature selection criteria in the training set using a 10-fold cross-validation method

Table 3. Formant based features selected using MaxARC, MaxRel and mRMR using the training set

| Arousal | | Valence | | Expectancy | | Power | |
| *MaxARC* | | *MaxRel* | | *MaxARC* | | *MaxRel* | |
Rank	Name	Rank	Name	Rank	Name	Rank	Name
26	F3 50%quantile	4	A3 50%quantile	24	F1 min	7	F3 50%quantile
28	BW2 1^{st}percentile	12	(A1-A3) 25%quantile			26	F1 flatness
29	BW2 min	25	A2 99^{th}percentile			28	(BW1/BW2) 25%quantile
36	(BW2/BW3) flatness	27	(BW1/BW3) min			31	BW2 25%quantile
						32	F1 linear reg. curve slope

Using the optimal feature subsets found in Section 3, the average recall as a function of feature number is plotted in Fig. 3. The highest ranked formant feature is "A3 50% quantile" for valence; it is ranked as the fourth most relevant feature. The formant feature that improves the average recall rate the most is "(A1-A3) 25% quantile"; it improves 0.2% recall rate. Table 3 shows more information on the selected formant based features in the subset. For each affective

Table 4. Average unweighted acuracy on the training set using the three selection criteria and a 10-fold cross-validation technique. *UA* represents unweighted accuracy.

	Arousal UA	Valence UA	Epxectancy UA	Power UA
Baseline	0.6593	0.5723	0.5778	0.6190
Formants	0.6142	0.5512	0.5315	0.5589
Baseline +formants	0.6614	0.5742	0.5782	0.6225

dimension, the detection was performed using the three feature selection criteria and a 10-fold cross-validation technique; this gives 30 detection trials on each affective dimension, and the average was taken as shown in Table 4.

5   Detection on Development Set

The training set corpus was used to train the four affective dimensions and their anti-models with 32 Gaussian mixtures, and detections were done on the development set. Once again, the selected feature sets from Section 3 were used to test the development set. The results are shown in Table 5, and the best unweighted accuracy for each affective dimension is in bold. It is consistent with Fig. 2 that the $MaxARC$ feature set produced the best unweighted accuracy on the development set for arousal, and $mRMR$ feature set for power; however, the $mRMR$ feature set produced the highest unweighted accuracy on the development set for valence and the $MaxRel$ feature set for expectancy.

Table 5. Classification results on the development set. *UA* represents unweighted accuracy while *WA* stands for weighted accuracy. *Base+form* is the combination of baseline and formant based features.

	Arousal		Valence		Expectancy		Power	
	UA	WA	UA	WA	UA	WA	UA	WA
Base+form Max Rel	64.40	64.35	51.31	54.31	**53.95**	60.67	**56.18**	63.96
Base+form mRMR	63.42	63.65	**54.19**	53.36	53.08	59.04	53.97	61.48
Base+form Max Recall	**65.62**	65.05	51.83	54.17	53.06	61.26	55.46	61.79

6   Conclusion

Our research has focused on exploring the possibility of using the formant based features to be included in the existing repertoire of baseline features for affective classification. It was shown that 14 formant based features were selected by the three feature selection algorithms; five formant frequency, three amplitude, and six bandwidth related features were selected. The inclusion of formant based features with the baseline features have shown an improvement in the average unweighted accuracy on the train set with a 10-fold cross-validation method compared to the average unweighted accuracy using only the baseline features for all the four affective dimensions.

References

1. Goodluck, H.: Language acquisition: A linguistic introduction, p. 162. Wiley-Blackwell (1991)
2. Petrushin, V.: Emotion in speech: Recognition and application to call centers. In: Artificial Neu. Net. In Engr. (ANNIE 1999), pp. 7–10 (1999)
3. McKeown, G., Valstar, M.F., Cowie, R., Pantic, M.: The SEMAINE corpus of emotionally coloured character interactions. In: IEEE International Conference on Multimedia and Expo. (ICME), pp. 1079–1084 (2010)
4. Schuller, B., Valstar, M., Eyben, F., McKeown, G., Cowie, R., Pantic, M.: AVEC 2011 - The First International Audio/Visual Emotion Challenge. In: D´Mello, S., et al. (eds.) ACII 2011, Part II, vol. 6975, pp. 415–424. Springer, Heidelberg (2011)
5. Bresch, E., Kim, Y.C., Nayak, K., Byrd, D., Narayanan, S.: Seeing speech: Capturing vocal tract shaping using real-time magnetic resonance imaging. IEEE Signal Processing Magazine, 123–132 (2008)
6. Ververidis, D., Kotropoulos, C.: Emotional speech recognition: Resources, features, and methods. Speech Communication 48(9), 1162–1181 (2006)
7. Liscombe, J., Venditti, J., Hirschberg, J.: Classifying subject ratings of emotional speech using acoustic features. In: EUROSPEECH-2003, pp. 725–728 (2003)
8. Oppenheim, A.V., Schafer, R.W., Buck, J.R., et al.: Discrete-time signal processing. Prentice hall, Englewood Cliffs (1989, 1999)
9. Peng, H., Long, F., Ding, C.: Feature selection based on mutual information: criteria of max-dependency, max-relevance, and min-redundancy. IEEE Transactions on Pattern Analysis and Machine Intelligence, 1226–1238 (2005)
10. Ding, C., Peng, H.: Minimum Redundancy Feature Selection from Microarray Gene Expression Data. Journal of Bioinformatics and Computational Biology 3(2), 185–205 (2005)
11. Ruiz, R., Aguilar, J.S., Riquelme, J.: Best agglomerative ranked subset for feature selection. In: JMLR Workshop and Conference Proceedings. New Challenges for Feature Selection in Data Mining and Knowledge Discovery, vol. 4, pp. 148–162 (2008)

Naturalistic Affective Expression Classification by a Multi-stage Approach Based on Hidden Markov Models

Hongying Meng and Nadia Bianchi-Berthouze

UCL Interaction Centre, University College London, London, UK
h.meng@ucl.ac.uk, n.berthouze@ucl.ac.uk

Abstract. In naturalistic behaviour, the affective states of a person change at a rate much slower than the typical rate at which video or audio is recorded (e.g. 25fps for video). Hence, there is a high probability that consecutive recorded instants of expressions represent a same affective content. In this paper, a multi-stage automatic affective expression recognition system is proposed which uses Hidden Markov Models (HMMs) to take into account this temporal relationship and finalize the classification process. The hidden states of the HMMs are associated with the levels of affective dimensions to convert the classification problem into a best path finding problem in HMM. The system was tested on the audio data of the Audio/Visual Emotion Challenge (AVEC) datasets showing performance significantly above that of a one-stage classification system that does not take into account the temporal relationship, as well as above the baseline set provided by this Challenge. Due to the generality of the approach, this system could be applied to other types of affective modalities.

Keywords: Emotion recognition, affective computing, multi-stage recognition, affective dimensions, spontaneous emotions, Hidden Markov Models.

1 Introduction

In the affective computing field [12], various studies have been carried out to create systems that can recognize the affective states of their user by analyzing their vocal [1], facial [11] [17], and body expressions [4], and even their physiological changes [6]. Most of the work has been carried out on acted or stereotypical expressions. More recently, there has been an increasing need to move towards naturalistic expressions in order to create systems that can interact with people in their everyday life. Naturalistic expressions, differently from acted ones, change slowly as a person interacts with the environment. The AVEC challenge [13] provides a unique dataset of naturalistic audio and facial expressions to help address this issue. These data have been recorded at a high sampling rate making it possible to capture and analyze the slow transition between affective expressions. The strong relationship between consecutive units (e.g., frames in

S. D'Mello et al. (Eds.): ACII 2011, Part II, LNCS 6975, pp. 378–387, 2011.

a video, utterance in a vocal expression) is an important source of information on the basis of which to decide what expression the unit belongs to.

In this paper, we propose to use Hidden Markov Models (HMM) to model this spontaneous process and create a system that is able to recognize the affective content of the expression. Whilst the proposed approach is general, in this paper we test it on the audio dataset in which the units of expression are the way verbal words are expressed. The AVEC dataset uses binary affective dimension levels to label each expression unit, however, our approach can be extended to deal with a larger set of discrete states.

2   Related Work

Our work is not the first work to propose to exploit the temporal relationship existing between recorded observations. Several methods have been proposed for building automatic affective expressions recognition systems from audio and video, with interesting results.

Long Short-Term Memory (LSTM) Recurrent Neural Networks have been successfully used for modelling the relationship between observations [15] [2] [9] [16]. Wöllmer et al. [15] first proposed a method based on LSTM recurrent neural networks for continuous emotion recognition that included modelling of long-range dependencies between observations. This method outperformed techniques such as Support Vector Regression (SVR). Eyben et al. [2] used it for audiovisual classification of vocal outbursts in human conversation and the results showed significant improvements over a static approach based on Support Vector Machines (SVM). Nicolaou et al. [9] also used LSTM networks to outperform SVR due to their ability to learn past and future contexts. Wöllmer et al. [16] used Bidirectional Long Short-Term Memory (BLSTM) networks to exploit long-range contextual information for modelling the evolution of emotions within a conversation.

Eyben et al. [3] proposed a string-based prediction model and multi-model fusion of verbal and nonverbal behavioral events for the automatic prediction of human affect in a continuous dimensional space. Recently, Nicolaou et al. [8] described a dimensional and continuous prediction method for emotions from naturalistic facial expression that augments the traditional output-associative relevance vector machine regression framework by learning non-linear input and output dependencies inherent to the affective data.

HMM is another method typically used to model processes characterized by temporal relationships. Nwe et al. [10] used a four-state fully connected HMM to recognize six archetypical emotions from speech, obtaining recognition performance comparable to subjective observers' ratings. A study by Lee et al. [5] showed that HMMs produce more interesting results when the modelling is not performed at the level of the emotional expression but at the level of the units composing them (phonemes in their case). In this paper, we propose to exploit HMMs to classify units of emotional expressions according to levels of affective dimensions. Differently from previous work, we propose to use the HMMs in a second stage of the classification process after a pre-decision has been made by exploiting other local methods. We also combine multiple classifiers into another HMM in the third stage to boost the overall performance. Indeed, it has been shown that multi-classifiers systems can outperform traditional approaches while simultaneously reducing computational requirements (see [1] for a review).

3   A Multi-stage Affective Dimension Level Classification System

3.1   System Overview

We propose the multi-stage automatic affective dimension level classification system shown in Figure 1. The system perform an initial pre-processing stage and three classification stages here described.

In the pre-processing stage, feature extraction and dimension reduction are implemented on each unit (e.g., uttered words in the experiments reported in this paper). Here, the dimension reduction is done by PCA.

In the first classification stage, the system aims to provide a classification of each unit according to the level of affective dimension the unit expresses. Each unit is treated independently from the other units. A set of different classifiers is used to improve the classification of each single unit. The output of each classifier is a set of decision values indicating the likelihood that the classified unit expresses a particular affective dimension level (e.g., the probability to express high arousal). For simplicity, we call this set of values the decision values.

Each classifier of the first stage is paired with an HMM in the second stage. The output of each first stage classifier is hence used as input to its HMM. Each HMM reclassifies each unit by taking into account the temporal relationship with the other units also classified at the first stage.

Finally, for the third stage, we propose to use a single HMM to combine the predicted labels from all the HMMs of the second stage and reclassify each unit in the sequence according to the affective dimension levels it expresses.

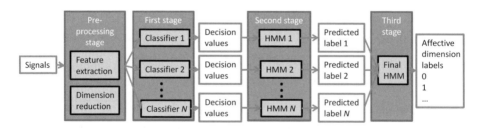

Fig. 1. Overview of the multi-stage automatic affective dimension level classification system. After the pre-processing stage, there are three classification stages, the last two of which are based on HMMs.

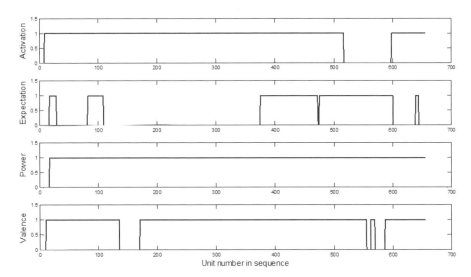

Fig. 2. Four affective dimension level labels (*activation, expectation, power and valence*) in an audio word sequence sample. Most of the affective dimension levels are changing very slowly. Only *expectation* tends to have some faster changes in the whole sequence.

3.2 First Stage Classification

This is a standard pattern recognition system in which every unit of the data is treated as sample. The temporal relationship between these units is not taken into account. For the classification itself, any classifier can be used here. The output of the classifier can be real values like the posterior probabilities in Naive Bayes classification, or the decision values in Support Vector Machines (SVM). Here, we propose to use the K-Nearest neighbour algorithm because it is simple and, as explained in section 4.2, can conveniently produce a very limited set of observed states for each sequence of units to be processed by an HMM in the second stage.

4 Hidden Markov Model

4.1 HMM Design

The main reason for considering HMM as modelling approach is that in a naturalistic affective expression labeled as a sequence of affective dimension levels we can observe the Markov property. Figure 2 shows an example of an audio recording whose units have been labeled according to levels over four different affective dimensions. Every expressed word (i.e., each unit) was labeled with a set of levels, one for each affective dimension. The levels considered in the AVEC database are binary: '0','1'. '1' means high level (e.g., high arousal) and '0' denotes low level (e.g., low arousal). The level of an affective dimension of one word is very likely to be the same as that of the previous word. In the case of a more

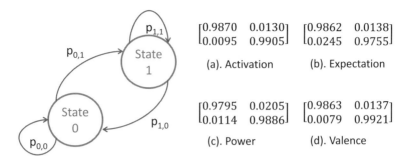

$$\begin{bmatrix} 0.9870 & 0.0130 \\ 0.0095 & 0.9905 \end{bmatrix} \quad \begin{bmatrix} 0.9862 & 0.0138 \\ 0.0245 & 0.9755 \end{bmatrix}$$

(a). Activation   (b). Expectation

$$\begin{bmatrix} 0.9795 & 0.0205 \\ 0.0114 & 0.9886 \end{bmatrix} \quad \begin{bmatrix} 0.9863 & 0.0137 \\ 0.0079 & 0.9921 \end{bmatrix}$$

(c). Power   (d). Valence

Fig. 3. Two hidden states in the HMMs and their transition matrices for four affective dimensions computed on a subset of the AVEC audio dataset. These two states are associated with the two levels of an affective dimension.

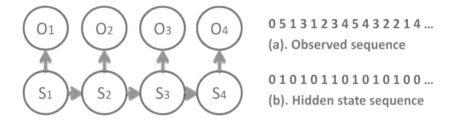

0 5 1 3 1 2 3 4 5 4 3 2 2 1 4 ...

(a). Observed sequence

0 1 0 1 0 1 1 0 1 0 1 0 1 0 0 ...

(b). Hidden state sequence

Fig. 4. HMMs used in the second stage. The observed values O_i are obtained from the decision values from the first classification stage. This example shows a possible observed sequence outputted by a KNN when K=5. The hidden states S_i are chosen from states '0' and '1' as the hidden state sequence illustrates.

refined description of number of levels per dimension, we could expect that the level assigned to two consecutive words would be highly identical or very similar.

Based on this typical Markov property presented in these sequences, for each affective dimension, we design HMMs with two hidden states: '0' and '1' as shown in Figure 3. These two states are exactly associated with the two levels of an affective dimension. These hidden states capture the temporal structure of the data. $p_{0,0}$ and $p_{1,1}$ are the probabilities the system remains in the current state and $p_{0,1}$ and $p_{1,0}$ are the transition probabilities between states. For each dimension, a typical transition matrix is represented in Figure 3.

4.2   HMMs in the Second Stage Classification

For the HMMs in the second stage, the observed sequence was obtained based on the decision values from the first stage classification. Each classifier of the first stage is paired with a HMM in this second stage. These decision values output by the first stage can be continuous values, or discrete values depending on the classifier used. When the decision values are continuous, Gaussian

Mixture Models can be used to estimate their probability distribution. When the decision values are discrete, discrete probability matrices can be estimated for each symbol on each state.

In this paper, KNN was used in the first stage. Discrete HMMs can be built based on the decision function from KNN as shown in Figure 4. For example, when K=5, the neighbours of a sample are 5 samples with label '1' or '0'. The probability of the label of this sample will be '0' depending on the number of '0' in its neighbours' labels. The number of '0' can be counted and there are only 6 possibilities: 0,1,2,3,4,5. Here, we simply choose this count number as observed value of the HMMs, as shown in Figure 4.

4.3   HMM in the Third Stage Classification

Another HMM was built for the third stage classification based on the predicted labels ('0' or '1') from the multiple HMMs in the second stage. This is a decision fusion stage where the Markov property of temporal relationships in the sequences is taken into account. As in the second stage, the count number of how many '0' were predicted is used as observed value. For example. a second stage with 5 HMMs is equivalent to a KNN with K=5 in the first stage for HMM modelling.

4.4   HMM Implementation

For the HMM training, the state transition matrix can be directly estimated from the labels in the training set. The state emission matrices can be estimated from the discrete probability distribution of the decision values from previous classifications. For the HMM testing, the classification problem is converted into a best path finding problem for the decision value sequence. The Viterbi algorithm [14] was used to produce the best match label sequence.

Although there are some commercial or free HMM software packages available from Internet, this paper did not use them because our model is simple and the matrices can be estimated directly from the data. The HMM can be designed to be more complex when the decision values are vectors. In the following experiments, only thess simple HMMs were used. They were trained separately for four affective dimensions as a possible relationship between these dimensions was not taken into consideration.

5   Experimental Results

5.1   Dataset and Features

The challenge data is constructed from the SEMAINE database, which consists of a large number of emotionally coloured interactions between a user and an emotionally stereotyped character. More specifically, the AVEC2011 dataset has been created from the first 140 operator-user interactions, which constitutes the

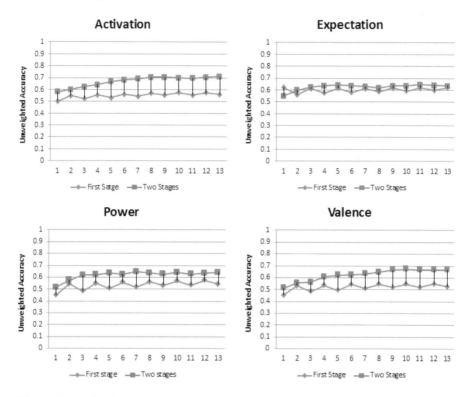

Fig. 5. Unweighted accuracy comparison for four affective dimension levels. 13 classifiers were trained and tested on stage one and two. The performance was improved significantly for affective dimensions *activation, power and valence*. There is only marginal improvement in *expectation*.

Solid-SAL partition of the SEMAINE database. The Solid-SAL partition consists of users interacting with another person who plays the role of the emotionally stereotyped character. The SEMAINE database is fully described in [7].

Only those features provided by the challenge organizer were used. For the audio dataset, each uttered word is described by a vector of 1941 features and a set of four labels representing the level of *activation, valence, expectation* and *power*. The detailed description of the features can be found in [13]. In order to reduce the dimension of the feature vector, PCA was used and only 100 principle components were selected in the following experiments as they covered most of the variance.

5.2   Results

The system was trained on the training dataset and firstly tested on the development dataset. 13 different KNN classifiers were used for the first stage classification tasks. The output of the KNN classifiers were inputted to the HMM models and their corresponding two-stage results were obtained. All samples in

Table 1. Unweighted accuracy for first stage and two-stage classifications on the development dataset. 13 KNN classifiers (K=2,3,...,14) were used in this experiment.

Accuracy	First stage classification				Two-stage classification			
%	activation	expectation	power	valence	activation	expectation	power	valence
KNN-02	50.00	62.09	44.90	45.36	58.21	54.84	51.49	51.09
KNN-03	54.96	55.99	54.30	53.36	60.13	59.74	57.54	55.74
KNN-04	52.31	61.34	48.45	47.94	62.35	62.37	61.72	56.18
KNN-05	55.82	57.17	55.18	53.49	64.28	63.80	62.06	60.61
KNN-06	53.41	61.52	50.74	49.45	66.65	64.21	63.64	62.14
KNN-07	56.47	57.98	55.90	54.42	68.02	63.56	62.60	62.45
KNN-08	54.65	61.37	51.89	50.88	69.10	62.96	64.57	63.30
KNN-09	57.00	58.67	56.33	54.75	70.47	61.94	63.56	64.83
KNN-10	55.50	61.79	53.39	51.91	70.39	63.75	62.83	66.38
KNN-11	57.48	59.38	56.88	54.71	69.77	63.69	64.38	67.06
KNN-12	55.56	61.90	53.48	52.02	69.63	64.75	62.77	66.59
KNN-13	57.26	60.06	57.12	55.04	70.55	64.37	63.65	66.72
KNN-14	56.09	62.16	54.44	52.78	70.94	63.82	64.28	66.76

Table 2. Comparison of recognition rates on test dataset between proposed method and baseline method

Accuracy	Activation		Expectation		Power		Valence	
%	WA	UA	WA	UA	WA	UA	WA	UA
baseline	55.0	57.0	52.9	54.5	28.0	49.1	44.3	47.2
our method	**64.3**	**66.2**	**57.0**	**58.6**	**41.3**	**54.4**	**50.5**	**51.4**

the training dataset were used for training and all samples in the development dataset were used for testing. In this first testing phase, only the first two stages of the system are considered and compared in order to evaluate the contribution made by the second stage to the first stage for each individual classifier.

The unweighted accuracy results for thirteen KNNs are shown in Figure 5. The maximum value of K (i.e., K=14) in the selection of the number of KNN classifiers was empirically determined. Any further increase did not provide an increase in performances. Detailed values are shown in Table 1. We can observe from the table a clear improvement in recognition rate between two-stage classification and first stage classification for *activation*, *power* and *valence* dimensions. Instead, there is only marginal improvement for the *expectation* dimension. A 1-tailed paired t-test and a 1-tailed non-parametric Wilcoxon signed-ranked test confirmed the significance of the improvement between first and second stage with p-values < 0.0001 for *activation*, *power* and *valence* dimensions and p-values $= 0.01$ for the *expectation* dimension.

The multi-stage method (including the third stage) was finally fully tested on the test dataset of the AVEC audio sub-challenge that contains 11 samples of audio sequences. The overall performances are shown in Table 2 and compared with the baseline performance provided with the AVEC dataset. Our results clearly show our method outperforms the baseline rates for all the affective dimensions.

6   Discussion and Conclusion

In this paper, HMMs were proposed to model the classification of a unit of affective expression by taking into account the naturally slow changes in terms of levels of affective dimensions occurring within an affective expression. A multi-stage automatic affective dimension level classification system was built. The process could be reduced into a two-stage system if the classifier in stage one was not used. In this case, the dimensionality of the feature vectors would have to be significantly reduced in order to be processed by the HMMs. The computing load would then be much higher than with the multi-stage system proposed here. Indeed, the classifier in the first stage reduces the dimensionality of the feature vector to one dimension, thus making the system faster.

The key idea of the paper is that the hidden states of the HMMs are associated with the levels of affective dimensions. Therefore, the classification problem is converted into a best path finding problem in HMMs. The Viterbi algorithm can be used to produce the best match label sequences. Our system was tested on the audio data of the AVEC challenge datasets and performance was shown to improve significantly in comparison to a one-stage classifier that does not consider the temporal information. In our tests with the development set, performance improved significantly for almost all 13 classifiers used. For the test dataset, our method outperformed the baseline method significantly.

An interesting development of this approach will be to take into consideration possible correlations between affective dimensions. Furthermore, given the generality of the approach, it will be interesting to test it on other modalities such as the video database, replacing words in audio with frames in videos.

Acknowledgments.   This   work   was   supported   by   EPSRC   grant EP/G043507/1: Pain rehabilitation: E/Motion-based automated coaching.

References

1. Ayadi, M., Kamel, M.S., Karray, F.: Survey on speech emotion recognition: Features, classification schemes, and databases. Pattern Recognition 44(3), 572–587 (2011)
2. Eyben, F., Petridis, S., Schuller, B., Tzimiropoulos, G., Zafeiriou, S.: Audiovisual classification of vocal outbursts in human conversation using long-short-term memory networks. In: Proceedings of IEEE Int'l Conf. Acoustics, Speech and Signal Processing (ICASSP 2011), Prague, Czech Republic (May 2011)
3. Eyben, F., Wollmer, M., Valstar, M.F., Gunes, H., Schuller, B., Pantic, M.: String-based audiovisual fusion of behavioural events for the assessment of dimensional affect. In: Proceedings of IEEE International Conference on Automatic Face and Gesture Recognition (FG 2011), Santa Barbara, CA, USA (March 2011)

4. Kleinsmith, A., Bianchi-Berthouze, N., Steed, A.: Automatic recognition of non-acted affective postures. IEEE Transactions on Systems, Man and Cybernetics, Part B (in press, 2011)
5. Lee, C.M., Yildirim, S., Bulut, M., Kazemzadeh, A., Busso, C., Deng, Z., Lee, S., Narayanan, S.: Emotion recognition based on phoneme classes. In: Proc. ICSLP 2004, pp. 889–892 (2004)
6. Mandryk, R.L., Inkpen, K.M., Calvert, T.W.: Using psychophysiological techniques to measure user experience with entertainment technologies. Behaviour & IT 25(2), 141–158 (2006)
7. Mckeown, G., Valstar, M.F., Cowie, R., Pantic, M.: The semaine corpus of emotionally coloured character interactions. In: Proceedings of IEEE Int'l Conf. Multimedia, Expo. (ICME 2010), Singapore, pp. 1079–1084 (July 2010)
8. Nicolaou, M.A., Gunes, H., Pantic, M.: Output-associative rvm regression for dimensional and continuous emotion prediction. In: Proceedings of IEEE International Conference on Automatic Face and Gesture Recognition (FG 2011), Santa Barbara, CA, USA (March 2011)
9. Nicolaou, M.A., Gunes, H., Pantic, M.: Continuous prediction of spontaneous affect from multiple cues and modalities in valence-arousal space. IEEE Transactions on Affective Computing 2, 92–105 (2011)
10. Nwe, T.L., Foo, S.W., De Silva, L.C.: Speech emotion recognition using hidden markov models. Speech Communication 41(4), 603–623 (2003)
11. Pantic, M., Rothkrantz, L.J.M.: Automatic analysis of facial expressions: The state of the art. IEEE Transactions on Pattern Analysis and Machine Intelligence 22, 1424–1445 (2000)
12. Picard, R.W.: Affective Computing. The MIT Press, Cambridge (1997)
13. Schuller, B., Valstar, M., Cowie, R., Pantic, M.: The first audio/Visual emotion challenge and workshop - an introduction (AVEC 2011). In: D'Mello, S. (ed.) ACII 2011, Part II. LNCS, vol. 6975, pp. 415–424. Springer, Heidelberg (2011)
14. Viterbi, A.: Error bounds for convolutional codes and an asymptotically optimum decoding algorithm. IEEE Transactions on Information Theory 13(2), 260–269 (1967)
15. Wöllmer, M., Eyben, F., Reiter, S., Schuller, B., Cox, C., Douglas-Cowie, E., Cowie, R.: Abandoning emotion classes - towards continuous emotion recognition with modelling of long-range dependencies. In: INTERSPEECH, pp. 597–600 (2008)
16. Wöllmer, M., Metallinou, A., Eyben, F., Schuller, B., Narayanan, S.S.: Context-sensitive multimodal emotion recognition from speech and facial expression using bidirectional lstm modeling. In: INTERSPEECH, pp. 2362–2365 (2010)
17. Zeng, Z., Pantic, M., Roisman, G.I., Huang, T.S.: A survey of affect recognition methods: Audio, visual, and spontaneous expressions. IEEE Trans. Pattern Anal. Mach. Intell. 31(1), 39–58 (2009)

The CASIA Audio Emotion Recognition Method for Audio/Visual Emotion Challenge 2011

Shifeng Pan, Jianhua Tao, and Ya Li

National Laboratory of Pattern Recognition, Institute of Automation,
Chinese Academy of Sciences, 95 Zhongguancun East Road, Beijing, China
{sfpan,jhtao,yli}@nlpr.ia.ac.cn

Abstract. This paper introduces the CASIA audio emotion recognition method for the audio sub-challenge of Audio/Visual Emotion Challenge 2011 (AVEC2011). Two popular pattern recognition techniques, SVM and AdaBoost, are adopted to solve the emotion recognition problem. The feature set is also simply investigated by comparing the performance of classifier built on the baseline feature set and the dimension reduced feature set. Experimental results show that the baseline feature set is better for the classification of *arousal* and *power* dimensions, while the reduced feature set is better for the other affective dimensions, and the average performance of AdaBoost slightly outperforms SVMs in our experiment.

Keywords: Emotion recognition, SVM, AdaBoost, principle component analysis.

1   Introduction

The Audio/Visual Emotion Challenge and Workshop (AVEC2011) is the first competition event aimed at comparison of automatic audio, visual and audiovisual emotion analysis [1]. In this challenge, four affective dimensions, namely arousal, expectancy, power and valence are adopted to describe emotion other than the frequently studied emotional states such as happy, sad, anger. These affective dimensions are those that psychological evidence suggests are best suited to capture affective colouring in general [2]. Each of these four dimensions needs to be classified as binary problem in the challenge. The challenge data is constructed from the SEMAINE database [3], which consists of a large number of emotionally coloured interactions between a user and an emotionally stereotyped character. There are three sub-challenges, i.e., audio sub-challenge, video sub-challenge and audiovisual sub-challenge. We only participate in the audio sub-challenge. Different from the general emotion recognition task where emotional state needs to be classified on utterance level, the affective dimensions need to be classified on word level in the audio sub-challenge.

Many pattern recognition techniques have been utilized in the field of emotion classification, which can be generally divided into two categories. One category is those employing prosody and acoustic contours (namely the sequences of short-time

S. D´Mello et al. (Eds.): ACII 2011, Part II, LNCS 6975, pp. 388–395, 2011.

prosody and acoustic features) as features, e.g., Womack used a technique based on artificial neural networks (ANNs) to classify speech in 1996 [4] and a multi-channel hidden Markov Model to classify speech in 1999 [5], Fernandez used the mixture of hidden Markov models to classify drivers' speech [6]. The other category is those employing statics of prosody and acoustic contours as features, e.g., the Bayes classifiers with different probability distribution function modeling on statics of many feature contours were built to classify speech in literature [7–9], and a support vector machines (SVMs) classifier was built on the statistics of many feature contours to perform emotion classification [10], and an ANNs classifier was also utilized in [11]. In this challenge, we prefer to the latter category, and two popular and effective pattern recognition techniques are adopted to solve the classification problem, namely SVMs and AdaBoost, for their strong learning and discriminant ability.

The rest of this paper is organized as follows. In section 2, the algorithm of SVM and AdaBoost is briefly introduced. The feature set is simply investigated in section 3. In section 4 the experimental result is presented. The conclusion is given in section 5.

2 SVM and AdaBoost

The SVM-based classifier, which separates different classes with a maximal margin, has empirically been shown to give good generalization performance on a wide variety of problems. The margin is defined by the width of the largest 'tube' not containing utterances that can be drawn around a decision boundary. The measurement vectors that define the boundaries of the margin are called support vectors. By employing non-linear kernels, it can be extended to non-linear boundaries. In particular, SVMs show a competitive performance on problems where the data are sparse, namely too many features and relatively few data, as is the case with the data-base of the audio sub-challenge [12].

The AdaBoost algorithm is a general method for generating a strong classifier out of a set of weak classifiers, and has been reported to be very effective in many pattern recognition applications [13] [14]. The algorithm is briefly described as follows.

The boosting algorithm calls weak learner repeatedly in a series of rounds. On round t, the booster provides the weak learner with a distribution D_t over the training set S. Then the weak learner computes a classifier or hypothesis h_t which minimizes the training error on distribution D_t. This process continues for T rounds, and finally the booster combines the weak hypotheses $h_1,..., h_T$ into a single final hypothesis h_f. There are still two unspecified terms in the above process. One is the manner in which D_t is computed on each round, the other is how h_f is computed. Different boosting schemes have different methods to solve them. The detailed algorithm can be found in [14], where two versions of AdaBoost algorithm are described in detail.

3 Feature Set

The baseline feature set of audio data consists of 1941 features, composed of low-level descriptors (LLD) related to energy, spectral, voicing, etc, and their statistics.

For that the set of LLD covers a standard range of commonly used features in audio signal analysis, the whole feature set could be used to build a baseline classifier.

However, the dimension of baseline features is so large that it possibly makes the training data sparse, which will degrade the performance of classifier. Therefore, it is necessary and maybe better to perform feature selection to decrease the dimension of features, and further compare the classification results on these two feature sets. In this paper, the principle component analysis (PCA) is adopted to perform reduction of feature dimension, which leads to a reduction of feature dimension from 1941 to 621.

4   Experiment

In the experiment on SVM classifier, three types of kernels were investigated, which are polynomial kernel, RBF kernel and sigmoid kernel. In the experiment on AdaBoost classifier, the version of AdaBoost.M1 [14] were adopted, with decision stump used as weak classifier. Since the number of weak classifier has influence on the performance of AdaBoost classifier, the number of weak classifier also needs to be investigated. Weighted accuracy (WA) rate is computed here to evaluate the performance of the above classifiers.

4.1   Experiment on the Baseline Feature Set

In this section, the whole features in the baseline feature set were used to train classifiers and perform the test. The weighted accuracy of these two classifiers on the development set is given in Fig. 1 and Fig. 2, respectively, where the "average" column represents the average classification accuracy of the four affective dimensions, and the digits in the legend keys represent the numbers of weak classifiers.

Firstly, as we can see from Fig. 1, the weighted accuracy on dimension *arousal* is visibly higher than that of other dimensions. Secondly, the three kernels have very close performance on *arousal* and *power* dimension. As the other two dimensions, RBF kernel shows the worst performance while sigmoid kernel shows the best performance. Finally, the average weighted accuracy column shows that SVM with sigmoid kernel achieves the best overall performance.

From Fig. 2, we can find the weighted accuracy of *expectancy* dimension is visibly higher than other dimensions. As to the number of weak classifiers, it has some influence on the performance of AdaBoost classifier. However, there's no consistent relationship between them. The average weighted accuracy column shows that the AdaBoost classifier with 10 weak classifiers achieves the best overall performance.

The best results of SVM and AdaBoost classifiers for classifying the four dimensions are listed in Table 1 separately. As we can see, SVM classifier achieves better performance on *arousal* and *valence* dimensions, while AdaBoost classifier achieves better performance on other two dimensions. Nevertheless, AdaBoost classifier achieves a slightly better overall performance than SVM classifiers.

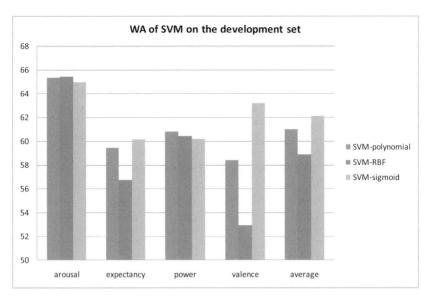

Fig. 1. The weighted accuracy of SVM classifiers on the development set with the baseline feature set

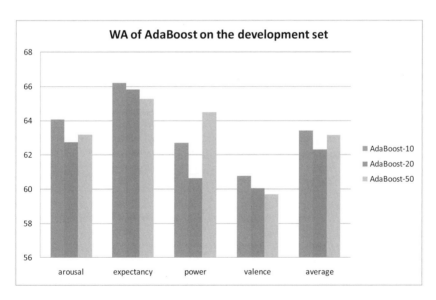

Fig. 2. The weighted accuracy of AdaBoost classifiers on the development set with the baseline feature set

Table 1. The best results of SVM and AdaBoost classifiers for classifying each affective dimension

Affective dimension	Best WA of SVM (%)	Best WA of AdaBoost (%)
Arousal	**65.43**	64.98
Expectancy	60.16	**66.20**
Power	60.82	**64.49**
Valence	**63.18**	60.76
average	62.40	**64.11**

4.2   Experiment on the Dimension Reduced Feature Set

In this section, the classifiers are rebuilt on the dimension reduced feature set. The weighted accuracy of the rebuilt classifiers on the development set is demonstrated in Fig. 3 and 4.

As we can see from Fig. 3, the weighted accuracy of SVM classifier on dimension *expectancy* is visibly higher than that of other dimensions. Another interesting result is that the performance of the three kernels are very close at each of the four affective dimensions, which might indicates that the reduced features by PCA are more generalized for different kernels to discriminate the classes.

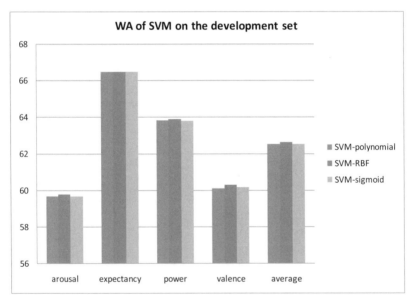

Fig. 3. The weighted accuracy of SVM classifiers on the development set under the reduced feature set

From Fig 4, we can find a similar phenomenon that the accuracy of AdaBoost classifier on *expectancy* dimension is higher than that of other dimensions. Still, there's no consistent relationship between the number of weak classifiers and the performance of AdaBoost classifier, as it is under the baseline feature set. The Adaboost classifier with 100 weak classifiers achieves the best overall performance.

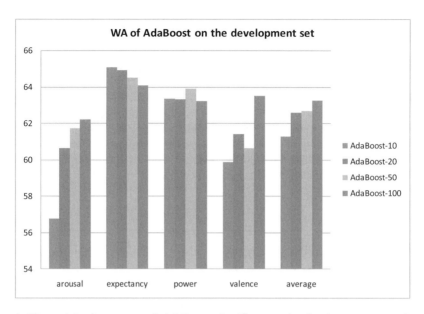

Fig. 4. The weighted accuracy of AdaBoost classifiers on the development set under the reduced feature set

Table 2. The best results of SVM and AdaBoost classifiers for classifying each affective dimension

Affective dimension	Best WA of SVM (%)	Best WA of AdaBoost (%)
Arousal	59.80	**62.20**
Expectancy	**66.49**	65.09
Power	**63.89**	**63.89**
Valence	60.31	**63.51**
average	62.62	**63.67**

The best results of these two classifiers for classifying the four dimensions are listed in Table 2 separately. AdaBoost classifier achieves a better performance at dimension *arousal* and *valence*, which is opposite to the result under the baseline feature set. Again, AdaBoost classifier achieves a better overall performance than SVM, though the difference is very small.

4.3   Summarization of the Experiment

According to the results of the above experiment, the overall performance of Adaboost classifier is slightly better than that of SVM classifier. Furthermore, by comparing Fig. 3 and 4 with Fig. 1 and 2 it is easy to find that:

- The classification performance on *arousal* dimension declines a lot for all classifiers after PCA was performed, which indicates that some clues which are important for discriminating different classes of *arousal* dimension are lost after the dimension reduction by PCA.

- For SVM classifier, the classification performance on *expectancy* and *power* dimension has a visible improvement after PCA was performed, which probably indicates that the noise in training data for these two affective dimensions is not negligible. The PCA can reduce the noise in data and alleviate the data sparseness problem, which leads to a better classifier for these two dimensions.

According to the experimental results on the baseline and the reduced feature set, the best classifier of the above utilized classifiers for this classification task can be obtained, which is shown in Table 3 including the corresponding feature set and the classification accuracy on the development set. We will further use these best classifiers to perform the emotion recognition on test set.

Table 3. The best classifier of the above utilized classifiers

Affective dimension	Classifier	Feature set	WA(%)
Arousal	SVM with RBF kernel	Baseline	65.43
Expectancy	SVM with sigmoid kernel	Reduced	66.49
Power	AdaBoost with 50 weak classifiers	Baseline	64.49
Valence	AdaBoost with 100 weak classifiers	Reduced	63.51

5   Conclusion

In this paper, two popular and effective patter recognition techniques, namely SVMs and AdaBoost, are utilized to solve the audio emotion recognition problem. For SVMs, the performance of three kernels is investigated. For AdaBoost, the influence of the number of weak classifiers on classification performance is investigated. Furthermore, the feature set is simply investigated by comparing the performance of classifier built on the baseline feature set and the reduced feature set by PCA. Experimental results show that the baseline feature set is better for the classification of *arousal* and *power* dimensions, while the reduced feature set is better for the other affective dimensions. It is also shown that the overall performance of AdaBoost slightly outperforms that of SVMs in our experiment.

Acknowledgments. The work was supported by the National Science Foundation of China (No. 60873160, 61011140075 and 90820303) and China-Singapore Institute of Digital Media (CSIDM).

References

1. Schuller, B., Valstar, M., Eyben, F., McKeown, G., Cowie, R., Pantic, M.: AVEC 2011 – The First International Audio/Visual Emotion Challenge. In: D´Mello, S., et al. (eds.) ACII 2011, Part II, vol. 6975, pp. 415–424. Springer, Heidelberg (2011)
2. Fontaine, J.R.J., Scherer, K.R., Roesch, E.B., Ellsworth, P.C.: The world of emotions is not two-dimensional. Psychological Science 18(2), 1050–1057 (2007)

3. McKeown, G., Valstar, M.F., Cowie, R., Pantic, M.: The SEMAINE corpus of emotionally coloured character interactions. In: 2010 IEEE International Conference on Multimedia and Expo. (ICME 2010), pp. 1079–1084 (July 2010)

4. Womack, B.D., Hansen, J.H.L.: Classification of speech under stress using target driven features. Speech Comm. 20, 131–150 (1996)

5. Womack, B.D., Hansen, J.H.L.: N-channel hidden Markov models for combined stressed speech classification and recognition. IEEE Trans. Speech Audio Processing 7(6), 668–677 (1999)

6. Fernandez, R., Picard, R.: Modeling drivers' speech under stress. Speech Comm. 40, 145–159 (2003)

7. Dellaert, F., Polzin, T., Waibel, A.: Recognizing emotion in speech. In: Proc. International Conf. on Spoken Language Processing (ICSLP 1996), vol. 3, pp. 1970–1973 (1996)

8. France, D.J., Shiavi, R.G., Silverman, S., Silverman, M., Wilkes, M.: Acoustical properties of speech as indicators of depression and suicidal risk. IEEE Trans. Biomed. Eng. 7, 829–837 (2000)

9. Slaney, M., McRoberts, G.: Babyears: A recognition system for affective vocalizations. Speech Comm. 39, 367–384 (2003)

10. McGilloway, S., Cowie, R., Douglas-Cowie, E., Gielen, C.C.A.M., Westerdijk, M.J.D., Stroeve, S.H.: Approaching automatic recognition of emotion from voice: a rough benchmark. In: Proc. ISCA Workshop on Speech and Emotion, vol. 1, pp. 207–212 (2000)

11. Petrushin, V.A.: Emotion in speech recognition and application to call centers. In: Proc. Artificial Neural Networks in Engineering (ANNIE 1999), vol. 1, pp. 7–10 (1999)

12. McGilloway, S., Cowie, R., Douglas-Cowie, E., Gielen, C.C.A.M., Westerdijk, M.J.D., Stroeve, S.H.: Approaching automatic recognition of emotion from voice: a rough benchmark. In: Proc. ISCA Workshop on Speech and Emotion, vol. 1, pp. 207–212 (2000)

13. Freund, Y., Shapire, R.: A decision-theoretic generalization of on-line learning and an application to boosting. In: Proceedings of the Second European Conference on Computational Learning Theory, pp. 23–37 (1995)

14. Freund, Y., Schapire, R.E.: Experiments with a new boosting algorithm. In: Thirteenth International Conference on Machine Learning, San Francisco, pp. 148–156 (1996)

Modeling Latent Discriminative Dynamic of Multi-dimensional Affective Signals

Geovany A. Ramirez[1], Tadas Baltrušaitis[2], and Louis-Philippe Morency[3]

[1] Computer Science Department, University of Texas at El Paso, USA
garamirez@miners.utep.edu
[2] Computer Laboratory, University of Cambridge, United Kingdom
tadas.baltrusaitis@cl.cam.ac.uk
[3] Institute for Creative Technologies, University of Southern California, USA
morency@ict.usc.edu

Abstract. During face-to-face communication, people continuously exchange para-linguistic information such as their emotional state through facial expressions, posture shifts, gaze patterns and prosody. These affective signals are subtle and complex. In this paper, we propose to explicitly model the interaction between the high level perceptual features using Latent-Dynamic Conditional Random Fields. This approach has the advantage of explicitly learning the sub-structure of the affective signals as well as the extrinsic dynamic between emotional labels. We evaluate our approach on the Audio-Visual Emotion Challenge (AVEC 2011) dataset. By using visual features easily computable using off-the-shelf sensing software (vertical and horizontal eye gaze, head tilt and smile intensity), we show that our approach based on LDCRF model outperforms previously published baselines for all four affective dimensions. By integrating audio features, our approach also outperforms the audio-visual baseline.

Keywords: audio-visual emotion recognition, multi-modal fusion, latent variable models, conditional random fields.

1 Introduction

Automated recognition and analysis of human emotions is an important part of the development of affect sensitive AI systems [18]. Humans display affective behaviour that is multi-modal, subtle and complex. People are adept at expressing themselves and interpreting others through the use of such non-verbal cues as vocal prosody, facial expressions, eye gaze, various hand gestures, head motion and posture. All of these modalities contain important affective information that can be used to automatically infer the emotional state of a person [23,7].

Majority of work in automated emotion recognition so far [23] has focused on analysis of the six discrete basic emotions [4] (happiness, sadness, surprise, fear, anger and disgust), even though in everyday interactions people exhibit non-basic and recognisable mental/affective states such as interest, boredom, confusion etc. [20].

S. D´Mello et al. (Eds.): ACII 2011, Part II, LNCS 6975, pp. 396–406, 2011.
© Springer-Verlag Berlin Heidelberg 2011

Furthermore, because a single label (or multiple discrete labels from a small set) might not describe the complexity of an affective state well, there has been a move to analyse emotional videos/audio along a set of small number of latent dimensions, providing a continuous rather than a categorical view of emotions. Examples of such affective dimensions are power (sense of control), valence (pleasant vs. unpleasant), activation (relaxed vs. aroused), and expectancy (anticipation). Fontaine et al. [6] argue that these four dimensions account for most of the distinctions between everyday emotion categories, and hence form a good set to analyse.

Automatic affect sensing and recognition researches have started exploring this venue as well [7]. The problem of dimensional affect recognition is often posed as a binary classification problem [7] (active vs. passive, positive vs. negative etc.) or even as a four-class one (classification into quadrants of a 2D space) rather than a regression one, although there are some exceptions (see Section 2 for more details). In our work we represent the problem as a separate binary classification one along each of the four dimensions.

In addition, most of the work so far has concentrated on analysing different modalities in isolation rather than looking for ways to fuse them   [23,7]. This is partly due to the limited availability of suitably labeled multi-modal datasets and the difficulty of fusion itself, as the optimal level at which the features should be fused is still an open research question [23,7].

We present a Latent-Dynamic Conditional Random Field [13] (LDCRF) based model to infer the dimensional emotional labels from multiple high level visual cues and a set of auditory features. This approach has the advantage of explicitly learning the sub-structure of the affective signals as well as the extrinsic dynamic between emotional labels. The dimensions analysed in our work are power, valence, expectancy, and activation. Our model is evaluated on the First International Audio/Visual Emotion Challenge (AVEC 2011) dataset. A complete description of the challenge and the dataset can be found in Shuller et al. [21]. For the challenge the originally continuous dimensions were redefined as binary ones based on whether they were above or below average, this reduced a regression problem into a classification one.

We evaluate our method on all of the three challenge datasets: video, audio and audio-visual. This allows us to examine the suitability of our approach for analysing audio, visual and audio-visual data. We see an improvement in performance over all of the selected baselines (Support Vector Machines, Conditional Random Fields and Decision Trees) when evaluating our approach on the development set. Furthermore, when evaluated on the test set our approach improves the baseline results for video and audio-visual data.

2   Previous Work

As this paper concentrates on recognition of emotion in dimensional space we present the previous work on this specific task. For recent surveys of dimensional and categorical affect recognition see Zeng et al. [23], and Gunes and Pantic [7].

Of special relevance to our work is the work done by Wöllmer *et al.* [22] that uses Conditional Random Fields (CRF) for discrete emotion recognition by quantising the continuous labels for valance and arousal based on a selection of acoustic features. In addition, they use Long Short-Term Memory Recurrent Neural Networks to perform regression analysis on these two dimensions. Both of these approaches demonstrate the benefits of including temporal information when approaching emotion recognition in dimensional space.

Nicolaou *et al.* [14] present experiments for classification of spontaneous affect based on Audio-Visual features using coupled Hidden Markov Models that allow them to model temporal correlations between different cues and modalities. They also show the benefits of using the likelihoods produced from separate (C)HMMs as input to another classifier, rather than picking the label with a maximum likelihood for audio-visual classification of affective data. Interestingly, their experiments show that visual features contribute more in spontaneous affect classification in the valence dimension. As in our work the task is approached as a classification rather than regression one.

Nicolaou *et al.* [15] propose the use of Output-Associative Relevance Vector Machine (OA-RVM) for dimensional and continuous prediction of emotions based on automatically tracked facial feature points. Their work poses the dimensional labeling problem as a regression and not a classification one. Their proposed regression framework exploits the inter-correlation between the valence and arousal dimensions by including in their mode the initial output estimation together with their input features. In addition, OA-RVM regression attempts to capture the temporal dynamics of output by employing a window that covers a set of past and future outputs.

Eyben *et al.* [5] fuse both visual (head motion, facial action units) and audio modalities in order to analyse human affect in valence and expectation dimensions. Their results show improved performance when using high-level event-based features such as smiles, head shakes or laughter rather than low-level signal-based ones such as facial feature points or spectral information when predicting affect from audiovisual data in valence and expectation dimensions.

3   Approach

When approaching the challenging problem of recognizing affective dimensions in un-segmented video and audio sequences, one valid approach is to experiment with an extensive set of visual or audio features, where each feature is a low-level representation of the instantaneous appearance of the face or a low level descriptor of the audio signal. The problem with this approach is that the feature space will end up extremely large (5900 dimensions of visual and 1941 of audio features in the case of Schuller *et al.* [21]). This high dimensionality issue can be partially solved by performing dimensionality reduction or feature selection.

For audio features we employ a standard approach of selecting a subset of features using Correlations-based Feature Selection (CFS) [8]. For visual features however, we propose to take advantage of the existing visual sensing techno-

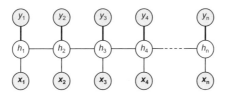

Fig. 1. Graphical representation of the LDCRF model. x_j represents the jth observation (corresponding to the jth observation of the sequence), h_j is a hidden state assigned to x_j , and y_j the class label of x_j (i.e. positive or negative). Gray circles are observed variables.

logy such as Omron OKAO Vision [17] and SHORE[1], to automatically compute higher-level visual features. These commercial and open-source software packages can detect visual features (e.g., eye corners) and recognize high-level communicative signals (e.g., smile intensity). We selected a subset of communicative signals which were shown to be useful when analyzing dyadic interactions [2,11,1] and could be estimated robustly: eye gaze, smile and head tilt (see Section 4.2 for more details). By using higher-level visual features, we have the advantage of lower dimensionality, which allows us to learn the interaction between features.

To recognize affective dimensions, we propose to explicitly learn the hidden dynamics between input features (e.g., gaze and smile) using the Latent-Dynamic Conditional Random Field(LDCRF) model [13] (see Figure 1). LDCRF offers several advantages over previous discriminative models. In contrast to Conditional Random Fields(CRFs) [12], LDCRF incorporates hidden state variables which model the sub-structure of gesture sequences. The CRF approach models the transitions between gestures, thus capturing extrinsic dynamics, but lacks the ability to represent internal sub-structure. LDCRF can learn the dynamics between gesture labels and can be directly applied to labeled unsegmented sequences.

As described in Morency *et al.* [13], the task of the LDCRF model is to learn a mapping between a sequence of observations $\mathbf{x} = \{x_1, x_2, ..., x_m\}$ and a sequence of labels $\mathbf{y} = \{y_1, y_2, ..., y_m\}$. Each y_j is a class label for the jth observation in a sequence and is a member of a set $\mathcal{Y}$ of possible class labels, for example, $\mathcal{Y} = \{\texttt{positive-valence}, \texttt{negative-valence}\}$. Each frame observation x_j is represented by a feature vector $\phi(x_j) \in \mathbf{R}^d$, for example, the eye gaze, smile and head tilt at each frame. For each sequence, we also assume a vector of "substructure" variables $\mathbf{h} = \{h_1, h_2, ..., h_m\}$. These variables are not observed in the training examples and will therefore form a set of hidden variables in the model.

Given the above definitions, we define a latent conditional model:

$$P(\mathbf{y} \mid \mathbf{x}, \theta) = \sum_{\mathbf{h}} P(\mathbf{y} \mid \mathbf{h}, \mathbf{x}, \theta) P(\mathbf{h} \mid \mathbf{x}, \theta). \qquad (1)$$

where θ are the parameters of the model.

---

[1] http://www.iis.fraunhofer.de/en/bf/bv/ks/gpe/demo/

Given a training set consisting of n labeled sequences $(\mathbf{x_i}, \mathbf{y_i})$ for $i = 1...n$, training is done following Lafferty $et\ al.$ [12] using this objective function to learn the parameter θ^*:

$$L(\theta) = \sum_{i=1}^{n} \log P(\mathbf{y}_i \mid \mathbf{x}_i, \theta) - \frac{1}{2\sigma^2} ||\theta||^2 \qquad (2)$$

The first term in Eq. 2 is the conditional log-likelihood of the training data. The second term is the log of a Gaussian prior with variance σ^2, i.e., $P(\theta) \sim \exp\left(\frac{1}{2\sigma^2}||\theta||^2\right)$.

For a more detailed discussion of LDCRF training and inference see Morency $et\ al.$ [13].

4   Experimental Setup

In this section we first introduce the dataset used for validating and testing our approach. We follow with a discussion of the audio and video features selected for our experiments. We then describe the audio-visual fusion methods used in our experiments. Finally, the training and the validation of the models is described.

4.1   Dataset

For all our experiments we used the dataset provided by Schuller $et\ al.$ [21]. The dataset consist of 95 video and audio recorded dyadic interaction sessions between human participants and a virtual agent operated by a human. The dataset consists of upper body video segments with per frame and audio and audio-visual segments with per word binary labels along the four affective dimensions (activation, expectation, power and valence).

4.2   Visual Features

As discussed in Section 3, we selected a subset of visual communicative signals which were shown to be useful when analyzing dyadic interactions [2,11,1] and could be estimated robustly by an off-the-shelf sensing software. In our experiments, we processed each video sequence with the Omron OKAO Vision software library [17] to automatically extract the following facial features: horizontal eye gaze direction (degrees), vertical eye gaze direction (degrees), smile intensity (from 0-100) and head tilt (degrees). We reason that the visual features that play an important role in face-to-face communication are potentially good for affective signal recognition. In addition, the use of higher-level visual features of low dimensionality allows us to learn the interaction between features better.

4.3   Audio Features

For our original audio feature set we used the 1941 features provided with the dataset [21]. Each of the features were sampled over a duration of a single word

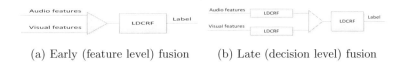

(a) Early (feature level) fusion   (b) Late (decision level) fusion

Fig. 2. The two multimodal fusion techniques used in our experiments

(mean word length is 263ms). As the dimensionality of the feature set is very high we applied Correlation-based Feature Selection (CFS) [8] to select a subset of features relevant for the task. Due to memory limitations of WEKA [9] toolkit a subsample of the audio training set was taken for feature selection (every third word). On the resulting subset a 10-fold cross validation CFS was performed on each of the four emotion labels (valence, activation, expectancy, and power) independently. That is, leaving a 10th of the training set out and running CFS on the remaining data. Features that were chosen in at least 5 of 10 folds were chosen as input features for our model, with the exception of arousal where only the features selected in all of the ten folds were chosen as the 5 out of 10 approach lead to 91 features. This was done in order to keep the dimensionality low, and have a roughly similar number of features across the different affective dimensions. This resulted in 19 features for arousal, 7 for expectancy, 22 for power, and 15 for valence dimensions.

4.4   Audio-Visual Features

In the case of fusion we needed to align the visual with audio features. Audio features were sampled over a longer and varying period of time as opposed to per frame sampling of video features. For computing the visual features at the word level, we used the mean values of all the frames happening during a specific word. This resulted in same length sequences for both video and audio features.

The optimal level of fusion is still an open research question. In our work we explore several approaches fusion (illustrated in Figure 2). The most straightforward one is to concatenate the audio and visual features and train a classifier on them (Figure 2a). An alternative to that is to concatenate the marginal probabilities output from the unimodal models (Figure 2b) and use that as an input to another classifier.

4.5   Baseline Models

In addition to the baseline provided by Shuller *et al.* [21], we decided to evaluate our approach (LDCRF) against Conditional Random Fields (CRF), which were already used in an affective dimension classification task by Wöllmer *et al.* [22]. We also compare our approach to decision trees due to their simplicity and speed of training, and also to provide us with an additional non-temporal model as a baseline.

SVM. The baseline proposed by Shuller et al. [21] uses Support Vector Machine (SVM) classification without feature selection. For the audio data a linear kernel SVM was used, while for the video a radial basis function kernel SVM. Both were trained on the training dataset. For the audiovisual data, they used late (decision level) fusion using a linear SVM trained on the development set.

Decision Trees. We used the Java implementation of C4.5 algorithm for decision trees as our first baseline model [19]. The decision tree is created based on the information entropy of each feature in a given training set.

Conditional Random Field. For our third baseline we trained a single Conditional Random Field (CRF) for each affective dimension using the visual input features [12]. The CRF model has a similar structure as the LDCRF model but without the hidden variables. No latent dynamic is explicitly learned with the CRF model.

4.6   Methodology

For all the experiments we use the data provided by Schuller *et al.* [21]. The data is divided into 3 subsets: training, development and testing. The training set consists of 31 sessions, while the development set consists of 32 sessions that were used for validation of the model parameters. The test set consists of 11 video only sequences, 11 audio only sequences, and 10 audio-visual sequences. All of the 32 test sequences did not have any publicly available labels. The same validation and testing methodology was applied to audio, video and audio-visual data. In the case of late fusion the training was again performed on the training dataset and validated on development one (same technique used for the unimodal models). In each case a separate binary classifier is trained for each of the dimensions rather than one giving multiple-label output. We automatically validated the following model parameters: for CRF and LDCRF the L2-norm regularization term was validated with values $10^k, k = -2..3$, for LDCRF we validated the number of hidden states (2-4), no validation was performed for decision trees. We used weighted accuracy as the measure of performance for all of our experiments.

For the decision tree experiments we used the WEKA toolkit [9]. For training CRF and LDCRF we used the freely available hCRF library [10].

5   Results and Discussion

5.1   Visual Data

The goal of our experiments on visual data were two fold: evaluating the selected visual features (gaze, smile and head tilt) and comparing our approach based on LDCRF with other baseline models. First, we performed a comparison of our selected set of features (see Section 4.2) with the Local Binary Patterns [16] used in Schuller *et al.* [21]. For fair comparison, we trained a Support Vector Machine (SVM) with a radial basis function (RBF) kernel as was performed by Schuller

Table 1. Visual feature evaluation: comparison between the use of Local Binary Patterns features [21] and our set of features described in Section 4.2 on the development set

Weighted accuracy (%)	**Activation**	**Expectancy**	**Power**	**Valence**
SVM + LBP [21]	60.2	58.3	56.0	63.6
SVM + Our features	**58.7**	**60.3**	**54.0**	**63.6**

Table 2. Classification results of our approach (LDCRF) and the baselines on the development dataset for audio and video modalities. A stands for activation, E for expectancy, P for power and V for valence.

Weighted accuracy	Audio					Video				
(%)	A	E	P	V	Average	A	E	P	V	Average
Baseline [21]	63.7	63.2	65.6	58.1	62.7	60.2	58.3	56.0	63.6	59.5
Decision trees	60.8	65.9	63.1	**64.3**	63.5	62.1	55.4	49.3	64.1	57.7
CRF	62.9	67.3	67.0	44.6	60.4	72.3	53.8	46.2	69.5	60.5
LDCRF	**74.9**	**68.4**	**67.0**	63.7	**68.5**	**74.5**	**60.0**	**60.3**	**72.9**	**66.9**

et al. [21], who used a 5900 dimensional visual feature vector, while our feature vector was only 4 dimensional (horizontal and vertical gaze, smile and head tilt). The performance of using our features can be seen (Table 1) to be similar to those used by Shuller *et al.* [21], showing that our selected features are at at least as good as theirs.

We compare our approach with the three selected baselines (described in Section 4.5) on the development set. It can be seen from Table 2, video sub-challenge, that our LDCRF approach outperforms all of them in all of the affection dimensions. We also evaluate our LDCRF model on the test set, it can be seen to outperform the baseline [21] in all of the affective dimensions (Table 4, video sub-challenge). We only compare the LDCRF method on the test set due to a limited number of five attempts of result submissions per sub-challenge.

5.2   Audio Data

Similarly to the video data experiments we first evaluate the approach on audio data against all three of the baselines on the development set (Table 2, audio sub-challenge), and only the LDCRF model on the test set (Table 4 audio sub-challenge). On the development set our model can be seen outperforming other approaches. On the test set, LDCRF performance is similar to the SVM baseline. The low performance of both SVM and LDCRF approaches (e.g. the best performance on the Power labels is 28%) on this test set suggests a significant difference in the data distribution of the audio-only sub-challenge test set.

Table 3. Fusion methods using LDCRF classifiers on the development set

Weighted accuracy (%)	Activation	Expectancy	Power	Valence	avg.
Early Fusion (LDCRF)	79.3	63.4	66.9	62.8	68.1
Late Fusion (LDCRF)	**81.7**	**73.1**	**73.3**	**73.5**	**75.4**
Late Fusion (SVM)	75.4	69.4	65.3	72.1	70.5

Table 4. Official results on the test set

Weighted accuracy (%)	Activation	Expectancy	Power	Valence	avg.
Video sub-challenge					
Baseline [21]	42.2	53.6	36.4	52.5	46.2
LDCRF	**65.5**	**61.7**	**47.1**	**69.8**	**61.0**
Audio sub-challenge					
Baseline [21]	55.0	**52.9**	**28.0**	44.3	**45.1**
LDCRF	**55.8**	50.1	19.8	**46.5**	43.0
Audiovisual sub-challenge					
Baseline [21]	**67.2**	36.3	62.2	**66.0**	57.9
LDCRF	65.6	**53.4**	**62.9**	59.5	**60.3**

5.3 Audio-Visual Data

For audio-visual fusion two experiments were performed, comparing the fusion methods and evaluating them on the test dataset. From Table 3 we can see that the late fusion using LDCRF as a model to fuse the outputs of uni-modal classifiers performed best in all of the affective dimensions, so only this approach was evaluated on the test set.

We can see in Table 4 the results of our approach on the audio-visual test set. Our LDCRF based approach gives results that are always better than 50% (chance level) while the SVM baseline approach performs below chance level for expectancy. Our LDCRF based approach outperforms the SVM-based baseline on the average over all 4 emotion labels.

6   Conclusion

In this paper, we proposed an approach that models the interaction between the high level perceptual features using Latent-Dynamic Conditional Random Fields. We evaluated our approach on the Audio-Visual Emotion Challenge (AVEC 2011) dataset. By using visual features easily computable using off-the-shelf software, we showed that our approach based on LDCRF model outperforms the previously published baseline for all four affective dimensions on both the development and test datasets. Integrating this with audio data we are able to improve performance of the baseline on audio-visual data on average.

LDCRF model seems to be suitable for late feature fusion outperforming the SVM model for fusion. Looking at the results from video and audio sub-challenges, they did not seem to generalise very well on the audio-visual sub-challenge data (both in the case of baseline and our approach), this might have been due to the differences between the test subsets. This points to the need of future work looking into using semi-supervised domain adaptation techniques (such as proposed by Blitzer et al. [3]) to learn the distribution of features in unseen data allowing the methods to generalise better.

References

1. Argyle, M., Dean, J.: Eye-contact, distance and affiliation. Sociometry 28, 233–304 (1965)
2. Bavelas, J.B., Coates, L., Johnson, T.: Listeners as co-narrators. Journal of Personality and Social Psychology 79(6), 941–952 (2000)
3. Blitzer, J., McDonald, R., Pereira, F.: Domain Adaptation with Structural Correspondence Learning. In: EMNLP, pp. 120–128 (2006)
4. Ekman, P.: An argument for basic emotions. Cognition & Emotion 6(3), 169–200 (1992)
5. Eyben, F., Wollmer, M., Valstar, M., Gunes, H., Schuller, B., Pantic, M.: String-based audiovisual fusion of behavioural events for the assessment of dimensional affect. In: IEEE FG 2011 (2011)
6. Fontaine, J.R., Scherer, K.R., Roesch, E.B., Ellsworth, P.: The world of emotion is not two-dimensional. Psychological Science 18, 1050–1057 (2007)
7. Gunes, H., Pantic, M.: Automatic, dimensional and continuous emotion recognition. Int'l Journal of Synthetic Emotion 1(1), 68–99 (2010)
8. Hall, M.: Correlation-based Feature Selection for Machine Learning. Ph.D. thesis, University of Waikato (1999)
9. Hall, M., Frank, E., Holmes, G., Pfahringer, B., Reutemann, P., Witten, I.H.: The weka data mining software: an update. SIGKDD Explor. Newsl. 11, 10–18 (2009)
10. HCRF: library for crf and ldcrf, http://sourceforge.net/projects/hcrf/
11. Krämer, N.C.: Nonverbal Communication. In: Human Behavior in Military Contexts, pp. 150–188. The National Academies Press, Washington (2008)
12. Lafferty, J., McCallum, A., Pereira, F.: Conditional random fields: probabilistic models for segmenting and labelling sequence data. In: ICML 2001 (2001)
13. Morency, L.P., Quattoni, A., Darrell, T.: Latent-dynamic discriminative models for continuous gesture recognition. In: CVPR 2007 (2007)
14. Nicolaou, M., Gunes, H., Pantic, M.: Audio-visual classification and fusion of spontaneous affective data in likelihood space. In: ICPR 2010 (2010)
15. Nicolaou, M., Gunes, H., Pantic, M.: Output-associative rvm regression for dimensional and continuous emotion prediction. In: IEEE FG 2011 (2011)
16. Ojala, T., Pietikainen, M., Maenpaa, T.: Multiresolution gray-scale and rotation invariant texture classification with local binary patterns. TPAMI 24(7) (2002)
17. OKAO: Software, http://www.omron.com/r_d/coretech/vision/okao.html
18. Pantic, M., Rothkrantz, L.: Toward an affect-sensitive multimodal human-computer interaction. Proceedings of the IEEE 91(9), 1370–1390 (2003)
19. Quinlan, J.R.: C4.5: programs for machine learning. Morgan Kaufmann Publishers Inc., San Francisco (1993)

20. Rozin, P., Cohen, A.B.: High frequency of facial expressions corresponding to confusion, concentration, and worry in an analysis of naturally occurring facial expressions of Americans. Emotion 3(1), 68–75 (2003)
21. Schuller, B., Valstar, M., Eyben, F., McKeown, G., Cowie, R., Pantic, M.: Avec 2011– the first international audio/visual emotion challenge. In: D′Mello, S., et al. (eds.) ACII 2011, Part II. LNCS, vol. 6975, pp. 415–424. Springer, Heidelberg (2011)
22. Wöllmer, M., Eyben, F., Reiter, S., Schuller, B., Cox, C., Douglas-Cowie, E., Cowie, R.: Abandoning emotion classes - towards continuous emotion recognition with modelling of long-range dependencies. In: INTERSPEECH. ISCA (2008)
23. Zeng, Z., Pantic, M., Roisman, G.I., Huang, T.S.: A survey of affect recognition methods: Audio, visual, and spontaneous expressions. TPAMI 31(1) (2009)

Audio-Based Emotion Recognition from Natural Conversations Based on Co-Occurrence Matrix and Frequency Domain Energy Distribution Features

Aya Sayedelahl, Pouria Fewzee, Mohamed S. Kamel, and Fakhri Karray

Pattern Analysis and Machine Intelligence Lab, Electrical and Computer Engineering,
University of Waterloo, Canada
{asayedel,fewzee,mkamel,karray}@pami.uwaterloo.ca

Abstract. Emotion recognition from natural speech is a very challenging problem. The audio sub-challenge represents an initial step towards building an efficient audio-visual based emotion recognition system that can detect emotions for real life applications (i.e. human-machine interaction and/or communication). The SEMAINE database, which consists of emotionally colored conversations, is used as the benchmark database. This paper presents our emotion recognition system from speech information in terms of positive/negative valence, and high and low arousal, expectancy and power. We introduce a new set of features including Co-Occurrence matrix based features as well as frequency domain energy distribution based features. Comparisons between well-known prosodic and spectral features and the new features are presented. Classification using the proposed features has shown promising results compared to the classical features on both the development and test data sets.

Keywords: Speech Emotion Recognition, Co-Occurrence Matrix, Frequency Domain Energy Distribution.

1 Introduction

A sizable portion of the research reported in the field of emotion recognition was based on acted emotional speech with predefined well-expressed emotions [1], [2]. Recently, the focus was directed towards detection of emotions from natural spontaneous speech conversations, especially in the field of human/machine communication and human/robot communication. One of the main difficulties facing this research, using real life data, is the fact that it is hard to exactly know what emotions the speakers were actually experiencing [3]. Furthermore, real life conditions are more challenging because emotions are usually mixed and less intense in natural speech [4].

This work presents the detection and classification of emotions from audio information in the following four dimensions: positive/negative valence, and high and low arousal, expectancy and power, for the Audio Sub-Challenge category. This challenge represents an initial step towards recognizing emotions from natural human/human emotionally colored conversations. The motivation behind this challenge, as stated in [5], is the need to build an emotion recognition system that is capable of dealing with

S. D´Mello et al. (Eds.): ACII 2011, Part II, LNCS 6975, pp. 407–414, 2011.

naturalistic emotional behavior in large volumes of un-segmented, non-prototypical and non-preselected data.

In this work, we propose a new set of features employing the concept of Co-Occurrence matrix and energy distribution in frequency domain. Co-Occurrence matrix has been widely used in image processing to provide information about the texture of an image. In [6], it was shown that Co-Occurrence matrix features provided better representation of the signal characteristics with high classification performance which indicates the potential advantage of such features. On the other hand, the use of energy-related features for the recognition of emotions in audio signals has been reported previously. This includes the use of energy progression in time [7], estimation of energy for different frequency bands [7-9], total energy as a local feature [10], and low and high frequency energy calculation [11].

In addition, and to provide basis for comparison, we also investigate some classical prosodic and spectral features which include; fundamental frequency, formants, short-time energy, and mel-frequency cepstral coefficient (MFCC) features. These well-known and widely used features were shown in previous studies to provide reliable indication of the emotion.

In the classification part of the system, support vector machines (SVM) and k-nearest neighborhood (K-NN) classifiers are employed to test the classification performance based on the proposed features compared to the well-known prosodic and spectral features. This paper is organized as follows. In Section 2, description of extracted features is presented. In Section 3, classification is described in more details. In section 4, experimental results and discussion are presented. Finally, conclusions are given in Section 5.

2   Feature Extraction

Past studies in the field of pattern recognition in general revealed that the performance of any designed system is greatly influenced by both features and classification schemes depending on the application. Our work concentrates on the feature part where the main goal is to exploit the effectiveness of these features on the problem at hand. This section introduces the features that are used for the Audio Sub-Challenge category. We employed some of the well-known prosodic and spectral feature as our base features (MFCC, energy, fundamental frequency, and formants). In addition, a new utilization of the concept of Co-Occurrence matrix in the field of emotion recognition and novel features employing the energy distribution of the signal in the frequency domain, are introduced. A brief description of the proposed features is given below.

2.1   Co-Occurrence Matrix Features

Co-Occurrence matrices have been utilized and widely used in the field of digital image processing as a tool for analyzing and recognizing different textures in images [12]. The use of Co-Occurrence matrices in digital speech analysis was proposed in [13]. They demonstrated their potential in a number of applications (e.g. estimation of pitch period of voiced speech, and voiced-unvoiced-silence classification). In [6] features based on occurrence patterns of zero crossing rate (ZCR) and short time energy (STE) of an audio signal were used for speech/ Music classification and showed the potential of these features in discriminating music signals from speech signals.

Here we investigate the effectiveness of using Co-Occurrence matrix based features in the field of emotion recognition from speech. In this work, the Co-Occurrence matrix is a square matrix representing the occurrences of ZCRs and STE amplitudes in neighboring frames. ZCR and STE were extracted from the frames of each word with frame size of 10msec and a 5msec overlap. The window size and overlap were chosen such that they guarantee the existence of multi-frames even in the cases where some of the words are very short yielding a single frame. This choice avoided that specific problem, as the Co-Occurrence matrix must be calculated along several frames. In addition, the dimension of the matrix is greatly influenced, in some cases, by the wide range of energy values between successive frames as well as the large number of zero crossings in some parts of the speech. This results in an increase in the computation time. To overcome this problem, the ZCR/STE values along all the frames are scaled to values between [0, 1], then these values are mapped into discrete number of levels. The number of levels will represent the dimension of the Co-Occurrence matrix. Four descriptor functionals are then calculated as given in equations (1-4).

$$Variation = \sum_{i,j} (i - j)^2 C(i, j) \tag{1}$$

$$Energy = \sum_{i,j} C(i, j)^2 \tag{2}$$

$$Correlation = \sum_{i,j} \frac{(i - \mu_i)(j - \mu_j) C(i, j)}{\sigma_i \sigma_j} \tag{3}$$

$$Homogeneity = \sum_{i,j} \frac{C(i, j)}{1 + |i - j|} \tag{4}$$

Where $C(i, j)$ represents the Co-Occurrence matrix, μ_i and σ_i are the mean and standard deviation of the rows of the Co-Occurrence matrix, while μ_j and σ_j are the mean and standard deviation of its columns. These functionals summarize the important contents in each word and represent our feature vector for the binary classification problems.

2.2 Frequency Domain Energy Distribution Features

In this work we propose the distribution of the speech in the frequency domain as a framework of features for emotional speech modeling. We have extracted the energy distribution of the signal in the frequency domain [7], [14]. We call these features FED (frequency-energy-distribution) and define them as follows.

$$FED_x^i = \int_{Li}^{Ui} X(w)dw \tag{5}$$

Where $x(t)$ is a continuous-time signal in the time domain and $X(w)$ is the Fourier transform of the signal $x(t)$. L_i and U_i are the lower and upper bounds of the ith region. According to this definition, one should consider setting the lower and upper bounds of regions, as they have an explicit effect on the extracted features. We are dealing with the discrete-time signals, so we can also define the FEDs as follows:

$$FED_x^i = \sum_{k=-\infty}^{\infty} X[k]\left(u[k-L_i]-u[k-U_i]\right) \tag{6}$$

Where $X(k)$ is the discrete-time Fourier transform of the discrete-time signal $x[k]$, and the function $u[k]$ is the discrete-time step function.

In this work, we define this set of features on a word basis rather than windows. In other words, calculation of the FEDs has been done for all of the words regardless how the words are defined locally in the time domain. The FEDs were calculated globally for each word. This is mainly due to the small time span that uttering each word takes (the average length of spoken words in the train data set of the challenge database is about 260 milliseconds). By extracting the FEDs globally on the word level, we introduce a simpler model, eliminating the need to calculate the statistical measures of the local features over multiple frames within the same word. This reduces the required computational efforts. Therefore, we define x as the speech signal of a spoken word. The regions boundaries L_i and U_i are parameters that have to be carefully chosen according to the task at hand.

We have set the length of all frequency regions equal to 40Hz, spanning the frequencies of 0-1000Hz. These parameters were set arbitrarily. Optimal settings for these parameters need further study and optimization. These parameters may be set adaptively as well, (e.g. multipliers of the mean fundamental frequency, F_0, as the boundaries).

This new set of features is capable of describing emotional states in spoken language, as it is a fine coding of the speech in frequency domain. At one extreme, if one sets the length of each region as small as the sampling frequency, the feature vector will basically contain the discrete Fourier of the x in whole. Even though such a small frequency span for each region makes it possible to reproduce the original signal, it yields a very long vector of features and on the other hand will not convey much useful information about the emotional contents of speech. On the other extreme, the energy of the whole signal is a much reduced feature vector of this sense, but it will not be very informative feature for our classification problem. One of the challenges of using FEDs as the features is the proper choice of L_i and U_i pairs of parameters, over all i.

3   Classification

3.1   SVM

Support vector machines (SVM) are one of the most popular algorithms used in machine learning [15]. They simply try to find the maximum margin hyper-plane between two classes by finding those sample points that can contribute to that hyper-plane the most. What makes SVM very favorable to the machine learning specialists is the fact that it is built upon the kernel functions. In other words, in the design of SVM, it has been considered that the data may not be linearly separable and one may need to map it into a higher space, in order to make it linearly separable. This is what kernel functions are good for.

In this work the classification was primarily done using SVM with linear kernel. For the data used in this paper linear kernel yielded more favorable results than the radial basis function kernel. The package LibSVM [16] was employed in the classification of the problem at hand. Five-fold cross validation was performed on the training data set using the prosodic and spectral features to obtain the optimum penalty parameter C. Then the best C was used to retrain the classifiers with the whole training data set for all the features in this work.

3.2 K-NN

The K-nearest neighbor (K-NN) classifier is a very simple algorithm: an object is classified based on the majority of its neighbors, resulting in the object being assigned to the class most common amongst its k nearest neighbors. K-NN was mainly used to allow us to investigate the effectiveness of the proposed features without the influence of complex classification schemes.

4   Experimental Results and Discussion

This section presents the results for the audio-based emotion recognition sub-challenge. The Solid-SAL partition of the SEMAINE database, which consists of emotionally colored conversations, is used as the benchmark database. Detailed information about the database is found in [5]. The database provided for the challenge consists of three main partitions: training, development, and testing sets. Our systems are trained using the training data set and the results are reported on the development data set. In the Audio Sub-Challenge, the recognition is done on word level. First, each word in the data set is divided into overlapping frames. We investigated the performance of the system by using three sets of features. For the first set of features, 12 MFCC, fundamental frequency, energy, and first 3 formants (F1, F2, F3) are extracted from each frame and statistical measures (min, max, mean, median, standard deviation) are calculated along all the frames to produce the final feature vector, prosodic - spectral feature vector, (FV_P-S). The second set of features is the Co-Occurrence matrix features (FV_CO). The statistical measures in equations (1-4) are calculated from Co-Occurrence matrices of ZCRs and STE which represent the final feature vector. The third set of features is the frequency domain energy distribution features (FV_FED). The final feature vector was extracted using a length of 40 Hz for the frequency windows and the windows cover the range of 0-1000Hz.

Table (1) shows the accuracy results on the development data set in the four dimensions; Arousal, Expectancy, Power, and Valence, using SVM classifiers with linear kernel.

Table 1. Accuracy results using SVM with linear kernel

Accuracy%	Arousal	Expectancy	Power	Valence
FV_P-S	60.39	66.60	64.65	65.36
FV_CO	53.27	66.57	66.96	65.36
FV_FED	59.31	64.74	63.48	63.67
Base-Line	63.7	63.2	65.6	58.1

The results in Table 1 show that the Co-Occurrence based feature (FV_CO), and the frequency domain energy distribution feature (FV_FED) offer adequate if not promising performance compared to the prosodic and spectral features. This is due to the use of the same optimum parameter C, which was optimized using the prosodic and spectral features, to train all the classifiers. However, comparing our results with the base line results provided in [5] on the development set, we achieved higher weighted accuracies in the Expectancy and Valence dimensions using all three feature vectors, and in the Power dimension using FV_CO. It's worth noting that these are preliminary results. Further optimization and training of the classifiers may improve the performance of the system considerably.

Table 2 shows the best accuracies for the K-NN classifier, with K values ranging from 1 to 1000.

Table 2. Accuracy results using K-NN classifier

Accuracy%	Arousal	Expectancy	Power	Valence
FV_P-S	57.23	66.62	64.63	62.92
FV_CO	54.96	66.57	66.91	65.35
FV_FED	61.12	66.50	67.36	65.44
Base-Line	63.7	63.2	65.6	58.1

The results in Table 2 show that higher performance was achieved in the Arousal, Power and Valence dimensions using the proposed features compared to the prosodic and spectral ones. Comparable performance in the Expectancy dimension is noticed using the proposed features compared to the prosodic and spectral ones. This reveals the potential of those features as discriminators for emotions in different dimensions given this challenging data set.

Comparing our results with the base line results provided in [5] on the development data set, we achieved higher weighted accuracies in the Expectancy, Power, and Valence dimensions. While in the Arousal dimension, our accuracy results didn't exceed the baseline result on the development data set. Further investigation is needed to identify the reasons behind the degraded performance in these cases.

The difference in the accuracy results using different classification schemes is influenced by the choice of parameters in each of the classifiers , for example ; the range of k in the K-NN classifier and the choice of kernel functions in SVM classifiers . Further investigation is needed to explain the reasons why some features work well in certain domains and performs poorly in others. More experimentation on the database is needed for better understanding and evaluation of the designed emotion recognition system using these types of naturalistic data.

5 Conclusion

In this work, an audio-based emotion recognition system; in four categorical dimensions; Arousal, Expectancy, Power and Valence; is presented for the AVEC2011 Audio Sub-Challenge. The main focus of our work was on the feature extraction part. Two new sets of features are proposed and their performance is evaluated and compared to classical features that are frequently used in the emotion recognition problem from speech.

Some differences were noticed when evaluating the results on the test data set versus the development data set. Although our results were below the base line results on the development data in the Arousal dimension, we achieved higher weighted accuracies on the test data set compared to the baseline results for all our feature sets with the highest weighted accuracy of 58.62% compared to 55.0% using the prosodic and spectral features.

The opposite was noticed in the Expectancy dimension, where the highest weighted accuracy of 48.18% was achieved using the FED features compared to 52.9%. For the Valence dimension, we achieved higher weighted accuracies for both the test and development data sets using all our features with the highest weighted accuracy of 51.93% using the FED features compared to 44.3% on the test data set. Finally, for the Power dimension, we achieved higher weighted accuracies for both the development and test sets for at least one or more features described in this paper. Slight improvement was achieved with the highest weighted accuracy of 28.45% using the prosodic and spectral features compared to 28% on the test data set.

Given this challenging database, we achieved promising results using the Co-Occurrence matrix based features with only eight feature vectors. Also, the proposed frequency domain energy distribution (FED) features showed promising results. Further improvement can be obtained by combining all the features and selecting the best combination that will give the highest performance. These preliminary results can be refined by further optimization of the parameters of the SVM classifier, which is a substantially time consuming step given the size of the provided data base.

References

1. Nicholson, J., Takahashi, K., Nakatsu, R.: Emotion recognition in speech using neural networks. In: International Conference on Neural Information Processing, vol. 2, pp. 495–501 (1999)
2. El Ayadi, M., Kamel, M.S., Karray, F.: Speech emotion recognition using gaussian mixture vector autoregressive models. In: ICASSP, vol. 4, pp. 957–960 (2007)
3. Schuller, B., Steidl, S., Batliner, A.: The INTERSPEECH 2009 Emotion Challenge. In: Proc. Interspeech, pp. 312–315. ISCA, Brighton (2009)
4. Tarasov, A., Delany, S.J.: Benchmarking Classification Models for Emotion Recognition in Natural Speech: a Multi-Corporal Study. In: IEEE International Conference on Automatic Face & Gesture Recognition and Workshops (2011)
5. Schuller, B., Valstar, M., Eyben, F., McKeown, G., Cowie, R., Pantic, M.: AVEC 2011–The First International Audio/Visual Emotion Challenge. In: D´Mello, S., et al. (eds.) ACII 2011, Part II. LNCS, pp. 415–424. Springer, Heidelberg (2011)

6. Ghosal, A., Chakraborty, R., Chakraborty, R., Haty, S., Chandra Dhara, B., Kumar Saha, S.: Speech/Music Classification Using Occurrence Pattern of ZCR and STE. In: Third International Symposium on Intelligent Information Technology Application, pp. 435–438 (2009)

7. Cichosz, J., Ślot, K.: 'Emotion recognition in speech signal using emotion extracting binary decision trees. In: Doctoral Consortium. ACII 2007. ACM, Springer, Lisbon (2007)

8. Pierre-Yves, O.: The production and recognition of emotions in speech: features and algorithms. Int. J. Human-Computer Studies 59 (2003)

9. ten Bosch, L.: Emotions, speech and the ASR framework. Speech Communication 40 (2003)

10. Ververidis, D., Kotropoulos, C.: Emotional speech recognition: Resources, features, and methods. Speech Communication 48 (2006)

11. Cowie, R., Cowie, E.D., Tsapatsoulis, N., et al.: Emotion Recognition in Human-Machine Interaction. IEEE Signal Processing Magazine, 32–80 (January 2001)

12. Haralick, R.M., Shanmugam, R., Dinstein, I.: Textural features for image classification. IEEE Trans. Syst., Man, Cybern. SMC-3, 610–621 (1973)

13. Terzopoulos, D.: Co-Occurrence analysis of speech waveforms. IEEE Transactions on Acoustics, Speech and Signal Processing, Trans. 33(1), 5–30 (1985)

14. Yacoub, S., Simske, S., Lin, X., Burns, J.: Recognition of Emotions in Interactive Voice Response Systems. In: 8th European Conference on Speech Communication and Technology, EUROSPEECH 2003, Geneva, Switzerland, pp. 729–732 (2003)

15. Vapnik, V.N.: The Nature of Statistical Learning Theory. Springer, Heidelberg (1995)

16. Chang, C.C., Lin, C.J.: LibSVM: a library for support vector machines (2001) Software, http://www.csie.ntu.edu.tw/~cjlin/libsvm

AVEC 2011–The First International Audio/Visual Emotion Challenge*

Björn Schuller[1], Michel Valstar[2], Florian Eyben[1], Gary McKeown[3],
Roddy Cowie[3], and Maja Pantic[2,4]

[1] Technische Universität München
Institute for Human-Machine Communication, Munich, Germany
[2] Imperial College London, Intelligent Behaviour Understanding Group, London, UK
[3] Queen's University, School of Psychology, Belfast, BT7 1NN, UK
[4] Twente University, EEMCS, Twente, The Netherlands
http://sspnet.eu/avec2011

Abstract. The Audio/Visual Emotion Challenge and Workshop (AVEC 2011) is the first competition event aimed at comparison of multimedia processing and machine learning methods for automatic audio, visual and audiovisual emotion analysis, with all participants competing under strictly the same conditions. This paper first describes the challenge participation conditions. Next follows the data used – the SEMAINE corpus – and its partitioning into train, development, and test partitions for the challenge with labelling in four dimensions, namely activity, expectation, power, and valence. Further, audio and video baseline features are introduced as well as baseline results that use these features for the three sub-challenges of audio, video, and audiovisual emotion recognition.

Keywords: Audiovisual Emotion Recognition, Speech Emotion Recognition, Facial Expression Analysis, Challenge.

1   Introduction

The Audio/Visual Emotion Challenge and Workshop (AVEC 2011) is the first competition event aimed at comparison of multimedia processing and machine learning methods for automatic audio, visual, and audiovisual emotion analysis, with all participants competing under strictly the same conditions. The goal of the challenge is to provide a common benchmark test partition for individual multimodal information processing and to bring together the audio and video emotion recognition communities, to compare the relative merits of the two approaches to emotion recognition under well-defined and strictly comparable conditions and establish to what extent fusion of the approaches is possible and beneficial. A second motivation is the need to advance emotion recognition systems to be able to deal

---

* The authors would like to thank the sponsors of the challenge, the Social Signal Processing Network (SSPNet) and the HUMAINE Association. The responsibility lies with the authors.

S. D´Mello et al. (Eds.): ACII 2011, Part II, LNCS 6975, pp. 415–424, 2011.

with naturalistic behaviour in large volumes of un-segmented, non-prototypical and non-preselected data as this is exactly the type of data that both multimedia retrieval and human-machine/human-robot communication interfaces have to face in the real world. As the benchmark database the SEMAINE database of naturalistic dialogues will be used. Three Sub-Challenges are addressed:

- In the *Audio Sub-Challenge*, exclusively audio feature information is used at the word level.
- In the *Video Sub-Challenge*, exclusively video feature information is used at the frame level.
- In the *Audiovisual Sub-Challenge*, audiovisual feature information is used at the word level.

Four classification problems need to be solved for Challenge participation: the originally continuous dimensions ACTIVITY (arousal), EXPECTATION, POWER, and VALENCE were redefined as binary classification tasks by testing at every frame whether they were above or below mean. The Challenge competition measure is classification accuracy averaged over all four dimensions. All Sub-Challenges allow contributors to find their own features and use them with their own classification algorithm. However, standard feature sets (for audio and video separately) are given that may be used. The labels of the test partition remain unknown to the participants, and participants have to stick to the definition of training, development, and test partition. They may freely report on results obtained on the development partition, but have only a limited number of five trials per Sub-Challenge to submit their results on the test partition, whose labels are unknown to them. To ensure that unimodal results on test are really based on this modality, the test partition has been further split into three test sub-partitions, one for each Sub-Challenge, with either exclusively the audio or video or, for the audiovisual task, both tracks available.

To be eligible to participate in the challenge, every entry has to be accompanied by a paper presenting the results and the methods that created them, which will undergo peer-review. Only contributions with an accepted paper will be eligible for the Challenge participation. The organisers preserve the right to re-evaluate the findings, but will not participate themselves in the Challenge. Participants are encouraged to compete in all Sub-Challenges.

We next introduce the Challenge corpus (Sec. 2) and labels (Sec. 3), then audio and visual baseline features (Sec. 4), and baseline results (Sec. 5), before concluding in Sec. 6.

2   SEMAINE Database

The SEMAINE corpus [11], freely available for scientific research purposes from http://semaine-db.eu, was recorded to study natural social signals that occur in conversations between humans and artificially intelligent agents, and to collect data for the training of the next generation of such agents. The scenario used is called the Sensitive Artificial Listener (SAL) [4]. It involves a user interacting

Table 1. Overview of dataset make-up per partition

# / (h:m:s) / [ms]	Train	Development	Test	Total
Sessions	31	32	32	95
Frames	501 277	449 074	407 772	1 358 123
Words	20 183	16 311	13 856	50 350
Total duration	2:47:10	2:29:45	2:15:59	7:32:54
Avg. word duration	262	276	249	263

with emotionally stereotyped "characters" whose responses are stock phrases keyed to the user's emotional state rather than the content of what (s)he says.

For the recordings, the participants are asked to talk in turn to four emotionally stereotyped characters. These characters are Prudence, who is even-tempered and sensible; Poppy, who is happy and outgoing; Spike, who is angry and confrontational; and Obadiah, who is sad and depressive.

Video was recorded at 49.979 frames per second at a spatial resolution of 780 x 580 pixels and 8 bits per sample, while audio was recorded at 48 kHz with 24 bits per sample. To accommodate research in audio-visual fusion, the audio and video signals were synchronised with an accuracy of 25 μs using the system developed by Lichtenauer et al. [10].

The part of the database used in this challenge consists of 24 recordings, with approximately 4 character conversation sessions per recording. This part was split into three partitions for the AVEC challenge: a training, development, and test partition each consisting of 8 recordings. Because the number of character conversations varies somewhat between recordings, the number of sessions (and thus audio and video files) is different per set: The training partition contains 31 sessions, while the development and test partitions contain 32 sessions. Table 1 shows the distribution of data in sessions, video frames, and words for each partition. A separate website was set up for the AVEC 2011 competition data[1].

3   Challenge Labels

For the challenge, we selected the affective dimensions for which all character interactions of the Solid-SAL part are annotated by at least two raters. These are the dimensions ACTIVITY, EXPECTATION, POWER, and VALENCE, which are all well established in the psychological literature. An influential recent study [7] argues that these four dimensions account for most of the distinctions between everyday emotion categories.

ACTIVITY is the individual's global feeling of dynamism or lethargy. It subsumes mental activity as well as physical preparedness to act as well as overt activity. EXPECTATION (Anticipation) also subsumes various concepts that can be separated as expecting, anticipating, being taken unaware. Again, they point to a dimension that people find intuitively meaningful, related to control in the

---

[1] http://avec2011-db.sspnet.eu/

Table 2. Overview of class balance: fraction of positive instances over total instances of video frames and words in training and test partition

Ratio	ACTIVITY	EXPECTATION	POWER	VALENCE
Frames training	0.466	0.455	0.512	0.547
Frames development	0.555	0.397	0.588	0.636
Words training	0.496	0.409	0.560	0.554
Words development	0.581	0.334	0.670	0.654

domain of information. The POWER (Dominance) dimension subsumes two related concepts, power and control. However, people's sense of their own power is the central issue that emotion is about, and that is relative to what they are facing. VALENCE is an individual's overall sense of "weal or woe": Does it appear that on balance, the person rated feels positive or negative about the things, people, or situations at the focus of his/her emotional state?

All interactions were annotated by 2 to 8 raters, with the majority annotated by 6 raters: 68.4% of interactions were rated by 6 raters or more, and 82% by 3 or more. The raters annotated the four dimensions in continuous time and continuous value using a tool called FeelTrace [3], and the annotations are often called *traces*. This resulted in a set of trace vectors $\{\mathbf{v}_i^a, \mathbf{v}_i^e, \mathbf{v}_i^p, \mathbf{v}_i^v\} \in \mathbb{R}$ for every rater i and dimension a (ACTIVITY), e (EXPECTATION), p (POWER), and v (VALENCE). To attain binary labels, we first computed the average value of each dimension over all raters, resulting in a set of continuous time, real valued variables $\{\hat{\mathbf{v}}^a, \hat{\mathbf{v}}^e, \hat{\mathbf{v}}^p, \hat{\mathbf{v}}^v\} \in \mathbb{R}$. We then computed the mean of these average ratings over all interactions in the dataset, resulting in the scalar values $\{\mu^a, \mu^e, \mu^p, \mu^v\} \in \mathbb{R}$. The binary labels $\{\mathbf{y}^a, \mathbf{y}^e, \mathbf{y}^p, \mathbf{y}^v\} \in \{\pm 1\}$ are then found by thresholding $\hat{v}_t^j > \mu^j$ for each dimension j at every frame t.

For the *Video Sub-Challenge*, the original traces are binned in temporal units of the same duration as a single frame (i.e., 1/49.979 seconds), resulting in a binary label per frame. For the audio, the traces are binned over the duration of the words uttered by the user, resulting in a single binary label per word. The word timings were obtained by running an HMM-based speech recogniser in forced alignment mode on the manual transcripts of the interactions. The recogniser uses tied-state cross-word triphone left-right (linear) HMM models with 3 emitting states and 16 Gaussian mixture components per state. Monophones with 1 Gaussian mixture component per state were bootstrapped on all available speech data (user and operator) of the SEMAINE corpus. The tied-state triphone models were created from these initial monophone models by decision tree based state clustering and the number of Gaussian mixture components was increased to 16 in four iterations of successive mixture doubling. In order to use accessible standard tool kits for maximum reproducibility of results, the Hidden Markov Toolkit (HTK) [18] was used to train the models and create the alignments.

Tables 1 and 2 provide an overview of the AVEC 2011 competition dataset. Table 1 lists the number of interactions per data partition, and the number of video instances (i.e., frames) and audio/audio-visual instances (i.e., words). It

Table 3. Correlation coefficients (CC) for the dimensions at the word and frame level. (E) denotes EXPECTATION, (P) POWER, and (V) VALENCE.

CC	Word level			Frame level		
[%]	E	P	V	E	P	V
ACTIVATION	-3.2	22.4	20.7	-3.2	24.5	24.9
EXPECTATION		-35.8	-10.4		-37.3	-7.7
POWER			29.7			29.6

also reports the average word duration, in milliseconds. Table 2 lists the fraction of positive instances per partition and per dimension. It shows that the data is fairly balanced – owed to the design choice of the two classes positive/negative being defined as above/below mean. This led to the use of the classification accuracy (weighted average accuracy, WA) as the performance measure in this Challenge.

Some of the dimensions are highly correlated. For example, in the training and development partitions, at the frame-level, expectation and power are negatively correlated by a factor of 0.373. The full correlation matrices for both word-level and frame-level labels are given in Table 3. All correlations have a p-value << 0.01.

4   Baseline Features

In the following sections we describe how the publicly available baseline feature sets are computed for either the audio or the video data. Participants could use these feature sets exclusively or in addition to their own features.

4.1   Audio Features

In this Challenge, an extended set of features with respect to the INTER-SPEECH 2009 Emotion Challenge (384 features) [13] and INTERSPEECH 2010 Paralinguistic Challenge (1 582 features) [14] is given to the participants, again using the freely available open-source Emotion and Affect Recognition (open-EAR) [5] toolkit's feature extraction backend openSMILE [6].

The audio baseline feature set consists of 1 941 features, composed of 25 energy and spectral related low-level descriptors (LLD) x 42 functionals, 6 voicing related LLD x 32 functionals, 25 delta coefficients of the energy/spectral LLD x 23 functionals, 6 delta coefficients of the voicing related LLD x 19 functionals, and 10 voiced/unvoiced durational features. Details for the LLD and functionals are given in tables 4 and 5 respectively. The set of LLD covers a standard range of commonly used features in audio signal analysis and emotion recognition. The functional set has been based on similar sets, such as the one used for the IN-TERSPEECH 2011 Speaker State Challenge [15], but has been carefully reduced to avoid LLD/functional combinations that produce values which are constant, contain very little information, and/or high amount of noise.

Table 4. 31 low-level descriptors

Energy & spectral (25)
loudness (auditory model based),
zero crossing rate,
energy in bands from $250 - 650$ Hz, 1 kHz $- 4$ kHz,
25%, 50%, 75%, and 90% spectral roll-off points,
spectral flux, entropy, variance, skewness, kurtosis,
psychoacousitc sharpness, harmonicity,
MFCC 1-10
Voicing related (6)
F_0 (sub-harmonic summation (SHS) followed by Viterbi smoothing),
probability of voicing,
jitter, shimmer (local), jitter (delta: "jitter of jitter"),
logarithmic Harmonics-to-Noise Ratio (logHNR)

Table 5. Set of all 42 functionals. [1]Not applied to delta coefficient contours. [2]For delta coefficients the mean of only positive values is applied, otherwise the arithmetic mean is applied. [3]Not applied to voicing related LLD.

Statistical functionals (23)
(positive[2]) arithmetic mean, root quadratic mean,
standard deviation, flatness, skewness, kurtosis,
quartiles, inter-quartile ranges,
1%, 99% percentile, percentile range 1%–99%,
percentage of frames contour is above: minimum $+ 25\%$, 50%, and 90% of the range,
percentage of frames contour is rising,
maximum, mean, minimum segment length[3], standard deviation of segment length[3]
Regression functionals[1] (4)
linear regression slope, and corresponding approximation error (linear),
quadratic regression coefficient a, and approximation error (linear)
Local minima/maxima related functionals[1] (9)
mean and standard deviation of rising and falling slopes (minimum to maximum),
mean and standard deviation of inter maxima distances,
amplitude mean of maxima, amplitude mean of minima, amplitude range of maxima
Other[1,3] (6)
LP gain, LPC $1 - 5$

The audio features are computed on short episodes of audio data of variable duration. To wit, one instance is recorded for every word uttered by the user in a SAL interaction. Since the timings of the word boundaries were estimated by a speech recogniser with forced alignment using the manually created transcripts of the interactions, it is possible that some of the word boundaries are calculated incorrectly. In particular, some of the words were found to be so short that it is impossible to compute the audio features. To alleviate this problem, for words that were found to be too short we artificially changed the start and end time of the word to attain a segment with a minimum length of 0.25 s. The actual annotated word thereby was placed in the centre of this segment.

4.2   Video Features

The bulk of the features extracted from the video streams of the character interactions are computed by dense local appearance descriptors. These descriptors are most informative if they are applied to frontal faces of uniform size. Since the head pose and distance to the camera varies over time in the SEMAINE recordings, we detect the locations of the eyes to help remove this variance. The information describing the position and pose of the face and eyes are valuable for detecting the dimensional affect in themselves and are thus added to the set of video features, too.

To obtain the face position, we employ another open-source available implementation – OpenCV's Viola & Jones face detector. This returns a four-valued face position and size descriptor, to wit, the x and y position of the top-left corner of the face area, and the width and height of the face area. The height and width output of this detector is rather unstable: Even in a video in which a face hardly moves the values for the height and width vary significantly (approximately 5 % standard deviation). Also, the face detector does not provide any information about the head pose. To refine the detected face region, and allow the appearance descriptor to correlate better with the shown expression instead of with variability in head pose and face detector output, we proceed with detection of the locations of the eyes. This is again done with the OpenCV implementation of a Haar-cascade object detector, trained for either a left or a right eye. After the left eye location p_l and right eye location p_r are determined, the image is rotated to set the angle α, defined as the angle between the line connecting the eyes and the horizontal, to be 0 degrees, scaled to make the distance between the eye locations 100 pixels, and then cropped to be 200 by 200 pixels, with p_r at position $\{p_r^x, p_r^y\} = \{80, 60\}$ to obtain the registered face image. The eye locations are included as part of the video features provided for candidates.

As dense local appearance descriptors we chose to use uniform Local Binary Patterns (LBP) [12]. They have been used extensively for face analysis in recent years, e. g., for face recognition [1], emotion detection [16], or detection of facial muscle actions (FACS Action Units) [9]. They were also used as the baseline features for the recently held challenge on facial expression recognition and analysis (FERA 2011, [17]). Consisting of 8 binary comparisons per pixel, they are fast to compute. By employing uniform LBPs instead of full LBPs and aggregating the LBP operator responses in histograms taken over regions of the face, the dimensionality of the features is rather low (59 dimensions per image block). In our baseline method and feature extraction implementation we divided the registered face region into 10 x 10 blocks, resulting in 5 900 features.

Not provided, but used in the baseline method, are the head tilt α, and the distance between the eyes in the original image $d = ||p_r - p_l||^2$. p_r and p_l thereby are the position of the right and left eyes, accordingly.

5   Challenge Baselines

For transparency and easy reproducibility, we use Support Vector Machines (SVM) classification without feature selection. For the *Audio Sub-Challenge*, we used SVMs with linear Kernel, Sequential Minimal Optimization (SMO) for learning, and optimised the complexity on the development partition of the corpus. The SMO implementation in the WEKA toolkit is used [8]. For the *Video Sub-Challenge*, a SVM with a radial basis function (RBF) kernel was used instead implemented in the LibSVM tool [2]. For the *Audiovisual Sub-Challenge*, we first obtained predictions of the audio and video classifiers separately on both the development set and the audio-visual test set, in terms of posterior probabilities per word. We then fused the two modalities by concatenating the two posterior probabilities and trained a linear SVM on the development set data.

Because of the large number of data (over 1.3 million frames) and relatively high feature dimensionality (5 908 features per frame), due to memory constraints it is impossible to train a model using all data on a desktop PC. Instead, we sampled 1 000 frames from the training partition and 1 000 frames from the development partition. These were evenly divided over training/development videos (e.g., $k = \lfloor 1\,000/31 \rfloor = 32$ for training and $k = \lfloor 1\,000/32 \rfloor = 31$ for test). Within a video of n frames length, instances sampled had index $\lfloor i * n/k \rfloor$ with $i \in \{1 \ldots k\}$. For audio, training with the full data set is possible, however, to reproduce similar conditions as for video, we sub-sampled the data by using only every third word from the training and development partition.

Results per Sub-Challenge are given in Table 6 for training on the train partition and testing on the development partition – this can be freely done by participants – as well as for training on the unification of the training and the development partition and testing on the test partition sub-set for each Sub-Challenge. These results can be uploaded five times by the participants. To allow a comparison between the different approaches, we have provided the results of using only audio, only video, and using both for the *Audiovisual Sub-Challenge*.

The baseline results show that, while reasonable results are attained on the development set, a fair amount of overfitting appears to occur. Note that some scores are below chance. Further note that, the test sets for the *Audio* and the *Video Sub-Challenge* are different, and their results can thus not be used to compare the performance of audio vs. video based methods.

For the *Audiovisual Sub-Challenge*, we show the results of using only the audio baseline classifiers, video baseline classifiers, and fusing the audio and video modalities (last three rows of Table 6). The results show that, on the audio-visual test set, video has a better performance for all dimensions except for EXPECTATION. Fusing the audio and video results shows mixed results: for POWER and VALENCE we observe a marked improvement. For ACTIVITY and EXPECTATION the results are lower than the maximum of either audio or video, though.

Table 6. Baseline results per Sub-Challenge: (*A*) denotes *Audio*, (*V*) *Video*, and (*AV*) *Audiovisual Sub-Challenge*. WA stands for weighted accuracy, UA for unweighted accuracy. The mean over the four dimensions in the last coloumn is the overall competition measure used to rank participants in the three Sub-Challenges as typeset in boldface.

Accuracy [%]	ACTIVITY **WA**	UA	EXPECTATION **WA**	UA	POWER **WA**	UA	VALENCE **WA**	UA	**Mean** **WA**
Audio Sub-Challenge									
Development	63.7	64.0	63.2	52.7	65.6	55.8	58.1	52.9	62.7
Test	**55.0**	57.0	**52.9**	54.5	**28.0**	49.1	**44.3**	47.2	**45.1**
Video Sub-Challenge									
Development	60.2	57.9	58.3	56.7	56.0	52.8	63.6	60.9	59.5
Test	**42.2**	52.5	**53.6**	49.3	**36.4**	37.0	**52.5**	51.2	**46.2**
Audiovisual Sub-Challenge									
Test (*A*)	51.2	51.2	59.2	49.5	52.7	45.9	55.8	46.5	54.7
Test (*V*)	77.1	77.2	36.8	45.5	53.7	52.9	60.8	47.6	57.1
Test (*AV*)	**67.2**	67.2	**36.3**	48.5	**62.2**	50.0	**66.0**	49.2	**57.9**

6   Conclusion

We introduced AVEC 2011 – the first combined open Audio/Visual Emotion Challenge, its conditions, data, baseline features and results. By intention, we had preferred open-source software and highest transparency and realism for the baselines by refraining from feature space optimisation and optimising on test data. These baseline results indicate that this is a challenging problem indeed: On the test partitions, the official baseline sur-passes chance-level on average over binarised dimensions only for the *Audiovisual Sub-Challenge*.

Following the Challenge, we plan to combine all participants' results of the challenge by voting or meta-learning.

References

1. Ahonen, T., Hadid, A., Pietikäinen, M.: Face description with local binary patterns: Application to face recognition. IEEE Transactions on Pattern Analysis and Machine Intelligence 28(12), 2037–2041 (2006)
2. Chang, C.C., Lin, C.J.: LibSVM: a library for support vector machines (2001), software available at http://www.csie.ntu.edu.tw/~cjlin/libsvm
3. Cowie, R., Douglas-Cowie, E., Savvidou, S., McMahon, E., Sawey, M., Schröder, M.: Feeltrace: An instrument for recording perceived emotion in real time. In: Proc. ISCA Workshop on Speech and Emotion, Belfast, UK, pp. 19–24 (2000)
4. Douglas-Cowie, E., Cowie, R., Cox, C., Amier, N., Heylen, D.: The sensitive artificial listener: an induction technique for generating emotionally coloured conversation. In: LREC Workshop on Corpora for Research on Emotion and Affect, pp. 1–4. ELRA, Paris (2008)
5. Eyben, F., Wöllmer, M., Schuller, B.: OpenEAR - Introducing the Munich Open-Source Emotion and Affect Recognition Toolkit. In: Proc. ACII, Amsterdam, The Netherlands, pp. 576–581 (2009)

6. Eyben, F., Wöllmer, M., Schuller, B.: OpenSMILE – The Munich Versatile and Fast Open-Source Audio Feature Extractor. In: Proc. ACM Multimedia (MM), Florence, Italy, pp. 1459–1462 (2010)

7. Fontaine, J., Scherer, K.R., Roesch, E., Ellsworth, P.: The world of emotions is not two-dimensional. Psychological Science 18(2), 1050–1057 (2007)

8. Hall, M., Frank, E., Holmes, G., Pfahringer, B., Reutemann, P., Witten, I.H.: The weka data mining software: An update. SIGKDD Explorations 11(1) (2009)

9. Jiang, B., Valstar, M., Pantic, M.: Action unit detection using sparse appearance descriptors in space-time video volumes. In: Proc. IEEE Int. Conf. on Automatic Face and Gesture Recognition, Santa Barbara, USA, pp. 314–321 (2011)

10. Lichtenauer, J., Valstar, M.F., Shen, J., Pantic, M.: Cost-effective solution to synchornized audio-visual capture using multiple sensors. In: Proc. IEEE Int. Conf. on Advanced Video and Signal Based Surveillance, pp. 324–329 (2009)

11. McKeown, G., Valstar, M., Pantic, M., Cowie, R.: The SEMAINE corpus of emotionally coloured character interactions. In: Proc. IEEE Int. Conf. Multimedia & Expo., pp. 1–6 (2010)

12. Ojala, T., Pietikainen, M., Maenpaa, T.: Multiresolution gray-scale and rotation invariant texture classification with local binary patterns. IEEE Transactions on Pattern Analysis and Machine Intelligence 24(7), 971–987 (2002)

13. Schuller, B., Steidl, S., Batliner, A.: The INTERSPEECH 2009 Emotion Challenge. In: Proc. INTERSPEECH 2009, Brighton, UK, pp. 312–315 (2009)

14. Schuller, B., Steidl, S., Batliner, A., Burkhardt, F., Devillers, L., Müller, C., Narayanan, S.: The INTERSPEECH 2010 Paralinguistic Challenge. In: Proc. INTERSPEECH 2010, Makuhari, Japan, pp. 2794–2797 (2010)

15. Schuller, B., Steidl, S., Batliner, A., Schiel, F., Krajewski, J.: The INTERSPEECH 2011 Speaker State Challenge. In: Proc. INTERSPEECH 2011. ISCA, Florence (2011)

16. Shan, C., Gong, S., Mcowan, P.W.: Facial expression recognition based on local binary patterns: A comprehensive study. Image and Vision Computing 27(6), 803–816 (2009)

17. Valstar, M., Jiang, B., Mehu, M., Pantic, M., Scherer, K.: The first facial expression recognition and analysis challenge. In: Proc. IEEE Int. Conf. on Automatic Face and Gesture Recognition, pp. 921–926 (2011)

18. Young, S., Evermann, G., Gales, M., Hain, T., Kershaw, D., Liu, X., Moore, G., Odell, J., Ollason, D., Povey, D., Valtchev, V., Woodland, P.: The HTK book (v3.4). Cambridge University Press, Cambridge (2006)

Investigating Glottal Parameters and Teager Energy Operators in Emotion Recognition

Rui Sun and Elliot Moore II

Georgia Institute of Technology
School of Electrical and Computer Engineering
210 Technology Circle, Savannah, GA, 31407
rsun7@gatech.edu, em80@mail.gatech.edu

Abstract. The purpose of this paper is to study the performance of glottal waveform parameters and TEO in distinguishing binary classes of four emotion dimensions (activation, expectation, power, and valence) using authentic emotional speech. The two feature sets were compared with a 1941-dimension acoustic feature set including prosodic, spectral, and other voicing related features extracted using openSMILE toolkit. The comparison work highlight the discrimination ability of TEO in emotion dimensions activation and power, and glottal parameters in expectation and valence for authentic speech data. Using the same classification methodology, TEO and glottal parameter outperformed or performed similarly to the prosodic, spectral and other voicing related features (i.e., the feature set obtained using openSMILE).

Keywords: Speech, Emotion detection, Glottal waveform parameters, Teager energy operator, SEMAINE, openSMILE.

1   Introduction

Automated emotion detection is the attempt to quantify an abstract interpretation into objectively measured components of recorded human interaction. Literature shows that prosodics (e.g., pitch, energy, speaking rate, etc.) and spectral acoustics (e.g., MFCC) are the most common form of speech analysis [1,2,3]. Researchers have been focusing on emotion detection using the well-studied prosodic and spectral features [1,4,5,6,7,8,9]. However, speech is a rich source and complex structure carrying many other aspects of description and measurements. Glottal waveform parameters and Teager Energy Operators (TEO) are two sets of the features characterizing the emotional speech. Work on the use of glottal features [10,11,12,13,14,15] (i.e., features extracted from the estimated signal representing the air-flow through the vocal folds) and TEO [16,17] in classifying emotion has shown that these features can provide valuable insight into distinguishing different types of emotional expression. This motivates the study of emotion recognition performance using glottal parameters and TEO, comparing with other prosodic, spectral, and voicing related acoustics (e.g., openSMILE [18,19]). Additionally, emotion recognition using glottal and TEO features has

S. D'Mello et al. (Eds.): ACII 2011, Part II, LNCS 6975, pp. 425–434, 2011.

been mainly focused on using acted speech in a lab environment and labeled with emotion words (e.g., happy, sad) or 1-3 emotion dimensions (e.g., activation, valence, power) [14,15,20], while little work has been reported using authentic emotional speech in more than three emotion dimensions. Real-life application is the goal of emotion research. Therefore, it's interesting to examine the discrimination ability of glottal parameters and TEO using *real* emotional speech data in more dimensions. The purpose of this paper is to study the performance of glottal waveform parameters and TEO in distinguishing binary classes in four emotion dimensions (activation, expectation, power, and valence) using the authentic emotional speech from SEMAINE corpus.

2   Data and Feature

The speech data used in this study is from the SEMAINE corpus [21]. The speech is the recording of conversations between humans (the user) and artificially intelligent agents (the operators). The emotion labels of the speech are provided in four emotion dimensions: activation, expectation, power, and valence. In each dimension, a binary label 1/0 represents the emotion possessing a higher/lower degree than the averaged. The provided corpus is divided into three parts: the training (for train model), the development (to test model), and the test (the challenge data, see [22]). More information about this data is available in [22]. Because of the large size of data, the speech data was down-sampled from 48kHz to 16kHz in this study.

This paper studied three sets of acoustic features, the given openSMILE feature set [18,19], glottal waveform parameters, and Teager Energy Operators (TEO). The given openSMILE features consist of prosodic related, spectral related, and other voice related (e.g., probability of voicing, jitter, and shimmer) features extracted using the openSMILE toolkit [18,19] and provided with the speech data. The 1941-dimensional acoustic feature set was created at the word-level (more information in [22]).

The second acoustic set used in this study is the glottal waveform parameter. The glottal waveform provides a representation of the shaping of the volume velocity of airflow *through* the vocal folds during voiced speech. Research has shown that the glottal waveform dynamics can play an important role in voice characterization [10,11,12,13,14,15]. Fig. 1 shows an example of the glottal waveform (Fig. 1(b)) and glottal waveform derivative estimate (Fig. 1(c)) for one cycle of voiced speech (Fig. 1(a)). One total cycle (TC) consists of an open phase (O) and closed phase (C). The open phase is divided into an opening phase (OP) (i.e., abduction) and closing phase (CP) (i.e., adduction). The opening phase may sometimes be further divided into the length of the primary opening (T_{o1}, i.e. OP) and a secondary opening (T_{o2}). The distinction between T_{o1} and T_{o2} is marked by a an increase in the slope during the opening phase (i.e. smaller slope for (T_{o1}, larger slope for T_{o2}).

The extraction of the glottal features for each speech utterance was processed in four steps [15]: (1) each utterance was divided into frames four pitch periods

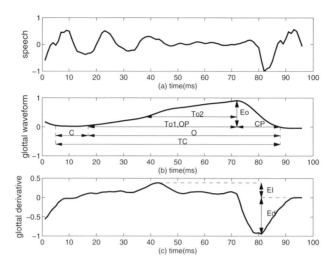

Fig. 1. Example of the time-based parameters extracted from the glottal waveform during a single speech cycle. (a) One-pitch cycle of speech (b) Glottal waveform estimate (c) Glottal waveform derivative.

long for feature extraction purposes (2) glottal closure instants (GCI's) were obtained using the DYPSA algorithm [23] on each frame (3) glottal waveform estimates were obtained for each frame using the Rank-Based Glottal Quality Assessment (RBGQA) algorithm [14], which iterates around approximate locations of GCI's to find the optimal analysis window position for deconvolution via the covariance method of linear predictive analysis (LPA) (for simplicity, an LPA order of 16 was used for all speakers) (4) for each frame, the 11 glottal features (the time-based nine features listed in Table 1 followed by two spectral-based features described below) were computed using version 0.3.1 of the APARAT toolbox [24]. All features were quantified using seven statistics (i.e, the mean, median, minimum, maximum, standard deviation, range, and inter-quartile) across all frames of a word to form the representation of this utterance. The feature extraction produced 77 glottal waveform features.

Spectral-based features calculated by APARAT on the glottal waveform included: *DH12* (the difference in the first and second glottal formants, in dB [26]) and *HRF* (the Harmonic Richness Factor, in dB [27]). These parameters were calculated as shown in Eq. 1 and Eq. 2, where $X(F0)$ is the spectral amplitude at the fundamental frequency ($F0$), $X(2*F0)$ is the amplitude at two times the fundamental frequency, and $X(f_i)$ is the spectral amplitude in the ith harmonics (f_1 is the fundamental frequency $F0$).

$$DH12 = 10\log\frac{|X(F0)|^2}{|X(2*F0)|^2}, \tag{1}$$

$$HRF = 10\log\frac{\sum_{i>1}|X(f_i)|^2}{|X(f_1)|^2}. \tag{2}$$

Table 1. Time-based glottal features extracted from the glottal waveform estimations (see Fig. 1)

Abbr.	Explanation	Equation
OQ1	(open quotient, from primary glottal opening)	$OQ1 = \frac{T_{o1}+CP}{TC}$
OQ2	(open quotient, from secondary glottal opening)	$OQ2 = \frac{T_{o2}+CP}{TC}$
AQ	(amplitude quotient)	$AQ = \frac{E_o}{E_d}$
NAQ	(normalized amplitude quotient)	$NAQ = \frac{AQ}{TC}$
ClQ	(closing quotient)	$ClQ = \frac{CP}{TC}$
OQa	(open quotient based on Liljencrants-Fant model)	$OQa = \frac{E_o}{TC}(\frac{\pi}{2EI} + \frac{1}{E_d})$
SQ1	(speed quotient, from primary glottal opening)	$SQ_1 = \frac{T_{o1}}{TC}$
SQ2	(speech quotient, from secondary glottal opening)	$SQ_2 = \frac{T_{o2}}{TC}$
QOQ	(quasi-open quotient)	[25]

The third domain of acoustic features in this study is the measurements of Teager Energy Operator (TEO) [16]. The TEO $\Psi[x(n)]$ of discrete-time speech signal $x(n)$ can be calculated following Eq. 3 derived by Kaiser [28],

$$\Psi[x(n)] = x^2(n) - x(n+1)x(n-1). \tag{3}$$

Three sets of measurements of TEO [17] were calculated: 1) Variation of FM component (FM-Var), given the FM demodulation component $\omega(n)$ obtained by Eq. 4 [29,30,31] , eight statistics (mean, minimum, maximum, range, log-range, standard deviation, median, and inter-quartile) were calculated for each frame to form FM-Var feature set; 2) Normalized TEO autocorrelation envelope area (Auto-Env), TEO was applied with four-band filters (0-2kHz, 2-4kHz, 4-6kHz, 6-8kHz) and the normalized area under envelope of TEO autocorrelation was computed for each band, respectively; 3) Critical band based TEO autocorrelation envelope (CB-Auto-Env), 16-critical band filterbank [32] was applied to TEO and the normalized area under envelope of TEO autocorrelation was computed for each band, respectively.

$$\omega(n) = arcsin\sqrt{\frac{\Psi[x(n+1)] - \Psi[x(n-1)]}{4 * \Psi[x(n)]}}. \tag{4}$$

All TEO features were quantified using seven statistics (i.e, the mean, median, minimum, maximum, standard deviation, range, and inter-quartile) across all frames of a word to obtain 196 TEO features. Together with the first two sets, 2214-dimension acoustic features were extracted at the word-level. Due to the algorithm for feature extraction, some words did not produce valid glottal parameters or TEO (e.g., impulsive phoneme). Therefore, the number of words with all three features sets available is smaller than the given speech data. The number of words in the training dataset and development dataset is summarized in Tabel 2. These datasets were used in the following analysis including the recalculated baseline of openSMILE (instead of the baseline given in [22]).

Table 2. Number of words in the training dataset ('Train') and the development dataset ('Develop') in total and in each binary class ('class-1/0')

	Train				Develop			
	activate	expect	power	valence	activate	expect	power	valence
total	15307	15307	15307	15307	12663	12663	12663	12663
class-1	7695	6253	8611	8357	7275	4240	8595	8131
class-0	7612	9054	6696	6950	5388	8423	4068	4532

3   Methodology

The purpose of this study was to evaluate the discrimination ability of glottal and TEO features on binary categories in four emotion dimensions using authentic emotion speech SEMAINE corpus.

First, the feature was subjected to a Kruskal-Wallis (KW) significance test individually for a fundamental sight of the distinguishing possibility. The significant test was conducted using the combination of the training data and the test data. Number of features showing statistically significant difference (i.e., $p < 0.01$) in each feature set was counted and the percentage of feature showing significant difference was calculated. The purpose of this test was to assess the individual discrimination ability of features in each feature set.

Although features showing statistically significant difference individually have been selected in the above test, features in subset may exhibit more discrimination ability than individually. To compare the classification results between three feature sets in subset, this experiment built a model on training data using a Support Vector Machine (SVM) and tested it on the development data using one set of features at a time (using LibSVM tool [34] in WEKA [33]). Due to the large number of features in each feature set, feature selection using Sequential Forward Floating Selection (SFFS) was applied to each feature set using WEKA [33] before classification. The evaluator of SFFS was to select the features possessing higher correlation with the emotion labels and lower inter-correlation ('CfsSubsetEval' option in WEKA), which was not classifier related.

Finally, the discrimination ability of feature sets was compared by using a Sequential Feature Selection (SFS) algorithm for selecting any subset of features out of the combination of three feature sets together. SFS starts with an empty feature set and sequentially adds features that have not yet been selected. Every feature combination set is evaluated until there is no improvement in the criterion function. For this study, the criterion was set to the accuracy rate from a quadratic discriminant computed as the number of correct classifications divided by the total number of observations (i.e., words). The SFS algorithm added features in an effort to increase the accuracy rate as much as possible. Due to the large size of feature dimension (2214), this study 1) chose SFS instead of SFFS for feature selection, and 2) SFS was applied onto features showing statistically significant difference obtained in the Kruskal-Wallis test instead of the full set (2214 dimensions). The SFS was run on the feature subset 20 times (20 trials) to ensure enough randomization.

4   Result

The percentage of features with statistically significant difference between the binary classes for four dimensions is shown in Fig. 2. Considering the percentage for each feature set across the four dimensions, the percentage of openSMILE is fairly similar across all dimensions. TEO possesses a much higher percentage in expectation and power than activation. For glottal parameters, the percentage for expectation is highest followed by valence. This observation indicates the discrimination power of TEO in expectation and power and glottal parameters in expectation. This discrimination power is further evaluated by classification experiments using the three feature sets individually.

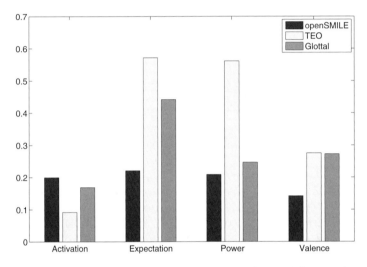

Fig. 2. Percentage of features with statistically significant difference between two classes in each feature set

The binary classification experiments were conducted using one feature set at a time. The accuracy rate (AR) and F-measure [35] of binary classification is calculated and shown in Table 3. The highest AR (in bold) is from TEO in activation and power, and glottal parameters in valence, while TEO and glottal features yielded equal ARs in expectation. This result is reasonable for the higher percentage of TEO showing significant difference in expectation and power and glottal in expectation and valence than other dimensions (in Fig. 2). Except for activation, the F-measures of other dimensions show the bias of classification results (i.e., expectation-1, power and valence-0). This could be the reason to cause the AR of activation lower than other three dimensions.

To get a closer look at the performance of glottal parameters and TEO comparing with openSMILE, the feature selection result using SFS on the combination of three feature sets was conducted. Because of the large dimension of

Table 3. The accuracy rate (AR) and F-measure (F-1/0) of classification using three sets of features separately (%) (op: openSMILE as the *baseline*, glo: glottal parameters, F-1/0: F-measure for class 1/0)

	activation			expectation			power			valence		
	op	TEO	glo	op	TEO	glo	op	TEO	glo	op	TEO	glo
AR	*55.0*	**59.3**	56.5	*66.0*	**66.3**	**66.3**	*66.3*	**67.4**	66.8	*62.9*	63.7	**64.1**
F-1	51.2	46.4	56.8	79.3	79.7	79.7	8.5	17.2	8.8	9.3	4.0	0.2
F-0	58.3	67.2	56.2	5.3	1.0	1.3	79.4	79.7	79.7	76.7	77.6	78.1

Table 4. The feature selected result: the averaged accuracy rate (AR %) over 20 trials and the number of features selected in all 20 trials

	activation	expectation	power	valence
AR	64.3	62.3	61.2	58.6
No. OpenSMILE	4	5	2	1
No. TEO	0	3	2	0
No. glottal	0	1	0	1

feature set, the original 2241 features were represented by a subset consisting of features showing significant difference in the KW test. Table 4 shows the resulting mean accuracy rates from the SFS procedure along with the number of features selected over 20 trials. From Table 4, fewer features were selected in valence than others. This result supports the previous work that valence is less captured by acoustics than other dimensions (e.g., arousal [36]). Comparing the three sets, more TEO features were selected for activation and power, and more glottal parameters were selected for expectation and valence. This indicates the stronger discrimination ability of TEO in activation and power, and of glottal parameters in expectation and valence. This also explains the highest AR in Table 3 achieved by TEO in activation and power and by glottal in expectation and valence. The AR by using SFS shows that combining three feature sets, the accuracy rate of activation is increased. The AR of other three dimensions is lower. This could be explained that the bias of classification results is reduced for the other three dimensions.

5   Conclusion

This paper examined the performance of glottal waveform parameters and TEO in distinguishing binary classes in four emotion dimensions (activation, expectation, power, and valence) using authentic emotional speech SEMAINE corpus. The result highlights the discrimination ability of TEO in emotion dimensions activation and power, and glottal parameters in expectation and valence for the authentic speech data. In the same classification experiment, TEO and glottal parameter outperformed or performed similarly to the prosodic, spectral and other voicing related features (i.e., the feature set obtained using openSMILE). Future work for this continuing study will involve the study of detailed aspect of each feature set using more complex classifier structure.

References

1. Cowie, R., Douglas-Cowie, E., Tsapatsoulis, N., Votsis, G., Kollias, S., Fellenz, W., Taylor, J.G.: Emotion recognition in human-computer interaction. IEEE Signal Processing Magazine 18, 32–80 (2001)
2. Tao, J., Tan, T.: Affective computing: A review. In: Tao, J., Tan, T., Picard, R.W. (eds.) ACII 2005. LNCS, vol. 3784, pp. 981–995. Springer, Heidelberg (2005)
3. Calvo, R.A., D'Mello, S.: Affect detection: An interdisciplinary review of models, methods, and their applications. IEEE Transactions on Affective Computing 1, 18–37 (2010)
4. Busso, C., Sungbok, L., Narayanan, S.: Analysis of emotionally salient aspects of fundamental frequency for emotion detection. IEEE Transactions on Audio, Speech, and Language Processing 17, 582–596 (2009)
5. Litman, D.J., Forbes-Riley, K.: Recognizing student emotions and attitudes on the basis of utterances in spoken tutoring dialogues with both human and computer tutors. Speech Communication 48, 559–590 (2006)
6. Fragopanagos, N., Taylor, J.G.: Emotion recognition in human-computer interaction. Neural Networks 18, 389–405 (2005)
7. Nicolaou, M., Gunes, H., Pantic, M.: Continuous prediction of spontaneous affect from multiple cues and modalities in valence-arousal space. IEEE Transactions on Affective Computing, 1–1 (2011)
8. Espinosa, H.P., Garcia, C.A.R., Pineda, L.V.: Bilingual acoustic feature selection for emotion estimation using a 3d continuous model. In: 2011 IEEE International Conference on Automatic Face and Gesture Recognition and Workshops, pp. 786–791 (2011)
9. Wu, C.H., Liang, W.B.: Emotion recognition of affective speech based on multiple classifiers using acoustic-prosodic information and semantic labels. IEEE Transactions on Affective Computing 2, 10–21 (2011)
10. Cummings, K.E., Clements, M.A.: Analysis of the glottal excitation of emotionally styled and stressed speech. The Journal of the Acoustical Society of America 98, 88–98 (1995)
11. Moore, E., Clements, M., Peifer, J., Weisser, L.: Investigating the role of glottal features in classifying clinical depression. In: Proceedings of the 25th Annual International Conference of the IEEE Engineering in Medicine and Biology Society, vol. 3, pp. 2849–2852 (2003)
12. Ozdas, A., Shiavi, R.G., Silverman, S.E., Silverman, M.K., Wilkes, D.M.: Investigation of vocal jitter and glottal flow spectrum as possible cues for depression and near-term suicidal risk. IEEE Transactions on Biomedical Engineering 51, 1530–1540 (2004)
13. Moore, E., Clements, M.A., Peifer, J.W., Weisser, L.: Critical analysis of the impact of glottal features in the classification of clinical depression in speech. IEEE Transactions on Biomedical Engineering 55, 96–107 (2008)
14. Moore, E., Torres, J.: A performance assessment of objective measures for evaluating the quality of glottal waveform estimates. Speech Communication (2007) (in press)

15. Sun, R., Moore, E., Torres, J.: Investigating glottal parameters for differentiating emotional categories with similar prosodics. In: IEEE International Conference on Acoustics, Speech and Signal Processing, ICASSP 2009, Taipei, Taiwan (2009)

16. Caims, D., Hansen, J.H.L.: Nonlinear analysis and classification of speech under stressed conditions. The Journal of the Acoustical Society of America 96, 3392–3399 (1994)

17. Zhou, G., Hansen, J.H.L., Kaiser, J.F.: Nonlinear feature based classification of speech under stress. IEEE Transactions on Speech and Audio Processing 9, 201–216 (2001)

18. Eyben, F., Wollmer, M., Schuller, B.: Openear - introducing the munich open-source emotion and affect recognition toolkit. In: 3rd International Conference on Affective Computing and Intelligent Interaction and Workshops, ACII 2009, pp. 1–6 (2009)

19. Eyben, F., Wollmer, M., Schuller, B.: Opensmile-the munich versatile and fast open-source audio feature extractor. In: ACM Multimedia (MM), Florence, Italy, pp. 1459–1462 (2010)

20. Sundberg, J., Patel, S., Bjorkner, E., Scherer, K.: Interdependencies among voice source parameters in emotional speech. IEEE Transactions on Affective Computing, 1–1 (2011)

21. McKeown, G., Valstar, M.F., Cowie, R., Pantic, M.: The semaine corpus of emotionally coloured character interactions. In: 2010 IEEE International Conference on Multimedia and Expo. (ICME), pp. 1079–1084 (2010)

22. Schuller, B., Valstar, M.F., Eyben, F., McKeown, G., Cowie, R., Pantic, M.: Avec 2011-the first international audio/visual emotion chanllenge. In: D´Mello, S., et al. (eds.) ACII 2011, Part II. LNCS, vol. 6975, pp. 415–424. Springer, Heidelberg (2011)

23. Patrick, A.N., Anastasis, K., Jon, G., Mike, B.: Estimation of glottal closure instants in voiced speech using the dypsa algorithm. IEEE Transactions on Audio, Speech, and Language Processing 15, 34–43 (2007)

24. Airas, M., Pulakka, H., Backstrom, T., Alku, P.: A toolkit for voice inverse filtering and parametrisation. In: INTERSPEECH (2005)

25. Laukkanen, A.M., Vilkman, E., Alku, P., Oksanen, H.: Physical variations related to stress and emotional state: a preliminary study. Journal of Phonetics 24, 313–335 (1996)

26. Titze, I.R., Sundberg, J.: Vocal intensity in speakers and singers. The Journal of the Acoustical Society of America 91, 2936–2946 (1992)

27. Childers, D.G.: Vocal quality factors: Analysis, synthesis, and perception. The Journal of the Acoustical Society of America 90, 2394–2410 (1991)

28. Kaiser, J.F.: On a simple algorithm to calculate the 'energy' of a signal. In: International Conference on Acoustics, Speech, and Signal Processing, ICASSP-1990, vol.1, pp: 381–384 (1990)

29. Maragos, P., Kaiser, J.F., Quatieri, T.F.: Energy separation in signal modulations with application to speech analysis. IEEE Transactions on Signal Processing 41, 3024–3051 (1993)

30. Hanson, H.M., Maragos, P., Potamianos, A.: A system for finding speech formants and modulations via energy separation. IEEE Transactions on Speech and Audio Processing 2, 436–443 (1994)

31. Potamianos, A., Maragos, P.: Speech formant frequency and bandwidth tracking using multiband energy demodulation. In: International Conference on Acoustics, Speech, and Signal Processing, ICASSP-1995, vol. 1, pp. 784–787 (1995)

32. Lippmann, R., Martin, E., Paul, D.: Multi-style training for robust isolated-word speech recognition. In: IEEE International Conference on Acoustics, Speech, and Signal Processing, ICASSP 1987, vol. 12, pp. 705–708 (1987)
33. Hall, M., Frank, E., Holmes, G., Pfahringer, B., Reutemann, P., Witten, I.H.: The weka data mining software: An update. SIGKDD Explorations 11 (2009)
34. Chang, C.C., Lin, C.J.: LIBSVM: A library for support vector machines. ACM Transactions on Intelligent Systems and Technology 2, 27:1–27:27 (2011) Software, http://www.csie.ntu.edu.tw/~cjlin/libsvm
35. Batliner, A., Steidl, S., Schuller, B., Seppi, D., Laskowski, K., Vogt, T., Devillers, L., Vidrascu, L., Amir, N., Kessous, L., Aharonson, V.: Combining efforts for improving automatic classification of emotional user states. In: Proc. IS-LTC 2006, Ljubljana, pp. 240–245 (2006)
36. Hirschberg, J., Liscombe, J., Venditti, J.: Experiments in emotional speech. In: ISCA and IEEE Workshop on Spontanous Speech Processing and Recognition, Tokyo, Japan, pp. 119–125 (2003)

Affective Brain-Computer Interfaces (aBCI 2011)

Christian Mühl[1], Anton Nijholt[1], Brendan Allison[2], Stephen Dunne[3], and Dirk Heylen[1]

[1] Human Media Interaction, University of Twente, Enschede, The Netherlands
{muehlc,anijholt,heylen}@cs.utwente.nl
[2] Technical University, Graz, Austria
allison@tugraz.at
[3] Starlab, Barcelona, Spain
stephen.dunne@starlab.es

Abstract. Recently, many groups (see Zander and Kothe. Towards passive brain–computer interfaces: applying brain–computer interface technology to human–machine systems in general. *J. Neural Eng.*, 8, 2011) have worked toward expanding brain-computer interface (BCI) systems to include not only active control, but also passive mental state monitoring to enhance human-computer interaction (HCI). Many studies have shown that brain imaging technologies can reveal information about the affective and cognitive state of a subject, and that the interaction between humans and machines can be aided by the recognition of those user states. New developments including practical sensors, new machine learning software, and improved interaction with the HCI community are leading us to systems that seamlessly integrate passively recorded information to improve interactions with the outside world.

To achieve robust passive BCIs, efforts from applied and basic sciences have to be combined. On the one hand, applied fields such as affective computing aim to develop applications that adapt to changes in the user states and thereby enrich interaction, leading to a more natural and effective usability. On the other hand, basic research in neuroscience advances our understanding of the neural processes associated with emotions. Similar advancements are made for more cognitive mental states such as attention, workload, or fatigue.

This is the second workshop on affective brain-computer interfaces. The first one was held at ACII 2009 in Amsterdam. Like the first workshop, this one explores the advantages and limitations of using neurophysiological signals as a modality for the automatic recognition of affective and cognitive states, and the possibilities of using this information about the user state in innovative and adaptive applications. Whereas in 2009 the focus was on affective and cognitive state estimation alike, in this 2011 workshop we focus more on the induction, measurement, and use of affective states, i.e. emotions and moods. Hence, the main topics of this workshop are (1) emotion elicitation and data collection for affective BCI, (2) detection of mental state via electroencephalography and other modalities, and (3) adaptive interfaces and affective BCI.

This workshop also seeks to foster interaction among researchers with relevant interests, such as BCI, affective computing, neuro-ergonomics, affective and cognitive neuroscience. These experts present state-of-the-art progress and their visions on the various overlaps between those disciplines.

Keywords: affective brain-computer interfacing, passive brain-computer interfacing, affective computing, user state, mental state, cognitive state estimation, emotions, mood, adaptive interfaces, EEG.

S. D´Mello et al. (Eds.): ACII 2011, Part II, LNCS 6975, p. 435, 2011.
© Springer-Verlag Berlin Heidelberg 2011

Online Recognition of Facial Actions for Natural EEG-Based BCI Applications

Dominic Heger, Felix Putze, and Tanja Schultz

Cognitive Systems Lab (CSL)
Karlsruhe Institute of Technology (KIT), Germany
{dominic.heger,felix.putze,tanja.schultz}@kit.edu

Abstract. We present a system for classification of nine voluntary facial actions, i.e. NEUTRAL, SMILE, SAD, SURPRISE, ANGRY, SPEAK, BLINK, LEFT, and RIGHT. The data is assessed by an Emotiv EPOC wireless EEG head-set. We derive spectral features and step function features that represent the main signal characteristics of the recorded data in a straightforward manner. With a two stage classification setup using support vector machines we achieve an overall recognition accuracy of 81.8%. Furthermore, we show a qualitative evaluation of an online system for facial action recognition using the EPOC device.

1 Introduction

There has been a great research interest on non-invasive BCI systems over the last couple of years. Numerous systems have been created that are successfully used as communication devices for people with disabilities, for prostheses control, in rehabilitation, or for mind-games. More recently, passive BCIs gain raising attention [14]. Passive BCIs are expected to provide computer systems with information about a user's cognitive and affective mental states. States such as attention, workload, or emotions have been recognized successfully by BCI systems. While BCIs can enhance the efficiency and user satisfaction (e.g. [10]), the integration of passive BCIs into human-machine interfaces causes many challenges which need to be overcome.

First and foremost, those parts of the EEG signal that do not origin from neurological phenomenons are considered as artifacts. Artifacts generated by the user's muscle activity, movements of the eyes, tongue, or electrical potentials caused by body movements may impact the complete frequency range of EEG signals. Therefore, they can interfere with the features used for BCI systems and cause misleading results. To avoid such artifacts, experimental setups are heavily controlled and often force the users to restrict their natural movement (e.g. refrain from muscle activity or eye blinks). However, for intuitive interaction with BCI systems, this is not acceptable and thus, artifacts are unavoidable and have to be dealt with.

Many current BCI systems simply ignore these effects, which causes poor recognition results when artifacts are present. One approach to deal with those

S. D´Mello et al. (Eds.): ACII 2011, Part II, LNCS 6975, pp. 436–446, 2011.

influences is to try to clean the signals using automatic rejection, frequency filtering, regression techniques using EOG signals, or blind source separation [7]. However, the impact of such techniques on the signals strongly depends on the user's activity causing them. A blind use of artifact removal techniques may have effects that can be as harmful as the original artifacts themselves (e.g. due to overestimation of artifacts or removal of relevant brain activity). In order to avoid deteriorating effects by blind artifact removal we propose to use explicit classification of non-brain activity to enable specialized artifact reduction methods.

From a user's perspective, one may unconsciously learn to control a system that is susceptible to artifacts by mimicking EEG activity, for example by raising the eyebrows or producing eye blinks [13]. Furthermore, there is a strong relationship between facial actions and natural communication signals, such as social cues and emotions [2]. In addition to that, interesting behavioral information can be assessed from eye movements or the eye blinking rate. Both, facial activity and eye movement can be recognized by a passive BCI system from systematic artifacts to get additional information about the user. Therefore, for BCIs, recognition of non-brain activity is important to be removed when unwanted, but to be interpreted when it contains relevant information.

Facial activity can also be assessed using video or EMG electrodes. However, deriving it directly from the EEG signal comes with the benefit of avoiding additional sensors. Furthermore, it yields the most direct connection between the facial activity and the influence on the EEG signal which is important when artifact removal is of interest. Consequently, we present in this paper the explicit recognition of facial actions and thus to provide a means to directly reduce artifacts of facial mimics and eye movements in a passive BCI system. For this purpose we describe a new approach for recognition of 9 different facial actions including facial mimics and eye activity from data recorded by the Emotiv EPOC, a low-cost EEG head-set designed for the consumer market.

2 Related Work

Recognition of facial expressions using visual information is widely researched. Ekman and Friesen developed the Facial Action Coding System (FACS) [6], a taxonomy to characterize nearly any facial activity. The fundamental atomic facial muscles or small muscle groups involved in facial expressions are called Action Units (AUs).

Some articles (e.g. [2], [11]) reviewed findings on the neural basis of spontaneous and voluntary expression of facial actions. The reported activation patterns strongly depend on which facial action is performed and involve several parts of the brain, such as motor cortex, frontal cortex, and areas involved in emotional processing. EEG has only rarely been used to investigate brain activity associated with the expression of facial actions because of the artifact problems [11].

Only few works have addressed classification of facial actions by EEG. The first research paper that proposed a recognizer for voluntary facial expressions in the context of EEG based BCIs was Chin et al. [4]. They presented an extension of the Filter Bank Common Spatial Pattern algorithm to multiclass classification and showed very good classification performance of 86%. They evaluated the system on 6 types of facial expressions, i.e. smile, straight, wince, agape, stern, and frown. Data was recorded using a standard EEG system with 34 electrodes. For classification they used a Naive Bayes Parzen Window classifier which was extended by a decision threshold based classification mechanism, which increased the recognition results for classes with lower accuracies.

Boot [3] presented a system for facial expressions recognition from EEG. They used an EEG cap with 32 electrodes to discriminate between four expression classes corresponding to neutral, angry, smile, and angry-pout. They applied Common Spatial Patterns and used Linear Discriminant Analysis for classification. They found that predominantly muscle activity was classified and that frontal EEG electrodes are most important for classification performance.

The Emotiv EPOC neuro head-set is a low cost EEG acquisition system for the consumer market [1]. In contrast to traditional EEG caps it allows for rather unobtrusive EEG recordings. The wireless device can be attached by the user himself or herself within a very short amount of time. It is comfortable to wear and uses saline electrodes which do not require electrode gel in the user's hair. However, the data acquired by such a consumer device may be more challenging for automatic processing due to the lower signal quality. Emotiv provides software that aims to recognize facial expression of the user. The system can discriminate eye blinks, winks, clenching of teeth, movement of eye brows, smiling, smirking, and laughing [1]. The growing user community of the EPOC has built numerous applications with the device including the control of a wheelchair using mimics. However, the Emotiv software is only available as a black-box and no published information are available which describe the functionality and performance of the algorithms.

In this work, we extend on the existing systems by including classes which describe facial actions such as speaking and different types of eye movement typically appearing in less controlled experimental setups. We also use a much more comfortable recording device with less electrodes than a standard EEG cap to foster more natural setups.

3   Data Acquisition

3.1   Facial Actions

In our experiment participants executed the 9 different facial action classes listed in Table 1. We selected these facial actions because they are relevant for human-machine interaction and occur frequently as social signals in natural interaction (e.g. [2]). Furthermore, they have a significant influence on the EEG signal, which makes artifact handling necessary to obtain the brain signal.

The NEUTRAL facial action class is characterized by relaxed muscles and eyes focused on a point on the screen. SMILE corresponds to a broad smile that mainly involves muscles around the mouth and the cheek. It may be related to happy

Table 1. Facial expression classes and corresponding Action Units

Class name	Action Units involved
Neutral	AU0 (Neutral)
Smile	AU6 (Cheek raiser), AU12 (Lip corner puller)
Sad	AU15 (Lip corner depressor), AU17 (Chin raiser)
Surprise	AU4 (Eyebrow lowerer)
Angry	AU1 (Inner brow raiser) AU2 (Outer brow raiser)
Speak	AU50 (Speaking)
Blink	AU45 (Eye blink with both eyes)
Left	AU61 (Eye movement to the left)
Right	AU62 (Eye movement to the right)

social signaling, however it is well known that the relationship between smiling and affective states is much more complex. A prototypical Sad expression moves the mouth corners downwards and the lower lip upwards. This pout expression can be related to a depressed or offended state. The Angry facial mimic moves the inner eyebrows into direction of the face center and gives an evil or angry impression. For the Surprise class subjects were instructed to tear up the eyebrows so that it creates wrinkles on the forehead. The expression gives the notion of being skeptical, surprised or puzzled. The Speak class contains speech produced by counting numbers aloud. Blink corresponds to one eye blink with both eyes. Left contains horizontal eye movement to the left and Right horizontal eye movement to the right.

Multiple of these classes share the same face region and muscle groups, which is expected to make the classification task more challenging and to give insights on the possible limitations of the assessment of facial actions by EEG technology. As we see from the involved AUs (see table 1), Smile and Sad mainly involve muscles around the mouth, Angry and Surprise movement of the eyebrows, and Blink, Left and Right contain eye movements. Speak also involves complex activity of the facial muscles and additionally movement of the tongue.

3.2   Experiment Design

For development and evaluation of the system, data from five subjects have been recorded at the Karlsruhe Institute of Technology (KIT). Before the experiment all subjects were instructed shortly and practiced to perform the different facial actions according to the descriptions in section 3.1. To reduce 'artifacts' in the data, subjects were asked to avoid unrelated muscle and eye activity during the recording parts of the trials. The execution of the facial actions was very intuitive and natural for the subjects. However, small deviations from the FACS and variability in the execution of the facial actions might occur as the data has not been filtered for correct execution using validated EMG or video recordings.

For each trial an icon and the class name were presented on the computer screen. Subjects started the expression phase on their own by a key press. After

2 seconds of recording, a gray bar was shown for 4 seconds to avoid influences of the previous trial. Subsequently, the next trial started.

This procedure was repeated for 190 trials, i.e. 20 trials for each class, except for NEUTRAL which had 30 trials. To avoid temporal effects in the classification the facial action classes were randomly ordered.

3.3   Spectral Data Analysis

Biological artifacts, such as potentials caused by muscle activity, movements of eye or tongue, cause significant distortions on the electric fields over the scalp, which can easily be recognized in the measured signals by visual inspection. Figure 1 shows log spectrograms for the different classes averaged over all channels and all subjects. The first plot shows the eye activity related classes BLINK, LEFT, and RIGHT in contrast to the NEUTRAL class (dashed curve). A strong increase of power for frequencies below 15 Hz due to the eye activity can be observed. These potentials are caused by the movement of the retinal or cornea-retinal dipole and the eyelids [5]. They produce high-amplitude patterns in time-domain predominantly at the frontal electrodes. The second plot shows the mimics activity related classes SMILE, SAD, SURPRISE, ANGRY, and SPEAK in contrast to the NEUTRAL class (dashed curve). Muscle activity has a strong influence on a wide frequency range, with greatest amplitude between 20 and 30 Hz [8]. For the SPEAK class, we expected influences at low frequencies by movement of the dipole at the tongue (glossokinetic potentials) [12], as well as muscle activity from articulation at higher frequency bands. However, the spectrogram

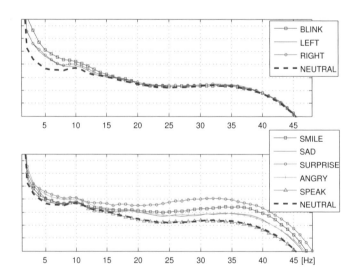

Fig. 1. Log power spectra of the facial action classes. Top: BLINK, LEFT, and RIGHT in contrast to NEUTRAL. Bottom: SMILE, SAD, SURPRISE, ANGRY, and SPEAK in contrast to NEUTRAL.

of SPEAK matches the one of NEUTRAL very closely at frequencies above 10 Hz. This indicates that muscle activity due to articulation had only a small impact in our experiment. The frequency characteristics of all activity classes differ significantly from the NEUTRAL class. Due to the characteristic impact of muscle, eye, and tongue movements on the signals, we expect that brain signals play a minor role in this classification task.

4 Recognition System

Figure 2 shows a block diagram of the system components involved in the recognition process. First, data is acquired from the Emotiv EPOC device using our recording software BiosignalsStudio [9]. The EPOC headset has 16 saline electrodes at positions AF3, F7, F3, FC5, T7, P7, O1, O2, P8, T8, FC6, F4, F8, AF4 referenced to P3 and P4. The raw sensor data from the device has a sampling rate of 128 Hz and is notch filtered at 50 Hz and 60 Hz. We use the raw signal data of each trial, re-reference it to common average montage and remove baseline offsets and linear trends from each channel. Then 3 different types of features are extracted that model the main characteristics of the classes as described in section 3.3:

1. We estimate the spectral density in the rage 0-45 Hz using Welch's method. This results in a feature vector of 34 elements for each channel when using a window length of 0.75 seconds. Including higher frequencies showed no increase of recognition accuracy, which appears to be caused by a strong attenuation of spectral power above 45 Hz due to the notch filters of the EPOC device at 50 Hz and 60 Hz (see Figure 1).
2. Additionally we calculate the ratio between the frequency bands 0-10 Hz and 25-45 Hz as feature.
3. To calculate features that are able to describe horizontal eye movement activity, we use the potentials from electrodes left of the left eye and subtract them from the potentials assessed right of the right eye:

$$X_{HEOG} = (AF3 + F7) - (AF4 + F8)$$

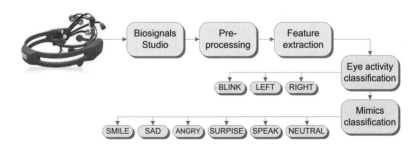

Fig. 2. Block diagram of the recognition process

To this time series, we optimally match two simple step functions, each consisting of two piecewise constant segments, by finding the largest local increase and decrease h_{up} and h_{down} of the level of the time series:

$$h_{up} = \arg\max_k \frac{1}{l} \sum_{i=1}^{l} X_{HEOG}[k - i] - \frac{1}{l} \sum_{i=1}^{l} X_{HEOG}[k + i],$$

$$h_{down} = \arg\min_k \frac{1}{l} \sum_{i=1}^{l} X_{HEOG}[k - i] - \frac{1}{l} \sum_{i=1}^{l} X_{HEOG}[k + i],$$

where l is the length of the interval before and after the step approximated by a constant function. For the experiments in this paper we chose $l = 20$ samples.

We apply a two stage classification scheme to recognize the facial actions. In the first stage, a linear support vector machine (SVM) discriminates the eye activity classes BLINK, LEFT, and RIGHT from a class consisting of the remaining facial actions. If the latter class is classified, the second stage uses a linear SVM to discriminate NEUTRAL, SMILE, SAD, ANGRY, SURPRISE, and SPEAK. Within both stages a one-vs-one approach is used for multiclass classification. SVMs with radial basis function kernels gave slightly worse classification results, which can be accounted to a higher robustness of the linear models when training with a small amount of data.

The two stage classification scheme allows to calculate specialized features for each of the two stages. In the first stage we use a feature vector composed of the spectral density features for each channel (1), h_{up}, and h_{down} (3). In the second stage, we use a feature vector composed of the spectral density features for each channel (1) and the power density ratio (2).

5   Evaluation and Results

We evaluated the two stage classification system using 10-fold cross-validations. This resulted in the following recognition accuracies for the five subjects:

S1 86.8% (SD=5.1%), S2 71.1% (SD=7.6%), S3 81.1% (SD=11.2%), S4 89.5% (SD=10.2%), S5 80.5% (SD=6.6%) (means and standard deviations over the 10 iterations). The overall recognition accuracy was 81.8% (SD=7.1%).

Figure 3 shows precision and recall for each of the facial action classes averaged over the five subjects. Precision is the ratio between the number of times the class was correctly classified and the number of times the class was predicted by the classifier. Recall is the ratio of the number of times the class was correctly classified and the number of times the class should be classified according to the ground truth.

Table 2 shows the classification results in form of a confusion matrix summed over all iterations of the cross-validation of all subjects. The most frequent confusions occur between NEUTRAL and SAD (19% off all misclassifications). For most facial action classes confusions occurred rarely in the experiment or are rather

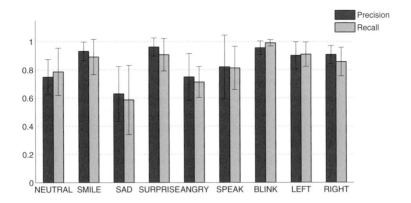

Fig. 3. Precision and recall for each facial action class averaged over the five subjects

Table 2. Confusion matrix of the five subjects using the two stage classifier. Facial action classes are NEUTRAL (N), SMILE (Sm), SAD (Sa), SURPRISE (Su), ANGRY (A), SPEAK (Sp), BLINK (B), LEFT (L), and RIGHT (R).

	true N	true Sm	true Sa	true Su	true A	true Sp	true B	true L	true R
pred. **N**	119	3	23	1	6	10	0	2	6
pred. **Sm**	0	89	5	1	0	1	0	0	0
pred. **Sa**	10	5	56	2	12	4	0	3	0
pred. **Su**	1	0	0	90	2	0	0	0	0
pred. **A**	7	1	8	3	71	1	2	1	2
pred. **Sp**	11	0	6	1	1	80	0	0	3
pred. **B**	0	0	2	0	3	1	98	0	0
pred. **L**	1	0	0	1	3	1	0	90	5
pred. **R**	1	2	0	1	2	2	0	4	84

equally distributed across subjects. However, the confusions of SAD and SPEAK are predominantly caused by single subjects: The results of S2 account for 16 of 21 confusions between NEUTRAL and SPEAK, and S5 causes 18 of 33 confusions between NEUTRAL and SAD. This results in a high inter-subject variance for these classes, which can also be observed in the error bars of Figure 3.

An evaluation using only the frontal electrodes AF3, F7, F3, F4, F8, AF4 (to investigate the possibility of electrode reduction) shows considerably more confusions among the classes NEUTRAL, SMILE, and SAD, which results in a drop of average recognition accuracy from 81.8% to 67.7%. In contrast to Chin et al. [4], who associated the lower recognition results with missing information on activity of the motor cortex, we assume that in our case this is caused by muscle and eye movement activity measured at the non-frontal locations with the full electrode setup. This is indicated by the low coverage of the motor cortex by the EPOC device. Additionally, visual inspection of the temporal channels T7 and

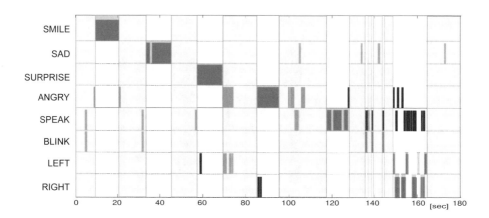

Fig. 4. Online classification results of a sequence of facial actions. Binary classification results are shown as green and blue bars for each second. Green overlays indicate time periods where a particular facial action should have been recognized, yellow overlays indicate time periods where NEUTRAL should have been recognized. Therefore, dark-green bars indicate correct classifications, light-green regions indicate false negatives, light-blue and dark-blue bars indicate false positives.

T8 of SMILE shows strong muscle activity which dominates any activity emitted by the motor cortex.

To test the online capabilities of the facial action recognition system described in this paper, subject S1 performed each of the facial mimics for about 10 seconds. After that, 3 eye blinks were recorded, followed by 2 times moving the eyes to the left and back to center and 2 times to the right and back to the center. We modified the two stage classifier to output the recognition result of the second stage (for mimics classification) in addition to the first stage result (for eye activity recognition), when eye activity is recognized. This enables the system to recognize eye activity and facial mimics at the same time.

Figure 4 shows the online recognition results. Green overlays indicate the periods of time when a particular facial action should have been recognized, yellow overlays indicate periods of time when NEUTRAL should have been recognized. A high precision of all facial action classes can be observed. However, recognition of BLINK always implied a simultaneous recognition of SPEAK by the second classification stage. A similar effect can be found for LEFT and ANGRY. This indicates that the second stage classifier is influenced by the eye activity, which has not occurred in the training data. Removal of eye activity, e.g. by Independent Component Analysis, before classification by the second stage could mitigate this effect. Most recognition errors occur at start and end of an expression. This can be associated with the missing alignment in online recognition (i.e. windows can partly contain facial activity). Furthermore, the onset and offset of a facial actions can cause strong low frequent potentials. To cope with such effects, sequential classifiers, such as Hidden Markov Models, might be used to better model the dynamic character facial expressions.

6 Conclusion

In this paper, we showed that it is possible to use an EEG-based system for the effective classification of a large number of different facial actions. We showed that high recognition rates can be achieved using straightforward spectral features and step function features in a two stage classification scheme. Furthermore, we extended the system for online application and the more challenging recognition of parallel occurring facial actions. Such a recognition system can give additional insights on the user's behavior, as well as on the acquired signals that may be useful for artifact handling.

Further experiments are needed to investigate how the findings transfer to spontaneous facial actions in natural situations. In such a setup the ground truth of the performed facial actions could be assessed by EMG or video recordings.

References

1. Emotiv Software Development Kit User Manual for Release 1.0.0.4
2. Blair, R.: Facial expressions, their communicatory functions and neuro–cognitive substrates. Philosophical Transactions of the Royal Society of London. Series B: Biological Sciences 358(1431), 561 (2003)
3. Boot, L.: Facial expressions in EEG/EMG recordings. Master's thesis, University of Twente (2009)
4. Chin, Z., Ang, K., Guan, C.: Multiclass voluntary facial expression classification based on filter bank common spatial pattern. In: 30th Annual International Conference of the IEEE Engineering in Medicine and Biology Society, EMBS 2008, pp. 1005–1008. IEEE, Los Alamitos (2008)
5. Croft, R., Barry, R.: Removal of ocular artifact from the eeg: a review. Neurophysiologie Clinique/Clinical Neurophysiology 30(1), 5–19 (2000)
6. Ekman, P., Friesen, W.: Facial action coding system. Consulting Psychologists Press, Stanford University, Palo Alto (1977)
7. Fatourechi, M., Bashashati, A., Ward, R., Birch, G.: Emg and eog artifacts in brain computer interface systems: a survey. Clinical Neurophysiology 118(3), 480–494 (2007)
8. Goncharova, I., McFarland, D., Vaughan, T., Wolpaw, J.: Emg contamination of eeg: spectral and topographical characteristics. Clinical Neurophysiology 114(9), 1580–1593 (2003)
9. Heger, D., Putze, F., Amma, C., Wand, M., Plotkin, I., Wielatt, T., Schultz, T.: BiosignalsStudio: A flexible framework for biosignal capturing and processing. In: Dillmann, R., Beyerer, J., Hanebeck, U.D., Schultz, T. (eds.) KI 2010. LNCS, vol. 6359, pp. 33–39. Springer, Heidelberg (2010)
10. Heger, D., Putze, F., Schultz, T.: An adaptive information system for an empathic robot using EEG data. In: Ge, S.S., Li, H., Cabibihan, J.-J., Tan, Y.K. (eds.) ICSR 2010. LNCS, vol. 6414, pp. 151–160. Springer, Heidelberg (2010)

11. Korb, S., Grandjean, D., Scherer, K.: Investigating the production of emotional facial expressions: a combined electroencephalographic (eeg) and electromyographic (emg) approach. In: 8th IEEE International Conference on Automatic Face Gesture Recognition, FG 2008, pp. 1–6 (September 2008)
12. Vanhatalo, S., Voipio, J., Dewaraja, A., Holmes, M., Miller, J.: Topography and elimination of slow eeg responses related to tongue movements. Neuroimage 20(2), 1419–1423 (2003)
13. Wolpaw, J., Birbaumer, N., McFarland, D., Pfurtscheller, G., Vaughan, T.: Brain-computer interfaces for communication and control. Clinical Neurophysiology 113(6), 767–791 (2002)
14. Zander, T., Kothe, C., Jatzev, S., Gaertner, M.: Enhancing human-computer interaction with input from active and passive brain-computer interfaces. Brain-Computer Interfaces, 181–199 (2010)

What You Expect Is What You Get? Potential Use of Contingent Negative Variation for Passive BCI Systems in Gaze-Based HCI

Klas Ihme[1,2] and Thorsten Oliver Zander[1,3]

[1] Team PhyPA, Chair of Human-Machine Systems, TU Berlin, Germany
[2] Clinic for Psychosomatic Medicine and Psychotherapy,
University Hospital Leipzig, Germany
[3] Max-Planck-Institute for Biological Cybernetics, Tuebingen, Germany

Abstract. When using eye movements for cursor control in human-computer interaction (HCI), it may be difficult to find an appropriate substitute for the click operation. Most approaches make use of dwell times. However, in this context the so-called Midas-Touch-Problem occurs which means that the system wrongly interprets fixations due to long processing times or spontaneous dwellings of the user as command. Lately it has been shown that brain-computer interface (BCI) input bears good prospects to overcome this problem using imagined hand movements to elicit a selection. The current approach tries to develop this idea further by exploring potential signals for the use in a passive BCI, which would have the advantage that the brain signals used as input are generated automatically without conscious effort of the user. To explore event-related potentials (ERPs) giving information about the user's intention to select an object, 32-channel electroencephalography (EEG) was recorded from ten participants interacting with a dwell-time-based system. Comparing ERP signals during the dwell time with those occurring during fixations on a neutral cross hair, a sustained negative slow cortical potential at central electrode sites was revealed. This negativity might be a contingent negative variation (CNV) reflecting the participants' anticipation of the upcoming selection. Offline classification suggests that the CNV is detectable in single trial (mean accuracy 74.9 %). In future, research on the CNV should be accomplished to ensure its stable occurence in human-computer interaction and render possible its use as a potential substitue for the click operation.

Keywords: passive brain-computer interfaces, gaze-based human-computer interaction, Midas-Touch-Problem, contingent negative variation.

1 Introduction

Human beings usually direct their attention to an object by looking at it before pointing at it [1]. However, in human-computer interaction (HCI), users generally use the mouse instead of gaze direction as cursor. Formerly this was due to

S. D'Mello et al. (Eds.): ACII 2011, Part II, LNCS 6975, pp. 447–456, 2011.

technical limitations, but as nowadays eye tracking technologies become more exact and affordable, these techniques are of great interest for HCI researchers. To make HCI more natural and intuitive, it would be of great help to provide hands-free interaction possibilities. Thus, direct interaction between human and computer using gaze direction was proposed in the 1990s to extend the bandwidth from user to computer and provide a more natural and hands-free way of interaction [2][3][4].

Still, when using eye gaze as cursor input, an appropriate substitute for the click operation has to be found. Blinking and dwell time provide just limited solutions. The former has the disadvantage of involuntary blinks leading to a large amount of unintended selections. When using the latter, one faces the problems that fixations not related to the intention to select are interpreted as command. Unintended fixations can occur due to spontaneous dwellings at random objects [5]. Moreover, it is hard to find an optimal dwell time for different stimulus complexities. The stimulus processing time might exceed the dwell time leading to an involuntary selection. This problem of unintended selections is called *Midas-Touch-Problem* because the user tends to feel comparable to the ancient King Midas who had the gift that everything he touched, even his food, turned into gold and because of this almost starved to death [2][3]. One can try to solve the problem by prolonging the dwell time, however then experienced users might become annoyed because the speed of the system is too slow leading to a speed-accuracy-trade-off.

With the rise of brain-computer interfaces (BCIs) in the last decades [6] [7], a new communication channel independent from standard human output channels was introduced that seems to bear good prospects for the application in human-computer interaction for healthy users [8]. Especially active and passive BCI systems have the potential to enhance HCI [9]. Zander et al. [10] presented a system in which the cursor control was provided by eye gaze and the click operation was accomplished by an active BCI. In this study, the users had to look at the object they want to select and then imagine a hand movement to elicit the selection. The system was appreciated by the users but due to its active nature loaded extra effort on the user. Passive BCIs, which solely rely on brain potentials generated in the common interaction, might be even more promising in this area as they can improve the human-computer interaction without any extra cost for the user [8].

The current study investigates human electroencephalogram (EEG) activity occurring during gaze-based HCI to find relevant potentials which can be used as input for a passive BCI to elicit the selection. Therefore, it was decided to choose a task, in which participants had to find a target object and select this with a dwell-time-based system. EEG potentials occurring during the dwell time could give rise to processes related to the intention to select or the expectation of the selection. In future BCI systems, these potentials then may give additional information about the user's intent, which could enhance gaze-based HCI. For these potentials to be used in a BCI, it is a must that they are detectable in single trial.

2   Methods

2.1   Participants

Ten volunteers (five male) aged between 24 and 30 (mean 27) participated in the experiment. All of them had normal or corrected-to-normal vision and none of them reported physical or mental illness for the time of the experiment. Participants gave written consent to take part in the study.

2.2   Experimental Set-Up

Brain activity was recorded with a 32-channel-EEG system (Brain Products BrainAmp DC, actiCap, Gilching, Germany) with a sampling rate of 250 Hz. Electrodes were placed at standard positions according to the 5% system of electrode placement [11]. Grounding was established with electrode FCz and electrodes were referenced to nasion. Impedances of all electrodes were lowered to 5 kΩ. Eye movements were tracked with the remote eye tracker IG-30 (IntelliGazeTM System, alea technologies, Teltow, Germany) which was mounted below a 19" monitor with a resolution of 1280 x 1024 pixels (Lenovo Thinkvision, Stuttgart, Germany). The eye tracker is equipped with a video and an infrared camera allowing for eye and head tracking. Eye tracker data were recorded with a sampling rate of 32 Hz. Participants sat in a comfortable chair at a distance of 60 cm away from the screen. Lighting conditions were held constant during the experiment.

2.3   Stimuli

Two different line drawings of black geometric figures, a triangle and a hexagon, with a size of 74x74 pixel served as stimuli. Only one of these stimuli was presented at a time at eight different locations on the screen. See Figure 1a for the possible locations on the screen.

2.4   Task

For the task, one of the two objects was assigned to be the target, while the other was the non-target. Participants' task was to find a target and select it via a dwell time of two seconds. For it was intended to examine the signal during the selection phase, it was decided to choose a rather long dwell time[1], so that possible ERP signals could evolve in this period. Randomly one of the two objects was randomly presented at one of the possible locations. In case the non-target was presented, participants had to fixate a cross hair for two seconds, which was visible all the time in the center of the screen. A trial continued with a presentation of a new object until either a target (or a non-target) was correctly (incorrectly) selected. Participants were given feedback in case their

---

[1] Commercial gaze-based systems generally use shorter dwell times.

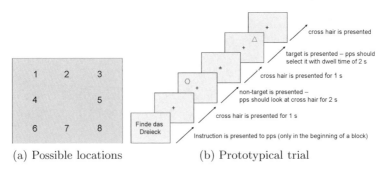

(a) Possible locations   (b) Prototypical trial

Fig. 1. (a) Possible locations of the objects. For each trial, one of the objects was randomly presented at one of these locations. (b) A prototypical trial (pps = participants). "Finde das Dreieck" literally translates to find the triangle. First, pps get instructed, then a cross hair occurs in the center of the screen. After 1 s, one object occurs. If this is the target, pps had to select it with dwell time; in case it is the non-target the cross hair had to be fixated.

selection was incorrect. Participants were not informed that the cross hair was an interactive object (so that the presented objected vanished after dwelling on the cross for 2 s); they were just asked to fixate the cross if the non-target occurs. See Fig. 1b for a prototypical trial. Participants got no visual feedback about their locus of fixation, because Velichkovsky & Hansen [4] stated that this is not necessary in gaze-based systems. Moreover, it was intended not to have an effect of a jumping cursor when fixations are not detected stably at one object due to a possible degrading of the calibration of the eye tracker.

2.5   Structure and Design

Participants had to accomplish eight blocks with ten trials of correct selection each. That means when participants selected the non-target an additional trial was appended at the end of the block. The target stayed constant in each block, so that participants had four blocks for each target. Before each block, participants were informed about the target by a message on the screen. The order of the blocks was randomized in the beginning. A block lasted approximately two minutes. All in all, participants accomplished 80 trials;, i.e., 40 for each of the two targets (triangle, hexagon). The whole procedure including electrode preparation, instruction and eye tracker calibration took roughly 1.5 hours.

2.6   Data Analysis

The data were referenced to a common average reference and filtered to a range between 0.1 and 15 Hz with a fast fourier transform (FFT) for ERP analysis. EEG data was analysed using the open-source toolbox EEGLAB [12]. Single-trial classification was accomplished using the PhyPA Toolbox [13] [14].

To analyse the event-related potentials, epochs of 5 s length were extracted relative to selection: these started 4 s before selection or vanishing of the non-target respectively. Since the dwell time lasted 2 s, the baseline was set to -4 to

-2.5 s before selection as no selection-related processing should take place in this period. Epochs relative to the end of the dwell time were compared to epochs of fixating the fixation cross. The grand average was exploratorily checked for ERP components showing distinct characteristics in the different conditions. In order to compare the amplitude of the components, representative time windows were defined and their averages in the two conditions were compared to each other using a repeated-measures ANOVA (with Greenhouse-Geisser corrected degrees of freedom as proposed in [15]) with the factors condition (target, non-target) and site (left, right, frontal, central; representatively, one electrode was chosen per site, namely C3, C4, Fz, and Cz, respectively). The sites were chosen because no ad-hoc-hypotheses about the possible potentials were generated.

Single-trial offline classification was performed to estimate the expected classification accuracy of an online application. For feature extraction, the pattern matching algorithm for slow cortical potentials proposed by [16] was used. Here, each channel was filtered. Then, the signal representing the potential was partitioned into (possibly overlapping) time windows [16]. The mean of each of these time windows was calculated and concatenated to a feature vector with dimensionality of channels x time windows. The feature vectors were then classified using a regularized linear discriminant analysis (rLDA) [17], as LDA has been shown to provide best possible results on slow cortical potentials [18]. In order to minimize overfitting, classification results were validated using 3 times a 10-fold (5-fold nested) cross-validation [19]. Classification was accomplished on the raw EEG data. Classification was accomplished on the potential elicited during the dwell time. For this, epochs of 3000 ms length (from -3 s to selection) were extracted from the signal and filtered to 0.1 to 8 Hz. Then, the time window between -1900 ms and 0 ms was subdivided into five overlapping time windows (-1.9 to 0 s, -1.9 to -1 s, -1.9 to -1.45 s, -1.9 to -1.65 s and -1.9 to -1.8 s) and classified. The time windows (one comprising the complete negativity and shorter time windows) were to chosen to account for the baseline shift induced by the negativity. Thus, the feature vector taken for classification had a dimensionality of 5 (time windows) x 32 (channels) = 160.

As the two conditions require different eye movements, it is possible that these have an influence on the ERP. In order to check this, horizontal and vertical eye movements (as measured by deflection in X and Y direction of the eye tracking data) during the two conditions were correlated with the EEG signal at the electrodes Cz and Fz across all participants and trials using the MATLAB function corrcoef.

3   Results

Participants committed on average 0.4 errors during the whole experiment. Being afterwards asked why they committed the errors, participants stated two different reasons: either they forgot which object was target or the calibration accuracy of the eye tracker at the target position was low at that moment, so that the target could not be selected. Erroneous trials were excluded from later analysis.

Table 1. Grand average amplitudes (and standard deviation) in μV during dwell time and looking at the cross hair, respectively, at electrodes Fz, Cz, C3, and C4

	Fz	Cz	C3	C4
Negativity selection	-15.4 (14.7)	-17.3 (15.9)	-5.0 (16.2)	-0.1 (23.7)
look at cross hair	-0.2 (14.8)	-2.0 (6.2)	-4.3 (8.3)	-3.7 (7.9)

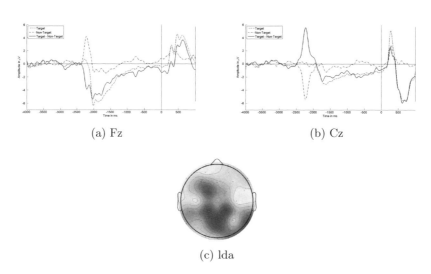

(a) Fz   (b) Cz

(c) lda

Fig. 2. Grand average ERP during selection (red dashed line, 800 epochs) compared to ERP when looking at the cross hair (blue dashed-dotted line, 961 epochs) at electrodes Fz (a) and Cz (b). The difference target minus non-target is plotted in black (solid). 0 marks the time point of selection. Baseline is between -4000 and -2500 ms. For visualization purposes, the signal is low-pass filtered to 8 Hz. (c): Absolute LDA weights averaged across time windows and participants. High weightings are displayed in red. Electrode positions are depicted by a cross.

The grand average ERP during the dwell time (depicted in Fig. 2 for the electrodes Fz and Cz and the two conditions) showed a negative deflection in the target condition which evolves after the begin of the selection and ends shortly before the selection is accomplished. In a time window between 1800 ms before and 0 ms after selection, this negativity is almost constantly at one level reaching zero shortly after selection. Therefore this time window (1800-0 ms) was chosen for ANOVA analysis. Table 1 lists the average amplitude values in this time window for the two conditions at the electrodes Fz, C3, C4, and Cz.

The ANOVA comparing the amplitude of the potentials occurring during the dwell time resulted in a significant main effect condition ($F(1, 9) = 6.926$, $p = 0.027$); no significant main effect site ($F(2.265, 20.386) = 1.550$, $p > .05$) and no significant interaction condition x site ($F(2.110, 18.992) = 3.047$, $p > .05$) were revealed.

Table 2. Correlation (p values) between eye movements in horizontal (Eye X) and vertical (Eye Y) direction and the ERP in electrode Cz and Fz during dwell time (left) and when looking at the cross hair (right).

	Eye X	Eye Y		Eye X	Eye Y
Fz	-0.0787 ($p <.05$)	-0.2364 ($p <.05$)	**Fz**	-0.0133 ($p <.05$)	-0.0289 ($p <.05$)
Cz	-0.0238 ($p <.05$)	-0.0205 ($p <.05$)	**Cz**	-0.0191 ($p <.05$)	-0.0202 ($p <.05$)

Mean classification accuracy was 74.9% with an average variance of 10.3%. According to [20], a classification accuracy above 65 % at 80 trials per class is above chance level with an error probability of p <0.01. This is fullfilled for every participant. Figure 2c displays the average absolute LDA weighting of the EEG channels used by the classifier across time windows and participants. It shows a high weighting of centro-parietal electrodes, namely Pz, CP1 and CP2, as well as fronto-central FC1 and parietal P8.

Regarding the relationship between the ERPs at electrode Fz and Cz and eye movements, significant correlations between the two electrodes and eye movements in horizontal and vertical direction have been revealed. Correlations appear to be stronger with electrode Fz than with Cz during the dwell time. The results of the correlation analysis are displayed in Table 2.

4   Discussion

In this study, participants task was to find a target object and select it via a dwell time of 2 s. The low error rate of 0.4 errors per participant suggests that the difficulty of the task was appropriate and participants had no problems accomplishing it. During the dwell time a sustained negativity occurs over fronto-central electrodes. An ANOVA showed that this negativity is significantly stronger than in case participants were merely fixating a cross hair while a non-target was presented on the screen. It is well possible that this negativity is a contingent negative variation (CNV). A CNV is a slow cortical potential generally thought to evolve between to stimuli, where the first stimulus (S1) announces the occurrence of a second stimulus (S2) that can for example prompt the participants to accomplish a motor response [21]. If the interval between S1 and S2 is long enough, the CNV is composed of is composed of two slow waves: an early or initial component (iCNV) and a late or terminal component (tCNV). The iCNV persists until approximately 1.2-1.5 s after S1 onset, is most prominent at frontal electrode sites and considered to mirror stimulus processing of S1 [22]. The tCNV was traditionally seen as mirroring motor preparation towards the required action after S2 [23]; however this view has been questioned by recent work reporting the late component of the CNV being present albeit smaller in time estimation tasks [22] [24], before stimuli giving knowledge of results and instruction stimuli without any motor response [25] [26]. Thus, the tCNV is rather seen as a reflection of anticipatory attention to the upcoming stimulus which is, in case there is a motor response, mixed with motor preparation. The origin of the CNV probably lies in the thalamo-cortical information flow [26][27].

In the current study, it seems likely that participants experience their dwell to be contingent to the later selection, which could in turn mean that the observed negativity reflects their expectation or anticipatory attention to the selection. A significantly lower negativity can be observed when the participants were looking at the fixation cross and wait until the trial (with a non-target presented) is over. This observation was interesting as the fixation cross was an interactive object, too: behaviorally, participants were doing the very same thing, i.e., they were fixating a spot and were waiting for something to happen. The difference was however that the participants were not informed about the fact, that the fixation cross was an interactive object. So, it seems that they experience the selection to be different from staring at the cross. If this CNV always occurs when participants are dwelling on objects they want to select, this potential might be used in a passive BCI to discriminate between dwellings to select something and spontaneous dwellings on random objects. It was possible to classify the negativity with an average accuracy of 74.9 %. This means that the state of selecting and the state of looking at the cross hair can be separated from each other on a modest level. The average weights of the linear discriminant analysis show the highest weighting of centro-parietal electrodes and a high weighting of frontal electrodes which is in line with literatur saying that a CNV has a initial frontal component and a later central component. Although it is possible that the weighting of the frontal electrodes includes a portion of eye movement, the high weighting of central electrodes suggests that the classifier uses brain activity to classify between the two classes. Recently, new methods for the classification of slow cortical potanials, especially the CNV, have been introduced by Garipelli et al., [28]. Applying these to the detected potential could improve the classification accuracy.

A limitation of the study is that there is a significant correlation of horizontal and vertical eye movements with the EEG. This suggests that the detected ERPs are influenced by eye movements, however as no electrooculogram (EOG) was recorded, the extent of this influence cannot be clarified in this study. The LDA weights indicate though that the information gets more coherent in parietal parts of the electrode set. Hence, even if the frontal electrodes are influenced by eye movements this might not be relevant for classification, even though the amplitude of the negativity is stronger in frontal electrodes. Nevertheless, the results of this study do not lead to a clear conclusion. Therefore future studies should use a paradigm where both conditions are accompanied by eye movements and simultaneously record EOG to check the occurrence of the CNV independent of eye movements. Furthermore, only the selection of the target was always followed by an upcoming eye movement, so that is not clear if a proportion of the tCNV is due to motor activity. This should also be clarified in upcoming studies by uncoupling the selection and subsequent eye movements.

The following step would be to design an experiment where this potential can be detected online. Then, this potential might be used to discern dwell times with the intend of selection from sporadic dwellings and long fixations due to stimulus complexity with the help of a passive BCI.

References

1. Prablanc, C., Echallier, J.F., Komilis, E., Jeannerod, M.: Optimal response of eye and hand motor systems in pointing at a visual target. I. Spatio-temporal characteristics of eye and hand movements and their relationships when varying the amount of visual information. Biological Cybernetics 35, 113–124
2. Jacob, R.J.K.: The use of eye movements in human-computer interaction techniques: what you look at is what you get. ACM Transactions on Information Systems 9(2), 152–169 (1991)
3. Jacob, R.J.K.: Hot topics-eye-gaze computer interfaces: what you look at is what you get. Computer 26(7), 65–66 (1993)
4. Velichkovsky, B.M., Hansen, J.P.: New technological windows into mind: there is more in eyes and brains for human-computer interaction. In: Proceedings of the SIGCHI Conference on Human Factors in Computing Systems: Common Ground, pp. 496–503 (1996)
5. Yarbus, A.L.: Eye movements during perception of complex objects. Eye Movements and Vision 7, 171–196 (1967)
6. Farwell, L.A., Donchin, E.: Talking off the top of your head: toward a mental prosthesis utilizing event-related brain potentials. Electroencephalography and Clinical Neurophysiology 70(6), 510–523 (1988)
7. Wolpaw, J.R., Birbaumer, N., McFarland, D.J., Pfurtscheller, G., Vaughan, T.M.: Brain–computer interfaces for communication and control. Clinical Neurophysiology 133(6), 767–791 (2002)
8. Zander, T.O., Kothe, C.: Towards passive brain–computer interfaces: applying brain–computer interface technology to human–machine systems in general. Journal of Neural Engineering 8, 025005 (2011)
9. Zander, T.O., Kothe, C., Jatzev, S., Gaertner, M.: Enhancing human–computer interaction with input from active and passive brain–computer interfaces. In: Tan, D., Nijholt, A. (eds.) The Human in Brain–Computer Interfaces and the Brain in Human–Computer Interaction, pp. 24–29 (2010)
10. Zander, T.O., Gaertner, M., Kothe, C., Vilimek, R.: Combining Eye Gaze Input with a Brain-Computer Interface for Touchless Human-Computer Interaction. International Journal of Human-Computer Interaction 27(1), 38–51 (2011)
11. Oostenveld, R., Praamstra, P.: The five percent electrode system for high-resolution EEG and ERP measurements. Clinical Neurophysiology 112(4), 713–719 (2001)
12. Delorme, A., Makeig, S.: EEGLAB: an open source toolbox for analysis of single-trial EEG dynamics including independent component analysis. Journal of Neuroscience Methods 134(1), 9–21 (2004)
13. Kothe, C.: Design and Implementation of a Research Brain-Computer Interface. Diploma's Thesis, Berlin Technical University, Berlin, Germany (September 2009)
14. Delorme, A., Kothe, C., Vankov, A., Bigdely-Shamlo, N., Oostenveld, R., Zander, T.O., Makeig, S.: MATLAB-based tools for BCI research. In: Tan, Nijholt (eds.) (B+H)CI: Brain-Computer Interfaces Applying our Minds to Human-Computer Interaction, pp. 241–259. Springer, Berlin (2010)
15. Luck, S.J.: An introduction to the event-related potential technique. MIT Press, Cambridge (2005)

16. Blankertz, B., Curio, G., Müller, K.R.: Classifying Single Trial EEG: Towards Brain Computer Interfacing. In: Advances in Neural Information Processing Systems: Proceedings of the 2002 Conference, vol. 157 (2002)

17. Friedman, J.H.: Regularized discriminant analysis. Journal of the American Statistical Association 84(405), 165–175 (1989)

18. Zander, T.O., Ihme, K., Gaertner, M., Roetting, M.: A public data hub for benchmarking common brain–computer interface algorithms. Journal of Neural Engineering 8, 025021 (2011)

19. Duda, R.O., Hart, P.E., Miley, J.: Pattern Classification, 2nd edn. Wiley Interscience, Hoboken (2001)

20. Müller-Putz, G.R., Scherer, R., Brunner, C., Leeb, R., Pfurtscheller, G.: Better than random? A closer look on BCI results. International Journal of Bioelectromagnetism 10(1), 52–55 (2008)

21. Walter, W.G.: Slow potential waves in the human brain associated with expectancy, attention and decision. European Archives of Psychiatry and Clinical Neuroscience 206(3), 309–322 (1964)

22. Ruchkin, D.S., Sutton, S., Mahaffey, D., Glaser, J.: Terminal CNV in the absence of motor response. Electroencephalography and Clinical Neurophysiology 63(5), 445–463 (1986)

23. Gaillard, A.W.K.: The late CNV wave: Preparation versus expectancy. Psychophysiology 14(6), 563–568 (1997)

24. Pfeuty, M., Ragot, R., Pouthas, V.: Relationship between CNV and timing of an upcoming event. Neuroscience Letters 382(1-2), 106–111 (2005)

25. Van Boxtel, G.J.M., Brunia, C.H.M.: Motor and non-motor aspects of slow brain potentials. Biological Psychology 38(1), 37–51 (1994)

26. Brunia, C.H.M., Van Boxtel, G.J.M.: Wait and see. International Journal of Psychophysiology 43(1), 59–71 (2001)

27. Nagai, Y., Critchley, H.D., Featherstone, E., Fenwick, P.B.C., Trimble, M.R., Dolan, R.J.: Brain activity relating to the contingent negative variation: an fMRI investigation. NeuroImage 21(4), 1232–1241 (2004)

28. Garipelli, G., Chavarriaga, R., del R Millan, J.: Single trial recognition of anticipatory slow cortical potentials: The role of spatio-spectral filtering. In: Proceedings of the 5th International IEEE/EMBS Conference on Neural Engineering (NER), Cancun, pp. 408–411 (2011)

EEG Correlates of Different Emotional States Elicited during Watching Music Videos

Eleni Kroupi, Ashkan Yazdani, and Touradj Ebrahimi

Multimedia Signal Processing Group,
École Polythechnique Fédérale de Lausanne-EPFL
CH-1015 Lausanne, Switzerland

Abstract. Studying emotions has become increasingly popular in various research fields. Researchers across the globe have studied various tools to implicitly assess emotions and affective states of people. Human computer interface systems specifically can benefit from such implicit emotion evaluator module, which can help them determine their users' affective states and act accordingly. Brain electrical activity can be considered as an appropriate candidate for extracting emotion-related cues, but it is still in its infancy. In this paper, the results of analyzing the Electroencephalogram (EEG) for assessing emotions elicited during watching various pre-selected emotional music video clips have been reported. More precisely, in-depth results of both subject-dependent and subject-independent correlation analysis between time domain, and frequency domain features of EEG signal and subjects' self assessed emotions are produced and discussed.

Keywords: Emotion, electroencephalogram, power spectral density, normalized length density, non-stationarity index.

1 Introduction

Although it is difficult to define, emotion can be considered as an overall psychophysiological process, influenced by many external and internal stimuli, such as personality, past experiences, affect and contextual environment to mention a few. Therefore, emotion is a continuous adaptive mechanism and serves the purpose of human interaction and expression, reaction to stimuli or events and re-evaluation of several circumstances. Since emotion is involved in every aspect of human life, it has gained a great deal of interest and attention in many research fields, such as neurology, psychology, sociology and computer science. In computer science, many researchers have endeavored to alter the "user-centered" orientation of human-computer interactions (HCI) systems and develop instead "human-centered" HCIs. This new term is more appropriate as it considers the overall human experience which is embodied in human emotions and interactions with machines. Nevertheless, current HCIs are still quite deficient in interpreting this affective information of emotion and they are still unable to take actions based on human emotion. Therefore, further insight has to be provided in this

S. D´Mello et al. (Eds.): ACII 2011, Part II, LNCS 6975, pp. 457–466, 2011.

research area in order to equip machines with an affective functionality, which could make them more user-friendly, more sensitive to human beings and more efficient.

Until today, various theories for emotion modeling have been proposed, which mainly fall into categorical and dimensional modeling of emotions. The categorical models investigate and study different quasi-independent categories of emotions, and provide a list of basic emotions. These models are mainly represented by the basic six emotions proposed by Ekman and Friesen [1]. On the other hand, many dimensional theories for emotion modeling have been proposed, which investigate independent component and dimensions of emotion. Russell [2] describes emotions quantitatively using the valence-arousal space and argues that all emotions can be placed in this space. In other words, this is a two-dimensional model, with valence and arousal being the horizontal and the vertical axes, respectively. Although these two dimensions can describe most of the emotional variations, there is at times a third dimension of dominance included in the model [2]. Valence ranges from negative to positive (or unpleasant to pleasant), whereas arousal ranges from inactive (or calm) to active (or excited). Dominance ranges from weak (or without control) to an empowered and strong feeling (with control of everything).

Implicit assessment of emotion can be carried out through analysis of human expressions and physiological reactions. Human expressions comprise of verbal and non-verbal cues that can be processed using speech and face recognition systems. Physiological signals are also known to convey traces of emotion, but they have received less attention . Generally, physiological signals originate from the central nervous system (CNS) and the peripheral nervous system (PNS). Regarding the signals from the CNS, brain electrical activity has gained great interest for studying emotions. Thanks to the reasonable prices and the decent time resolution, EEG has become the main tool in brain research. Among other physiological signals, EEG has gained special interest because emotion is considered as a psychophysiological process which is directly reflected in brain activities.

Many scientists have tried to explore the correlations between different emotions and brain regions, but unfortunately, there is not much consistency among different studies [3]. For instance, according to Davidson's motivational model of emotion [4], left frontal brain activity indicates a positive emotion (high valence) whereas right frontal activity indicates a negative emotion (low valence). This is the phenomenon of "frontal EEG asymmetry", that has played a prominent role in affective EEG research. Moreover, Coan and Allen [5] have published a review of over 70 studies that examine the relationship between emotion and EEG frontal asymmetry. They argue that emotion correlates with EEG asymmetry are predominant and can be observed with different elicitation procedures. However, some studies, such as [6], failed to produce the similar expected results. On the other hand, several studies have reported that bilateral EEG activity can be also supported and mostly associated with negative emotions [7].

In the current study, we explore the EEG changes during different emotional states based on subjective and subject-independent analysis. Emotion elicitation is performed by watching music videos. In particular, subjective analysis is performed in order to estimate how different emotions contribute to brain region activation among different subjects. Subject-independent analysis is performed in order to investigate the common behavior of all subjects and draw general conclusions on how brain is affected by emotions while watching music videos. Emotion modeling is performed by using a three dimensional model of valence, arousal and liking (VAL). Liking dimension is added in order to capture the additional variations that cannot be identified by the other two dimensions. The analysis of the signals is performed both in time and in frequency domains. More specifically, for time domain we use two indexes that capture the complexity of the EEG time series, namely the normalized length density (NLD) [8] and the non-stationarity index (NSI) [9]. Furthermore, for the frequency domain we use the power spectral density (PSD) of the signals. Hence, the goal of the current study is twofold. First, to investigate how different EEG sub-bands and regions are affected by different emotional states, considering specific characteristics of the signals that are captured by features both in time and frequency domains. Second, to explore how these regions are affected in different subjects while they watch music video clips.

The paper is organized as follows. Section 2 describes the data and signal processing techniques used in this study. The results and further discussion are detailed in Section 3. Finally, the conclusions are presented in Section 4.

2   Materials and Methods

2.1   Dataset

The experiments were performed in a laboratory environment with controlled temperature and illumination. EEG signals were recorded using a Biosemi ActiveTwo system through 32 active AgCl electrodes at sampling frequency of 512 Hz. Six participants were asked to view the 20 music videos, displayed in a random order. These music video clips were carefully selected using a subjective test. More information about the selection procedure can be found in [10]. Before displaying each video a 5-second long baseline was recorded. After each video was finished the participant was asked to perform a self-assessment of their levels of valence, arousal, and like/dislike which was later used as the ground truth.

2.2   PSD Estimation

Before estimating the PSD of EEG signals, the data was re-referenced to the common average, down-sampled to 256 Hz and high-pass filtered with a cutoff frequency of 3 Hz using a Butterworth filter of third order. The eye-blinking artifacts were removed using RunICA algorithm implemented in EEGLAB toolbox[1]. Furthermore, in order to remove the influence of the stimulus-unrelated

---

[1] http://sccn.ucsd.edu/eeglab/

variations, a five second baseline was recorded before each trial. We processed the final one second of each baseline.

The frequency power of the signals and the baselines were extracted for frequencies between 4 and 47 Hz, using Welch's method with windows of 128 samples. The logarithm of the mean baseline power was then subtracted from the logarithm of the mean trial power, in order to extract the power changes without considering the pre-stimulus period. These power changes were captured for different brain bands, namely theta band (4-7 Hz), alpha band (8-13 Hz), beta band (14-29 Hz) and gamma band (30-47 Hz).

2.3 Complexity

Living organisms consist of complex structures and functions. In particular, parameters of the physiological signals of such organisms, for instance the amplitude of the EEG signals, appear to vary over time in a complex manner. These temporal variations result from intrinsic disturbances and actions, such as the activity of an organism or the process of aging. In physiological signals these fluctuations are non-periodic. In the past years, the properties of the physiological signals used to be described by the mean value, whereas the fluctuations around the mean were discarded as noise. However, research over the recent years revealed that these fluctuations exhibit long-range correlations over many time scales, indicating the presence of self-invariant and self-similar structures. Such structures can be captured with fractal or non-linear analysis.

In the current study, we explore the behavior of the temporal fluctuations that are generated by different emotional states. More specifically, NLD index is used in order to capture the self-similarities of the EEG signals and to explore how they are correlated with the dimensions of valence, arousal and liking. NLD is estimated by

$$\text{NLD} = \frac{1}{N} \sum_{i=2}^{N} |y_n(i) - y_n(i-1)|, \qquad (1)$$

where $y_n(i)$ and N represent the ith sample after amplitude normalization and the length of the signal respectively [8]. NLD index is very accurate and easy to implement and it is related to the actual fractal dimension of the time series through a power law [8].

The other measure of complexity used in this study is NSI, which segments the signals into small parts and estimates the variation of the local averages [9]. NSI is also easy to implement and it is related to the signal's complexity through the fact that it captures the degree of the signal's non-stationarity. The mean values of both NLD and NSI were used to estimate the correlation between EEG fluctuations over time and the subjective ratings of valence, arousal and liking.

2.4 Correlation Analysis

For the correlation analysis we computed the Spearman coefficients between the PSD, NLD and NSI features, and the subjective ratings of valence, arousal and

Table 1. Inter-correlations between the different dimensions of ratings for each subject

	Subject 1			Subject 2			Subject 3		
	Valence	Arousal	Liking	Valence	Arousal	Liking	Valence	Arousal	Liking
Valence	1	0.13	-0.46	1	0.33	-0.95*	1	0.75*	-0.77*
Arousal	0.13	1	-0.56*	0.33	1	-0.4	0.75*	1	-0.79*
Liking	-0.46	-0.56*	1	-0.95*	-0.4	1	-0.77*	-0.79*	1
	Subject 4			Subject 5			Subject 6		
	Valence	Arousal	Liking	Valence	Arousal	Liking	Valence	Arousal	Liking
Valence	1	0.4	-0.41	1	0.55*	-0.5*	1	0.61*	-0.88*
Arousal	0.4	1	-0.12	0.55*	1	-0.94*	0.61*	1	-0.58*
Liking	-0.41	-0.12	1	-0.5*	-0.94*	1	-0.88*	-0.58*	1

liking for each electrode. In terms of the subjective correlation analysis, the most significant electrodes were selected as those with p-value, $p < 0.05$, for each subject. Then the common most significant electrodes were selected by considering independency among the subjects and combining the individual p-values using Fisher's meta-analysis method. Briefly, Fisher's method assumes that a set of p-values obtained from independent studies testing the same null hypothesis may be combined to overally verify the null hypothesis. Finally, subject-independent correlation analysis was performed by treating all subjects as one. Hence, all features were concatenated in one matrix and the significant electrodes were selected as those with $p < 0.05$.

3   Results and Discussion

3.1   Subjective Analysis

The inter-correlation values between each subject's ratings for valence, arousal, and liking are presented in Table 1. The significant correlations are indicated with a star and they are selected as those with $p < 0.05$. The correlation values between the logarithmic mean PSD and the ratings, mapped into the corresponding brain regions, are presented in Figure 1 for each subject respectively. Significant electrodes are represented by black spots.

Regarding the EEG behavior of different subjects, as can be seen in Figure 1, subject 1 shows the highest correlation between the ratings and the logarithmic mean PSD. For this subject, the maximum correlation value reaches 0.8. Such high correlations appear mainly in theta and alpha bands, indicating positive correlation between logarithmic mean PSD and arousal, as well as between logarithmic mean PSD and valence. High positive correlation also appears in gamma band, between logarithmic mean PSD and liking.

Observing the correlations of the Figure 1(a), it is obvious that arousal and liking follow opposite correlation patterns, especially in theta band. This behavior is certified by the fact that there is significant negative correlation between arousal and liking for the first subject, which is presented in Table 1. Negative

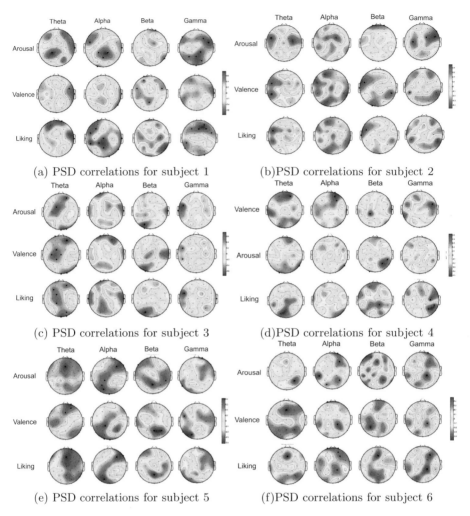

(a) PSD correlations for subject 1   (b) PSD correlations for subject 2

(c) PSD correlations for subject 3   (d) PSD correlations for subject 4

(e) PSD correlations for subject 5   (f) PSD correlations for subject 6

Fig. 1. Brain region mappings of the correlations between the logarithmic mean PSD and the ratings for each subject

correlation between arousal and liking indicates that subject 1 shows preference for music videos that elicit low arousal values regardless of the value of valence.

For subject 2, a significant negative correlation value between valence and liking appears, which is clearly presented in Figure 1(b) due to the fact that they are very high ($r = 0.95$). These negative correlations indicate that subject 2 has a preference for music videos that elicit negative values for valence, independent of the values of arousal. For subject 3 there are significant correlations among all ratings, which can be obviously seen in Figure 1(c). More specifically, valence and arousal appear to follow similar correlation patterns, whereas arousal and

Table 2. Common significant electrodes using Fisher's meta-analysis test

	Theta	Alpha	Beta	Gamma
Valence	FC1, CP5, P8, CP6 Oz, Fz, F4, AF4	CP6, Oz	O1, Pz, PO4	CP5
Arousal	Fz, PO4, AF4	CP5, Oz, Pz, Cz O2, F8, Fz, F4	O2, Fp1	FC5, CP5, P7 C4, FC2, F8
Liking	-	Fp1, CP5, Oz, O2	-	FC5, CP5, F8, Fz, AF4

liking, as well as valence and liking, follow opposite correlation patterns. This behavior indicates that subject 3 prefers music videos that elicit low arousal values and negative valence values (sad videos). Finally, subjects 5 and 6 show similar correlation behavior, indicating that they both prefer music videos that elicit low arousal and negative valence values (sad music video clips), whereas there are no significant inter-correlations among the ratings of subject 4.

Since emotion is a very complex phenomenon and is influenced by different structures, situations and contextual environment, it is expected to see different activated brain regions for different subjects even if their affective states seem to be similar. Nevertheless, there is occasionally some level of affective consistency among the activated brain regions of different subjects. In order to capture these common activated regions, Fisher's meta-analysis method was applied. Fisher's method combines the p-values of independent tests which share the same null hypothesis. The null hypothesis for this case is the hypothesis that the logarithmic mean PSD is uncorrelated with the ratings of valence, arousal and liking for each electrode and subject. Hence, if the null hypothesis is rejected, there must be significant correlations between the logarithmic mean PSD and the corresponding rating, for the specific electrode and subject. The common significant electrodes for all the subjects after applying Fisher's test are presented in Table 2.

As it is shown in Table 2, only 15 electrodes out of 32 show significant activation in the overall affective process, some of which are activated with more than one ratings or for more than one brain bands. For instance, CP5 electrode shows activation with valence, arousal and liking but for different brain bands. Moreover, it is observed that, for all emotion dimensions, the CP5 region is activated in gamma band. Another example is the Fz electrode, which demonstrates activation for valence and arousal in theta band, for arousal in alpha band and for liking in gamma band. Hence, there are some electrodes that show significance for more than one affective dimension (valence, arousal or liking) and for the same brain frequency bands. Therefore, these electrodes might not be able to distinguish the variations in each of the dimensions. If, thus, significant electrodes are used as features to infer for the status of each rating, the analysis should be better based on the electrodes which are exclusively related with one affective dimension for each brain band.

3.2   Subject Independent Analysis

Subject independent analysis is performed by concatenating all features and ratings in one vector, which from now on will be referred to as overall features and ratings, respectively. The inter-correlations between the overall rating dimensions of valence, arousal and liking are all significant with values $r = 0.6$ for arousal and valence, $r = -0.68$ for valence and liking, and $r = -0.67$ for arousal and liking. The correlations between the overall logarithmic mean PSD and the subjective ratings of valence, arousal and liking are shown in Figure 2(a). Significant electrodes are presented by black spots.

In consistency with the overall subjective ratings, alpha and gamma bands of Figure 2(a) show similar correlation patterns for arousal and valence, and opposite correlations for arousal and liking as well as valence and liking. These significant correlations indicate that subjects had a tendency to prefer music videos that elicit low arousal and negative valence values.

Regarding the analysis of the brain regions of interest, in Figure 2(a) high positive correlation appears between arousal and logarithmic mean PSD in theta band, especially on the right side of the cortex. In alpha band, left dorsolateral prefrontal cortex is activated with arousal, whereas right central region is positively correlated with arousal.

Moreover, left temporal region is positively correlated with arousal in beta band, indicating that the left auditory region is activated when arousal becomes lower and consequently when the subjects are more calm. Since arousal and liking are oppositely correlated, left auditory region in beta band is activated with high

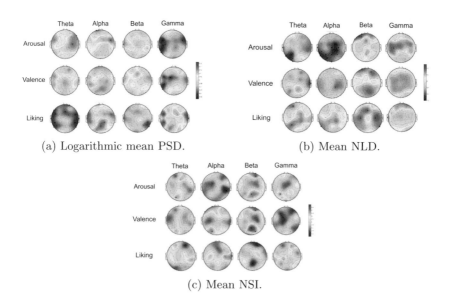

(a) Logarithmic mean PSD.   (b) Mean NLD.

(c) Mean NSI.

Fig. 2. Brain region mappings of the correlations between the overall frequency and time features with the ratings

liking. This is consistent with the findings of the correlations among the overall subjective ratings. Temporal lobe is also related to memory and understanding of language. Therefore, it is normal that this lobe is activated when liking is high.

Furthermore, in gamma band, somatosensory motor cortex is activated with high arousal, high valence and low liking, indicating that the subjects are willing to move when arousal and valence are high, although this is not necessarily related to whether they like the specific music clip. However, somatosensory motor cortex is also activated with high liking in theta band, regardless of the values of arousal and valence.

Finally, ventral stream of the left lateral parietal lobe shows similar behavior with the somatosensory motor cortex. In particular, it yields activation with high arousal and valence in gamma band, whereas it is being activated with high liking in theta band, independently of the values of arousal and valence. Ventral stream is highly associated with object recognition and form representation, indicating that these processes take place with high arousal and valence in gamma band and with high liking in theta band.

Regarding the analysis in the time domain, the correlations between the overall mean NLD and the subjective ratings are shown in Figure 2(b) and the correlations between the overall mean NSI and the subjective ratings are shown in Figure 2(c). Although NLD does not follow the patterns of the correlations among the overall subjective ratings, these patterns are obviously shown in almost all bands of NSI. In NSI, frontal and parietal cortex seem to be associated with low arousal, negative valence and high liking. More specifically, in alpha and beta bands, frontal lobe is positively correlated with valence and arousal, and negatively correlated with liking, whereas in gamma band frontal lobe is negatively correlated with valence. Considering that frontal lobe is associated with attention, different brain bands of the frontal lobe are activated depending on whether the attention emanates from liking issues or issues associated with high valence.

3.3   Conclusions

In this paper, the changes of EEG signal during different emotions elicited by watching various music video clips were studied. To this end, time domain and frequency domain features of the EEG signal were extracted and the analysis of correlation between these features and subject's self assessed emotions was performed. These self assessments were verified to make sure they are expanded on the arousal-valence plane. Subject-dependent analysis revealed that there are differentiations among the subjects' brain activation patterns, due to the difference in age, personality, different contextual environment and general preferences. Nevertheless, there are similarities regarding the activation of several electrodes, which were captured using Fisher's method. Finally, subject-independent analysis explored the general behavior of the different brain bands, depending on the overall features and ratings. It revealed that frequency and time features are complementary, so they are both needed for the correlation analysis.

Acknowledgement. The research leading to these results has been performed in the frameworks of Swiss National Foundation for Scientic Research (FN 200020-132673-1), European Community's Seventh Framework Program (FP7/2007-2011) under grant agreement no. 216444 (PetaMedia), and the NCCR Interactive Multimodal Information Management (IM2). Last but not least, the authors would like to thank Christian Mühl, Mohammad Soleymani, Sander Koelstra, and Jong-Seok Lee for their participation in data acquisition.

References

1. Ekman, P., Friesen, W.V., O'Sullivan, M., Chan, A., Diacoyanni-Tarlatzis, I., Heider, K., Krause, R., LeCompte, W.A., Pitcairn, T., Ricci-Bitti, P.E.: Universals and cultural differences in the judgements of facial expressions of emotion. Journal of Personality and Social Psychology 53, 712–717 (1987)

2. Russell, J.A.: A circumplex model of affect. Journal of Personality and Social Psychology 39, 1161–1178 (1980)

3. Sammler, D., Grigutsch, M., Fritz, T., Koelsch, S.: Music and emotion: Electrophysiological correlates of the processing of pleasant and unpleasant music. Psychophysiology 44(2), 293–304 (2007)

4. Davidson, R.J.: Cerebral asymmetry and emotion: conceptual and methological conundrums. Cognition and Emotion 7, 115–138 (1993)

5. Coan, J.A., Allen, J.J.B.: Frontal eeg asymmetry as a moderator and mediator of emotion. Biological Psychology 67, 7–49 (2004)

6. Mller, M.M., Keil, A., Gruber, T., Elbert, T.: Processing of affective pictures modulates right hemisphere gamma band eeg activity. Clinical Neurophysiology 110, 1913–1920 (1999)

7. Dennis, T., Solomon, B.: Frontal eeg and emotion regulation: Electrocortical activity in response to emotional film clips is associated with reduced mood induction and attention interference effects. Biological psychology (2010)

8. Kalauzi, A., Bojic, T., Rakic, L.: Extracting complexity waveforms from one-dimensional signals. Nonlinear Biomedical Physics 3 (2009)

9. Hausdorff, J.M., Lertratanakul, A., Cudkowicz, M.E., Peterson, A., Kaliton, D., Golberger, A.L.: Dynamic markers of altered gait rhythm in amyotrophic lateral sclerosis. Journal of Applied Physiology 88 (2000)

10. Koelstra, S., Yazdani, A., Soleymani, M., Mühl, C., Lee, J.-S., Nijholt, A., Pun, T., Ebrahimi, T., Patras, I.: Single trial classification of EEG and peripheral physiological signals for recognition of emotions induced by music videos. In: Yao, Y., Sun, R., Poggio, T., Liu, J., Zhong, N., Huang, J. (eds.) BI 2010. LNCS, vol. 6334, pp. 89–100. Springer, Heidelberg (2010)

Classifying High-Noise EEG in Complex Environments for Brain-Computer Interaction Technologies

Brent Lance[1], Stephen Gordon[2], Jean Vettel[1], Tony Johnson[2], Victor Paul[3],
Chris Manteuffel[2], Matthew Jaswa[2], and Kelvin Oie[1]

[1] U.S. Army Research Laboratory – Human Research & Engineering Directorate,
RDRL-HRS-C, Aberdeen Proving Ground, MD, USA
[2] DCS Corporation
[3] U.S. Army Tank & Automotive Research, Development, & Engineering Center
{brent.j.lance,jean.vettel,victor.paul,
kelvin.oie}@us.army.mil
{sgordon,tjohnson,cmanteuffel,mjaswa}@dcscorp.com

Abstract. Future technologies such as Brain-Computer Interaction Technologies (BCIT) or affective Brain Computer Interfaces (aBCI) will need to function in an environment with higher noise and complexity than seen in traditional laboratory settings, and while individuals perform concurrent tasks. In this paper, we describe preliminary results from an experiment in a complex virtual environment. For analysis, we classify between a subject hearing and reacting to an audio stimulus that is addressed to them, and the same subject hearing an irrelevant audio stimulus. We performed two offline classifications, one using BCILab [1], the other using LibSVM [2]. Distinct classifiers were trained for each individual in order to improve individual classifier performance [3]. The highest classification performance results were obtained using individual frequency bands as features and classifying with an SVM classifier with an RBF kernel, resulting in mean classification performance of 0.67, with individual classifier results ranging from 0.60 to 0.79.

Keywords: EEG, affect, self-relevant, classification, noise.

1 Introduction

Brain-Computer Interaction Technologies (BCIT) aim to use electroencephalography (EEG) and other physiological measures to enhance a healthy user's performance with a system [4]. These technologies, and similar technologies such as affective brain-computer interfaces (aBCI), have promising applications such as monitoring fatigue or recognizing extreme negative affect (i.e. stress or anger). These applications could provide important and relevant information about the performance of a Soldier in real time, ideally allowing the identification and mitigation of performance degradation before tragic mistakes occur. However, for these technologies to achieve their full potential, they will need to function in an environment with higher noise and complexity than currently seen in traditional laboratory settings. Further, many traditional experiments use a reductionist approach of studying a single task performed in isolation. For these systems to be viable, they

S. D´Mello et al. (Eds.): ACII 2011, Part II, LNCS 6975, pp. 467–476, 2011.

must detect relevant user states or emotions when an individual is performing multiple concurrent tasks.

In this paper, we begin to address these noise and complexity challenges by describing preliminary results derived from an experiment in a complex virtual environment. In this experiment, teams of two Soldiers performed Vehicle Commander (VC) and Driver roles in a simulated Stryker vehicle on a six degrees-of-freedom (DOF) ride motion platform. The focus of the EEG and behavioral data collection was on the VC, who interacted with the Driver and performed multiple overlapping tasks, such as route planning, maintaining local situational awareness, and monitoring and responding to radio communications. Additionally, the EEG data collected from the VC in this experiment has large amounts of noise artifacts, including those caused by reaching and speaking, unconstrained eye and head movements, and the movements of the motion platform. EEG collected in this environment will provide a test bed for evaluating data processing methods for real-world applications.

For this preliminary analysis, we are attempting to classify between a Soldier hearing and reacting to a self-relevant audio stimulus, and the same Soldier hearing a irrelevant audio stimulus. Reliably accomplishing this task would demonstrate a capability for extracting physiological information in a complex environment, and potentially provide the capability for performing minor optimizations of a vehicle crew station interface. The complexity of the environment will likely result in high classification error percentages, leading us to perform an individual-based analysis. However, by performing this analysis we obtain a baseline performance metric that demonstrates the potential for analyzing this complex data set. In addition, by performing classifier training on individuals we hope to improve classifier performance for particular individuals, instead of using classifiers trained across groups or on normative data [3].

This paper is organized as follows: section 2 will discuss work relevant to the goals of this paper. Section 3 will describe the experimental methodology. Sections 4 and 5 will describe the analysis methods and discuss the results, and the paper concludes in section 6.

2   Related Work

In this preliminary analysis, we aim to classify the neural processing related to self-relevant auditory communications compared to irrelevant auditory communications. The self-relevance of an event has considerable effects on its ability to catch our attention, and to the emotional value assigned to that event [5], [6]. Prior research indicates that self-relevant communication has particular underlying neural and physiological codings that classification can be based on. While much of the research demonstrating neural correlates of self-relevance has focused on fMRI studies [7], there is some research showing the relationship between self-referential stimuli and electrophysiological correlates. For example, Gray et al. [8] have shown that self-relevant visual stimuli have a significant effect on event-related P300 latency and amplitude, and Tanaka et al. [9] report a focal response (N250) in right posterior channels when viewing pictures of oneself. In addition to these studies of self-relevant

Fig. 1. Vehicle Commander (VC) Warfighter-Machine Interface (WMI), consisting of a 180° field-of-view banner across the top, a 60° field-of-view window on the left hand side, and an overhead map on the right hand side.

visual stimuli, several researchers have shown neural correlates of auditory recognition using both fMRI and EEG, while Krause et al. [10] showed a statistically signification relationship between an auditory recognition task and event-related desynchronizations in the upper (10-12 Hz) and lower (8-10 Hz) alpha frequency bands of the EEG signal. In short, these studies collectively suggest a differentiation in the neural processing of self-referential stimuli, whether visual or auditory, and it is this differentiation in the brain signal that our classification approach seeks to identify despite the noise in the recorded EEG signal and the complexity of the task environment.

3   Experimental Methodology

3.1   Subjects

The subjects were 14 U.S. Army Sergeants, all male, ranging from age 27 to age 50, with mean age 34.5 from Military Occupational Specialty (MOS) 11B (Infantryman), MOS 19D (Cavalry Scout), and MOS 19K (Armor Crewman). The Soldiers were all combat veterans of Iraq or Afghanistan, and all from the U.S. Army Maneuver Center of Excellence at Fort Knox, KY and Fort Benning, GA. Two of the subjects were excluded from the analysis due to technical difficulties during the data collection, and two subjects were excluded due to failure to accomplish experimental tasks, resulting in 10 subjects being utilized for the analysis.

3.2   Design and Procedure

The goal of the experiment was to study commander task performance under varying task load conditions during team operations in a complex Army-relevant virtual environment. During the experiment, teams of two Soldiers performed six simulated missions consisting of traveling in a Stryker vehicle from a Forward Operating Base (FOB) to a nearby small desert metropolitan area, visiting three sequential checkpoints in the city area, and then returning to the FOB. One Soldier was assigned the role of the Vehicle Commander (VC), while the other Soldier was assigned to be the Driver. Each Soldier would spend one day as VC, and one day as the Driver. The simulated Stryker was equipped with a Closed-Hatch Local Situational Awareness (LSA) system, consisting of six external cameras covering a 360° area around the vehicle that were accessible from the VC crew station (Fig. 1).

During each mission, the VC performed numerous tasks that can be categorized into three main task groupings:

1. Overseeing mission progress and ensuring that the vehicle arrived at each checkpoint within a specific time range. This included supervising the Driver and providing turn-by-turn directions through the city, halt/resume commands, and immediate command driving around difficult obstacles in the environment.
2. Maintaining visual LSA, which included detecting road obstacles and traffic conditions relevant to navigating the environment, and reporting the position of uniformed local forces and objects identified as threats over the radio network to a simulated Tactical Operating Commander (TOC).
3. Maintaining auditory LSA, which included monitoring and responding to radio communications about mission status from the TOC and verbally interacting with the Driver.

In order to explore differential effects of task loading, the portion of the mission consisting of the ride from the FOB into the metro area was designed to induce much lower cognitive load than the portion of the mission taking part inside the metro area. There were considerably more audio and visual stimuli, and more pedestrian and vehicle traffic within the metro area than there were outside of it.

3.3 Auditory Stimuli

While there are many potential aspects of this data set that could be mined for results, including neural or physiological correlates of visual targets or error-related signals induced by driver mistakes such as vehicle-vehicle or vehicle-pedestrian contact, the focus of this preliminary analysis is on the auditory stimuli. The VC monitored four audio channels during the course of the experiment: primary audio stimuli, background audio stimuli, all-listener audio stimuli, and Driver communications.

Primary audio stimuli consisted of pre-recorded messages from a single radio operator (a simulated TOC) that were directed to the VC's call sign, "Blue 4." The primary audio stimuli were directly associated with the mission being performed, and were triggered either by trip lines in the virtual environment or when specific scenario conditions were met. For the purposes of this analysis we have divided the primary audio stimuli into three categories (Table 1): (1) messages that tell the VC to change between radio communication nets, which the VC would perform by pressing a button on the crew station; (2) messages that ask a question of the VC, which the VC would respond to by pressing a push-to-talk button and speaking; and (3) messages that require minimal response from the VC (i.e. the VC would respond by pressing the push-to-talk button and saying "roger").

Table 1. Audio Stimuli Categorizations

Category Label	Stimulus Type	Total Quantity
A1	Primary: Change between radio nets	625
A2	Primary: Asking question of Soldier	321
A3	Primary: Other primary communication	1563
B1	Background: Messages to Blue 12	634
B2	Background: Other background communications	501
C1	All Listeners: Change radio net status	93
C2	All Listeners: other communications	293

Background audio stimuli consisted of pre-recorded messages from various other speakers which were not directed to the VC, were not mission-relevant, and were randomly triggered. We have divided the background audio stimuli into two categories: (1) messages to the call sign 'Blue 12', which is similar to the VC's call sign; and (2) other background communication.

All-listener audio stimuli consisted of pre-recorded messages that were directed to all listeners on the channel, were not mission-relevant, and were randomly triggered. We have divided these stimuli into two categories: (1) messages that tell all of the listeners (including the VC) to change the radio net status, which the VC would perform by pressing a button on the crew station; and (2) messages that provide information to all listeners (including the VC).

Relevant and irrelevant audio stimuli were clearly defined through the use of call signs. All Army radio messages are prefaced with the call sign of the Soldier to whom they are directed. Thus, within the first 0.5 to 1.0 seconds of the radio message, the VC was able to determine the relevancy of the audio stimulus. The Soldiers successfully responded to almost all relevant primary audio stimuli (i.e., all communications that began with "Blue 4" followed by the question or directive from the Tactical Operating Commander), which indicates successful identification and comprehension of the VC-directed auditory communications. The driver communications were less controlled since the Driver was a live participant rather than a recorded voice like the Tactical Operating Commander. For this preliminary analysis, the VC communication with the Driver was ignored.

3.4 Experimental Setup

EEG was collected from the VC using a 64-channel BioSemi active-electrode EEG system placed according the 10-20 international system, referenced to averaged mastoids, and recorded at 256 Hz. In addition, horizontal EOG was collected from two electrodes placed on the outer canti of the eyes and vertical EOG was collected from two electrodes placed above and below the right eye.

The Driver viewed the simulated environment through a 60° straight-ahead field of view, and interacted with it through a yoke, and two pedals (gas and brake). The VC interacted with the simulated environment through a crew station with 2 touchscreens, through which he had access to the full 360° LSA system, a digital map of the area, and the ability to perform any mission-relevant tasks (Fig 1). The VC also had a paper map for planning the mission route.

The VC performed the experiment while riding on the 6-DOF servo-hydraulic Ride Motion Simulator (RMS) platform at the U.S. Army Tank and Automotive Research, Development, and Engineering Center (TARDEC).   The RMS platform was developed at TARDEC for simulating the ride of military vehicles, and it provides motion cues to the occupant derived from physics-based dynamics models of the vehicle and its interaction with the terrain.

The simulated environment consisted of a FOB near a small desert metropolitan area.   Within the metro area, there were six checkpoints.   Three checkpoints were used in each of the six missions performed by the subjects.   Pedestrian and vehicle traffic also served as distracters and obstacles.   Behavioral data was collected from the simulated environment, including but not limited to: all of the VC's crew station interactions, timing and audio of all communications, what camera the VC used at any given time, and the position and heading of the simulated Stryker in the environment.

4 Feature Extraction and Classification

For this preliminary analysis we performed two separate sets of offline classifications between a Soldier hearing and reacting to a self-relevant audio stimulus, and between the same Soldier hearing an irrelevant audio stimulus.   The first classification set was performed using BCILab [1], an open-source tool for BCI development in MATLAB (Mathworks; Natick, MA) developed at the Swartz Center for Computational Neuroscience at the University of California, San Diego.   The second set of classifications was performed using the support vector machine (SVM) library LibSVM [2], developed at National Taiwan University, Taipei, Taiwan.   Distinct classifiers were trained for each individual Soldier taking part in the experiment.   It has been our experience that, on data such as this, individually-trained classifiers tend to outperform classifiers trained on group or normative data [3].

4.1 BCILab Procedure

The BCILab analysis was performed using BCILab's built-in epoching, filtering, feature extraction, and classification capabilities to analyze the data.   The data was downsampled to 100 Hz, bandpass filtered to 1-50 Hz, and epoched from 0.5 seconds to 4.5 seconds after the audio stimulus, with baseline removal performed for each epoch.   This epoch size provided the best performance of those tried. Feature extraction was performed using BCILab's log bandpower paradigm, which uses the log variance of the spectral power over the entire 1-50 Hz frequency for each channel for each epoch as the features passed to the classifier, which in this case was a linear discriminant analysis (LDA) classifier.   Classifiers were trained and tested for each individual using 10-fold classification validation.

4.2 LibSVM Procedure

For the LibSVM analysis, the data was bandpass filtered to 1-50 Hz, and epoched from 0.5 seconds to 4.5 seconds after the audio stimulus, after which the epochs were detrended.   Feature extraction consisted of the bandpower of multiple frequency bands for each channel at each epoch.   The frequency bands used were those defined by Andreassi [11], consisting of the delta (1-3 Hz), theta (4-7 Hz), alpha (8-13 Hz), low beta (14-20 Hz), high beta (21-30 Hz), and the gamma (31-50) bands. The features were scaled on a 0 to 1 range, and classified using an SVM with a radial basis function (RBF) kernel and 10-fold validation. SVM parameters were defined by manual search through the space of possibilities.

Table 2. Mean classifier performance across all subjects

Condition	BCILAB	LibSVM	Actual
A (all) vs. B (all) + C(all)	0.54±0.038	0.60±0.038	0.60 / 0.40
A (all) vs. B (all)	0.57±0.044	0.62±0.048	0.67 / 0.33
A (all) & C (all) vs. B (all)	0.57±0.033	0.67±0.048	0.70 / 0.30
A1 & A2 & C1 vs. B (all)	0.64±0.066	0.65±0.054	0.47 / 0.52
A1 & A2 vs. B (all)	0.66±0.073	0.67±0.053	0.45 / 0.55

4.3 Results

Classifications were performed based on the previously-defined categories of audio stimuli, shown in Table 1. The performance value provided is the mean of the true positive and true negative result percentages across the 10-fold results of the classifiers trained for all subjects. We performed five primary classifications (Table 2): stimuli directly addressed to the VC vs. stimuli that were not (shown in row 1), stimuli directly addressed to the VC vs. irrelevant audio stimuli addressed neither to the VC nor to all listeners of the channel (row 2), stimuli directly or indirectly addressed to the VC vs. irrelevant audio stimuli (row 3), stimuli that required a major response (i.e. crew station interaction or complex verbal response) vs. irrelevant audio stimuli (row 4), and stimuli directly addressed to the VC that required a major response vs. irrelevant audio stimuli (row 5). To show individual classifier performance, the 10-fold performance values for each individual subject for the primary audio that required a major response vs. irrelevant audio stimuli condition are shown in Table 3.

Table 3. 10-fold individual classifier performance for the A1 & A2 vs. B (all) condition

Subject	BCILab	LibSVM	Actual A1 & A2
1	0.78	0.79	0.46
2	0.66	0.64	0.47
3	0.59	0.67	0.49
4	0.61	0.60	0.51
5	0.66	0.62	0.46
6	0.60	0.65	0.47
7	0.69	0.67	0.42
8	0.78	0.72	0.4
9	0.61	0.66	0.48
10	0.61	0.67	0.45

5 Discussion

The highest classification performance results were obtained by classifying the recognition of relevant audio with a major response to irrelevant audio, with both BCILab and LibSVM providing similar results in the 0.65-0.67 range. However, one potential concern regarding the results arises from the fact that during each scenario there were high-activity time periods (those within the urban area, which had increased tasks and distracters) and low-activity time periods (those outside the urban area). In order to ensure that the results were not showing a distinction between high activity and low activity, we ran two additional sub-classifications, one comparing relevant audio with a response vs. irrelevant audio in low-activity time periods, and another comparing the audio stimuli that occurred in high-activity time periods. The results were comparable to the overall classification (Table 5), indicating that we are classifying based on the audio stimuli conditions, not on the low vs. high-activity condition.

Table 4. Mean classifier performance across all subjects for the A1 & A2 vs. B2 & B4 condition with low-activity and high-activity conditions

Condition	BCILab	LibSVM	Actual
Low-Activity	0.64±0.077	0.64±.097	0.47 / 0.53
High-Activity	0.64±0.046	0.62±.081	0.45 / 0.55

Another potential concern with the analysis is that the 4-second epoch starting ½ second after the auditory stimuli could be long enough that the classifier was based entirely on EMG noise related to the spoken response to the stimuli. While there is certainly some noise used in the classification, the mean length of the primary audio stimuli is 4.85 seconds (stdev = 0.996, min = 3.62, max = 7.19), suggesting that we are not classifying solely based on EMG noise related to speaking.

6 Conclusion

To begin developing aBCIs and related systems such as BCITs that function in noisy environments in which individuals are responsible for multiple concurrent tasks, we have demonstrated a basic ability to classify when a Soldier is listening to a relevant audio com, i.e. one that is addressed to them, and to which they later respond. It is clear that performance must be improved before using this classifier in an application. As such, we are exploring ways to improve and further our analysis through the use of multiple methods for extracting information from EEG data. For example, Independent Components Analysis (ICA) can remove eye [12] and other artifacts [13] from the EEG data, while connectivity measures such as Phase-Lag Index (PLI, [14]) can be insensitive to many movement artifacts [15]. Finally, we will need to evaluate the resulting performance in real-time in order to explore providing minor optimizations to crew station interfaces.

However, one remaining question is whether the classifier is learning from true brain data, or if it is primarily keying off of other physiological artifacts, such as EMG or EOG activity in the EEG recording. From the perspective of better understanding the cognitive processes associated with attending relevant audio stimuli such a question raises a clear, valid point. From the point of view of developing functional systems that operate robustly in complex environments, we would argue that, given the state of current technology, limiting research exploration to only explicitly demonstrated brain signals is neither pragmatic nor beneficial. It is not yet clear how much useful information is contained in the "noise" of the EEG data, and if the presence of this information improves, or at least does not hinder, the overall operation of an aBCI or similar system it may not be practical or even possible to completely remove such noise in real time.

In this paper, we described an experiment in a complex, high-noise, simulated environment, and we demonstrate that we are able to classify relevant audio coms with an intended response from irrelevant audio coms using EEG data collected during this experiment. In addition, we have described a planned analysis pipeline that should provide improved results over the performed preliminary analysis. By successfully processing complex, noisy data such as that described in this paper, we move closer towards being able to develop capabilities for detecting cognitive and affective states from EEG and other physiological data in real-world environments.

Acknowledgements. This work was funded under the High-Definition Cognition for Operational Environments (HD-Cog) Army Technology Objective (ATO).

References

1. Delorme, A., et al.: MATLAB-Based Tools for BCI Research. In: (B+H)CI: The Human in Brain-Computerss Interfaces and the Brain in Human-Computer Interaction, pp. 241–259 (2010)
2. Chang, C.C., Lin, C.J.: LIBSVM: a library for support vector machines (2001)
3. Kerick, S., et al.: 2010 Neuroscience Director's Strategic Initiative. Army Research Laboratory, pp. 1–32 (2011)
4. Lance, B., Capo, J., McDowell, K.: Future Soldier-System Design Concepts: Brain-Computer Interaction Technologies. In: Designing Soldier Systems: Current Issues in Human Factors (in press)
5. Scherer, K.R.: Appraisal Considered as a Process of Multilevel Sequential Checking. In: Appraisal Processses in Emotion: Theory, Methods, Research, pp. 92–120. Oxford University Press, Oxford (2001)
6. Schupp, H.T., Junghöfer, M., Weike, A.I., Hamm, A.O.: Attention and emotion: an ERP analysis of facilitated emotional stimulus processing. Neuroreport 14(8), 1107 (2003)
7. Northoff, G., Heinzel, A., de Greck, M., Bermpohl, F., Dobrowolny, H., Panksepp, J.: Self-referential processing in our brain–a meta-analysis of imaging studies on the self. Neuroimage 31(1), 440–457 (2006)
8. Gray, H.M., Ambady, N., Lowenthal, W.T., Deldin, P.: P300 as an index of attention to self-relevant stimuli. Journal of Experimental Social Psychology 40, 216–224 (2004)
9. Tanaka, J.W., Curran, T., Porterfield, A.L., Collins, D.: Activation of pre-existing and acquired face representations: The N250 ERP component as an index of face familiarity. Journal of Cognitive Neuroscience 18, 1488–1497 (2006)

10. Krause, C.M., Heikki Lang, A., Laine, M., Kuusisto, M., Pörn, B.: Event-related. EEG desynchronization and synchronization during an auditory memory task. Electroencephalography and Clinical Neurophysiology 98(4), 319–326 (1996)
11. Andreassi, J.L.: Psychophysiology: Human behavior and physiological response. Lawrence Erlbaum Assoc. Inc., Mahwah (2006)
12. Kelly, J.W., Siewiorek, D.P., Smailagic, A., Collinger, J.L., Weber, D.J., Wang, W.: Fully Automated Reduction of Ocular Artifacts in High-Dimensional Neural Data. IEEE Transactions on Biomedical Engineering 58(3), 598–606 (2011)
13. Onton, J., Makeig, S.: Information-based modeling of event-related brain dynamics. In: Progress in Brain Research, vol. 159, pp. 99–120 (2006)
14. Stam, C.J., Nolte, G., Daffertshofer, A.: Phase lag index: assessment of functional connectivity from multi channel EEG and MEG with diminished bias from common sources. Human Brain Mapping 28(11), 1178–1193 (2007)
15. McDowell, K., Kerick, S.E., Oie, K.: Non-Linear Brain Activity in Real-World Settings: Movement Artifact and the Phase Lag Index. In: Proceedings of the 27th Army Science Conference 2010 (2010)

Neural Correlates of Mindfulness Practice for Naive Meditators

An Luo[1], Dyana Szibbo[1], Julie Forbes[2], and Thomas J. Sullivan[1]

[1] NeuroSky Inc., 125 S Market St., Suite 900, San Jose, CA, 95113, USA
{aluo,dyana,tom}@neurosky.com
http://www.neurosky.com
[2] Minding Your Stress, Principal, 165 East O'Keefe St., Suite 7, Menlo Park, CA,
94025, USA
julie@julieforbes.com
http://www.julieforbes.com

Abstract. Mindfulness-Based Stress Reduction (MBSR), a widely-used form of mindfulness-based meditation, has shown positive effects on reducing psychological stress, and helping the immune system and a variety of disorders. So far little is known as to how neurophysiological activity is affected by MBSR and how it changes over time as a meditator becomes more experienced with MBSR. In this study we investigated naive meditators' EEG activity during an eight-week MBSR program. We developed easy-to-use and portable dry-sensor EEG devices and the participants recorded data by themselves. We investigated the effect of concentration level on EEG power spectrum, and tracked how EEG changed over time during the program. Significant results were found between EEG and concentration, and between EEG and amount of experience. We discussed our findings in the context of EEG rhythmic activity in relation to meditation. Our findings provided insight into developing a BCI system to guide meditation practice.

Keywords: mindfulness meditation, stress reduction, EEG power spectrum, dry-sensor, ANOVA.

1 Introduction

There has been a growing awareness of the negative effects from long-term stress and anxiety. Studies have shown chronic stress can lead to decreased health, and increased propensity to illness [1–3]. Meditation has been widely accepted as an effective and affordable way to manage stress without significant side-effects [4–6].

An educationally-based program designed by Dr. Jon Kabat-Zinn, Mindfulness-Based Stress Reduction (MBSR) focuses on training mindfulness practices, including meditation and yoga, to relieve stress and help reduce chronic pain [7]. Its main concept is to bring attention to moment-by-moment experience with a compassionate, nonjudgmental attitude. MBSR has been shown to have a positive effect on the immune system response [8, 9], and to reduce psychological

S. D'Mello et al. (Eds.): ACII 2011, Part II, LNCS 6975, pp. 477–486, 2011.

distress of student subjects as well as their ruminative thoughts [10]. It has also been employed extensively in hospitals and stress clinics.

In over 100 scientific articles about MBSR [11], most studies measured efficacy in terms of effect on the population of patients and the effect of the training on their symptoms, and only few of them addressed the neural correlates of MBSR. A related study by Lutz et al. [12] showed that long-term meditation could induce short-term and long-term neural changes. For example, long-term Buddhist practitioners self-induced high-amplitude gamma synchrony during mental practice, and their ratio of gamma-band activity (25-42 Hz) to slow oscillatory activity (4-13 Hz) was higher before, during and after meditation than the controls. It was also shown that during meditation there was an increase in both theta and alpha EEG patterns in long-term Acem meditation [13]. A recent paper by Hözel et al. reported changes in gray matter concentration after an eight-week MBSR program [16]. Despite all these efforts, little is known about how engagement during meditation may affect EEG, and how neurophysiological activity progresses as the meditator becomes more experienced. To study this, EEG data collected from naive meditators are desired. For naive subjects, it is preferred for them to practice in a group setting under the direction of a qualified coach. Due to the high cost of EEG devices and the long time to prepare a subject before EEG recording, the data collection is especially hard since multiple subjects' EEG has to be recorded simultaneously.

For this study, we designed and manufactured our own EEG devices that were both easy to use and low cost. The device was housed in a comfortable headband form factor with two dry sensors placed on the forehead, so subjects could easily record on their own. It also came with an on-board memory and Bluetooth so the EEG could be stored on the on-board memory during meditation and later downloaded to a computer. In this way no computer was needed during data acquisition so any electrical noise from computer was reduced. With these devices, we recorded EEG from a group of naive subjects while they were performing daily MBSR practice. Each subject obtained an EEG device and either participated in group practice or practiced on their own.

2   Methods

2.1   Subjects

Nineteen subjects (5 females and 14 males, mean age 37 years) volunteered for the experiment. No subjects had previous experience with MBSR or other mindfulness-based meditation. None of the subjects had known psychiatric illnesses or mental disabilities, and none used recreational drugs. Informed consent was obtained from all participants in accordance with the guidelines and approval of the NeuroSky Institutional Review Board.

After the program started, four subjects quit due to schedule conflicts. The rest of the subjects recorded a various number of sessions. Among them, eight subjects recorded at least half of the sessions, these eight subjects' EEG data were used for the data analysis.

2.2   Experimental Paradigm

The MBSR was extensively described in [7]. A formal MBSR program consists of eight weekly classes each lasting 2.5 hours, and one full day (6.5 hours) of retreat between the sixth and the seventh week of the program. Also, participants practice 45 minutes of guided mindfulness exercises daily, including sitting meditation, body scan, and mindful yoga. They are also taught to do their everyday activities such as eating, walking, or driving in a mindful way to facilitate the concept of mindful living.

In our study, we designed a slightly shortened version of the regular MBSR class for our data collection. The weekly classes were changed from 2.5 hours to 2 hours, and the retreat lasted for four hours instead of 6.5 hours. For the daily practice, the duration was changed to 35 minutes and only guided sitting meditation was practiced, although all MBSR exercises were taught and practiced during the weekly classes and the retreat. One of the authors of this article, Julie Forbes, Ph.D., is a senior MBSR instructor, who guided the whole program and recorded an instruction CD for the daily practice.

During each 35-minute daily session, the subjects followed the instruction CD and went through five blocks of sitting meditation: breathing, hearing, body sensations, emotions/thoughts, and choiceless awareness. More detailed information about these sitting meditation methods can be found in [7]. The duration of each block ranged from 4 to 6 minutes, and between every two successive blocks there was a transition period lasting one to two minutes.

After each daily practice session, the subjects filled out a short questionnaire in which they rated their level of concentration and level of mind-wandering on a scale of one to five (five being highest). A high concentration rating indicated that the subject was more engaged in the meditation, thus was more mindful of their breathing, sensations, or thoughts. In this questionnaire they also wrote down whether their eyes were closed and whether they were drowsy and/or sleeping during each block.

After the whole program was finished, the subjects filled out a qualitative total meditation outcome (TMO) questionnaire where they provided feedback about the program, such as if they have experienced any change in concentration, creativity and stress.

2.3   EEG Data Acquisition

EEG data were recorded while the subjects were performing daily meditation practice. The subjects either practiced in their own home or joined the group practice in a conference room in NeuroSky's San Jose office with other subjects. Under both situations they were instructed to stay away as much as possible from any electrical devices such as power lines, computers, or fluorescent lights.

The EEG were recorded using NeuroSky's prototype two-channel EEG system. A picture of the EEG device is shown in Figure 1. The two channels are located on the forehead of the subject, corresponding to FP1 and FP2 of the International 10-20 system. The two sides of the ear clip attached to the left

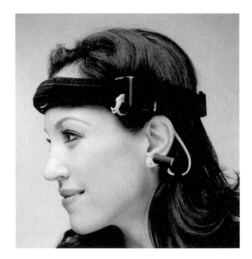

Fig. 1. Two-channel dry-sensor EEG device. The EEG device is housed in a headband form factor with two dry sensors placed at the inner side of the headband on the forehead (FP1 and FP2). The EEG circuitry is located inside the black case at the left side of the head. A power switch at the bottom of the case serves to turn on/off the device. A mini-USB port, also at the bottom of the case, is for charging a lithium-ion battery that provides power to the device. A blue light outside the case will start to flash when the device is turned on; and it stays on continuously when the device is communicating to a computer via Bluetooth connection. An on-board 8MB flash memory inside the case can store up to 3.5 hours of EEG data.

ear lobe served as the reference and the ground. The EEG was recorded with a 128Hz sampling rate at 12-bit precision.

During each daily session, the subjects followed the instruction CD to turn on their EEG device, go through all five blocks of MBSR sitting practice, and then turn the device off. The acquired EEG data were first stored in the device's on-board memory during practice and then downloaded to a computer via Bluetooth connection afterwards. In this way no computer was needed by the subject during the practice.

2.4   EEG Data Preprocessing

After the EEG data were downloaded to a computer, a set of software-based filters were applied to the raw data, which included:

- An eightieth-order band-pass FIR digital filter between 0.3Hz and 60Hz to remove the DC drift and high-frequency noise.
- An eightieth-order band-stop FIR digital filter between 58Hz and 62Hz to further remove the 60Hz power line noise.

Following these steps the EEG data were shifted to compensate for the delay introduced by the filtering.

2.5 Eye Blink Removal

Even though during the practice most subjects' eyes were kept closed, there was still a considerable amount of artifacts caused by eye blinks or eye movements. A Savitzky-Golay smoothing filter based eye blink removal procedure was used to detect and remove these artifacts [17].

2.6 Frequency Decomposition

After eye blink removal, three minutes of EEG data in the middle of each meditation block were extracted from each daily session. They were further divided into many four-second EEG traces, and our data analysis was based on these traces. Namely, the power spectral density (PSD) of each of these traces was calculated using Welch's method [18], a widely-used PSD estimation method. Then the logarithm of the PSD was derived for each four-second EEG trace for the next step.

2.7 Mixed ANOVA

In this paper we not only study how EEG changes as a function of concentration level during meditation, but also study how experience with meditation affects EEG. We did this via a three-way mixed ANOVA (analysis of variance) with repeated measures[19]. The dependent variable was the log EEG PSD; the independent variables included the self-reported concentration level, the session ID (starting from one), and the subject ID. Among them, the concentration level and the session ID were both fixed effects, while the subject ID was treated as a categorical variable and as a random effect. In this way the within-subject correlation was accounted. All the main effects from the independent variables and all the interactions between each pair of variables were included in the ANOVA model.

Moreover, since EEG shows different patterns between eyes-open and eyes-closed, and between awake and drowsy conditions, we only included the data for analysis if: 1) the eyes were closed when the data were recorded; 2) the subject was not drowsy and did not fall asleep. This information was available to us from the questionnaires that the subjects filled after each daily session.

3 Results

3.1 Behavioral Results

The progress that the subjects made over the eight weeks was tracked by their self ratings during the program. The correlation analysis between concentration level during meditation and amount of experience (indexed by session ID) showed no significant correlation between these two variables (correlation coefficient = 0.03, p=0.37). This result may suggest that overall the subjects did not make significant progress after the eight-week training in terms of their ability to engage in meditation. However, it is also possible that the subjects' skills have improved, so they were able to catch their mind-wandering moments more often, thus their self-evaluation did not truly reflect their progress. Furthermore, in [16] the authors reported significant progress after an eight-week MBSR program for naive subjects. They used mindfulness scores to measure the subjects's progress and reported significantly increased scores on three (acting with awareness, observing, and non-judging) out of the five mindfulness scales.

In our experiment some subjects dropped out during the program or only finished a small portion of the whole program. In the end ten subjects returned their TMO questionnaires. Among them, eight people experienced different levels of reduction in stress, anxiety and depression, and eight people reported improved concentration or creativity on different level. Based on this feedback, their general experience with MBSR was positive.

3.2   EEG Results

After the ANOVA procedure, p-values for all main and interaction effects were calculated, which were used to decide the significance of each effect's contribution. From ANOVA we also obtained the coefficients for the concentration level and the session ID, which provided a quantitative measure of these two variable's effects on EEG.

Figure 2 shows the estimated coefficients for concentration level during meditation at each frequency across subjects. The ANOVA was based on Channel FP1. A false discovery rate (FDR) control procedure [20] was used to correct for multiple comparisons of the p-values. If the effect at a frequency is significant under a 0.05 significance level, the corresponding estimated coefficient value is displayed as a black circle in the figure, otherwise it is marked in gray.

In this way we studied the neural correlates of engagement in the MBSR meditation. A significantly positive coefficient value indicated that the EEG power increased when the engagement level was higher, and a significantly negative coefficient indicated that the EEG power decreased with higher engagement level. From Figure 2 the concentration level shows a significantly positive effect on EEG below 10Hz (delta, theta, and low alpha bands) and above 29Hz (gamma band), and a significantly negative effect between 13Hz to 22Hz (beta band).

We also tracked the change of EEG power over time by studying the estimated coefficient for session ID across subjects using ANOVA. Figure 3 shows the result. A FDR control procedure was also used during the statistical significance test. Similarly, the coefficient value is shown as a black circle in the figure only if the effect is significant. From this figure we see that the EEG power increased between 6 to 14Hz (mainly alpha band) as the subjects became more experienced with MBSR. Also the EEG power decreased between 16 to 44Hz (beta and low gamma) as the subjects were more experienced. We also notice this effect is much weaker than that of concentration level on EEG.

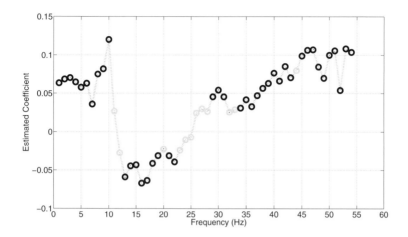

Fig. 2. ANOVA's estimated coefficients for concentration level during meditation on Channel FP1. A false discovery rate (FDR) control procedure was used to correct for multiple comparisons in the statistical significance test. If the effect is significant at a frequency under a 0.05 significance level, the corresponding coefficient is shown as a black circle in the figure, otherwise it is gray.

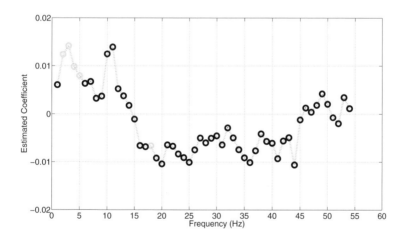

Fig. 3. ANOVA's estimated coefficients for session ID on Channel FP1. A false discovery rate (FDR) control procedure was used to correct for multiple comparisons in the statistical significance test. If the effect is significant at a frequency under a 0.05 significance level, the corresponding coefficient is shown as a black circle in the figure, otherwise it is gray.

4   Discussion

Subjects' self-reported concentration level during mindfulness-based meditation reflected how engaged they were during the practice. Subjects also reported that they engaged better when there was less stress and when they were not tired. Therefore a higher concentration during meditation would be related to a more relaxed brain state. Since alpha (8–13Hz) activity in EEG is known to be associated with relaxation and a lack of active cognitive processes [14, 15], initial stages of meditation research focused primarily on alpha band effects. Several investigators also proposed that EEG theta (4–7Hz) activity correlates positively with the level of meditation experience [13]. In this study we found that EEG in theta and low alpha domain both increased significantly as subjects were more concentrated in the meditation task. A study by Takahashi et al. [21] on twenty novice meditators also reported increased theta and alpha activity in frontal areas during meditation. They further suggested that alpha and theta waves were independently involved in mental processing during meditation. In [13] the authors reported that EEG in these two bands increased in long-term Acem meditators during meditation compared to rest condition. Our result is in line with these studies.

In [13], a significant increase in delta power was reported in the temporal-central region in the meditation condition compared to rest. However in that study no significant difference in the frontal region in delta was found. In contrast, our result showed an increase of EEG power in delta band in the frontal region when the subjects were more engaged in meditation. We also found significant decrease of EEG power in beta domain, which is, again, in contrast to [13] where no significant difference was found in EEG beta activity between meditation and rest conditions for long-term Acem meditators.

In [12], it was shown that long-term Buddhist practitioners self-induce high-amplitude gamma synchrony during mental practice. Although our study only involved novice subjects, a similar result was found that EEG gamma activity is positively correlated with concentration level during meditation. This is consistent with [12]'s suggestion that the endogenous gamma-band synchrony may reflect a change in the quality of moment-to-moment awareness.

Another interesting finding from this study is an increase in alpha and a decrease in beta power as the subjects became more experienced with MBSR. This change in EEG has a similar trend to when the concentration level was higher. However, the EEG gamma activity decreased with experience, which is in contrast to its increase with higher concentration level. We also note that the effect of experience on EEG is much weaker than that of concentration in this eight-week program, and an extended longitudinal study may help verify these results.

The next step of this study would be to build an EEG-based meditation aid system, which can be used to monitor one's EEG during meditation, and to track their progress over time. The EEG device contains only one active dry sensor on the forehead, so it can be easily used by anyone at any place.

5 Conclusion

MBSR has been widely used for stress management and has shown positive effects on psychological and physiological well-being. In this study we investigated EEG power spectrum as a function of concentration and experience for a group of naive subjects in an eight-week MBSR program. The EEG devices we used were both low cost and easy to use so the participants were able to record data by themselves. Significant effects were found between EEG and concentration on meditation, and between EEG and experience. Based on these findings it is possible to build a BCI system that a meditator can use to monitor and guide his/her practice on an everyday basis.

References

1. Kiecolt-Glaser, J.K., Glaser, R., Gravenstein, S., Malarkey, W.B., Sheridan, J.: Chronic Stress Alters the Immune Response to Influenza Virus Vaccine in Older Adults. PNAS 93(7), 3043–3047 (1996)
2. McEwen, B.S.: Protection and Damage from Acute and Chronic Stress: Allostasis and Allostatic Overload and Relevance to the Pathophysiology of Psychiatric Disorders. Annals of the New York Academy of Sciences 1032, 1–7 (2004)
3. Dhabhar, F.S., Mcewen, B.S.: Acute Stress Enhances while Chronic Stress Suppresses Cell-Mediated Immunityin Vivo: A Potential Role for Leukocyte Trafficking. Brain, Behavior, and Immunity 11(4), 286–306 (1997)
4. Jin, P.: Efficacy of Tai Chi, Brisk Walking, Meditation, and Reading in Reducing Mental and Emotional Stress. Journal of Psychosomatic Research 36(4), 361–370 (1992)
5. Shapiro, S.L., Bootzin, R.R., Figueredo, A.J., Lopez, A.M., Schwartz, G.E.: The Efficacy of Mindfulness-based Stress Reduction in the Treatment of Sleep Disturbance in Women with Breast Cancer: An Exploratory Study. Journal of Psychosomatic Research 54(1), 85–91 (2003)
6. Alexander, C.N., Swanson, G.C., Rainforth, M.V., Carlisle, T.W., Todd, C.C., Oates Jr., R.M.: Effects of the Transcendental Meditation Program on Stress Reduction, Health, and Employee Development: A Prospective Study in Two Occupational Settings. Anxiety, Stress and Coping: An International Journal 6(3), 245–262 (1993)
7. Kabat-Zinn, J.: Full Catastrophe Living: Using the Wisdom of Your Body and Mind to Face Stress, Pain, and Illness. Delta Trade Paperbacks, New York (1990)
8. Davidson, R.J., Kabat-Zinn, J., Schumacher, J., Rosenkranz, M., Muller, D., Santorelli, S.F., Urbanowski, F., Harrington, A., Bonus, K., Sheridan, J.F.: Alterations in Brain and Immune Function Produced by Mindfulness Meditation. Psychosom Med. 65(4), 564–570 (2003)
9. Robinson, F.P., Mathews, H.L., Witek-Janusek, L.: Psycho-endocrine-immune Response to Mindfulness-based Stress Reduction in Individuals Infected with the Human Immunodeficiency Virus:a Quasiexperimental Study. J. Altern. Complement. Med. 9(5), 683–694 (2003)
10. Jain, S., Shapiro, S.L., Swanick, S., Roesch, S.C., Mills, P.J., Bell, I., Schwartz, G.E.: A Randomized Controlled Trial of Mindfulness Meditation versus Relaxation Training: Effects on Distress, Positive States of Mind, Rumination, and Distraction. Ann. Behav. Med. 33(1), 11–21 (2007)

11. Rapgay, L., Bystrisky, A.: Classical Mindfulness: an Introduction to its Theory and Practice for Clinical Application. Ann. NY Acad. Sci. 1172, 148–162 (2009)
12. Lutz, A., Greischar, L.L., Rawlings, N.B., Ricard, M., Davidson, R.J.: Long-term Meditators Self-induce High-amplitude Gamma Synchrony during Mental Practice. Proceedings of the National Academy of Sciences USA 101(46), 16369–16373 (2004)
13. Lagopoulos, J., Xu, J., Rasmussen, I., Vik, A., Malhi, G.S., Eliassen, C.F., Arntsen, I.E., Sæther, J.G., Hollup, S., Holen, A., Davanger, S., Ellingsen, Ø.: Increased Theta and Alpha EEG Activity During Nondirective Meditation. The Journal of Alternative and Complementary Medicine 15(11), 1187–1192 (2009)
14. Pfurtscheller, G., Stancak Jr., A., Neuper, C.: Event-related Synchronization (ERS) in the Alpha Band-an Electrophysiological Correlate of Cortical Idling: A Review. Int. J. Psychophysiol. 24, 39–46 (1996)
15. Jensen, O., Mazaheri, A.: Shaping Functional Architecture by Oscillatory Alpha Activity: Gating by Inhibition. Front. Hum. Neurosci. 4, 186 (2010)
16. Hözel, B.K., Carmody, J., Vangel, M., Congleton, C., Yerramsetti, S.M., Gard, T., Lazar, S.W.: Mindfulness Practice Leads to Increases in Regional Brain Gray Matter Density. Psychiatry Research: Neuroimaging 191, 36–43 (2011)
17. Savitzky, A., Golay, M.J.E.: Smoothing and Differentiation of Data by Simplified Least Squares Procedures. Analytical Chemistry 36(8), 1627–1639 (1964)
18. Welch, P.D.: The Use of Fast Fourier Transform for the Estimation of Power Spectra: A Method Based on Time Averaging Over Short, Modified Periodograms. IEEE Trans. Audio Electroacoustics AU-15, 70–73 (1967)
19. Hogg, R.V., Ledolter, J.: Engineering Statistics. MacMillan, New York (1987)
20. Yoav, B., Yosef, H.: Controlling the False Discovery Rate: a Practical and Powerful Approach to Multiple Testing. Journal of the Royal Statistical Society, Series B (Methodological) 57(1), 289–300 (1995)
21. Takahashi, T., Murata, T., Hamada, T., Omori, M., Kosaka, H., Kikuchi, M., Yoshida, H., Wada, Y.: Changes in EEG and autonomic nervous activity during meditation and their association with personality traits. Int. J. Psychophysiol. 55(2), 199–207 (2005)

First Demonstration of a Musical Emotion BCI

Scott Makeig, Grace Leslie, Tim Mullen, Devpratim Sarma,
Nima Bigdely-Shamlo, and Christian Kothe

Swartz Center for Computational Neuroscience, Institute for Neural Computation,
University of California San Diego, 9500 Gilman Drive, La Jolla, California, USA 92093-0559
smakeig@ucsd.edu

Abstract. Development of EEG-based brain computer interface (BCI) methods has largely focused on creating a communication channel for subjects with intact cognition but profound loss of motor control from stroke or neurodegenerative disease that allows such subjects to communicate by spelling out words on a personal computer. However, other important human communication channels may also be limited or unavailable for handicapped subjects -- direct non-linguistic emotional communication by gesture, vocal prosody, facial expression, etc.. We report and examine a first demonstration of a musical 'emotion BCI' in which, as one element of a live musical performance, an able-bodied subject successfully engaged the electronic delivery of an ordered sequence of five music two-tone bass frequency drone sounds by imaginatively re-experiencing the human feeling he had spontaneously associated with the sound of each drone sound during training sessions. The EEG data included activities of both brain and non-brain sources (scalp muscles, eye movements). Common Spatial Pattern classification gave 84% correct pseudo-online performance and 5-of-5 correct classification in live performance. Re-analysis of the training session data including only the brain EEG sources found by multiple-mixture Amica ICA decomposition achieved five-class classification accuracy of 59-70%, confirming that different voluntary emotion imagination experiences may be associated with distinguishable brain source EEG dynamics.

Keywords: BCI, affective computing, emotion, music, ICA.

1 Introduction

Cognitive neuroscience now recognizes that the human mind and brain do indeed have parallel perceptual and communication channels for rational / objective versus emotional / affective awareness [1]. Emotional expression and communication with others is viewed as being strongly linked to health and sense of well-being – however, until recently direct emotional communication has not been a major part of computer-based communications. The field of affective computing [2] has arisen recently to address the challenge of incorporating affective communication into information and communication technologies. Various measures can be used to track related physiological responses [3], such as electromyography (EMG), blood volume pressure (BVP), and galvanic skin response (GSR). Some researchers [4] have defined basic emotions (such as fear, anger,

S. D´Mello et al. (Eds.): ACII 2011, Part II, LNCS 6975, pp. 487–496, 2011.
© Springer-Verlag Berlin Heidelberg 2011

sadness, happiness, disgust, surprise) based on facial expressions, among others. These and other measures are now being incorporated into consumer products, so far mainly for video gaming.

Linking emotion, EEG and music. This demonstration project was based on the assumption that spontaneous emotional associations of a musically sensitive and accultured listener with a given musical interval are to a significant degree stimulated by properties of the musical interval itself and by a web of associations common across a musical culture. Relationships between the perceived affective character of the intervals and the harmonic ratios underlying them have long been examined [5]. Here, five whole-ratio (just) frequency ratio combinations of two low cello tones were used to create five continuous drone sounds with differing affective characters.

Although earlier efforts to differentiate emotional reactions and states via average event-related potential (ERP) measures have had limited success [6], recent efforts in these directions using more adequate measures of larger parts of the recorded electroencephalographic (EEG) dynamic information have proved more successful. As an example, real-time recognition of emotions from EEG was recently demonstrated by Liu et al. [9] using fractal dimension analysis. Recently as well, Onton and Makeig [7] reported orderly changes in the spectral character of source-resolved high-density (248-channel) EEG activity during imagination of 15 different emotions using a method of guided imagery [8]. The dynamic state differences were stable across imagination periods of 1-5 min. Further, separable features of both brain and scalp/neck muscle activities were linked to the nature of the imagined emotion.

Most previous attempts to use EEG signals to drive musical sound have attempted to sonify the EEG directly, as first reported in 1934 by Adrian and Matthews though Alvin Lucier's 1965 *Music for Solo Performer* is widely considered the first actual EEG-based musical performance. More recently, adaptation of a standard P300 BCI speller by Grierson [10] allowed users to produce a note sequence by selectively attending to symbols on a computer display. Others have attempted passive sonification of cognitive state [11], hoping that feelings engendered by the resulting soundscapes would in turn affect participant EEG. In a recent offline study, Lin et al. [12] were able to recognize music-induced emotions using Support Vector Machines and spectral EEG features. However, the production of explicitly feeling-dominated musical expression via a brain-computer interface is still largely unexplored.

A Musical emotion BCI. These results suggest the possibility of creating brain-computer interface (BCI) systems that communicate a user's feelings non-verbally, for instance via affective musical communication. So far, the nascent field of BCI systems based on EEG signals has focused on providing subjects with profound loss of motor control with the ability to perform binary or smooth prosthetic device control [13] and to communicate by spelling-out words [15] or actuating musical tones [10].

Here, we provide an account and further *post hoc* analysis of a first demonstration of the potential feasibility of an EEG-based BCI system that attempted to directly express, by musical sound production, the feeling states of its operator. We describe an experimental musical production produced for and performed at the Fourth International BCI Meeting in Pacific Grove, California. In this piece, a subject wearing an EEG cap, the 'brainist' (TM), contributed to the live musical performance by a violinist (SM), flautist (GL), and cellist by imaginatively *re*-experiencing the emotions or affective qualities that he had spontaneously associated with five musical two-tone combinations delivered to him, during previous training sessions, under computer control as continuous, unvarying, two-tone 'drone' sounds. During the live performance, an online EEG classifier first attempted to identify which emotional or affective state the brainist intended to convey, then initiated production of the corresponding drone sound. As this drone sound continued, the three musicians performed an original music composition composed (SM) for the occasion 'over' it.

Following a more detailed account of this performance, we report re-analysis of a part of the training session EEG data collected from the brainist subject using a new method for constructing BCI classification models that may be resolved into spatially localizable brain and non-brain source features amenable to neuroscientific interpretation. Finally, we discuss the potential for both brain and non-brain information to be used in emotion BCI applications.

2 Methods

Training protocol. Following two preliminary subject training sessions, four BCI training sessions (Sessions A to D) were recorded over three days. In the two preliminary training sessions, nine different musical 'drone sounds,' each comprised of two recorded, pitch adjusted cello tones, were presented to the subject who was asked to spontaneously imagine emotional associations with each one. During the four BCI training sessions, this number was reduced to five drone sounds for which five associated musical pieces were composed and rehearsed out of brainist hearing.

In all sessions, the subject sat with eyes closed in a comfortable chair facing three loudspeakers. The first section of pre-recorded audio instructions asked the subject to fully relax into an emotionally neutral state. Next, the subject was asked to listen to the first musical drone sound, while imagining it to be a human emotional expression (for instance, an expressive sigh or moan). The subject was asked to attempt to empathize with the human they imagined to be the source of the sound, while also paying attention to their own somatic sensations associated with their experience. The latter suggestion was made to create a somatic feedback loop stabilizing and prolonging the subject's empathetic experience.

The subject was asked to press a hand-held button once when he began to experience a definite feeling or emotion he spontaneously imagined as associated with the drone sound, to then attempt to strengthen and maintain this feeling for as long as possible, and to press the button a second time when the experienced emotion waned. After the second button press, the drone sound faded out and another recorded instruction asked the subject to return to their previous relaxed, emotionally neutral state in preparation for hearing and imaginatively emotionally experiencing the next drone sound. EEG recordings of the BCI training sessions were retained for model development and *post hoc* analysis, each of which comprised a sequence of extended (and not further partitioned) blocks, where each block comprised continuous data associated with the subject's experience of an imagined empathetic feeling.

The BCI training sessions A and B were recorded on a single day in the laboratory to serve as calibration data for subsequent real-time testing. Session C was recorded for additional pseudo-online testing; Session D was the BCI training session used to train the model used in the dress rehearsal and live performance.

Performance protocol. The live performance protocol represented a verifiable attempt to demonstrate an emotion BCI operating under constraints of time and social pressure, while (hopefully) delivering a satisfying musical experience for the musical performers and audience of roughly 200 BCI researchers. The brainist sat in a comfortable chair at stage center wearing a high-density EEG cap. Right and left of the stage, elevated speakers presented a recorded audience introduction and subject instructions. These included a brief (few word) description of the feeling the brainist had used to described the feeling he associated with each drone sound following training sessions. These descriptions were, respectively: "*uncertain, quiet, shy and sensitive*" (for the 5/4 frequency ratio, musical just major third); "*frustrated, sullen and angry*" (45/32, just tritone); "*hopeful longing*" (15/8, just major seventh), "*at peace and surrounded by love*" (3/2, perfect fifth), and "*triumphant, grandiose and exultant*" (2/1, perfect octave). These few-adjective cues constituted, in effect, the musical 'score' for the brainist to realize by re-capturing and experiencing the intended feeling, thereby initiating the associated drone sound that began each musical piece.

A few seconds after the affective cue, the BCI computer began processing brainist EEG signals until a sufficiently certain classification decision was reached. At that point, the previously associated drone sound was produced by the computer through a speaker facing the brainist. The task of the three musicians was to recognize the selected drone sound and then to play the piece written to accompany it. (In the event the computer made an unintended interval selection, the musicians would have needed to quickly bring the unexpected score to the front on their music stands; fortunately, during the performance this was never necessary). The BCI-selected drone sound continued playing throughout the performance of the musical selection, then was terminated by the BCI operator. A photograph of the performance scene is available at http://sccn.ucsd.edu/events/just_carmel10.html.

Music production and EEG recording. The drone sounds initiated by BCI classification were based on a recording of a cellist playing a series of long bowed notes on the open 'G' string. The upper notes were tuned to so-called "just" ratios (identified above) of the lower-note frequency (near 98 Hz). A Max/MSP software patch seamlessly looped playback of the BCI-selected musical intervals. Five (1-3 min) pieces were composed (by SM) in twentieth-century chamber music styles intended to convey feelings and harmonies compatible with each of the five drone intervals. The brainist heard these pieces only at the final rehearsal and performance, in each case after the BCI classification was complete and with thus no effect on the outcome. In all sessions, EEG was recorded from 128 scalp channels via a Biosemi ActiveTwo system (Amsterdam) at a sampling rate of 512 Hz with 24-bit resolution. In training sessions, additional peri-ocular electrodes were placed at the right and left mastoids, at the outer corner of the right eye, and below the mid line of the left eye.

Online BCI learning and classification. For live performance, a classifier was trained on previously recorded training session data using a rather conventional BCI approach, then was applied online with additional application-specific post-processing. The training data used for the performance (lasting in all 35 minutes) contained five blocks (102s +/- 12s each), one per class of emotion beginning 5 s after the first subject button press for each drone, and ending 5-s before the second press; 2-s time windows with 1.5-s overlap were extracted from these blocks and used as training trials, yielding a total of 1512 training trials. The data in each window were notch-filtered between 55-65 Hz and band pass filtered between 8-200 Hz, as suggested by the recent report of Onton and Makeig [7] in which broadband high-frequency (30-200 Hz) EEG power was found to be informative for classification of imagined emotions. Subject-specific spatial filters were then learned using the Common Spatial Patterns (CSP) method ([15] and references therein). Since standard CSP operates on only two classes, here a CSP contrast was learned separately for each pair of classes, yielding *nchoosek*(5,2)=10 CSP pair contrasts each comprised of six spatial filters. Subsequent log-variance feature extraction and classifier training was done separately for each CSP solution. As classifiers we used Linear Discriminant Analysis (LDA) with shrinkage regularization, using an analytically derived regularization parameter. The total number of features used across classifiers was 60.

During online operation, incoming EEG was classified every 200 ms using the most recent 2-s data window. This window was spatially filtered using the CSP-derived filters, and spectrally filtered as in the calibration phase. Log-variance features were then extracted and passed to the respective binary LDA classifier, whose gradual outputs were mapped onto per-class (pseudo-)probabilities. The probabilities assigned to each class were summed across classifiers according to a 1-vs-1 voting scheme. Multiple successive outputs were aggregated and averaged in a growing window. A classification decision was reached (within at most 45 s) when the estimated probability of a class exceeded a threshold that was lowered at a constant rate from 1 to 0, allowing for a quick prediction in clear cases and more lengthy accumulation of sufficient evidence in other cases. To prevent any musical selection from being selected twice in live performance, the admissible classes were those intervals that had not been played before. Thus, the online classification was effectively five-class for the first interval, then four-class, and so on.

Refined post-hoc analysis. While the emotion detector used in live performance and described above could (and did) make sufficiently accurate predictions on new data, it was not clear to what extent its performance relied on measures of brain versus non-brain source activities. Exclusion of non-brain data is less important in BCI applications for healthy users (e.g., in gaming or other HCIs), but is of practical interest when considering users who lack muscle control. During a post-hoc analysis, calibration Session A was used for advanced model calibration and Session B for model testing, as both were measured on the same day using the same electrode montage. Since for technical reasons data from the online performance was not stored, it could not be included in the post-hoc analysis.

Since each EEG channel measures a linear superposition of signals from sources distributed across brain, head and environment, it is not generally possible to interpret single sensor signals as a measure of the activity of a distinct cortical source. This limitation can be lifted or at least minimized when spatial filters are optimized to recover source signal components that are mutually statistically independent. Following data pre-processing and automated artifact rejection using the default pipeline for Independent Component Analysis (ICA) [16] in our open-source BCILAB toolbox [17], we employed a recently-developed extension of ICA, Adaptive Mixture ICA (Amica) [18], to derive a set of maximally independent source signals, as a mixture of multiple (here six) full-rank signal decompositions (each decomposition with different, possibly overlapping, temporal support).

The components of each model (here 92 each) were then visually screened for clear brain components (see [7]) indicated by the close resemblance of their cortical maps to the projection of a single equivalent dipole or cortical patch. Non-brain (muscle, heart, eye) component processes were also identified, based on temporal and spectral properties, and eliminated, leaving a total of 38 brain component processes. A single (or in some cases dual-symmetric) equivalent current dipole model was fit to each brain component using a four-shell spherical head model. All components were localized within or on the periphery of the brain volume and above the neck or lower head region that contributes the majority of electromyographic (EMG) artifacts.

Next, trial epochs and features were extracted from the unmixed continuous multi-component signal, separately for each Amica decomposition. Epoch extraction was analogous to the original analysis: the continuous unmixed data were low-pass filtered below 90 Hz, sub-sampled to 180 Hz and then high-pass filtered above 2 Hz using a causal minimum-phase FIR filter. From these data, 3-s windows overlapping by 2.5 s were extracted and the discrete Fourier power spectral densities in each window were used as features, giving 1,183 trials in total each with 10,260 spatio-spectral features.

On these data, a weighted l1-regularized logistic regression classifier (realized by 1-vs-1 voting of binary classifiers) selected a sparse, best-classifying subset of spatially- and spectrally-localized features. The trials were weighted according to the temporal support of the respective underlying Amica model, and individual features were standardized similarly to the first-order model introduced in [19] and further weighted using a (here 0/1-valued) masking of brain vs. non-brain components.

During pseudo-online evaluation, the data were then causally pre-processed and mapped to per-model features as described above, and the classifiers for each model were applied to yield a discrete probability distribution over the five possible outcomes. The final probabilities were obtained as a weighted average of the classifer outputs under each Amica model, where the weight was the total probability of the respective model under the training dataset (a measure of the model's relative temporal support in the data).

3   Results

Initial offline analysis results. To determine the method to be used for the live performance, the across-session prediction accuracies of a variety of methods – CSP (see Section 2), Spectrally weighted CSP, and an implementation of Independent Modulators [7] – were assessed using data from Sessions A and B. The CSP-based classification gave the best across-session performance, reaching a single-time window, between-session classification accuracy of 84% (chance level 20%), so was chosen for all real-time analyses. A subset of its spatial filters is shown in Fig. 2(a)).

Live performance. In the concert performance, the BCI classification selected the brainist- (and composer-) intended drone sound in all five cases, though the BCI classification monitor showed that one of the selections was nearly mis-classified. BCI performance level (>70%) was thus as expected from numerical experiments on the data from the four pilot sessions. Anecdotally, in the rehearsal performance the intended first interval (major third, described by the brainist as 'uncertain, quiet, shy, and sensitive') was substituted by its near opposite (tritone; 'frustrated, sullen, and angry'); the brainist later said he actually did feel frustrated at the time by the presence of unwelcome noise in the rehearsal hall.

Post-hoc data analysis. In a pseudo-online analysis, the classifier described above achieved a single-time window, between-session classification accuracy of 59%-70% when trained on Session A and applied on Session B, depending on the length of the time window (windows up to 15 s in length were tested, with longer windows giving better results). The model used approximately 1/3 of all features. Figure 1 shows a smoothed (5-s moving-average window) time course of the predicted probability distribution over the 1-s time windows of this session. The fitted dipole locations for each component in Figure 2(b)-(c) included across-models clusters of near-identical component processes in or near primary and lateral visual cortex, somatomotor cortex, dorsolateral prefrontal cortex, superior parietal cortex, middle temporal gyrus, and anterior and posterior cingulate cortex. For each brain source, we identified the coordinates of equivalent dipoles and corresponding Brodmann Area designations of the nearest gray matter using the Talairach Daemon. Figure 2(e) lists these results sorted in descending order by average absolute classifier weight of each independent component (IC). The learned spectral weights of the classifiers for these components (Fig. 2(d)) show a clear focus on alpha band amplitudes of many components, as well as sensitivity to high-frequency broadband (HFB) activity in some somatomotor and occipital components, as in previous emotion imagination results in [7].

time course of BCI-predicted 5-class probabilities in test session (white frames mark the correct class)

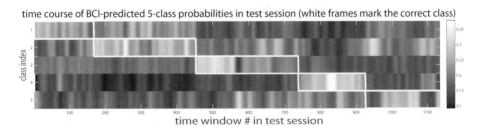

time window # in test session

Fig. 1. Predicted probability distribution across test session (B) time windows in the post-hoc analysis. The ordinate separates the five possible outcomes of the classification. Light shades indicate high probability of the respective outcome; dark shades indicate low probability. White rectangles mark the five (true) conditions the subject was asked to imaginatively experience during the five training sessions.

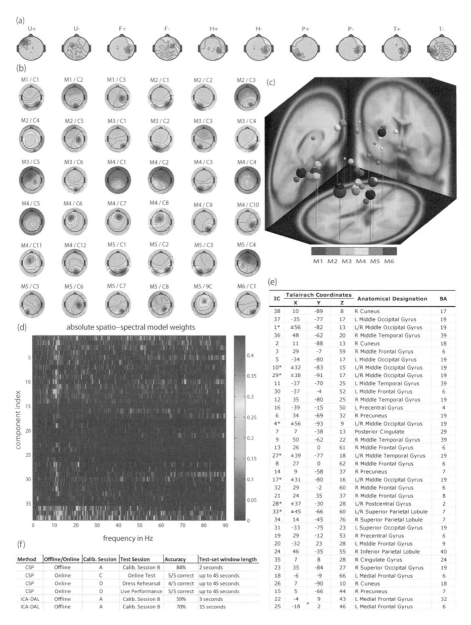

(e)

IC	X	Y	Z	Anatomical Designation	BA
38	10	-89	8	R Cuneus	17
37	-35	-77	17	L Middle Occipital Gyrus	19
1*	±56	-82	13	L/R Middle Occipital Gyrus	19
36	48	-62	20	R Middle Temporal Gyrus	39
2	11	-88	13	R Cuneus	18
3	29	-7	59	R Middle Frontal Gyrus	6
5	-34	-80	17	L Middle Occipital Gyrus	19
10*	±32	-83	15	L/R Middle Occipital Gyrus	19
29*	±38	-91	17	L/R Middle Occipital Gyrus	19
11	-37	-70	25	L Middle Temporal Gyrus	39
30	-37	-4	52	L Middle Frontal Gyrus	6
12	35	-80	25	R Middle Temporal Gyrus	19
16	-39	-15	50	L Precentral Gyrus	4
6	34	-69	32	R Precuneus	19
4*	±56	-93	9	L/R Middle Occipital Gyrus	19
7	7	-38	13	Posterior Cingulate	29
9	50	-62	22	R Middle Temporal Gyrus	39
13	26	0	61	R Middle Frontal Gyrus	6
27*	±39	-77	18	L/R Middle Temporal Gyrus	19
8	27	0	62	R Middle Frontal Gyrus	6
14	9	-58	37	R Precuneus	7
17*	±31	-80	16	L/R Middle Occipital Gyrus	19
32	29	-2	60	R Middle Frontal Gyrus	6
21	24	35	37	R Middle Frontal Gyrus	8
28*	±37	-30	28	L/R Postcentral Gyrus	2
33*	±45	-66	60	L/R Superior Parietal Lobule	7
34	14	-45	76	R Superior Parietal Lobule	7
31	-33	-75	23	L Superior Occipital Gyrus	19
19	29	-12	53	R Precentral Gyrus	6
20	-32	23	28	L Middle Frontal Gyrus	9
24	46	-35	55	R Inferior Parietal Lobule	40
35	7	8	28	R Cingulate Gyrus	24
23	35	-84	27	R Superior Occipital Gyrus	19
18	-6	-9	66	L Medial Frontal Gyrus	6
26	7	-90	10	R Cuneus	18
15	5	-66	44	R Precuneus	7
22	-4	9	43	L Medial Frontal Gyrus	32
25	-18	2	46	L Medial Frontal Gyrus	6

(f)

Method	Offline/Online	Calib. Session	Test Session	Accuracy	Test-set window length
CSP	Offline	A	Calib. Session B	84%	2 seconds
CSP	Online	C	Online Test	5/5 correct	up to 45 seconds
CSP	Online	D	Dress Rehearsal	4/5 correct	up to 45 seconds
CSP	Online	D	Live Performance	5/5 correct	up to 45 seconds
ICA-DAL	Offline	A	Calib. Session B	59%	3 seconds
ICA-DAL	Offline	A	Calib. Session B	70%	15 seconds

Fig. 2. Original (a) and post-hoc (b-e) classifier structure. (a) Highest-weighted CSP filters per emotion class (letter matching the leading description word), from both ends of the eigenvalue spectrum (+/-). (b) Scalp projections of leading 36 (of 38) selected independent components, grouped by Amica model. (c) Equivalent dipole locations for components in (b), surface area proportional to total weight under the classifier and colored by Amica model. (d) Absolute spectral weights for the selected components and frequencies, order corresponding to (b) when read from left to right, top to bottom. (e) Anatomical labels for equivalent dipole locations, sorted by descending total classifier weight. (f) Overview of BCI analyses and obtained results.

4 Discussion

The classification accuracy of both the CSP classifier and the ICA classifier are remarkably high, given that the chance level was 20% in both cases. The successful live performance produced its intended result of demonstrating the potential feasibility of a direct emotion BCI, here in the form of a system that used a learned vocabulary of musical sounds to express feeling states of the 'brainist' subject. Such a system might be usable by paralyzed users, by users limited in emotional expression, or in ordinary social settings to augment emotional communication.

Using ICA decomposition methods, we separated the scalp data into physiologically localizable brain and non-brain source process features weighted by a classifier. Localization of the involved IC sources implicated a number of anatomical regions known to be involved in visual and somatomotor imagery, self-reflection, emotion and music processing. The predominance of visual cortical areas among localized sources is not surprising given the use of visual imagery as reported by the subject. Alpha power modulation of ICs localized to bilateral occipital cortex has also been linked to changes in music structure (mode/tempo) as well as emotional responses to music [20]. Some dependence on sources localized in or near premotor cortex (MFG), precentral gyrus, and postcentral gyrus (IC 28) might also be expected since the subject was asked to pay attention to somatic sensations associated with the emotional experience, and reported significant somatomotor imagery associated with his emotional state. The precuneus has been implicated in episodic memory (including those related to the self), visuospatial processing and imagery, self-referential processing, and is thought to be the core hub of the "default mode (resting) network" [21]. Changes in regional blood flow as well as theta- and alpha-band power modulation of ICs localized to precuneus have also been linked to musical dissonance and major/minor mode distinctions [20] also tied to musical frequency ratios.

5 Conclusion

We have demonstrated the potential feasibility of a novel emotion-classification and augmented emotional communication system via a live musical performance in which EEG-based BCI classification played an artistic role, intended to suggest the development of BCI technology to enable or augment direct non-verbal emotional communication. In *post hoc* analysis of the training session data we successfully applied a novel method to learn ICA source-resolved BCI models that allow use of anatomical source constraints (here to eliminate non-brain sources) and can be interpreted in terms of localizable cortical dynamics.

Acknowledgments. We thank an anonymous donor and The Swartz Foundation (Old Field, NY) for gifts supporting this research, Theresa Vaughan for encouraging our efforts, and Julie Onton for key contributions to our emotion research.

References

1. Adolphs, R.: Cognitive Neuroscience of Human Social Behaviour. Nat. Rev. Neurosci. 4, 165–178 (2003)
2. Picard, R.: Affective Computing. MIT Press, Cambridge (1997)

3. Cacioppo, J.T., Bernston, G.G., Larsen, J.T., Poehlmann, K.M., Ito, T.A.: The psychophysiology of emotion. In: Lewis, R., Haviland, J.M. (eds.) The Handbook of Emotion, pp. 119–142. Guilford Press, New York (1993)
4. Ekman, P., Friesen, W.V.: Facial Action Coding System: A technique for the measurement of facial movement. Consulting Psychologists Press, Palo Alto (1978)
5. Makeig, S.: Theory of Interval Affect. Monograph submitted for the Master's Thesis in Music, University of South Carolina, Columbia, SC (1979)
6. Olofsson, J., Nordin, S., Sequeira, H., Polich, J.: Affective picture processing: An integrative review of ERP findings. Biolog. Psycholog. 77, 247–265 (2008)
7. Onton, J., Makeig, S.: High-frequency broadband modulation of electroencephalographic spectra. Frontiers In Human Neurosciences 3, 61 (2009)
8. Bonny, H.L., Savary, L.M.: Music and your mind: listening with a new consciousness. Harper & Row, New York (1973)
9. Liu, Y., Sourina, O., Nguyen, M.K.: Real-time EEG-based Human Emotion Recognition and Visualization. In: Proc. 2010 Int. Conf. on Cyberworlds, Singapore (2010)
10. Grierson, M.: Composing with brainwaves: minimal trial P300b recognition as an indication of subjective preference for the control of a musical instrument. In: Proc. Int. Cryog., Mat. Conf., Seoul, Korea (2008)
11. Hinterberger, T., Baier, G.: Parametric orchestral sonification of EEG in real time. IEEE Multimedia 12(2), 70–79 (2005)
12. Lin, Y.P., Wang, C.H., Wu, T.L., Jeng, S.K., Chen, J.H.: EEG-based emotion recognition in music listening: A comparison of schemes for multiclass support vector machine. In: ICASSP 2009, pp. 489–492 (2009)
13. Kübler, A., Nijboer, F., Mellinger, J., Vaughan, T.M., Pawelzik, H., Schalk, G., McFarland, D.J., Birbaumer, N., Wolpaw, J.R.: Patients with ALS can use sensorimotor rhythms to operate a brain-computer interface. Neurology 64(10), 1775–1777 (2005)
14. Pfurtscheller, G., Müller-Putz, G.R., Scherer, R., Neuper, C.: Rehabilitation with Brain-Computer Interface Systems. Computer 41, 58–65 (2008)
15. Blankertz, B., Tomioka, R., Lemm, S., Kawanabe, M., Müller, K.-R.: Optimizing spatial filters for robust EEG single-trial analysis. IEEE Signal Processing Mag. 25, 41–56 (2008)
16. Bell, A.J., Sejnowski, T.J.: An information-maximization approach to blind separation and blind deconvolution. Neural Computation 7, 1129–1159 (1995)
17. Delorme, A., Mullen, T., Kothe, C., Acar, Z.A., Bigdely-Shamlo, N., Vankov, A., Makeig, S.: EEGLAB, SIFT, NFT, BCILAB, and ERICA: New tools for advanced EEG/MEG processing. In: Computational Intelligence and Neuroscience: Special Issue on Academic Software Applications for Electromagnetic Brain Mapping Using MEG and EEG (2011)
18. Palmer, J.A., Makeig, S., Kreutz-Delgado, K., Rao, B.D.: Newton Method for the ICA Mixture Model. In: Proc. 33rd IEEE International Conference on Acoustics, Speech and Signal Processing, Las Vegas, NV, pp. 1805–1808 (2008)
19. Tomioka, R., Müller, K.-R.: A regularized discriminative framework for EEG analysis with application to brain-computer interface. Neuroimage 49(1), 415–432 (2010)
20. Lin, Y.P., Duann, J.R., Chen, J.H., Jung, T.P.: Electroencephalographic dynamics of musical emotion perception revealed by independent spectral components. Neuroreport 21(6), 410–415 (2010)
21. Bullmore, E., Sporns, O.: Complex brain networks: graph theoretical analysis of structural and functional systems. Nature Reviews Neuroscience 10(3), 186–198 (2009)

Emotion in Games

Georgios N.Yannakakis[1], Kostas Karpouzis[2], Ana Paiva[3], and Eva Hudlicka[4]

[1] IT University of Copenhagen, Denmark
yannakakis@itu.dk
[2] ICCS-NTUA, Greece
kkarpou@cs.ntua.gr
[3] Instituto Superior Técnico/INESC-ID, Portugal
ana.paiva@inesc-id.pt
[4] Psychometrix Associates, USA
Hudlicka@ieee.org

Abstract. Computer games are unique elicitors of emotion. Recognition of player emotion, dynamic construction of affective player models, and modelling emotions in non-playing characters, represent challenging areas of research and practice at the crossroads of cognitive and affective science, psychology, artificial intelligence and human-computer interaction. Techniques from AI and HCI can be used to recognize player affective states and to model emotion in non-playing characters. Multiple input modalities provide novel means for measuring player satisfaction and engagement. These data can then be used to adapt the gameplay to the player's state, to maximize player engagement and to close the affective game loop.

The Emotion in Games workshop (EmoGames 2011 http://sirenproject. eu/content/acii-2011-workshop-emotion-games) will bring together researchers and practitioners in affective computing, user experience research, social psychology and cognition, machine learning, and AI and HCI, to explore topics in player experience research, affect induction, sensing and modelling and affect-driven game adaptation, and modelling of emotion in non-playing characters. It will also provide new insights on how gaming can be used as a research platform, to induce and capture affective interactions with single and multiple users, and to model affect- and behaviour-related concepts, helping to operationalize concepts such as flow and engagement.

The workshop will include a keynote, paper and poster presentations, and panel discussions. Selected papers will appear in a special issue of the IEEE Transactions on Affective Computing, "Emotion in Games", in mid-2013.

The EmoGames2011 workshop is organized in coordination with the newly formed 'Emotion in Games' Special Interest Group (SIG) of the Humaine Association and the IEEE Computational Intelligence Society (CIS) Task Force on Player Satisfaction Modelling. We would like to thank all participants, as well as the members of the Program Committee, for their reviews of the workshop submissions: Elisabeth André, Ruth Aylett, Nadia Bianchi-Berthouze, Antonio Camurri, Marc Cavazza, Jonathan Gratch, Hatice Gunes, Dirk Heylen, Katherine Isbister, Stefanos Kollias, Maurizio Mancini, Anton Nijholt, Julian Togelius, Asimina Vasalou, Gualtiero Volpe, Catherine Pelachaud, and Tom Ziemke.

Keywords: emotion, games, affective gaming.

S. D´Mello et al. (Eds.): ACII 2011, Part II, LNCS 6975, p. 497, 2011.
© Springer-Verlag Berlin Heidelberg 2011

Improvisation, Emotion, Video Game

Josephine Anstey

Department of Media Study,
University at Buffalo
http://josephineanstey.com

Abstract. Actors are increasingly used by the video game industry to give life to non-player characters. Models are animated based on face and body tracking. Voices are dubbed. This paper argues that it is now time to tap into the improvising expertise of actors. To create games with rich, emotional content, improvisation with a group of actors is a necessary part of game-play development. *abstract* environment.

Keywords: improvisation, emotional game-play, common-sense psychology.

1 Introduction

Since 1995 I have worked on interdisciplinary and collaborative productions that focus on interactive, user-centered experiences designed to put the player in emotionally rich territory. These productions have included virtual reality fiction; networked virtual reality drama; intermedia performance incorporating video games; and the deployment of non-player characters. The productions have explicitly fore-fronted the structuring of emotional situations such that players can conduct psychological explorations of the self. To create such situations I have used techniques based in "common sense psychology" and narrative and dramatic manipulation. In the earliest work non-playing characters talked to the player, and relied on software interpretation of the player's tracked physical gestures and movement to judge her emotional state and respond appropriately. In later work I experimented with natural-language-using non-player characters and actors using puppet avatars, to create the same supporting roles. These experiences have led me to the conclusion that improvisation with live actors is a necessary step in the development of emotional game-play, both as a process for the modeling of non-player characters, and for construction of experiential situations where the players are empowered to feel and act.

After a brief description of my collaborative group and our project history, in Section 3 I discuss the techniques relying on "common sense psychology" and in Section 4 narrative and dramatic manipulation that form the basis of my approach to the structuring of emotional game-play. In Section 5 I discuss lessons learned from tracking the user to judge emotional state and in Section 6 our experiences with natural language using agent- versus human- actors. In Section 7 I lay out my argument for the inclusion of improvisation with live actors

S. D'Mello et al. (Eds.): ACII 2011, Part II, LNCS 6975, pp. 498–507, 2011.

as a necessary, formal step in the creation of emotionally charged interactive experiences. The experiences I am personally interested in generating tend to be on the fringe of game development; my experimental arena has been virtual reality, mixed-reality and intermedia performance; the content domain I circle is the creation of identity, a gendered self and power dynamics; but I believe that including improvisation expertise is crucial for all projects interested in pushing the boundaries of emotional content in games.

2 Collaboration History

I have collaborated on a series of interactive productions that have explored issues of identity: how identity is structured and gendered; cyber-identity; post-human identity; questions of virtual bodies and remote bodies. These collaborations led in 2005 to the formation of The Intermedia Performance Studio (IPS), an interdisciplinary group, whose members have expertise in interactive fiction and game studies (Anstey), performance theory and directing (Sarah Bay-Cheng), virtual reality and computer graphics (Dave Pape), and artificial intelligence (Stuart C. Shapiro). Productions have included: *The Thing Growing* (2000), a virtual reality drama with intelligent agents; *PAAPAB* (2004), networked VR with puppet avatars; *The Trial The Trail/Human Trials* (2005-2007), networked VR, intelligent agents, puppet avatars; *365 Days/365Plays* (2007), intermedia performance with live and virtual performers, interactive sets; *Workers of the World* (2008) & *Office Diva* (2008), robot/virtual character performances *WoyUbu* (2009), intermedia performance with live performers, computer-controlled actors, robots, improvisation, game-like interaction, interactive and mixed-reality sets; *play/share beyond/in* (2010), pervasive game. Developing effective emotional game-play has been central to this work.

3 Common Sense Psychology

"Common Sense Psychology" is folk wisdom about how people will react to physical and emotional stimuli. Its use in media is best described by Bernard Perron, who extended Ed Tan's work on films as "emotion machines" to video games [18]. Perron suggests that many authors of films and games are superb common sense cognitive psychologists, able to set up scenarios that stimulate emotion, and sequences that create emotional roller-coasters. They intersect the techniques of their media with typical psychological, behavioral, and social rules, patterns, and interactions. Alfred Hitchcock is the paradigmatic common sense psychologist/film-maker. His work demonstrates how evoking emotion rather than telling a story can be the central creative concern and driver: the germ of his films was not a narrative concept but emotional territory that he wanted to explore and to lead the audience through. He was supremely cavalier with the plot - using the term McGuffin to describe the plot pretext which got his characters into appropriate emotional dilemmas [22]. Horror film makers created a language of audio and visual techniques to indicate: someone is following the protagonist; a monster is around the corner; the panic of the protagonist as she flees etc. All of which make the viewer's heart pound and palms sweat. Perron argues that game developers, most specifically in the horror/suspense genre amended these tropes for an interactive form, and similarly depend on the players ability to decode them and react emotionally. For example, in film, emotions are empathetic, and often evoked by reaction shots. Perron points out that players are represented by avatars in games, but we don't tend to see reaction shots of the avatar. Instead the players own emotions are stimulated by the visuals, the sound effects, the non-diegetic music.

Perron also introduces the idea of game-play emotions, refering to the work of psychologist Nico Frijda who describes emotions as action tendancies [11]. This implies that if an interactive environment evokes a certain emotion, the user will be motivated to act in a certain way. The idea that emotion can determine action is vitally important. It implies that the job of the emotional game developer is to stimulate emotions with a certain calculation about the kind of action that may result. The author should be creating emotional snares that spur the user to action without full awareness of the implications of the act until she has acted. Agency and action are constrained by an emotional logic. The next section explores this process of manipulation, and what it can mean for interactive media more fully.

4   Manipulation and Constraint

S. Nath writes: "Producing a narrative is ... an act of directly (and successively) manipulating narrative elements to indirectly (and successively) manipulate audience knowledge, feeling and action ..."[17]. In [3] I argued that this kind of manipulation is also crucial for interactive forms, that it is the author's work to create in the position of player the kind of emotional agent she wants. To avoid the negative connotations of the word manipulation for a moment, let us use the more value neutral word constraint. The work of the author is to set up the structures of constraint that allow meaning, emotion and agency to emerge. All the elements in the virtual world enable play but also serve as the constraints: audio, visuals, narratives, non-playing characters provide the context, the tools and the motivations for the player. The author manipulates these constraints so that a user watching or interacting with the spectacle can decode and interpret events, react to them and act. Within this framework, interaction can work by trapping the user, so that her actions implicate her ever more strongly in an unfolding emotional and semiotic process. However apparently simple the interaction, the results can be powerful.

As an example, I will give my own reaction to the interactive art installation *Items 1-2000*, by Paul Vanouse. Video monitors are placed around an object that suggests a surgical table or a coffin. The table is covered with thick wax with the life-size imprint of a man in it. A naked male performer can lie in the imprint. A pane of glass is set above the table with bar codes strips aligned with each of the major organs. A bar code scanner lies on the glass. The initial set up evokes curiosity, what happens if I scan? It may evoke a certain sense of transgression, what if I scan across the genitals? If the viewer swipes the scanner across the bar codes, the video moves through the data set of the Visible Human Project until it reaches the image which corresponds to that organ. Entranced and made curious by technology we act, and our action ties us into an economy that executes a man, cuts him up into hundreds of fine slices and photographs each slice. We have benefited, we are complicit. Interaction leads to an Ah Ha! moment that says, I did this. I am part of this. This is about me, my curiosity, my ghoulishness, my scientic inquiry, my medical establishment, my society. My own reaction differed depending on whether the performer was lying in the wax imprint or not. Without the performer I felt a great sadness, a loss, perhaps mourning for the man who had been sliced up. When the performer was present, I felt much more strongly the generally invasive behavior that surrounds western medical practice - the treatment of the patient as a commodity.

I consider this work a completely successful example of the way the elements of an interactive composition can constrain thought, emotion and action: my emotions see-sawed as I became aware of the literal manipulation and its metaphorical reverberations. I manipulate the scanner. I am manipulated by this installation. My society manipulated the prisoner who donated this body.

5   Tracking Emotions

Manipulating emotion and emotion-action-emotion sequences by setting up constraining scenarios based in common sense pyschology are fundamental building blocks in my work. This section and the next give two examples.

The Thing Growing [4] [6], is a CAVE VR experience where the tracked user encounters an abstract virtual character, the *Thing*, in a story-book landscape. The goal of the application is to give the user an emotional experience of coping with a difficult and cloying relationship. An early design decision was to use a dancing activity to build the relationship. Common sense psychology tells us that humans are very apt to physically mimic the movements of other humans, and that physical mimicry and dancing both signify intimacy. In our application this translates into the *Thing* demonstrating dance steps and encouraging the user to copy them. We backchain from the data received from the tracking system, to the action that caused it, to the probable emotional state of the user. Feedback data tells the application if the user is dancing or not, or if the user is trying to drive away from the *Thing*. The *Thing* responds with words of encouragement, praise or criticism. If the user runs away the *Thing* persistently follows and tries to persuade her to stay still and dance.

The dancing activity also creates a second order of meaning for the information we receive from the tracking system - the numbers we receive can be interpreted as attempts to dance and therefore please the virtual creature, or as a refusal to co-operate. Common sense psychology tells us about the patterns of abusive relationships: the victim is kept off balance as the abuser alternates praise and condemnation, love and abandonment. The dance trope creates a constrained space for the *Thing* to deploy these patterns. Having to dance makes some people uncomfortable and therefore more vulnerable to the *Thing* as it praises or criticizes them. The user (victim) quickly or slowly recognizes the *Thing's* dominating character and squirms to cope with the kind of clinging, intrusive relationship which it is trying to foist on her as it begs, whines, threatens, and flatters her with the single intention of making her dance. Because this is an immersive 3D experience and the *Thing* is approximately the same size as the user, it can also use its physical presence to intimidate and to harass by literally getting into the user's face, and invading her space. This ability to manipulate a sense of physical over-proximity in the VE feeds into the project's theme of creating a claustrophobic relationship. The aim of the dancing section is to stimulate a variety of emotional reactions from the user as she reacts to the *Thing's* demands and moods.

At the earliest demonstrations of the project, we had not implemented a system to analyze the feedback from the tracking system, instead we networked a spying human into the loop, who activated buttons that told the *Thing* whether the user was dancing well or badly or not even trying to dance. This Wizard of Oz experience totally altered and simplified how we built the detection system. We had originally assumed that we would have to build a virtual 3D grid around the user to detect her gestures at quite a fine degree of granularity and reveal whether she was accurately copying the dance steps she was shown. But as we watched the interactions of real users, we noticed that the "monkey see, monkey do" common sense psychology idea was very powerful. If they danced at all, the great majority of people tried very hard to copy the *Thing* . We also noticed that if they they appeared timid, we pushed the "danced-well" button, so the *Thing* could be encouraging. The final detection system only tested how vigorously the user was moving, not how accurately. A lesson in not building something complicated until you have tested what is necessary.

6   Experiments with Natural Language and Performance

The Trial The Trail [5] [21] was another VR drama with intelligent agents. The basic experience was a warped quest narrative which would draw a participant into a series of strategic alliances with two characters, one representing a careless cynicism and the other responsible caring. We bogged down in the complexity of creating virtual humans that could walk and talk: navigate the landscape and correctly stage confrontations and events; follow a script but respond to the user with correct emotion; understand natural language. An ex-puppeteer and performance theorist joined our group, and we used our prior experiences with networked VR to make the autonomous agents into puppet avatars, controlled by actors, renaming the project *Human Trials* [2]. Rather than involving solely human actors, as in a traditional drama, or entirely computer-driven agents, as in a video game, the final performance combined both. This gave the advantages of actors, to improvise and to adapt to an unpredictable human participant, while allowing agents to fill out the world and take the roles of minor characters. We made use of a networked virtual environment to bring the actors, participant and agents together, all of them appearing as avatars in the shared world.

The final version of *Human Trials* was an intermedia spectacle for a participant of one and a larger audience. The audience saw two actors with VR helmets and tracking systems sitting in front of three large projections. Above each actor's head was their own view into the virtual world. The third projection was the view of a participant, who took part from a CAVE-like VR system, screened for privacy. The actors and participant interacted with voice and gesture as they navigated the virtual scenes. The scenes were also inhabited by completely virtual characters who spoke and reacted to the user, but could not understand natural language, - monkat creatures that played with her but then clung to her and would not let go, bad-guys (red, pawn-like, enormous) who jostled and taunted her.

The production of *Human Trials* was intense and the use of actors offered useful insights; the performances were enjoyable but problemmatic. The main insight was that in rehearsal the director and actors worked to codify a set of gestures for each puppet avatar, a constrained set that grounded the personality of each character. Then, as far as possible, the actors worked with the existing script to discover strategies to lead the participant from point to point in the unfolding experience, folding her responses back into the narrative and interactive world of our virtual scenes and its inhabitants. Difficulties arose because our attempts to create language-using agents had led us to tie down and formalize script choices before we had really tested them with participants. Although the humans could be flexible and cope with anything the user might say or do, sometime their spur of the moment reactions took us away from the content domain of the piece. Another difficulty was that adding actors, had moved us into the realm of performance and audience. An interesting experience for one, does not necessarily translate into an interesting spectacle for many, and the actors had to push the pace to keep it interesting, which made the participant feel harried and manipulated. This experience has became the basis for other experiments in intermedia performance for our group (*36Days/ 365Plays*, *WoyUbu*), productions incorporating mixed reality, virtual sets, agent and robot actors, interactive sets; and prioritizing the handling of large audience rather than personal interactive experience.

However, for me the main lesson of *Human Trials* was that for a game-like work of participatory drama the production process had essentially been backwards - it should have started with actors and moved to computers not vice versa. If we want to create a game or interactive fiction with strong emotional content conveyed by language-using computer agents, the place to start is with an improvising group of actors. To create emotional interactive scenarios we need to start with our common sense psychology and an idea of the manipulations we are interested in and use a group of improvisers to play out the psychological situations. Their fast and flexible iterations on the themes of our content domain will serve as the basis for building the game in the computer. In the next section I turn to a more detailed discussion of the idea.

7 Adding Improv to the Toolset

The problem of creating believable intelligent agents capable of interacting dramatically is one of the major issues long identified by a lively academic community of AI researchers focusing on interactive story-telling [9] [10] [16] [12] [20]. An especially difficult part of this problem is building agents that can converse. Piece by piece, the elements of using natural language are being formalized, but the pieces are many (analyzing sound-streams; detecting words; using semantics, semiotics, pragmatics to understand them; synthesizing speech), and the process is imperfect as anyone who has hurled imprecations at a service chat bot knows.

One successful technique for conversational agents is to constrain the content domain, so that the agent has a higher chance of responding correctly even with imperfect knowledge about what is said. Human beings also use this tactic, employing schemas or scripts that assume what the other person has said, and that are based/built from the typical patterns that emerge from social or psychological settings. The famous Eliza, used the constrained setting of therapy, detected key words and responded with therapy-speak strategies including repetition, general questions about keywords, evasive generalities [23]. Zubeck and Horswill's conversational agent in *The Break Up Conversation*, has an area of competence in the domain of "breaking up" [24]. The NICE project used the content area of Hans Anderson and his fairy tales to program their Hans Anderson agent [7]. In the first two cases conversation was conducted in text, only in the third case is the agent designed to respond to natural oral language. An early part of the construction of such agents is a thorough study the kind of scripts and schemas that operate in this domain [8]. If the domain is fictional (whether interactive story or game), I believe that any initial script needs to be workshopped with improvising actors, so that the typical language patterns, schemas, scripts and strategies can be a) evolved and refined and b) collected and formalized for use by the AI agent builders.

Although some critics have stated categorically that the freedom of choice of game and authorial control of story are fundamentally irreconcilable [1], it is clear that story genres such as science fiction, suspense-horror, action-adventure, are well established in video games and story-lines, plots and even relationships with computer-based characters are routine [19]. Players are very clear about what they have to do in these games: explore, collect things, shoot. But if the game were to include the negotiation of social, emotional or psychological situations, things would become more difficult not only for the AI, but for the player. Free and open improvisation is all but impossible for a novice, it is a learned skill [13] [14]. Moreover, Torunn Kjolner and Niels Lehmann argue, improvisation is never free and open but relies heavily on rules and conventions [13]. If the improvisational situation can be carefully structured, such that the rules of engagement are clear to the player, and s/he is supported during the improvisation by more experienced actors, a successful, interactive dramatic experience is possible. By successful we mean that the participant knows what to do, is empowered to take part actively, and in effect feels freer with a lot of rules than without them [13]. Two improvisation tasks must be accomplished in order to create a player-friendly, structured-improvisation setting. First given basic scenarios, actors must work until possible avenues of reply, of verbal tactic and strategy become clear. Second an actor must take the part of the novice player in order to define the best supportive tactics for the other actors.

8   Conclusion

Work on *The Thing Growing's* tracking detection, taught me the value of using Wizard of Oz experiments to see exactly how complex a computer-based solution needs to be. I believe that a fast and flexible, technology-free, improvisation-based, production stage for game development will similarly indicate where effort must be spent in creating supportive, emotionally rich, interactive scenarios and the computer agents that will deliver them. I do not think that such a strategy is appropriate for building non-player characters that can handle generic transactions in a sprawling sand-box world, but in creating much more constrained and encapsulated scenarios delivered at the correct dramatic moment and handling a very domain-specific interaction.

The IPS's next production, working title *meNOme*, a work based on an original script and specifically designed for participatory drama, will implement such a stage. Following in the footsteps of Brenda Laurel and her virtual reality work PLACEHOLDER [15], the production will be iteratively developed starting with improvisation workshops. My first step for this production was to write a text that explores cognition as historically contingent by immersing a participant in a series of scenarios, each of which operates according to a different theory of mind. A series of conversations with collaborator Bay-Cheng, has started the process of moving from a word-heavy script that explains theories of mind, to a series of ideas, scenarios, and character descriptions, that we can use as the basis for experimental improvisations/script workshopping. This process has already been eye-opening. Bay-Cheng has introduced me to a central tenet of successful improv, each actor needs to have a clear goal and obstacle. Ideally the with two actors, each is the other's obstacle. The script needs to be heavily revised!! The improvisation workshop stage will be observed by AI researchers and recorded and, I hypothesize, serve a key role for the development of the computer-controlled actors .

In the shorter term the project will result in mixed reality performances for an audience/participant of one. The long term goal, if the experiment with an improvisation stage proves successful, is to create a video game populated with sophisticated, emotion-evoking agents. The production of "meNOme" will serve as a site of development/experimentation/proof-of-concept for the hypothesis that instituting improvisation with live actors as a formal step in the production process will lead to emotion-rich interactive media.

Acknowledgments. I would like to thank and acknowledge the support and input of the other members of the The Intermedia Performance Studio, Sarah Bay-Cheng, Dave Pape and Stuart C. Shapiro. I would also like to thank those institutions that have funded our work: the Office of the Vice President for Research, The Digital Humanities Initiative at Buffalo, the Gender Institute, and the Honors Program all at the University at Buffalo; The Robert and Carol Morris Fund for Visual Expression and the Performing Arts; Beyond/In Western New York 2010

References

1. Aarseth, E.: Genre Trouble: Narrativism and the Art of Simulation. In: Wardrip-Fruin, N., Harrigan, P. (eds.) First Person: New Media as Story, Performance and Game. The MIT Press, Cambridge (2004)
2. Anstey, J., Bay-Cheng, S., Pape, D., Shapiro, S.C.: Human Trials: An Experiment in Intermedia Performance. Computers in Entertainment Magazine 5(3) (2007), http://www.acm.org/pubs/cie.html
3. Anstey, J., Pape, D.: Being there: Interactive fiction in virtual reality. In: Consciusness Reframed 3. CAiiA. University of Wales College, Newport (2000)
4. Anstey, J., Pape, D.: Scripting the interactor: An approach to VR drama. In: The Fourth Conference on Creativity and Cognition. ACM SIGCHI, pp. 150–158. ACM Press, New York (2002)
5. Anstey, J., Pape, D.: The trial the trail: Building a VR drama. In: Technologies for Interactive Digital Storytelling and Entertainment Conference, pp. 394–402. Fraunhofer IRB Verlag (2003)
6. Anstey, J., Pape, D., Sandin, D.: The Thing Growing: Autonomous characters in virtual reality interactive fiction. In: IEEE Virtual Reality 2000. IEEE, Los Alamitos (2000)
7. Bernsen, N.O., Dybkjr, L.: Meet Hans Christian Andersen. In: 6th SIGdial Workshop on Discourse and Dialogue, pp. 237–241 (2005)
8. Bernsen, N.O., Dybkjr, L., Killerich, S.: Evaluating Conversation with Hans Christian Andersen. In: Proc. of the Fourth International Conference on Language Resources and Evaluation (LREC), pp. 1011–1014 (2004)
9. Charles, F., Lozano, M., Mead, S.J., Bisquerra, A.F., Cavazza, M.: Planning formalisms and authoring in interactive storytelling. In: Technologies for Interactive Digital Storytelling and Entertainment Conference, pp. 216–225. Fraunhofer IRB Verlag (2003)
10. Fencott, C.: Agencies of interactive digital storytelling. In: Technologies for Interactive Digital Storytelling and Entertainment Conference, pp. 152–163. Fraunhofer IRB Verlag (2003)
11. Frijda, N.H.: The Emotions, Editions de la Maison des Science de L'Homme. Cambridge University Press, London (1986)
12. Ibanez, J., Aylett, R., Ruiz-Rodarte, R.: Storytelling in virtual environments from a virtual guide perspective. Virtual Reality, Special Edition on Storytelling in Virtual Environments 7(1), 30–42 (2003)
13. Kjolner, T., Lehmann, N.: Uses of Theatre as Model:Discussing Computers as Theatre - some additional perspectives. In: Qvortrup, L. (ed.) Virtual Interactions: Interaction in Virtual Inhabited 3D Worlds, pp. 76–93. Springer, Heidelberg (2001)
14. Laurel, B.: Computers as Theater. Addison-Wesley, Reading (1993)
15. Laurel, B., Strickland, R., Tow, R.: Placeholder: Landscape and narrative in virtual environments. In: Dodsworth, C. (ed.) Digital Illusion, pp. 181–208. ACM Press, New York (1998)

16. Mateas, M.: Expressive AI - A hybrid art and science practice. Leonardo 34(2), 147–153 (2001)
17. Nath, S.: Story, Plot & Character Action: Narrative Experience as an Emotional Braid. In: Technologies for Interactive Digital Storytelling and Entertainment Conference, pp. 1–18. Fraunhofer IRB Verlag (2003)
18. Perron, B.: Silent Thrills in Silent Hill, lecture (2005)
19. Perron, B.: Horror Video Games: Essays on the Fusion of Fear and Play. McFarland (2009)
20. Sengers, P.: Designing comprehensible agents. In: International Joint Conference on Artificial Intelligence (1999)
21. Shapiro, S.C., Anstey, J., Pape, D.E., Nayak, T.D., Kandefer, M., Telhan, O.: The Trial The Trail, Act 3: A Virtual Reality Drama using Intelligent Agents. In: First Annual Artificial Intelligence and Interactive Digital Entertainment Conference, pp. 157–158. AAAI, Menlo Park (2005)
22. Spoto, D.: The Dark Side of Genius, The Life of Alfred Hitchcock. Little, Brown and Company, Boston (1983)
23. Weizenbaum, J.: ELIZA - A Computer Program for the Study of Natural Language Communication between Man and Machine. Communications of the Association for Computing Machinery 9, 36–45 (1966)
24. Zubek, R., Horswill, I.: Hierarchical Parallel Markov Models of Interaction. In: AI and Interactive Digital Entertainment Conference, pp. 141–146 (2005)

Outline of an Empirical Study on the Effects of Emotions on Strategic Behavior in Virtual Emergencies

Christian Becker-Asano, Dali Sun, Birgit Kleim, Corinna N. Scheel,
Brunna Tuschen-Caffier, and Bernhard Nebel

Freiburg Institute for Advanced Studies, Albert-Ludwigs-Universität Freiburg,
Starkenstraße 44, 79104 Freiburg, Germany
{basano,sun,nebel}@informatik.uni-freiburg.de,
b.kleim@psychologie.uzh.ch, {corinna.scheel,
brunna.tuschen-caffier}@psychologie.uni-freiburg.de

Abstract. The applicability of appropriate coping strategies is important in emergencies or traumatic experiences such as car accidents or human violence. In this context, emotion regulation and decision making are relevant. However, research on human reactions to traumatic experiences is very challenging and most existing research uses retrospective assessments of these variables of interest. Thus, we are currently developing and evaluating novel methods to investigate human behavior in cases of emergency. Virtual reality scenarios of emergencies are employed to enable an immersive interactive engagement (e.g., dealing with fire inside a building) based on the modification of Valve's popular Source™ 2007 game engine.

This paper presents our ongoing research project, which aims at the empirical investigation of human strategic behavior under the influence of emotions while having to cope with virtual emergencies.

Keywords: Coping, virtual reality, empirical study, head-mounted display.

1 Introduction

The necessity of appropriate coping strategies for emergency situations has become apparent to the public by catastrophes such as the ICE accident in Enschede 1998 or terror attacks like the one on the World Trade Center in 2001. Also in common place emergencies or traumatic experiences such as car accidents or human violence coping strategies, comprising of emotion regulation and decision making, are relevant. In general, research on human reactions to traumatic experiences is very challenging. Thus, we aim to develop and evaluate novel means to investigate human behavior in cases of emergency.

In order to let people engage in emergency situations, we make use of state-of-the-art Virtual Reality (VR) equipment. At the same time we measure physiological indices online and relate them with questionnaire results with respect to the emotional impact of the emergency scenario presented interactively.

Our project faces the following three challenges arising from our aim to evoke natural emotional effects in emergency situations that can also be assessed at runtime:

S. D'Mello et al. (Eds.): ACII 2011, Part II, LNCS 6975, pp. 508–517, 2011.

- The VR hardware technology has to allow for a high degree of "immersion" (Slater & Willbur, 1997) as it is a mandatory prerequisite for achieving "presence", i.e. a user's strong feeling of "being there" in the virtual world. At the same time, it needs to be compatible with the presentation software and should be affordable in price, because the system is planned to be used to train coping strategies in the public later on.
- The VR software framework has to permit the creation and simulation of detailed, high-quality, interactive scenarios in order to allow for high "plausibility" (Rovira, Swapp, Spanlang, & Slater, 2009). In this respect, simulated, physically correct movements of objects are as important as believable and situation-appropriate behaviors of virtual characters.
- In order to assess the emotional effects of being immersed in virtual emergencies, a number of psychological measures need to be applied both on the level of subjective report and on the physiological level. The latter will be used during exposure, whereas the former can only be applied before and after the VR experience, because its assessment is based on questionnaires.

The paper is organized as follows. First, we give an overview of related work on VR research in general and the use of VR in the context of applied research on emotions in particular. This is followed by an outline of the decisions we had to take in order to achieve the highest possible degree of immersive VR experience using relatively inexpensive and flexible of-the-shelf hard- and software components in light of the interdisciplinary research goal. Section 4 will describe the overall design of an ongoing empirical study, before in Section 5 preliminary conclusions will be drawn.

2 Related Work

Over the last ten years VR technology has been used, for example, to train surgeons (Seymour, 2008), to treat posttraumatic stress disorder (PTSD) in veterans of the Iraq war (Reger & Gahm, 2008; Kenny, Parsons, Gratch, & Rizzo, 2008), or as a means to evaluate emotion simulation architectures driving virtual humans (Becker-Asano & Wachsmuth, 2010; Gratch & Marsella, 2005). Furthermore, a VR setup has evoked similar responses to violent incidents in human observers as can be expected in real world situations (Rovira, Swapp, Spanlang, & Slater, 2009) given that a high degree of plausibility could be achieved and maintained.

All these applications are realized with different simulation software, ranging from game engines such as Epic's Unreal Tournament (Reger & Gahm, 2008; Kenny, Parsons, Gratch, & Rizzo, 2008; Gratch & Marsella, 2005) to a number of custom made installations (Dunkin, Adrales, Apelgren, & Mellinger, 2007; Becker-Asano & Wachsmuth, 2010) with proprietary software components. They are combined with different display technologies such as panoramic, auto-stereoscopic, or head-mounted displays (HMDs), or even CAVEs (Brooks, 1999). Notably, according to Slater (2009) one can, in principle, simulate a CAVE with a (head-tracked) HMD and a CAVE, in turn, enables one to simulate a panoramic screen. Thus, if the field-of-view of an HMD is sufficiently big and head movements of its user are taken into account, an HMD can be considered the best choice, because it is also least expensive and easiest to transport. Of course, the weight of the HMD and the according discomfort of wearing it over a longer period of time can be considered a clear disadvantage of such technology.

The VR-related aspects of a project for PTSD treatment are meant to teach the patient "coping skills" (Riva, et al., 2010) through virtual exposure, similarly to our project goal. For an empirical study on the link between presence and emotions Riva and colleagues (2007) used an HMD with head-tracking and a joystick for navigation. They successfully induced an anxious mood in participants only by systematically changing visual and auditory components of a virtual park scenery.

In applied research on emotions with Virtual Humans coping is mostly understood as an agent's ability to deal with its emotions in either a problem-focused or an emotion-focused way (Marsella & Gratch, 2009). In this sense, emotions as a product of situation appraisal either cause behavioral change or a process of (internal) reappraisal. As for now, we are merely interested in assessing the behavioral changes caused by fearful emotions, which we are hopefully able to induce in our participants by means of our newly developed VR setup.

3 Outline of the Research Project

3.1 Research Goal

We aim to develop novel technological means to assess emotional reactions of people online while they are interactively exposed to potentially life-threatening emergencies. In a second step, we would like to use this technology to train coping strategies in these emergencies.

At first, however, it needs to be assured that the emotions evoked by employing our technical setup are not only similar to, but also similarly intense as those emotions that can be expected to arise in similar real world emergencies. In the worst case, participants will simply treat the VR situation as if they were playing a computer game, in which their actions and corresponding emotions might be driven by the playful aim to explore the artificial world and its rules, rather than to cope with the emergency in a realistic way. Previous research on fire simulation in VR and subjects' behaviors (Smith & Trenholme, 2009) has shown that, first, the type of interface the user is provided with, and, second, his or her previous experience with computer games seems to have major impact on this undesired effect. As we opted for the rather uncommon use of a tracked HMD in combination with a joystick controller, even experienced players of computer games will most likely not treat our setup similarly to a computer game.

Furthermore, our setup allows us to investigate, how strategic behavior might change under the influence of emotions. Accordingly, as a first step we decided to test, if our VR scenario has a similar emotional effect on participants as a video clip, which has already been evaluated to induce fear. Therefore, we designed an empirical study with one group of participants, who watched a fear-inducing movie clip before entering the VR scenario, and control group that watched a neutral video instead.

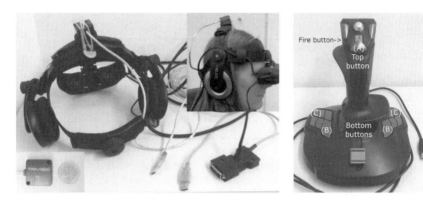

Fig. 1. (left) TriVisio's "VRVision" HMD with the "Colibri" tracker (down left) attached; (right) The "Thrustmaster T-16000M" joystick for navigating the virtual emergency scenario

Fig. 2. (left) An example of the complete setup; (middle) The experiment room with HMD, joystick, physiological sensors, fan, and desktop monitor; (right) The "VarioPort" biometrical device with sensors for skin conductance, ECG, finger pulse, and chest measurement, plus remote marker buttons

3.2 Hardware Setup

At first, the VR-related setup will be described in detail, before also the physiological devices are explained.

Virtual Reality Setup. For the immersive setup we opted for Trivisio's "VRvision HMD" **(Trivisio)**, which features two SVGA AMLCD 800x600 color displays with 24 bit color depth, 60 Hz video frame rate, and a field of view of 42° diagonally and 25° vertically, cp. Fig. 1. The HMD is powered via USB, by which a pair of built in Sennheiser HD 205 headphones are connected to the PC as well. An ATI Sapphire Radeon 5870 together with an Intel Core-i5-760 CPU drives the HMD via its two distinct DVI inputs making use of the iZ3D driver under Windows 7 (64bit). A USB-powered "Colibri" tracker—mounted on top of the HMD—provides information on the user's head movements including yaw and pitch, which allow the user to look around in the virtual world.

Table 1. Joystick configuration for moving in and interacting with the virtual environment

In-game movement / action	Joystick configuration
Forward / backward	Push / pull (pitch)
Turn	Turn handle (yaw)
Side step	Tilt left / right (roll)
Use (pick up / release / open)	Top button
Duck	Base button
Throw object / use tool	Fire button (front)

In 3D first-person computer games, such as the one we modified, the default user navigation is achieved by means of keyboard and mouse and a considerable amount of training is needed to get accustomed to it. As our participants can be expected to have diverging levels of gaming experience, and, thus, to avoid that experienced players might treat the setup similar to a computer game, we decided to implement a rather unusual navigation method by means of a Thrustmaster T-16000M joystick; cp. Fig. 1, right, and Table 1. This joystick can easily be adjusted for left-handed use.

The user can move forward and backward through the virtual world by pushing and pulling the joysticks handle, respectively (cf. Table 1 and Fig. 2, left). By leaning the handle left or right the user can step sideways, whereas turning the handle itself slightly to the left or right makes the user turn accordingly inside the virtual world. Finally, by pressing and holding "base button B" the user can duck to crouch below an obstacle, for example. As soon as "base button B" is released, the user returns to a standing position in the VR world again. In addition, two more of the joystick's buttons are programed to let the user interact with the virtual world. "Top button A" lets the user pick up an object (any small physical object, which does not qualify as a tool) or a tool (in terms of the game engine also called a "weapon"), which he or she is looking at. While holding an object, pressing "top button A" again will result in dropping the object. While holding a tool, however, the user can still open and close doors or push buttons (such as for calling an elevator) with "top button A" the same way as without holding any object or tool in his or her hands. By pressing the "fire button" on the front of the joystick, the user either throws an object or uses the tool he or she is holding. For example, a spray can is implemented as a tool, which emits white paint when being used. If he or she wants to throw a tool away, the user can press "base button C."

Although the participants wear an HMD (cp. Fig. 2, left), they were also provided with a standard desktop monitor (cp. Fig. 2, middle) for online questionnaire assessment before, between, and after the experimental sessions. The electrical fan (cp. Fig. 2, middle) was used to distribute artificial smell of burning fire at a certain moment during the experiment.

Physiological Sensors Setup. The following physiological indices (cp. Fig. 2, right) are taken from each participant using a "VarioPort" biometrical device in order to assess physiological arousal whilst participants are in the virtual world:

- Skin conductivity taken from the non-dominant hand's palm
- Heart rate variability, i.e. the variation in beat-to-beat intervals in the heart rate signals, based on the electrocardiogram recorded from the participant's chest
- Breath rate variability derived from chest measurement at a high and a low position on the participants chest

These sensors are recorded in parallel for later analysis. In order to relate the physiological indices with certain events in the virtual emergency, a number of markers are set manually by the experimenter from a remote location, which is separated from the participant by a black curtain during the experiment.

3.3 Software Setup

A large number of game engines allow for rapid prototyping of virtual worlds that feature both high-level graphical as well as interactive realism. In choosing Valve's Source™ Engine (Valve Corporation) as our software framework we follow the conclusions provided by Smith and Trenholme (2009). This game engine exists in three versions, two of which are available as open source, namely Source 2006 and Source 2007. The newest 2007 engine version of the Software Development Kit (SDK) is included on the Orange Box edition of Valve's Half Life 2 computer game. A number of modifications are based on either the single- or multiplayer part of the source code. In at least one of them, namely "Missing Information" (Gabe), a fire extinguisher has been reactivated from an early, abandoned version of Half Life 2. This allows the player to extinguish a virtual fire by shooting white smoke at it.

To implement this project's virtual emergency scenario the source code of the Source™ 2007 engine had to be modified. In addition, an underground parking lot needed to be designed that features signs, doors, stairways, elevators, cars, and additional models such as a coke vendor machine to make it look most convincingly.[1]

4 Design of the Empirical Study

4.1 Overall Design

The overall design of our study can be split up into five parts (cp. Fig. 3):

1. Socio-demographical data and personality profiles as well as previous experience with computer games and VR technology are acquired through questionnaires. A five minute physio-baseline is recorded. A rating of felt fear, anger, shame, sadness, happiness, boredom, guilt, and tension is acquired on a ten point scale each ("EMO-Rating").
2. Participants are guided acoustically and visually through a training course, which starts at their own car in the parking lot and ends after exiting an elevator on the ground floor. This training allows them to get used to the interface and it is being followed by another rating of felt emotions, see above.
3. After a control of the physiological measurement the participant either watches a neutral video clip (control) or a fear inducing video clip (experimental manipulation). Both are around five minutes long and the latter is a clip taken from the movie "Blair Witch Project." Then the participants rate their feelings again.
4. The experimental session starts with the participant standing in front of the elevator on the ground floor inside the same virtual world as the one used for training in step two. They are instructed to go down to their red sports car and drive it out of

---

[1] Videos of this VR scenario can be found at http://bit.ly/pc7Ou6

the parking lot. They are also told to react adequately in any situation that they might get into. (For a more detailed description see Section 4.2.) After the VR experiment the participant has to rate his or her felt emotions again.

5. Finally, the physiological measurement is being controlled again and the participant is asked to fill another questionnaire and to report one last time on his or her felt emotions.

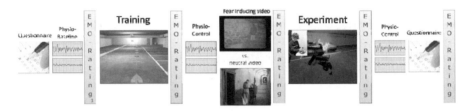

Fig. 3. Outline of the overall design of the empirical study

4.2 The VR Experiment

In the experimental session the participant is instructed to get back to his or her red sports car, which he or she was introduced to in the beginning of the training session.

First, the participant has to call the elevator and wait for it to arrive. Then, after pressing any of the elevator's buttons inside, the "P5" button is lit and the elevator starts moving down to level five accompanied by some machinery sounds. After the doors opened again, the participant has to step out of the elevator and open the blue door to get from the elevator room into the parking lot; cp. Fig. 4 (a).

While walking back in the direction of the red sports car, which is hidden behind one of the walls (cp. Fig. 4 (b)), the light configuration is the same as during the training session, i.e., all lights are on and the participant has a good overview of the parking lot. Suddenly, however, a loud noise is played together with some male scream and the lights in the parking lot are dimmed to nearly dark; cp. Fig. 4 (c).

If the participant does not give up on approaching the red sports car, he or she finds a male person lying beneath a number of heater elements, which seemingly prevent him from escaping the dangerous situation; cp. Fig. 4 (d). When approaching him, the injured person raises his head and shouts "help!" once, before fainting and stopping to move. In fact, the participant has no chance to help this person other than by extinguishing the fire behind him (cp. Fig. 4 (e)) and starting the alarm by pressing one of the emergency buttons; cp. Fig. 4 (f). The fire, however, can only be extinguished (cp. Fig. 4 (g)) after one of the fire extinguishers has been picked up from a wall; cp. Fig. 4 (f). While the fire is burning, the area of the emergency is gradually filling with smoke (cp. Fig. 4 (h)) making it not only increasingly more difficult for the participant to find his or her way out, but also more dangerous, because in a standing posture the smoke is programmed to have a negative health effect. This is made clear to the participant by periodically appearing red flashes on the screen together with different coughing sounds being played at the same time. Only by keeping in a kneeling posture the participant can avoid this negative effect. The experimental session ends when the participant either takes one of the emergency exits (cp. Fig 4 (i)), or a car exit, or calls the elevator.

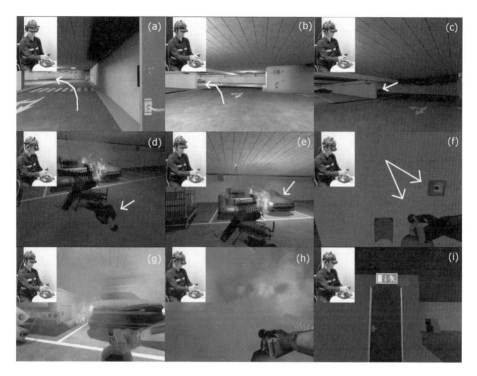

Fig. 4. An example run of an experimental session

5   Preliminary Results and Conclusions

At the time of writing, the data of 19 participants have been collected. Ten of them participated in the control condition (one male, nine female) and nine of them in the experimental condition (four male, five female). The time that participants stayed in the VR scenario were not significantly different (ctrl: 323 secs, STD 134 secs; exp.: 302 secs, STD 130 secs; two-tailed t-test (unequal variances): p>0.73, n.s.).

Table 2. Performance points and actions per experimental group

	points	call emerg.	take fire exting.	address person	exting. fire	take elevator	take stairs	take car exit
Exp. (9)	⌀ 32	78%	89%	44%	78%	22%	67%	11%
Ctrl (10)	⌀ 26	50%	50%	60%	50%	20%	70%	10%
f (14)	⌀ 25	64%	57%	50%	50%	21%	71%	7%
m (5)	⌀ 38	60%	100%	60%	100%	20%	60%	20%

Table 2, however, reveals that a greater percentage of the nine participants, who had watched the fear inducing video, pressed the emergency button (78%) and extinguished the fire (78%) as compared to the control group participants (50%). Grouping the participants according to their resp. gender, however, shows that all five male participants took a fire extinguisher and extinguished the fire in contrast to only approx. half of all 14 female participants.

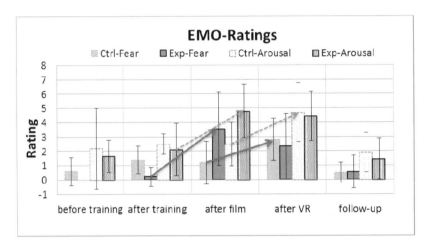

Fig. 5. Mean values with standard deviations for the emotion ratings of "fear" and "arousal" for 19 participants (nine experimental group and ten control group)

Figure 5 presents the means and standard deviations of the subjective ratings of felt "fear" and "arousal" after each part of the experiment. Concerning fear, as indicated by the two bold arrows in Fig. 5, our VR scenario seems to have a similar fear-inducing effect as the movie. The same holds for the increase of general arousal levels as can be derived from the positive slopes of both of the dashed arrows in Fig. 5. Notably, however, we also find that the high level of fear reached by the experimental group after watching the fear-inducing movie seems to diminish during the VR experiment. Thus, our preliminary conclusion is that we might not need to induce a fearful mood before the VR sessions. We are aware, however, that a higher number of participants is needed to consolidate this finding.

In the long run, we aim at a more detailed analysis that includes the personality questionnaire and physiological data, which will be analyzed in correlation with the trajectories of the participants in the VR emergency. Accordingly, we are confident that we can derive more meaningful conclusions in the future.

Acknowledgments. We would like to thank Maria Mustafina for their great help in conducting the experiments. This research project is partly supported by a return fellowship of the Alexander von Humboldt foundation.

References

Becker-Asano, C., Wachsmuth, I.: Affective computing with primary and secondary emotions in a virtual human. Autonomous Agents and Multiagent Systems 20(1), 32–49 (2010)

Brooks, F.: What's real about virtual reality? Computer Graphics and Applications (19), 16–27 (1999)

Dunkin, B., Adrales, G., Apelgren, K., Mellinger, J.: Surgical simulation: a current review. Surgical Endoscopy 21, 357–366 (2007)

Gabe: Missing Information: Half Life 2 MOD, http://www.love-tub.net/ (retrieved April 18, 2011)

Gratch, J., Marsella, S.: Evaluating a Computational Model of Emotion. Autonomous Agents and Multi-Agent Systems 1(11), 23–43 (2005)

Kenny, P., Parsons, T.D., Gratch, J., Rizzo, A.A.: Evaluation of Justina: A Virtual Patient with PTSD. In: Prendinger, H., Lester, J.C., Ishizuka, M. (eds.) IVA 2008. LNCS (LNAI), vol. 5208, pp. 394–408. Springer, Heidelberg (2008)

Marsella, S.C., Gratch, J.: EMA: A process model of appraisal dynamics. Cognitive Systems Research 10(1), 70–90 (2009)

Reger, G.M., Gahm, G.A.: Virtual reality exposure therapy for active duty soldiers. Journal of Clinical Psychology (64), 940–946 (2008)

Riva, G., Mantovani, F., Capideville, C.S., Preziosa, A., Morganti, F., Villani, D., et al.: Affective Interactions Using Virtual Reality: The Link between Presence and Emotions. CyberPsychology & Behavior (1), 45–56 (2007)

Riva, G., Raspelli, S., Algeri, D., Pallavicini, F., Gorini, A., Wiederhold, B.K., et al.: Interreality in Practice: Bridging Virtual and Real Worlds in the Treatment of Posttraumatic Stress Disorders. Cyberpsychology, Behavior, and Social Networking 13, 55–65 (2010)

Rovira, A., Swapp, D., Spanlang, B., Slater, M.: The Use of Virtual Reality in the Study of People's Responses to Violent Incidents. Frontiers in Behavioral Neuroscience 59(3), 1–10 (2009)

Seymour, N.: VR to OR: A Review of the Evidence that Virtual Reality Simulation Improves Operating Room Performance. World Journal of Surgery 32, 182–188 (2008)

Slater, M.: Place illusion and plausibility can lead to realistic behaviour in immersive virtual environments. Philosophical Transactions of the Royal Society B: Biological Sciences 364, 3549–3557 (2009)

Slater, M., Willbur, S.: A Framework for Immersive Virtual Environments (FIVE) - Speculations on the role of presence in virtual environments. Presence: Teleoperators and Virtual Environments 6(6), 603–616 (1997)

Smith, S.P., Trenholme, D.: Rapid prototyping a virtual fire drill environment using computer game technology. Fire Safety Journal 44(4), 559–569 (2009)

Trivisio: VRvision HMD product website (Trivisio). Trivisio Prototyping GmbH, http://www.trivisio.com/index.php/products/hmdnte/vrvision-hmd (retrieved February 17, 2011)

Valve Corporation: Half-Life 2, http://www.valvesoftware.com/games/hl2.html (retrieved February 17, 2011)

Assessing Performance Competence in Training Games

Hiran Ekanayake[1,2,3], Per Backlund[1], Tom Ziemke[1],
Robert Ramberg[2], and Kamalanath Hewagamage[3]

[1] University of Skövde, P.O. Box 408, SE-541 28 Skövde, Sweden
[2] Stockholm University, Forum 100, SE-164 40 Kista, Sweden
[3] University of Colombo School of Computing, 35, Reid Avenue, Colombo 7, Sri Lanka
hiran@dsv.su.se, {per.backlund,tom.ziemke}@his.se,
robban@dsv.su.se, kph@ucsc.cmb.ac.lk

Abstract. In-process assessment of trainee learners in game-based simulators is a challenging activity. This typically involves human instructor time and cost, and does not scale to the one tutor per learner vision of computer-based learning. Moreover, evaluation from a human instructor is often subjective and comparisons between learners are not accurate. Therefore, in this paper, we propose an automated, formula-driven quantitative evaluation method for assessing performance competence in serious training games. Our proposed method has been empirically validated in a game-based driving simulator using 7 subjects and 13 sessions, and accuracy up to 90.25% has been achieved when compared to an existing qualitative method. We believe that by incorporating quantitative evaluation methods like these future training games could be enriched with more meaningful feedback and adaptive game-play so as to better monitor and support player motivation, engagement and learning performance.

Keywords: Serious Games, Performance Evaluation, Motivation, Driver Training.

1 Introduction

There is an increasing demand for the use of computer and video games for purposes other than pure entertainment – for example, education, skill training and health care. Proponents of such "serious games" claim three major benefits: they are intrinsically motivating, they provide immediate feedback to users and they provide ample learning opportunities [1].There is no doubt that advancement in rendering of graphics and realistic simulation of real-world aspects in games from the viewpoint of the player character (referred to as the first-person perspective) have contributed to this tremendous growth in the game play community. However, the use of game-based technologies for education and training purposes is still hindered by lack of methods and tools to measure and relate its learning effect to other, more conventional types of training/learning. For instance, in classroom-based learning, assessment is conducted in two ways called *formative* and *summative*. However, in game-based learning these assessment methods become inappropriate in the same sense, because negative feedback could cause a cautious learner to lose motivation and to stop playing. Despite the abovementioned benefits, however, misconceptions

S. D´Mello et al. (Eds.): ACII 2011, Part II, LNCS 6975, pp. 518–527, 2011.

and lack of awareness have caused a wide public opinion that educational use of computer and video games is not a valid alternative to classroom-based learning.

The purpose of this paper is to propose an automated, formula-driven quantitative method to measure the learning effect, especially in the psychomotor skills domain, in serious training games, which is based on performance-oriented achievement motivation of a learner. Currently, assessment of performance competence in training games is often conducted by human instructors using subjective qualitative methods [6][22]. These methods have their own drawbacks in addition to not scaling enough to one instructor per student vision in game-based learning. We believe that our method provided a first step towards future research on adaptive game-play and real-world effects of learning.

The paper is organized as follows: In section 2, we discuss the evolution of learning theories and aspects relevant to learning, such as the context and transfer, concerned to game-based learning environments and real-world. Section 3 focuses mainly on assessment methods, the connection between classroom-based learning and game-based learning, and a psychological perspective on the crucial role of motivation in learning. In section 4, we present the proposed formula-driven approach to assessing performance competence of a learner. Section 5 presents the steps involved in the empirical validation of the proposed formula-driven approach. In section 6, we discuss the results, findings, limitations and future work.

2 The Validity of Game-Based Simulator Training

Shuell (as interpreted by [2]) defined learning as follows:

"Learning is an enduring change in behavior, or in the capacity to behave in a given fashion, which results from practice or other forms of experience."

The above definition accounts for behaviorist view of learning which virtually denies the existence of the mind. Therefore, it fails to give an account of internal cognitive processes involved [3] or acquisition of higher level skills, such as language development and problem solving [2]. On the contrary, contemporary school of learning theories falls in cognitive and constructivist camps which accounts for internal mental processes involved and environmental conditions [3]. Constructivism differs from cognitivism in its subjectivistic assumption, i.e. "[knowledge] is a function of how the individual creates meaning from his or her own experiences" [2]. According to constructivism the memory is always evolving with new uses and new situations through three processes known as externalism, internalism and incongruousness, and learning must include three crucial factors: activity (practice), concept (knowledge) and culture (context). Although Bloom's taxonomy identifies three domains in which learning could occur, namely cognitive, affective and psychomotor [4], from the constructivist point of view any type of learning is explained as a change in a corresponding mental model [3].

Learning is successful if what is learnt can be successfully transferred to new situations and contexts. [5] explains two types of transfer mechanisms of learning in such contexts: low-road transfer and high-road transfer. The low-road transfer involves triggering of well-practiced semi-automatic responses (reflexive) as a result of similarities between prior and transfer learning contexts. The high-road transfer, on the other hand, is more likely to happen when the learning contexts are more remote and it involves mindful and searching of deliberate connections between the two learning contexts.

A recent trend in learning is to use computer games for educational purposes. The formal study into this aspect is called serious games and it studies the use of computer games for purposes beyond pure entertainment, such as for education, skills training, health care, and military [1][6][7][8]. Among the other advantages, serious games with advanced simulator technologies offer repeating of critical situations, such as operation on slippery roads and night driving, which are otherwise dangerous with ordinary training sessions [7]. According to [9], the four primary learning principles in serious games are practicing skills, knowledge gain through exploration, cognitive problem solving, and social problem solving. Here our focus is mainly on skills training using serious training games.

From a general perspective, all computer games represent alternate realities like in dreams [10]. Therefore, the serious games initiative is challenged by various parties either criticizing its theoretical foundation or practical usage. The primary advantage of serious games is in its entertainment value which serves to engage and motivate the learner to the gaming task. However, the entertainment value of a serious game depends on both the subject's performance and the complexity of the game [11]. Three complexity factors, physical realism of the environment and characters, affective realism of characters, and social complexity and realism of their interactions determine the complexity of the game [12]. For subject's performance the engagement to the gaming task is crucial, for which adaptive challenge is a necessity. [7] identifies this adaptive challenge and appropriate feedback as the two essential aspects in promoting self-efficacy. Moreover, engagement is considered as an important parameter which can improve the learning performance [13].

Although uncertainty remains on the validity of simulator-based training, [14] and [15] using two sufficiently complex game-based simulator training environments, a fire-fighter training simulator and a driving simulator, show that simulator-based training is indeed a valid alternative for classroom-based training. Simulator-based learning has also been characterized as facilitating model-based thinking, because it helps bridge between concrete experiences and more abstract and systematic understanding [16].

3 Learning Goals and Performance Evaluation in Game-Based Simulator Training

Assessment is a powerful tool that can be used to direct students' attention to what matters in their learning [17]. Conventional assessment methods designed for classroom-based learning cannot be applied in game-based learning systems in the same sense. According to [18], educational serious games and classroom-based learning have connections between intersections of feedback, aesthetics and mechanics. In classroom-based learning feedback can be given in two forms: summative and formative. Summative feedback comes as a quantitative measure of the learner's performance after a summative assessment in the completion of a learning session. In games, summative feedback is typically a kind of a scoring system, such as experience points, level progression, item collection, different endings, or just simple points. Experience point systems are considered very motivational in games; however, [18] find it difficult to convert a course grade system into an experience point system. The difference exists as games usually offer quick early leveling to motivate the players to stay within the game, whereas in courses the students have a failing grade through much of the course. Achievement-based systems can work well in both games and classroom, such as unlock special features in games or incentives in the classroom.

Formative feedback is often a qualitative feedback given during the process of learning and it allows the learner to formulate opinions, share problem areas and reflect on how to accomplish his/her goals. In games formative feedback can result in adaptive game play, in which the game will become easier or harder depending on the player's game play behavior. One important factor facilitating this adaptive game play is called the "flow" experience, in which the learner loses track of time and the outside world while completely absorbed by the activity he/she is currently engaged in [19][20]. Interruptions in flow cause the learner to leave the game. The flow is a result of constant cycle of cognitive disequilibrium and resolution, and this is to be created without foiling the expectations and exceeding the capacity of the player.

Since the focus of this paper is on assessment of psychomotor performance in serious training games more emphasis is put towards aspects important for such games. Simulation games invite experimentation and exploration while improving strategic thinking and insight, psychomotor skills, analytical and spatial skills, iconic skills and visual selective attention [8][21]. However, when it comes to assessment, there is no appropriate computer-based assessment methodology designed for the needs of simulation-based serious training games. Currently the only valid assessment method is by an expert teacher monitoring the learner constantly or by inspecting application logs of user interactions [6][22], which becomes inappropriate when considering the expected benefits of digital game-based learning as reducing instructional time and costs [20] and facilitating an adaptive challenge.

From the constructivist point-of-view learning is a subjectivistic mental process and achievement motivation plays a major role in its success. Although entertainment value of serious games is considered to serving motivation for gameplay, motivational researchers contrast this individual interest as intrinsic and situational. Intrinsic interest is a stable motivational construct that orients the individual to develop competence and task mastery, while situational interest is a transitory motivational construct which orients one's focus to a certain condition or stimuli in the environment which may or may not last for a longer period [19][23]. Since digital games are basically designed for situational interest, suitability of using digital games for practicing skills is questionable [9]. Several researchers aim to identify the current emotional state, physiological state and many other aspects of the player and use these information in game dynamics to improve the game interaction which is studied under themes of affective feedback games and biofeedback games [24][25[26][27].

In a learning setting, learners adopt to different achievement goals. The specific type of achievement goal the learner has been adopted triggers relevant behavioral patterns including how an individual approach, engage in, and respond to achievement tasks [23][28]. This creates differences between learners. As discussed in the theory of academic risk taking [19], an adventuresome learner is a learner typically with high ability and want to be challenged with difficult tasks, take risks of failure, and even stable on the face of negative emotions. In contrast, a cautious learner prefers fewer and easier tasks and takes fewer risks. Achievement goal theorists contrast this difference as to which goals learners have adopted to: a performance goal focused on the demonstration of competence relevant to others, or a mastery goal focused on the development of competence and task mastery [28]. Further to their discussion, [28] identify three achievement orientations: mastery goal, performance-approach goal and performance-avoidance goal. Both mastery and performance-approach goals are characterized as self-regulation according to potential positive outcomes while performance-avoidance goal is characterized as self-regulation according to potential negative outcomes.

4 The Proposed Formula for the Assessment of Performance Competence

Our proposed method for the assessment of performance competence in training (assumed as an indirect way to measure the task mastery) is based on an evaluation of behavioral patterns of the player. We hypothesize that the achieved performance (P) of a player depends on favorable outcomes (F), unfavorable outcomes (U) and the physical effort (E), as given by the following formula,

$$P = (F - U)/E \qquad (1)$$

Formula 1 distinguishes one learner who achieves a certain performance putting in less effort as compared to another learner who achieves the same training outcome putting in a greater effort. To account for an 'expert' level of effort, which is characterized as neither more than required nor less than required effort, a measurement of optimal effort (O) is introduced to the formula 1, which now becomes,

$$P = (F - U)/(E' - O) \qquad (2)$$

Further, a threshold value is used to avoid division by zero and higher peaks when the divisor reaches zero.

5 The Empirical Validation of the Proposed Method

5.1 Data Collection

The virtual driving environment was designed using the VDrift open source racing simulator game engine [29]. Physically realistic steering wheel and pedals were used as the game controller and the video output has been projected to a large white-board using a multimedia projector. The player was sitting about two meters away from the screen. Two web cameras recorded the front screen with player's position from back and the player's position from front.

A total of seven volunteers (four male and three female) of age between 25 and 44 with a mean age of 32 participated in the experiment. All of them have obtained their driving license, but differences exist in their driving experience. They were asked to play in the driving simulator considering it as a real-world like driving situation. Each participant played at least two sessions in the simulator, where each session consisted of three laps and taken approximately ten minutes to complete. Differences were made by changing the type of track between two possibilities.

The VDrift game engine has been customized to render data representing the current game state to an external data logging program. The program recorded the player's pressure to throttle, brake and steering wheel, as well as, speed of the car, crashes to walls and other cars, and off-the-track driving.

5.2 Data Analysis

The data analysis has been started by annotating recorded videos into segments of two types, straight road ahead (type 1) and turn/bend ahead (type 2) , as how the player would see the situation ahead, using Transana annotation tool [30]. Although, 14 sessions were recorded, one recording was dropped due to some errors in the recording, which resulted in 13 session recordings for the seven subjects. The evaluation of each player's driving behavior has been obtained using two methods: a qualitative method and the proposed formula-driven quantitative method.

The qualitative assessment has been carried out by an author of this paper who has about 15 years of driving experience, which otherwise should have been done by an independent expert or a panel of evaluators. Table 1 lists the guidelines followed in the qualitative assessment of performance.

Table 1. Guidelines for the Qualitative Assessment

Code	Value	Guidelines
Very good	2	No observable mistake; near expert level of driving
Good	1	Car balancing not good; drive very closer to road boundary or slightly drift beyond boundary
Average	0	Car balancing is very bad; Crosses into boundaries, but not much disturbance on velocity/speed of the car; no damage to the car
Bad	-1	Go off the track and disturbances to driving; minor damage to the car and objects in the environment
Very bad	-2	Crash into walls or other cars

The Formula-Driven Quantitative Method

The idea was to analyze each player's driving behavior for each session within the identified situation types. For example, player A's driving behavior in straight roads against player B's. However, data showed that the time spent on each situation differs significantly, because of different track geometries and player's condition at that period of time. To overcome this problem, segments of each type (1 and 2) have been further categorized into three categories (named as A, B and C) considering their length of time. All data processing has been done with the assistance of Matlab [31].

When substituting values in the formula 2, it was assumed that a player's favorable outcome is to achieve a good speed while minimizing unfavorable outcomes, such as crashes or car to go off-the-road. Effects of priority incidents (e.g. crash in to a wall) has been multiplied in the formula. A way to study psychologically significant learner behaviors and situations in game simulator-based driver training is presented in [32]. The player's effort has been determined using the physical pressure the player puts in the game controller to control the situation in the game world, i.e. pressure to the throttle, the brake and the steering wheel. Since the current study has not been designed to find an accurate measurement for the optimal effort and the threshold, they have been determined by trial and error, for which both has lead to 0.1.

5.3 Results

Fig. 1 represents the relationships between qualitative method and proposed formula-driven method for two categories 1C and 2C.

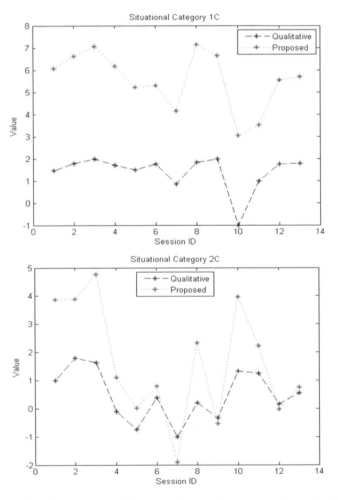

Fig. 1. Relationships between the qualitative method and the proposed formula-driven method for the situation categories 1C and 2C

The correlation coefficients for the relationships between the qualitative method and the formula-driven method for the four situation categories 1B, 1C, 2B and 2C are 13.52%, 82.69%, 55.84% and 90.25%, respectively. The category A has been omitted from further analysis, because the number of segments was not sufficient.

6 Discussion and Conclusion

This paper has presented a formula-driven method to obtain a quantitative assessment of performance competence in serious training games. The proposed method has been validated against a qualitative method using 13 sessions and seven subjects in a driving simulator game. In addition to the formula, the paper has discussed its empirical validation, which has included the following steps: identify different types of situations and categories, determine values for variables in the formula, and compare obtained results against an existing qualitative approach. However, for simplicity, only a certain number of game and user action variables have been considered. Moreover, the two parameters, optimal performance and threshold, were determined using trial and error. However, the comparison has reported as high as 82.69% and 90.25% correlation coefficients respectively for 1C and 2C cases and low to moderate 13.52% and 55.84% correlation coefficients respectively for 1B and 2B cases. The low values for correlation coefficients may be because fewer numbers of situations to compare with or the length of segments is shorter than that for the category C. On the other hand, it may be because less accuracy of the qualitative method.

Future research is planned to improve the formula and validate it against different types of training games, learning aspects, situations, learners and applicability in real-world. Another improvement in the formula to stand in general-purpose games is to extend the definition of favorable and unfavorable outcomes and their means of verification (which also depends on the particular game in question). Moreover, we are in the process of collecting psychophysiological signals to determine learner's mindful interaction and effort to accurately determine the engagement and effort. Apart from that, our method could be improved to include learner's affect or satisfaction, as measured by their facial expressions or other indicators, or by questionnaires. Thereby, we hope that the method can be enhanced to capture more learning aspects into the formula, such as exploration, experiencing, self-efficacy and flow.

Acknowledgments. The authors wish to sincerely thank the staff of InGaMe lab at University of Skövde and all participants in the experiment.

References

1. Ritterfeld, U., Cody, M., Vorderer, P.: Serious Games: Explication of an Oxymoron: Introduction. In: Ritterfeld, U., Cody, M., Vorderer, P. (eds.) Serious Games: Mechanics and Effects, pp. 3–9. Routledge, New York (2009)
2. Ertmer, P., Newby, T.: Behaviorism, cognitivism, constructivism: comparing critical features from an instructional design perspective. Performanc. Improvement Quarterly 6(4), 50–72 (1993)

3. Goel, L., Johnson, N., Junglas, I., Ives, B.: Situated Learning: Conceptualization and Measurement. Decision Sciences Journal of Innovative Education 8(1), 215–240 (2010)
4. Clark, D.: Bloom's Taxonomy of Learning Domains: The Three Types of Learning, http://www.skagitwatershed.org/~donclark/hrd/bloom.html
5. Perkins, D.N., Salomon, G.: Transfer of learning. In: International Encyclopedia of Education, 2nd edn. Pergamon Press, Oxford (1992)
6. Brennecke, A.: A General Framework for Digital Game-Based Training Systems. Doctoral thesis, University of Rostock (2009)
7. Backlund, P., Engström, H., Johannesson, M., Lebram, M.: Games for traffic education: An experimental study in a game-based driving simulator. Simulation & Gaming 41(2) (2010), doi:10.1177/1046878107311455
8. Mitchell, A., Savill-Smith, C.: The use of computer and video games for learning: A review of the literature. In: Learning and Skills Development Agency, London, pp. 1–93 (2004)
9. Ratan, R., Ritterfeld, U.: Serious Games: Explication of an Oxymoron: Classifying Serious Games. In: Ritterfeld, U., Cody, M., Vorderer, P. (eds.) Serious Games: Mechanics and Effects, pp. 10–24. Routledge, New York (2009)
10. Hsu, J.: Video Games and Control Dreams, Study Suggests, http://www.livescience.com/culture/video-games-control-dreams-100525.html
11. Piselli, P., Claypool, M., Doyle, J.: Relating Cognitive Models of Computer Games to User Evaluations of Entertainment. In: 4th International Conference on Foundations of Digital Games, Orlando, Florida (2009)
12. Hudlicka, E.: Affective Game Engines: Motivation and Requirements. In: 4th International Conference on Foundations of Digital Games, Orlando, Florida (2009)
13. Carini, R.M., Kuh, G.D., Klein, S.P.: Student Engagement and Student Learning: Testing the Linkages. Research in Higher Education 47(1), 1–32 (2006)
14. Backlund, P., Engstrom, H., Hammar, C., Johannesson, M., Lebram, M.: Sidh - a Game Based Firefighter Training Simulation. In: 11th International Conference Information Visualization (IV 2007), pp. 899–907 (2007)
15. Backlund, P., Engström, H., Johannesson, M., Lebram, M., Sjödén, B.: Designing for self-efficacy in a game based simulator: An experimental study and its implications for serious games design. In: Bannatyne, M., et al. (eds.) Vis 2008, London, UK, pp. 106–113 (2008), ISBN: 978-0-7695-3271-4
16. Gee, J.P.: Theories and Mechanisms: Deep Learning Properties of Good Digital Games: How Far Can They Go? In: Ritterfeld, U., Cody, M., Vorderer, P. (eds.) Serious Games: Mechanics and Effects, pp. 67–82. Routledge, New York (2009)
17. Gibbs, G., Habeshaw, T.: Preparing to Teach: An Introduction to Effective Teaching in Higher Education. Technical and Educational Services Ltd., Bristol (1992)
18. Bayliss, J.D., Schwartz, D.I.: Instructional Design as Game Design. In: 4th International Conference on Foundations of Digital Games, Orlando, Florida (2009)
19. Graesser, A., Chipman, P., Leeming, F., Biedenbach, S.: Theories and Mechanisms: Deep Learning and Emotion in Serious Games. In: Ritterfeld, U., Cody, M., Vorderer, P. (eds.) Serious Games: Mechanics and Effects, pp. 83–102. Routledge, New York (2009)
20. Eck, R.V.: Digital Game-Based Learning: It's Not Just the Digital Natives Who Are Restless. EDUCAUSE Review 41(2), 16–30 (2006)
21. Debul, P.: Game on!: Game-based learning. T.H.E. Journal 33(6), 41, 30–33, http://www.thejournal.com/articles/17788

22. Picard, R., Papert, S., Bender, W., Blumberg, B., Breazeal, C., Cavallo, D., et al.: Affective learning: A manifesto. BT Technology Journal 22(4), 253–264 (2004)
23. Hidi, S., Harackiewicz, J.M.: Motivating the academically unmotivated: A critical issue for the 21st century. Review of Educational Research 70(2), 151–179 (2000)
24. Gilleade, K.M., Dix, A., Allanson, J.: Affective Videogames and Modes of Affective Gaming: Assist Me, Challenge Me, Emote Me. In: DiGRA 2005, Vancouver, BC, Canada (2005)
25. Bersak, D., McDarby, G., Augenblick, N., McDarby, P., McDonnell, D., MdDonald, B., Karkun, R.: Intelligent Biofeedback using an Immersive Competitive Environment. In: Designing Ubiquitous Computing Games Workshop at UbiComp 2001, Atlanta, GA, USA (2001)
26. Kim, J., Bee, N., Wagner, J., André, E.: Emote to win: affective interactions with a computer game agent. In: GI Jahrestagung, vol. (1), pp. 159–164 (2004)
27. Fairclough, S.H.: Psychophysiological Inference and Physiological Computer Games. In: Brainplay 2007: Brain-Computer Interfaces and Games. Advances in Computer Entertainment, Salzburg, Austria (2007)
28. Elliot, A.J., Church, M.A.: A hierarchical model of approach and avoidance achievement motivation. Journal of Personality and Social Psychology 72(1), 218–232 (1997)
29. VDrift.net, http://vdrift.net/
30. Transana version 2.42, http://www.transana.org/
31. MATLAB version 7.6.0. Natick. The MathWorks Inc., Massachusetts (2003)
32. Ekanayake, H., Backlund, P., Ziemke, T., Ramberg, R., Hewagamage, K.: Game Interaction State Graphs for Evaluation of User Engagement in Explorative and Experience-based Training Games. In: International Conference on Advances in ICT for Emerging Regions (ICTer), Colombo, Sri Lanka (2010)

Affective Preference from Physiology in Videogames: A Lesson Learned from the TORCS Experiment

Maurizio Garbarino, Matteo Matteucci, and Andrea Bonarini

Politecnico di Milano, IIT Unit, Dipartimento di Elettronica e Informazione,
Piazza Leonardo da Vinci, 32, 20133 Milano, Italy
{garbarino,bonarini,matteucci}@elet.polimi.it

Abstract. In this paper we discuss several issues arisen during our most recent experiment concerning the estimation of player preference from physiological signals during a car racing game, to share our experience with the community and provide some insights on the experimental process. We present a selection of critical aspects that range from the choice of the task, to the definition of the questionnaire, to data acquisition.

Thanks to the experience gained during the mentioned case study, we can give an extensive picture of which aspects can be considered in the design of similar experiments. The goal of this contribution is to provide guidelines for analogous experiments.

Keywords: preference evaluation, physiological signals, emotion in games, experimental setting.

1 Introduction

A number of critical issues need to be addressed during the design of an experiment involving physiological signals, that affect estimation and human-computer interaction. Some theoretical and general guidelines about design methodologies regarding psychophysiology are described by Cacioppo et al. [1]. Other generic advices, more oriented to an affective computing perspective, are proposed by Picard et al. [2] and Calvo et al. [3]. However, many of these advices are often quite generic and they can hardly be applied to a practical experiment. For example, one of the point issued by Picard is gathering good affective data: while the problem of ground truth assessment is clearly stated, guidelines for a number of practical issues are missing.

This paper takes as reference our most recent experiment [4], whose original purpose was to assess whether physiological measurements could discriminate the preference between two different game experiences, namely races in the TORCS (The Open Racing Car Simulator [5]) car driving videogame. The answer to this question is a fundamental aspect for the development of an adaptive video game that is able to offer different game experiences according to the preferences inferred from the players (e.g., from their physiological status). In principle,

S. D´Mello et al. (Eds.): ACII 2011, Part II, LNCS 6975, pp. 528–537, 2011.

different players have different preferences, given their experience, their mood, the emotions they feel, and many other factors. If we could identify the player preference on-line, we might adapt the game to match it.

We are investigating whether physiological response could provide a more robust and interesting insight, since game performance is not necessarily a good estimate of the preference of a generic player,

This paper analyzes the most important and critical issues we had to face in our TORCS experiment when trying to minimize the possibility of a failure; with "failure" we do not mean a negative answer to the above-mentioned question (i.e., "Could physiological measurements discriminate the preference between two different affective game experiences?"), but the impossibility to answer properly to such a question due to a wrong protocol or to underestimation of some critical aspects.

Given the usual lack of space, authors of papers presenting their experimental work often are not able to report and discuss all the precious lessons learned during every single phase of the experimental process. Many common mistakes could be avoided by other colleagues if systematically reported. Having this kind of information would speed up the research process and improve the quality of future works. Knowledge about the details behind the reason of a choice is often more valuable than the sole knowledge about the choice itself. Knowledge about things that did not go as expected is also very valuable. Too often, this kind of knowledge does not find a way to be reported to the community.

Thanks to the experience gained in our case study, in this paper we can give an extensive picture of which aspects we have considered as fundamental, and we provide practical considerations about our a priori choices and a posteriori analysis. The goal of this contribution is to provide guidelines for future experiments with similar settings and purposes, not to show which results could be extracted from the data (we point the interested reader to [6,4,7]).

In the next sections, for each presented critical aspect, we describe the logic behind our choices, we discuss the underestimated problems risen during all the project (from design of the experiment to data analysis), and suggest possible variants to adopt in future experiments.

2   The TORCS Experiment

The cognitive task in the experiment concerned playing a video game. This made it possible to reach a high repeatability and a high level of involvement among participants. The Open Racing Car Simulator (TORCS) was chosen as reference. Being a video game that requires the player to sit in front of a computer, subjects can experiment emotionally different situations characterized by a similar physical activity and the effects of movement artifacts, or physical activity, on acquired data are negligible.

During a game session (about 30 minutes), each participant played 7 races lasting 3 minutes each against one computer driver, which is the only opponent during the race. The opponent skill has been changed among races. We

Fig. 1. TORCS experimental setting

hypothesize that this can influence the preference for one race with respect to another.

The environment where the experiment took place has been conceived with the purpose of isolating the player and maximizing the game immersion so that no external event could influence the subject physiological state. The setting was a small room with a computer placed on a desk. The player was sitting in front of the monitor and was interacting with the computer through standard mouse and keyboard. No other people were in the same room and the operator monitored the experiment from an external site.

To avoid the effect of covert communication, no interaction between operator and subject occurred during the experiment. The protocol was carried on by an automatic script on the computer that started each race and managed the questionnaire. At the end of each race, starting from the second one, the participants were asked by a script to express, via a computer-based form, the preference between the race just played and the previous one.

The duration of each race was 3 minutes. This provided enough time to eliminate past race effects on physiological signals and to produce a new one, potentially different, enjoyment level before the overcoming of boredom caused by excessive race length.

2.1 Videogame Choice

For our experiment we needed a fully customizable videogame, which would be possible to play with just one hand, because the other hand had to be fitted with physiological sensors. Therefore, all games that required a joypad or mouse & keyboard were rejected. A second strong constraint was on the physical involvement level: we did not want the physical involvement to influence the physiological responses. Therefore, physical games such as the one used in previous works [8] have not been considered. Moreover, since the subjects had to play several variants of the game during the acquisition session, a single play of the game had to last at most 3-5 minutes, to reduce the effects f fatigue. The Open Racing Car Simulator (TORCS) was chosen among the suitable open source games because it fitted all the constraints. In addition, it was easy enough to play, even for inexperienced players, which could, thus, be included in the trials.

We decided to reduce the amount of details of the graphic environment (e.g., no crowd surrounding the track, no buildings, no stickers on the cars) to let the player focus on the task (driving the car) rather then look around. Even the number of opponents was reduced to only one to maximize the controllability of the game experience. A simple track, an oval with 2 "s" curves (showed in Figure 1), was chosen to minimize the learning time for inexperienced players. In general, every game parameter has been adjusted to minimize the effect of external, not controllable events.

While these changes were fundamental to have a controlled experimental environment, after all these tuning, the quality of the game did not look appealing to players anymore. Some players stated that the game was not on par of other recent car racing game and therefore they did not enjoy playing such a old looking game. The game experience was certainly compromised not only because the players were fitted with sensors, but also because they where more concerned to the experiment rather then just trying to enjoying playing a videogame.

2.2 Task Choice

We proposed 3 different gaming experiences considering the following 3 categories of players:

- P_W is a player who likes to win (even easily)
- P_L is a player who does not really care to win. For example, he/she can be a novice who cares more about learning how to play.
- P_C is a player who enjoys to have a balanced fight against an opponent that matches his/her skills.

Therefore, the considered game experience, obtained by implementing a customized opponent driver matching the skill of the player, are the following:

- R_W where the player competes against a weaker opponent (i.e., the computer opponent is programmed to always stay behind the player). The player always wins and virtually there is no interaction with the opponent which can never reach player.
- R_L where the player competes against a stronger opponent (i.e., the computer opponent is programmed to always stay ahead the player). The player always loses and virtually there is no interaction with the opponent since the player can never reach the opponent.

– R_C where the player races against an equally skilled opponent (the computer opponent is programmed to match the player skill level and to engage a challenging race). The interaction between player and opponent is higher and the winner of the race cannot be determined a priori.

Our initial hypothesis was that players $\{P_W, P_L, P_C\}$ respectively would enjoy more races $\{R_W, R_L, R_C\}$. Unfortunately, as described in Section 3.2, the participant distribution was biased towards R_C, therefore our a posteriori analysis had to take into account this. We tried to build a model for the classification of these 3 categories of players using the following information: data from general personal info questionnaire (age, sex, game experience, TORCS game prior knowledge), data from in-game logs and data from physiology. Unfortunately the resulting model could not classify the player with enough accuracy to be used for preference estimation. The reason is because many subjects did not express a coherent preference among races.

2.3   Self Report Preference Questionnaire

A 2 Alternative Forced Choice (2AFC) pairwise preference scheme was proposed at the end of each race with the following question: "Which race did you like most?". The following set of possible answers to choose from: "1) The last race 2) The previous race?". The player was thus forced to express a simple preference (i.e., either the last race or the previous one) without being asked to rank the strength of such preference. 2AFC offers a main advantage to acquire objective enjoyment: it normalizes the different personal conception of enjoyment among players and it allows a fair comparison between the answers of different subjects. On the other hand, a problem arises when the player does not experience a real difference between races: there is no way to discriminate such situation and, therefore, a number of noisy answers might be generated. However, this preference scheme was successfully used in previous work in the field [8].

A better method, that reduces the noise of the answers, is 4 Alternative Forced Choice (4AFC). In addition to the answers proposed by 2AFC scheme, the subject can also choose "3) Both races 4) Neither race". With this technique, during the estimation of a differential preference model, it is possible to ignore the races whose preference could not be determined even by the player itself.

Moreover, the knowledge of the main reason behind the answers might be crucial for having a more detailed explanation of the preference patterns and for creating clusters of players. For example, an inexperienced player could report a preference that is evolving during the races due to the learning process. On the other hand, a skilled player might report a preference that is just related to the in–game performance. A way to obtain this is to introduce an open question asking the player to describe the reason of his/her answer. Other open questions (e.g, "What did you enjoy most/least during the last game?") can also improve the level of knowledge of the task.

A main drawback of open questions is that they stop the flow of the session because the subject has to focus on thinking and typing the answer. This might not be a problem if the questions concern independent pairs of games (the players play 2 games and at the end of the second they answer the questionnaire and then they continue with the second pair of races and so on).

Very often, reviewers are concerned about the unreliability of self-reported measurements to assess the ground truth of user preference. We are aware of different problems related to the poor reliability of self-reported emotions, but note that, in this experiment, we are asking the subjects to express a preference between two situations and not to asses a level of emotion. Alternative methods such as expert judgment of user preference would be even less reliable.

3 Participants to the Experiment

When working at an affective computing acquisition session, one of the hardest collateral task is to find a reasonable amount of volunteers willing to join the experiment. One of the most common resources, especially when a project is developed within the university, are students. For example, in our TORCS experiment, 80% of participants were students. It is clear that this uneven distribution of the sample population might lead to biased results. Every statement regarding the generality of the learned affective model have to be considered valid for a population represented by the sample. Moreover, a lot of characteristics of the players may influence the findings, and it is not easy to evaluate all of them with a relatively small sample as the one that can usually be recruited for these experiments. Learning a model able to reliably predict the preference for a generic population is a very challenging task, in these conditions. Instead, having a number of less general, but more accurate models might be a better choice.

3.1 Motivating Participants

To enhance participants involvement during the experiment, players have been told that they were competing for a prize. Prizes were given basing on a series of parameters including in–game performance, but also on physiological responses, so that potential advantages of skilled players were reduced. While the competition actually kept high the motivation of players, and, therefore, the competitive level, on the other hand, it distorted the genuine concept of enjoyment. Actually, for most subjects, having fun is not related to win, as demonstrated by the results. Unfortunately, for some of them, the motivation given by winning induced behavior the goal of the game was not just"having fun", but, instead, playing to win the race, also when this lead to behaviors incompatible with having fun. This drawback can be overcome by specifying that the score for the prize will not take into account the in–game score, but other intangible factors such as the "enjoyment level" or the physiological response, so that the motivation to play for the prize is kept, but the in–game performance has not to be achieved at any cost.

Table 1. Distribution of player typology obtained trough the analysis of reported preference between race pairs. The total number of players is 75.

Preference	# Players
$R_C \succ R_W \succ R_L$	32
$R_C \succ R_L \succ R_W$	6
$R_W \succ R_C \succ R_L$	1
incoherent	36

Preference	# Players
$R_W \succ (R_C, R_L)$	2
$R_W \prec (R_C, R_L)$	8
incoherent	65

Preference	# Players
$R_C \succ (R_W, R_L)$	52
$R_C \prec (R_W, R_L)$	1
incoherent	22

Preference	# Players
$R_L \succ (R_W, R_C)$	0
$R_L \prec (R_W, R_C)$	35
incoherent	45

3.2   Classification of Participants

In Section 2.2 we introduced a hypothesis on players typology. Unfortunately we have not considered the possibility that a player could not always like the same race typology. For example, at the beginning of the session, a player could prefer a typology of race where there is no much interaction with the opponent because he/she is more concerned to learning how to control the car. On the other hand, at the end of the session the player could have learned how to control the car and enjoy more a race versus a challenging opponent. A player that reports to prefer one typology of race over another and then he/she reports the opposite, is labeled as "incoherent" because different preferences are expressed for the same pairs. Moreover, as suggested by the theory of flow [9], the player game experience migth differ according to her involvement. To verify the initial hypothesis we analyzed the reported preference between race pairs. The distribution of players among different categories has been identified and it is summarized in Table 1.

The 2AFC protocol adopted in this experiment forces the player to express a preference, even if actually there is no relevant preference between the two races. The incoherent answers coming from the need to select between two alternative when no precise preference was established could have been avoided by using a different answer scheme (i.e., 4AFC) that provides a way to express the concept of "no preference". Some other incoherent answers might come from a learning effect during the session, and should have been investigated, although we hypothesized that this effect was negligible, due to the relatively short experience done in the trial. A randomization of the game sequence would have also helped in reducing some inter–subject inconsistency.

A second analysis, which does not consider the full order among the 3 variants of game, is done by comparing only the preferred race variant versus the remaining 2. Table 1 reports that, for most of the players, R_C is preferred over R_W and R_L.

4 Data Acquisition

Physiological data were gathered using the ProComp Infiniti. This device acquires 5 physiological signals: Blood Volume Pulse (BVP), Electrocardiogram (ECG), Galvanic Skin Response (GSR), Respiration (RESP) and Temperature (TEMP). Moreover, an additional channel was used to acquire a synchronization signal coming from an optical sensor attached to the computer screen. A sample rate of 256Hz has been used except for ECG and BVP signals that were sampled at 2048Hz. The hand not used for interacting with the game was fitted with GSR, BVP and TEMP sensors. The 3 terminal ECG sensors were placed around the chest, as well as the RESP sensor. Our analysis reported ECG and TEMP sensor does not bring any additional information to the model of preference. Therefore, due to the high level of invasivity of the ECG sensor, we suggest to not use it in a similar experiment especially since the heart rate could be determined by using the less invasive BVP sensor, which is adequate in this case, due to the trial settings. In particular, as statistically verified in the experiment, the information needed to classify the signal and brought by ECG was less relevant than that brought by BVP.

A log file containing time-stamp and some game status information was saved during each race. Unlike the work presented in [10] where events from the game are sent to the acquisition hardware (with a jitter of 200ms), the data logs have been continuously saved at 10Hz on the local computer. Note that information regarding the TORCS state has not been used to obtain the results reported in this paper, but the timestamps have been used for synchronization between races and physiological data.

Two video cameras recorded the environment in which the player acted too. A frontal camera captured the player's face, the second camera was placed at the top right back corner of the room, with respect to player, and captured the player actions and the game output from the monitor. Data from camera are used during data analysis to detect and validate eventually present strange signals behaviors. For example, we were able to find out whether a singularity in signals was related to an in–game event or an external event. In particular, we were able to identify the parts of the experiment where the player was moving the sensorized hand generating an unexpected noisy behavior in the physiological signals that was not related to physiology in any way. Other sensors (e.g., accelerometers) could have been used for this specific purpose, but cameras provide much more information for different purposes.

5 Conclusion

In a previous paper [4], we showed that it was possible to discriminate the preference between two races with up to 74% accuracy by looking at the physiological responses. But are we sure that this is the answer that we were actually looking for when we planned the experiment? During the data analysis, as described above, we had to face a number of issues: biased population have influenced the estimation of performance for the model; noisy questionnaire answers have introduced a certain amount of noise in model estimation; and very different race variants could have influenced the physiology more than expected.

If the goal is to estimate the player enjoyment at runtime, is it really necessary to exploit physiology? More in detail, the game designers already have some tools to estimate the enjoyment: they can rely to some reasonable hypothesis (e.g., most of the people prefer a challenging opponent to an always winning one; most of the people prefer a certain ratio of success over failure) that could be verified by using in-game features as metrics (e.g., number of overtakes, distance from the opponent or number of lives lost). Could physiology improve the estimation of enjoyment by providing a set of metrics that work better than the ones extracted from games? In our recent work [7] we addressed whether the in-game metrics could estimate the preference among races better than physiological responses, and how the performed tasks (in our case the race variants) were related to those two aspects. Applying the proposed methodology, we find out that in-game logs could predict the preference (80% Correct Classification Rate) better than physiological measures. However, a deeper analysis showed that a model based on a simple ranking of races (in particular $R_C \succ R_W \succ R_L$) had the same exact performance of classification than the model based on in-game logs. In addition, we found out that race types and some in-game features had an extremely high correlation (in particular, the average distance from the opponent can discriminate 3 classes of races with 100% of accuracy). Therefore, in this experiment, we could not find any way of exploiting physiological measurement or in-game logs that performed better than the a priori hypothesis "most of the players will prefer a challenging race rather than a race where they always win, rather than a race where they always lose".

For the next experiment, we plan to let users play a videogame (even against a friend as in [11]) in a non-controlled environment. Ideally the player will wear a set of non-invasive sensors that will reduce the awareness of being recorded. No a priori hypotheses will be made on player "category". The questionnaire scheme will be a 4AFC with some open question about on the detail of why a version of the game was preferred. We expect to have many "equally preferred" answers and a few of strong preferences and this will be used as an advantage. We will know that for those answers, the player could really state that he/she enjoyed more that particular game experience. Therefore we expect to see a stronger impact on physiology during such races.

Acknowledgments. The research activity described in this paper has been partially supported by IIT - Italian Institute of Technology.

References

1. Cacioppo, J., Tassinary, L., Berntson, G.: Psychophysiological science. In: Handbook of Psychophysiology, vol. 2, pp. 3–23 (2000)
2. Picard, R., Vyzas, E., Healey, J.: Toward machine emotional intelligence: Analysis of affective physiological state. IEEE Transactions on Pattern Analysis and Machine Intelligence, 1175–1191 (2001)

3. Calvo, R., D'Mello, S.: Affect detection: An interdisciplinary review of models, methods, and their applications. IEEE Transactions on Affective Computing, 18–37 (2010)

4. Tognetti, S., Garbarino, M., Bonarini, A., Matteucci, M.: Modeling player enjoyment from physiological responses in a car racing game. In: Proceedings IEEE International Conference on Computational Intelligence and Games (August 2010)

5. The open racing car simulator website, http://torcs.sourceforge.net/

6. Tognetti, S., Garbarino, M., Bonarini, A., Matteucci, M.: Enjoyment recognition from physiological data in a car racing game. In: Proceedings of the 3rd International Workshop on Affective Interaction in Natural Environments, AFFINE 2010, pp. 3–8. ACM, New York (2010)

7. Tognetti, S., Garbarino, M., Bonarini, A., Matteucci, M.: The affective triad: stimuli, questionnaires and measurements. In: D´Mello, S., et al. (eds.) ACII 2011, Part II. LNCS, vol. 6975, pp. 101–110. Springer, Heidelberg (2011)

8. Yannakakis, G., Hallam, J., Lund, H.: Entertainment capture through heart rate activity in physical interactive playgrounds. User Modeling and User-Adapted Interaction 18(1), 207–243 (2008)

9. Csikszentmihalyi, M.: Flow: The psychology of optimal experience. Harper & Row, New York (1990)

10. Nacke, L., Lindley, C., Stellmach, S.: Log whos playing: psychophysiological game analysis made easy through event logging. Fun and Games, 150–157 (2008)

11. Mandryk, R., Inkpen, K., Valvert, T.: Using psychophysiological techniques to measure user experience with entertainment technologies. Behaviour & Information Technology 25(2), 141–158 (2006)

Analysing the Relevance of Experience Partitions to the Prediction of Players' Self-reports of Affect

Héctor Perez Martínez and Georgios N. Yannakakis

Center for Computer Games Research,
IT University of Copenhagen,
Rued Langgaards vej 7, 2300, Denmark
{hpma,yannakakis}@itu.dk

Abstract. A common practice in modeling affect from physiological signals consists of reducing the signals to a set of statistical features that feed predictors of self-reported emotions. This paper analyses the impact of various time-windows, used for the extraction of physiological features, to the accuracy of affective models of players in a simple 3D game. Results show that the signals recorded in the central part of a short gaming experience contain more relevant information to the prediction of positive affective states than the starting and ending parts while the relevant information to predict anxiety and frustration appear not to be localized in a specific time interval but rather dependent on particular game stimuli.

Keywords: preference learning, post-experience self-reports, heart rate, skin conductance, blood volume pulse, games.

1 Introduction

Video games, even the most simple ones, have the potential of providing engaging episodes in which the player might experience a plethora of psychological states from fear and frustration to excitement and fun. A game able to recognize those psychological states could offer tailored and optimized experiences to each different player according to her preferences and motivations to play without the need of asking directly [1,2].

A predictor of affect can be trained on data gathered across several game sessions in which players report their experience during or after the game ([3,4,5] among others) resulting in a computational model that receives as inputs the objective (measurable) part of the experience (e.g. achievements on the game, buttons pressed on the game pad, heart rate and facial expression) and outputs a value estimating the subjective part (e.g. valence and arousal or frustration). Typically, the inputs of the model consist of *statistical features* (e.g. score, keys pressed per second and average heart rate) calculated on a time interval before the player responds to online (i.e. during play) or post-experience questionnaire [6,7]. According to some theories, when humans report past emotional experiences, they have to retrieve specific thoughts, event-specific details or beliefs [8] that relate to the past experience. Consequently, we expect that certain parts of the experience are more relevant than others to predict self-reported affect. To the best of our knowledge there exists no study that suggests an optimal time interval that maximizes

S. D'Mello et al. (Eds.): ACII 2011, Part II, LNCS 6975, pp. 538–546, 2011.

the predictability of computational models for recognition of affect. The common practice followed is to either choose an arbitrary time window (e.g. the complete game [5]) or run preliminary experiments to determine the most appropriate one for the task at hand [9].

This paper examines the relevance of different experience time windows with respect to the prediction accuracy of seven self-reported affective/cognitive preferences — players report after a pair of games whether the first or the second felt more *anxious*, *boring*, *challenging*, *exciting*, *frustrating*, *fun* and *relaxing* — in a short (90 seconds) 3D prey/predator game. Features calculated on different time intervals of three physiological signals, namely heart rate (HR), skin conductance (SC) and blood volume pulse (BVP), are compared as inputs to artificial neural network (ANN) models of affect.

The rest of the paper is organized as follows: Section 2 reviews the literature in psychophysiology, games and affect, Section 3 and 4 , respectively, present the dataset and the methodology followed in this study and Section 5 and 6 discuss the results and conclusions of the study.

2   Related Work

Research in game psychophysiology has gained interest in recent years [10] resulting in studies exploring different modalities, emotions and affective states of players. Some affective gaming researchers attempt to draw the mappings between physiology and affect by analysing the correlations between statistical features extracted from the physiological signals of participants while playing and their affective post-experience self-reports. For example, Nacke and Lindley [11] investigate the correlations between flow, boredom and immersion, and the cumulative averages of jaw electromyography (EMG) and SC over the complete playing time in a first person shooter while Rani et al. [12] explore the correlations between anxiety, engagement, boredom and frustration self-reports after playing Pong and various statistical features extracted from the physiological signals (HR and SC among others) recorded during the entire game.

Another approach to the same problem consists of training computational models that predict self-reports of affect relying on features of the physiological signals. Kapoor et al. [9] implement different computational predictors of frustration based on the average value over 150 seconds of 14 features extracted from a SC sensor, a pressure mouse, a posture sensor and a face tracker. The time window is calculated just before the participant reports to be frustrated or 225 seconds after the game has started if the participant does not report frustration during the experience. McQuiggan et al. [4] aim to maximize the time for a correct early detection of frustration based on BVP and SC features (among other modalities). The best models reported predict the frustration self-reports 35 seconds before they are introduced by the user. Mandryk et al. [13] use fuzzy rules to map HR, SC, respiration and EMG of the jaw muscles continuously (i.e. every physiological recording is transformed) to an arousal-valence space and further to levels of fun, boredom, challenge, excitement and frustration during a hockey computer game. This model is validated by analysing the correlation between the average value of the predicted psychological states along the entire game session and the post-experience emotional ratings of the players. Yannakakis et al. [14,15] model the fun pairwise preferences of children playing physical interactive games from an extensive set of statistical features extracted from HR and SC recorded during the 90-second long games using neuroevolutionary preference learning. On the same basis, Martinez et al. [16,5] trained predictors of seven self-reported affective states in a 3D prey/predator game using statistical features of HR, BVP and SC recorded during 90-second long games. Tognetti et al. [17] apply Linear Discriminant Analysis to map a large number of features calculated on the last minute recordings of HR, BVP, respiration and SC to player preferences in a racing game.

In the aforementioned studies, either the complete signals over the full length of a game or an interval selected after preliminary — not reported — studies are used to calculate the statistical features. On the contrary, McQuiggan et al. [18] explore different time window lengths and positions in HR and SC signals to calculate the statistical features that feed a predictor of self-efficacy in a 3D learning environment. A large number of features are calculated covering overlapping parts of the experience. Unfortunately, the relevance of each feature for the prediction is not analysed. Broekens et al. [19] present a brief analysis of five window lengths in eye-gaze data. That analysis shows that features calculated in shorter windows (1, 2, 4 and 6 seconds) prior a player action predict more accurately the type of action than longer time windows (10 seconds). That study differs from this paper both in the signals analysed and more importantly the prediction target.

It is worth mentioning other psycho-physiological studies in games with a focus on short signal intervals associated to game events. Conati and Maclaren [20] propose a probabilistic model of joy and distress of students and their admiration and reproach towards an agent based on Dynamic Decision Networks. For each game event, the model takes as input the difference between the average EMG signal in the corrugator muscle over the whole experience (30 minutes) and the average EMG in the four seconds following the event. Hazlett [21] studies the correlations between positive and negative events and the mean value of corrugator and zygomaticus muscles EMG during those events and one second following the event. Ravaja et al. [22] examine the effect of game events on zygomatic and orbicularis oculi EMG, SC and HR by analysing statistically the changes on the mean value of the signals in eight 1-second windows (2 before the event and 6 after). On these studies, the time windows are selected to allow enough time to detect a physiological response while minimizing overlapping windows among subsequent events. This paper does not explore event-associated time windows and instead focuses on models of post-experience affective reports that are based on physiological signals gathered during play.

3 Data Recording

The dataset used in this paper was gathered during an experimental game survey in which 36 participants (80% males, aged from 21 to 47 with mean and standard deviation of age equal 27.2 and 5.84, respectively) played four pairs of different variants of the same video-game. The test-bed game named *Maze-Ball* is a 3D prey/predator game that features a green ball inside a maze controlled by the arrow keys. The goal of the player is to maximize her score in 90 seconds by collecting the pellets scattered in the maze while avoiding the red enemies that wander around. The eight available variants of the game differ only on the virtual camera profile used which defines how the virtual world is presented on screen.

Blood volume pulse, b, and skin conductance, s, were recorded at 32Hz during the session using the IOM biofeedback device. Heart rate, h, is inferred by the BVP signal every 5 seconds and the magnitude (SM), m, and the duration (SD), d, of signal variation have been derived from SC [23]. The players filled in a 4-alternative forced choice questionnaire after completing a pair of variants reporting whether the first or the second game of the pair felt more anxious, boring, challenging, exciting, frustrating, fun and relaxing, or whether both felt equally, or none of them did. The details of the Maze-Ball game design and the experimental protocol followed can be found in [24,5].

The following set of features is extracted from different time intervals — full game (90 seconds), two overlapping windows of 60 seconds (0 to 60 and 30 to 90), two non-overlapping windows of 45 seconds, three non-overlapping windows of 30 seconds and four non-overlapping windows of 22.5 seconds — of each signal ($\alpha \in \{b, s, h, m, d\}$) inspired by previous studies on physiological feature extraction [15,25]:

- average ($E\{\alpha\}$) and variance ($\sigma^2\{\alpha\}$) of the signal;
- initial (α_{in}) and final (α_{last}) recording and difference between them (Δ^α);
- minimum ($min\{\alpha\}$) and maximum ($max\{\alpha\}$) signal recording and difference between them (D^α);
- time when maximum ($t_{max}\{\alpha\}$) and minimum ($t_{min}\{\alpha\}$) samples were recorded and difference between those times (D_t^α);
- average first and second absolute differences ($\delta_{|1|}^\alpha$ and $\delta_{|2|}^\alpha$, respectively);
- Pearson's correlation coefficient (R_α) between raw α recordings and the time t at which data were recorded;
- autocorrelation (lag equals the sampling rate of α) of the signal (ρ^α);

All features are normalized to the [0,1] interval using standard min-max normalization.

4   Method

Neuroevolutionary preference learning is applied in order to train computational models that learn the players' pairwise self-reports of affect. The inputs to the models are selected automatically through Genetic Feature Selection (GFS). The two algorithms are briefly described in the following subsections.

4.1   Genetic Feature Selection

Feature selection (FS) is essential in scenarios where the available features do not have a clear relationship and, thus, impact to the prediction of a target output (i.e. it is not easy to decide *a priori* which features are useful and which are irrelevant for the prediction). Moreover the computational cost of testing all available feature sets is combinatorial and exhaustive search might not be computationally feasible in large feature sets. Under these conditions, FS is critical for finding an appropriate set of model input features that can yield highly accurate predictors [5].

Genetic feature selection [16] is a global search FS algorithm guided by a genetic search. The search starts by evaluating the fitness of several subsets with one feature; in subsequent iterations combinations of the fittest subsets from the previous iterations are evaluated. The algorithm stops after a fixed number of iterations or when highly fit feature subsets are found. The fitness function is calculated as the average cross validation performance of a model trained on the selected features on unseen folds of classification data. More details about GSF can be found in [16].

4.2   Neuroevolutionary Preference Learning

We apply preference learning [26] to build affective models that predict users' self-reported emotional preferences based on the subsets of features selected by the GFS algorithm. In this study, the models are implemented as single layer perceptrons (SLPs) that are trained via neuroevolutionary preference learning (as in [27,5]) to map the selected features to a predictor of the reported pairwise emotional preferences.

Note that the pairwise preference relationship of the training data is known (e.g. game A is preferred to game B) but the value of the target output is not (i.e. the magnitude of the preference is unknown). Thus, any gradient-based optimization algorithm is inapplicable to the training problem since the error function under optimization is not differentiable. The trained model learns for each pair of games a higher output value for the preferred game than for the non preferred.

5   Experiments

Ten ANN-models are trained for each affective state and time window using 3-fold cross validation and their average accuracy is depicted on Figure 1. For the 45 and 60 second long intervals, all affective states but challenge are predicted with higher accuracy in the second interval. By further subdividing the windows, boredom and the three positive affective states — excitement, fun and relaxation — are predicted with the highest accuracy using statistical features of the physiological signals calculated in the central 30-second interval and the second or third quarter of the game (22.5 second long intervals). Furthermore, these models built on small time intervals yield, on average, significantly higher prediction accuracies than the models trained on the full-length experience — difference in accuracy of 3.15% for boredom ($t(18) = 3.43$), 6.0% for excitement ($t(18) = 7.31$), 4.75% for fun ($t(18) = 4.52$) and 7.22% for relaxation ($t(18) = 10.82$); p-values < 0.01 for all four states. This suggests that the information more relevant for predicting self-reports of positive experiences and boredom in Maze-Ball is located at time windows which are in the middle of the short (90 s) gaming experience.

The anxiety models built on 45 and 60 second-long windows suggest that the second half of the game is more relevant to define the experience; however, the smaller windows do not show a clear trend. Similarly, frustration models present the same average accuracy in the last 60 seconds and in the first 30 seconds. This points out that self-reports of these two negative affective states are not significantly related to a specific

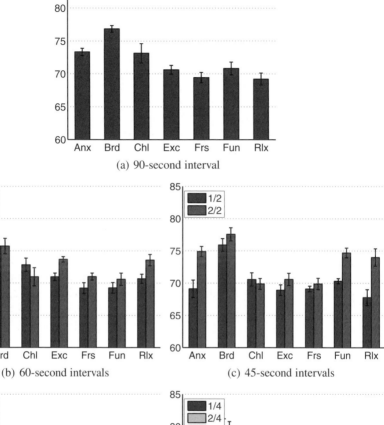

Fig. 1. Average and standard error of ten models trained on the 7 affective states — anxiety (Anx), boredom (Brd), challenge (Chl), excitement (Exc), frustration (Frs), fun (Fun) and relaxation (Rlx) — using statistical features calculated in different time-intervals of the experience

part of the Maze-Ball experience and instead possibly linked to concrete asynchronous events in the game. It is possible that when players report fun, excitement, relaxation and boredom they build an overall assessment of the experience which is better approximated by the events occurring in the middle of the game while the reports of anxiety and frustration might be determined by punctual events in the game that elicited those affective states.

The predictors built for self-reports of challenge present, consistently across different time-window sizes, higher accuracies when trained on the first parts of the experience although no significantly different from the models trained on the complete 90 seconds of the game (higher difference equal to 1.81%; $t(18) = 1.18, ns$). It appears that in such short experience with a constant level of challenge — all elements in the level remain the same during each level — the first half of the game is enough to assess the difficulty of the level. Perceived challenge, opposite to the other six user states investigated, is not considered an affective state but rather a cognitive state which might be remembered more accurately than affect having an impact on which parts of the experience are taken into account while reporting the experience via questionnaires.

Despite the fact that only some states appear to be related to a specific interval of the experience, there exists at least one time interval for each of the seven states investigated that yields, on average, more accurate models than the complete game (not significant for challenge and anxiety). This suggests that statistical features calculated in small parts of the signals highlight better the differences on the experience than physiological features calculated in the full-length of the game.

6   Conclusions

The most common approach to create predictors of players' affective states based on their physiological states consists of applying machine learning algorithms to find mappings between reports of affect and statistical features extracted from the physiological signals recorded during play. This paper examines the effect of using different fractions of the physiological signals to the prediction of seven self-reported affective/cognitive states in a short 3D prey/predator game. Results show that features extracted from middle parts of the signals yield more accurate predictors of positive affective states and boredom than features extracted from the complete signals. Moreover, self-reports of perceived challenge are predicted more accurately by parts of the signals located at the beginning of the experience. Finally, reports of anxiety and frustration are not clearly related to a specific time window in the experience. Even though the games played are short (90 seconds), results show that more accurate models can be built when using a fraction instead of the complete physiological signals recorded during the game.

Future work will attempt to validate these results across more players and different casual games, i.e. short games with simple rules, that can provide comparable experiences. Additionally, this paper only uses information from the physiological state of the player leaving out game play events and game metrics which provide relevant information for the prediction of reported emotions (see [16] among others); an extended study will explore whether the most informative intervals of that modality correspond to the same intervals of the physiological signals.

References

1. Gilleade, K., Dix, A., Allanson, J.: Affective videogames and modes of affective gaming: assist me, challenge me, emote me. In: Proc. DIGRA 2005 (2005)
2. Hudlicka, E.: Affective game engines: motivation and requirements. In: Proceedings of the 4th International Conference on Foundations of Digital Games, pp. 299–306. ACM, New York (2009)
3. Mandryk, R., Inkpen, K., Calvert, T.: Using psychophysiological techniques to measure user experience with entertainment technologies. Behaviour & Information Technology 25(2), 141–158 (2006)
4. McQuiggan, S.W., Lee, S.Y., Lester, J.C.: Early prediction of student frustration. In: Paiva, A.C.R., Prada, R., Picard, R.W. (eds.) ACII 2007. LNCS, vol. 4738, pp. 698–709. Springer, Heidelberg (2007)
5. Yannakakis, G.N., Martínez, H.P., Jhala, A.: Towards affective camera control in games. User Modeling and User-Adapted Interaction 20, 313–340 (2010), doi:10.1007/s11257-010-9078-0
6. Picard, R., Vyzas, E., Healey, J.: Toward machine emotional intelligence: Analysis of affective physiological state. IEEE Transactions on Pattern Analysis and Machine Intelligence, 1175–1191 (2001)
7. Cacioppo, J., Berntson, G., Larsen, J., Poehlmann, K., Ito, T., et al.: The psychophysiology of emotion. In: Handbook of Emotions, pp. 119–142 (1993)
8. Robinson, M., Clore, G.: Belief and feeling: Evidence for an accessibility model of emotional self-report. Psychological Bulletin 128(6), 934 (2002)
9. Kapoor, A., Burleson, W., Picard, R.: Automatic prediction of frustration. International Journal of Human-Computer Studies 65(8), 724–736 (2007)
10. Kivikangas, J., Ekman, I., Chanel, G., Järvelä, S., Salminen, M., Cowley, B., Henttonen, P., Ravaja, N.: Review on psychophysiological methods in game research. In: Proc. of 1st Nordic DiGRA
11. Nacke, L., Lindley, C.: Flow and immersion in first-person shooters: measuring the player's gameplay experience. In: Proceedings of the 2008 Conference on Future Play: Research, Play, Share, pp. 81–88. ACM, New York (2008)
12. Rani, P., Sarkar, N., Liu, C.: Maintaining optimal challenge in computer games through real-time physiological feedback. In: Proceedings of the 11th International Conference on Human Computer Interaction, pp. 184–192 (2005)
13. Mandryk, R., Atkins, M.: A fuzzy physiological approach for continuously modeling emotion during interaction with play technologies. International Journal of Human-Computer Studies 65(4), 329–347 (2007)
14. Yannakakis, G.N., Hallam, J., Lund, H.H.: Entertainment capture through heart rate activity in physical interactive playgrounds. User Modeling and User-Adapted Interaction 18(1), 207–243 (2008)
15. Yannakakis, G.N., Hallam, J.: Entertainment modeling through physiology in physical play. International Journal of Human-Computer Studies 66(10), 741–755 (2008)
16. Martínez, H., Yannakakis, G.: Genetic search feature selection for affective modeling: a case study on reported preferences. In: Proceedings of the 3rd International Workshop on Affective Interaction in Natural Environments, pp. 15–20. ACM, New York (2010)
17. Tognetti, S., Garbarino, M., Bonanno, A., Matteucci, M., Bonarini, A.: Enjoyment recognition from physiological data in a car racing game. In: Proceedings of the 3rd International Workshop on Affective Interaction in Natural Environments, pp. 3–8. ACM, New York (2010)

18. Mcquiggan, S., Mott, B., Lester, J.: Modeling self-efficacy in intelligent tutoring systems: An inductive approach. User Modeling and User-Adapted Interaction 18(1), 81–123 (2008)

19. Broekens, J., Kosters, W., de Vries, T.: Eye movements disclose decisions in set. BNAIC (2009)

20. Conati, C., Maclaren, H.: Modeling user affect from causes and effects. User Modeling, Adaptation, and Personalization, 4–15 (2009)

21. Hazlett, R.: Measuring emotional valence during interactive experiences: boys at video game play. In: Proceedings of the SIGCHI Conference on Human Factors in Computing Systems, pp. 1023–1026. ACM, New York (2006)

22. Ravaja, N., Saari, T., Laarni, J., Kallinen, K., Salminen, M., Holopainen, J., Järvinen, A.: The psychophysiology of video gaming: Phasic emotional responses to game events. In: Proceedings of the DiGRA Conference Changing Views: Worlds in Play

23. Tognetti, S., Garbarino, M., Bonarini, A., Matteucci, M.: Modeling enjoyment preference from physiological responses in a car racing game. In: 2010 IEEE Symposium on Computational Intelligence and Games (CIG), pp. 321–328. IEEE, Los Alamitos (2010)

24. Martinez, H.P., Jhala, A., Yannakakis, G.N.: Analyzing the Impact of Camera Viewpoint on Player Psychophysiology. In: Proceedings of the Int. Conf. on Affective Computing and Intelligent Interaction, pp. 394–399. IEEE, Amsterdam (2009)

25. Tognetti, S., Alessandro, C., Bonarini, A., Matteucci, M.: Fundamental issues on the recognition of autonomic patterns produced by visual stimuli. In: 3rd International Conference on Affective Computing and Intelligent Interaction and Workshops. ACII 2009, pp. 1–6. IEEE, Los Alamitos (2009)

26. Fürnkranz, J., Hüllermeier, E.: Preference learning. Künstliche Intelligenz 19(1), 60–61 (2005)

27. Yannakakis, G.N.: Preference Learning for Affective Modeling. In: Proceedings of the Int. Conf. on Affective Computing and Intelligent Interaction, ACII 2009, Amsterdam, The Netherlands (September 2009)

A Game-Based Corpus for Analysing the Interplay between Game Context and Player Experience

Noor Shaker[1], Stylianos Asteriadis[2], Georgios N. Yannakakis[1],
and Kostas Karpouzis[2]

[1] IT University of Copenhagen, Rued Langaards Vej 7, 2300 Copenhagen, Denmark
[2] National Technical University of Athens, 157 80 Zographou, Athens, Greece
{nosh,yannakakis}@itu.dk, {stiast,kkarpou}@image.ntua.gr

Abstract. Recognizing players' affective state while playing video games has been the focus of many recent research studies. In this paper we describe the process that has been followed to build a corpus based on game events and recorded video sessions from human players while playing *Super Mario Bros*. We present different types of information that have been extracted from game context, player preferences and perception of the game, as well as user features, automatically extracted from video recordings. We run a number of initial experiments to analyse players' behavior while playing video games as a case study of the possible use of the corpus.

Keywords: game-based corpus, player behavior, player's affective state, player experience.

1 Introduction

Many theories exist regarding why we play games and what makes computer games engaging and immersive environments [4,8,9,11,2]. Studying player's behavior and recognizing players' affective state while playing video games has been the focus of attention of recent research. Closing the affective loop [10] is one of the ultimate aims of the research carried out in the field of affective computing [16]. Closing the affective loop within games context entails recognizing/modeling players affective state and identifying game events that elicit certain players' behavior. The next step is the generation of player-adaptive content by incorporating players' emotions into the game in a closed-loop manner using models of player emotion built from the interaction between the player and the game [19,27].

Recognition of emotion, such as entertainment, is considered a hard problem mainly because of the multi-modal nature of emotion which makes sensing, recognizing and modeling emotion a hard task [6]. Traditional evaluation methods such as subjective and objective techniques have been adopted to detect affective states [13,14,24,19,20]. Although subjective reporting is a good approach for

S. D'Mello et al. (Eds.): ACII 2011, Part II, LNCS 6975, pp. 547–556, 2011.

affective capturing and modeling, there are limitations to this methodology [13]. Other input sources, including biofeedback and additional context-based game metrics, could be used for further analysis but do not supplant the self-reports.

Physiological measures have been used to assess users emotional experience when engaged with HCI systems [12,3,26]. Physiological data is a very powerful source for assessing affective state as it can continuously and objectively provide a quantitative metric of user experience [12]. Although physiological measurement devices have been used extensively within the affective computing research for emotion recognition [17] and despite the great efforts that have been devoted to make these devices wearable, their use in commercial computer games is still limited. Facial expressions [7] and head movements [1] are rich non intrusive sources of information regarding the issue of capturing the emotional or behavioral state of a person while interacting with a machine or undertaking certain tasks. A lot of work has been done in recent bibliography for modeling such cues in a variety of environments. For example, Asteriadis et al. in [1] investigate the issue of using head movements, as well as gaze patterns in order to achieve a mapping between these and a child's state towards learning material, aiming at the adaptation of the learning process to the child's needs. Smith et al. [22] propose a scheme for mapping gaze and eye blinks to driver state, in the context of driving conditions, utilizing Finite State Automata. Sidner et al. in [21] investigate those head movements that imply high degree of engagement with a robot utilizing head nods, gaze patterns, as well as head gestures declaring user familiarization with the environment.

The focus and main contribution of this paper is the design of a game-based corpus derived from the popular Super Mario Bros platform game. The corpus contains information about the game context, different game events, players' preferences and perception of the game, as well as visual feedback of players' faces, taken with video recordings. The design of this corpus is an important step towards a more in-depth analysis of the relationship between game context, players' behavior and players' affective state. Findings out of the presented corpus are expected to play a significant role in the game adaptation and personalization procedure. We are not aware of any other similar corpus that has been designed within games context.

Together with the presentation of the corpus, in this study, we present initial findings for correlating a set of game events, a set of features extracted from the corresponding video recordings and/or questionnaires; the results obtained here, are an indicate of the validity of our corpus and the findings that can be extracted from it. The idea of correlating human behavior with interaction context has been studied before in a variety of problems, aiming especially at interpreting attention levels of a user towards specific events. Thus, the same behavioral cue can be interpreted differently under different conditions. For example, although one person might appear to be attentive towards his or her computer screen, his real levels of engagement are low if there is nothing being exposed on it. Furthermore, a person sitting in front of a computer monitor, at the start of an interaction should be expected to be "excused" if he or she is looking around. As

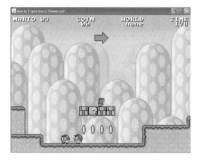

Fig. 1. Snapshot from Super Mario Bros game

the authors in [21] state, this is not necessarily a sign of indifference, but could declare a high degree of engagement, as it can be translated into the person's curiosity to familiarize himself with the environment. Following these ideas, the presented dataset and the accompanying information aim at correlating what is actually taking place in the game with people's reactions and their perception of game quality. The results obtained by such an analysis can be further employed for game adaptation for personalization which is expected to increase the level of engagement.

2   Testbed Platform Game

The testbed platform game used for our study is a modified version of Markus Perssons Infinite Mario Bros (see Fig. 1), which is a public domain clone of Nintendos classic platform game Super Mario Bros. The original Infinite Mario Bros and its source code is available on the web [1].

The gameplay in Super Mario Bros consists of moving the player-controlled character, Mario, through two dimensional levels. Mario can walk, run, duck, jump, and shoot fireballs. The main goal of each level is to get to the end of the level. Auxiliary goals include collecting as many coins as possible, and clearing the level as fast as possible.

While implementing most features of Super Mario Bros, the stand out feature of Infinite Mario Bros is the automatic generation of levels. Every time a new game is started, levels are randomly generated. In our modified version, we concentrated on a few selected parameters that affect gameplay experience.

3   Dataset Design

To assess the players' affective state during play, the following experiment was set up: We seated 36 volunteers (28 male) in front of a computer screen for video recording. Players' age varied from 23 to 39 years old, while experiments were

---

[1] http://www.mojang.com/notch/mario/

carried out in Greece and Denmark. Lighting conditions were typical of an office environment, and for capturing players' visual behavior, a HD camera was used.

We designed a game survey study to collect subjective affective reports expressed as ranking and pairwise preferences of subjects playing different variants (levels) of the test-bed game by following the experimental protocol proposed in [24]. A detailed description of the procedure followed is described.

- An introduction scene presents the game to the player and contains information about the procedure that will be followed. The player is being told that during the session she will play two short games and will be asked to answer a few questions about her game experience.
- Then, a demographics scene is presented which is used to collect the demographics data.
- The player is introduced to the keys that can be used to control *Mario* and their functionality.
- The player is then informed that her game sessions will be video recorded and analysed.
- After these introductory steps the player is set to play the first game (game *A*). The player is given three chances to complete the short game level of Super Mario Bros. If she fails in the first trial the game is reset to the starting point and the player is set to try again. The game ends either by winning one of the three trials or by failing the third one.
- After finishing game *A* a Likert questionnaire scheme is presented to the player. The player is asked to express her emotional preferences of the played game across the three different emotional states (engagement, frustration and challenge). The questionnaire is inspired by the game experience questionnaire (GEQ) [18] according to which a likert scale from 0 to 4 represents the strength of the emotion (4 means "extremely"; 0 means "not at all").
- A second short game (game *B*) is then presented to the player and the player is set to play. The player is given three chances (i.e. Mario lives) to complete the level and the same rules apply as in game *A*.
- After finishing game *B* the GEQ questionnaire is presented to the player (as in game *A*).
- After completing a pair of two games *A* and *B*, the player is asked to report the preferred game for the three emotional dimensions through a 4-alternative forced choice (4-AFC) questionnaire protocol (i.e. A is preferred to B, B is preferred to A, both are preferred equally, neither is preferred (both are equally unpreferred)) [23]. Please note that the questionnaire presented to the players is the following: "Which game was more *x*" where *x* is one of the three emotional states under investigation.
- The player then has the choice to either end the session or to continue. In the latter case, a new pair of two games is presented and the procedure is repeated.

Each participant played three pairs on average. The game sessions presented to players have been constructed using a level width of 100 Super Mario Bros units (blocks), about one-third of the size usually employed when generating levels for Super Mario Bros game in previous experiments [15,19]. The selection of this length was due to a compromise between a window size that is big enough to allow sufficient interaction between the player and the game to trigger the examined affective states and a window which is small enough to set an acceptable frequency of an adaptation mechanism applied in real-time aiming at closing the affective loop of the game [5].

4   Recorded Variables

The following sections describe the data that has been included in the corpus.

4.1   Controllable Features

The level generator of the game has been modified to create levels according to the following six controllable features:

- The number of gaps in the level.
- The average width of gaps.
- The number of enemies.
- Enemies placement: The way enemies are placed around the level is determined by three probabilities which sum to one; around horizontal boxes; Around gaps and random placement.
- The number of powerups.
- The number of boxes.

Two states (low and high) are set for each of the controllable parameters above except for enemies placement which has been assigned three different states allowing more control over the difficulty and diversity of the generated levels. The selection of these particular controllable features was done after consulting game design experts, and with the intent to cover the features that have the most impact on the investigated affective states [15,19]. Other features of the levels have been given fixed values such as the number of cannon and flower tubes = 1, the type of background = over ground, the number of coins = 7, the number of coins hidden in boxes = half the total number of boxes and the number of stairs around the gaps = half the number of gaps.

The analysis presented in this paper is based on 36 players playing 120 game pairs chosen randomly by varying the above-mentioned controllable parameter values. Readers may refer to [20] for more detailed information about these features and the level generation process.

4.2   Gameplay Events

While playing the game, different player actions and their corresponding timestamps have been recorded. These events are categorized in different groups according to the type of the event and the type of interaction with the game objects.

- Winning: This even is generated when the player wins.
- Losing: This event is generated when the player loses. An extra attribute is associated with this event to define the type of object that causes the death. This attribute can take one of the following values (turtle, goompa, flower, cannon ball and gap).
- Interaction with game items: This event is generated when the player collects items or interacts with intractable game objects. The event has an attribute that defines the type of the object that can take one of the values: free coins, empty rock, coin block/rock and power-up rock/block.
- Interaction with enemies: This event is generated when the player kills different types of enemies using different possible actions. The event has two attributes that defines the type of the action performed (stomp, shoot fire balls or unleash a turtle shell) and the type of the enemy killed (red/green/armored turtle, goompa, flower or cannon ball)
- Changing Mario mode: Mario can be in one of the following modes; little, big and fire. Whenever Mario mode is changed, an event is generated with the information about the type of the new mode.
- Changing Mario state: An event is generated whenever Mario changes his state between: moving left/right, jumping, running and ducking.

Note that for each of the above-mentioned events the associated time within which this event occurred is also recorded. Also note that for the last two events two time-stamps are saved marking the start and the end of the event.

4.3   Player Experience

Player experience is measured through rankings presented to the player after each game, and a 4-alternative forced choice questionnaire, presented to the player after playing a pair of games with different controllable features. The questionnaire asks the player to report the preferred game for three user states: *engagement, challenge* and *frustration*. The selection of these states is based on earlier game survey studies [15] and our intention to capture both affective and cognitive/behavioral components of gameplay experience [25]. Moreover, we want to keep the self-reporting as minimal as possible so that experience disruption is minimized.

4.4   Demographics

Each subject has been asked to give information about the following:

- Nationality, gender and age.
- Whether or not the player plays video games (yes and no).
- The weekly time spent playing video games (0-2 hours per week; 2-5 hours per week; 5-10 hours per week and 10+ hours per week).
- Whether or not the player has played Super Mario before (yes and no).

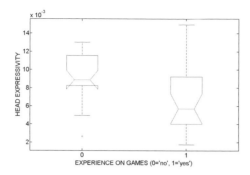

Fig. 2. Experienced game players' and non-experienced players' average head expressivity during game sessions

5 Experiments

5.1 Correlating Player Movements with Self Reported Data

Discovering game events that trigger particular player reactions is expected to highlight instances of personalized preferences or lack of interest. In the following, we present an initial experiment that has been conducted to demonstrate how data from the corpus can be used to analyze this relationship.

A series of head movement parameters have been extracted [1] (please note that these parameters are not part of the data included in the corpus, but rather, features extracted from the video recordings). More specifically, the parameters extracted for each player were: Horizontal H_h and Vertical V_h components of head pose, the horizontal component of eye gaze H_e, head roll H_r and the fraction of the inter-ocular distance with regards to a frame where the algorithm starts. This last indicator is a variable standing for player movements back and forth.

Experiments have shown that all players, regardless of their sex, nationality or experience, tend to adopt high head expressivity (here, defined as the absolute derivative of head rotation) when they lose. More specifically, all 36 players pose fast head movements, on average almost twice (1.8 times) as fast as their head rotation speed during the whole session.

Furthermore, analyzing the players' video sessions has shown that head expressivity is less intense, as experience on game playing increases. Figures 2 and 3 show box plots of average head expressivity per player and reported experience on game playing, as well as average head expressivity and amounts of hours spent on video game playing on a weekly basis.

The respective one-way anova tests also illustrate the fact that head expressivity is an indicator of how experienced one is on games ($F(1,34) = 4.27$, $p = 0.049$) or the amount of hours they spend on game-playing, on a weekly basis ($F(3,32) = 3.46$, $p = 0.028$).

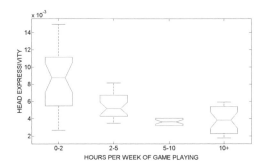

Fig. 3. Average head expressivity as a function of the hours spent on game playing on weekly basis

Table 1. Within-game percentage of agreement between self-reported user states: Engaging (E); Frustrating (F) and Challenging (C)

	E	Not E	F	Not F	C	Not C
E			44%	56%	69%	30%
F	44%	56%			76%	24%
C	69%	29%	78%	22%		

5.2 Analysis of Self Reported Data

On another front of the analysis we attempt to make some initial experiments in order to see how self-reports relate to each other and derive conclusions about the interplay between self-reported, engagement, challenge and frustration in Super Mario. Table 1 presents the pairwise comparison of the percentage of the preferred games across the three emotional states examined. The data presented in the table has been extracted from the players' answers to the preference questionnaires in which the players showed a clear preference for one game over the other. Based on these results it appears that, 30% of the players were engaged in a game that is not challenging while 56% of them found a frustrating game not engaging. These findings suggest that a game can be engaging if it contains the right level of challenge and frustration. It seems that, on average, a game that is too frustrating for the player is not engaging and so is a game with too high or too low level of challenge. This means that the challenge level in the game should meet each individual players' skill. The results from the relationship between engagement and the level of challenge show a consistency with Csikszentmihalyis theory of *flow* [4].

6 Conclusions and Future Work

In this paper, we presented a dataset built for capturing player behavior and preferences during gameplay. The participants covered the whole gamut of experience levels, and attention was paid so that players were from a multinational background. Ground truth of the dataset comes in the form of visual feedback of players' behavior, answers to questionnaires and demographical information.

Initial results from experiments that demonstrate the use of the corpus suggest that there is a significant affect of players' expertise on average head expressivity. Additional findings indicate that self-reported engagement, challenge and frustration are linked, in part, to the theory of flow. The work presented in this paper is the first important step to our future work that will focus on a more in-depth analysis of the relationship between behavioral, game events, game parameters and experience variables. Successfully defining this relationship constitutes a very important step in any adaptation mechanism applied aiming at closing the affective loop in games.

Acknowledgments. We would like to thank the participants in the experiments. This research was supported, in part, by the FP7 ICT project SIREN (project no: 258453) and by the Danish Research Agency, Ministry of Science, Technology and Innovation project *AGameComIn*; project number: 274-09-0083.

References

1. Asteriadis, S., Tzouveli, P., Karpouzis, K., Kollias, S.: Estimation of behavioral user state based on eye gaze and head pose - application in an e-learning environment. In: Multimedia Tools and Applications, vol. 41(3), pp. 469–493. Springer, Heidelberg (2009)
2. Calleja, G.: In-Game From Immersion to Incorporation. MIT Press, USA (2011)
3. Conati, C.: Probabilistic assessment of users emotions in educational games. Applied Artificial Intelligence 16, 555–575 (2002)
4. Csikszentmihalyi, M.: Flow: The Psychology of Optimal Experience. Harper Perennial (March 1991)
5. Höök, K.: Affective loop experiences – what are they? In: Oinas-Kukkonen, H., Hasle, P., Harjumaa, M., Segerståhl, K., Øhrstrøm, P. (eds.) PERSUASIVE 2008. LNCS, vol. 5033, pp. 1–12. Springer, Heidelberg (2008)
6. Hudlicka, E.: Affective computing for game design. In: GAMEON-NA 2008: Proceedings of the 4th Intl. North American Conference on Intelligent Games and Simulation, Montreal, Canada, pp. 5–12 (2008)
7. Ioannou, S., Caridakis, G., Karpouzis, K., Kollias, S.: Robust Feature Detection for Facial Expression Recognition. EURASIP Journal on Image and Video Processing 2007(2), 1–23 (2007)
8. Isbister, K., Schaffer, N.: Game Usability: Advancing the Player Experience. Morgan Kaufmann, San Francisco (2008)
9. Koster, R.: A theory of fun for game design. Paraglyph press, Scottsdale (2004)
10. Leite, I., Pereira, A., Mascarenhas, S., Castellano, G., Martinho, C., Prada, R., Paiva, A.: Closing the loop: from affect recognition to empathic interaction. In: Proceedings of the 3rd International Workshop on Affective Interaction in Natural Environments, AFFINE 2010, pp. 43–48. ACM, New York (2010)

11. Malone, T.: What makes computer games fun (abstract only). In: Proceedings of the Joint Conference on Easier and More Productive Use Of Computer Systems (Part - II): Human Interface and the User Interface, CHI 1981, p. 143. ACM, New York (1981)
12. Mandryk, R.L., Inkpen, K.M.: Physiological indicators for the evaluation of co-located collaborative play. In: Proceedings of the 2004 ACM Conference on Computer Supported Cooperative Work, CSCW 2004, pp. 102–111. ACM, New York (2004)
13. Pagulayan, R.J., Keeker, K., Wixon, D., Romero, R.L., Fuller, T.: User-centered design in games. In: The Human-Computer Interaction Handbook, pp. 883–906. L. Erlbaum Associates Inc., Hillsdale (2003), http://portal.acm.org/citation.cfm?id=772072.772128
14. Pedersen, C., Togelius, J., Yannakakis, G.N.: Modeling player experience in super mario bros. In: CIG 2009: Proceedings of the 5th International Conference on Computational Intelligence and Games, pp. 132–139. IEEE Press, Piscataway (2009)
15. Pedersen, C., Togelius, J., Yannakakis, G.N.: Modeling player experience for content creation. IEEE Transactions on Computational Intelligence and AI in Games 2(1), 54–67 (2010)
16. Picard, R.W.: Affective Computing. The MIT Press, Cambridge (1997)
17. Picard, R.W., Vyzas, E., Healey, J.: Toward machine emotional intelligence: Analysis of affective physiological state. IEEE Transactions on Pattern Analysis and Machine Intelligence 23, 1175–1191 (2001)
18. Poels, K., IJsselsteijn, W.: Development and validation of the game experience questionnaire. In: FUGA Workshop Mini-Symposium, Helsinki, Finland (2008)
19. Shaker, N., Yannakakis, G.N., Togelius, J.: Towards Automatic Personalized Content Generation for Platform Games. In: Proceedings of the AAAI Conference on Artificial Intelligence and Interactive Digital Entertainment (AIIDE). AAAI Press, Menlo Park (2010)
20. Shaker, N., Yannakakis, G.N., Togelius, J.: Feature Analysis for Modeling Game Content Quality. In: IEEE Transactions on Computational Intelligence and AI in Games. IEEE Press, Los Alamitos (2011)
21. Sidner, C., Lee, C., Kidd, C., Lesh, N., Rich, C.: Explorations in engagement for humans and robots. Artificial Intelligence 166(1-2), 140–164 (2005)
22. Smith, P., Shah, M., da Vitoria Lobo, N.: Determining driver visual attention with one camera. IEEE Transactions on Intelligent Transportation Systems 4(4), 205–218 (2003)
23. Yannakakis, G.N.: Preference Learning for Affective Modeling. In: Proceedings of the Int. Conf. on Affective Computing and Intelligent Interaction, pp. 126–131. IEEE, Amsterdam (2009)
24. Yannakakis, G.N., Maragoudakis, M., Hallam, J.: Preference learning for cognitive modeling: a case study on entertainment preferences. Trans. Sys. Man Cyber. Part A 39, 1165–1175 (2009)
25. Yannakakis, G.N., Togelius, J.: Experience-driven Procedural Content Generation. IEEE Transactions on Affective Computing (in print, 2011)
26. Yannakakis, G., Hallam, J.: Real-time adaptation of augmented-reality games for optimizing player satisfaction. In: IEEE Symposium on Computational Intelligence and Games, CIG 2008, pp. 103–110 (December 2008)
27. Yannakakis, G., Hallam, J.: Real-time Game Adaptation for Optimizing Player Satisfaction. IEEE Transactions on Computational Intelligence and AI in Games 1(2), 121–133 (2009)

Effect of Emotion and Articulation of Speech on the Uncanny Valley in Virtual Characters

Angela Tinwell[1], Mark Grimshaw[1], and Debbie Abdel-Nabi[2]

[1] University of Bolton, Faculty of Arts and Media Technologies, Bolton, UK, BL3 5AB
{A.Tinwell,M.N.Grimshaw}@bolton.ac.uk
[2] University of Bolton, Faculty of Well Being & Social Sciences, Bolton, UK, BL3 5AB
A.Nabi@bolton.ac.uk

Abstract. This paper presents a study of how exaggerated facial expression in the lower face region affects perception of emotion and the Uncanny Valley phenomenon in realistic, human-like, virtual characters. Characters communicated the six basic emotions, anger, disgust, fear, sadness and surprise with normal and exaggerated mouth movements. Measures were taken for perceived familiarity and human-likeness. The results showed that: an increased intensity of articulation significantly reduced the uncanny for anger; yet increased perception of the uncanny for characters expressing happiness with an exaggeration of mouth movement. The practical implications of these findings are considered when controlling the uncanny in virtual characters.

Keywords: Emotion, Video Games, Uncanny Valley, Characters, Expression.

1 Introduction

The Uncanny Valley [1] provides a rationale as to the variations in emotional response humans can experience when interacting with synthetic agents [2-6]. Mori observed that as the human-likeness for a robot increases, the viewer will maintain a positive emotional response to that robot (measured as perceived familiarity), until the robot appears close to full human-likeness. At this point, inconsistencies in the robot's appearance and behavior from the human norm evoke a more negative response from the viewer and the robot is regarded as strange [1].

The Uncanny Valley is now also recognized as a phenomenon not only in android science, but in realistic, human-like characters featured in film and video games [2], [3], [4], [7], [8]. Much work has been carried out to examine which factors may exaggerate the uncanny. Humans can experience a more positive affective response towards androids and realistic, human-like, virtual characters when the level of behavioral fidelity matches their human-like appearance [9], [10]. Empirical evidence collected so far shows that, various factors including: facial expression [6], [11]; proportion of facial features, [5], [7]; characteristics of speech [11], [12]; lip-synchronization [11], [12]; gesture, timing, quality of motion [9], jerkiness of movement [13]; and contingency of interaction when responding to others and events [14] can contribute to perception of the uncanny. The uncanny was also exaggerated for empathetic and antipathetic characters with a perceived over-exaggeration of

S. D´Mello et al. (Eds.): ACII 2011, Part II, LNCS 6975, pp. 557–566, 2011.

mouth movement during speech [11]. This effect (and others) can work to the advantage of antagonist characters intended to be frightening [11].

Perception of the uncanny can vary depending on which emotion is being communicated [6]. This may be due to the adaptive function of that emotion (i.e. physical survival or social interaction) [6]. The results of a previous study show that the uncanny was exaggerated for realistic, human-like characters when emotional expressivity had been limited in the upper face region, including the brows and forehead, when expressing the emotions fear, sadness, surprise and disgust. However, a lack of upper facial animation had a less noticeable effect on perceived 'uncanniness' for the emotions anger and happiness [6].

Given these findings, it was recommended that if designers wished to avoid the uncanny, particular attention should be paid to modeling the upper face region for the emotions fear, sadness and surprise [6]. Overall sadness was regarded more favorably than the other emotions when presented in virtual characters with full or restricted animation in the upper face. This was attributed to people's ability to anthropomorphize virtual characters and express sympathy towards them despite perceived flaws in facial expression [6]. Despite that disgust can serve as a warning signal to avoid an unpleasant object, it was assumed more likely that limitations in the graphical fidelity of the 'nose wrinkler' action [15] in facial animation software accounted for the significant increase in perceived uncanniness for this emotion [6]. It was suggested that disgust may remain significantly more uncanny than other emotions until the graphical realism for this distinctive facial feature is improved [6].

As the lower facial features are of greater importance when communicating the emotions anger and happiness [16-18], these emotions were less noticeably affected by a lack of expressivity in the upper face region. Surprisingly, despite happiness being a more positive emotion, it was rated most uncanny in characters with full facial animation [6]. It was suggested this may have been due to a person's sensitivity to a false smile [19] thus, increasing the uncanny for this emotion [6].

1.1 Articulation and the Expression of Emotion

During speech, facial movement is primarily driven by articulation and one's intensity of articulation is influenced by the desired intensity of emotion that one wishes to communicate [16]. Importantly, this intensity of articulation differs depending on which emotion is being presented [16]. When compared to neutral speech, lower facial features were found to be significantly more active for anger and happiness, while less active for sadness [16].

Facial expression is used in primates to communicate how they feel and their likely, intended behavior [20], [21]. Primates can use the mouth to communicate anger either when the jaws are clenched, lips pressed tightly together (referred to as *Anger Type 1*), or when the lips are retracted, jaws open, exposing the teeth (referred to as *Anger Type 2*) [15], [20]. For example, a monkey can display a round or open mouth with exposed teeth to communicate intense fear, blended with anger [21]. Both these expression-types serve the same functions, regarded as a subordinate threat.

Due to the muscular constraints of the smile shape on the inner and outer lip features, the pronunciation of vowels during smiled speech necessitates the use of physiological mechanisms that are also involved in speech production [22]. In non-smiled speech, lip protrusion lengthens the vocal tract, aiding the pronunciation of rounded vowels [22], [23]. However, in smiled speech, a shortened vocal tract occurs as the lips retract and the mouth shape widens; resulting in a conflicting demand placed upon the lip shape when pronouncing rounded vowels [22]. Both larynx lowering [22] and the position of the tongue [22] can compensate for a reduction of lip rounding in the pronunciation of speech. When comparing non-smiled to smiled speech, the stretched lips that create a smile shape, result in a smaller difference of lip movement between vowels and the vertical lip opening is significantly reduced on vowel pronunciation [22], [23].

1.2 Articulation of Speech in Video Games

One of the most complex challenges for designers when creating realistic, human-like, virtual characters is modeling the mouth and lower face region during speech [3], [12], [24]. The dynamics of each individual muscle in the lower face region may be well understood [15], yet their combined effect is more difficult to simulate accurately. High-fidelity facial expression and animation can be recorded using motion capture techniques; however the mouth area remains one of the more intricate areas to modify once the recorded motions are applied to a 3D model [3], [12]. A designer may take a substantial amount of time to edit individual key frames of recorded motion capture data for parts of a video game that use full motion video, such as cut scenes and trailers. However, visual material for in-game play is generated in real time. Automated processes are required for facial animation and the synthesis of lip movement with speech. A predetermined set of visual mouth shapes (visemes) is available for each phoneme sound modeled on the International Phonetic Alphabet. As default, a viseme class entitled *normal* is available where mouth shapes represent a normal articulation of speech. In the facial animation software *FacePoser* (as part of the SDK video game engine developed by Valve) classes, entitled *strong* and *weak* are also available to represent mouth shapes used for an increased or reduced emphasis of articulation. Interpolated motion is then generated automatically between each phoneme animating the character's speech.

This present study investigated the implications of exaggerating mouth movement during speech across the six basic emotions [17], on perception of the uncanny in virtual characters. On the basis of results from previous studies investigating the uncanny it was predicted that, humans would be perceived as more familiar and human-like (less uncanny) than those virtual characters in the normal and over condition across all emotions (H1). Also, as the results of previous experiments have revealed that the lower facial features may be of greater importance in the successful communication of the emotions anger and happiness [6], [15], [16], [18], the emotions anger and happiness would be rated more familiar and human-like (less uncanny) in the over state than when compared to the normal condition (H2).

2   Method

A 3 x 6 repeated-measures analysis of variance (ANOVA) design was used. The independent variables were: (1) the type of character (a) human (a male human actor),

(b) normal (a male, virtual character with normal articulation of speech), and (c) over (the same virtual character with an increased intensity of articulation); and (2) the emotion type (anger, fear, disgust, happiness, sadness, and surprise [17] expressed facially and orally by the human or virtual character (Figure 1). A neutral state, in which the human and virtual character presented a neutral facial expression and tone of voice, was included as a seventh level of emotion type. This was employed as a control measure with the purpose to ensure participants could identify neutrality within a face and that they were responsive to different emotions when presented in the stimuli. Apart from analysis of participant accuracy and selection, neutral data was not included as an independent variable in the statistical model. The dependent variables were ratings of perceived: (1) familiarity and; (2) human-likeness as the characters presented the six emotions (and neutral) in the videos. Nine-point scales were used so that results could be compared with previous experiments that used 9-point scales to measure viewer response to the uncanny [6], [8], [11], [25].

Fig. 1. A human and Barney from *Half-Life 2*, pronouncing "c" in the 3 conditions for anger

2.1 Participants

Previous experiments have revealed conflicting evidence that perception of the uncanny differs between gender and levels of experience in interacting with synthetic agents. Some previous studies found no significant effect of gender on perception of the uncanny in robots [14], yet others found that females were more likely to rate robots as more human-like than males [7]. It has also been found that female participants were more accepting and tolerant of realistic, human-like, virtual, female characters than male participants [13]. Previous authors suggested that sensitivity to the uncanny would be reduced for those used to interacting with realistic, human-like characters on a regular basis [2]. However, another study found no significant difference in perception of the uncanny between participants with a high level of experience in playing video games and using 3D modeling software compared to those with none or a lesser amount of experience [25]. Male participants were used only in this present study to control potential disparities in gender. Forty, male, university students took part with a mean age of 20.9 years (SD = 5.50 years). To control the potential confounding impact of levels of experience in interacting with synthetic agents on perception of the uncanny, students were selected from the areas of: video game art, video game design and video game software development. It was expected that students from these subject areas would have an equivalent level of experience in exposure to realistic, human-like virtual characters.

2.2 Procedure

Video footage was taken of the actor reciting the line, "The cat sat on the mat", whilst using appropriate facial expressions and intonation of speech for each emotion. Apart from the neutral state (for which the actor was instructed to show no facial expression or intonation of voice), the actor portrayed moderate to high intensity facial expression and prosody for each emotion. The software *FacePoser* was used to synchronize the actor's speech with the character's mouth movement and replicate the actor's facial movement for each emotion. The same choreographed facial animations and sound files were used as in the normal condition for the over condition, but the phoneme class *strong* was used instead of *normal* for all phonemes extrapolated within the sentence. For example, in the over condition, mouth shapes in the *strong* class were used to replace mouth shapes from the *normal* class for the sounds "m" "ae" and "t" in the word mat. A dark background was used in all videos.

The survey was conducted in a computer lab with an individual computer station available for each participant. Experience levels of both playing video games and using 3D modeling software were taken with participants required to rate their level of experience as either, (1) *none*, (2) *basic*, or (3) *advanced*. Participants were then presented with a total of twenty videos, played in random order, via an online questionnaire. Participants used *Speed Link, Ares*[2] *Stereo PC* headphones for the sound and *Dell E207WFPc 20.1 inch Widescreen* monitors to watch the videos. Eighteen videos presented the six basic emotions: anger, disgust, fear, happiness, sadness and surprise [16], in the human, normal and over conditions. Two showed a neutral expression of the virtual character and human. On watching each video, participants selected which facial expression best described the character from: (a) *anger*, (b) *disgust*, (c) *fear*, (d) *happiness*, (e) *sadness*, (f) *surprise*, and (g) *neutral*. Participants then rated the character using a 9-point likert scale for perceived familiarity[1] from 1 (*very strange*) to 9 (*very familiar*) and how human-like or non-human-like they judged it to be from 1 (*nonhuman-like*) to 9 (*very human-like*).

3 Results

Ninety percent of participants had an advanced level of playing video games, with 10% a basic level of experience. For experience of using 3D modeling software: 47.5% had no experience, 32.5% had a basic level, and 20% an advanced level. Despite that emotion recognition was not the main purpose of this study, the recognition rates of perceived emotion were compared for both the human and virtual character to ensure that the animation in the virtual characters replicated (as accurately as possible) that of the human stimuli. A mean recognition rate of 88.33%

---

[1] As the word familiarity is the common translation of the Japanese neologism that Mori originally used to describe the uncanny (*shinwakan*) and previous authors have used this word as a dependent variable to measure the uncanny [11], [14], the word familiarity was also used in this experiment.

(SD = 12.62%) was achieved for the human, with a mean recognition rate of 78.33% (SD = 20.10%) achieved for the animated character with a normal articulation of speech. Participants also demonstrated the ability to recognize when no emotion was being presented with high recognition rates achieved for the neutral state in both the human (97.5%) and virtual character (95%). Due to restrictions of facial movement with current facial animation software, it was expected that the virtual character would achieve a lower mean value for emotion recognition than the human.

The mean ratings (and SD) for familiarity and human-likeness associated with each emotion for each condition are represented in Table 1. Consistently, videos of humans were rated as more familiar and human-like across the six emotions than virtual characters with normal and an over articulation of speech (see Table 1). The mean ratings for each dependent variable are also shown in Figures 2 & 3 with standard error bars. Inspection of the mean values for perceived familiarity (Figure 2) and human-likeness (Figure 3), show that: anger was the only emotion to be rated as more familiar and human-like in the over condition; happiness was rated as the most uncanny (least familiar and human-like) in the normal and over conditions; and disgust was rated highest for human-likeness in the human, though achieved the second lowest rating for human-likeness in the virtual character with normal articulation. Whilst rated as one of the least familiar and human-like emotions in the human, sadness achieved the highest ratings for perceived familiarity and human-likeness in the virtual character with normal articulation of speech, and the highest rating for familiarity in the over condition (see Figures 2 & 3). To assess the significance of these results, two 3 x 6 repeated-measures ANOVA were applied to the data. A main effect of character type was shown for both familiarity, $F_{(1.34, 52.08)} = 155.55$, $p < .001$, and human-likeness, $F_{(1.08, 42.01)} = 182.01$, $p < .001$. Regardless of emotion type, Bonferroni post-hoc tests revealed that human videos were rated higher for familiarity and human-likeness when compared to virtual characters with normal articulation (both $ps < .001$) and when compared to characters with an over articulation of speech (both $ps < .001$). This finding shows the existence of the uncanny in virtual characters, as was expected (H1).

Table 1. Mean familiarity and human-likeness ratings for each character ($N = 40$)

Condition	Familiarity						Human-likeness					
	Human		Normal		Over		Human		Normal		Over	
	M	SD	M	SD	M	SD	M	SD	M	SD	M	SD
Emotion												
Anger	7.64	1.44	3.80	1.87	4.10	1.68	8.30	1.02	4.05	2.02	4.40	1.81
Disgust	7.75	1.37	4.05	1.87	3.80	2.07	8.55	0.68	3.95	1.80	3.83	2.00
Fear	7.32	1.70	3.98	1.69	3.78	1.90	8.20	1.42	4.08	1.99	4.08	2.04
Happiness	7.13	1.99	3.73	2.05	3.38	2.02	8.03	1.78	3.93	1.89	3.78	2.06
Sadness	7.34	1.53	4.93	1.80	4.50	2.10	8.05	1.34	4.80	2.09	4.35	2.15
Surprise	7.60	1.61	4.20	1.71	4.18	1.78	8.35	1.10	4.43	1.92	4.20	1.86

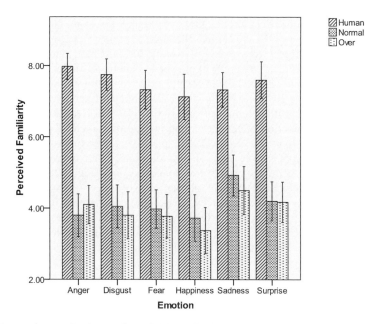

Fig. 2. Mean ratings and std. error bars (95% confidence level) for perceived familiarity for the three conditions, across emotion types

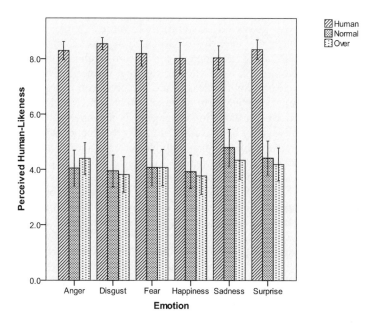

Fig. 3. Mean ratings and std. error bars (95% confidence level) for perceived human-likeness for the three conditions, across emotion types

A significant main effect of emotion was found for both familiarity, F (4.33, 168.90) = 5.751, p < .001, and human-likeness, F (4.44, 173.25) = 2.925, p < .05, indicating that emotions were rated differently for familiarity and human-likeness irrespective of character type. Within-subject contrasts revealed a significant difference between the overall experimental effect and the emotion: happiness for both familiarity, F (1, 39) = 12.296, p < .001, and human-likeness, F (1, 39) = 6.695, p < .05; and sadness, just for familiarity, F (1, 39) = 10.901, p < .05.

A significant interaction effect was found between Character Type x Emotion for both familiarity, F (8.56, 333.84) = 2.857, p < .05, and human-likeness ratings, F (5.31, 207.004) = 2.503, p < .05. This finding indicates that emotion type had different effects on people's ratings for familiarity and human-likeness depending upon which type of character (human, normal or over) was presented. Within-subject contrasts showed that anger was perceived as significantly more familiar in the over state, F (1, 39) = 4.377, p < .05, offering partial support for the second hypothesis (H2). Disgust was regarded as significantly less human-like in the normal condition when compared to the human, F (1, 39) = 7.005, p < .05.

4   Discussion

This study investigated how the magnitude of mouth movements during speech influenced perception of the Uncanny Valley phenomenon in realistic, human-like virtual characters and has revealed that this factor significantly affects expressions of anger and happiness. It was predicted that, due to the importance of the lower facial features in communicating the emotions anger and happiness, that the uncanny would be reduced for anger and happiness for characters with exaggerated mouth movement. As expected, anger was perceived as significantly more familiar (and considerably more human-like) when the intensity of articulation was increased in the virtual character (see Figures 2 & 3). An increased exposure of the teeth and exaggerated lower facial movement sends a clear warning sign that intense anger is felt [15], [17], [20]. When anger is clearly communicated, the perceiver can respond accordingly to this emotion to prevent potential harm or threat. More subtle communication of this emotion (i.e. with a normal articulation of speech) is potentially more unsettling for the viewer. The perceiver may be uncertain as to how to react or what the anticipated behavior of that character will be. Such ambiguity raises alarm and exaggerates the uncanny for that character. Based on this finding, designers hoping to reduce the uncanny may exaggerate mouth movement during speech when communicating anger. Such modifications increase the salience of this emotion so it is perceived as more conspicuous and human-like, and less uncanny. A normal articulation of speech is recommended when portraying anger, if a designer wishes to increase the uncanny for an antipathetic character, as this is likely to make the viewer feel more uncomfortable. A reduced intensity of articulation that displays a clenched jaw with gritted teeth and lips pressed together (characteristic of *Anger Type 1* behavior) [15], [20] may also be perceived as less uncanny than characters with normal articulation when communicating anger. Reduced lip movement may be recognized as a more salient display of anger, hence increasing perceived familiarity and human-likeness.

A surprising finding was that not only was happiness perceived as less familiar and human-like when intensity of articulation was increased in the virtual character, but, overall, happiness was rated significantly as the most uncanny emotion (least familiar and human-like) across all three conditions: human, normal and over. This result was unexpected, given that happiness is renowned as a positive emotion and that lower facial features are predominantly more important when communicating this emotion than the upper face [15], [16], [18]. Humans find alternate ways to compensate for reduced lip rounding (protrusion) during smiled speech such as a lowering of the larynx and positioning of the tongue [22], [23]. Perception that the character's lip movement was exaggerated whilst maintaining a smile shape may have appeared strange and possibly 'wrong'. For example, an increased protrusion of the lips when pronouncing the vowel "a", when one may otherwise expect a widening of the mouth shape and decrease in vertical lip opening. However, it is more likely that this finding supports the previous notion that happiness is regarded less favorably as a viewer suspects they are being presented with a false smile [6]. Despite full muscle movement and animation in the upper face, low-polygon counts in the character's skin texture results in a lack of detail around the eye area, reducing the appearance of wrinkles or bugles below and beside the eye. Without this detail, the viewer cannot distinguish if a spontaneous emotion is actually felt [19]. Even when the smile is extreme (as with an increased articulation of speech), the absence of the wrinkled skin below and around the eyes indicates that the eyes are not involved in the smile. This may confuse the viewer as a deliberate attempt to communicate a positive emotion when other more negative emotions may be felt [19], thus exaggerating the uncanny. Until the graphical realism of skin texture is improved around the eye area, happiness may continue to be perceived as uncanny despite strategic design modifications to the lower face. To prevent the uncanny, it may be recommended to reduce the intensity of mouth movement and animation in the lower facial features when expressing happiness. However, exaggerated articulatory motion during speech may make an antipathetic character appear more insincere. Perception of fabricated versus spontaneous facial expression may influence perception of the uncanny for other emotions as well as happiness. This is a matter for future investigation.

Disgust was perceived as significantly less human-like in virtual characters with normal articulation, than in humans. This finding supports the previous notion that the realism of the 'nose wrinkler' action, characteristic of disgust, is not sufficient to communicate this emotion in virtual characters [6]. Sadness was found to be regarded more favorably when presented in a virtual character than in a human. This finding supports previous evidence that this emotion is regarded less uncanny due to a human's ability to anthropomorphize virtual characters [6]. Increasing the range of characters used within the experiment by age and gender would provide greater support for this assumption as other faces communicating this emotion may have differential levels of response. Including male and female actors and characters in future experiments may also increase validity and allow further investigation into the effect of gender, emotion and perception of the uncanny. The range of sentences can also be increased. The word 'familiarity' could be construed as how well-known a character is in popular culture [25]. Alternative measures of the Uncanny Valley may be used in future experiments to avoid potential misinterpretation of this word. Words such as coldness and eeriness [4] may be better descriptors in this context.

References

1. Mori, M.: Bukimi No Tani (The Uncanny Valley). Energy 7, 33–35 (1970)
2. Brenton, H., Gillies, M., Ballin, D., Chatting, D.: The Uncanny Valley: does it exist? In: HCI Annual Conference: Animated Characters Workshop, Edinburgh, UK (2005)

3. Plantec, P.: Crossing the Great Uncanny Valley (December 19, 2007),
   `http://www.awn.com/articles/production/`
   `crossing-great-uncanny-valley`
4. Ho, C.-C., MacDorman, K.F.: Revisiting the uncanny valley theory: Developing and validating an alternative to the Godspeed indices. CHB 26, 1508–1518 (2010)
5. MacDorman, K.F., Green, R.D., Ho, C.-C., Koch, C.T.: Too real for comfort? Uncanny responses to computer generated faces. CHB 25, 695–710 (2009)
6. Tinwell, A., Grimshaw, M., Abdel-Nabi, D., Williams, A.: Facial expression of emotion and perception of the Uncanny Valley in virtual characters. CHB 27, 741–749 (2011)
7. Green, R.D., MacDorman, K.F., Ho, C.-C., Vasudevan, S.K.: Sensitivity to the proportions of faces that vary in human likeness. CHB 24, 2456–2474 (2008)
8. Tinwell, A.: Uncanny as Usability Obstacle. In: Ozok, A.A., Zaphiris, P. (eds.) OCSC 2009. LNCS, vol. 5621, pp. 622–631. Springer, Heidelberg (2009)
9. Ho, C.-C., MacDorman, K.F., Pramono, Z.A.: Human emotion and the uncanny valley. A GLM, MDS, and ISOMAP analysis of robot video ratings. In: The Third ACM/IEEE International Conference on Human-Robot Interaction, Amsterdam, pp. 169–176 (2008)
10. Vinayagamoorthy, V., Steed, A., Slater, M.: Building characters: Lessons drawn from virtual environments. Cog. Sci., 119–126 (2005)
11. Tinwell, A., Grimshaw, M., Williams, A.: Uncanny behaviour in survival horror games. J. of Gaming and Virtual Worlds 2, 23–25 (2010)
12. Tinwell, A., Grimshaw, M., Williams, A.: Uncanny speech. In: Grimshaw, M. (ed.) Game Sound Technology and Player Interaction, pp. 213–234. IGI Global, Hershey (2011)
13. MacDorman, K.F., Coram, J.A., Ho, C.-C., Patel, H.: Gender differences in the impact of presentational factors in human character animation on decisions in ethical dilemmas. Presence: Tel. and Vir. Env. 19, 213–229 (2010)
14. Bartneck, C., Kanda, T., Ishiguro, H., Hagita, N.: My robotic doppelganger - A critical look at the Uncanny Valley theory. In: 18th IEEEIS, Japan, pp. 269–276 (2009)
15. Ekman, P., Friesen, W.V.: Facial action coding system: A technique for the measurement of facial movement. Consulting Psychologists Press, Palo Alto (1978)
16. Busso, C., Narayanan, S.S.: Interplay between linguistic and affective goals in facial expression during emotional utterances. In: 7th ISSP, Brazil, pp. 549–556 (2006)
17. Ekman, P.: An argument for basic emotions. Cognition and Emotion 6, 169–200 (1992)
18. Ekman, P.: About brows: emotional and conversational signals. In: Von Cranach, M., Foppa, K., Lepenies, W., Ploog, D. (eds.) Human Ethology: Claims and Limits of a New Discipline, pp. 169–202. CUP, New York (1979)
19. Ekman, P., Friesen, W.V.: Felt, false and miserable smiles. J. of NVB 6, 238–252 (1982)
20. Darwin, C.: The expression of the emotions in man and animals. University of Chicago Press, Chicago (1965) (Original work published 1872)
21. Chevalier-Skolnikoff, S.: Facial expression of emotion in nonhuman primates. In: Ekman, P. (ed.) Darwin and Facial Expression, pp. 11–83. Academic Press, New York (1973)
22. Fagel, S.: Effects of Smiling on Articulation: Lips, Larynx and Acoustics. In: COST 2102 Training School, pp. 294–303 (2009)
23. Shor, R.E.: The production and judgment of smile magnitude. Gen. Psy. 98, 79–96 (1978)
24. Cao, Y., Faloustsos, P., Kohler, E., Pighin, F.: Real-time Speech Motion Synthesis from Recorded Motions. In: ACM SIGGRAPH/Eurographics, France, pp. 345–353 (2004)
25. Tinwell, A., Grimshaw, M.: Bridging the uncanny: an impossible traverse? In: Sotamaa, O., Lugmayr, A., Franssila, H., Näränen, P., Vanhala, J. (eds.) 13th Int. MindTrek Conf.: Everyday Life in the Ubiquitous Era, pp. 66–73. ACM, New York (2009)

Machine Learning for Affective Computing

Mohammed Hoque[1], Daniel J. McDuff[1], Louis-Philippe Morency[2],
and Rosalind W. Picard[1]

[1] MIT Media Lab, Cambridge, MA 02139, USA
{mehoque,djmcduff,picard}@media.mit.edu
[2] Institute for Creative Technologies, University of Southern California,
Marina del Ray, CA 90292, USA
morency@ict.usc.edu

Abstract. Affective computing (AC) is a unique discipline which includes modeling affect using one or multiple modalities by drawing on techniques from many different fields. AC often deals with problems that are known to be very complex and multi-dimensional, involving different kinds of data (numeric, symbolic, visual etc.). However, with the advancement of machine learning techniques, a lot of those problems are now becoming more tractable.

The purpose of this workshop was to engage the machine learning and affective computing communities towards solving problems related to understanding and modeling social affective behaviors. We welcomed participation of researchers from diverse fields, including signal processing and pattern recognition, statistical machine learning, human-computer interaction, human-robot interaction, robotics, conversational agents, experimental psychology, and decision making.

There is a need for a set of high standards for recognizing and understanding affect. At the same time, these standards need to take into account that the expectations and validations in this area may be different than in traditional research on machine learning. This should be reflected in the design of machine learning techniques used to tackle these problems. For example, affective data sets are known to be noisy, high dimensional, and incomplete. Classes may overlap. Affective behaviors are often person specific and require temporal modeling with real-time performance. This first edition of the ACII Workshop on Machine Learning for Affective Computing will be a proper venue to invoke such discussions and engage the community towards design and validation of learning techniques for affective computing.

Keywords: spontaneous affective states, automated recognition of affect, multimodal data fusion, probabilistic modeling, feature selection.

S. D'Mello et al. (Eds.): ACII 2011, Part II, LNCS 6975, p. 567, 2011.
© Springer-Verlag Berlin Heidelberg 2011

Large Scale Personality Classification of Bloggers

Francisco Iacobelli[1], Alastair J. Gill[2], Scott Nowson[3], and Jon Oberlander[4]

[1] Northeastern Illinois University, Chicago, Illinois 60625 USA
f-iacobelli@neiu.edu
[2] University of Surrey, Guildford, Surrey GU2 7HX, UK
A.Gill@surrey.ac.uk
[3] Appen Pty Ltd, Chatswood NSW 2067, Australia
snowson@appen.com.au
[4] University of Edinburgh, Edinburgh, EH8 9AB, UK
J.Oberlander@ed.ac.uk

Abstract. Personality is a fundamental component of an individual's affective behavior. Previous work on personality classification has emerged from disparate sources: Varieties of algorithms and feature-selection across spoken and written data have made comparison difficult. Here, we use a large corpus of blogs to compare classification feature selection; we also use these results to identify characteristic language information relating to personality. Using Support Vector Machines, the best accuracies range from 84.36% (openness to experience) to 70.51% (neuroticism). To achieve these results, the best performing features were a combination of: (1) stemmed bigrams; (2) no exclusion of stopwords (i.e. common words); and (3) the boolean, presence or absence of features noted, rather than their rate of use. We take these findings to suggest that both the structure of the text and the presence of common words are important. We also note that a common dictionary of words used for content analysis (LIWC) performs less well in this classification task, which we propose is due to their conceptual breadth. To get a better sense of how personality is expressed in the blogs, we explore the best performing features and discuss how these can provide a deeper understanding of personality language behavior online.

Keywords: Machine Learning, Personality Classification.

1 Introduction

Personality traits, which are intimately linked to affect [3], and their detection is of high interest for systems that target users by personalising content (e.g., online stores, recommender systems, social media and search engines; cf. [22]). Personal weblogs (blogs) are a popular way to write freely and express preferences and opinions on anything that is of interest to the author [9], and therefore provide a useful resource for investigating personality. Indeed, personality has been shown to relate to writing style in blogs and more generally (e.g.,[19,17,16,25]), blogger motivation [6], as well as influencing the content that a user prefers to read [23]. However, despite studies indicating linguistic cues of personality, attempts to classify personality from essays or emails have yielded modest results [11,4]. In the case of blogs, although classification of author personality has been successful on small corpora, the performance of features on larger corpora has degraded, possibly as a result of overfitting [14].

S. D'Mello et al. (Eds.): ACII 2011, Part II, LNCS 6975, pp. 568–577, 2011.

Direct comparison between these previous personality classification studies is difficult given inconsistencies in algorithms, feature-selection, and data sources (ranging from speech to essays, emails and blogs). Thus, in this paper we use a very large corpus of blogs with associated author personality information to provide the first systematic comparison of feature sets used by machine learning algorithms in the task of personality classification. In addition, by exploring the features that are more informative for a classifier, we are able to build a deeper picture of how personality behavior is *actually* realised linguistically.

In the following section, we review previous findings of studies exploring and classifying personality and language. In the method section, we describe in more detail the feature and data sets used in this comparison study. We then present our classification results and discussion, where we also present some of the most predictive bigram features relating to the different personality types. The presentation of such features is important, since they can increase our understanding of how personality is expressed in language. We conclude the paper with a summary of our main findings, future directions and pointers to build a better theoretical understanding of personality and its relationship with language.

2   Background

Like other studies relating to personality and language (e.g. [16,19]), we adopt the five-factor model of personality [2], which describes the following traits on a continuous scale: neuroticism, extraversion, openness to experience, agreeableness and conscientiousness. General behaviors characteristic of high and low scorers for each of the traits are listed in Table 1, along with previous findings for personality and language.

These previous results reported for personality and language relate specifically to written language (although other studies have examined speech, e.g., [12]), and have applied both data-driven words and phrases (e.g., [16,13]) and lexical features grouped by psychological categories (e.g., [19,6]). Both approaches have been applied to classification tasks for personality. Studies using psychological groupings of lexical features have adopted the LIWC dictionary (Linguistic Inquiry and Word Count; [18]) to compare baseline classification algorithms to Naïve Bayes and SMO (sequential minimal optimization algorithm for a support vector classifier [24,20]). Applying such feature groupings to written texts [1] obtained optimal results of around 57-60% accuracy for extraversion and neuroticism using SMO; similar analysis of conversational data resulted in accuracies of around 65% [11].

Other features have included structural and lexical features of corpus of email (approximately 9,800 messages) which were used to classify several dimensions, including the five personality traits [4]. Although accuracies were in the range of 53–57%, this study used the largest corpus for personality classification of which we are aware.

In another case, n-grams were used to assemble features for classifying four of the five personality traits: in a small corpus of blogs, SMO gave the best accuracies (of around 83–93%) [17]. However, when these trained classifiers were applied to a much larger corpus, the accuracies dropped to approximately 55%, which may have been a result of overfitting [14].

Table 1. Personality traits –neuroticism (N), extraversion (E), openness to experience (O), agreeableness (A) and conscientiousness (C)– with behavioral and linguistic characteristics

Trait	Type	High Score	Low Score
N	Behavior	Emotional instability; anxious; hostile; prone to depression	Emotional stability; calm; less easy upset
	Linguistic	*Use of first person singular and negative emotion words (on essays) [19]; talk of discrepancies, jobs, and physical states (on blogs) [13]; exclusive and inclusive connectives, use of multiple-punctuation expressions (on emails) [16].*	*Use of refererences to other people (on blogs) [13]; more nouns and adverbs (email) [16].*
E	Behavior	Extraverts; warm; assertive; action-oriented; thrill-seeking	Introverts; low key; deliberate; easily stimulated
	Linguistic	*Use of social words, self and other references, positive emotion words, greater certainty (on emails and essays) [16,19]; greater complexity, conjunctions and adjectives (on email) [16]; present tense verbs, references to communication (on blogs) [13].*	*Use of negations and negative emotion expressions, exclusive, inclusive, causation words, articles (on essays) [19]; greater tentativity (on email) [16]; achievements, discrepancies (on blogs)[13].*
O	Behavior	Appreciate art and ideas; imaginative; aware of feelings	Straightforward interests; conservative; resist change
	Linguistic	*Use of articles, longer words and insight words (on essays) [19]; use longer words, express positive feelings, inclusive words (on blogs) [13].*	*use of first person singular, present tense, and causation words (on essays) [19]; negations, references to school (on blogs) [13]*
A	Behavior	Compassionate; cooperative; considerate; friendly	Suspicious; unfriendly; wary; antagonistic; uncooperative
	Linguistic	*Use of first person singular, positive emotion words (on essays) [19].*	*Use of articles, negative emotion words (on essays) [19]; discrepancies, talk about body states (on blogs) [13].*
C	Behavior	Disciplined; dutiful; persistent; compulsive; perfectionist	Spontaneous; impulsive; achievement less important
	Linguistic	*Use of positive emotion words (on essays) [19].*	*Use of negations, negative emotion, causation, exclusive words, discrepancies (essays) [19]; topics concerned with death (on blogs) [13].*

As these studies show, a variety of features and algorithms have been applied to personality classification tasks, however their application to different data sets makes comparison difficult (see e.g., [15] which compares the contextuality of blogs against genres of the British National Corpus) . Therefore, in the following study, we use a single, large blog corpus upon which to compare a variety of features for personality classification. We aim to be able to identify the best features for classification and also describe how these features give us new insight into personality as expressed through written language.

3   Method

This study is concerned with the linguistic characteristics of personality (rather than structural or design features of blogs), and therefore compares feature sets derived from 1- and 2-grams. In addition, we include features based upon psychological categories (from LIWC [18]), as they are extensively used in previous studies, to compare them to n-gram derived features.

3.1   Data Preparation

The corpus used was drawn from a large collection of around 3000 bloggers writing over several months. The corpus was processed to give one file per author per month. Each file contains all the postings for each author in each month. HTML tags, embedded and quoted text were removed. Each author completed a self-administered on-line personality questionnaire with five items measuring each of the Big 5 personality types. The items are simple yes/no questions and so personality scoring was rather coarse. The questionnaire gave low, middle and high scores for each trait (for more details see [14])

For inclusion in subsequent analysis, authors had to write a minimum of 1000 words in a month, with any month's contribution capped at 5000 words. When authors contributed in more than one month, their most recent month was used. Following the approach of Argamon et al. [1], only authors who scored high or low on these personality dimensions were included for analysis. Mairesse [11] also tested this approach and reported a 2–3% increase in overall accuracy scores compared to datasets that included middle scorers. However, he suggests that removing the middle scorers "potentially [increases] precision at the cost of reducing recall." Because case data is gathered from online sources, large quantities of data are more likely to result in problems of low precision than low recall.

Finally, to prepare the data for classification, we balanced the size of the high-low groups for each trait, by randomly discarding authors from the larger set to match the number in the smaller set. The number of authors originally within each class, along with the total used in experiments, can be seen in Table 2.

3.2   Feature Selection

For each of the several data sets compared, texts were further processed as follows: (a) words were stemmed using Porter's stemming algorithm [21]; (b) *proper names* (naive detection of continuous sets of words with initial letters capitalised) were replaced by a

Table 2. Number of authors in each class considered for each personality trait by level. Numbers applied to both high *and* low groups and used for experimentation are in **bold**.

Level	N	E	O	A	C
High	**553**	669	1465	892	884
Low	840	**637**	**137**	**372**	**323**
Total	**1106**	**1274**	**274**	**744**	**646**

common token; (c) *laughter* (variants, of different lengths and spellings, of *haha*, *hehe*, etc.) were also replaced by a common token; and (c) *apostrophes* (words containing an apostrophe were tagged).

Data sets were built for each personality trait using all variations of the following features: (a) words window size. Namely single words (size 1) vs. bigrams (size 2) used by five or more authors; and (b) including stop words ("sw") or omitting ("wo") stop words. In addition, each of these features were represented using one of two scores: (i) boolean (score of 1 or 0 to represent the presence or absence of a word) or (ii) importance (TF*IDF scores for each word). Combining features and weighting schemes resulted in 8 data sets per personality trait. In addition, we created one extra data set per trait not based on individual words, but on the psychologically defined categories of the Linguistic Inquiry and Word Count (LIWC) tool [18], as implemented using TAWC [10].

By deriving a number of different data sets, we are able both to compare their features in terms of relevance to the task of personality classification, and also to derive a greater understanding of the linguistic behavior of different personality types. Further, by implementing some of the classification and feature extraction techniques used in analogous data sets [13,11,1] we can also begin to understand the relative utility of the different approaches.

After building the data sets, Weka's Cfs-Subset selector [8] with Subset forward selection [7] was applied to each one in order to include only the features that contribute most to accurate classification.

To provide a comparison of features, texts were classified using the LibLinear [5] Support Vector Machines (SVM) classifier in Weka [24] (Weka's wrapper for LibLinear was faster and generally more accurate than the SMO, the standard Weka SVM). Following experimentation on a small training dataset we use the default parameters: $C = 1$; $\epsilon = 0.01$. In each case 10 fold cross validation was used to classify the data sets.

Baseline classification which assigns the majority class (ZeroR) produced 50% in each case since high-low groups were balanced. Classification using Weka's [24] default implementation of Naïve Bayes (NB) were in each case outperformed[1] by the SVM algorithm, and therefore are also omitted.

4   Classification Results and Discussion

Table 3 compares the performance of SVM using the feature sets achieving greatest accuracy (boolean scoring with 2-grams including stop-words; "b-2-sw") with the

---

[1] Statistically significantly in most cases.

Table 3. Accuracy scores by trait and feature sets using SVM. Feature sets were coded as *(b)ool* or *(f)requency* scoring; *1 or 2* grams; include stopwords (sw) or not (wo). Classification with the LIWC feature set is also included.

Dataset	b-2-sw	b-1-sw	b-1-wo	b-2-wo	f-1-sw	f-1-wo	f-2-sw	f-2-wo	LIWC
N	**70.51**	70.47	70.12	67.77	67.77	67.25	67.83	65.24 ∘	59.56 ∘
E	**71.68**	67.80 ∘	68.40	63.99 ∘	64.84 ∘	65.22 ∘	69.42	64.15 ∘	54.86 ∘
O	**84.36**	81.44	79.14	77.49 ∘	74.74 ∘	74.74 ∘	77.93 ∘	73.77 ∘	56.86 ∘
A	**78.31**	69.98 ∘	69.49 ∘	71.09 ∘	66.01 ∘	64.78 ∘	72.61 ∘	68.07 ∘	61.09 ∘
C	**79.18**	75.17	72.74 ∘	76.41	68.79 ∘	68.34 ∘	73.87 ∘	73.98 ∘	56.11 ∘

∘ statistically significant degradation, $p < 0.05$ compared to **b-2-sw**

performance of SVM on the other data sets. The table shows that for openness, when features contain a boolean scoring system, there are no significant differences in accuracy. However, when features contain TF*IDF scores, the accuracy of the classifier becomes significantly worse.

This suggests that openness can be inferred by checking for the occurrence of individual words. The accuracies for conscientiousness suggest that besides boolean scoring resulting in better accuracies, it may be that stop words are relevant for classification. Because the score with bigrams and excluding stopwords produced no significant difference from the accuracy obtained with bigrams including stopwords, it may be that when some structural information is captured (bigrams), stop words become less relevant for classification.

In the case of extraversion, the accuracy produced by bigrams with stop words using boolean scores was not significantly different from bigrams that included stopwords but were scored using TF*IDF. In addition, it was not different from unigrams that excluded stop words. Agreeableness accuracy scores show clearly that the mere presence or absence of bigrams that include stop words (bool-2-sw) produced the most accurate classification. Lastly, the accuracies for neuroticism did not vary significantly except in the case of the use of TF*IDF frequencies on bigrams that did not include stopwords. Also included in Table 3 are results from the data sets based on LIWC's thematic categories. As described earlier, the accuracy across all traits is a significant degradation from that of the best data sets. Considering words in context, as bigrams to a degree allow, is apparently a more reliable indicator of personality than thematic grouping of words. We therefore note that even though these thematic categories appear to be theoretically justifiable, for such a classification task, they appear to overgeneralize.

In sum, we notice that the presence or absence of bigrams including stop words produced the most accurate classification, although this difference was not always significant with respect to other methods.

4.1   Bigrams Characteristic of Personality

An analysis of the features that best classified our data provides a view of the linguistic features that reveal the bloggers' personalities. In this section we provide a first analysis of these features by presenting (a) their average precision of classification; and (b) the Big 5 personality traits and how they are classified by individual features (bigrams).

To examine which of the bigrams classified high or low scorers of each personality trait, we looked at each bigram ($bigram_i$) within the set of bigrams that best classified each trait (c.f. Section 3.2) and retrieved the set of documents (D_i) that contained it. Then, we counted how many of these documents corresponded to high and low scorers, the highest number determining which score level was more precisely classified by the bigram. We call this the "majority classification" for this bigram. For example, for openness, if the bigram *the hell* was present in 50 documents of which 14 were high scorers and 36 were low scorers, we conclude that the majority classification for this bigram is low scorers. We then compute precision using the following formula: $precision_i = \frac{|tp|}{|tp+fp|}$, where $precision_i$ is the precision score for the ith bigram. In this context, true positives (tp) are the documents from D_i that correspond to the majority classification of $bigram_i$. $|tp|$ is, then, the size of the set of true positives. False positives fp is the set of documents from D_i that do not correspond to the majority classification. In other words, $D_i = tp + fp$. Note that we talk about precision, and not accuracy, because we are measuring fidelity only among the documents that contain each bigram.

Table 4 shows the mean precision for bigrams on each trait on each score level. For example, for neuroticism, the bigrams that best classified low scorers had, on average, a precision of 0.9. As we can see, the bigrams, when present, classified scores for each trait with high precision.

Table 4. Mean precision of classification of bigrams for low and high scorers on each personality trait

Trait	High	Low
N	0.90	0.90
E	0.86	0.92
O	0.88	0.91
A	0.91	0.86
C	0.88	0.89

We can consider a representative subset of the features that classified each score level on each personality trait. For the present paper we did not analyse the words surrounding the bigrams. Therefore, they cannot be reliably grouped into sub categories within each trait (cf. Table 1). In addition, because the bigrams were stemmed, in some cases it is not possible to determine which words they correspond to. However, in some cases we can reverse the stemming to obtain the exact words (e.g. *onli i = only I*) or, at least, a naive, but plausible interpretation (*am excit = am excited*, versus other tenses of the verb *excite*). Table 5 presents the subset of bigrams, from those that best classify our data, that are easily translated into the words that likely generated them.

Neuroticism's high and low scorers seem to use some problem talk (*only problem, depressed you, be sad*). The use of these kinds of words had been documented for low extravert scorers only [19]. On the other hand, low scorers of neuroticism use thoughtful words (*reflect on, choose to*). High extraverts use strong curse words (*you f**k, b**ch I, was f**k*), talk (possibly figuratively) about location (*i'm at*), and, and as described in previous literature [16,19], they use social words and words suggesting positive emotional valence (*dance i, a club, fun anyway, most social*) and more self references than

Table 5. Stemmed bigrams that drive classification

Trait	High	Low
N	hope.thei; punish.for; get.work; onli.problem; you.onli; depress.you; drunk.i; i.wasnt;	mental.togeth; be.sad; am.excit; we'v.had; reflect.on; then.look group.of; chose.to; the.winner
E	more.excit; i.hang; im.at; im.too; b**ch.i; danc.i; love.me; i.miss; you.f**k; wa.f**k; fun.anywai; hear.you; friend.were; love.me; a.club;	wai.so; my.regular; increas.my; my.flower; didn't.need; coupl.year; each.year; bond.slowli; favourit.charact; most.social; other.job;
O	is.beauti; like.s**t; be.held; think.he's; unabl.to; and.fun; danc.and; pick.me; i.lost; the.hell;	to.church; prai.for; at.church; laid.back; mondai.and; not.bad; you.belong; not.exactli; over.time;
A	even.better; of.beauti; compromis.with; hold.you; the.colleg; keep.myself; me.sigh; no.point; from.peopl;	like.it's; comment.about; like.it'; ex-cus.to; later.if; suppos.to; wa.worri; my.offic; sai.thing; goal.is; remain.in; return.of; send.the; unfortun.the; self.interest;
C	and.reliabl; prior.to; succe.in; so.hopefulli; got.caught; the.obviou; do.after; made.for; our.own; of.tear; on.track; to.drag; i.studi; hope.i'm; forget.that; realli.look;	episod.of; be.treat; not.thi; thi.just; pat-tern.is; real.reason; am.also; i.laugh; how.i'm; dare.to; of.why;

low scorers. In terms of self references, high extraverts use the first person singular more often, whereas low scorers use the possessive *my* more often. Low extraverts seem to use more time related language (*couple years, each year, bond slowly*).

Low openness scorers seem to use words for religious institutions and activities in their blogs (*to church, pray for, at church*). High scorers use weaker cursing than extraverts (*like s**t, the hell*). Also, as previously described [19], our data shows that high agreeableness scorers display more positive words (*even better, of beauty*). Lastly, high conscientiousness scorers seem to use language that denotes planning, outcome and evaluation (*to study, on track, prior to, succeed in*). Low scorers, in contrast, seem to use justification language more often (*real reason, of why*).

Because there were so few bigrams in each personality trait, the classification may overfit the data. However, we consider that given the size of the corpus, these features provide a reliable insight into the kinds of lexical choices that people with different personality traits make when writing.

Because personality classification is a multi-class classification problem (i.e. personality traits are not mutually exclusive), there are methods that are better suited for this task such as conditional random fields –which consider the influences of the various classes over each other. We also note that future work is likely to harness greater linguistic information from natural language processing tools such as shallow parsers.

In this paper, we did not attempt to compare classification algorithms, but use the best performing one so far and explore the types of features that will lead to better classification and to provide a theoretical insight into the personality of bloggers.

5   Conclusion

In this paper we have presented a systematic examination of feature sets, both data-driven as well as categories derived from psychological dictionaries, to classify personality. Our best results ranged from 70.51% for neuroticism to 84.36% for openness to experience. Choosing bigrams as features yielded the best results. Our LIWC-based results are similar to those of previous studies that used LIWC for this task, but our best results with bigrams significantly improve upon them.

The superior performance of bigrams over word categories suggests that, at least to some degree, language structure is important when classifying personality traits. Similarly, Functional stopwords are also important in this context. Moreover, the presence or absence of features resulted in more accurate classification than frequency related scores for these features.

Based on preliminary analysis, we suggest that the thematic categories of words often used to analyse personality data may be too broad and future work might choose to refine them for this particular task. Future work will also consider classification using different corpora, different features such as topic distributions, and different kind of classifiers such as conditional random fields, in order to gain a better theoretical framework of personality in bloggers.

References

1. Argamon, S., Dhawle, S., Koppel, M., Pennebaker, J.W.: Lexical predictors of personality type. In: Proceedings of the 2005 Joint Annual Meeting of the Interface and the Classification Society of North America (2005)
2. Costa, P.T., McCrae, R.R.: Neo PI-R Professional Manual. In: Psychological Assessment Resources, Odessa, FL (1992)
3. Eid, M., Diener, E.: Intraindividual variability in affect: Reliability, validity, and personality correlates. Journal of Personality and Social Psychology 76(4), 662–676 (1999)
4. Estival, D., Gaustad, T., Pham, S.B., Radford, W., Hutchinson, B.: Author profiling for english emails. In: 10th Conference of the Pacific Association for Computational Linguistics (PACLING 2007), pp. 262–272 (2007)
5. Fan, R.E., Chang, K.W., Hsieh, C.J., Wang, X.R., Lin, C.J.: Liblinear: A library for large linear classification. J. Mach. Learn. Res. 9, 1871–1874 (2008)
6. Gill, A.J., Nowson, S., Oberlander, J.: What are they blogging about? personality, topic and motivation in blogs. In: ICWSM 2009 (2009)
7. Gütlein, M.: Large scale attribute selection using wrappers. Master's thesis, Albert-Ludwigs-Universitat, Freiburg (2006)
8. Hall, M.A., Smith, L.: Practical feature subset selection for machine learning. In: Proc. 21st Australian Computer Science Conference, Perth, Australia, pp. 181–191. Springer, Heidelberg (1998)
9. Herring, S., Scheidt, L., Bonus, S., Wright, E.: Weblogs as a bridging genre. Information, Technology & People 18(2), 142–171 (2005)
10. Kramer, A.D.I., Fussell, S.R., Setlock, L.D.: Text analysis as a tool for analyzing conversation in online support groups. In: Extended Abstracts of the 2004 Conference on Human Factors and Computing Systems, pp. 1485–1488 (2004)

11. Mairesse, F., Walker, M.A., Mehl, M.R., Moore, R.K.: Using linguistic cues for the automatic recognition of personality in conversation and text. Journal of Artificial Intelligence Research 30, 457–500 (2007)
12. Mehl, M.R., Gosling, S.D., Pennebaker, J.W.: Personality in its natural habitat: manifestations and implicit folk theories of personality in daily life. Journal of Personality and Social Psychology 90(5), 862–877 (2006)
13. Nowson, S.: The Language of Weblogs: A study of genre and individual differences. PhD thesis, University of Edinburgh (2006)
14. Nowson, S., Oberlander, J.: Identifying more bloggers: Towards large scale personality classification of personal weblogs. In: Proceedings of the International Conference on Weblogs and Social (2007)
15. Nowson, S., Oberlander, J., Gill, A.J.: Weblogs, genres and individual differences. In: Proceedings of the 27th Annual Conference of the Cognitive Science Society, pp. 1666–1671 (2005)
16. Oberlander, J., Gill, A.J.: Language with character: A stratified corpus comparison of individual differences in e-mail communication. Discourse Processes 42(3), 239–270 (2006)
17. Oberlander, J., Nowson, S.: Whose thumb is it anyway? Classifying author personality from weblog text. In: Proceedings of COLING/ACL-2006: 44th Annual Meeting of the Association for Computational Linguistics and 21st International Conference on Computational Linguistics (2006)
18. Pennebaker, J.W., Francis, M.E.: Linguistic Inquiry and Word Count, 1st edn. Lawrence Erlbaum, Mahwah (1999)
19. Pennebaker, J.W., King, L.A.: Linguistic styles: language use as an individual difference. Journal of Personality and Social Psychology 77(6), 1296–1312 (1999)
20. Platt, J.C.: Fast training of support vector machines using sequential minimal optimization, pp. 185–208. MIT Press, Cambridge (1999)
21. Porter, M.F.: An algorithm for suffix stripping. Program 14(3), 130–137 (1980)
22. Reeves, B., Nass, C.: The media equation: how people treat computers, television, and new media like real people and places. Cambridge University Press, New York (1996)
23. Schutte, N.S., Malouff, J.M.: University student reading preferences in relation to the big five personality dimensions. Reading Psychology an International Quarterly 25(4), 273–295 (2004)
24. Witten, I.H., Frank, E.: Data Mining: Practical Machine Learning Tools and Techniques, 2nd edn. Morgan Kaufmann Series in Data Management Systems. Morgan Kaufmann, San Francisco (2005)
25. Yarkoni, T.: Personality in 100,000 Words: A large-scale analysis of personality and word use among bloggers. Journal of Research in Personality 44, 363–373 (2010)

Smartphones Get Emotional: Mind Reading Images and Reconstructing the Neural Sources

Michael Kai Petersen, Carsten Stahlhut, Arkadiusz Stopczynski,
Jakob Eg Larsen, and Lars Kai Hansen

DTU Informatics, Cognitive Systems
Technical University of Denmark, Building 321, DK-2800 Kgs. Lyngby, Denmark
{mkp,cs,arks,jel,lkh}@imm.dtu.dk

Abstract. Combining a wireless EEG headset with a smartphone offers
new opportunities to capture brain imaging data reflecting our everyday
social behavior in a mobile context. However processing the data on a
portable device will require novel approaches to analyze and interpret
significant patterns in order to make them available for runtime interaction. Applying a Bayesian approach to reconstruct the neural sources
we demonstrate the ability to distinguish among emotional responses reflected in different scalp potentials when viewing pleasant and unpleasant pictures compared to neutral content. Rendering the activations in a
3D brain model on a smartphone may not only facilitate differentiation
of emotional responses but also provide an intuitive interface for touch
based interaction, allowing for both modeling the mental state of users
as well as providing a basis for novel bio-feedback applications.

Keywords: affective computing, mobile EEG, source reconstruction.

1 Motivation

Only recently affordable wireless EEG headsets capturing the electric potentials
of neuronal populations through electrodes resting on the scalp have
become available. Originally designed as cognitive game interfaces they have
subsequently been applied as brain machine interfaces to directly manipulate
robotic arms [1], drive a car [2] or mentally select images using the P300 oddball
paradigm to call contacts by mentally selecting their image from the phonebook
of an iPhone [3]. Scott Makeig et al. [4] have summarized the many benefits of
brain monitoring under naturalistic conditions, emphasizing the need for moving
beyond gauging how a few bits of information are transported through the brain
when tapping a finger, and widen the focus to map out how we perceive our
surroundings reflected in embodied cognition and real life emotional responses.
Cognitively speaking our feelings can be thought of as labels that we consciously
assign to the emotional responses triggered by what we perceive [5]. While we
often think of affective terms as describing widely different states, these can
be represented as related components in a circumplex model framed by the
two psychological primitives: valence and arousal [6]. When viewing affective

S. D´Mello et al. (Eds.): ACII 2011, Part II, LNCS 6975, pp. 578–587, 2011.

pictures, earlier neuroimaging studies have established that emotional content trigger not only autonomic responses of increased heart rate and electrodermal skin conductance, but also distinct brain potentials characterizing pleasant or unpleasant feelings compared to neutral imagery [7]. These event related responses ERPs covary with autonomic arousal and self report [8], and a data set of affective images, international affective picture system IAPS, has experimentally been validated by users to define how pleasant or intense the emotional content is perceived as being, measured along the psychological dimensions of valence and arousal [9]. Previous brain imaging studies of emotional responses when viewing affective pictures [8] have identified distinct differences in the ERP amplitudes elicited by pleasant and unpleasant compared to neutral images. An early component emerge most pronounced for pleasant content at 150-200 ms termed early posterior negativity EPN, triggering a relative negative shift over temporal occipital areas and a positive potential over central sites [10]. Followed by yet another ERP component; a late positive potential LPP at 300-500 ms, characterized by an enhanced posterior positivity over central parietal sites for affective compared to neutral content, with left hemisphere enhanced for pleasant pictures while activation appeared right lateralized for unpleasant images [7]. However the obvious question remains whether the limited number of electrodes and the quality of consumer priced EEG sets make it feasible to capture brain imaging data in noisy environments. We therefore decided to combine a wireless neuroheadset with a smartphone for presenting media, gauge the emotional responses by capturing the EEG data and subsequently process and visualize the reconstructed patterns of brain activity on the device. And in the following sections outline the mobile EEG system design, experimental setup, results based on ICA analysis and source reconstruction, which are discussed in relation to earlier neuroimaging findings obtained in laboratory settings using conventional EEG equipment.

2 Materials and Methods

2.1 Mobile EEG System

Our setup is based on a portable wireless Emotiv Research Edition neuroheadset (http://emotiv.com) which transmits the EEG and control data to a receiver USB dongle, originally intended for a Windows PC version of the Emotiv research edition SDK. We instead connect the wireless receiver dongle to a USB port on a Nokia N900 smartphone with Maemo 5 OS. Running in USB hostmode we decrypt the raw binary EEG data transmitted from the wireless headset, and in order to synchronize the stimuli with the data we timestamp the first and last packets arriving at the beginning and end of the EEG recording. While the 128 Hz sample rate of the neuroheadset turns out to be 126-127 Hz when averaged over several minutes of recording. Timestamps saved during the experiments indicate that a resolution of 10 ms can be achieved with the current Python implementation. Designed as a client-server architecture, computationally expensive data analyses can be performed on a remote server and results are

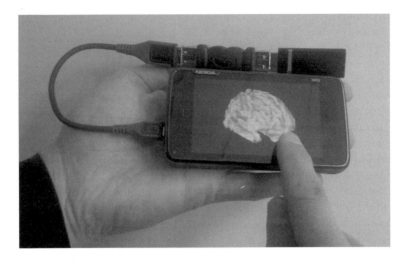

Fig. 1. The wireless neuroheadset transmits the brain imaging data via a receiver USB dongle connected directly to a Nokia N900 smartphone. Reconstructing the underlying sources realtime from the EEG data in a sparse 3D model improves decoding of the signal and potentially provides relevant neurofeedback for brain machine interfaces.

transmitted back to the phone for presentation. Server-side, the neural sources are reconstructed from the EEG scalp maps and presented on the phone in a 3D brain model that contains 1028 vertices and 2048 triangles. Stored as a mobile application on the device the brain activity is rendered at approximately 30 fps allowing for fluent touch-based interaction. The current design of the system has a delay of approximately 150 ms between the signal appearing in the brain and the subsequent visualization on the smartphone.

2.2   Experimental Setup

Eight male volunteers from the Technical University of Denmark, between the ages of 26 and 53 (mean age 32,75 years) participated in the experiment. Replicating the setup for identifying neural correlates of emotional responses triggered by affective pictures, originally performed using a high density 129 electrode array [7], we in the present study applied a simplified approach based on the portable wireless 14 channel neuroheadset to capture the signal from electrodes positioned at AF3, F7, F3, FC5, T7, P7, O1, O2, P8, T8, FC6, F4, F8, AF4 according to the international 10-20 system. Channels were recorded at a sampling rate of 122 Hz. using the electrodes P3/P4 as CMS reference and DRL feedback respectively. Based on earlier studies showing that late emotional responses to affective pictures remain unaffected when varying the size of images [11], the participants viewed a randomized sequence of 60 IAPS images presented at approximately 50 cm distance on the 3.5" display (800 x 480 screen resolution) of

N900 Nokia smartphones rather than on a standard monitor. Combining earlier experimental designs for eliciting emotional responses when viewing affective pictures, we selected 3 x 20 images from the user rated international affective picture system IAPS [9] identical to the subset used in [7] representing categories of pleasant (erotic and family photos) unpleasant (mutilated bodies, snakes and spiders) and neutral images (simple objects as well non-expressive portraits of people). Taking into consideration findings establishing that the ERP neural correlates of affective content in images can be distinguished even when the exposure of target pictures are limited to 120 ms [10], we opted for adopting the experimental picture viewing paradigm outlined in [12], where a randomized sequence of images from the 3 x 20 IAPS picture categories are presented with 0.5 second prestimulus consisting of a white fixation cross on black background, before a 1 second visual stimulus presentation of a picture followed by a subsequent 1 second poststimulus black screen.

2.3   Source Reconstruction

The inverse problem of estimating the distribution of underlying sources from a scalp map is severely ill-posed with multiple solutions, as the electrodes are placed at a distance and therefore sum the volume conducted brain activities from cortical areas throughout the scalp [13]. However, computing a sparse 3D representation may not only provide relevant neurofeedback for brain machine interfaces, but also facilitate decoding and interpretation of EEG signals by reducing redundancy and thus retrieve the most informative features constituting the functional network dynamics [14]. The forward propagation is considered linear and written in terms of a matrix A, relating the measured electrode signals $Y = AX + E$ to the source signals X where E is a noise term [15]. Here the forward model depends on electrode positions based on a head model approximating the spatial distribution of tissue and conductivity values. Assuming the noise to be time independent Gaussian distributed, the observation model becomes $p(y_t|x_t, \Sigma_E) = N(y_t|Ax_t, \Sigma_E)$ where Σ_E is the noise spatial covariance matrix. We here apply a Bayesian formulation of the widely used minimum norm MN method for solving the inverse problem [16], which allows for fast computation of the inverse solution. In a MN setting a multivariate Gaussian prior for the sources with zero mean and covariance $\alpha^{-1} I_{N_d}$ is assumed. Moreover, it is assumed that the forward propagation model is fixed and known. With Bayes rule the posterior distribution is maximized by

$$\Sigma_{\mathbf{y}} = (\alpha^{-1}\mathbf{A}\mathbf{A}^T + \beta^{-1}\mathbf{I}_{N_c})^{-1} \tag{1}$$

$$\hat{\mathbf{X}} = \alpha^{-1}\mathbf{A}^T\Sigma_{\mathbf{y}}\mathbf{Y} \tag{2}$$

where the inverse noise variance is estimated from the hyper parameters α and β using a Bayesian EM approach.

2.4   ICA Data Analysis

Even when electrodes are accurately placed the recorded potentials may still vary due to individual differences in cortical surface and volume conduction. To further analyze the coherence in the neuroheadset data, we clustered 14 ICA independent components generated from continuous EEG trial data in order to identify common patterns of brain activity across the eight subjects. While the rows of the matrix of EEG data initially consist of voltage differences measured over time between each electrode and the reference channel, they come to represent temporally independent events that are spatially filtered from the channel data by applying ICA independent component analysis [17]. Even though neither the location of electrodes or aspects of volume conductance in the brain are part of the equation, the ICA decomposition of the original data matrix often results in independent components resembling scalp projections of brain dipoles, as they reflect synchronous brain activity of local field potentials projected through volume conduction throughout the scalp [18]. As part of the recorded potentials are induced by muscle activity and noise we followed the approach in [13] to cluster ICA components retrieved from each subject to isolate the components representing information sources based on the EEGLAB plug-in (v9.0.4.4) for Matlab (R2010b). Initially by reducing the N dimensionality of the feature space to N=10 by applying PCA principal component analysis [19], which as a pre-clustering function computes a vector for each component to define normalized distances in a subspace representing the largest covariances within scalp maps and power spectra. Subsequently, we applied a K-means algorithm choosing K=10 to cluster similar ICA components and separate outliers that remain more than three standard deviations removed from any cluster centroids.

3   Results

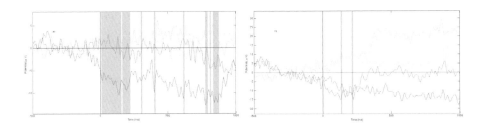

Fig. 2. Event related potentials ERP of channel amplitudes averaged across eight subjects viewing four different types of affective images outlined in red: arousing (erotic couples), green: unpleasant (mutilated bodies), blue: neutral (people and faces), turquoise: pleasant (families with kids). The differences remain statistically significant based on a repeated one-way ANOVA analysis at p < 0.05 marked in the grey time intervals for the neuroheadset electrodes P7 (left) and F8 (right).

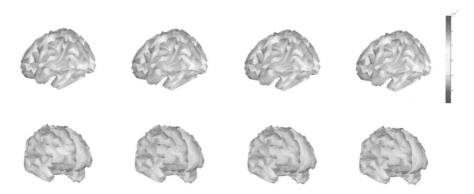

Fig. 3. Activations in the 8-13 Hz alpha frequency band at 148-156 ms after stimulus, based on MN reconstructed sources generated from scalp maps averaged across subjects viewing pictures of (from left to right): erotic couples, mutilated bodies, neutral people and families with kids. Consistent with earlier neuroimaging findings at the 150 ms time window related to the early posterior negativity EPN component [7] [10], the reconstructed sources reflect increased activity for pleasant versus unpleasant and neutral content.

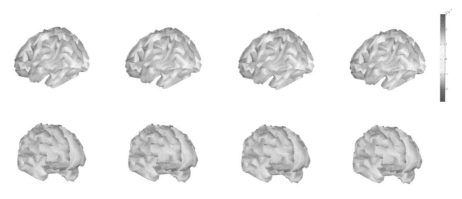

Fig. 4. Activations in the 8-13 Hz alpha frequency band at 451 ms after stimulus, based on MN reconstructed sources generated from scalp maps averaged across subjects viewing pictures of (from left to right): erotic couples, mutilated bodies, neutral people and families with kids. Consistent with earlier neuroimaging findings at the 450 ms time window related to the late positive potential LPP component [7] [10], the reconstructed sources reflect increased activity for pleasant versus unpleasant and for affective versus neutral content.

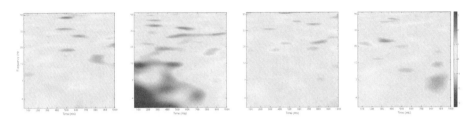

Fig. 5. Spectograms of event related spectral perturbation ERSP [18] across the frequencies 3-60 Hz for neuroheadset electrode F8, signifying the mean changes in power spectrum at a given frequency and latency averaged across subjects viewing pictures of (from left to right): erotic couples, mutilated bodies, neutral people and families with kids, visualizing the contributions of theta, alpha, beta and gamma brain waves elicited by the emotional content

4   Discussion

Combining a wireless neuroheadset with a smartphone to process brain imaging data, our findings indicate we can distinguish among emotional responses reflected in different scalp potentials when viewing pleasant and unpleasant pictures and thereby replicate results previously obtained using conventional high density 129 electrode EEG equipment [7] [10]. Analyzing the event related potentials ERP averaged across eight subjects when viewing affective images (Fig.2), allows for differentiating between affective and neutral images as well as pleasant and unpleasant content, which based on a repeated one-way ANOVA analysis remain statistically significant at $p < 0.05$ for the neuroheadset electrodes P7 and F8. Even though the neuroheadset has only a limited number of channels and no central electrodes, including electrode positions like F7/F8, P7/P8 and O1/O2 which have been shown to contribute significantly to the differentiation between affective and neutral pictures [7], might thus allow for replicating results previously obtained using standard EEG setups. Although at the same time raising the question as to whether the electrode positions can be considered similar, as the form factor of the neuroheadset will provide a slightly different fit for each subject depending on the shape of the head in contrast to traditional EEG caps. We therefore clustered the 8 x 14 ICA components based on power spectrum and scalp maps generated from continuous EEG trial data in order to identify common patterns of brain activity across the eight subjects. Here four clusters captured 7, 12, 17 and 15 ICA components respectively, all positioned within 3 standard deviations from the centroids. Indicating an ability to consistently capture common patterns of brain activity across subjects even when taking into account the less accurate positioning and limited number of electrodes. While the clustered ICA components do not represent absolute scalp map polarities as such, they indicate common sources of synchronous brain activity, consistent with activities in central, temporal and parietal cortex previously observed to differentiate responses when viewing affective pictures compared to neutral content [7] [10].

Taking a Bayesian approach we estimate the parameters for applying the minimum norm MN method and thus reconstruct the underlying sources from the recorded scalp potentials. Initially exploring the 3D brain model at 150 ms after picture onset we identified activations averaged across subjects viewing pictures of: erotic couples, mutilated bodies, neutral people and families with kids. Consistent with earlier neuroimaging findings related to the early posterior negativity EPN component [7] [10], our reconstructed sources also reflected increased activity for pleasant versus unpleasant and neutral content (Fig.3). This early component thought to reflect allocation of attentional resources has earlier been found to be more significant for erotic relative to neutral content. Our MN source reconstruction here adds further details as it highlights a number of frontal cortical areas such as the dorsomedial prefrontal cortex which has previously been found to be co-activated and closely associated with core limbic structures involved in generating emotional states. While at the same time triggering activations from the visual cortex through the temporoparietal junction along the superior temporal sulcus. Activations well aligned with earlier studies of affective pictures, in which they have been associated with attention directed towards inferring the conceptual relevance of emotional content [20]. Also the pleasant pictures of family and kids show a stronger activation in this early time window compared to neutral content, suggesting that not only arousing images but positive valence in general may enhance the activations. Within the later time window we found a strong activation at 451 ms after picture onset which based on the reconstructed sources may represent the late positive potential LPP previously observed using a conventional EEG setup. Consistent with earlier neuroimaging findings at the 450 ms time window related to the LPP component [7] [10], our reconstructed sources also reflected increased activity for pleasant versus unpleasant and for affective versus neutral content. It has been suggested that the LPP component signifies increased allocation of neural resources for processing emotionally salient relative to neutral content. The MN source reconstruction here again provides further details as the unpleasant pictures appear to activate the dorsomedial prefrontal cortex which is considered an interface for projecting the cognitive context to the underlying subcortical structures related to core affect. Whereas the pleasant content to a higher degree seems to activate posterior areas for high-level visual processing and orbitofrontal areas associated with evaluating emotional stimuli and forming motivational states [20].

Earlier studies of emotional face expressions indicate that the EEG signals can be differentiated based on brain wave oscillations, with angry faces increasing the amplitude in the high end of the 8-13 Hz alpha oscillations, while happy expressions enhance amplitudes in the low end of the alpha frequency band [21]. Analyzing the spectograms of event related spectral perturbation ERSP (Fig.5) constituting the mean changes in power spectrum at a given frequency and latency [18], across the frequencies 3-60 Hz for the neuroheadset electrode F8, it seems feasible to similarly differentiate among the four image categories based on the complementary contributions of theta, alpha, beta and gamma brain waves elicited by the emotional content. As a consequence when subdividing the activations in the alpha band previously discussed (Fig. 4), it is also here evident that the responses triggered by unpleasant pictures are enhanced within the 11-13 Hz upper end of the alpha oscillations, whereas the cortical areas activated by pleasant content are more pronounced within the lower 8-11 Hz end of the frequency band. This emotional bias towards positive or negative valence within the alpha frequency band might be utilized in brain machine interfaces, as participants undergoing neurofeedback training likewise report evoking emotions as the best strategy to consciously control alpha brain waves [22].

Applying a Bayesian approach to reconstruct the underlying neural sources may thus provide a differentiation of emotional responses based on the raw EEG data captured online in a mobile context, as our current implementation is able to visualize the activations on a smartphone with a latency of 150 ms. The early and late ERP components are not limited to the stark emotional contrasts characterizing images selected from the IAPS collection. Whether we read a word with affective connotations, come across something similar in an image or recognize from the facial expression that somebody looks sad, the electrophysical patterns in the brain seem to suggest that the underlying emotional processes might be the same [23]. The ability to continuously capture these patterns by integrating wireless EEG sets with smartphones for online processing of brain imaging data may offer completely new opportunities for modeling the mental state of users in real life scenarios as well as providing a basis for novel bio-feedback applications.

Acknowledgments. This work is supported in part by the Danish Lundbeck Foundation through CIMBI Center for Integrated Molecular Brain Imaging.

References

1. Ranky, G.N., Adamovich, S.: Analysis of a commercial eeg device for the control of a robot arm. In: IEEE 36th Annual Northeast Bioengineering Conference, IEEE Explore (2010), doi:10.1109/NEBC.2010.5458188
2. Squatriglia, C.: Thinking your way through traffic in a brain-controlled car. Wired (2011),
   http://www.wired.com/autopia/2011/03/braindriver-thought-control-car/
3. Campbell, A.T., Choudhury, T., Hu, S., Lu, H., Mukerjee, M.K., Rabbi, M., Raizada, R.D.S.: Neurophone: brain-mobile phone interface using a wireless eeg headset. In: ACM MobiHeld, pp. 1–6 (2010)
4. Makeig, S., Gramann, K., Jung, T.-P., Sejnowski, T.J., Poizner, H.: Linking brain, mind and behavior. Int. J. Psychophysiol. 73(2), 95–100 (2009)
5. Damasio, A.: Feelings of emotion and the self. Annals of the New York Academy of Sciences 1001, 253–261 (2003)
6. Russell, J.A.: A circumplex model of affect. Journal of Personality and Social Psychology 39(6), 1161–1178 (1980)
7. Keil, A., Bradley, M.M., Hauk, O., Rockstroh, B., Elbert, T., Lang, P.J.: Large-scale neural correlates of affective picture processing. Psychophysiology 39, 641–649 (2002)

8. Cuthbert, B.N., Schupp, H.T., Bradley, M.M., Birbaumer, N., Lang, P.J.: Brain potentials in affective picture processing: covariation with autonomic arousal and affective report. Biological Psychology 52, 95–111 (2000)
9. Lang, P.J., Bradley, M.M., Cuthbert, B.N.: International affective picture system (iaps): Affective ratings of pictures and instruction manual. Tech. Rep. A-8, University of Florida, Gainesville, FL (2008)
10. Schupp, H.T., Junghöfer, M., Weike, A.I., Hamm, A.O.: The selective processing of briefly presented affective pictures: An erp analysis. Psychophysiology 41, 441–449 (2004)
11. de Cesarei, A., Codispoti, M.: When does size not matter? effects of stimulus size on affective modulation. Psychophysiology 43, 207–215 (2006)
12. Frantzidis, C.A., Bratsas, C., Papadelis, C.L., Konstantinidis, E., Pappas, C., Bamidis, P.D.: Toward emotion aware computing: an integrated approach using multichannel neurophysiological recordings and affective visual stimuli. IEEE Transactions on Information Technology in Biomedicine 14(3), 589–597 (2010)
13. Delorme, A., Mullen, T., Kothe, C., Acar, Z.A., Bigdely-Shamlo, N., Vankov, A., Makeig, S.: Eeglab, sift, nft, bcilab and erica: new tools for advanced eeg processing. Computational Intelligence and Neuroscience, 1–12 (2011), doi:10.1155/2011/130714
14. Besserve, M., Martinerie, J., Garnero, L.: Improving quantification of functional networks with eeg inverse problem: Evidence from a decoding point of view. NeuroImage 55(4), 1536–1547 (2011)
15. Baillet, S., Mosher, J.C., Leahy, R.M.: Electromagnetic brain mapping. IEEE Signal Processing Magazine 18, 14–30 (2001)
16. Hämäläinen, M.S., Ilmoniemi, R.J.: Interpreting magnetic fields of the brain: minimum norm estimates. Medical and Biological Engineering and Computing 37(1), 35–42 (1994)
17. Comon, P.: Independent component analysis, a new concept? Signal Processing 36, 287–314 (1994)
18. Delorme, A., Makeig, S.: Eeglab: an open source toolbox for analysis of single-trial eeg dynamics including independent component analysis. Journal of Neuroscience Methods 134(1), 9–21 (2004)
19. Jolliffe, I.T.: Principal Component Analysis. Springer Series in Statistics. Springer, Heidelberg (1986, 2002)
20. Kober, H., Barrett, L.F., Joseph, J., Bliss-Moreau, E., Lindquist, K., Wager, T.D.: Functional grouping and cortical–subcortical interactions in emotion: a meta-analysis of neuroimaging studies. NeuroImage 42, 998–1031 (2008)
21. Güntekin, B., Basar, E.: Emotional face expressions are differentiated with brain oscillations. International Journal of Psychophysiology 64, 91–100 (2007)
22. Zoefel, B., Huster, R.J., Hermann, C.S.: Neurofeedback training of the upper alpha frequency band in eeg improves cognitive performance. NeuroImage (in press, 2011), doi:10.1016/j.neuroimage.2010.08.078
23. Schacht, A., Sommer, W.: Emotions in word and face processing - early and late cortical responses. Brain and Cognition 69, 538–550 (2009)

Generalizing Models of Student Affect in Game-Based Learning Environments

Jennifer Sabourin, Bradford Mott, and James C. Lester

Department of Computer Science, North Carolina State University,
Raleigh NC 27695
{jlrobiso,bwmott,lester}@ncsu.edu

Abstract. Evidence of the strong relationship between learning and emotion has fueled recent work in modeling affective states in intelligent tutoring systems. Many of these models are designed in ways that limit their ability to be deployed to a large audience of students by using expensive sensors or subject-dependent machine learning techniques. This paper presents work that investigates empirically derived Bayesian networks for prediction of student affect. Predictive models are empirically learned from data acquired from 260 students interacting with the game-based learning environment, CRYSTAL ISLAND. These models are then tested on data from a second identical study involving 140 students to examine issues of generalizability of learned predictive models of student affect. The findings suggest that predictive models of affect that are learned from empirical data may have significant dependencies on the populations on which they are trained, even when the populations themselves are very similar.

Keywords: Affective modeling, Intelligent tutoring systems, Dynamic Bayesian networks.

1 Introduction

Affect has begun to play an increasingly important role in intelligent tutoring systems. The intelligent tutoring systems community has seen the emergence of work on affective student modeling [1], detecting frustration and stress [2,3], modeling agents' emotional states [4,5], detecting student motivation [6], and diagnosing and adapting to student self-efficacy [7]. All of this work seeks to increase the fidelity with which affective and motivational processes are understood and utilized in intelligent tutoring systems in an effort to increase the effectiveness of tutorial interactions and, ultimately, learning.

This level of emphasis on affect is not surprising given the effects it has been shown to have on learning outcomes. Student affective states impact problem-solving strategies, the level of engagement exhibited by the student, and the degree to which he or she is motivated to continue with the learning process [8,9]. All of these factors have the potential to impact both how students learn immediately and their learning behaviors in the future. Consequently, the ability to understand and model affective behaviors in learning environments has been a focus of recent work [1,10,11].

S. D´Mello et al. (Eds.): ACII 2011, Part II, LNCS 6975, pp. 588–597, 2011.
© Springer-Verlag Berlin Heidelberg 2011

However, the detection and modeling of affective behaviors in learning environments poses significant challenges. Among these challenges is the issue of subject independence and developing models that can generalize well to new student users. Emotional experiences may be highly individual [12,13] and developing models that are able to utilize individualized information are often desirable. However, in order to reach a wider population, affect models that are subject-independent are preferable. This is especially true in educational systems, which are designed to reach a wide population. Affect models in these systems must be able to generalize well to students who have never interacted with the environment before.

A related issue is the consideration of which channels to use for emotion recognition. Facial expressions and physiological data can offer insight into the experience of individuals but also have significant limitations for educational systems designed for widespread use. First, collection of this data often requires expensive or intrusive equipment that may limit the ability to deploy the learning environments when sensors are unavailable or inappropriate. Additionally, some features such as facial expression and speech prosody are highly dependent on an individual and limits the ability of the models to generalize well to future populations. One way to avoid these limitations is to build models that are more focused on the use of context information, such as students' current actions and progress during learning activities, for informing affect prediction.

In this paper we investigate empirically derived Bayesian models of student affect based on a theoretical model of learning emotions that focus on students' contexts and goals. Student self-reports of emotion were collected in a study in which students at a local middle school interacted with an exploratory game-based learning environment, CRYSTAL ISLAND. After learning and evaluating the predictive models of student affect with data from the first study, an identical second study was conducted with a different population of students. Further analyses examined the extent to which the learned models could generalize to future populations.

2   Background

Currently, there is an active debate in the emotional psychology community about the universality of emotions [12]. The community is attempting to identify to what extent affective experiences (including expression and recognition) are culturally or individually dependent. This debate mirrors the issue in affective computing on whether to learn models of affect recognition that are dependent or independent of the subjects on which they are trained. Affect recognition models trained on physiological or facial expression data have been shown to benefit significantly from subject dependent data [14,15]. These findings are not unexpected given the uniqueness of individual faces and physiological experiences. However, subject dependent models will have limited abilities to extend to future populations.

To date, many models of affect detection have been developed for use in computer-based learning environments. For instance, Conati and Maclaren have incorporated physical sensors into a complex model based on OCC theory [1]. This model estimates student goals based on personal traits and behaviors in the environment as well as evidence from physical feedback channels that further support the model's prediction. Similarly, Arroyo et al. have found benefits of multiple channels of physical evidence of affect [10]. By adding features such as facial expressions, skin conductivity, posture, and pressure they were able to account for much more variance over using contextual features of the tutoring environment alone. As in other environments, the incorporation of physiological feedback data offered substantial improvement over models without this feature; however, the reliance on these sensors limits the ability to deploy the learning environments when sensors are unavailable or inappropriate.

The models explored in this paper are designed to focus on contextual information rather than data from physiological sensors in order to increase the possible reach of the educational system. Theoretical models of learner emotion [16,17] are used to inform the design of Bayesian networks. These models are initially evaluated for subject independence within the same population. Further analyses examine how well learned models are actually able to generalize to a new population.

3   Method

The predictive models of learner emotions were built using data from students' interactions with CRYSTAL ISLAND (Figure 1), a game-based learning environment being developed for the domain of microbiology that follows the standard course of study for eighth grade science in North Carolina. CRYSTAL ISLAND features a science mystery set on a recently discovered volcanic island. Students play the role of the protagonist, Alex, who is attempting to discover the identity and source of an unidentified disease plaguing a newly established research station. The story opens by introducing the student to the island and the members of the research team for which her father serves as the lead scientist. As members of the research team fall ill, it is her task to discover the cause and the specific source of the outbreak. Typical gameplay involves navigating the island, manipulating objects, taking notes, viewing posters, operating lab equipment, and talking with non-player characters to gather clues about the disease's source. To progress through the mystery, a student must explore the world and interact with other characters while forming questions, generating hypotheses, collecting data, and testing hypotheses.

Fig. 1. CRYSTAL ISLAND environment   **Fig. 2.** Self-report device

In order to empirically build and validate models of student affect, data from a study involving 296 eighth grade students from a rural North Carolina middle school was collected (School 1). After removing instances with incomplete data or logging errors, there were 260 students remaining.

Pre-study materials were completed during the week prior to interacting with CRYSTAL ISLAND. The pre-study materials included a demographic survey, researcher-generated CRYSTAL ISLAND curriculum test, and measures of several personal characteristics including goal orientation, personality, and emotion regulation tendencies. Details of the study are provided in [17].

Students were given approximately 55 minutes to work on solving the mystery. Students' affect data was collected during the learning interactions through regular self-report prompts. Students were prompted every seven minutes to self-report their current mood and "status" through an in-game smartphone device (Figure 2). This report was described to students as being part of an experimental social network being developed for the island's research camp. Students selected one emotion from a set of seven options, which included *anxious, bored, confused, curious, excited, focused,* and *frustrated*. This set of cognitive/affective states is based on prior research identifying states that are relevant to learning. After selecting an emotion, students were instructed to briefly type a few words about their current status in the game, similarly to how they might update their status in an online social network. The seven minute intervals between self-reports was selected to balance a desire for a rich picture of affective experience and to avoid irritating the students. Future work may investigate the use of other techniques of affect detection to avoid issues with self-report such as honesty of the student and interruption from the learning environment.

4 Results

In total 1863 emotion self-reports were collected from 260 students, an average of 7.2 reports per student. These reports covered the range of available emotion choices with *focused* (22.4%) being the most frequent. Following this were reports of *curiosity* (18.6%), *frustration* (16.3%), *confusion* (16.1%), *excitement* (13.5%), *boredom* (8.5%) *and anxiety* (4.6%). Overall emotions with positive valence (*focused, curious,* and *excited*) accounted for 54.5% of emotion self-reports. These totals inform the baseline accuracy against which the predictive models were compared: 22.4% for emotion prediction and 54.5% for valence prediction.

4.1 Predictive Modeling

Because of the inherent uncertainty in predicting student emotion, Bayesian networks were used to model the cognitive appraisal process. Bayesian networks are graphical models used to model processes under uncertainty by representing the relationship between variables in terms of a probability distribution [18]. In this study, each Bayesian network was specified using the GeNIe modeling environment developed by the

Decision Systems Laboratory of the University of Pittsburgh (http://dsl.sis.pitt.edu). The variables and their dependencies were informed by Elliot and Pekrun's model of learner emotions [17]. After the structure of the model had been specified, the parameters, or probability distributions of each dependency, were learned using the Expectation-Maximization (EM) algorithm provided within GeNIe. Each model was trained using 10-fold cross-validation, in which the model is trained on data from 90% of the students and is then tested for accuracy on the remaining 10%. This technique is commonly used to provide an estimate of how well a model can be expected to generalize to future users. However, each user in this case is from the same population which may prove to be a limitation in overall generalizability.

The models contained three types of variables:

(1) **Personal Attributes.** These static attributes were taken directly from students' scores on the surveys prior to the interaction. Included were all four attributes for goal orientation and three personality attributes expected to be relevant to the student's appraisal: *conscientiousness, openness*, and *agreeableness*.

(2) **Observable Environment Variables.** These dynamic attributes capture a snapshot of the student's activity in the learning environment at the time of the self report. They provide a summary of important actions taken, such as *TestsRun, BooksViewed,* and *GoalsCompleted*. They also include information about how well the student is doing in the environment based on certain milestones, such as *SuccessfulTest* and *WorksheetChecks*.

(3) **Appraisal Variables**. These variables are not directly observable in the environment. Instead they are the result of the student's cognitive appraisal of many factors. The selected appraisal variables and their relation to observable variables are informed by the model of learning emotions.

4.2 Bayesian Networks

In order to provide an additional baseline of comparison a naïve Bayesian network was learned. A naïve Bayesian network operates under the "naïve" assumption that all variables are directly related to the outcome variable but are conditionally independent of each other [18]. The learned naïve Bayesian network achieved a predictive accuracy of 18.1% on emotion label and 51.2% on valence. This performance is less accurate than the most frequent label baseline, but provides an additional baseline measure. By comparing carefully constructed Bayesian networks against the naïve assumption we can make better inferences about how affective models benefit from theoretically informed structure.

Next, a Bayesian network (Figure 3) was designed with the structure informed by the proposed relationships described within Elliot and Pekrun's model of learner emotions [16]. After the structure was designed, the parameters of the model were learned using the EM algorithm. Evaluation of the model showed that the Bayesian network could predict the emotion label with 25.5% accuracy and could predict the valence of the emotional state with 66.8% accuracy (Table 1). Both of these predictions offer a statistically significant gain over the most frequent baseline and the naïve Bayesian network ($p<0.05$). This improvement highlights the benefits of using a theoretical model of learner emotions to guide the model's structure.

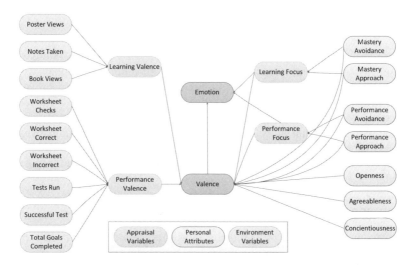

Fig. 3. Structure of static Bayesian network

However, the simple Bayesian network has no explicit representation of how emotions change over time. For instance, while poor performance at a task may merely be *frustrating* early in the interaction, for highly performance-oriented students this could turn into *anxiety* as more and more time passes. In order to capture dynamic nature of emotions as they occur over time, the structure of the simple Bayesian network was used as the foundation of a series of dynamic Bayesian networks.

Dynamic Bayesian networks extend Bayesian networks by representing changes of the phenomena modeled over time. In this way, observations at time t_n are able to inform observations at time t_{n+1} [18]. A variety of representations of the dynamic nature of appraisal and the resulting affective states were tested. Of these, the model with the highest accuracy was able to predict emotional state with 32.6% accuracy and valence with 72.6% accuracy. This model included a dynamic link between both emotion and valence, where the values of these two variables at t_{n+1} are partially informed by the emotion and valence at time t_n.

Table 1. Prediction accuracies

	Emotion Accuracy	Valence Accuracy
Baseline	22.4%	54.5%
Naïve Bayes	18.1%	51.2%
Bayes Net	25.5%	66.8%
Dynamic BN	32.6%	72.6%

Table 2. Frequency and proportion of emotion reports

Emotion	School 1		School 2	
	Freq	Per	Freq	Per
anxious	86	4.6%	41	4.0%
bored	159	8.5%	84	8.2%
confused	300	16.1%	167	16.3%
curious	347	18.6%	203	19.8%
excited	251	13.5%	126	12.3%
focused	417	22.4%	252	24.6%
frustrated	303	16.3%	150	14.7%
Total	**1863**	-	**1023**	-

5 Validation

To ensure that models of student affect could generalize well to future students interacting with CRYSTAL ISLAND an independent 10-fold cross-validation scheme was used. However, since all 260 students used to train and test the data were from the same school and likely have similar prior exposure to content it is interesting to test on students from an unseen population. For this purpose, a second study was conducted with 154 eighth grade students from a middle school in same rural school district as the first study (School 2). After cleaning the data, 140 students' data remained in the test data set. From these students 1023 affect self-reports were collected.

5.1 Comparing Populations

The first step in examining how well the learned affect models are expected to extend to future populations was to compare the emotional experiences of the two populations. Therefore, we compared the relative frequency of emotional states for each school. An initial comparison of the two populations indicated some striking similarities. The student populations from both schools covered a similar range of the personality attributes selected. It was also important to compare the emotional experiences of students. The frequency for each school is presented in (Table 2). The relative frequencies appear very similar for each emotional state and a chi-squared analysis indicates that there are not statistically significant differences in the frequencies, $\chi 2$ (6, N=400) = 4.368, p=0.627.

Perhaps even more interesting than the similarity in the frequencies of emotional states is how these frequencies change over time. Since each student was prompted at routine intervals, we can measure students' states at approximately the same times across studies. The two graphs of Figure 4 show the change in proportion of self-reports at each time interval. It is interesting to examine the striking similarities between the two graphs. For instance, for both populations *curiosity* is the most frequent report in the first interval and drops rapidly and steadily from there. While students are initially *curious* at the beginning of the interaction, this curiosity wanes over time, being replaced by other emotions. Interestingly, both *frustration* and *excitement* increase over time. It is likely that two different groups of students are responsible for these rises. Students experiencing more *frustration* after time have likely been struggling throughout the interaction and have reached their limit. *Excited*

Table 3. Prediction accuracies

	Emotion Accuracy	Valence Accuracy
Baseline	24.6%	56.7%
Bayes Net	17.9%	45.6%
Dynamic BN	25.9%	52.9%

students on the other hand likely feel they are near to the completion of the mystery and are excited about their progress. *Boredom* appears to increase slightly over time,

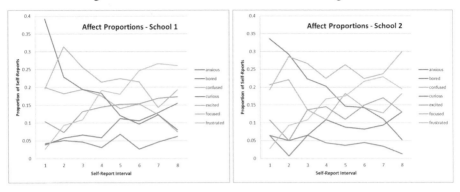

Fig. 4. Graphs of the proportion of affect self-reports across time

while emotions like *confusion, anxiety,* and *focused* remain relatively steady throughout the gameplay. The similarities in the frequency and dynamics of students' emotional states between populations suggest that models learned from School 1 ought to generalize well to School 2.

5.2   Generalization to New Populations

The ability of the models to generalize to future populations was determined by learning a model on the full data set from School 1 and using the entire data set from School 2 for evaluation. Predictive performance was compared against the most frequent baseline of emotion (24.6%) and valence (56.7%). Both a Bayesian network and a dynamic Bayesian network were trained on the full data set from School 1 (Table 3). Interestingly, though the original models were evaluated in a way that was designed to promote generalizability, neither model was able to provide additional accuracy over baseline. The static Bayesian network had a predictive accuracy significantly lower than baseline for both emotion and valence. Alternatively, the dynamic Bayesian network was able to offer a slight improvement over baseline for prediction of emotional state, but was unable to outperform baseline at prediction of valence.

It is particularly interesting how poorly these models were able to generalize to new populations given the striking similarities in the emotional frequencies between schools and the high predictive accuracy of the models when evaluated against unseen students from the original population. One possibility may be that the populations at each school vary significantly, but examination of the distribution of personality traits at each school suggested that the populations were similar in this manner. Another possibility is that students had different levels of prior exposure to the content, but a t-test analysis indicated that students did not significantly differ on their pre-test performance, $t(398) = 0.56, p = 0.576$. On average students at **School 1** answered 6.7 out of 19 questions correctly, while students at **School 2** answered an average of 6.5 questions correctly.

Though the populations are similar, there are many reasons why the learned models may not generalize the second population. First, though cross-validation yielded significant gains in predictive accuracy, the models may still be overfit to the training data. Additionally, the selected Bayesian networks and theoretical model may not be appropriately general for predicting affect in future populations. Investigation into these possibilities is an important next step for understanding why the learned models did not generalize well. Hopefully, the answers to these questions may be used to guide more robust models of student affect prediction that can be utilized with a broad range of future students.

6   Conclusion

This work presents Bayesian networks for predicting student affect with a structure informed by a theoretical model of learning emotions. Models were learned using empirical data from one middle school population and were able to achieve predictive accuracy significantly greater than chance. However, though these models were evaluated in a subject-independent manner, they were not successfully able to extend to a future population. This finding is particularly interesting given the strong similarities between the two populations.

The findings suggest that predictive models of affect that are learned from empirical data may have significant dependencies on the populations on which they are trained. Further work is necessary to determine under which circumstances predictive models of affect are unable to generalize to future populations. One possible solution may be training on data from multiple and varied populations in order to increase the chances that the models may extend to future users. This approach will involve significant research effort but will hopefully improve the ability of affect-sensitive learning environments to reach a large audience of students.

Acknowledgments. The authors wish to thank members of the IntelliMedia Group for their assistance, Omer Sturlovich and Pavel Turzo for use of their 3D model libraries, and Valve Software for access to the Source™ engine and SDK. This research was supported by the National Science Foundation under Grants REC-0632450, DRL-0822200, IIS-0812291, and CNS-0739216. This material is based upon work supported under a National Science Foundation Graduate Research Fellowship.

References

1. Conati, C., Maclaren, H.: Empirically Building and Evaluating a Probabilistic Model of User Affect. User Modeling and User-Adapted Interaction 19(3), 267–303 (2010)
2. Burleson, W.: Affective Learning Companions: Strategies for Empathetic Agents with Real-Time Multimodal Affective Sensing to Foster Meta-Cognitive and Meta-Affective Approaches to Learning, Motivation and Perseverance. PhD thesis, Massachusetts Institute of Technology (2006)
3. McQuiggan, S., Lee, S., Lester, J.: Early prediction of student frustration. In: Paiva, A.C.R., Prada, R., Picard, R.W. (eds.) ACII 2007. LNCS, vol. 4738, pp. 698–709. Springer, Heidelberg (2007)
4. Marsella, S., Gratch, J.: EMA: A Process Model of Appraisal Dynamics. Cognitive Systems Research 10(1), 70–90 (2009)

5. Paiva, A., Dias, J., Sobral, D., Aylett, R., Sobreperez, P., Woods, S., Zoll, C., Hall, L.: Caring for Agents and Agents that Care: Building Empathetic Relations with Synthetic Agents. In: Proc. of the 3rd Intl. Joint Conf. on Autonomous Agents and Multiagent Systems, pp. 194–201 (2004)

6. de Vicente, A., Pain, H.: Informing the detection of the students' motivational state: An empirical study. In: Cerri, S.A., Gouardéres, G., Paraguaçu, F. (eds.) ITS 2002. LNCS, vol. 2363, pp. 933–943. Springer, Heidelberg (2002)

7. Beal, C., Lee, H.: Creating a Pedagogical Model That Uses Student Self Reports of Motivation and Mood yo Adapt ITS Instruction. In: AIED 2005 Workshop on Motivation and Affect in Educational Software (2005)

8. Kort, B., Reilly, R., Picard, R.: An Affective Model of Interplay Between Emotions and Learning: Reengineering Educational Pedagogy—Building a Learning Companion. In: Proc. IEEE Intl. Conf. on Advanced Learning Technology: Issues, Achievements and Challenges. IEEE Computer Society, Madison (2001)

9. Picard, R., Papert, S., Bender, W., Blumberg, B., Breazeal, C., Cavallo, D., Machover, T., Resnick, M., Roy, D., Strohecker, C.: Affective Learning – A Manifesto. BT Technology Journal 22(4) (2004)

10. Arroyo, I., Cooper, D., Burleson, W., Woolf, B., Muldner, K., Christopherson, R.: Emotion Sensors Go to School. In: Proc. of the 14th 'Intl. Conf. on Artificial Intelligence in Education, pp. 17–24 (2009)

11. D'Mello, S., Graesser, A.: Multimodal Semi-Automated Affect Detection from Conversational Cues, Gross Body Language, and Facial Features. User Modeling and User-Adapted Interaction 20(2), 147–187 (2010)

12. Elfenbein, H., Ambady, N.: On the Universality and Cultural Specificity of Emotion Recognition: A Meta-Analysis. Psychological Bulletin 128, 203–235 (2002)

13. Picard, R., Vyzas, E., Healey, J.: Toward Machine Emotional Intelligence: Analysis of Affective Physiological State. IEEE Transactions on Pattern Analysis and Machine Intelligence 23(10), 1175–1191 (2001)

14. Kolodyazhniy, V., Kreibig, S., Gross, J., Roth, W., Wilhelm, F.: An Affective Computing Approach to Physiological Emotion Specificity: Toward Subject-Independent and Stimulus-Independent Classification of Film-Induced Emotions. Psychophysiology 48, 908–922 (2011)

15. Chen, L.: Joint Processing of Audio-Visual Information for the Recognition of Emotional Expressions in Human-Computer Interaction. Ph.D. Thesis, University of Urbana-Champaign (2000)

16. Elliot, A., Pekrun, R.: Emotion in the Hierarchical Model of Aproach-Avoidance Achievement Motivation. In: Schutz, P., Pekrun, R. (eds.) Emotion in Education, pp. 57–74. Elsevier, London (2007)

17. Sabourin, J., Mott, B., Lester, J.: Modeling Learner Affect with Theoretically Grounded Dynamic Bayesian Networks. In: ACII 2011, Part II. LNCS, vol. 6975, pp. 286–295. Springer, Heidelberg (2011)

18. Russell, S., Norvig, P.: Artificial Intelligence: A Modern Approach, 2nd edn. Pearson, London (2003)

A Spatio-Temporal Probabilistic Framework for Dividing and Predicting Facial Action Units

A.K.M. Mahbubur Rahman, Md. Iftekhar Tanveer, and Mohammed Yeasin

Electrical and Computer Engineering, The University of Memphis

Abstract. This paper proposed a probabilistic approach to divide the Facial Action Units (AUs) based on the physiological relations and their strengths among the facial muscle groups. The physiological relations and their strengths were captured using a Static Bayesian Network (SBN) from given databases. A data driven spatio-temporal probabilistic scoring function was introduced to divide the AUs into : (i) frequently occurred and strongly connected AUs (FSAUs) and (ii) infrequently occurred and weakly connected AUs (IWAUs). In addition, a Dynamic Bayesian Network (DBN) based predictive mechanism was implemented to predict the IWAUs from FSAUs. The combined spatio-temporal modeling enabled a framework to predict a full set of AUs in real-time. Empirical analyses were performed to illustrate the efficacy and utility of the proposed approach. Four different datasets of varying degrees of complexity and diversity were used for performance validation and perturbation analysis. Empirical results suggest that the IWAUs can be robustly predicted from the FSAUs in real-time and was found to be robust against noise.

Keywords: Affective computing, Spatio-Temporal AU relations.

1 Introduction

Autonomous analysis and synthesis of facial expressions and emotions are emerging issues in affective computing and agent-human communication. Facial action units (AUs) defined in Facial Action Coding System (FACS) [2] has been widely used in recognizing facial expressions (i.e., [12]), emotions (i.e., [14]), and affective states [8] to compute description of facial behavior. Despite the recent surge of computational methods, robust and real-time recognition of AUs remains challenging due to inaccuracies in measurements of subtle facial deformation and pose.

State-of-the art methods in recognition of AUs are limited to subset of *posed expressions* that are inadequate for recognition of spontaneous facial expressions, modeling blended emotions and also unsuitable for real-time applications. For example, the number of AUs recognized by Tong *et al.* [12], Lucey *et al.* [5], Zhang *et al.* [15], and Bartlett *et al.* [1] were 14, 17, 18, and 20, respectively. The choices of subset of AUs in the reported literatures were done mostly by *adhoc*-principles for a variety of reasons (that include but are not limited to): (i) skewed and non-uniform distribution of "representative examples" in existing

S. D'Mello et al. (Eds.): ACII 2011, Part II, LNCS 6975, pp. 598–607, 2011.

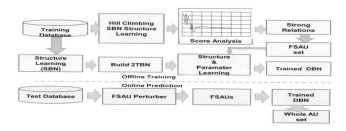

Fig. 1. Proposed Approach

emotion databases [5], (ii) lack of systematic approaches to determine significant subset of AUs even in the context of a niche application to characterize facial behavior, and (iii) lack of framework for real-time processing of full set of AUs. It is easy to note that methods based on *heuristics* and *adhoc* rules preclude important relationships between AUs.

The problems mentioned above can be addressed by logically dividing the AUs into two subsets: **f**requently occurred and **s**trongly connected **AUs** (FSAUs) and **i**nfrequently occurred and **w**eakly connected **AUs** (IWAUs). By exploiting the physiological constraints, the IWAUs can be predicted from the FSAUs in real time. In addition to physiological constraints, AUs are evolved over time when facial expressions evolves from onset to apex to offset. By modeling both the spatial and temporal relations, it is possible to rely on a smaller significant subset of AUs to infer the occurrences of other AUs.

1.1 Proposed Approach

This paper introduces a probabilistic mechanism that captures the spatio-temporal evolution of AUs to logically divide them into FSAUs and IWAUs and to predict the IWAUs from the FSAUs in real-time. The full set containing (m) AUs is divided into two subsets: (i) subset $P = \{p_1, p_2, \ldots, p_n\}$ containing FSAUs and (ii) subset $S = \{s_1, s_2, \ldots, s_{m-n}\}$ containing IWAUs. The key objective is to keep the size of P as small as possible while maintaining robustness in inferring the set S. The spatial relations and physiological constraints among the AUs were modeled and synthesized with SBN while their temporal evolution was modeled using DBN. The scoring mechanism was defined using an optimized SBN that captures the strength of AU relations learned from the database. The figure 1 shows the conceptual framework for proposed solution.

1.2 How Is It Different?

Adhoc selection of AUs [12], [6],[15] bypass the problem of finding of significant AUs. A number of closely related works (i.e., [15,12,13]) use Bayesian analysis with frequent AUs. The proposed approach is significantly different from these techniques in a number of ways. The key difference is the use of AU relations obtained using the "scoring mechanism" as opposed to "frequency" that clearly separates this work from reported related works. Since the combination of AUs and their temporal evolutions are mostly responsible for spontaneous facial behavior, the proposed solution incorporates a spatio-temporal statistical approach to capture the *AU relations* from the evidences. The scoring process defined using the SBN is novel (to the best of our knowledge) though it uses existing tools and was found to be very robust. Moreover, the prediction performance of IWAUs outperformed the contemporary related works.

Additionally, perturbation (noise) analysis was performed at AU level as well as at the level of categorical emotion recognition. At first, robustness in predicting IWAUs against perturbation in the FSAUs were analyzed. It was observed that the proposed approach is stable in the presence of varying degrees of perturbation in the FSAUs while maintaining reasonable IWAU recognition performance. However, different IWAUs have different level of noise tolerance. Also, empirical analysis was performed to characterize the effect of perturbation at FSAUs on the robust prediction of facial expressions.

2 Analysis of AU Relations

The relations between AUs are functions of physiological constraints as well as facial expressions. Physiological constraints that are resulted from the anatomy of the human face are critical for analyzing relations between AUs. A number of examples of physiological constraints are described in brief for the sake of clarity. AU 15 pulls the corners of the lips down that have been affected by AU 17 (Chin Raiser). Both AUs are connected through *Orbicularis oculi* and *Mentalis* resulting in a stronger relation. Conversely, *Zygomaticus Minor* and *Risoricus* are not connected to each other but the muscles *Zygomaticus*, *Orbicularis Oculi*, and *Masseter* are responsible for weaker relation between AU 11 and AU 20. Relations between AUs are also functions of facial expressions. Though AU 6 and AU 12 are related to the different facial regions, they are involved in happy expressions frequently resulting strong relation among themselves. Relations between AU 2 (Outer brow raiser) and AU 27 (mouth stretch) possess a mixture of the both kinds of relations.

Using a linguistic analogy, one can define the AU tree and the root based on frequently occurred strong relations that are present in the expressions database(s). The main objective here is to separate the strong relations between AUs from weaker ones.

3 Identify Strong AU Relations

We developed a proposition to identify strong relations between AUs based on a scoring mechanism while empty SBN is used as the initial network in the hill climbing algorithm. For detail proof and derivation of the proposition, please refer to [9].

Proposition: Strong relations are modeled in the earlier iterations while weak relations are modeled at the later iterations of the SBN structure learning process using hill climbing algorithm.

3.1   Strong Relations vs. Weak Relations

Following the proposition, the entire structure learning process is divided into two parts, where the first part ("Buildup Area") contains iterations which are involved to model stronger edges and the later part "Tuning Area" is responsible for modeling weak relations. In the "Buildup Area", the stronger AU relation increases the score at a very high rate of change albeit one at a time. Therefore, the main portion of score buildup has occurred in "Buildup Area". In "Tuning Area", the structure is being tuned with weaker edges.

Initially, Extended Cohn-Kanade dataset (CK+) [5] has been used to build the SBN structure to identify the strong relations. 23 AUs are used in the experiments. In figure 2, before the 8th iteration, rates of change of network score are high. Alternately, after the 8th iteration, rates of change of score are very low. A sharp transition is observed at iteration 8. Using the proposition, we would say that up to iteration 8, all strong relations are modeled in SBN structure. Weaker relations are added in later iterations. Therefore, the SBN structure shown in figure 3 obtained at iteration 8 gives us all strong or frequent edges.

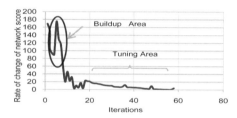

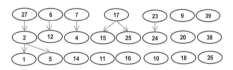

Fig. 2. Rate of Change of scores   **Fig. 3.** Strong relations between AUs

3.2   FSAUs

Figure 3 shows that particular AUs are involved in building the strong relations. The responsible AUs to build strong relations are defined as FSAUs as they are the building blocks of root relations. Now, the right side in figure 4 shows the final structure of SBN where boxed nodes represent FSAUs. The status of node 1 and node 5 do not affect any other nodes. Consequently, AU 1 and AU 5 are removed from FSAU set and are considered as members of IWAUs.

3.3   Temporal Relationships among AUs

In spontaneous behavior, facial expressions involves a muscle group or a subset of action units that evolves over time.

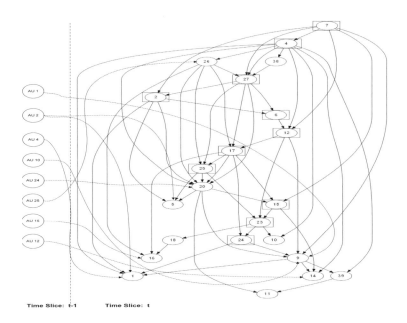

Fig. 4. Two Slice DBN

Modeling Temporal Evolution of AUs with DBN: A 2TBN is a very good framework with two connected SBN to represent the temporal evolution where a AU node in time slice t depends on AUs at time $t-1$ as well as other AUs at time t. Figure 4 shows the final 2TBN where temporal edges from time slice $t-1$ to time slice t represent the temporal evolution. Temporal edges between same IWAUs are not shown here. In inference procedure, nodes for corresponding FSAUs (boxed nodes) act as observed nodes while IWAUs are hidden.

4   Experimental Results

Empirical analyses using a number of different datasets consisting of varying degrees of variabilities were used to illustrate the utility of the proposed approach. In particular, four different datasets, **CK+** dataset (posed expressions [5]), Bosphorus dataset (posed 3D expressions [10]), M and M Initiative (**MMI**) dataset (mixture of posed and natural expressions [7]), and Emotion Elicitation (**EE**) dataset (natural expressions [14]) were used for empirical analyses.

4.1   Utility of Scoring Algorithm in Logical Division of AUs

It is widely acknowledged that the FACS provides a mechanism for analysis and synthesis of facial behavior that is consistent across culture, ethnicity, gender, and age groups. Hence, relations among the AUs are expected to be similar across datasets. The scoring proposition described in the Section 3 was used to compute the relations among AUs. The trends in the rate of change of scores over iterations were used as an indicator to divide the AUs into FSAUs and IWAUs. Figure 5 shows the 2nd derivative of the scores over iterations computed during the SBN structure learning process. From the figure 5 it is easy to note that the "Buildup Area" and "Tuning Area" were divided after 8th iteration. All four datasets were used in the experimentation to check consistency in dividing the AUs into FSAUs and IWAUs. It was observed that the strong relations were found after 8th iteration - these were **identical** across the datasets.

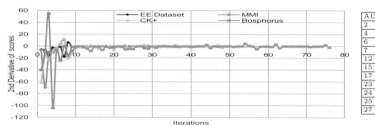

Fig. 5. 2nd derivative of scores

Fig. 6. ROCA of FSAUs in [11]

4.2 IWAUs Predictions

Three different validation experiments were performed. Firstly, performance evaluation and comparison with recently reported literature were performed using the CK+ dataset. Secondly, generalization of the proposed approach was tested using MMI dataset while the DBN had been trained with the CK+. Furthermore, EE dataset [14] was used to illustrate the suitability of the proposed approach in dealing with spontaneous emotion in an uncontrolled environment.

Empirical Analysis using Posed Expressions: The CK+ was used to quantify the performance of the proposed system and also to perform comparative analysis with [11]. The area under the Receiver Operating Characteristic (ROC) Curve was used as a metric and was abbreviated as ROCA. FSAUs from CK+ were perturbed to add noise in such a way that their recognition performance followed the figure 6 that is reported in [11].

Figure 7 showed the comparative analysis of prediction accuracies of IWAUs. Numbers within the blue bars indicated the ratios between positive and negative samples. Figure 7 suggests that ROCAs for AU 1, 5, 10, 11, 16, 20, and 26 were increased compared to [11]. Particularly, performance of AU 10 was increased by 19%, AU 11 by 9%, AU 16 by 8.64%, and AU 26 by 12.5%. It indicates that the performance of the proposed approach is significantly better compared to concurrent methods even though IWAUs were predicted without any computer vision techniques. The key observation is that the particular AUs that are difficult AUs (AU 10, 11, 14, 16, 20, and 26) were predicted with significant ROCA. Another comparative analysis was performed with the work reported by Tong

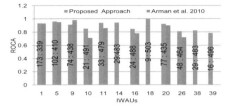 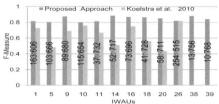

Fig. 7. ROCA for 3-fold cross validation with CK+

Fig. 8. Recognition Performance of
IWAUs for MMI dataset

et al. [12] to provide additional perspectives in the light of dynamic modeling
of AUs where the True Positive rate (TPR) of AU 1, 5 and 9 are 0.8, 0.75 and
0.9, respectively. The corresponding number for the proposed approach are 0.93,
0.97, and 0.98, respectively.

Generalization using Mixed Expressions: MMI dataset was used to test
the generalization of the proposed approach. This experiment used CK+ dataset
for training the DBN and the MMI dataset for testing. In this experiment, F-
measure was used as performance metric. The input to the DBN were corrupted
to produce FSAUs with F-measures reported in [3].

Comparative results between the proposed approach and [3] were shown in
the figure 8. It was found that all IWAUs achieved significant increase in F-
Measure. The average F-measure for the proposed approach was 0.8429 whereas
[3] got 0.6404. The F-measure of the difficult AUs AU 11, 14, 18, and 20 were
reasonable enough compared to the state-of-the-art techniques.

Analysis with Natural Expressions: To further illustrate the utility of the
proposed method in the real life scenario, an experiment was performed using
the EE dataset [14]. In this experiment, CK+ database was used for training
while the EE dataset was used for testing. Comparison of the performance was
made with spontaneous facial expression dataset (FACS-101) collected by Mark
Frank [1] while FSAUs followed the ROCAs from [4]. Particularly, ROCAs of
AU 14, 20, and 26 have been increased 14%, 33.8% and 21.45%, respectively
although these AUs are considered error prone.

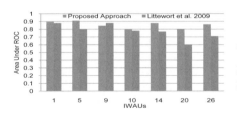 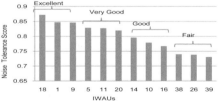

Fig. 9. Performance evaluation for
IWAUs in spontaneous datasets

Fig. 10. Noise Tolerance Scores for
IWAUs

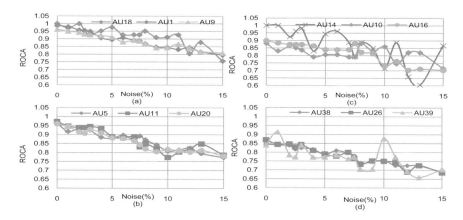

Fig. 11. Performance of IWAU Prediction against Noise

4.3 Performance Analysis with Perturbation

Though state of the art technologies have achieved significant improvement in the AU recognition, noise is added due to the inaccuracies in measurements of subtle facial deformation, pose, and out of plane head movements. A number of studies were performed to study the effect of perturbation both at the AU level as well as in predicting categorical emotion.

Noise Analysis in Predicting IWAUs: In the context of FSAUs, noises are propagated through the proposed DBN while inferring the IWAUs. However, the proposed method makes the IWAUs less susceptible to noise due to spatio-temporal relations between AUs. CK+ and MMI database were used for these experiments with three fold cross validations.

Noises from identical uniform distribution were added to each of the FSAUs and subsequently noisy FSAUs were used for IWAU prediction. Figure 11 depicts the prediction results of IWAUs with varying degrees of noise. To provide a better insight, a measure to calculate the "noise tolerance" was introduced. The approach was to find the RMS error of the performance graph from the baseline performance (with noise 0%). After that, RMS error was subtracted from theoretically maximum possible RMS error for each IWAU. Thus, the result can be interpreted as a measure of noise tolerance where ideal score should be 1.00. To provide better insight and visualization, IWAUs were grouped into four clusters (excellent, very good, good, and fair) based on the tolerance score (fig 10).

It was observed that AU 18, 1, and 9 had excellent noise tolerance in figure 11a. Among them, AU 18 seemed to be mostly tolerant against noise. It was also noted that noise had linear effect on the prediction of AU 1 and 9. The degradation of their performance was gradual as the ROCA remained above 0.90 and above 0.85 while the noise were increased to 7% and to 12%, respectively. AU 5, 11, and 20 showed very good noise tolerance as observed from the figure 11b. Average ROCA of this group remained above 0.9 for noise up to 4% while average ROCA went below 0.80 after 10% noise. The AU 14, 10, and 16 was found to have good tolerance (fig 11c) and the other AUs showed fair tolerance.

For fair tolerant IWAUs (fig 11d), more than 4% noise resulted inferior ROCA on average.

Noise Analysis in Facial Expression Recognition: An additional experiment was performed to analyze the effects of perturbation/noises in FSAUs on recognition of six categorial emotions. CK+ and MMI database were used for this experiment while emotion recognition was performed on 18 AUs (11 FSAUs and 7 IWAUs). FSAUs are perturbed accordingly to generate noisy FSAUs as earlier experiments. Then, IWAUs were inferred using proposed technique while another Bayesian net [15] had been used to predict the emotions.

It was observed from figure 12 that '**Happy**' emotion had the best noise tolerance against noisy FSAUs. The performance was found to be almost consistent as the ROCA remained above 0.95 up to 29% noise in FSAUs with one exception. '**Surprise**' expression showed convincing error tolerance as well. It maintained ROCA more than 0.90 across the whole noise range. Though '**Disgust**' had inferior performance after 9% noise compared to Happy and Surprise expressions, its ROCA was more than 0.85 up to 23% noise level with two exceptions only. Performance in predicting '**Anger**' found to be somewhat better than 'Disgust'. The ROCA of Anger recognition was more than 0.90 where noise increased from 0% to 7% and ROCA remained more than 0.80 up to 28% noise. '**Sad**' has reasonable noise tolerance up to 24% noise while more than 0.85 ROCA has been maintained.

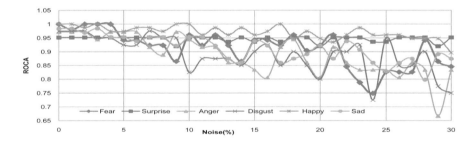

Fig. 12. Performance of Facial Expression Recognition against Noise

5   Conclusions

Reliable estimation of affective states and continuous categorical emotion spotting require all AUs or a majority of them. However, automated, robust, and real-time recognition of all AUs are computationally expensive and error prone. To address such issues, this paper proposed a spatio-temporal data driven probabilistic scoring function to divide the AUs into FSAUs and IWAUs. SBN was used to capture the relations among AUs and the DBN was used to capture their temporal evolution. A framework was implemented to predict the IWAUs on the fly from the FSAUs with very high accuracy. The proposed approach improved robustness in predicting IWAUs. In addition, perturbation anaylsis was performed to understand the effect of noise at both the AU level as well as recognition of categorical emotion. These contributions will enable real-time analysis, synthesis, and tracking of complex and natural facial behaviors.

References

1. Bartlett, M.S., Littlewort, G., Frank, M.G., Lainscsek, C., Fasel, I.R., Movellan, J.R.: Automatic recognition of facial actions in spontaneous expressions. Jour. of Multimedia 1(6) (2006)
2. Ekman, P., Friesen, W.V.: Facial action coding system: A technique for the measurement of facial movement (1978)
3. Koelstra, S., Pantic, M., Patras, I.: A dynamic texture-based approach to recognition of facial actions and their temporal models. IEEE Tran. on PAMI (2010)
4. Littlewort, G.C., Bartlett, M.S., Lee, K.: Automatic coding of facial expressions displayed during posed and genuine pain. Image Vi. Comput. 27, 1797–1803 (2009)
5. Lucey, P., Cohn, J., Kanade, T., Saragih, J., Ambadar, Z., Matthews, I.: The extended cohn-kanade dataset (ck+): A complete dataset for action unit and emotion-specified expression. In: CVPR Workshops (June 2010)
6. Lucey, S., Ashraf, A., Cohn, J.: Investigating spontaneous facial action recognition through aam representations of the face. I-Tech Ed. and Pub. (2007)
7. Pantic, M., Valstar, M.F., Rademaker, R., Maat, L.: Web-based database for facial expression analysis. IEEE, Los Alamitos (2005)
8. Picard, R.W.: Affective computing: challenges. Int. J. Hum.-Comp. Stud. 59 (2003)
9. Mahbubur Rahman, A.K.M.: Using probablistic graphical model in finding significant subset of facial action units. MS Thesis (2011)
10. Savran, A., Alyüz, N., Dibeklioğlu, H., Çeliktutan, O., Gökberk, B., Sankur, B., Akarun, L.: Bosphorus database for 3D face analysis. In: Schouten, B., Juul, N.C., Drygajlo, A., Tistarelli, M. (eds.) BIOID 2008. LNCS, vol. 5372, pp. 47–56. Springer, Heidelberg (2008)
11. Savran, S., Sankur, B., Bilge, M.T.: Facial action unit detection: 3d versus 2d modality. In: CVPR Workshop on Human Comm. Behavior Anal., USA (2010)
12. Tong, Y., Liao, W., Ji, Q.: Facial action unit recognition by exploiting their dynamic and semantic relationships. IEEE Trans. on PAMI (29), 1699 (2007)
13. Tong, Y., Chen, J., Ji, Q.: A unified probabilistic framework for spontaneous facial action modeling and understanding. IEEE Trans. on PAMI 32(2), 258–273 (2010)
14. Yeasin, M., Bullot, B., Sharma, R.: Recognition of facial expressions and measurement of levels of interest from video. IEEE Trans. on Multimedia (2006)
15. Zhang, Y., Ji, Q.: Active and dynamic information fusion for facial expression understanding from image sequences. IEEE Trans. on PAMI (27), 699–714 (2005)

Author Index